THE
AMERICAN
PEOPLES

ENCYCLOPEDIA
YEAR BOOK
1972

ISBN 0-7172-0403-0

Library of Congress Catalog Card Number: 48-171

Contributors

HELMUT A. ABT, astronomer at Kitt Peak National Observatory, is managing editor of *The Astrophysical Journal.*   ASTRONOMY

FRANK BALDWIN is assistant professor of Korean in the Department of East Asian Languages and Cultures, Columbia University.   KOREA

CLIVE BARNES, ballet and drama critic of *The New York Times*, has written *Ballet in Britain since the War, Frederick Ashton and His Ballets* and *Dance Scene: U.S.A.*   DANCE

CHARLES W. BELL reports for United Press International as news editor and chief correspondent for Italy.   AUSTRIA; GREECE; ITALY; SWITZERLAND

DAVID BINDER is chief correspondent of *The New York Times* for Germany.   GERMANY; ERICH HONECKER

ALTON BLAKESLEE, science editor of The Associated Press, New York, has recently written *What You Can Do about Dangerous Drugs*, published by The Associated Press.   MEDICINE: DRUG ABUSE

GEORGE A. W. BOEHM, free-lance science writer, member of the National Association of Science Writers, was special assistant to the United States Metric Study Group of the Department of Commerce.   METRIC SYSTEM; PHYSICAL SCIENCES; TECHNOLOGY ASSESSMENT

PETER BROCK is news editor of *World Medicine*, published in London, newspaper medical columnist of the *London Evening News* and a BBC contributor.   MEDICINE AND HEALTH

BOB BROEG, sports editor of the *St. Louis Post-Dispatch*, was awarded the 1971 Missouri University medal for distinguished service to journalism and has most recently written *Super Stars of Baseball.*
    SPORTS: FOOTBALL; PAN-AMERICAN GAMES

STEPHENS BROENING is news editor of the Moscow Bureau of The Associated Press.
    UNION OF SOVIET SOCIALIST REPUBLICS

ALLAN YALE BROOKS, electrical engineer, acts as communications consultant and project engineer for the Western Union Corporation.   COMPUTERS

RICHARD BUTWELL, chairman of the Department of Political Science at the State University of New York, Brockport, has written, among other books, *Southeast Asia Today and Tomorrow.*
    PHILIPPINE REPUBLIC; TAIWAN; THAILAND

LEON CARNOVSKY is a professor in the Graduate Library School of the University of Chicago.   LIBRARIES

DINK CARROLL serves as sports columnist of *The Gazette*, Montreal.   SPORTS: ICE HOCKEY

DWIGHT CHAPIN is a sportswriter for the *Los Angeles Times.*   SPORTS: SWIMMING; TRACK

MARQUIS CHILDS, awarded a Pulitzer Prize for distinguished commentary, serves as a contributing editor for the *St. Louis Post-Dispatch.*
    SPIRO T. AGNEW; RICHARD M. NIXON

HAROLD (SPIKE) CLAASSEN is a free-lance sportswriter.   SPORTS: BOXING; GOLF

LYDIA COHEN, staff writer.   MIGRATION

BOB COLLINS, sports editor of *The Indianapolis Star*, has written *What's It Like Out There* (with Mario Andretti).   SPORTS: AUTO RACING

NELSON H. CRUIKSHANK, president of the National Council of Senior Citizens, Inc., serves or has served as a member of a number of organizations such as the Health Insurance Benefits Advisory Council.   AGING, CONFERENCE ON

DEREK DAVIES is editor of the *Far Eastern Economic Review*, published in Hong Kong.   HONG KONG; INDONESIA; MALAYSIA; SINGAPORE

WILLIAM DAVIS is travel editor of *The Boston Globe.*   TRAVEL

PETER DESBARATS is Ottawa editor and political columnist of the *Toronto Star* and frequently comments or writes for the Canadian Broadcasting Corporation.
    CANADA; PIERRE ELLIOTT TRUDEAU

LAWRENCE DeVINE is entertainment editor for *The Detroit Free Press*, drama critic and film reviewer.   MOTION PICTURES

ROBERT W. DIETSCH, business-economics editor of Scripps-Howard Newspapers, contributes to *The New Republic* and *Saturday Review.*
    HOUSING; STATES, U.S.; WELFARE

RICK DU BROW writes the "Television in Review" column for United Press International.   TELEVISION

DIANE DURYEA is editorial assistant of *Yachting Magazine* and is a member of the Navy League of the United States.
    SHIPPING; SPORTS: YACHTING

DEAN EAGLE, sports editor of *The Courier-Journal* (Louisville, Ky.) is a former president of the National Turf Writers Association.
SPORTS: HORSE RACING

WILLIAM J. EATON, Washington correspondent of the *Chicago Daily News*, won a Pulitzer Prize for national reporting and a Sidney Hillman award. With Frank Cormier, Mr. Eaton wrote a biography of Walter Reuther.
DEFENSE; FOREIGN AID

JERRY C. EDGERTON is environmental reporter in the Washington Bureau of McGraw Hill Publications.
ENVIRONMENT

CORTEZ F. ENLOE, JR., M.D., is editor and publisher of *Nutrition Today* and has written numerous articles on medicine and other scientific subjects for national magazines.
NUTRITION

SAM J. ERVIN, JR., "best-known defender of the citizen's right to be let alone," has served as U.S. senator from North Carolina since 1954 and is chairman of the Subcommittee on Constitutional Rights.
THE RIGHT TO PRIVACY

LARRY EVANS is a chess grand master and international authority on the game.
GAMES: CHESS

HARRY FLEISCHMAN is executive secretary of the National Alliance on Shaping Safer Cities and race-relations coordinator of the American Jewish Committee.
CRIME

JACK FOISIE serves as Southeast Asia correspondent and Bangkok Bureau chief of the *Los Angeles Times*.
INDOCHINA; PRISONERS OF WAR

RICHARD FREEDMAN, associate professor of English at Simmons College, Boston, Mass., reviews books for such magazines as *Life*, *The New Republic*, *The Nation* and *Book World*.
LITERATURE IN ENGLISH

ERIK J. FRIIS is editor of *The American-Scandinavian Review*.
DENMARK; FINLAND; NORWAY; SWEDEN

LILLIAN N. GERHARDT serves as editor in chief of the *School Library Journal*, as adviser to R. R. Bowker Co. Juvenile Projects and as second vice-president of the Women's National Book Association.
LITERATURE, JUVENILE

BRIAN GLANVILLE, British journalist, has written *Soccer: A History of the Game.* SPORTS: SOCCER

NATHAN GLAZER, professor of education and social structure at Harvard University, wrote the influential *The Lonely Crowd* (with D. Riesman) and *Beyond the Melting Pot* (with D. P. Moynihan).
MINORITIES, AMERICAN ETHNIC

CHARLES H. GOREN is the world-famous bridge expert.
GAMES: BRIDGE

FRED P. GRAHAM, U.S. Supreme Court correspondent of *The New York Times*, wrote *The Self-Inflicted Wound.*
LAW

PHILIP GREER, New York financial correspondent of *The Washington Post*, won the G. H. Loeb Award in 1971.
ECONOMY

JAMES J. HAGGERTY, former editor of *Aerospace Year Book*, has written numerous books on aerospace subjects; among the most recent was *Apollo Lunar Landing.*
SPACE

JOSEPH W. HALL, JR., is a member of the U.S. Senate staff, Washington Bureau, The Associated Press.
ACTION; DISTRICT OF COLUMBIA; WILBUR DAIGH MILLS; VETERANS

VERN HAUGLAND is aviation editor of The Associated Press.
AVIATION

EARL O. HEADY, professor of economics, Curtiss Distinguished Professor, and executive director of the Center for Agricultural and Economic Development, Iowa State University, has written numerous books and hundreds of articles.
AGRICULTURE

FRED M. HECHINGER, member of the editorial board and former education editor of *The New York Times*, has also served as president of the Education Writers' Association.
EDUCATION

WALTER HERBERT, Fellow of the Royal Society of Arts, is a self-employed consultant on Canadian cultural matters.
CANADA: ARTS AND LETTERS

STEPHEN HESS was national chairman of the White House Conference on Children and Youth.
YOUTH

RONALD HILTON helped found and is the executive director of the California Institute of International Studies; he is also a professor at Stanford University, and founded and edited *Hispanic American Reports* 1948–64.
LATIN AMERICA

MARVINE HOWE, special correspondent of *The New York Times*, wrote *One Woman's Morocco.*
PORTUGAL

FREDERIC HUNTER, stationed in Nairobi, Kenya, is Africa correspondent of *The Christian Science Monitor*.
AFRICA, BLACK

MARY E. JESSUP, retired, was news editor of *Civil Engineering* magazine, published by the American Society of Civil Engineers.
ENGINEERING, CIVIL; HIGHWAYS

5

STEPHEN W. KANN is editor and publisher of *Industrial World* magazine. **INDUSTRY**

SANKA KNOX reports on archeological subjects for *The New York Times*. **ARCHEOLOGY**

JACK C. LANDAU acts as U.S. Supreme Court correspondent for the Newhouse Newspapers. **LAW: THE PENTAGON PAPERS CASE**

RUBEN LEVIN is editor and manager of *Labor*, weekly newspaper published by the Labor Co-operative Educational and Publishing Society. **LABOR**

F. ROY LOCKHEIMER is associate executive director of the Japan Society, Inc., after a number of years service as associate for Japan with the American Universities Field Staff. He has written many articles on Japanese politics, history and so on, published in both Japanese and English. **JAPAN**

SIDNEY G. LUTZIN is director of communications and development of the (U.S.) National Recreation and Park Association. **PARKS**

COLMAN McCARTHY serves as a member of the editorial page staff of *The Washington Post*. **POLITICAL PRISONERS**

SIGURDUR A. MAGNUSSON acts as editor of *Samvinnan*, a bimonthly cultural and political magazine published in Reykjavik, Iceland. **ICELAND**

DAVID MASON, foreign correspondent for The Associated Press, is stationed in Paris. **EUROPEAN ECONOMIC COMMUNITY; FRANCE; NORTH ATLANTIC TREATY ORGANIZATION**

JOHN ALLAN MAY, a member of the Economic Research Council of Great Britain, serves as chief of the London bureau of *The Christian Science Monitor*. **BELGIUM; IRELAND, REPUBLIC OF; LUXEMBOURG; THE NETHERLANDS; UNITED KINGDOM**

ARTHUR C. MILLER is senior editor of *The Asia Letter*, an authoritative newsletter on Asian affairs published in Hong Kong. **AFGHANISTAN; BURMA; CEYLON; PAKISTAN**

NORVAL MORRIS, professor of law and criminology at the University of Chicago, is one of America's leading criminologists. Among his many books are *Studies in Criminal Law* (with Colin Howard) and *The Habitual Criminal*. **PRISON REFORM**

DANIEL B. MOSKOWITZ, correspondent in the Washington Bureau of McGraw-Hill World News, specializes in economic subjects. **FUELS AND ENERGY**

BRUCE W. MUNN has been chief United Nations correspondent of United Press International since 1949. **DISARMAMENT; UNITED NATIONS**

MARTIN C. NEEDLER, director of the Division of Inter-American Affairs of the University of New Mexico, has written numerous books and articles on Latin American affairs. **MEXICO**

EDWARD NEILAN is a correspondent for the Copley News Service. **POSTAL SERVICE**

DEANNE E. NEUMAN serves as managing editor of International Trade Reporter, published by The Bureau of National Affairs, Inc. **TRADE**

JAMES V. O'GARA is editor of *Advertising Age* magazine. **ADVERTISING**

WILFRED OWEN is a senior fellow of The Brookings Institution, Washington, D.C. **CITIES**

HENRY POPKIN, drama critic of *The Herald* (N.Y.) weekly, is professor of English at the State University of New York at Buffalo. He served as editor of *The Concise Encyclopedia of Modern Drama*. **THEATER**

SHIRLEY POVICH is sports editor of *The Washington Post;* he is a former president of the Baseball Writers of America. **SPORTS: BASEBALL**

ROBERT REINHOLD, a national correspondent of *The New York Times*, specializes in scientific subjects. **ANTHROPOLOGY**

ALAN RICH, music critic of *New York* magazine, won an ASCAP Deems Taylor award for his book *Music, Mirror of the Arts*, published in 1969. **MUSIC, CLASSICAL**

JOHN RODERICK, foreign correspondent of The Associated Press, spent some years in China before the communist take-over and was one of the few correspondents allowed to enter China with the U.S. table tennis team in 1971. **COMMUNIST CHINA AFTER 22 YEARS**

ALBERT J. ROSENTHAL, professor of law at Columbia University, has made a special study of campaign spending. **CAMPAIGN SPENDING**

NORMAN ROTHSCHILD is senior editor of *Popular Photography* magazine. **PHOTOGRAPHY**

LOUIS RUKEYSER, news commentator and economic editor for the American Broadcasting Company, conducts a daily ABC radio program, "Rukeyser's Week," and is the host of a public-TV series, "Wall Street Week." **CONSUMER AFFAIRS, U.S.; TAXATION, U.S.**

DENNISON RUSINOW is associate for Yugoslavia, American Universities Field Staff. **YUGOSLAVIA**

DANIEL SCHORR, Washington correspondent of CBS News, wrote *Don't Get Sick in America,* based on an award-winning TV documentary.
HEALTH CARE

EUGENE L. SCOTT, a member of the 1963–65 Davis Cup team, has written on tennis for numerous publications. SPORTS: TENNIS

HENRY J. SELDIS, art critic of the *Los Angeles Times,* has served in a variety of posts as art director or consultant and is a regular contributor to art magazines and such newspapers as *The Christian Science Monitor.* His numerous catalogue prefaces include *Sculpture of Jack Zajac.*
ARTS

EUGENIA SHEPPARD writes a widely syndicated column on fashion and for such magazines as *Harper's Bazaar* and *Travel and Leisure.*
FASHION: DRESS OPTIONAL

SIR PHILIP SHERLOCK, secretary-general of the Association of Caribbean Universities, has written such books as *Short History of the West Indies* and *Land and People of the West Indies.*
CARIBBEAN ISLANDS

JOHN E. SHIELDS is editor of the *Congressional Digest.* INSURANCE, AUTO

HERMAN SINGER serves as editor of *East Europe* magazine. ALBANIA; BULGARIA; HUNGARY; RUMANIA

MARC SLONIM, professor emeritus of English, Sarah Lawrence College, has written widely on European literature. His many books include *The Epic of Russian Literature* and, as editor, *Modern Italian Short Stories.*
LITERATURE, NON-ENGLISH

JEANNETTE A. SMYTH is a reporter on the "style" staff of *The Washington Post.* WOMEN

WILLIAM SPENCER, professor of history at Florida State University, has written about and traveled extensively in North Africa and the Middle East.
ARAB STATES; IRAN; ISRAEL; TURKEY

RICHARD F. STAAR, associate director of the Hoover Institution on War, Revolution and Peace, is an authority on Eastern Europe affairs and edits the Hoover Press' *Yearbook on International Communist Affairs.*
CZECHOSLOVAKIA; POLAND

HARRY A. STARK serves as editor of Wards Automotive Reports, published in Detroit.
AUTOMOBILES

FRED B. STAUFFER was transportation editor of the former *New York Herald Tribune.*
RAILROADS

WILLIAM H. TAFT, professor of journalism at the University of Missouri, has written extensively about his field. Among his most recent works is *Newspapers as Tools for Historians.*
PUBLISHING

LAWRENCE E. TAYLOR is a Washington correspondent of the *St. Louis Post-Dispatch.*
MINE SAFETY

J. F. terHORST, chief of the Washington Bureau of *The Detroit News,* also writes a twice-weekly syndicated column for the North American Newspaper Alliance. UNITED STATES

JENNY TESAR is senior editor of *The Book of Popular Science* and the *Encyclopedia Science Supplement.*
BIOLOGICAL SCIENCES: OCEANOGRAPHY

JACK C. THOMPSON, professor of meteorology at San Jose (Calif.) State College, wrote *Elements of Meteorology* (with Albert Miller).
METEOROLOGY

JACK TWYMAN, former all-star player for the Cincinnati Royals basketball team, served as commentator on ABC's *NBA Game of the Week* during the 1970–71 season.
SPORTS: BASKETBALL

WOLF VON ECKARDT, author of *A Place to Live: The Crisis of the Cities,* is architecture critic of *The Washington Post.* ARCHITECTURE

WELDON WALLACE is religion editor of *The Sun* (Baltimore). RELIGION

JAMES WARGO serves as bureau chief in Detroit for McGraw-Hill World News.
VEHICLES, ALL-TERRAIN

GEOFFREY WHEELER is the editor of *Craft, Model & Hobby Industry,* published by Hobby Publications, Inc. HOBBIES

WAYNE WILCOX, professor and chairman (on leave) of the Department of Political Science at Columbia University, wrote, among other books, *Asia and United States Policy.* INDIA

JOHN S. WILSON reviews popular music and jazz for *The New York Times.* MUSIC, POPULAR

J. TUZO WILSON, principal of Erindale College of the University of Toronto is coauthor of *Physics and Geology;* in 1971 he made a scientific trip to mainland China. GEOLOGY

R. M. YOUNGER, former director of the Australian News and Information Bureau in New York City, wrote *Australia and the Australians.*
AUSTRALIA; NEW ZEALAND; OCEANIA

ILLUSTRATION JOHN A. LIND

TABLE OF CONTENTS

Pages 60-496 *Alphabetical Section*
(partial listing)

© Göksin Sipahioglu-Jocelyne Benzakin

Massed flags and hovering balloons, in October anniversary parade in Peking's Tienamen Square, are enjoyed by relaxed soldiers.

Table-tennis match with U.S. team was held in Peking's sports stadium before 18,000 spectators.

Frank Fischbeck, "Life" magazine © Time Inc.

ENCYCLOPEDIA YEAR BOOK FEATURE:

COMMUNIST CHINA AFTER 22 YEARS

by John Roderick

Foreign Correspondent, Tokyo Bureau

The Associated Press

© Göksin Sipahioglu-Jocelyne Benzakin

Serious school tots, each one clutching a little red book of Communist Party Chairman Mao's thoughts, recite in unison from the works of their country's leader.

For practically the first time since 1949, Western visitors were allowed to see the Great Wall in 1971.

© Göksin Sipahioglu-Jocelyne Benzakin

The Chinese have a saying that a journey of 10,000 li begins with a single step. I took that step in April 1971, returning to China after an absence of a little more than 22 years. It was no ordinary journey. Taken in conjunction with the visit of the U.S. table-tennis team to mainland China, it marked a breakthrough in long-hostile U.S.-China relations. We were the first ordinary Americans invited to the People's Republic since it was established in 1949.

In Peking, Chinese Premier Chou En-lai wrung my hand and said, "Welcome back to China. It's been a long time." Later, speaking to the assembled table-tennis players and journalists in the Great Hall of the People, he said: "Mr. Roderick, you opened the door."

That door, which had been slammed so firmly in American faces two decades before, now opened a few inches to let in a trickle of newsmen, students, scientists and intellectuals.

Then, in mid-July, the incredible happened. Henry Kissinger, President Richard Nixon's chief aide for national security affairs, made a secret trip to the Communist Chinese capital. When he returned, Nixon and Chou jointly announced that the American chief executive would be going to Peking sometime before May 1972 to discuss "normalization of relations" and other subjects of concern to both countries.

Textiles (l) are most important light industry; China is world's largest cotton exporter. Women workers are now almost as common in heavy industry (below, turning steel parts on a lathe) as in light. Slogan on Mao poster above means: "The working class must take the leadership in everything." Chinese theater and opera have long been famous; today they are major propaganda instruments as in a modern revolutionary dance drama "Red Detachment of Women" (upper r). Modern surgery has a place in health care (lower r).

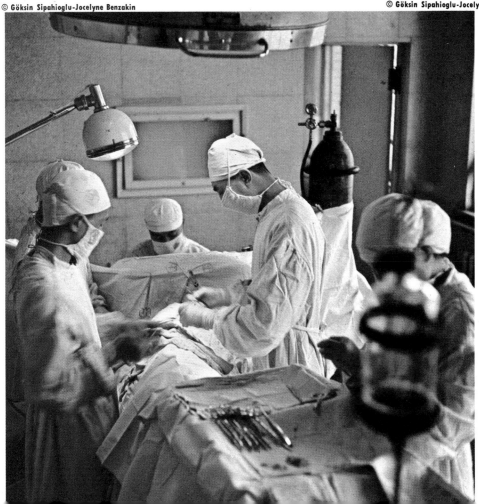

15

Traditional crafts, such as exquisitely painted pottery, are still carried on, but only in Peking. Strictly for export, the lovely wares are rarely seen by the Chinese people; domestic pottery is utterly utilitarian.

Although small gas-driven cultivators are beginning to appear in the rice fields, traditional, painstaking hand cultivation remains the general rule. As a view of a commune near Canton indicates, the riceland of southern China is still richly productive.

© Göksin Sipahioglu-Jocelyne Benzakin

Frank Fischbeck, "Life" magazine © Time Inc.

The Nixon initiative was hailed in many quarters as a significant move toward peace in the Pacific; the more cautious warned that the grapes could turn to ashes in the mouth. The critics feared its impact on Chiang Kai-shek's Republic of China on Taiwan. Their anxieties were justified. Late in the night of Oct. 25, the General Assembly of the United Nations voted by a crushing 76-35 margin (with 17 abstentions) to oust Taiwan from all organs of that international body and to seat the People's Republic instead. Peking's "Ping-Pong diplomacy" had paid off in rich dividends.

From 1945 through 1948 I was a foreign correspondent in China. A month after establishing myself in the wartime capital, Chungking, I received a rare assignment: Yenan. Yenan, in northwest China, was the capital of the Chinese Communists. It lies near the edge of the Gobi, the vast desert, and camel caravans plodded through it like sedate land ships en route to Mongolia and North China. The Communists had reached Yenan in 1935 after a terrible 6,000-mile retreat from the Chinese east-coast province of Kiangsi, a withdrawal carried out under the pounding guns of Chiang Kai-shek's Nationalist armies. Of the 100,000 men, women and children who had set out, on what now is known as the Long March, scarcely more than 30,000 survived.

In the years that followed, Yenan became a city of mystery, blockaded from the outside world by Nationalist troops. It had been visited by American reporters only once before. For six months I lived in one of the 10,000 caves that made up Yenan. During that time I met, interviewed and got to know the men and women who now rule China.

Yenan was a point in time, the halting place on the road to a future only dimly perceived. The Communists who inhabited it were united in a common objective; the conquest, peacefully or otherwise, of all China. They had endured suffering, privation, hunger and disappointment to reach their position as the second most powerful force in China. Their life was austere. Their morale was high. And they were drawn together by their shared goal. Mao Tsetung, a peasant's son who had led the Communists to Yenan, strove over the years to keep the guerrilla spirit of that time alive.

I found widespread evidence of that mood wherever I went in 1971. It seemed to me that in many ways China was a vast extension of the Yenan of 1945-47. From the Hong Kong border to Canton, Peking, Shanghai and back, I was reminded of the distant, former communist capital. There were the same enthusiasms, the same dedication to hard work, the same austerity, the same Spartan way of life, and the same apparent confidence in the future. And like the Yenan of a quarter century earlier, there were smiles and words of friendship for Americans. Wherever I went the words echoed in my ears: *Meiguo ren, hao, hun hao* (Americans are good, very good).

It had taken a long time for the wheel to come full circle. But that it has done so seems beyond question. Peking is now the capital of all China; Yenan is a cherished memory. Peking is a city of ancient palaces, graceful pagodas and tile-roofed temples.

Mao, Premier Chou En-lai and the members of Chou's Government live and work behind the high crimson walls of the old Forbidden City, once the home of China's emperors. The Communists show none of the imperial love of display but are aware of the value of symbolism. For centuries the Chinese masses have turned their eyes toward this center of power. Today, instead of emperors there is Mao, China's proletarian ruler in a cotton tunic.

Wherever I went in Peking I saw the round face of Mao smiling down from enormous paintings on the sides of buildings, dominating railroad stations, airport terminals, even whole mountainsides. Heroic-size statues, in white plaster, of Mao welcome the visitor in hotel lobbies and the entrances to public buildings.

Why this cult of the individual? The answer is that during the 1966-69 Great Proletarian Cultural Revolution, Mao relied almost totally on his immense prestige as a weapon to bludgeon his enemies. The then President, Liu Shao-chi, and his followers controlled nearly every mass organization, including the Government, the Army and the Communist Party.

But in April 1971 there were signs that the Mao cult was abating. In my Canton hotel room I noted two nails on the wall, and a German businessman told me they had once carried portraits of Mao. In the recreation hall on the top floor the outline of missing Mao cameos could be seen on the red canopies over the billiard tables. In the downstairs dining room, paintings turned to the wall proved to be of Mao. Mao himself subsequently told a Western newsman that he felt the need had passed for such enormous personal public exposure. The return of a more normal way of life in China following the excesses of the cultural purge may mean that the leadership cult is on the way out. The day could well come when Mao will be one among equals rather than raised above his political associates and venerated, as he has been for years, as a demigod.

The Peking of 1971 had a purposeful air, in contrast with the easy anarchy of 1947 when I lived on Ta Tien Shui Ching (the Lane of the Great Sweet Water Well) for a year. The city is laid out in straight lines in a grid pattern. Wide boulevards run east and west, north and south. Today the pattern appears to have become a part of men's lives. The doctrines of Mao, and of Chinese communism, demand that the people take the shortest and straightest course to their work or schools. They do not meander on the way as they did in the past.

In Mao's China, conformity is the most cherished virtue; individuality is a dirty word. The Chinese told me that without teamwork nothing could be accomplished in a nation that must keep 750,000,000 people alive each day. Anyone who decides to defy the mass and move against the human tide is branded a pariah. The Chinese frontiers have already been reached. There is no room for the sturdy adventurer in search of a personal fortune. The goal is survival, not private wealth.

I revisited the Summer Palace, a few miles outside Peking, which was favored by the old Empress Dowager, Tzu Hsi (1835-1908), whose ruthless rule earned her the nickname, the Old Buddha. She often went there to escape the summer heat among its graceful pavilions and airy rooms. Once when she wished to carry out extensive repairs, she appropriated money earmarked for the Imperial Navy. Anticipating public criticism, she ordered a huge and immovable marble boat built which she had placed on the banks of the big artificial lake. Thousands of ordinary Chinese spend their leisure hours at the Summer Palace today. In the hot weather they often plunge into the cool waters of the lake.

Under Mao, the palace has been turned into a museum of recent Chinese history. The exploits of the Red Guards and of the Liberation Army are depicted in the pavilions, lending them a startling air of contemporaneity. The inevitable portraits and statues of Mao are encountered at every turn. Yet the overall impression has not been damaged. The palace retains its air of park and pleasure garden.

The combination of ancient art and present-day propaganda seen in the Summer Palace reflects Mao's ideas of culture. As a classical poet, calligrapher and historian, he is interested in preserving the old arts and works of literature. But as chairman of the Communist Party and a theoretical Marxist, he sees the need to educate all China's people rather than a literate few. So he has decreed that there can be no art for art's sake. All culture must communicate with the peasant and the worker. It must teach a lesson. It must instill love for, and loyalty to, the new state of affairs.

For the Communists, the Chinese worker-peasant is a simple man. He cannot understand complicated themes. Abstract ideas are lost on him. In order to reach him, Chinese writers and artists must speak his language, understand how he thinks and talks. For this reason, I was told, Mao has ordered writers and artists to "learn from the people," to serve an apprenticeship working on farms or in factories.

The idea has its merits. Both Western and Oriental literature have profited from efforts to speak the popular tongue and portray life realistically. But the Chinese today do not recognize the validity of any art that does not point a moral, teach a lesson or fulfill the demands of propaganda. The result is banality. China's modern art is little better than poster art, complete with slogans. Its theater is reminiscent of medieval English morality plays. Villains are pure Evil, heroes are untarnished Good. There is no room for subtlety, once a Chinese virtue. Madame Mao, the moving force in present-day Chinese culture, speaks of "revolutionary romanticism." It is a phrase that recalls both the good and the bad in modern political violence.

Education is undergoing drastic change. Many years ago, Chinese students would not deign to soil their hands. They studied the gentlemanly arts: literature, philosophy, economics, history. Mechanics and engineers were in desperately short supply. In the first twenty years of the People's Republic, the educational system wavered between the philosophical and the practical.

Since the end of the Cultural Revolution, the emphasis has been almost entirely on the practical. I visited Tsinghua University, which had reopened its doors only six months earlier. Like all the schools of China, it had been closed during the three years of the cultural purge. There are only 2,800 students there now compared with 15,000 before the Cultural Revolution began. Those admitted take no entrance examinations. Graduates of middle schools, they have worked for a time in the fields and factories and were chosen by their coworkers. Party committees certify their loyalty to Mao.

Instead of spending four or five years in college they now take two years, and only a third of this time is spent in the classroom. The rest goes toward building factories and laboratories.

China has a long way to go economically, and it needs all the skilled labor and engineers it can get. Philosophy is expendable. The only kind encouraged is Marxism-Leninism-Maoism. To be accurate, Maoism should perhaps be listed first.

One of the things that struck me in today's China was the unisex look. Men and women dress alike, in trousers and jackets. There were few differences. The men wore their hair cut short; the women sometimes braided theirs in twin pigtails tied at the back with bits of colored yarn. There were no smart shops displaying styles a non-Chinese woman might wear.

With time all this could change. Since turning a smiling face to the outside, China has made some hesitant steps toward providing its people with more attractive and original clothes. However, it is only the smallest beginning.

If life is less colorful than it was 25 years ago, it also appears to be more balanced. In the 1940's, existence in China was precarious. The poor were at the mercy of illness, joblessness, and natural calamities which left floods, shattered homes and famine in their wake. Countless millions of Chinese died in disasters before the People's Republic was established in 1949. Death and illness were private matters, of no public concern. I often saw Chinese dead or dying in the streets a quarter century ago, ignored by passersby. To have extended a helping hand would have increased their own terrible burden.

In the cities this time—Shanghai, Canton and Peking—there were no beggars or dead and dying. The people appeared healthy and energetic. The threat of famine appears to have been brought under control. Large reserves of grain are maintained for emergencies; when a disaster occurs, the stored food is moved to the stricken areas. Public ownership, a stake in the fate of the poor, and better communication systems have contributed to the fight against starvation, once the scourge of China.

Perhaps most astonishing of all was that the three big cities I visited were all spotlessly clean. There were no flies, no dogs, no cats and no rubbish. All this is a consequence of Chinese belief in preventive medicine. In the past, epidemics produced by accumulated filth and bad hygiene were common. To eliminate them the new China makes almost a fetish of cleanliness.

How does it get the masses to carry out its orders? The answer: organization. Chinese cities are run by citizen committees at the street and neighborhood level. The committees are responsible for keeping their areas tidy, watching out for criminals, political or otherwise, and reporting strangers.

What impressed me most about China revisited? It was the leveling of society. In the old days, China had its very poor, its poor, its small middle class, its intellectuals and its very rich. Today the very poor, the middle class and the very rich have disappeared. Instead there are the poor, the intellectuals and the bureaucrats. In the past the intellectuals and bureaucrats might be comfortably well-off. Today they are on a level with the poor. In China no one eats much better than the other fellow. Each person wears about the same kind of clothing, replaceable twice a year, in winter and summer. Houses or apartments are modest and barely furnished. Luxury is nonexistent.

Yet this is beginning to change, ever so slowly. The status symbol is a bicycle. I saw thousands of shiny new ones on the streets. But it will be a long, long time before the average Chinese ponders having one or two automobiles in his garage.

When the U.S. table-tennis team met with Chou En-lai in the Great Hall of the People on Apr. 14, 1971, there still was some doubt about the official attitude of the Government toward the United States. Chou dispelled it in a sentence. A new page, he said, has been turned in U.S.-China relations.

Chou is the man perhaps most responsible for this unexpected *rapprochement* with China's bitterest enemy. I first met him in Chungking in 1945 and on many other occasions afterward in Yenan, Nanking and Shanghai. The Chou of 1971 was 73. He had a few deeper lines on his face; his hair was touched with gray; and he carried one arm at an angle as the result of an old illness. But he was as bouncy, personable and charismatic as ever.

The son of a mandarin family, he might in earlier times have gone on to take the imperial examinations and spend his life at court. But the days of his youth were not ordinary. The Emperor had been overthrown, and nationalism was emerging. The young Chou, handsome and willowy—he had played female roles in the Peking Opera—joined the Nationalists, spent a year in prison, then went to France to study the ways of the West. There he became a Communist. Returning, he was named by Chiang Kai-shek, then commanding the joint Nationalist-Communist military forces seeking to unite the country, to soften up Shanghai for attack. Chou had never talked to workers, but within weeks he organized the 800,000 Shanghai "proletariat" into a powerful force. He obtained arms for a handful of them who seized the police stations, the military barracks and the arsenals. The warlord governor fled. Chiang's army walked in unopposed.

Within a month, however, Chiang had put a price on Chou's head. The Generalissimo, seeking more money for his northward advance, made a deal with Shanghai's bankers and industrialists: in exchange for a break with the Communists, they would give him the financial backing he needed. Thousands were killed in the bloodbath that followed.

Chou has been premier since 1949, once was concurrently foreign minister. He is regarded as one of the world's leading diplomats. His reputation for moderation springs from the fact that he prefers negotiation to confrontation.

China's man for all seasons, he was the mediator in the Cultural Revolution, seeking to prevent the antagonists from indulging in excesses. When it ended, he took the initiative to restore China's diplomatic image abroad. He sent ambassadors back to the posts from which they had been withdrawn, and made overtures to both the West and the communist bloc. Finally, backed by the Army, he introduced "Ping-Pong diplomacy."

ENCYCLOPEDIA YEAR BOOK FEATURE:

THE RIGHT TO PRIVACY

by U.S. Senator Sam J. Ervin, Jr.
Chairman
Subcommittee on Constitutional Rights

"The right to one's person," said Justice Thomas M. Cooley of the Michigan Supreme Court in 1878, "may be said to be a right to be let alone." This idea was echoed half a century later by U.S. Supreme Court Justice Louis D. Brandeis in the famous *Olmstead* case:

> "The makers of our Constitution undertook to secure conditions favorable to the pursuit of happiness. They recognized the significance of man's spiritual nature, of his feelings and of his intellect. They knew that only a part of the pain, pleasure and satisfaction of life is to be found in material things. They sought to protect Americans in their beliefs, their thoughts, their emotions and their sensations. They conferred, as against the Government, the right to be let alone—the most comprehensive of rights and the right most valued by civilized man."

As these statements suggest, the rights and liberties we have long recognized as inherent in the idea of individual freedom may also be regarded as aspects of a fundamental human "right of privacy." Indeed, the Supreme Court, in the 1964 case of *Griswold* v. *Connecticut,* declared that the right to privacy is a constitutional right. The court said that the rights incorporated in the Constitution demonstrate that the Founding Fathers recognized the importance of individual privacy and sought to protect it from government intrusion. Among the specific constitutional safeguards that serve to protect privacy are freedom of speech, of the press, of conscience, of thought, of belief, of association and assembly, and the right to petition government for redress of grievances (First Amendment); the right not to have troops quartered in private homes (Third Amendment); the right to be secure in one's home and personal effects, and the freedom from unreasonable searches (Fourth Amendment); and the privilege against self-incrimination, and the right to due process of law (Fifth Amendment).

Although these individual rights have long been part of our heritage, recognition of privacy as a separate and distinct right is of relatively recent origin. This is largely because the technology and changing social patterns of the twentieth century have had a great impact on the way we live our lives and have made us more conscious of the privacy that we used to take for granted. Now there are psychological tests to find out what we are like; wiretaps, electronic bugs, and other technological marvels to find out what we are saying; and lie detectors to discover whether we are telling the truth. No-knock laws and fire, health and welfare inspectors invade our homes without notice or

Senator Ervin displays a two-inch square of microfilm that he said had 773,746 words on it, the same number as in the 1,245-page Bible in front of him.

warning. Questionnaires seek to discover what we are, what we have done, and what we think. Sensitivity sessions try to change the kind of people we are. Insurance companies, credit bureaus and retailers learn all about us, our finances and our family life. Government agents, local, state, Federal and even military, keep watch over our public activities—and sometimes our private, personal affairs—taking note of what we say, whom we meet, and what we think. Millions of dollars are involved in preparing and selling mailing lists which bombard our homes with tons of unwanted mail. Polling companies, marketing researchers and political groups visit our door and call us on the phone. The social-security number, once confidential, is now becoming a universal identifying number—no less a part of us than our name, address, telephone number, and date of birth—and we cannot get a driver's license, go to school, pay our taxes, get a job, serve in the Army, buy a car, or even get our poodle clipped without giving our number.

More and more, business and government display an eagerness to get all the facts on each of us, to record those facts, and then to make decisions that affect ourselves, our families, our livelihood, and our very way of life. Perhaps the most significant new factor modern man's desire for privacy must cope with is the computer. For while our privacy would still be endangered without this new miracle of technology, the computer has brought with it a host of new problems. The computer permits the storage, production and transmission of virtually unlimited amounts of information about people. The same wonderful invention that guides astronauts across hundreds of thousands of miles, lands them on the moon, and then returns them safely home, all the while collecting, storing, analyzing and communicating millions upon millions of pieces of information with split-second speed—that same computer can do the same thing with information about every man, woman and child in the United States. It has been estimated that a mere few hundred reels of magnetic tape, not unlike the magnetic tape used in home tape recorders, would serve to store information on every man, woman and child in the country. While it is highly unlikely that we will see one universal, master computer brain, the past decade has seen the creation or the planning of hundreds of computerized data banks containing personal information about individuals. Singly and totally, these data banks pose serious dangers to our personal privacy.

It has been estimated that the names of Americans are recorded 2,800,000,000 times in files kept by the Federal Government. Social-security numbers are listed 1,500,000,000 times. Police have 264,000,000 records on people. Federal and state officials have or have access to 323,000,000 medical records, and 279,000,000 psychiatric histories. Among the individual files and data banks maintained by the Federal Government are the following:

- A Secret Service computerized data bank containing 100,000 names and 50,000 dossiers of persons who "might" be a danger to the president. Included are persons who seek redress for "imaginary grievances," those who have "embarrassed" high officials, and those who have participated in "antigovernment" or "anti-U.S." demonstrations. None of the terms in quotations is defined, and the criteria for including a person's name are extremely vague.
- A Health, Education, and Welfare Department-sponsored computer data bank containing the school records and other personal information of 300,000 children of migrant workers.
- A National Driver Register computer containing information on 3,000,000 citizens who have had their licenses revoked or suspended.
- A "lookout" file in the Passport Office of the State Department containing 250,000 names, including 2,000 "runaway fathers" said to be involved in custody or desertion proceedings.
- A collection of 2,120,000 index cards held by the U.S. Civil Service Commission dealing with the political activity of individual American citizens. The commission also maintains 10,250,000 cards covering investigations of persons who have worked or applied for work with the Federal Government since 1939, as well as 625,000 current investigative reports and 2,100,000 noncurrent investigative files.
- A file in the Department of Housing and Urban Development with 325,000 cards containing information on individuals who have made FHA loan applications.

The foregoing is only a small sample of the Federal data banks in existence. It does not include files in the Census, the Federal Bureau of Investigation, the Internal Revenue Service, the Department of Defense and many other Federal agencies. In addition, state and local governments maintain uncounted files with information about taxes, education, dog licenses, motor-vehicle records, parking violations, marriages, births and deaths, employment, housing and almost any facet of human activity one can think of, and probably quite a few one wouldn't think of. The amount of information held by government on the citizens of this country is truly staggering, and more and more of these records are going on computers.

With a few exceptions, each of these data banks serves an important and often even an essential public purpose. Either they help to prevent or punish wrongs against society, or they enable government to perform beneficial services. Obviously, it would be difficult if not impossible to control crime if criminal records were not kept. And it would be difficult if not impossible to educate the children of migrant agricultural workers if the records of their schooling were not available to the new teachers they have as the family moves from community to community and job to job.

The choice, however, is not whether we accept these infringements on privacy totally and uncritically, or reject and eliminate them out of hand. We need not be like the Luddites, who viewed machines as the work of the devil and sought to destroy them. Instead, we must try to draw a fine line between need and abuse, between efficiency and liberty. For example, no one can quarrel with the need of local, state and Federal officials to prepare for civil disturbances and riots. Nor can one take issue with the need of the Army to be prepared to restore order if local officials cannot handle the situation. But this does not and should not justify permitting the Army to put thousands of citizens and churches, schools and private homes under surveillance. The peaceful political and social activity of Americans should not interest the Army. They should not be permitted to list as "subversive," "communist," "dissident" or "un-American" any person who happens to voice an opinion the Army finds distasteful, irritating or uncomfortable.

When the effort to guard against illegal activity expands to include surveillance of peaceful and legal political activity, then we run the risk of suppressing freedom and the individual's right to be free of government control over the mind. Such surveillance poses a mortal threat to every American's constitutional birthright to say what he likes, to criticize his government and to work for peaceful change. These rights—freedom of speech, of conscience, of thought and of association—must be preserved, even when it is displeasing to the Army and even when it is displeasing to a majority of Americans. The Constitution grants these rights to the wise and the foolish, the weak and the brave, the devout and the ungodly, and even to those who hate our country no less than to those who love it. Computers and data banks that gather, store and transmit what we say and do pose one of the greatest dangers to liberty and to the privacy of one's thoughts and beliefs. They must be carefully controlled and monitored so that we do not unthinkingly create a thought police that listens to our every thought and word.

There are also dangers in the other kinds of computers and data banks that are now being developed. Computer systems that contain the medical records of individuals pose the danger that untold numbers of people can, by pushing a button, learn all about our medical history and all the other personal and intimate facts that in simpler days were known only to our family physician. Our children's school records, which, in the days before computers, were known only to the principal and a few teachers, now are being put into computers that have a permanent record available to anyone who can use that computer. Our tax records, now on computers at the Federal level and in many states and localities, contain complete facts on our financial situation. They contain not only what we earn and spend but also many details of the financial transactions we have engaged in. Unfortunately, in each of these cases, the rules against unauthorized access or disclosure are not adequate to protect our privacy.

The increasing collection and computerization of information about individuals raises the specter of a "goldfish-bowl society." Everything we have ever done, all records about us, from birth to death, might be on computers. It would be possible to reconstruct a complete picture of any one of us from the records and facts we leave in our wake. Such a dossier society, even if it did not result in a terrible political tyranny, would certainly be a confining, unpleasant one in which to live. We would be judged not by what we are but by what the records show us to be. We would never escape our past. It would follow us inexorably in the form of computer memories that never forget. We could never do or say anything without knowing that it might be recorded in a computer for all time.

Although only a few experts see this "1984 society" as a real possibility, almost all people concerned about privacy agree that computers pose significant dangers to privacy. Errors that appear in computers are much more serious than mistakes in old-fashioned paper files. The improper listing of a citizen in a "security" or "criminal" computer can destroy his career and his reputation forever. The inclusion of irrelevant, inaccurate or incomplete data in a computer can mean loss of a job, or credit, or insurance, or a driver's license, or a government benefit. Very personal information, once on a computer, can be available to thousands of people who have no business knowing the intimate details of our lives. Because the computer can store more information, keep it indefinitely, and transmit it at the push of a button, the careless collection and distribution of information about individuals is a luxury we can no longer afford. We now run the risk that thousands and even millions of citizens will lose their right to life, liberty and the pursuit of happiness because their lives have literally become an open book.

It is often said that a person who has nothing to hide should not be concerned about invasions of his privacy. This is easy to say when it concerns another person. But nobody likes to have his personal affairs revealed for all the world to see. Everyone does or says things that can look very different in the cold light of day or when written down on paper. Sometimes the most innocent behavior seems sinister when reported on a government form and taken out of context. Even facts that are entirely innocent or inconsequential can take on added meaning and have unforeseen effects. When someone is refused credit because the computer says he has not paid a bill even though he actually has, or when he is refused insurance because of a neighbor's malicious gossip, or when a mix-up in identity results in a brush with the law that remains in the files years after and results in his losing a job, it is no consolation to tell him that he has nothing to hide and therefore should not worry about his privacy.

To guard against these dangers, we need strict laws at all levels of government and in private industry limiting the kinds and amounts of information that may be collected and stored. These laws should restrict the agency to only that information it truly needs for performing its function. We must take steps to ensure that the information is accurate, and that it is up-to-date. Equally important, we must make certain that old, useless or outdated information is removed, so that decisions about us are based on what we are, not on what we used to be. Every person should have the right to know exactly what information the agency has about him. If it is incorrect or incomplete, the individual should have the right to have it corrected or removed. If it is prejudicial or gives an inaccurate impression of the true story, the individual should have the right to explain the situation. Laws are needed to restrict the right of access to information about citizens to a very few officials. We cannot permit this information to become known to hundreds or thousands of government officials and bureaucrats.

Congress has already taken a first step toward controlling private data banks run by credit-bureau companies. Under a new law, every individual has a right to be told what information a credit company has about him, and if he has been refused credit, why. This is an important step toward ensuring that these companies do not gain absolute and arbitrary power over the economic existence of American citizens. Legislation has also been suggested to restrict the use of lie detectors, to prevent the sale by the government and otherwise restrict the use of mailing lists, and to limit the use of wiretaps, bugs and other kinds of electronic surveillance. Indiscriminate use of psychological testing, sensitivity training, and government questionnaires are other invasions of privacy that have attracted Congressional concern. Similar efforts are being made at the state and local level to deal with some of these problems. And, gradually, public officials and private citizens are beginning to grapple with the complex problem of controlling computers so that they do not turn into more of a curse than a blessing.

From the perspective of 1971, it sometimes appears that, as one observer has already put it, we will soon see the "death of privacy." Certainly, we will have to tolerate a lessening of our traditional notions of privacy as America becomes more crowded and more complex. Yet the future need not be as bleak as some have painted it. A greater appreciation of the dangers to privacy on the part of American citizens is the key to ensuring that the right to be left alone remains secure in the years ahead.

ENCYCLOPEDIA YEAR BOOK FEATURE:

HEALTH CARE

by Daniel Schorr
Washington Correspondent, CBS News
Author, *Don't Get Sick in America*

In 1971, health care was the third largest industry in the United States, with an estimated gross of $78,000,000,000, employing about one out of every twenty working Americans. It was also the nation's most inflationary industry, its prices rising twice as fast as the general cost of living, 60 per cent of its growth in a decade representing swollen costs. In Phase 2 of President Nixon's stabilization program, it was the only industry to rate a special watchdog committee.

To grapple with its complex problems, piecemeal or wholesale, more than 2,000 bills were introduced in the first session of the 92nd Congress. It was the only industry that political analysts scanned as having such a profound impact on the body politic as to loom as a 1972 presidential-campaign issue. Yet, most Americans are surprised to hear it called an industry at all. It is what used to be called "the healing arts."

What President Nixon called the "massive crisis" in health care has been developing for years: shortages and maldistribution of professionals, inefficient cost-plus hospitals, fragmented services, expensive new technology, hospital-canted private insurance, Medicare and Medicaid billions chasing scarce services in an upward spiral.

By 1971 the crisis was full-blown, acknowledged in a dozen books, in television documentaries, Congressional hearings, presidential messages and position papers for presidential candidates. They all centered on two main issues: broader new financing of health care and, because money alone has been found to contribute more to the problem than to the solution, the need for fundamental changes in the organization and delivery of medical services.

Less at issue was medical science, although the supporters of research complained that the quest for new breakthroughs was being shortchanged in tight budgets. There was also the question of how research should be organized: for example, should the conquest of cancer be pursued through an independent "crash" program, as the "cancer lobby" urged, or through the traditional National Institutes of Health, as the NIH-dependent "medical school lobby" urged?In July 1971 the Senate passed a bill establishing an independent cancer-research agency, connected in little but name with NIH. Four months later, a bill passed by the House of Representatives called for spending $1,600,000,000 in cancer research by 1974. The House bill tied such research to NIH. Commenting on a compromise bill agreed to by a Senate-House conference committee, Rep. Paul G. Rogers (D-Fla.) said: "The basic principles of the House bill did come out intact, including maintaining the integrity of the NIH."

However, the greater issue was not the flower of medical science but the marketing of its fruits. Millions of Americans—the poor and increasingly the middle class—complained of difficulty in finding convenient, personal, effective care at prices they could afford. The symptoms of the crisis were rural counties and urban ghettoes whose doctors had fled to greater rewards, of mothers who could not get attention for their children in emergencies, of rising insurance premiums and ruinous hospital bills.

What many Americans knew from their experience the statistics tended to confirm, that America was not getting adequate health care although spending, in absolute figures and relatively, a bigger slice of its national income and a larger amount per capita than any other advanced country. The statistics went like this: Between 1950 and 1970 health-care expenditures rose more than 5 times, from $12,100,000,000 to $67,200,000,000, from 4.6 to 6.9 per cent of the gross national product. The average person's health bill rose from $79 to $324 a year. Yet the end was not in sight. The Social Security Administration estimated that by 1974, with no change in the law, the cost would reach $105,400,-000,000.

Yet international statistics, though they reflect many factors apart from the state of medical care, displayed the world's wealthiest nation as being far from the healthiest. In 1969 the United States ranked 14th among industrial nations in infant mortality, with 20.7 deaths per 1,000 births. (In 1970, according to preliminary figures, the rate went below 20 per 1,000.) In life expectancy for males, the United States ranked 18th in 1968. At 66.8 years, life expectancy of the average white American male was 5 years shorter than that of the average Swedish male. In life expectancy for white females (73.7 years) the United States ranked 11th.

The statistics also displayed the inequality of health care in America. Infant-death rates for minorities were 80 per cent higher in 1969 (32.3 per 1,000) than for whites (18.8). The poor were consistently sicker than the nonpoor. Those with incomes under $3,000 a year were 4 times as likely as those in the over-$10,000 bracket to have chronic conditions limiting their activity. Days of disability because of illness or accident were 50 per cent higher for the poor than the nonpoor. Although more likely to be sick, the poor were not much more likely to see a doctor. The lowest-income category averaged 4.6 physician visits a year; in other income groups it ranged from 4.1 to 4.6. And for the poor, doctor visits were more likely to be for acute illness, less often for preventive care.

Through Medicare for the aging and Medicaid for the poor, the Government had tried, starting in 1966, to provide for the most vulnerable segments of the population. But with a legislated taboo against intervening in the pattern of delivery of services, the result was to increase the pressures and send costs spurting upward. Between 1966 and 1970 the public share of the health-care dollar rose from 26 cents to 37 cents, the spending from $7,900,000,000 to $20,500,000,000. In 1970 the Federal Government was spending $6,800,000,000 for Medicare, paying about two thirds of the health bill of the aging, and $3,300,000,000 in matching funds for state-operated Medicaid programs. The higher prices that these programs helped to generate returned to plague the programs—and their beneficiaries. Starting in January 1972, a senior citizen must pay the first $68 of his hospital bill instead of $40, as in 1966. Combined Federal-state expenditures for Medicaid rose 20 per cent between 1969 and

Edward M. Kennedy
U.S. Senator (D-Mass.)

Elliot Richardson
Nixon administration

Dr. Ernest B. Howard
American Medical Assoc.

In brief outline, the main proposals for a national health-insurance system were:

The Health Security Bill (Kennedy, labor). A government-operated insurance system would pay almost all hospital and medical bills for all Americans from the cradle to the grave. It would cover physician and institutional services without limit, and, with some limitation, dental care, drugs, nursing-home and private psychiatric care. The financing would come partly from the Treasury and partly from an increase in the Social Security tax. It would enforce specific cost controls on a regional basis and would provide specific incentives for the creation of organized medical groups.

The National Health Insurance Partnership Bill (Nixon administration). A three-part plan whose principal component would require employers to provide all employees and their families with specified benefits, including physician services, hospitalization and protection against catastrophic medical costs. Employers would eventually pay 75 per cent of the premiums. The plan would be administered by private insurance companies under state regulation. The second part would be a Family Health Insurance Plan for the poor, largely replacing Medicaid, financed from tax revenues, with more limited benefits than for the employed, and a sliding scale of beneficiary contributions—free only at the lowest end. The third element would be a vaguely defined "insurance pool," making available policies at group rates to individuals not covered by the other two plans.

1970, reaching $5,600,000,000 and accelerating the drive to cut back eligibility and benefits. At its peak Medicaid reached only about 12,000,000 of the poor and near-poor, little more than a quarter of its target population of 40,000,000.

As Medicare raised its deductibles and Medicaid cut its benefits, the question arose of why medical services were not keeping pace with requirements. The Carnegie Commission on Higher Education reported: "The United States today faces only one serious manpower shortage, and that is in health care personnel." In 1970, according to the U.S. Public Health Service, there was a shortage of nearly 500,000 persons, including physicians, osteopaths, dentists, nurses, optometrists, veterinarians, pharmacists and allied health professionals. The service estimated that the shortage could increase to 725,000 by 1980.

Sen. Edward M. Kennedy (D-Mass.) charged that it was the fault of the American Medical Association, which, "long after the doctor shortage was clear to every impartial expert, obstinately maintained that there was no shortage at all." The AMA admitted that, in the 1950's, it had miscalculated expanding needs, but said that it was "presently engaged on a broad front in expanding the supply of physicians and other key health personnel." It noted

UPI

**Leslie Hemry, Health
Insurance Assoc. of America**

**Dr. Edwin L. Crosby
American Hospital Assoc.**

**Jacob Javits
U.S. Senator (R-N.Y.)**

The Health Care Insurance Bill (Medicredit, AMA). The Federal Government would finance insurance premiums for the poor from tax revenues and allow income-tax credits for all others toward purchase of private insurance—the lower the income, the larger the credit. Benefits would include sixty days of hospitalization, all emergency and outpatient services, all physician services, drugs, psychiatric and physical therapy.

The National Health Care Bill (insurance industry). A system of health insurance through private companies, financed by direct payments, income-tax deductions and government contributions. Medicare and Medicaid would be retained, but the poor not covered by these Federal plans would be covered by state-assigned risk pools.

Ameriplan (American Hospital Association). Health-care corporations would be created, each to supervise a specific area, together overseeing health-care delivery for the area's entire population. There would be two basic benefit packages: health maintenance for short-term care, and catastrophic-illness benefits for chronic and long-term illness.

National Health Insurance and Health Services Improvement Bill (Sen. Jacob Javits, R-N.Y.). Basically, would expand Medicare, step by step, to include the entire population. Subscribers could use private or employer plans. Insurance would be financed through employer-employee contributions and through general tax revenues.

an improvement in the doctor-patient ratio from 1-to-712 in 1960 to 1-to-632 in 1970. This, though, had to be qualified by the dwindling proportion who remain in family practice and by the trend toward high urban concentration.

But beyond expanding the ranks of health professionals there was a more basic problem, summed up in *The Washington Post* by Alice M. Rivlin, on leave from the Brookings Institution: "The basic trouble is that everyone—doctors, hospital administrators, insurance executives—are caught in a system which they are individually powerless to alter, and that system has a whole web of perverse incentives built into it. It offers doctors irresistible monetary rewards for practicing in the suburbs rather than in the ghetto and for entering specialization rather than practicing family medicine. The fact that most people have hospital insurance rather than more comprehensive coverage encourages overuse of hospitals and emphasizes treatment rather than prevention of disease. The rules under which insurance companies and governments reimburse suppliers of medical services give the latter little or no incentive to hold costs down. The whole system is just too badly designed to deliver good care efficiently to those who need it."

31

The U.S. Government took steps in 1971 to set limits on the doctors' fees and hospital costs that it will reimburse, and it took one step toward redesign of the system of health care through its espousal of the Health Maintenance Organization (HMO). Previously called "prepaid group practice," it is based on a patient's annual contract with an organized medical group to receive a full range of health services. It is aimed at reversing the traditional incentive pattern, rewarding preventive care, efficient use of resources and a low rate of hospitalization. The oldest and biggest organization in the field is the Kaiser Foundation of California, going back more than thirty years to when industrialist Henry J. Kaiser offered to look after the health of workers at remote construction sites for five cents a day. Today, Kaiser has some 2,000,000 subscribers in five states, and other such medical organizations serve another 5,000,000. In 1970 the Federal Government sponsored Medicare-Medicaid amendments that permit beneficiaries to receive their reimbursed care through such organizations.

It seemed clear that the HMO would play an essential role in any national health plan, but the issue now was: what kind of nation's health plan? It was an issue that had long been settled in welfare-conscious Europe and in most other industrial countries. Great Britain has its National Health Service, with a system of public hospitals employing salaried doctors, and private family physicians serving panels of patients on a fixed-fee schedule. Sweden has its compulsory insurance system, with regional offices paying up to 75 per cent of physician fees negotiated with the Medical Association. Canada has a system under which the Federal Government and the provinces share the costs to provide universal coverage for all residents.

In the United States, national health insurance was broached by President Franklin Roosevelt as early as 1934, was proposed by President Truman and has been the subject of recurrent legislative proposals since the Wagner-Murray-Dingell bill of 1943. But attacked by the AMA and others with the emotion-laden epithet "socialized medicine," the idea made little headway until private insurance, staggering under price inflation, showed it could not meet the need adequately. The principal impetus toward a universal health-insurance system came from organized labor. When the Committee for National Health Insurance, fathered by the late Walter Reuther, president of the United Auto Workers, merged its proposals with those of the AFL-CIO, the stage was set for joining the issue.

The year 1971, which President Nixon had predicted would be "health year," became a year of controversy not resolution. Three times during the year Secretary of Health, Education, and Welfare Elliot Richardson signaled the opening of the debate. On Feb. 22, before the Senate health subcommittee, he said that we must "debate the issues meaningfully and productively." On Apr. 26, he told the Senate Finance Committee that "this distinguished committee has begun what I feel sure will be regarded as a historic dialogue." On Oct. 19, as the first of some 200 witnesses before the House Ways and Means Committee, he said: "Today this distinguished committee will begin a major debate that I am certain will culminate in a national health insurance program."

If 1971 brought no conclusion, it did help to sharpen the issues. For, as The New York Times reported: "Americans from all strata of society and all economic classes are swinging over to the idea that good health care, like a good education, ought to be a fundamental right of citizenship."

NUMBER OF PHYSICIANS, DENTISTS AND NURSES IN THE UNITED STATES

Per 100,000 resident population

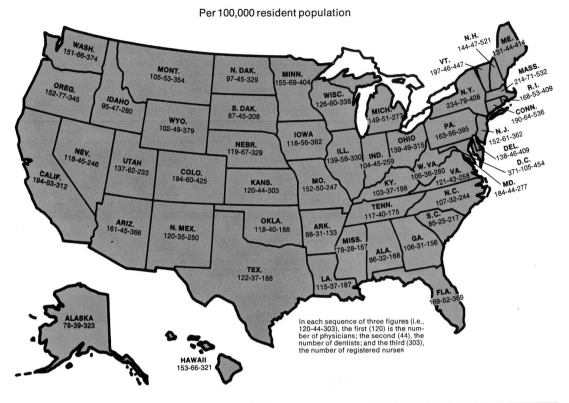

WASH. 151-66-374
OREG. 152-77-345
IDAHO 95-47-280
MONT. 105-53-354
N. DAK. 97-45-329
MINN. 155-69-404
WISC. 126-60-338
S. DAK. 87-45-308
WYO. 102-49-379
IOWA 118-56-362
NEBR. 119-67-329
NEV. 118-45-246
UTAH 137-62-233
COLO. 194-60-425
KANS. 120-44-303
MO. 152-50-247
CALIF. 194-63-312
ARIZ. 161-45-366
N. MEX. 120-35-250
OKLA. 118-40-188
ARK. 88-31-133
TEX. 122-37-188
ILL. 139-58-330
IND. 104-45-259
KY. 103-37-198
TENN. 117-40-175
MISS. 78-28-157
ALA. 86-32-168
GA. 106-31-156
LA. 115-37-187
FLA. 169-52-369
MICH. 149-51-277
OHIO 139-49-315
PA. 163-56-395
W. VA. 106-36-260
VA. 121-43-258
N.C. 107-32-244
S.C. 85-25-217
N.H. 144-47-521
VT. 197-46-447
ME. 131-44-414
MASS. 214-71-532
R.I. 168-53-409
CONN. 190-64-536
N.Y. 234-79-408
N.J. 152-61-362
DEL. 138-46-409
D.C. 371-105-454
MD. 184-44-277
ALASKA 78-39-323
HAWAII 153-66-321

In each sequence of three figures (i.e., 120-44-303), the first (120) is the number of physicians; the second (44), the number of dentists; and the third (303), the number of registered nurses

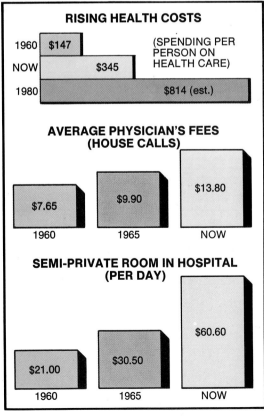

RISING HEALTH COSTS

(SPENDING PER PERSON ON HEALTH CARE)

1960 $147
NOW $345
1980 $814 (est.)

AVERAGE PHYSICIAN'S FEES (HOUSE CALLS)

$7.65 — 1960
$9.90 — 1965
$13.80 — NOW

SEMI-PRIVATE ROOM IN HOSPITAL (PER DAY)

$21.00 — 1960
$30.50 — 1965
$60.60 — NOW

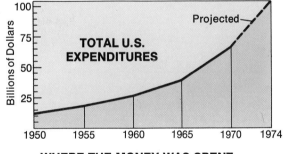

TOTAL U.S. EXPENDITURES

Billions of Dollars

Projected

100
75
50
25

1950   1955   1960   1965   1970   1974

WHERE THE MONEY WAS SPENT

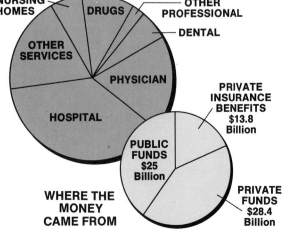

NURSING HOMES
DRUGS
OTHER PROFESSIONAL
DENTAL
OTHER SERVICES
PHYSICIAN
HOSPITAL

PRIVATE INSURANCE BENEFITS $13.8 Billion

PUBLIC FUNDS $25 Billion

PRIVATE FUNDS $28.4 Billion

WHERE THE MONEY CAME FROM

ENCYCLOPEDIA YEAR BOOK FEATURE:

FASHION: DRESS OPTIONAL

"Mademoiselle"

by Eugenia Sheppard
Syndicated Columnist
Publishers-Hall Syndicate

"Mademoiselle"   "Mademoiselle"

FASHION: DRESS OPTIONAL

A new kind of invitation was born in 1971. Instead of Black Tie or White Tie, the words Dress Optional appeared in the lower left-hand corner.

Dress Optional marked a final and official surrender to the wear-your-own-thing look that was once limited to costume parties. It meant that the hostess, though she might wear a square evening dress for the sake of a few conservatives, was ready to welcome unlimited flights of fancy from the rest of her guests.

She was rarely disappointed. Ladies came to the same dinner party wearing everything from Edwardian dresses with puffed sleeves and high-boned collars to Indian blankets and feathers. At a Sunday night dinner dance attended by a group of ambassadors in full regalia, one New York socialite arrived wearing a black, rib-knit body stocking. Instead of jewels, a cartridge belt was slung around her middle.

Looking around at the clothes, some, like Gloria Vanderbilt's, made by actual costume designers, one woman cried, "I feel so square. I'm going home to throw out all my evening dresses and start all over again." She did.

"Why are women deliberately making themselves so ugly?" complained a man, but he was lost in the minority.

Private parties were not the only ones that went costumy. Women began turning up in eighteenth-century velvet knee breeches, white stockings and buckled pumps for the opening of the opera. Others were happy in hot pants.

From the beginning, museum parties, especially the N.Y. Museum of Modern Art's, were breeding grounds for Dress Optional. It was there that artist Larry Rivers first appeared wearing a striped shirt and two neckties in different patterns. Parties brought out Andy Warhol's girls, one in a cotton undershirt and another dressed like a forties tart; gypsies in patchwork skirts; and a man gloriously got up like The Blue Boy in a velvet cavalier suit.

Just occasionally a Dress Optional party really came off, and it happened that way one night at the museum. There wasn't a genuine evening dress in the place as hundreds, in tie-dye chiffons, white-crochet playsuits, or three or four prints mixed together, sauntered in the garden or danced under a butterfly tent top with no sides and no visible means of support.

The breakdown in traditional fashion started way back with the Youth Revolution in London. The English girls looked so new

"Fun and games to the observer" (on pages 34-35): Tights, shorts and boots with a romantic hat and heavy makeup might once have indicated schizophrenia; the "camels" are coming; not to speak of hot pants, in satin, on the run.

FASHION: DRESS OPTIONAL

and amusing in their costumy granny skirts and droopy, floppy tops that they quickly cracked all the conventions about clothes and where to wear them that fashion had lived by for over a hundred years. Obviously, they had an audience that was ripe for the change.

Dress Optional was far from confined to parties. It was soon all over the streets. The year of the black crows, when teen-agers flapped along the sidewalks with coats brushing the ground, was followed by something much more uninhibited for all ages.

"Dress the way you feel; your clothes are your identification tag" became the new slogan. If you were a well-to-do matron or a successful businesswoman, you settled for shopping in a pantsuit as neither too square nor too far-out. If you were romantic, you wore ruffles. If you were young, you shuffled along in a granny skirt and a shawl. If you were a beauty, you strode along in hot pants with your long blond hair blowing in the wind. If you were a young man, you stuck to long hair, blue jeans and a bare chest. If you were a student at the Museum of Contemporary Crafts, you wound yourself in half a dozen skeins of brown wrapping twine and let it go at that. Fashion was chaos but it was a great show.

Dress Optional had far-reaching effects. Fun and games to the observer, it was no fun at all to retail stores.

When it came to creating fantasy, most designers fell flat on their faces, except a few of the whimsical like English Thea Porter and Ossie Clark, French Yves St. Laurent, and Americans Adolfo and Giorgio di Sant'Angelo. Giorgio slicked up the American Indian and put hundreds of socialites all over the United States into fringed leather, war paint, beads and feathers. Adolfo draped them in Spanish shawls.

Stores were equally bewildered, since the switch to be yourself killed all the well-known fashion categories, like the cocktail dress, that both they and the customers understood. How to find fantasy and where in the store to sell it were the big problems. Complications increased with the fall and rise of skirts. As hem lengths traveled 13 inches in less than a year, fashion went completely out of control.

The forecast was back to sanity. Experts were hopefully polishing all the good, safe phrases like "the return to elegance" and "back to the classics," but was it all only wishful thinking? Only 1972 will tell.

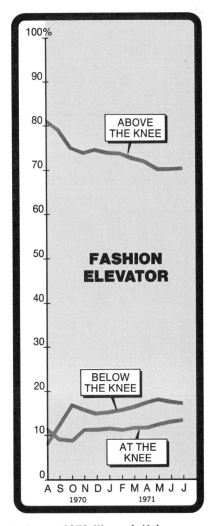

In August 1970, Woman's Haberdashers, a chain of women's apparel stores in New York City, began keeping track of the percentage of sales of the various skirt lengths. The results are charted above.

For the fancy free, some shops specialized in accessories. A mixture of two or more bold plaids provoked no cries of outrage (except perhaps from a Scot). Some clothes, like the leather skirt and the striped blouse, still required precise tailoring. Playsuits made a comeback; the one shown is stained sateen. A bridesmaid's dress was a froth of flowered and wallpaper-striped cotton; its matching gaiters bore the stamp of 1971.

TECHNOLOGY ASSESSMENT

by George A. W. Boehm
Free-Lance Science Writer
Member, American Association for
the Advancement of Science

For a whole generation, scientists and engineers were heroes of U.S. society. With radar and fantastic weapons they had done much to ensure victory in World War II. Then in the years that followed came a flood of new machines and new chemicals that seemed to be making life easier and more enjoyable for everyone, especially in the United States, the most technologically advanced country in the world. To point out just a few:

• Television and then color television provided home entertainment on a scale never before envisioned.

• Wonder drugs and polio vaccine saved thousands of lives.

• Cleaning agents spared housewives hours of drudgery each week.

• Insecticides and other new agricultural chemicals made it possible to grow food in abundance under almost any conditions.

• And as the decade of the 1960's got well under way, scientists and engineers were engaged in probably the most thrilling technological venture in history: putting man on the moon.

Almost overnight, a few years ago, the tide of public opinion began to turn. To many people, technology began to appear like a strong drug that gives the user a temporary "kick" but later an agonizing letdown. People have become increasingly aware of some of the high prices they have paid for progress in technology. Many lakes and rivers are so polluted that fish no longer swim in them. In most cities and towns the air is noticeably less fresh. Cans, bottles and other junk pile up in parks and on beaches. Traffic jams have become national problems. The list of ills sometimes seems to be growing endlessly.

Some thoughtful people are now so furious that they want to call a halt to technology advances. "Let's have no more inventions," they say, "until we can manage the shortcomings of those already in use."

But there are other equally sincere people—among them many scientists and engineers—who are confident that technology can and will be brought under

The atmosphere is fouled (opposite page, top) by an industrial complex, and a river (bottom) in a copper-mining area is polluted by an overflow pipe—ugly, destructive results that technological assessment could avoid or at least minimize.

control. They are in favor of a whole new approach to such problems, which they call "technology assessment"—or, for short, TA. Briefly, TA consists of studying a new development as it comes into widespread use, figuring out what troubles might arise, and then taking steps to eliminate the sources of trouble.

TA will probably be a major U.S. national effort for many years to come. It has been widely endorsed by congressmen and leading scientists and engineers. No one expects miraculous cures to result immediately, for assessments are bound to take a great deal of time and considerable money. Quite likely, some of the children who are today considering careers in science and engineering will spend at least half their lives helping with TA's. They will painstakingly analyze what is new and put the facts before legislators and others who make decisions for the public. In this way, TA can be a sort of "social radar" that gives early warning of danger.

While the U.S. Congress has been considering setting up an Office of Technology Assessment, a world organization has already been formed, the Organization for Economic Cooperation and Development. Most of the nations of Western Europe are participating. A committee headed by Professor Harvey Brooks, a noted Harvard physicist, is concentrating on improving productivity in education, health care, recreation, pollution abatement, housing and mass transit for cities.

To get an idea of how complicated a TA is likely to be, consider some of the problems that have arisen because TA was *not* applied. Consider also what solutions might involve.

Millions of passengers travel in jet airplanes that fly at about nine miles per minute. Yet sometimes a trip from, say, New York to Chicago (flying time a little more than an hour) can take easily five or six hours from door to door. In order to get to the airport a passenger has to fight his way through crawling traffic. Once he gets there and boards the plane, there may be a delay of half an hour while a line of planes wait their turns to take off. At the other end is a similar delay while planes circle and circle waiting their turns to land. Then in many airports during busy periods the passenger has to wait for his baggage. Finally, he may be caught in more heavy traffic on his way into the city.

What could TA have accomplished to prevent this ridiculous imbalance of terrific airspeed almost canceled out by snail-like movement on the ground? Presumably, a preliminary TA would have been started during the mid-1930's, when commercial flying was still young, and studies would have continued for at least twenty years. Cities that wanted to make efficient use of their airports would have been forewarned and prepared. They might, for instance, have installed express subways linking the airport with the midtown area, as Cleveland has recently done. They might also have bought much more land, when prices were low, so that the airport could have two runways in use at the same time. And the Federal Government might have put much more effort into developing automatic control of air traffic so that planes could safely take off and land in rapid procession.

Modern packaging is in some ways wonderful and in others almost disastrous. Twenty years ago we had steel cans that quickly rusted and disappeared; cardboard boxes that rotted away; and soda bottles that stores redeemed for two cents or a nickel. Today most bottles are stamped "no return." Many cans are made of aluminum, a metal that is almost rustproof. And various boxes and other containers are made of plastics that can hardly be destroyed by burning.

Cleveland Transit System

Thoughtful city planners are turning to modern, public rapid transit systems to whisk passengers between city hubs and airports, avoiding the long, frustrating rides by car or bus.

Harvey Brooks, distinguished American physicist, is a leader in the application of technological assessment to such fields as health care, pollution abatement, housing and mass transit.

Harvard University

Presumably, a TA on containers of all sorts could have prevented much litter if it had been started about 1950. The new materials would probably have come into use, but manufacturers and retailers would have been required to collect and dispose of them, perhaps through a sort of "garbage tax" such as some cities are now trying to levy.

Millions of dollars are being spent every year on ways of removing the salt from seawater. The hope is that limitless amounts of fresh water can be made available for the home, industry and agriculture in some arid places that are now scarcely habitable. So far, though, the efforts have come to very little. Fresh water made from seawater is simply too expensive except in a few corners of the world where a little more water is, so to speak, worth its weight in gold. A thorough TA study of this subject might have directed efforts in slightly different and more helpful directions. For example, it is not nearly so expensive to remove only *some* of the salt from seawater. Although slightly salty water might not be pleasant to drink, it should be possible to develop strains of useful plants that can use it for growth.

As these three examples show, most TA's are going to have to be studies of great breadth and depth, taking into account all aspects of a problem and examining all possible ways of relieving it. Without a TA, the "cure" is likely to be as bad as the "disease." There has been great public alarm about the contamination of air by the lead in high-test gasoline. Some congressmen and state legislators have demanded that leaded gasoline (which makes today's automobile engines perform well) be immediately outlawed. But some knowing scientists and engineers have pointed out that this simple measure is not likely to work. In order to get the same performance, gasoline manufacturers might enrich their products with certain petroleum chemicals that are suspected of being serious generators of smog and are also chemically related to some compounds suspected of causing cancer. Perhaps it would be better to settle for some lead in the air, or maybe the automobile engine will have to be thoroughly redesigned. Only an expert TA could provide the facts that will be needed to make such decisions.

The ideal time to begin a TA is when a new technology is just emerging. Later, after thousands of people have invested their money, their careers and their personal pride in a technology, it is hardly possible to develop an unbiased set of facts and judgments. Take, for example, the case of the SST, or U.S. supersonic transport. In 1971, Congress decided not to support further development of this 1,800-mile-an-hour airplane. At times the debates and public hearings almost degenerated into shouting matches. Dozens of experts were all for the SST, and dozens were dead set against it. The trouble was that work on the SST had already gone so far that there was no more time, nor little inclination, for qualified people to try to get realistic answers to the crucial questions, e.g., whether the plane would ever pay for itself financially, whether it might disturb the upper atmosphere so as to seriously alter the world climate, whether its noise could be reduced to an acceptable level. Right or wrong, the decision to abandon the SST for the time being was based more on emotions than on solid facts.

Many new technologies that have not yet fully emerged are now clearly ripe for preliminary TA's. There is the current debate about whether the United States should build a new and larger canal roughly paralleling the Panama Canal. Tentative plans call for a canal cut through Central America at sea level.

At Greenfield, Iowa, in the first such city-owned plant in the world, brackish water is forced through interconnected permeators— that is, through the walls of tiny hollow fibers. The treatment provides the town with 150,000 gallons a day of wholesome drinking water.

If carried out, this would result in the mixing of fish and other animals and plants at the Pacific and Atlantic ends of the canal. What would be the effects of this mixing on forms of life that have been separated for eons? Would commercial fishing prosper or be ruined?

The day when man can control weather to a great extent seems now to be approaching. But the important questions of what controls should be used and who would decide how weather is controlled have yet to be answered. In a limited area, for instance, some farmers might want rain while others would want a dry spell for harvesting hay. Picnickers, baseball players, and public officials who manage reservoirs might also have conflicting ideas on how much it should rain and when. Then, too, who can yet tell whether local modification of the weather might not in the long run greatly change the climate of a large region or even parts of another country? In addition to scientific study, this kind of TA might involve questions of international law.

Another prime candidate for TA today is a new field that has been called "genetic engineering." It seems theoretically possible to control human reproduction in ways that would hardly have been imaginable twenty years ago. Some biologists feel they are on the verge of the secrets of turning out babies "to order." They might be able to guarantee all girls or all boys to families who wanted them. Much further still, they might control inheritance so that each

45

child could be a "carbon copy" of Albert Einstein or Willie Mays or some other noted individual. Or they might manufacture a whole race of subhuman robots who would serve as sturdy and unfeeling slaves for menial work. Here again, TA would have to involve not only the most advanced science but also ethics, morality and the law.

Even seemingly simple technology problems deserve more thoughtful attention than they are now getting. Restrictions on the sulfur content of oil and gas are becoming increasingly severe. On the surface, this seems an obviously excellent idea, for high-sulfur fuels contaminate the air with fumes that irritate the lungs. Yet in the long run, prohibitions against high-sulfur fuels may create some serious problems. For one thing, a large part of our natural fuel reserves would become illegal to use or terribly expensive to process in order to reduce the sulfur content. This might result in an eventual energy shortage and a sharp rise in prices. The United States is already spending about $1,000,000,000 a year for the luxury of low-sulfur fuels, and the cost is going upward steadily. All things considered, how much sulfur in the air is too much? This is the kind of question that only a thorough TA can answer.

As a social and scientific movement, technology assessment is still in its infancy, but like a baby it has plenty of loving friends and no enemies. The concept of TA was born back in 1965 at a luncheon in Cambridge, Mass. The host was Connecticut Congressman Emilio Q. Daddario, who was deeply interested in problems of science and technology involving national policy. The guests were scientists and engineers, including a former presidential science adviser, Jerome Wiesner, who is now president of the Massachusetts Institute of Technology.

Daddario asked his friends to brief him on the outstanding problems in science and technology. During the course of the discussion, Wiesner pointed out that technology sometimes backfires. He suggested the creation of "an early warning system" to alert the nation to the unwanted and unexpected consequences of technologies.

The idea appealed to Congressman Daddario, and soon thereafter he began hearings that were held on and off until his retirement from Congress in the fall of 1970. Although there was little or no opposition, he was unable to get Congress interested enough to take immediate action. Nevertheless, the way in which the Federal Government may participate in TA began to take form. A bill that came up for consideration again in late 1971 called for a 13-man Technology Assessment Board, headed by a full-time director. The other members would consist of two senators, two members of the House of Representatives, the comptroller general, the director of the Legislative Reference Service of the Library of Congress, and six public members appointed by the U.S. president.

The detailed assessments, of course, would be done by experts in many fields, people familiar with social and legal problems, as well as those expert in engineering.

In the last year or two, many scientists have been deeply disturbed by a lack of opportunity to use their talents and training. One survey showed that nearly half of the young men and women who had recently become Ph.D.'s in physics were not employed in physics two years after graduation. When technology assessment becomes national policy, all these young people and many more like them will be needed to help solve some of the most bothersome problems of our times.

DIARY OF EVENTS 1971

Communist China joins the United Nations: Chiao Kuan-hua, deputy foreign minister, tells the General Assembly that UN affairs "must be handled jointly by all" its members and the superpowers must not "manipulate or monopolize" them.

UPI

3 A report by a task force of the U.S. Department of Defense states that increasing drug abuse among U.S. military personnel in Vietnam and elsewhere in Asia has become a "military problem" with no effective answer.

5 Representatives of Israel, Jordan and the United Arab Republic resume indirect peace talks at the United Nations.

11 Great Britain and the United States withdraw from the United Nations Colonialism Committee.

12 Six persons, including the Rev. Philip F. Berrigan, are indicted on charges of plotting to kidnap Henry A. Kissinger, assistant to President Richard M. Nixon for national security affairs, and on other counts.

In Great Britain, Selwyn Lloyd is elected speaker of the House of Commons.

15 U.S. Air Force fighter-bombers, escorting B-52 bombers on raids along the Laotian-North Vietnamese border, attack three antiaircraft missile sites inside North Vietnam.

President Anwar el-Sadat of the United Arab Republic and President Nikolai V. Podgorny of the Soviet Union formally dedicate Egypt's Aswan High Dam.

Sen. Robert J. Dole (Kans.) is appointed chairman of the Republican National Committee.

16 Giovanni Enrico Bucher, Switzerland's ambassador to Brazil, who was kidnaped by Brazilian guerrillas on Dec. 7, 1970, is released. In exchange, the Brazilian Government flew 70 political prisoners to asylum in Chile.

19 In the U.S. House of Representatives, Carl Albert of Oklahoma and Hale Boggs of Louisiana are chosen speaker and majority leader respectively.

Official sources in Saigon, South Vietnam, disclose that U.S. helicopter gunships are flying combat missions in Laos in support of Laotian ground troops.

20 In Singapore, representatives of the British Commonwealth nations agree that Britain can supply arms to South Africa, but a study group is named "to consider the question further."

21 As the 92d Congress convenes in Washington, Sen. Robert C. Byrd (D-W. Va.) defeats Sen. Edward M. Kennedy (D-Mass.) for the post of majority whip.

22 In his second State of the Union Message, President Nixon proposes a revenue-sharing program, a major reorganization of the executive branch of the Government, and a $100,000,000 program to combat cancer.

At Pnompenh, Cambodia, airport, a predawn raid by guerrillas kills at least 39 persons and leaves 170 wounded.

24 The National Assembly of Guinea sentences 92 persons to death, 34 *in absentia,* on charges of treason for alleged involvement in the invasion of Guinea on Nov. 21–22, 1970.

25 After deposing Milton Obote as president, Uganda's Army establishes a military Government.

In Los Angeles, Calif., a jury finds Charles M. Manson and three young women guilty of the murder of seven persons, including actress Sharon Tate.

26 The Soviet Union announces that its unmanned Venera 7 spacecraft made a soft landing on Venus in December 1970.

29 The U.S. Army drops all court-martial charges against Maj. Gen. Samuel W. Koster, divisional commander at Mylai in March 1968. (On Jan. 14 a jury of six Army officers acquitted Sgt. Charles E. Hutto of assault with intent to murder civilians at Mylai, and on Jan. 21–22 the Army dismissed all charges against the remaining four enlisted men accused of taking part in the alleged massacre.)

President Nixon proposes a Federal budget of $229,200,000,000 for fiscal 1972.

31 Apollo 14, with Comdr. Edgar D. Mitchell, Maj. Stuart A. Roosa and Capt. Alan B. Shepard, Jr., aboard, is launched from Cape Kennedy.

FEBRUARY 1971

1 Georgia Gov. Jimmy Carter appoints David H. Gambrell (D) to fill the unexpired Senate term of the late Richard B. Russell.

2 At the final session of a nine-day meeting in Washington, the foreign ministers of the Organization of American States adopt a convention condemning diplomatic kidnaping.

3 According to a study conducted by the Citizens Conference on State Legislatures, a nonpartisan private group, the states of California and New York have the most-effective legislatures, while Alabama and Wyoming have the least-effective ones.

4 Rolls-Royce Ltd., the British automobile and jet-engine manufacturers, declares bankruptcy.

5 Apollo 14 astronauts Shepard and Mitchell walk on the moon.

6 Following a night of rioting in Northern Ireland, in which at least 4 civilians and 1 soldier were killed, some 600 additional British troops are sent to Belfast.

8 Thousands of South Vietnamese troops, supported by U.S. aircraft and artillery, cross into Laos to attack Hanoi's main supply lines along the Ho Chi Minh trail.

9 Following a massive earthquake, Southern California is declared a major disaster area.

The crew of Apollo 14 splashes down safely in the Pacific Ocean.

As strife between Protestants and Catholics continues in Northern Ireland, a booby trap, apparently intended for British troops, kills five civilians in Belfast.

11 In ceremonies in London, Moscow and Washington, diplomats from 67 nations, including the Soviet Union, the United Kingdom and the United States, sign a treaty banning nuclear weapons from the ocean floor.

12 Because of "recent developments in the military situation," the Laotian Government declares a state of emergency and transfers security affairs from the police to the military.

14 The Soviet Union reveals a new five-year plan, which is to "ensure a considerable growth of the people's living and cultural standards on the basis of a high pace of production. . . ."

In Tehran, Iran, 23 Western oil companies agree to pay the 6 Persian Gulf states an increase amounting to more than $10,000,000,-000 over the next 5 years.

15 Great Britain switches to a decimal-currency system.

17 In Los Angeles, a Federal grand jury indicts William O. Wooldridge, the Army's former top-ranking enlisted man, and seven others on charges that they conspired to defraud noncommissioned officers' clubs in Vietnam.

23 The Senate Subcommittee on Constitutional Rights, under the chairmanship of Sen. Sam J. Ervin, Jr. (D-N.C.), opens nine days of hearings on the effect of government and private surveillance and computer-data banks on individual privacy.

24 Algeria President Houari Boumedienne announces that Algeria is taking a 51 per cent interest in all French oil companies in Algeria and is nationalizing the companies' natural-gas facilities and gas pipelines. The French companies are to be compensated.

In a series of raids on wholesale heroin dealers, U.S. Federal agents arrest 54 persons.

In a letter to West Berlin Mayor Klaus Schutz, East German Premier Willi Stoph proposes negotiations on permitting West Berliners to visit East Berlin and East Germany.

26 Following rioting in Cali, Colombia's third largest city, in which several persons were killed, President Misael Pastrana Borrero declares a state of siege (semimartial law).

28 In a referendum, male voters in the principality of Liechtenstein defeat a proposal that would have given women the right to vote. (On Feb. 7, Switzerland's male electorate approved a measure granting women the right to vote in Federal elections and to hold Federal office.)

1 A bomb explodes in the Senate wing of the U.S. Capitol in Washington, D.C., causing extensive damage but no injuries to anyone.

2 Dr. Claude L. Fry, U.S. soil expert who was kidnaped by Leftist guerrillas in Uruguay on Aug. 7, 1970, is released.

3 Communist China launches its second earth satellite.

7 The Arab-Israeli cease-fire, in effect since August 1970, officially expires.

8 British postal workers return to work after a 47-day strike.

Four U.S. airmen, kidnaped by Leftists in Turkey, are freed unharmed.

10 William McMahon becomes prime minister of Australia. Earlier McMahon had been elected to succeed John G. Gorton as leader of the nation's dominant Liberal Party.

12 As Turkish military leaders demand a government "above party politics" and warn that "if this is not speedily realized" the military will seize power, Premier Suleyman Demirel resigns.

13 In Montreal, Canada, Paul Rose, 27-year-old Quebec separatist on trial for his part in the murder of Pierre Laporte (in October 1970), is found guilty and sentenced to life imprisonment.

14 In West Berlin parliamentary elections, the Social Democratic Party of Chancellor Willy Brandt wins a slight majority.

For the first time since President Georges Pompidou came to power in 1969, municipal elections are held in France; voting patterns remain much the same as, in general, incumbent mayors are reelected.

15 Sheik Mujibur Rahman, leader of East Pakistan's largest political party, announces that he is assuming administrative control of East Pakistan.

17 President Nixon signs a bill increasing social-security benefits by 10 per cent.

In Norway, a minority Government, with Labor Party leader Trygve M. Bratteli as prime minister, is sworn in. (Prime Minister Per Borten had resigned on Mar. 2.)

18 In India, a new 36-member Cabinet, headed by Prime Minister Indira Gandhi, takes the oath of office. In elections for the lower house of Parliament, Mar. 1–10, India's ruling New Congress Party won an overwhelming victory; on Mar. 17, Mrs. Gandhi was reelected party leader.

23 Brian Faulkner, newly elected leader of Northern Ireland's Unionist Party, is asked to form a Government. Faulkner, a moderate Protestant, succeeds Maj. James Chichester-Clark, who resigned as prime minister on Mar. 20.

24 South Vietnam's drive against enemy supply routes in Laos officially ends.

The U.S. Senate rejects an amendment to provide $134,000,000 for continued Federal funding of the supersonic transport plane.

25 Civil war breaks out in East Pakistan as troops of the Pakistan central Government launch a widespread attack to quell East Pakistan's demands for autonomy.

In Brussels, Belgium, the ministers of the six European Economic Community nations agree to increase their farm prices by an average of 4 per cent, and to spend $1,480,000,000 to improve backward agricultural enterprises. (On Mar. 23, 1 person was killed and more than 100 were injured as some 80,000 farmers from the EEC members staged a protest demanding increased prices.)

26 Lt. Gen. Alejandro Agustin Lanusse is sworn in as president of Argentina. (On Mar. 23 the commanders of Argentina's armed services dismissed Roberto Marcelo Levingston as president.)

28 Ramon Ernesto Cruz is elected president of Honduras.

29 At Fort Benning, Ga., a jury of six officers finds First Lt. William L. Calley, Jr., guilty of the premeditated murder of at least 22 South Vietnamese civilians at Mylai in 1968.

2 The United States and Great Britain begin evacuating their citizens from East Pakistan.

Libya and 25 Western oil companies sign a 5-year agreement increasing the posted price of Libyan oil from $2.25 to $3.45 a barrel.

3 The White House announces that President Nixon will personally review and decide the case of First Lieutenant Calley, "before any final sentence is carried out." On Mar. 31, Calley was sentenced to life imprisonment.

6 Richard J. Daley (D) wins an unprecedented fifth term as mayor of Chicago, Ill.

7 President Nixon announces that 100,000 additional U.S. soldiers will be withdrawn from South Vietnam by Dec. 1, 1971. The reduction will leave 184,000 U.S. troops in the war zone.

In Turkey the coalition Government of Nihat Erim, which was sworn in on Mar. 26 to succeed that of Premier Demirel, wins a vote of confidence from the National Assembly.

9 At the concluding session of the 24th Soviet Communist Party Congress, meeting in Moscow, Party Secretary Leonid Brezhnev announces that all 25 members of the Politburo and Secretariat have been "reelected" and that four members have been added to the Politburo.

In Ceylon, security forces battle a group of insurgents led by militant young Leftists demanding the overthrow of Prime Minister Mrs. Sirimavo Bandaranaike; a 24-hour curfew is imposed.

10 Seven Western newsmen, including three Americans, are granted visas to enter Communist China.

Secessionist leaders of East Pakistan form a cabinet with the imprisoned Sheik Mujibur Rahman as president.

12 Ryokichi Minobe, 67-year-old former economics professor, is reelected governor of Tokyo.

14 President Nixon announces a series of "further steps" that the United States will take "to create broader opportunities for contacts between the Chinese and American peoples." Included is a relaxation of the twenty-year-old embargo on trade with Communist China.

17 Members of the U.S. table-tennis team conclude a seven-day visit to Communist China.

In Benghazi, Libya, President Sadat of the U.A.R., Col. Muammar al-Qaddafi of Libya and President Hafez al-Assad of Syria sign an agreement to form a federation of their three countries.

18 Earth Week, a series of activities aimed at improving man's environment, starts throughout the United States.

19 According to Nixon administration officials, the United States is in the process of selling 12 additional F-4 Phantom jets to Israel.

21 Following the death of Haiti's President François Duvalier, the dictator's 19-year-old son, Jean-Claude Duvalier, is sworn in as the nation's new president for life.

24 In Washington, D.C., a crowd of people estimated at 200,000 convenes at the Capitol, demanding that Congress end the war in Indochina immediately. (Also in Washington, on Apr. 19, about 1,000 veterans of the Vietnam conflict had begun a week-long demonstration against the war.)

25 Soyuz 10, Soviet spacecraft with three cosmonauts aboard, returns to earth following a 48-hour spaceflight. During the mission, Soyuz 10 docked with the unmanned Soviet orbital laboratory Salyut.

In Canada, David Lewis, Polish-born moderate, is elected leader of the New Democrats, the nation's third largest political party.

27 South Korea's President Chung Hee Park is reelected to a third four-year term.

29 A U.S. court-martial jury acquits Capt. Eugene M. Kotouc of guilt in the maiming of a Vietnamese prisoner at Mylai in 1968.

MAY 1971

1 The National Railroad Passenger Corporation (Amtrak), established by the U.S. Congress in 1970 to run the nation's intercity railroads, officially starts operations.

2 U.A.R. President Sadat dismisses Aly Sabry as vice-president.

3 Citing old age and ill health, Walter Ulbricht resigns as chairman of East Germany's Communist Party; Erich Honecker is named to the post.

Gen. Lon Nol, who for reasons of health resigned as premier of Cambodia on Apr. 20, agrees to serve as the nation's titular premier; Lt. Gen. Sisowath Sirak Matak will direct the ministerial Cabinet as Lon Nol's delegate.

Some 7,000 antiwar demonstrators are arrested in Washington, D.C.

The U.S. Supreme Court rules that states do not violate the Federal Constitution when they give "untrammeled discretion" to juries "to pronounce life or death in capital cases." The Court also upholds the practice by which juries decide guilt and immediately determine the penalty of death, without hearing further evidence.

5 The central banks of Austria, Belgium, West Germany, the Netherlands and Switzerland withdraw support of the U.S. dollar and close their foreign-exchange markets until May 10. Foreign-exchange markets are also closed in Finland and Portugal.

7 A Soviet military training mission arrives in Ceylon to help the Government quell the rebellion of ultra-Leftist youths. (On May 5 the Government had announced that about 4,000 rebels had surrendered during a May 1–4 amnesty period.)

9 West Germany and the Netherlands permit their currencies to float, within limits, in relation to the U.S. dollar; Austria and Switzerland increase the value of their currencies against the fixed price of the dollar.

14 U.A.R. President Sadat announces that an unsuccessful attempt to remove him from office led to the resignation on May 13 of six cabinet members and three members of the executive committee of the Arab Socialist Union, the nation's only political organization; a new Cabinet is sworn in.

18 President Nixon signs bill requiring striking railroad signalmen to return to work at once. The action ends a 41-hour national rail strike.

19 In Moscow, Soviet Premier Kosygin and Canadian Prime Minister Pierre E. Trudeau sign an agreement by which both nations will "enlarge and deepen consultations" to improve "friendship, good-neighborliness and mutual confidence."

The U.S. Senate rejects a series of proposals aimed at reducing the number of U.S. forces stationed in Western Europe.

Maj. Gen. Samuel W. Koster and Brig. Gen. George H. Young, Jr., are disciplined by the U.S. Army for failing to investigate adequately the slayings of civilians at Mylai in 1968.

21 Following two days of talks in Paris, French President Pompidou and British Prime Minister Edward Heath announce agreements paving the way for Britain's entry into the Common Market.

Stanley R. Resor resigns as U.S. secretary of the Army, a post he has held since 1965.

27 In Cairo, President Sadat and Soviet President Podgorny sign a 15-year treaty of friendship and cooperation.

In Riga, U.S.S.R., the Latvian Supreme Court finds 4 Jews guilty of anti-Soviet activity and sentences them to prison-camp terms of 1 to 3 years. (On May 20, a Leningrad court found 9 Soviet Jews guilty of similar charges and sentenced them to terms of 1 to 10 years.)

29 At the final session of the 14th Czechoslovak Communist Party Congress, Gustav Husak is reelected party chairman.

30 Mariner 9, an unmanned U.S. spacecraft, is launched from Cape Kennedy and joins two Soviet spaceships in an attempt to gather new information about the planet Mars.

1 In Istanbul, Turkey, police storm an apartment and rescue Sibel Erkan, 14-year-old girl held hostage by two Leftist guerrillas. The men —one was killed by police, the other wounded —were wanted in connection with the kidnaping and slaying in May of Ephraim Elrom, Israel's Consul General in Istanbul.

3 North Vietnam cancels arrangements to receive 13 sick and wounded prisoners of war from South Vietnam. A total of 660 such prisoners were asked by the International Committee of the Red Cross if they wished to be repatriated; 98 per cent said "no."

James R. Hoffa announces from prison that he will not seek reelection as president of the International Brotherhood of Teamsters. He endorses Frank E. Fitzsimmons as his successor.

4 At the conclusion of a two-day foreign-ministers meeting in Lisbon, the North Atlantic Treaty Organization decides to seek exploratory talks with the U.S.S.R. and the other Warsaw Pact nations concerning "mutual and balanced force reductions" in central Europe.

10 At least 9 students are killed and 160 people are injured during anti-Government demonstrations in Mexico City, Mexico.

12 With an estimated 100,000 refugees from East Pakistan -entering India daily, the U.S. Government urges India and Pakistan to use restraint, and to return to normalcy through "peaceful political accommodation."

13 *The New York Times* starts publishing a series of articles on and excerpts from a confidential Pentagon study of the origins of the U.S. involvement in the Vietnam war.

The Israeli Government announces that a Liberian tanker carrying seventy thousand tons of crude oil for Israel was shelled as it passed through the Strait of Bal el Mandeb off Southern Yemen. A Palestinian guerrilla group claims responsibility.

In Chile, two left-wing extremists, accused of assassinating Edmundo Perez Zukovic, a former right-wing cabinet minister, are killed in a gun battle with police.

15 In Washington, President Nixon confers with West German Chancellor Willy Brandt.

17 Japan's Foreign Minister Kiichi Aichi (in Tokyo) and U.S. Secretary of State William P. Rogers (in Washington) formally sign treaty returning Okinawa and the other Ryukyu islands to Japanese sovereignty sometime in 1972. Under the treaty, which must be ratified by the Diet and the Senate, the United States will retain 88 military installations on the islands.

Dr. Jerome H. Jaffe is named director of new U.S. Special Action Office of Drug Abuse Prevention.

After Malta's Labor Party wins a narrow victory in parliamentary elections, Dom Mintoff is sworn in as prime minister.

21 In an advisory ruling, the International Court of Justice holds that the "presence of South Africa in South-West Africa being illegal, South Africa is under the obligation to withdraw its administration from the territory immediately."

28 The U.S. Supreme Court declares unconstitutional the state programs that reimburse church-related schools for instruction in non-religious subjects, but upholds a 1963 Federal act under which church-related colleges may receive funds for building construction.

29 President Nixon vetoes a $5,600,000,-000 accelerated public-works-plan bill.

30 The Soviet Union announces that the three-man crew of Soyuz 11—Lt. Col. Georgi Dobrovolsky, Vladislav Volkov and Viktor Patsayev—was found dead when the spacecraft returned to earth after a record-setting 24-day spaceflight.

The U.S. Supreme Court rules that *The New York Times* and *The Washington Post* may resume publication of articles based on the Pentagon study of the Vietnam war. Court orders, obtained by the Nixon administration, had halted publication.

The 26th Amendment to the U.S. Constitution, lowering the voting age to 18 years in all elections, is ratified officially.

1 The new semi-independent U.S. Postal Service goes into operation, replacing the 182-year-old Post Office Department.

3 Millions of Indonesians vote in the nation's first national elections since 1955.

5 Japan's Prime Minister Sato appoints a new Cabinet; Finance Minister Takeo Fukuda and Kakuei Tanaka, secretary of the ruling Liberal-Democratic Party, are named foreign minister and minister of international trade and industry respectively. Shigeru Hori becomes new party secretary.

6 Queen Juliana of the Netherlands administers oath of office to a new Cabinet, headed by Prime Minister Barend W. Biesheuvel. (The preceding four-party Government of Premier Piet de Jong lost its parliamentary majority in national elections.)

11 The Congress of Chile unanimously adopts a constitutional amendment authorizing the Allende Government to nationalize the properties of three U.S. copper companies— Kennecott, Anaconda and Cerro—immediately.

13 In Morocco, ten high-ranking Army officers are executed by a firing squad for their part in an unsuccessful coup against King Hassan II. (On July 10, rebellious Army officers and cadets stormed the King's summer palace and killed 93 persons who were celebrating the King's birthday.)

14 In Iceland, a Leftist-coalition Government, with Olafur Johannesson as premier, is sworn in. (The preceding coalition Government resigned after losing its parliamentary majority in national elections on June 13.)

15 President Nixon announces that he will visit mainland China before May 1972 to "seek the normalization of relations between the two countries and also to exchange views on questions of concern to the two sides." (Henry A. Kissinger, the President's adviser for national security affairs, and China's Premier Chou En-lai discussed the trip during secret meetings in Peking, July 9–11.)

19 Britain's Chancellor of the Exchequer Anthony Barber announces tax cuts totaling $564,000,000 a year and the elimination of all consumer-credit controls.

Jordan's Premier Wasfi al-Tal claims that Jordanian troops have "rounded up" 2,300 Arab commandos during the preceding week and that only 200 commandos remain in Jordan. "Subversive" guerrilla groups will no longer be permitted to operate in Jordan. (The Jordanian Government launched an all-out campaign against the Palestinian commandos in the north on July 13.)

22 Maj. Gen. Gaafar al-Nimeiry, who was deposed as head of state of Sudan in a coup on July 19, is returned to power by officers and troops loyal to him.

23 Following the death of Liberia's President William V. S. Tubman, Vice-President William R. Tolbert is installed as president.

26 Apollo 15, with astronauts Col. David R. Scott, Lt. Col. James B. Irwin and Maj. Alfred M. Worden aboard, is launched from Cape Kennedy.

28 Officials of the Nixon administration reveal that all U.S. reconnaissance flights over mainland China have been suspended so as to avoid any incident that might mar the President's planned visit to Peking.

The executive body of Britain's Labor Party votes to oppose Britain's entry into the Common Market.

William J. Porter is nominated to succeed David K. E. Bruce as the chief U.S. delegate to the Paris peace talks.

The U.S. Government reports a budget deficit of $23,200,000,000 for fiscal year 1971.

U.S. Vice-President Spiro T. Agnew returns to Washington after a ten-nation diplomatic tour.

29 President Josip Broz Tito is elected chairman of Yugoslavia's newly established collective presidency.

31 Riding a four-wheel, battery-run vehicle, astronauts Scott and Irwin begin exploring the moon.

2 "Selective" strikes by various U.S. railroads, which began in July, end as negotiators for the railroads and the United Transportation Union agree to a new contract. (On Aug. 1, the United Steelworkers of America approved a three-year contract, averting a steel strike.)

3 President Nixon orders Attorney General John N. Mitchell to "work with individual school districts to hold busing [transporting children to and from a school some distance from home to achieve school integration] to the minimum required by law."

5 China and the Soviet Union sign a new trade and payments agreement.

6 Morocco's King Hassan II appoints a new Cabinet, headed by Premier Mohammad Karim Lamrani.

7 Ending an "epic scientific voyage," Apollo 15 splashes down in the Pacific Ocean.

9 Rioting erupts in Northern Ireland as the Government invokes emergency powers of preventive detention and internment.

In New Delhi, India, Andrei A. Gromyko, Soviet foreign minister, and Swaran Singh, India's foreign minister, sign a twenty-year Indian-Soviet friendship treaty.

11 New York City Mayor John V. Lindsay, a Republican, joins the Democratic Party.

12 Accusing Jordan of "continuing to engage in a policy inconsistent with Arab character and with the joint Arab confrontation against Israel," Syria breaks off diplomatic relations with Jordan.

Jack Lynch, prime minister of the Republic of Ireland, calls for abolition of the government of Northern Ireland and the formation of a new government in which the area's Roman Catholic minority would share power with the ruling Protestants.

14 Sheik Isa ibn Sulman al-Khalifa, ruler of Bahrain, declares the Persian Gulf island group an independent sovereign nation. (The new nation had rejected federation with eight neighbors.)

15 In a 20-minute televised address, President Nixon outlines a "new economic policy." It includes a 90-day freeze on wages and prices; a reduction of $4,700,000,000 in Federal expenditures during fiscal 1972; a 10 per cent surcharge on all imports not subject to quotas or quantitative limits; a request for Federal tax cuts; and temporary suspension of the convertibility of U.S. dollars into gold.

16 Malawi President Hastings K. Banda becomes first head of state to visit the Republic of South Africa since 1947.

18 The governments of Australia and New Zealand announce that all of their combat forces in South Vietnam will be withdrawn by the end of 1971.

20 Although representatives of the Red Cross societies of North Korea and South Korea meet for only four minutes, it is the first such direct contact since the Korean war.

21 At San Quentin Prison (Calif.), three prisoners and three guards are killed as George Jackson, one of the men charged with the killing of a guard at Soledad Prison (Calif.), attempts to escape.

22 Israel devalues its currency by 20 per cent.

Following a successful revolt against Gen. Juan Jose Torres Gonzales, Bolivia's left-wing president, Col. Hugo Banzer Suarez assumes the presidency. During four days of fighting, more than 120 people were killed and nearly 200 injured.

23 The European foreign-exchange markets, which closed after President Nixon's Aug. 15 speech, reopen; most currencies, with the exception of the French franc and the Japanese yen, are permitted to float.

26 Arriving in Jakarta, Indonesia, Queen Juliana of the Netherlands becomes the first ruling sovereign of the House of Orange to visit the former Dutch colony.

28 The Japanese Government permits the yen to float "provisionally" within unspecified limits.

SEPTEMBER 1971

1 U.S. Secretary of Defense Melvin R. Laird announces that the United States has agreed to sell West Germany 175 Phantom jet fighters for an estimated $750,000,000.

3 In Berlin the ambassadors of the United States, Soviet Union, Great Britain and France sign a treaty on the future status of West Berlin. Before the treaty goes into effect, East and West Germany must reach a subsidiary agreement on implementation of the treaty.

9 Addressing a joint session of Congress, President Nixon promises to take all the "steps needed to see that America is not again afflicted" with runaway inflation.

At the Attica State Correctional Facility in Attica, N.Y., more than 1,000 prisoners seize 32 guards as hostages and take control of part of the prison.

In Uruguay, the Tupamaros, a guerrilla group, release Geoffrey H. S. Jackson, Britain's ambassador to Uruguay, who had been held captive by the group since Jan. 8. (On Sept. 6, practically all the Tupamaros held by the Government had escaped from prison.)

11 Following an "unlucky" lunar landing, Luna 18—an unmanned Soviet spacecraft launched Sept. 2—loses contact with earth.

13 Some 1,000 New York State troopers, sheriff deputies and prison guards storm Attica prison as authorities regain control of the facility; 43 inmates and guards are killed in the rebellion.

17 An Israeli Air Force cargo plane is shot down by an Egyptian ground-to-air missile, 14 miles behind Israel's position on the Suez Canal. The incident occurs one week after Israeli ground fire downed an Egyptian jetfighter.

18 For the first time since August 1970, Egypt and Israel exchange rocket fire across the Suez Canal.

A communiqué on the meeting of Soviet Party Chairman Brezhnev and West German Chancellor Brandt emphasizes the need for an all-European security conference.

21 At the opening of its 26th session, the UN General Assembly elects Indonesia's Foreign Minister Adam Malik president.

22 A jury of five combat officers acquits Capt. Ernest L. Medina of all charges of involvement in the killing of civilians at Mylai in March 1968.

23 John M. Harlan becomes the second associate justice of the U.S. Supreme Court to resign within a week. (Hugo L. Black resigned on Sept. 17.)

The U.S. command in Saigon acknowledges that on Sept. 21, U.S. planes bombed stores of military oil, antiaircraft-gun and missile sites in North Vietnam.

24 Because of espionage activities, Great Britain orders ninety representatives of the Soviet Union expelled from Britain, and bars the return of 15 additional Soviet officials who are temporarily away.

25 Concluding three days of talks in Belgrade, Soviet Party Chairman Brezhnev and Yugoslavia's President Tito sign a declaration reaffirming Yugoslavia's political independence and right to develop its own form of communism.

26 At Elmendorf Air Force Base in Alaska, President Nixon greets Emperor Hirohito of Japan, who is beginning a tour of Europe.

28 Jozsef Cardinal Mindszenty—who had been in confinement, self-imposed or otherwise, in Hungary since 1949—arrives in Rome.

Following two days of talks near London, the prime ministers of Britain, the Republic of Ireland and Northern Ireland urge a "process of political reconciliation" in troubled Northern Ireland and condemn "any form of violence as an instrument of political pressure."

30 In Washington, Secretary of State Rogers and Soviet Foreign Minister Gromyko sign two nuclear-control agreements; they provide for the modernizing of the existing Washington-Moscow hot line, and for common procedures to prevent accidental nuclear war.

OCTOBER 1971

1 At the UN, the resignation (because of ill health) of Ralph J. Bunche as undersecretary for special political affairs is announced.

3 In South Vietnam's one-candidate election, President Nguyen Van Thieu wins a new term.

7 Outlining Phase 2 of his economic program, to take effect when the wage-price freeze expires on Nov. 13, President Nixon sets up an economic-control system to curb prices, wages, rents and "windfall profits."

The British Government orders 1,500 additional troops sent to Northern Ireland, raising Britain's troop strength in Ulster to 14,000.

8 China's Party Chairman Mao Tsetung meets with Emperor Haile Selassie of Ethiopia in Peking; it is Mao's first public appearance since Aug. 7.

In retaliation for Britain's expulsion of 105 Soviet officials, the Soviet Government orders the ouster from Soviet soil of 4 British diplomats and 1 businessman, revokes the entry visas of 3 other British businessmen, and cancels the planned 1972 visit to Moscow of British Foreign Secretary Sir Alec Douglas-Home.

9 In Argentina a revolt by two Army regiments against the Government of Gen. Alejandro Agustin Lanusse is quelled.

Soviet President Nikolai V. Podgorny concludes a visit to North Vietnam; a joint North Vietnamese-Soviet committee, to work out long-term economic, trade, cultural, scientific and technological relations between the two nations, is formed.

10 In Austria's Parliamentary elections, the Socialist Party of Chancellor Bruno Kreisky gains a narrow majority.

11 In a one-for-one prisoner exchange, U.S. officials release a North Vietnamese lieutenant; on Oct. 8, the Vietcong had freed John C. Sexton, Jr., a U.S. Army staff sergeant.

Denmark's Social Democratic leader Jens Otto Krag takes over as premier. The new minority Government succeeds the center-right coalition of Premier Hilmar Baunsgaard, which lost its majority in September elections.

12 President Nixon announces that he will visit Moscow in May 1972.

14 Following the release of figures showing a September unemployment rate of 7.1 per cent, the Canadian Government announces a program increasing Federal spending by $375,-000,000 and temporarily reducing personal and corporate income taxes.

Two-day celebrations in honor of the 2,500th anniversary of the founding of the Persian Empire by Cyrus the Great end in Iran.

15 Representatives of Japan and the United States initial a "memorandum of understanding" limiting for three years the flow of Japanese textiles to the U.S. market. Simultaneously, the United States agrees to remove its 10 per cent import surcharge on synthetic and woolen textiles.

18 In Ottawa a man shouting "Long live free Hungary!" attacks Soviet Premier Kosygin. The Premier, who began an eight-day tour of Canada on Oct. 17, is not injured.

20 In Peking, Henry A. Kissinger, President Nixon's assistant for national security affairs, and Premier Chou En-lai discuss President Nixon's forthcoming trip to China.

22 George H. Boldt, a Federal judge in Washington State, and C. Jackson Grayson, Jr., dean of Southern Methodist University's School of Business, are named chairmen of the Pay Board and Price Commission respectively. The agencies will create and administer Phase 2 of the administration's economic plan.

25 The UN General Assembly votes to admit Communist China and to expel Nationalist China.

27 During Soviet Party Chairman Brezhnev's six-day visit to France, France and the Soviet Union sign a ten-year economic agreement.

28 By a margin of 112 votes, Britain's House of Commons approves British membership in the European Economic Community.

2 In Mississippi's gubernatorial race, William L. Waller, a white Democrat, defeats Charles Evers, the Negro mayor of Fayette who ran as an independent; in Kentucky, Lt. Gov. Wendell Ford (D) is elected governor. Joseph L. Alioto (D), Ralph J. Perk (R), Frank Rizzo (D) and Kevin White (D) win the mayoralty races in San Francisco, Cleveland, Philadelphia and Boston respectively.

5 "In the first step in the expansion of [U.S.] trade with the Soviet Union," the Nixon administration announces the sale of $136,000,-000 worth of feed grain to the U.S.S.R.

6 At Amchitka, Alaska, a hydrogen bomb is exploded underground in largest U.S. test ever conducted. By a vote of 4–3, the U.S. Supreme Court had refused to issue a temporary injunction against the controversial test.

7 In general elections in Belgium, the coalition-government partners—the Christian Social and the Socialist parties—retain their majority.

After approving Albania's 1971–75 economic-development plan, the Sixth Congress of the Albanian Communist Party adjourns in Tirana.

10 Cuba's Premier Fidel Castro arrives in Santiago, Chile, on his first visit to South America in 11 years.

11 Peking's newly-appointed delegation to the UN arrives in New York City. Chiao Kuan-hua, deputy foreign minister, is head of the delegation; Huang Hua, ambassador to Canada, will serve as permanent representative.

The U.S. Price Commission announces an average yearly price-increase guideline of 2.5 per cent. (On Nov. 8, the U.S. Pay Board had voted to establish a 5.5 per cent standard for wage increases under the economic-stabilization program.)

12 President Nixon announces that 45,000 additional U.S. troops will be withdrawn from Vietnam by Feb. 1, 1972.

13 Mariner 9, unmanned U.S. spacecraft, goes into orbit around Mars, becoming the first man-made object to orbit another planet.

U.S. soft-coal miners sign a contract, ending a 44-day strike.

15 In a "speech to the nation," South Vietnam President Thieu outlines his economic-reform plan which includes devaluing the piaster.

17 To deal with "the dangers that have been threatening Thailand," a group of military and other leaders, headed by Premier Thanom Kittikachorn, organize a "revolutionary" council. The constitution is abolished, Parliament dissolved, the Cabinet disbanded and martial law declared.

18 China tests its twelfth nuclear bomb, the first since Oct. 14, 1970.

22 Indian and Pakistani sources report major military action in East Pakistan.

Responding to a Cambodian appeal for help against communist pressures northeast of Pnompenh, South Vietnamese forces begin a major drive into eastern Cambodia.

24 Paul W. McCracken resigns (effective Jan. 1, 1972) as chairman of the President's Council of Economic Advisers; Herbert Stein, a council member, is named to the post.

25 According to an agreement signed (Nov. 24) by Great Britain and Rhodesia, a revised Rhodesian constitution will offer Rhodesia's black majority new legal rights and economic aid.

27 In Northern Ireland's worst outbreak of violence in several weeks, a British soldier and two civilians are killed.

28 Returning from a meeting of the Arab League's Joint Defense Council in Cairo, Jordan's Premier Wasfi al-Tal is assassinated.

29 White House Press Secretary Ronald L. Ziegler announces that President Nixon's trip to China will begin on Feb. 21, 1972.

Jordan's King Hussein names Foreign Minister Ahmed al-Lawzi premier and Maj. Gen. Mohammed Rasoul al-Kallani national security adviser.

2 In Santiago, Chile, 150 persons are injured in an antigovernment demonstration, mainly of women; the Allende Government declares a state of emergency.

Six Persian Gulf sheikdoms form the Union of Arab Emirates and break all ties to Britain.

The U.S. Senate confirms the nomination of Dr. Earl L. Butz as secretary of agriculture. He succeeds Clifford M. Hardin, who resigned.

3 Prime Minister Gandhi declares that Pakistan has begun a "full-scale" war against India.

7 UN General Assembly approves a resolution calling for an India-Pakistan cease-fire and mutual troop withdrawals. (Debate on the issue switched to the General Assembly after the U.S.S.R. vetoed a similar plan in the Security Council.)

10 At a NATO meeting in Brussels, U.S. Secretary of State Rogers and West German Foreign Minister Walter Scheel sign an agreement under which Bonn will assume more of the costs of keeping U.S. troops in Germany.

By a vote of 68–26, the U.S. Senate approves the nomination of William H. Rehnquist as an associate justice of the U.S. Supreme Court. (The appointment of Lewis F. Powell was confirmed on Dec. 6.)

The U.S. State Department announces a U.S.-Portugal agreement, effective immediately, by which the United States will provide Portugal with up to $436,000,000 in economic credits and aid. In exchange, Portugal will permit the United States to use the Lajes military base in the Azores until 1974.

13 Peking releases two Americans held as prisoners in China—one since 1952 and the other since 1968.

15 In Bahamian waters, a Cuban gunboat seizes a Miami-based freighter of Panamanian registry. Three people are injured.

The U.S. Price Commission limits increases in doctors' fees and hospital charges to 2.5 per cent and 6 per cent respectively.

17 President Agha Mohammad Yahya Khan announces that Pakistan has agreed to a cease-fire, ending 15-day war with India.

A U.S. military jury finds Col. Oran K. Henderson not guilty of charges that he failed "to carry out a proper investigation" of the events at Mylai in March 1968.

The first session of the 92d Congress adjourns.

18 Meeting in Washington, the finance ministers of the world's ten leading noncommunist industrial nations agree on new currency-exchange rates, involving devaluation of the U.S. dollar.

20 President Nixon signs proclamation lifting 10 per cent import surcharge imposed Aug. 15.

In the wake of Pakistan's defeat in the war with India, President Yahya Khan is forced to resign; Zulfikar Ali Bhutto is sworn in as the new president and martial-law administrator.

22 The UN General Assembly elects Kurt Waldheim of Austria to succeed U Thant as secretary-general.

24 Italy's 1,008-member Electoral College elects Giovanni Leone the nation's president.

27 U.S. Secretary of Defense Laird announces that there will be no draft calls during January 1972.

28 At Key Biscayne, Fla., President Nixon meets with West German Chancellor Brandt. (Earlier in the month, the President conferred with Israel's Prime Minister Golda Meir, Canada's Prime Minister Trudeau, Brazil's President Emilio G. Medici, France's President Pompidou and Britain's Prime Minister Heath.)

29 Britain announces that it will withdraw all its military forces from Malta.

30 A U.S.-military-command spokesman in Saigon announces that the intensified U.S. bombing raids on North Vietnam, begun on Dec. 26, have ended.

60

the year 1971

61

ACTION

President Nixon, despite the opposition of liberal Democrats, created a new agency, ACTION, in mid-1971 to bring together many of the Government's volunteer service programs. The principal components of the agency are the Peace Corps and VISTA, the latter organization serving ghetto neighborhoods, Indian lands and Appalachia. Joseph H. Blatchford, head of the Peace Corps, was named by Nixon to administer ACTION.

The President submitted to Congress a reorganization plan to establish ACTION on Mar. 24. He declared "We need an increased effort to stimulate broader volunteer service, to involve more volunteers, and to involve them not simply as foot soldiers in massive enterprises directed from the top, but in those often small and local efforts that show immediate results, that give immediate satisfaction—those efforts that return to citizens a sense of having a hand in the business of building America."

Nevertheless, his message aroused fears that the administration planned to dismantle VISTA, which was why the plan was fought by many Democratic liberals in Congress. Sen. Edmund S. Muskie (D-Me.) charged that the proposal "substitutes bureaucratic shuffling for dynamic new initiatives" and declared that it would decrease the effectiveness of current volunteer programs. However, the House declined 224–131 to kill the plan on May 25, and the Senate upheld it 54–29 on June 3. The new agency came into formal existence on July 1.

Blatchford said that VISTA would continue. He announced that two of ACTION's first steps would be to enlist Army medics returning from Vietnam as domestic volunteers, and to initiate a program allowing college students to spend their junior year as domestic volunteers, for which they would earn full academic credit. In addition to the Peace Corps and VISTA, other programs placed under ACTION were: National Student Volunteers (from the antipoverty program), Foster Grandparents, Retired Senior Volunteers, Service Corps of Retired Executives, and Active Corps of Executives. Nixon said he would also ask Congress to transfer the Teacher Corps from the Office of Education to ACTION.

JOSEPH W. HALL, JR.
Washington Bureau, The Associated Press

ADVERTISING

The tempo of attacks on advertising and marketing from critics and regulators increased markedly in 1971. The Federal Trade Commission called on seven automobile manufacturers to document their advertising claims. In response to another FTC action, Continental Baking Co. agreed to devote 25 per cent of its advertising for a year to statements that, contrary to earlier ads, Profile bread was not effective for weight reduction. The FTC also indicated it planned to look into testimonial advertising where endorsements of a product were based primarily on "monetary consideration" and not personal use, preference or familiarity. It started to move against "uniqueness" claims in advertising; and it also came up with a study that reportedly charged breakfast-cereal makers with hiking prices to provide higher profits and increased advertising expenditures.

Ralph Nader assailed the Ford Motor Co. for advertising its doubts about the reliability of air bags as an automobile-safety feature. He attacked "clever" Volkswagen advertising that promoted "a seriously unstable Beetle." He charged that Volvo advertising was "monumentally misleading" and that its ads were better than the car's engineering. A U.S. senator offered a bill that would create a government institute to study the impact of advertising on society. The Food and Drug Administration called for hazard warnings on many of the new nonphosphate detergents. Government officials got ready to take action against what they saw as a national over-the-counter drug binge created by advertising for such "mood" drugs as tranquilizers, sleeping pills, and stimulants.

In October the FTC began an inquiry into how advertising works, so that commission members could get a fuller understanding of the business. But some advertising leaders were fearful that, as one of them expressed it, the "unparalleled hostility" evidenced in Washington toward business would cause the inquiry to "create hysteria and do much to bring our business into disrepute." The FTC replied that its aim was informational, not prosecutory.

A major attempt to make self-regulation of the advertising industry effective resulted in the creation of a National Advertising Review Board, headed by Charles W. Yost, former U.S. ambassador to the United Nations. The NARB was to serve as a court of last resort for complaints arising under a new all-industry code barring deception in advertising.

Marketers in foreign countries were also on the defensive. Moves were made against advertising by governments, consumers and intellectuals in Canada, Japan, Australia, Austria, Sweden, Greece and South Africa. Taxes were imposed on advertising in Sweden and Mexico. Canada was trying to put a stop to all cigarette advertising. The West German Government planned to phase out cigarette commercials. (In the United States the leading cigarette brands enjoyed a sales gain, although their advertising was no longer allowed on television.)

Meanwhile, advertising volume in the United States reached the $20,800,000,000 mark in 1970, only $330,000,000 above its 1969 level, the smallest increase since 1961. Responsible forecasters predicted "a pretty good chance that 1971 would be better than 1970" because of favorable economic factors.

In 1970, newspapers had an advertising volume of $4,940,000,000, television $2,850,000,000, direct mail $2,550,000,000, radio $1,280,000,000, and magazines $1,020,000,000. The leading 100 national advertisers reduced their promotional investments from $4,640,000,000 in 1969 to $4,620,000,000 in 1970. Procter & Gamble was the biggest advertiser, spending $265,000,000. Then came General Foods at $170,000,000; Sears, Roebuck at $130,000,000; General Motors at $129,764,000; and Warner-Lambert with $126,000,000.

JAMES V. O'GARA
Editor, *Advertising Age*

AFGHANISTAN

Drought and the threat of economic disaster occupied the mountainous Muslim kingdom of Afghanistan in 1971. The country's 17,400,000 people, who are among the poorest in the world, depend almost entirely on agriculture and livestock raising. For the second year running a severe drought hit Afghanistan, and the country's nearly 20,000,000 head of livestock faced starvation. The small economic progress that had been achieved in 1969 and 1970 was virtually wiped out in 1971.

With the Afghan plains devoid of fodder and with a drastic reduction in food-grain production, Afghanistan turned to the United Nations and "friendly" nations for help. The Soviet Union allowed hundreds of thousands of the country's famed Karakul sheep to pasture on Soviet territory. Aid also came from China, the United States and several other countries. Nevertheless, with 20,000,000 head of livestock to

feed, by the end of 1971 the task had become Herculean.

Afghanistan's exports, which are largely agricultural and livestock products, took a plunge in 1971. Karakul skins alone usually account for some US$25,000,000 of the country's US$90,000,000 annual exports. In addition to the loss of sheep due to famine, poor feeding conditions led to a further decline in the quality of Karakul pelts. Since it takes 75 per cent of Afghanistan's export earnings to service its international debts, the decline in exports was especially painful.

As if the drought were not causing enough suffering, a flood pouring out of a crack in a natural reservoir swept away almost a whole village in the Hindu Kush Valley; more than a hundred people were killed.

These troubles came after Afghanistan had started the year on a hopeful note. One important economic development was that after seven years of discussion, the country's House of the People—the lower house of the Afghan Parliament—approved the charter of an Industrial Development Bank (IDB). Afghanistan's fledgling industries are in considerable need of new capital and had been pegging their hopes to the creation of the IDB. Politics blocked its formation until 1971.

By year's end politics had taken a back seat, despite several pressing political matters, especially the long-delayed bill legalizing political parties. A new piece of legislation making political parties legal was given to King Mohammad Zahir Shah for his signature. However, the King appeared to be too worried, over a possible leftist political take-over if he legalized parties, to sign the measure. A number of parties already exist, the fastest-growing and most influential being the pro-Chinese Sholai Jawid (Eternal Flame).

Earlier, in May and June, a minor political crisis arose when the lower house of Parliament brought down the Government of Prime Minister Noor Ahmad Etemadi, who resigned on May 16. Etemadi's downfall was ostensibly over the result of a dispute about parliamentary procedure questions. Knowledgeable Afghans, however, suggest that it might have had more to do with Etemadi's refusal to hand out bribes.

In early June, Dr. Abdul Zahir, the then ambassador to Rome, was appointed prime minister and asked to form a new government. Zahir, 61, is a graduate of Columbia University in New York and was formerly speaker of the lower house, the first premier and health minister after 1964 constitution was promulgated.

ARTHUR C. MILLER
Senior Editor, *The Asia Letter*

AFGHANISTAN

Area: 250,000 sq. mi.
Population: 17,400,000
Capital: Kabul
Government: Mohammad Zahir Shah, king—1933; Abdul Zahir, prime minister—1971
Gross National Product: $1,400,000,000
Foreign trade: exports, $90,000,000; imports, $135,000,000
Armed forces: 83,000

Black-white dialogue in Johannesburg: Malawi President Banda (behind microphone) gives banquet at which guests include South Africa Prime Minister Vorster (speaking) and South Africa President Fouché.

AFRICA, BLACK

Dialogue and its ramifications dominated Africa's considerations in 1971. This dominance emphasized the failure of the quest for black African political unity which had stemmed from the ideal of pan-Africanism and found expression in the Organization of African Unity (OAU). It signaled a more realistic analysis in each country of its position in the world. It

Maj. Gen. Idi Amin drives jeep through jubilant crowds in Kampala, Uganda, after coup.

underlined the nations' increasing divergence in assessing black Africa's—and their own—political and economic self-interest.

The dialogue took two forms. Black Africa's major concern was the beginning of contacts across the black-white racial frontier roughly marked by the Zambezi River. At the same time, white-white dialogue between the British Government and the Ian Smith regime in Rhodesia figured importantly.

Black-White Dialogue. By the beginning of 1971 the Republic of South Africa had carefully laid the groundwork for its outward policy of making contact with the black African nations. Such contacts, suggesting African acceptance of the Republic's social system, were intended to lessen world pressure against South Africa and also to create badly needed new markets for South African goods.

From the viewpoint of those black African states interested in dialogue, the contacts offered potential trade-and-aid benefits, plus some possibility of exposing apartheid's contradictions by forcing the Republic's Government to accept foreign black Africans as equals.

The dialogue controversy threatened to split the OAU when the heads of state met in June. April had seen a vain South African attempt to use the controversy to discredit the OAU chairman for the year, Zambian President Kenneth Kaunda. In the South African Parliament, Prime Minister John Vorster announced that he and Dr. Kaunda had had secret contacts for three years.

The following week Ivory Coast President Félix Houphouet-Boigny told a large, international press conference that dialogue was one of the components of peace in Africa. He stated his intention of exploiting South Africa's willingness to meet black Africans "on a footing of equality."

The June OAU meeting ultimately passed an antidialogue resolution by a two-thirds majority. But enough (11) member states abstained from or opposed the resolution to ensure that black African diplomatic probing in quest of dialogue would continue.

In August, Malawi President Hastings Kamuzu Banda paid an official state visit to South Africa. The press reported him as making a tremendous impression in the Republic. Among other tributes, he received a standing ovation at Stellenbosch University, the seat of Afrikaner thought. Interpretations of the precise effect of the trip varied. Some South Africans claimed that it made a mockery of apartheid; others contended that it strengthened the Vorster Government by appearing to be a foreign-policy victory.

In late September, Uganda's new, military leader, Gen. Idi Amin, announced his desire to send a ten-man fact-finding mission to the Republic to investigate conditions there. Made with apparent guilelessness but without prior consultation, the announcement challenged South Africa to open apartheid to black African examination. In holding out for a delegation of government officials (rather than politicians, students, and prominent Ugandan personalities suggested by General Amin), the Republic lost whatever possibility had existed of winning a convert in East Africa.

In October, Ivory Coast officials visited Pretoria, following anniversary celebrations in Lesotho. The visit produced more press coverage in South Africa than the Ivory Coast

Presidents Kaunda (Zambia) and Nyerere (dark glasses; Tanzania) meet with Chinese officials who are building the Tan-Zam Railway, starting a few miles from Dar es Salaam. Below: Chinese earthmovers, with Chinese drivers, level the right-of-way.

Photos Africapix

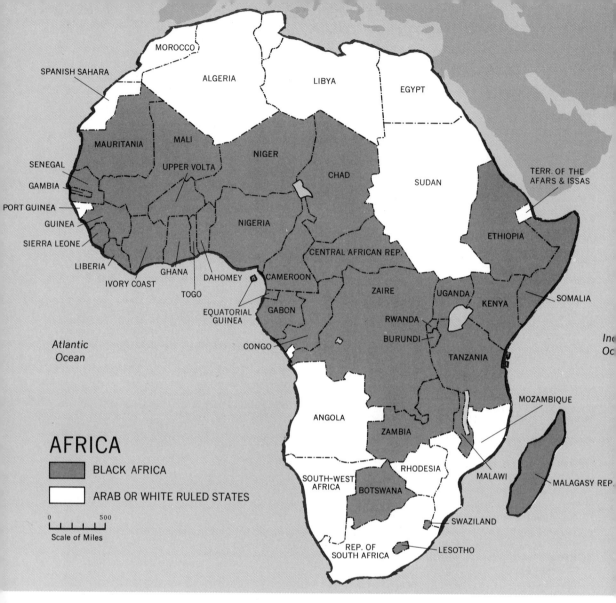

AFRICA

⬛	BLACK AFRICA
⬜	ARAB OR WHITE RULED STATES

0   500
Scale of Miles

Government had anticipated, and the delegation returned to Abidjan under a cloud. The incident gave the Ivory Coast a deeper understanding of South Africa's stake in the success of the dialogue.

At the same time, two leaders of the Republic's opposition Progressive Party, Helen Suzman and Colin Eglin, launched the first foray of white South Africans into black Africa. They held talks with leaders in six countries, advising them that any dialogue with South Africa should include discussions with nonwhite and opposition political leaders there.

At the year's end, the intense publicity surrounding dialogue had waned. Nonetheless, pro-dialogue states were continuing behind-the-scenes efforts to make further contacts with the white-ruled South.

Two factors, among others, motivated the pro-dialogue stance. One was fear of Communist Chinese influence in Africa. The other was the impotence of black African liberation movements to challenge white-ruled Africa effectively.

Peking in Africa. As its largest development-aid project anywhere, the Tanzania-Zambia railroad, is in Africa, Communist China was hardly a newcomer to the continent. In 1971 more black African states gave it diplomatic recognition than gave recognition to Taiwan.

China's entry into the United Nations made the more radical African nations regard it as the most likely world spokesman for the nonwhite, underdeveloped world. This potential role disquieted the politically conservative states, led by Ivory Coast. They saw communism

NATION	POPULATION (in millions)	CAPITAL	AREA (in sq. mi.)	HEAD OF STATE AND/OR GOVERNMENT, DATE INSTALLED (as of Jan. 1, 1972)
Botswana	0.6	Gaborone	231,804	Sir Seretse Khama, president—1966
Burundi	3.7	Usumbura	10,747	Michel Micombero, president—1966
Cameroon	5.9	Yaoundé	183,569	Ahmadou Ahidjo, president—1960
Central African Rep.	1.6	Bangui	240,535	Jean Bedel Bokassa, president—1966
Chad	3.8	Fort-Lamy	495,754	François Tombalbaye, president—1960
Congo	1.0	Brazzaville	132,047	Marien Ngouabi, president—1969
Dahomey	2.8	Porto-Novo	43,483	Hubert Maga, president—1970
Equatorial Guinea	0.3	Santa Isabel	10,830	Francisco Macias Nguema, president—1968
Ethiopia	25.6	Addis Ababa	471,777	Haile Selassie I, emperor—1930
Gabon	0.5	Libreville	103,346	Albert B. Bongo, president—1967
Gambia	0.4	Bathurst	4,361	Sir Dauda K. Jawara, president—1970
Ghana	9.3	Accra	92,099	Kofi A. Busia, prime minister—1969 Edward Akufo-Addo, president—1970
Guinea	4.0	Conakry	94,926	Sékou Touré, president—1958
Ivory Coast	4.4	Abidjan	124,503	Felix Houphouet-Boigny, president—1960
Kenya	11.2	Nairobi	224,959	Jomo Kenyatta, president—1963
Lesotho	1.1	Maseru	11,720	Leabua Jonathan, prime minister—1965
Liberia	1.2	Monrovia	43,000	William R. Tolbert, president—inaugurated Jan. 1972
Malagasy Rep.	7.1	Tananarive	226,657	Philibert Tsiranana, president—1959
Malawi	4.6	Zomba	45,747	Hastings K. Banda, president—1966
Mali	5.2	Bamako	478,765	Moussa Traoré, president—1969
Mauritania	1.2	Nouakchott	397,954	Moktar O. Daddah, president—1961
Mauritius	0.9	Port Louis	720	Sir Arthur Leonard Williams, governor-general—1968 Sir Seewoosagur Ramgoolam, prime minister—1967
Niger	4.0	Niamey	489,190	Hamani Diori, president—1960
Nigeria	56.5	Lagos	356,668	Yakubu Gowon, head of state—1966
Rhodesia	5.2	Salisbury	150,333	Ian D. Smith, prime minister—1964 Clifford Dupont, president—1970
Rwanda	3.7	Kigali	10,169	Gregoire Kayibanda, president—1961
Senegal	4.0	Dakar	75,750	Léopold Senghor, president—1960 Abdou Diouf, prime minister—1970
Sierra Leone	2.7	Freetown	27,699	Siaka Stevens, president—1971 Sorie I. Koroma, prime minister—1971
Somalia	2.9	Mogadishu	246,200	Mohammad Siad Barre, president, supreme revolutionary council—1969
South Africa, Rep. of	20.6	Pretoria Cape Town	471,444	J. J. Fouche, president—1968 Balthazar J. Vorster, prime minister—1966
Sudan	16.3	Khartoum	967,497	Gaafar al-Nimeiry, president—1969
Swaziland	0.4	Mbabane	6,704	Sobhuza II, king—1921 Makhosini Dlamini, prime minister—1967
Tanzania	13.6	Dar es Salaam	362,820	Julius K. Nyerere, president—1964
Togo	1.9	Lomé	21,622	Etienne Eyadema, president—1967
Uganda	8.8	Kampala	91,134	Idi Amin, president—1971
Upper Volta	5.5	Ouagadougou	105,869	Sangoulé Lamizana, president—1966
Zaire	17.8	Kinshasa	905,565	Joseph D. Mobutu, president—1965
Zambia	4.4	Lusaka	290,585	Kenneth D. Kaunda, president— 1964

as a greater threat to the continent than southern Africa's white-minority governments.

Liberation Movements. The various African guerrilla movements continued to prove themselves generally ineffective in efforts to overturn white rule by force. The one exception was the PAIGC (African Party for the Independence of Portuguese Guinea and Cape Verde). It claimed that it could attack all the urban centers, including Bissau. Moreover, it showed that it had good sources of information on the Portuguese side, and reported that the first eight months of 1971 were the best in its history.

Frelimo (Mozambique Liberation Front), however, seemed bogged down. Although it harassed road communications in Tete Province, it could not hinder construction of the Cabora Bassa hydroelectric project.

After months of dissension within the ranks of ZAPU and ZANU, the main Rhodesian liberation movements, splinter groups from the two organizations formed the Front for the Liberation of Zimbabwe (as they call Rhodesia) in early October. Frolizi, telescoped name of the new organization, intended to soft-pedal politics and to reactivate armed action inside Rhodesia. Its leaders predicted that the other two movements would wither away as it achieved its goal. The other groups considered Frolizi a tribal organization, however, based on the Zezuru clan of the Shona tribe. At year's end they had shown no signs of withering, although no estimate was available of their guerrilla strength.

Rhodesia. Africa's second important 1971 dialogue culminated in late November in British-

Rhodesian leader Smith and British Foreign Secretary Douglas-Home chat on arrival of latter in Salisbury for talks on independence.

Rhodesian proposals designed to end the six-year independence dispute. While the British Government claimed that the settlement terms lay well within the five negotiating principles it had enunciated, the proposals fell far short of even moderate African hopes for a settlement.

The terms themselves were highly complicated. On one side they provided for the reintroduction of a Declaration of Rights subject to test in the courts. They envisaged a joint, ten-year British-Rhodesian development program, involving some $260,000,000, designed to advance African education and develop the Tribal Trust Lands.

The terms also proposed a process of gradual African progress toward equal black-white representation in Parliament, based on economic development. An increase in African parliamentary representation was to depend on the size of a newly created "higher roll" of African voters in relation to the size of the European voters roll. Africans were to receive two new parliamentary seats every time voter registration on the higher roll increased by 6 per cent of the European roll. Once parity representation was reached, a commission would investigate procedures for establishing majority rule. However, the proposals provided mechanisms by which the white representatives could block such procedures. Thus they gave no guarantee of eventual African rule.

The settlement terms avoided any discussion of a schedule for reaching majority rule. Scholars, however, estimated that it would require fifty to sixty years. Thus the proposals left the structure and practice of racial discrimination in Rhodesia basically unchanged.

They also provided for a test of the settlement's acceptability to Rhodesians as a whole. The test was to be conducted by a commission appointed by the British; it allowed for neither a vote nor for a quantitative assessment of African reaction to the proposals.

Prior to announcement of the terms, observers had hoped that a British-Rhodesian settlement might make the building of a viable multiracial nation in Rhodesia easier and thus foster racial harmony in the region. The settlement terms, however, offered little prospect of such a result.

Coups. After 1970 had passed without a single African *coup d'état,* some observers talked—with more hope than reason—of the new nations as having reached a degree of political maturity that would make them see that coups hinder national development. The events of 1971 gave the lie to such speculation.

In Uganda the Government of Milton Obote was overthrown in late January by Army commander Gen. Idi Amin, a man of little education and no political experience. The coup occurred while Obote was out of the country. It stemmed from tribal jealousies within the national security structure and from Amin's fear that Obote was plotting his assassination. Amin set the country on a more conservative course, one dictated in part by the need for seeking friends wherever they could be found.

The coup triggered other acts. Old tribal scores were settled within the Uganda Army; as many as 1,000 men may have been killed. Recognition of the Amin regime threatened to split the OAU, along with the dialogue dispute. Although behind-the-scenes diplomacy resolved the matter, the Ugandans boycotted the June meeting of heads of state.

The coup put a severe strain on relations between Uganda and Tanzania, which offered Obote refuge and refused to recognize the Amin regime. In the year's third quarter the tension flared in clashes along the countries' common border west of Lake Victoria.

Tanzania-Uganda difficulties largely incapacitated the East African Community, of which both nations are members. They illustrated how political considerations hamper African attempts to achieve economic cooperation. Only after nine months of uncertainty did mediation by Kenya President Jomo Kenyatta pave the way to resuming normal community operations.

In late March, months of political instability in Sierra Leone came to a head with an abortive coup. It stemmed from fears that Prime Minister Siaka Stevens would try to manipulate Parliament in order to make the country a republic and himself an executive president. To

President Nyerere gives the "Uhuru" (Freedom) drum 10 strokes to signal the start of Tanzania's celebration of 10 years of independence, in December.

protect his position, Stevens called in troops from neighboring Guinea, detained his opponents, executed the coup leaders and had himself inaugurated as executive president on Apr. 21.

In July another coup, led by Army officers and Communists, seized power for three days in Sudan. It failed to generate popular support, however, and was overthrown by military forces loyal to Gen. Gaafar al-Nimeiry. Following the countercoup, 11 rebel officers were shot. Three communist leaders were hanged, including Abdul Khalek Mahgoub, general secretary of the Sudan Communist Party, and Joseph Garang, minister for southern affairs. The last executions seriously strained Russo-Sudan relations. General Nimeiry was subsequently elected president in a national referendum in September.

Other Events. The death in July of Liberia's longtime President, William V. S. Tubman, underlined the fact that a number of African leaders are elderly men who will soon pass from the scene. The death or resignation of some may trigger political violence. It need not be inevitable, however, as the case of Liberia showed. Vice-President William R. Tolbert, Jr., succeeded to the presidency and worked to give the Government a more modern flavor.

With the blessing of the Economic Commission for Africa and the six countries involved, the oft-mooted idea of a trans-African highway entered exploratory stages. The highway is planned to run from Mombasa (on the Indian Ocean coast of Kenya) through Uganda and Zaire (formerly Congo-Kinshasa) into Central African Republic and Cameroon and reach the Atlantic in Nigeria, probably via Kano and Lagos. A British team began to survey possible routes.

The Congo (Kinshasa) renamed itself in late October. It chose the name Zaire, a fifteenth-century Portuguese approximation of a local name for the Congo River. Henceforth, to Zairiens at least, both their country and the river would be called Zaire. The action eliminated what had been one of the continuing difficulties of African geography: the existence of two countries called the Congo.

FREDERIC HUNTER
Africa Correspondent
The Christian Science Monitor

Congo (Kinshasa) acquires new name, Zaire, and new flag, which features a flaming torch.

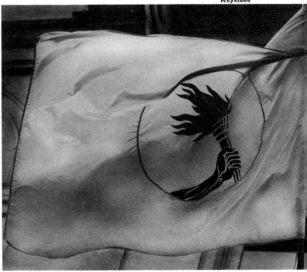

Victoria Beller

Keeping a zest for life in retirement, an active couple play shuffleboard in a "leisure village."

AGING, CONFERENCE ON

The 20,000,000 Americans age 65 or over are in a particularly vulnerable position because of the overwhelming social and economic changes that have occurred in their lifetime. They are the generation that helped America win two world wars, overcome the disastrous economic depression of the 1930's, and achieve a living standard measured by a gross national product of more than a trillion dollars a year.

Yet, growing old in America can be difficult —even heartbreaking—in spite of the nation's high living standard. Nearly 5,000,000 men and women age 65 or over exist at or below the poverty line, and millions more elderly are very close to it, according to a report by the U.S. Senate Special Committee on Aging.

A specific formula for making life meaningful for the retirement generation has been provided by 3,400 delegates to the White House Conference on Aging held Nov. 28 to Dec. 2, 1971, in Washington.

Here are the main White House conference recommendations.

Income. "There is no substitute for income if people are to be free to exercise choices in their style of living," the White House conference delegates agreed.

An elderly couple should be entitled to a minimum income standard based on the intermediate budget for an older couple prepared by the U.S. Labor Department (nationally averaging $4,500 a year as of the spring of 1970). For an elderly individual, a minimum income standard should be 75 per cent of the elderly couple's budget.

To achieve this floor of income, the basic financial features of the social-security system should be retained, but augmented by a supplementary payment based on an income test. The payment would be financed by Federal general revenues but disbursed as a single Social Security Administration payment to avoid the stigma attached to welfare or relief payments.

The need to ensure needy men and women age 65 or over an adequate level of living is urgent today. Unless the need is met now, it will become increasingly more urgent as the number of elderly grows to an estimated 25,-000,000 by 1980.

Health Care. Medicare, the Federal health-insurance program for those age 65 or over, was a notable social advance. It has relieved older Americans of some of the burden of medical costs, lessening their need to turn to relatives or apply for welfare to meet the costs of health care.

However, it pays much less than the total health costs of the elderly, and more and more eligibles are being excluded from Medicare benefits because of the rising out-of-pocket payments required for Medicare coverage. The United States can never attain a reasonable goal of income security as long as heavy and unpredictable health costs threaten the aged.

The conference delegates urged that priority consideration be given "to the establishment of a comprehensive national health security program" that would include all Americans, not only the aged. "Financing the program through wage and payroll taxes and contributions from Federal general revenues would ensure that health-care expenses would be a shared responsibility of the government, employers and individuals," the delegates agreed.

Pending establishment of a comprehensive system of health care for all Americans, substantial improvements were recommended in Medicare health insurance for the elderly and Medicaid health benefits for the needy at all age levels, including removal of all existing out-of-pocket charges (sometimes called deductibles, co-payments or co-insurance). Particularly, the conference urged expanded health services in the home and other alternatives to institutional care for the disabled elderly.

Nutrition. Approximately one third to half of the health problems of the elderly are believed related to nutrition, according to health experts.

The Federal Government should establish and enforce more strictly high standards with specific regulations for the food and nutrition services provided by institutions and home-care agencies that receive any direct or indirect Federal funds. It should require a high level of performance from state-government enforcement agencies, and, when necessary, provide financial assistance to bring nonprofit organizations up to standard. The standards should encompass such important areas as quality and nutritive value of food; methods of handling, preparing and serving foods; the special dietary needs of individuals; and accessibility to nutritional counseling.

Nutrition services and counseling should be a required component of all health delivery systems, including such plans as Medicare, Medicaid, health-maintenance organizations, home-health services, extended-care facilities, and prevention programs.

The Federal Government should assume responsibility for making adequate nutrition available to the elderly by assuring them of a minimum income of at least $4,500 a year for a couple, and $3,000 a year for a single person, and by financing low-cost meals in convenient locations and meals-on-wheels programs for the low- and moderate-income elderly.

Housing. A fixed proportion of all government funds—Federal, state or local—allocated to housing and related services should be set aside to provide housing for the elderly.

Housing construction for the elderly should be at the rate of 120,000 units a year, twice the present rate. Special attention should be given to the needs of those at or below the poverty level.

Housing funds impounded by the Nixon administration should be released for immediate use, and Federal aid for housing under the Federal Housing Act's Section 202 program, with its special guidelines relating to space, design, construction and financing (direct loans from the Federal Treasury at low interest rates), should be restored. (This 10-year-old program has been abandoned by the Department of Housing and Urban Development.)

The rent-supplement program of the present housing law should be expanded.

Employment and Retirement. The elderly should have a free choice between continuing in employment as long as a person wishes and is able to work or retiring on adequate income with opportunities for meaningful activity.

It is imperative that adequate funds based

Standing in the center, President Nixon welcomes the delegates to the White House Conference on Aging held Nov. 28 through Dec. 2, 1971.

The White House

on population, needs and special circumstances of the elderly be earmarked for employment programs for the elderly.

More vigorous enforcement of the law against age discrimination in employment is essential to reemployment of the elderly wishing to return to the labor force, and Congress should eliminate the age 65 limit under this law. Chronological age should not be the sole criterion for retirement. A flexible policy should be adopted that is based upon the worker's desires and needs and upon his or her physical or mental capacity. Policies and programs that provide employment opportunities after age 65 must be made available.

Federal-training programs should be provided to ensure reemployability of the elderly and to make retirement more meaningful.

Transportation. Meeting the transportation needs of the elderly is vital. Federal funds should be made available for improving existing transportation services and also for developing flexible and innovative systems, especially where transportation facilities exist.

Federal aid should encourage reduced or no fares for elderly persons. Transportation programs so financed should also encourage standards for design of equipment and facilities to ensure the safety, comfort and convenience of the elderly.

Nationwide standards should be established for licensing automobile drivers that do not discriminate against the elderly on the basis of chronological age alone.

The Federal Government and the states should forbid insurance companies from increasing auto-insurance premiums or canceling car-insurance policies on the basis of age alone.

Over and above these essential requirements, the elderly should be assured of services, including education and recreation, to enable them to stay in the mainstream of community life.

The first White House Conference on Aging, held in January 1961, helped promote public support for Medicare, the Older Americans Act, which is the enabling legislation for the U.S. Administration on Aging, and gave impetus to the enactment of housing programs for the elderly, legislation forbidding age discrimination in employment, and other significant acts. The 1961 conference also helped launch the 3,000,000-member National Council of Senior Citizens, the leading organization of older Americans.

The 1971 White House Conference on Aging was expected to generate new organizational activity among the elderly and to give new impetus to programs to make life better for the retirement generation.

NELSON H. CRUIKSHANK
President
National Council of Senior Citizens

NEW SOCIAL SECURITY BENEFITS

On Mar. 17, 1971, President Nixon signed a bill increasing Social Security benefits by 10 per cent, retroactive to Jan. 1, 1971. (The benefits are based on the average earnings covered by Social Security over a number of years.) In addition, the amount of annual earnings subject to the Social Security tax was increased from $7,800 to $9,000, effective Jan. 1, 1972. It had been increased to $7,800 in 1968. The figures below are the monthly benefits for which a worker becomes eligible at age 65 under the old and new laws.

Average Monthly Earnings in Working Years	Retired Worker Old Benefit	New Benefit	Retired Couple Old Benefit	New Benefit
$ 76 or less	$ 64.00	$ 70.40	$ 96.00	$105.60
$100	$ 82.30	$ 90.60	$123.50	$135.90
$150	$101.70	$111.90	$152.60	$167.90
$200	$116.90	$128.60	$175.40	$192.90
$250	$132.30	$145.60	$198.50	$218.40
$300	$146.20	$160.90	$219.30	$241.40
$350	$161.50	$177.70	$242.30	$266.60
$400	$176.70	$194.40	$265.10	$291.60
$450	$189.80	$208.80	$284.70	$313.20
$500	$204.20	$224.70	$306.30	$337.10
$550	$218.40	$240.30	$327.60	$360.50
$600	$234.60	$258.10	$351.90	$387.20
$650	$250.70	$275.80	$376.10	$413.70
$750	$250.70	$295.40	$376.10	$443.10

AGNEW, SPIRO

Following the precedent of previous vice-presidents, Theodore Spiro Agnew spent not a little of his time in 1971 in travel abroad and at home. On June 27 he flew from Honolulu on a visit to ten nations in Asia, Africa and Europe. His first mission was as President Nixon's representative to the inauguration in Seoul of Korea's President Chung Hee Park for a third term. At a stopover in Guam, Agnew told reporters he was interested in visiting Communist China but that he had doubts about Nixon's mission because China was essentially hostile to the United States.

Throughout the year, Agnew kept up his criticism of the news media. In a speech to radio station owners, he charged that the media had reacted to his "constructive" criticism over 18 months with a frenzy bordering on paranoia. This, he said, further damaged the credibility not only of the media but of government as well. In a series of speeches around the country, Agnew called for support of the President's economic policies.

Persistent rumors that he would be dropped from the ticket brought the Vice-President strong support from the right wing of his party. In some instances, as registered by the Young Americans for Freedom, support for Agnew was stronger than for the President. As for his own future, the Vice-President said he would do whatever Nixon asked. If the President wanted another running mate, Agnew would comply and step aside.

MARQUIS CHILDS
Contributing Editor
St. Louis Post-Dispatch

AGRICULTURE

As agriculture moves ahead into the 1970's it still has many characteristics of earlier decades. The 1970's represent a challenge to the developing countries still faced with problems of producing enough food to meet the demands of their rapidly growing populations. The decade also presents a challenge to certain developed countries of solving problems of surpluses, low farm incomes and underemployment in rural areas.

Late 1971 estimates indicated that worldwide food production for the year would be near record levels. Overall supplies were augmented by favorable weather in most major producing regions. Because of favorable weather and ever-stronger efforts to improve agriculture, India harvested its second successive record crop of cereals. Total cereals production amounted to 107,000,000 tons, nearly 8 per cent more than

in 1970. The bumper crop allowed the nation to put 5,000,000 tons into storage or buffer stocks.

The developing countries of Asia continued to make their greatest agricultural strides in wheat yields per acre and in production. Increases in wheat production came from the larger area planted to new high-yielding varieties of short-stemmed, or Mexican, wheats and from such auxiliary practices as fertilization and irrigation. Less spectacular but still substantial gains were achieved in rice production. Gains in rice production and exportable surpluses brought attention to potential problems for countries that have traditionally supplied the international market. For example, increased rice production and exports by such countries as the Philippine Republic along with

Before agricultural economist Earl L. Butz was confirmed as agriculture secretary, he was opposed as being too close to corporate farming.

Dennis Brack, Black Star

Shelled corn piles up in the open air on a Midwest farm after glut fills all storage space.

an approach to self-sufficiency in many other countries are beginning to make an impact on such "third countries" as Thailand. While its yields have improved very little, Thailand has always devoted a large area to rice, and a large portion of its foreign-exchange earnings has come from this crop. With an unfavorable trade balance developing, especially as a result of stronger competition in the rice-export market, Thailand began to emphasize crop diversification in 1971. It initiated a shift into production of soybeans, feed grains, livestock and industrial crops. Contracts were signed for the export of increased amounts of feed grains to Japan.

World wheat production, the major agricultural item in international trade, rose rather sharply in 1971 after two years of decline. The North American crop increased by 12 per cent to 1,600,000,000 bushels, and Canadian output by 53 per cent to 507,000,000 bushels. West Europe's wheat crop increased by nearly 10 per cent and exceeded the 1968 record. Wheat production in Australia and Argentina recovered from the low of 1970, and the crop in Eastern Europe increased by about 10 per

cent. The major exporters had huge stocks on hand at the beginning of the 1970–71 season. While these stocks were drawn upon during the year, international prices were depressed by the large 1971 wheat crop. In comparison with a year earlier, Rotterdam prices in mid-September 1971 were about 9 per cent lower for Canadian and U.S. wheat. Also, for the same dates, import levies by the European Economic Community (EEC) rose 17 per cent for wheat and 85 per cent for corn. Hence the larger world crop and the burden on imports by the EEC generally depressed world grain prices.

The virulent Southern corn blight had greatly reduced the 1970 U.S. corn crop. The possibility that the disease would again prevail in the major corn-producing states was considered likely. The U.S. Department of Agriculture therefore relaxed acreage control somewhat on production. The disease did not strike nationally, however. Consequently, the 1971 U.S. corn crop established records for yield per acre and total production. Production in 1970 was 4,100,000,000 bushels on 57,400,000 acres. In 1971 it was 5,400,000,000 bushels on 64,100,-000 acres. The Chicago corn price for December delivery dropped by 15 per cent. By November, farmers without storage space were forced to pile harvested corn on the ground. The size of the crop also burdened marketing facilities, and country-town streets were piled high with shelled corn as elevator space was filled. Local corn prices fell as low as 90 cents per bushel, the lowest level since 1942 when World War II demands were beginning to exhaust the large stockpile built up through the emergency programs of the 1930's depression. While government administrators had forecast higher meat and livestock prices as a result of corn blight and low corn yields in 1970, hog prices averaged 28 per cent lower in the first 8 months of 1971 than in the same period of 1970. Over the first 8 months of 1971, beef-cattle prices were only slightly higher than in the preceding year.

The sharp decline in farm prices and income, resulting from the large supplies of feed grains and livestock, provoked heated farmer criticism of government programs. Partly in answer to the criticism, Clifford M. Hardin resigned as secretary of agriculture in November. Dr. Earl Butz, a dean at Purdue University, was nominated to the post. Yet this move also provoked criticism because of Butz's association with large agribusiness firms and his tenure as assistant secretary of agriculture under Secretary Ezra Taft Benson in the Eisenhower administration. At that time, farm incomes fell to low levels, and large stocks of farm commodities accumulated in government hands. Following extensive hearings the Senate approved the nomination.

Exports of U.S. farm commodities were hampered by a prolonged dock workers' strike in the fall of 1971. Farm representatives blamed the strike for depressed grain prices. Somewhat offsetting the situation, however, was the sale of U.S. grain to the Soviet Union. Announced in November, the sale included 80,000,000 bushels of corn, 39,000,000 bushels of barley and 24,000,000 bushels of oats. The sale, handled by Continental Grain Co. of New York and Cargill Inc. of Minneapolis, drew grain from government-owned stocks held by the Commodity Credit Corporation. To be used by the Soviet Union for livestock production, the grain was sold at prices considerably lower than either its cost to the U.S. Government or prevailing market prices. On the one hand, the sale was criticized by U.S. livestock farmers who claimed that Soviet livestock production was being subsidized while home production was not, and by Canadian farmers who considered that the low prices excluded them from Eastern European markets. On the other hand, U.S. grain farmers favored the sale and price levels as a rein on depressed prices. As a further limit on future U.S. grain supplies and stocks, the Government announced a set-aside farm program in October 1971. It is designed to cut corn production back to about 4,500,000,000 bushels in 1972. To accomplish the cutback, farmers were offered additional inducement in the form of permissible idle land and the subsidy paid for keeping it idle.

Britain's decision to enter the EEC posed agricultural adjustments for member countries. EEC price levels for grain and livestock have been considerably higher than Britain's, where much of the farmers' income consists of government subsidies. Elimination of these subsidies is expected to increase food costs for British consumers, while EEC levies will be at the expense of Commonwealth farm exports to Britain. However, as grain prices are expected to jump upon full EEC entry, British farmers may devote a much larger acreage to grain production.

EEC countries, as well as others in Western Europe, continued to be glutted with a surplus of butter and milk products, even as low incomes for small farmers have persisted and farm subsidies have become more costly. In the absence of any price increases for farm commodities since 1968, EEC farmers demanded higher prices to keep abreast of inflation. At a meeting in Brussels the EEC agricul-

tural ministers moved to raise the prices of some farm commodities and to initiate a $1,500,000,000 fund to modernize the agriculture of member countries. Price increases (averaging 4 per cent for all commodities affected) were 3 per cent on wheat and rye, 5 per cent on barley, 6 per cent on milk and 10 per cent on beef. Emphasis was laid on shifting cattle production from butterfat (milk), where large surpluses and subsidized exports have long prevailed, to beef. The $1,500,-000,000 fund is to be used for pensions, to encourage early retirement from farming, and for low-interest loans to encourage expansion by the remaining farmers.

The EEC Executive Commission, led by EEC Vice-President Sicco Mansholt, continued to press for structural reforms in farm programs by member countries. The commission claimed that EEC farm programs have not solved the problems of the small farm but have benefited large farmers and have encouraged the growing surpluses of such commodities as butter and other dairy products. To many observers it is fairly evident that the many small farms of Western Europe are inefficient in relation to current technology and resource prices; that to maintain an adequate farm-family income, they require price levels that result in high consumer-food costs; that they hold too many people on farms, where labor is underemployed and economic opportunity restricted; and that they will eventually disappear under ongoing market forces anyway. The structural reforms recommended by the EEC commission were therefore directed toward phasing out the smaller farm units and reducing the number of people on farms.

Eastern European countries continued their efforts toward consolidating and increasing the size of collective farms. Hungary neared completion of the last phases of consolidation, halving the number of farms in the nation. The Soviet Union announced plans to expand still further the specialized production of livestock products in 1971–75. The 5-year plan calls for launching 1,170 specialized meat and dairy enterprises, and 585 broiler and hatchery enterprises. These large-scale units may parallel the mammoth hog-producing units in operation in Rumania and some very large dairy units in Yugoslavia. Soviet private home plots have accounted for about 35 per cent of meat and milk and 55 per cent of egg production in recent years. Most of the remainder has come from unspecialized state and collective farms.

Developing countries continued to bank on cotton as an export crop to acquire foreign exchange. In mid-October the world cotton crop for the 1971–72 crop year was estimated at 53,100,000 bales, up by 1,900,000 bales from 1970–71 and by 2,100,000 bales from the 1965–69 average. Substantial increases in 1971–72 production were noted in South America, Mexico, Turkey, India, Pakistan and the United States. Soviet production was down about 10 per cent. A large land area of the world is adapted to cotton production.

EARL D. HEADY
Executive Director
Center for Agricultural and Economic Development
Iowa State University

ALBANIA

After years of self-imposed isolation and devoted adherence to the People's Republic of China, Albania moved into the international spotlight on behalf of its massive ally. Albanian delegates to the United Nations guided to victory a resolution in the General Assembly bringing mainland China into the UN and expelling the Government on Taiwan headed by Chiang Kai-shek. (Rumania was the only other communist country that joined in sponsoring the resolution, adopted Oct. 25.) The Albanians had sponsored the pro-Chinese resolution for eight years.

Relations with China. Albania pledged its support of China under any circumstances on the 22d anniversary of the communist victory in China. This apparently included Albanian acceptance of the visit to China by President Nixon, whose policies have been vociferously condemned by Albanian ideologists.

Relations with the Soviet Union. There was no effort to achieve rapprochement with the Soviet Union. The Albanian party daily *Zeri i Popullit* dismissed out of hand First Secretary Leonid Brezhnev's offer, delivered at the 24th Soviet Communist Party Congress in March, to reestablish normal relations with Albania.

Other Foreign Ties. Albania continued to move cautiously toward friendlier ties with the outside world. Diplomatic relations with Greece were restored; contacts with Yugoslavia and

---

ALBANIA

Area: 11,100 sq. mi.
Population: 2,200,000
Capital: Tirana
Government: Enver Hoxha, Communist Party Secretary—1946; Mehmet Shehu, premier—1954
Gross National Product: $900,000,000
Foreign trade: exports, $80,000,000; imports, $143,000,000
Armed forces: 42,000

Rumania expanded; the first Swedish trade delegation toured Albania; and Albania's state film studio made an agreement with French film makers to produce a picture based on an Albanian novel, *The General of the Dead Army*.

Domestic Economy. Successive failures on the agricultural front—the output target was missed again in 1970—evoked a new set of directives. They called for additional mergers and still further centralized control of collective farms. The program "rotation of cadres"—sending office workers to work on farms—was again used in the effort to expand farm output. The 1971 plan called for a 25.8 per cent increase in agricultural production, and a 7.8 per cent rise in industrial output.

HERMAN SINGER
Editor, *East Europe*

ALBERT, CARL BERT

On Jan. 19, 1971, a caucus of the Democratic members of the U.S. House of Representatives chose Carl Bert Albert of McAlester, Okla., as the nation's 46th Speaker of the House, succeeding John W. McCormack. Albert, now second in the line of succession to the presidency, behind the vice-president, has served in the House since January 1947. During 1955–62 he was the House Democratic whip, and in January 1962 he was elected House majority leader.

Although Albert considers the job of Speaker that of a "party leader trying to put over the party program," he promised not to oppose presidential programs solely "for the sake of opposing." Albert's general views represent the middle ground between the party's Northern liberals and Southern conservatives. He was a friend and admirer of the late Speaker Sam Rayburn.

Born in McAlester on May 10, 1908, Carl Albert studied political science at the University of Oklahoma. The university's president called Albert "the brightest mind ever to come to the university." A Rhodes scholar, the future Congressman received two law degrees from Oxford University in 1934. After coming home from England, he practiced law until the outbreak of World War II. He then enlisted in the U.S. Army, where he rose to the rank of lieutenant colonel and was awarded the Bronze Star.

Speaker Albert is married to the former Mary Harmon; they have a son and a daughter. Although the Speaker suffered a heart attack in 1966, he usually spends at least 12 hours daily at the Capitol.

AMBASSADORS AND ENVOYS[a]

FROM U.S.	COUNTRIES	TO U.S.	FROM U.S.	COUNTRIES	TO U.S.
Robert G. Neumann	AFGHANISTAN	Abdullah Malikyar	G. McMurtrie	LAOS	Prince Khammao
John D. Lodge	ARGENTINA	Carlos M. Muniz	Godley		
Walter L. Rice	AUSTRALIA	James Plimsoll	William B. Buffum	LEBANON	Najati Kabbani
John P. Humes	AUSTRIA	Karl Gruber	Charles J. Nelson	LESOTHO	Mothusi T.
William A. Stoltzfus, Jr.	BAHRAIN	(vacant)			Mashologu
Eileen R. Donovan	BARBADOS	Valerie T. McComie	S. Z. Westerfield, Jr.	LIBERIA	S. Edward Peal
(vacant)	BELGIUM	Walter Loridan	Joseph Palmer 2d	LIBYA	Abdulla al Suwesi
Ernest V. Siracusa	BOLIVIA	Edmundo Valencia-	Kingdon Gould, Jr.	LUXEMBOURG	Jean Wagner
		Ibanez	(vacant)	MALAGASY	Jules Alphonse
Charles J. Nelson	BOTSWANA	Chief Linchwe 2d		REP.	Razafimbahiny
William M. Rountree	BRAZIL	J. A. de Araujo Castro	William C. Burdett	MALAWI	Nyemba W.
Horace G. Torbert, Jr.	BULGARIA	Luben Guerassimov			Mbekeani
Edwin W. Martin	BURMA	U San Maung	Jack W. Lydman	MALAYSIA	Tan Sri Yoke
Thomas P. Melady	BURUNDI	Nsanze Terence			Lin Ong
Emory C. Swank	CAMBODIA	Sonn Voeunsai	Robert Strausz-Hupé	MALDIVE IS.	Abdul Sattar
	(KHMER REP.)		Robert O. Blake	MALI	Seydou Traore
Lewis Hoffacker	CAMEROON	Francois X. Tchoungui	J. C. Pritzlaff, Jr.	MALTA	Joseph Attard
Adolph W. Schmidt	CANADA	Marcel Cadieux			Kingswell
Melvin L. Manfull	CENTRAL AFR.	Christophe Maidou	Richard W. Murphy	MAURITANIA	Moulaye El
	REP.				Hassen
Robert Strausz-Hupé	CEYLON	Neville Kanakaratne	William D. Brewer	MAURITIUS	Pierre G. G.
Terence A. Todman	CHAD	Lazare Massibe			Balancy
Nathaniel Davis	CHILE	Orlando Letelier	Robert H. McBride	MEXICO	Jose Juan de
Walter P. McConaughy	CHINA	James C. H. Shen			Olloqui
	(TAIWAN)		Stuart W. Rockwell	MOROCCO	Badreddine Senoussi
Leonard J. Saccio	COLOMBIA	Douglas Botero-	Carol C. Laise	NEPAL	Kul S. Sharma
		Boshell	J. W. Middendorf 2d	NETHERLANDS	R. B. Van Lynden
Walter C. Ploeser	COSTA RICA	Rafael A. Zuniga	Kenneth Franzheim 2d	NEW ZEALAND	Frank Corner
David H. Popper	CYPRUS	Zenon Rossides	Turner B. Shelton	NICARAGUA	Guillermo Sevilla-
(vacant)	CZECHOSLO-	Jaroslav Zantovsky[b]			Sacasa
	VAKIA		Roswell D. McClelland	NIGER	Georges M. Condat
M. J. Looram, Jr.	DAHOMEY	Wilfrid De Souza	John E. Reinhardt	NIGERIA	Joe Iyalla
Fred J. Russell	DENMARK	Eyvind Bartels	Philip K. Crowe	NORWAY	Arne Gunneng
Francis E. Meloy, Jr.	DOMINICAN	S. Salvador Ortiz	Joseph S. Farland	PAKISTAN	Nawabzada Agha
	REP.				Mohammad Raza
Findley Burns, Jr.	ECUADOR	C. Mantilla-Ortega	Robert M. Sayre	PANAMA	Jose A. de la Ossa
Henry E. Catto, Jr.	EL SALVADOR	Julio A. Rivera	J. Raymond Ylitalo	PARAGUAY	Roque J. Avila
Lewis Hoffacker	EQUATORIAL	(vacant)	Taylor G. Belcher	PERU	Fernando
	GUINEA				Berckemeyer
E. Ross Adair	ETHIOPIA	Ghebeyehou Mekbib[b]	Henry A. Byroade	PHILIPPINES	Eduardo Z. Romualdez
(vacant)	FIJI	Semesa K. Sikivou	Walter J.	POLAND	Witald Trampczynski
Val Peterson	FINLAND	Olavi Munkki	Stoessel, Jr.		
Arthur K. Watson	FRANCE	Charles Lucet	Ridgway B. Knight	PORTUGAL	Joao Hall Themido
John A. McKesson 3d	GABON	Gaston-Robert	W. A. Stoltzfus, Jr.	QATAR	(vacant)
		Bouckat-Bou-	Leonard C. Meeker	RUMANIA	Corneliu Bogdan
		Nziengui	Robert F. Corrigan	RWANDA	F. Nkundabagenzi
G. Edward Clark	GAMBIA	(vacant)	Nicholas G. Thacher	SAUDI ARABIA	Ibrahim Al-Sowayel
Kenneth Rush	GERMANY (W.)	Rolf Pauls	G. Edward Clark	SENEGAL	André Jean Coulbary
Fred L. Hadsel	GHANA	Ebenezer M. Debrah	(vacant)	SIERRA LEONE	Jacob A. C. Davies
Walter H. Annenberg	GREAT BRITAIN	Earl of Cromer	(vacant)	SINGAPORE	Ernest S. Monteiro
Henry J. Tasca	GREECE	Basil D. Vitsaxis	(vacant)	SOMALI DEM.	Abdullahi A. Addou
William G. Bowdler	GUATEMALA	Julio Asensio-		REP.	
		Wunderlich	John G. Hurd	SOUTH AFRICA	Johan S. F. Botha
Albert W. Sherer, Jr.	GUINEA	El Hadj Keita Mory	(vacant)	SPAIN	Jaime Arguelles
Spencer M. King	GUYANA	Rahman B. Gajraj	Charles J. Nelson	SWAZILAND	S. T. M. Sukati
Clinton E. Knox	HAITI	Rene Chalmers	Jerome H. Holland	SWEDEN	Hubert de Besche
Hewson A. Ryan	HONDURAS	Roberto	Shelby C. Davis	SWITZERLAND	Felix Schnyder
		Galvez Barnes	Claude G. Ross	TANZANIA	G. M. Rutabanzibwa
Alfred Puhan	HUNGARY	Karoly Szabo	Leonard Unger	THAILAND	Sunthorn
Luther I. Replogle	ICELAND	Gudmundur I.			Hongladarom
		Gudmundsson	Dwight Dickinson	TOGO	Epiphane A. Mawussi
Kenneth B. Keating	INDIA	Lakshmi Kant Jha	(vacant)	TRINIDAD AND	Ellis E. I. Clarke
Francis J. Galbraith	INDONESIA	Sjarif Thajeb		TOBAGO	
(vacant)	IRAN	Amir-Aslan Afshar	John A. Calhoun	TUNISIA	Slaheddine
John D. J. Moore	IRELAND	William Warnock			El-Goulli
Walworth Barbour	ISRAEL	Yitzak Rabin	William J. Handley	TURKEY	Melih Esenbel
Graham A. Martin	ITALY	Egidio Ortona	C. Clyde Ferguson, Jr.	UGANDA	Mustapha Ramathan
John F. Root	IVORY COAST	Timothée Ahoua	Jacob D. Beam	U.S.S.R.	Anatoly F.
Vincent de Roulet	JAMAICA	Sir Egerton R.			Dobrynin
		Richardson	Donald B. Easum	UPPER VOLTA	Paul Rouamba
Armin H. Meyer	JAPAN	Nobuhiko Ushiba	Charles W. Adair, Jr.	URUGUAY	Hector Luisi
Lewis D. Brown	JORDAN	Abdul Hamid	Robert McClintock	VENEZUELA	J. Sosa-Rodriguez
		Sharaf	Ellsworth Bunker	VIETNAM (S.)	Bui Diem
Robinson McIlvaine	KENYA	Leonard O. Kibinge	Malcolm Toon	YUGOSLAVIA	Toma Granfil
Philip C. Habib	KOREA (S.)	Dong Jo Kim	Sheldon B. Vance, Jr.	ZAIRE	Pierre Ileka
W. A. Stoltzfus, Jr.	KUWAIT	Shaykh Salim al	Oliver L. Troxel, Jr.	ZAMBIA	Unia Gostel Mwila
		Sabah al Salim			

[a] As of January 1972
[b] Chargé d'affaires

ANTHROPOLOGY

Ever since the emergence of Darwin's theory of evolution, man has wondered what kind of lives were led by the primitive human creatures from which he descended. While the broad outlines of human evolution have long been drawn, it was not until 1971 that the human species began to learn how old it really is and how remarkably clever its forefathers must have been. It was an extraordinarily productive year for anthropologists.

One of the most startling reports came from Harvard University, where a team of scientists announced the discovery in northern Kenya of a human jaw-bone fragment that is over 5,500,-000 years old. This is 1,500,000 years older than any previously known human remains and has compelled scholars to rethink some fundamental assumptions about human evolution. According to the leader of the expedition, Professor Bryan Patterson, the bone came from a creature much like *Australopithecus,* a five-foot-high upright-walking creature that was the first true man and that eventually evolved into *Homo sapiens,* or modern man. The age of the fragment, which consists of the right half of a lower jaw with one molar in place, was established by sophisticated radioactive dating and by archeological comparison with other sites of known age.

What excited experts about the find was that it seems to mean that the transformation of the "man-apes" into humans began much earlier than anyone had ever supposed before. It was formerly believed that *Australopithecus* had emerged largely during the Pleistocene epoch, which began about 2,000,000 years ago. But the Harvard discovery suggests that man was already evolving during the earlier Pliocene period, which began about 13,000,000 years ago. Anthropologists still do not know how the apes evolved the upright position and ground-living habit of man.

Anthropologists also were able to shed new light on modern man's more recent ancestors, Neanderthal men, who developed in Europe about 90,000 years ago, and Cro-Magnon men, who emerged about 34,000 years ago. Some of the mystery surrounding the evolution of Neanderthal man was dispelled in the summer of 1971 when French scientists discovered, in a huge ballroom-sized cave in southern France, the skull of a man who lived some 200,000 years ago. It was found amid numerous rhinoceros, horse, deer and other animal bones, which suggest he was a skilled hunter.

Extremely primitive, the skull has a flat sloping forehead, enormous eyebrows, massive jaws and a relatively small braincase. The teeth are twice the size of those in modern man and relatively unworn, indicating the creature was a youth of about twenty when he died. According to its discoverers, Henry and Marie-Antoinette de Lumley of the University of Aix-Marseilles, the skull is evidence that Neanderthal man in Europe developed altogether independently of his African and Asian contemporaries.

Meanwhile, a research worker at Harvard presented evidence suggesting that the prehistoric Cro-Magnon man had extraordinary mental capabilities. This cave-dwelling ice-age creature flourished throughout Europe from about 34,000 to 10,000 years ago, after which he evolved into modern man. He left thousands of artifacts for present-day archeologists, among them bones, stones and antlers covered with intricate notches, marks and scratches. Until very recently, these markings were generally regarded as mere decorations or grooves to permit stronger handle grip.

But the Harvard scientist Alexander Marshack contended in 1971 that the markings are in fact very sophisticated calendars used to keep track of the phases of the moon. If true —and a number of leading authorities have endorsed the interpretation—then it would appear that prehistoric man had already developed the ability to use abstract symbols, a stage in human cognition that was previously thought to have awaited the emergence of agriculture less than 10,000 years ago.

These findings have rekindled an old debate over the intellectual capabilities of primitive man. Some have even speculated that his mind was superior to ours because modern man, less dependent on brains for day-to-day survival, tends to preserve subnormally intelligent individuals in the population.

Anthropologists are as concerned with twentieth-century man as with his ancestors, and a growing army of specialists—ethnologists, linguistic anthropologists, physical anthropologists and others—are studying both isolated primitive societies and industrialized cultures. One of the leading experts, Margaret Mead of the American Museum of Natural History in New York, has spent much of the last 45 years studying the rich cultures of the South Pacific islands. In 1971 Dr. Mead opened a new museum exhibit, the Hall of the Peoples of the Pacific. It displays many items from the museum's priceless collection of tools, sculpture, tattooed heads, costumes, weapons and other artifacts of the native peoples of Polynesia, Indonesia, the Philippines, Australia, Melanesia and Micronesia.

In the remote mountain forests of the Philippine island of Mindanao, 650 miles south of Manila, a hunter named Dafal accidentally discovered a tribe of Stone Age human beings. The tribe, the most primitive group to be discovered in many years, has had the same life-style for centuries. Immediately after the hunter's find was reported, Philippine anthropologists began to live with the Tasadays (as the people call themselves) to study their customs before their primitive civilization disappears as they acquire some of today's habits from their new contacts.

Short and brown-skinned, the tribesmen have been isolated for between 700 and 2,000 years. They have survived by gathering rather than growing food, utilizing stones extensively and making various instruments, including containers and knives, from bamboo. Numbering only about 100, the Tasadays are extremely family-oriented, strongly fear *fugú* (epidemics such as smallpox) and have a generally short life-span.

According to Manuel Elizalde, Jr., an authority on Filipino minorities, "the survival of these singularly unique people is being threatened by plans of loggers to drive roads into their great forest sanctuary" and by disease. This is indeed unfortunate when you consider Elizalde's belief that the "Tasaday provide an unparalleled op-

portunity in the twentieth century to more fully understand man's culture and behavior before the appearance of agriculture and the domestication of animals; before the appearance among 'modern' man of a highly complex technology based upon metals."

Many anthropologists believe that their science holds important lessons for world leaders today. For example, Dr. Gerald C. Hickey, a Vietnamese-speaking American anthropologist, returned from Vietnam in 1971 after ten years of studying village life in that war-torn country. He came away feeling that the conflict could be ended only by the Vietnamese themselves "through a process of political accommodation between the central government and the numerous political movements and parties that exist in South Vietnam." He was critical of American officials for not being able to understand the cultures of the people whose lives they so deeply affected. "We never care about the ordinary people," he said. "We never see the necessity of understanding them. We are so ethnocentric."

ROBERT REINHOLD
National Correspondent
The New York Times

Wide World

Amid flowing water a monkey trap is set by Tasadays, a small group of Stone Age people, isolated until recently for hundreds of years, in the remote wilds of the Philippine island of Mindanao.

ARAB STATES

Except for Egypt, pressures within the Arab states for another trial of strength with Israel declined considerably as Arab governments turned their attention to internal political development and economic growth. Arab restraint toward Israel was conditioned partly by realism but also by the vanishing effectiveness of the Palestine guerrillas. Although a few Arab leaders, notably Libya's Col. Muammar al-Qaddafi, hammered at the theme of liberating Palestine by force, there was relatively little action. The guerrilla movement, already riddled with factional rivalries and unable to operate within Israel because of efficient Israeli countermeasures, was further weakened as it was systematically pursued by the Jordanian Army. King Hussein's forces drove the two main guerrilla brigades across the border and into Syria and Egypt, where they were interned. By midsummer the King felt confident enough of his control of Jordan to declare a national amnesty and proclaim a National Charter as the first step in the conversion of his country into a parliamentary one-party state. However, on Nov. 28, Jordanian Premier Wasfi Tal was assassinated in Cairo, where he was attending meetings of the Arab League's Joint Defense

Jordan's Premier Wasfi Tal studies a letter not long before he was assassinated in Cairo.

Charles Harbutt © Magnum Photos, Inc.

Council. His three slayers were said to be Palestinian terrorists. The next day, King Hussein appointed Finance Minister Ahmad al-Lawzi the new premier.

The question of an Arab-Israeli peace settlement continued to defy solution and to absorb a large proportion of Arab energies. Apart from the intransigence of Israeli leaders—deeply suspicious of Arab intentions and distrustful of international or major-power efforts toward peace—progress toward even a temporary Arab-Israeli *rapprochement* depended on the cooperation of Egypt. (In 1971 the United Arab Republic returned to its old, historic name, Egypt —in full, officially, the Arab Republic of Egypt.) President Anwar el-Sadat proved more adept than the late President Nasser at marshaling support abroad for Arab views and policy. Sadat had the strong backing of the U.S.S.R., emphasized by the signing of a 15-year treaty of friendship and cooperation between the two countries. Along with a reduction in deliveries of Soviet arms, the United States paradoxically found itself more or less on the Arab side, eager to avoid another round of conflict. Sadat's sweet reasonableness in the matter of concessions made better listening than Israeli trucu-lence.

Yet Sadat's carefully orchestrated policy of maximum diplomatic pressure on Israel and its chief ally, the United States, as the principal obstacles to peace placed the Egyptian leader in a difficult position in relation to his Arab allies. The cease-fire along the Suez Canal continued by tacit agreement after it had expired officially in March. Sadat had said that 1971 would be the year of decision for the Arabs— unless, as some wag put it, he converted Egyptian time to other calendars or abolished December. By late November he had begun to speak openly of "the battle at hand," although what form Egyptian military action against Israel would take was not made clear.

The formation in September of the Federation of Arab Republics, consisting of Egypt, Libya and Syria, marked another and potentially more positive step toward Arab political unity. The federation links three Arab states with a combined population of 42,000,000 and significant economic and social resources. (It was then that the U.A.R. changed its name to conform with the federal statutes.) Cairo became the federal capital, and President Sadat was chosen head of the three-man Presidential Council that would supervise trinational affairs. Yet the hoped-for adherence of other Arab nations did not materialize. Sudan, Egypt's southern neighbor, which had been expected to join next, deferred its decision after a **military**

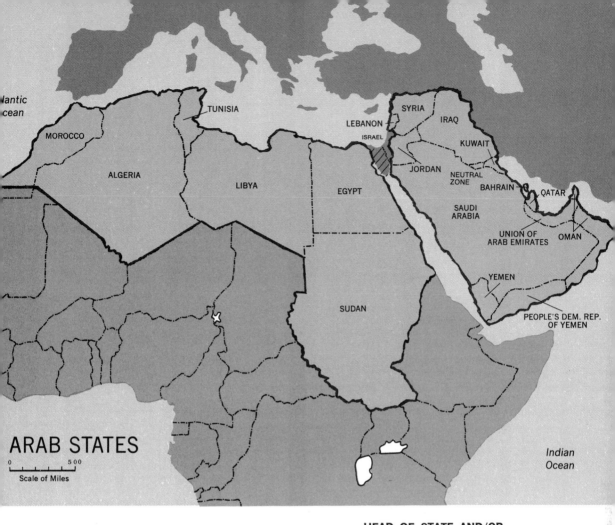

ARAB STATES

0 — 500
Scale of Miles

Indian Ocean

NATION	POPULATION (in millions)	CAPITAL	AREA (in sq. mi.)	HEAD OF STATE AND/OR GOVERNMENT, DATE INSTALLED (as of Jan. 1, 1972)
Algeria	14.5	Algiers	919,593	Houari Boumedienne, president—1965
Bahrain	.2	Manama	231	Isa ibn Sulman al-Khalifa, head of state—1961
Egypt	34.9	Cairo	386,660	Anwar el-Sadat, president—1970
				Mahmoud Fawzi, premier—1970
Iraq	10.0	Baghdad	167,925	Ahmad Hassan al-Bakr, president—1968
Jordan	2.4	Amman	37,738	Hussein I, king—1952
				Ahmad al-Lawzi, premier—1971
Kuwait	0.8	Kuwait	6,178	Sabah al-Salim al-Sabah, head of state—1965
				Jabir al-Ahmad al-Jabir, prime minister—1965
Lebanon	2.9	Beirut	4,015	Suleiman Franjieh, president—1970
				Saeb Salam, premier—1970
Libya	1.9	Tripoli	679,360	Muammar al-Qaddafi, president, Revolutionary Command Council—1969
Morocco	16.3	Rabat	172,997	Hussan II, king—1961
				Mohammad Karim Lamrani, premier—1971
Oman	.6	Muscat	82,030	Qabus ibn Said, sultan—1970
Qatar	8.7	Doha	35,553	Ahmad ibn Ali al-Thani, sheik—1960
Saudi Arabia	8.0	Riyadh	829,997	Faisal ibn Abdul Aziz, king—1964
Sudan	16.3	Khartoum	967,497	Gaafar al-Nimeiry, president—1969
Syria	6.4	Damascus	71,498	Hafez al-Assad, president—1971
Tunisia	5.3	Tunis	63,378	Habib Bourquiba, president—1957
				Hedi Nouira, prime minister—1970
Union of Arab Emirates	.3	Abu Dhabi	40,000	Zayd ben Sultan, president—1971
Yemen	5.9	Sana	75,290	Abdul Rahman al-Iryani, president—1967
Yemen, People's Dem. Rep. of	1.3	Medina al-Shaab	112,000	Salem Ali Rubaya, head of state—1969
				Ali Masir Mohammad, prime minister—1971

Egyptian President Sadat, Libyan President Qaddafi and Syrian President Assad sign agreement to establish the Federation of Arab Republics.

coup nearly overthrew the Government of Gen. Gaafar al-Nimeiry. The other Arab states expressed little serious interest.

The continued Arab inability to achieve overall political unity, despite the professed desire of both leaders and rank and file to do so, stemmed from the failure of most Arab governments to achieve consensus or broad national representation. There were attempted coups in Morocco and Sudan, growing intraparty friction in the one-party states of Tunisia and Iraq, and power struggles within such ill-established regimes as those of the People's Democratic Republic of Yemen (formerly Southern Yemen) and Yemen. Even Lebanon, with its mixed economy and multiparty parliamentary system, experienced considerable social discontent.

The coup in Morocco surprised many because it developed within the armed forces, traditionally regarded as the main support for the monarchy of King Hassan II. It was the King's failure to deal effectively with corruption in his Government that turned his top military commanders, except for Interior Minister General Oufkir (who later became defense minister), against him. Military cadets surrounded the royal palace at Skhirat, near Rabat, on July 10, during the King's 42d-birthday celebration, and opened fire. Hassan

himself was held captive briefly, and several hundred guests were killed or wounded. The bulk of the Army, however, remained loyal; and lacking its support and that of the general population, the revolt collapsed. The resultant wave of executions, including four generals, decimated the Moroccan armed forces and aroused concern that Morocco would become another Arab state cursed with chronic instability.

In August, Hassan began a long-overdue housecleaning. Six former ministers and lesser government officials were arrested on charges of misuse of funds and taking bribes for approval of foreign-exchange development projects. The King formed a new Cabinet of nonpolitical technicians. He met for the first time since 1965 with leaders of his civilian political opposition, in an effort to generate national support for his program of gradual constitutional monarchy.

In Tunisia a growing political crisis developed after the return of President Bourguiba from lengthy convalescence abroad. Bourguiba's absolute leadership was questioned by members of the Neo-Destour Socialist Party who believe that Tunisia needs collective leadership and broader participation at all levels. The crisis came out into the open during the October party congress, as Bourguiba's choices for members of the party's Political Bureau, the national governing body, were challenged by a faction that included two former cabinet members.

Disagreements within the ruling Revolutionary Command Council of Libya brought about the temporary resignation of President Qaddafi in September. His dissatisfaction was prompted by the slow pace of Libyan social reform, partly a result of the inexperience of the young officers who had seized control of the country in 1969. Another factor was Qaddafi's inability to promote his brand of puritan-Islamic Arab nationalism abroad. Subsequently Qaddafi withdrew his resignation, and in a cabinet shakeup, several RCC officers were replaced by competent civilian experts, including the Libyan Republic's first Foreign Minister, Salih Abu Yasir (Buwaysir).

Syria and Iraq fared better, although divergent views within the ruling Baath Party in Iraq led to the dismissal of several ministers. In November, Iraq's President Ahmad Hassan al-Bakr, apparently recovered from an unspecified illness, issued a call for national unity that would be built around a new "draft national charter" embodying the interests and the participation of all parties and groups. The Government also renewed its pledges to give the Kurds local autonomy and a voice in Iraqi affairs, and allocated funds for the development of the war-ravaged northern region of the country. In Syria, General Hafez al-Assad was elected president of the Republic for a seven-year term, under the provision of the provisional constitution, by 99 per cent of the votes cast. He was the only candidate. The Syrian Baath Party also set up a People's Council as the country's legislative body; it replaced the National Assembly dissolved in 1966 after a military coup.

The most significant domestic changes in the Arab lands occurred in Egypt. In May a power struggle within the Government of President Sadat was resolved in his favor. The struggle involved not only the direction of the Egyptian Arab state but also the succession to the late President Nasser. Encouraged by widespread concern within the Arab Socialist Union (ASU), Egypt's sole political organization, over the federation with Libya and Syria, Sadat's rivals determined to replace his leadership with that of a coalition Government. The chief rivals were Vice-President Ali Sabry and Interior Minister Gomaa. Learning of their plans, Sadat immediately dismissed Sabry. The subsequent resignations of Gomaa and other ministers failed to weaken popular or Army support for the President. The result, ironically,

Keystone

After the attempt to oust him fails, King Hassan II of Morocco holds a press conference.

Egypt's President Sadat gets a close view of the enemy on the east bank of the Suez Canal.

UPI

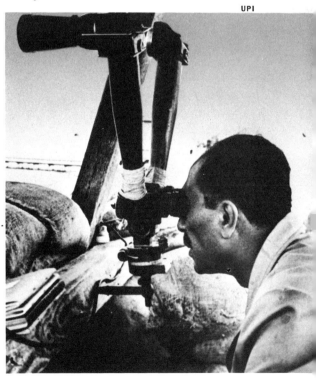

removed the basis for potential dissension within the Egyptian Government and gave Sadat a free hand for his own program of genuine reforms.

Along with the vigorous promotion of the Arab cause against Israel abroad, a series of "liberalization" measures inaugurated the Sadat program. Some three hundred government officials were arrested, and trials of the ringleaders of the plot resulted in a demand for death sentences for eight persons, including Sabry and Gomaa. Four, including Sabry and Gomaa, were so sentenced, but Sadat reduced the sentences to life imprisonment. The civil service was extensively purged, with numerous senior officials dismissed or retired and replaced by young, technically qualified university graduates. Four hundred political prisoners, mostly members of the outlawed Muslim Brotherhood, were released. Egyptians were promised that arbitrary police action would end and full personal rights be restored. Police dossiers were burned in public to demonstrate the Government's good faith.

Sadat also carried out his pledge to reinvigorate Egypt. Elections were held in several states for delegates from basic ASU units to a national congress. The requirement that urban

Amid fierce hostility, an interval of brotherhood: Israeli soldiers share food, water and cigarettes with Arab guerrillas who have surrendered.

Keystone

labor, rural peasants, teachers and all other groups be represented by candidates and a certain number of seats, and increases in the number of seats and candidates contesting them, gave the campaign an air of vigorous competition, as Egyptians responded to the appeal of free, secret elections.

Other aspects of Sadat's program were the creation of an Egyptian Development Bank, and compensation for foreigners whose land and businesses had been affected by the nationalization decrees of the 1960's. A ten-year "program of national action" was announced, to lift the standard of living. Whether the liberalization and aggressive economic action could move fast enough to meet Egypt's rising social aspirations or solve long-term problems was not clear, but the start was favorable.

The Arab oil-producing states benefited enormously from new price agreements signed at Tehran (Iran) and Tripoli (Libya) with the major international oil companies. Increases in the posted prices for Middle Eastern oil would bring royalties nearly double those of previous years, along with expanded production. However, on Dec. 7, Libya suddenly nationalized the British Petroleum Company's operations there, and withdrew all Libyan money from British banks.

Lebanon, Syria and Jordan also benefited, although they produce no oil, by subsidiary agreements that increased their fees from oil exported in pipelines across their territory to Mediterranean refineries. The continued flow of wealth from their oil industries enabled certain Arab countries, such as Kuwait and Saudi Arabia, to underwrite development projects for their less fortunate neighbors.

In spite of their access to elements of economic wealth, the Arab states remained marginally effective politically. For the least-favored ones, such as Yemen and Southern Yemen, the future was very bleak. They had minimal resources and bitterly divided governing factions. Their circumstances—Yemen faced an external debt of $186,000,000—gave added weight to the need for a regional Arab-Israeli federation, suggested by Tunisia's President Bourguiba in an interview, as the only possible solution to the Middle East's problems.

In the simmering Persian Gulf area another independent Arab state was born on Dec. 2, the Union of Arab Emirates. It consists of Abu Dhabi (richest in oil), Dubai, Sharja, Ajman, Fujaira and Umm al Qaiwain. (*See also* Bahrain; Qatar)

WILLIAM SPENCER
Professor of History
The Florida State University

Unknown until 1971, a civilization of about 3500 B.C. was uncovered in a mound in Iran.

ARCHEOLOGY

An unsuspected civilization of 4000–3001 B.C., having the art of writing and indicating trade connections with ancient Mesopotamia and the Indus Valley peoples, was revealed in 1971 in a huge mound in southeastern Iran. Tepe Yahya is the local name of the mound, 60 feet high and 600 feet in diameter, in the rugged Soghun Valley about 60 miles from the Persian Gulf. Archeologists are speculating that the ancient site may be the mysterious "Magan," recorded in a Sumerian text of 2500 B.C.

Archeologists, slowly coursing through the area's roadless mountains in 1967, were hunting for clues to commerce between westerly Mesopotamia (now in Iraq) and the distant Indus (1,000 miles to the east in present-day West Pakistan). Tepe Yahya was along a possible trade route, about equidistant from either. It could be dated very closely as inscribed tablets and associated material were discovered in subsequent probes. It was found that the newly discovered urban center existed in about 3500 B.C., 1,000 years before it was supposed that civilization appeared in the area. One of the revealing finds was 6 tablets inscribed in cuneiform in the writing known as proto-Elamite. It and Sumerian writing are the earliest known. Proto-Elamite was devised by the people of the Mesopotamian kingdom of Elam, about 500 miles west of Tepe Yahya.

Elam, whose geographic and cultural boundaries have been dim until now, is assuming significant proportions. A great quantity of proto-Elamite tablets form an archive from Susa, capital of Elam.

The invention of writing has been traditionally ascribed to the Sumerians of Mesopotamia. It appears now that literacy or, at least, the knowledge of writing was a simultaneous phenomenon among peoples that were widely separated.

Tepe Yahya's people appear to have developed a fairly sophisticated society. The administrative building indicates knowledgeable organization and use of the structure as a trading center. A quantity of blank tablets, found with the inscribed ones, suggests that records of transactions were written on the spot, as merchandise came or went.

Tools and pottery and more than a thousand whole and fragmentary steatite, or soapstone, vessels, bowls, figures, beads and cylinder seals, along with unworked blocks and partly fashioned pieces of soapstone were retrieved. Many are elaborately carved with geometric and curvilinear designs and human and animal figure motifs. Numerous steatite bowls with identical designs have been excavated from Mesopotamian and Indus Valley sites. One of the sources of Tepe Yahya's steatite—a strip mine—was about twenty miles from the mound. As Mesopotamia was poor in natural resources and Mohenjo-Daro, among other centers of the Indus culture, had to import materials, it is suggested that Tepe Yahya supplied the steatite.

In Sumerian writing names of places and of stones appear that have no present-day meaning. One text mentions "Dilmun," a site discovered in 1951; "Maluhha," which is conjectured to be somewhere in the Indus Valley; and "Magan" which, previous to the discovery of Tepe Yahya, was set in southeastern Iran. A fragmentary Sumerian text listing imports from "Magan," mentions "u-stone" and "shumash stone," now considered references to Tepe Yahya's bountiful commodity. Legend has it that Tepe Yahya was named for a king whose head was cut off and buried in the mound. The Government has posted a 24-hour guard on the site, the largest area of pre-Islamic times thus far discovered in Iran.

Official indignation and protest have been rising in archeologically rich countries with the increase of illicit digging and the smuggling of culturally and monetarily valuable objects to foreign depots for sale, keeping pace with the demand of a world market. Looting of ancient shipwrecks is another branch of illegal treasure hunting, and the looters' operations have destroyed invaluable archeological evidence. This happened to a merchantman of the fourth century B.C. that sank in the Strait of Messina, the victim of, perhaps, treacherous currents, a storm and a too heavy cargo. Looters made away with many pottery plates, cups, bowls, pitchers and animal-shaped rhytons before they were caught. They also cut up into manageable pieces three large anchor stocks and about twenty loaf-shaped lead ingots with foundry stamps, which were sold as scrap. The stamps could not be reconstituted and the identity of the foundry was lost. A cargo of amphorae, indicating ports of call, shows that the ship had traveled from somewhere in Greece to Italy or Sicily before it met disaster. One highly unusual amphora, of cigar shape, possibly for dried fish, was Punic.

Diving archeologists brought up ingots and pancake shapes of pure silver that had eluded the plunderers; and lead sheathing, now in fragments, that once covered the ship's bottom, wholly or in part. This is believed to be the earliest ship yet found and examined scientifically to have used protective sheathing. The vessel is estimated to have been about seventy feet long. The most spectacular cargo recovered were broken parts of two life-size bronze male statues. All fragments, except a head that had been sold by the robbers and later purchased by the Antike Museum in Basel, Switzerland, were placed in Italy's museum at Reggio in Calabria.

Underwater archeology, still in its infancy, studies the construction of shipwrecks and makes theoretical reconstructions, attempts to plot routes and trading points and has developed elaborate techniques and equipment for, ofttimes, hazardous undertakings.

Slowly, the Bronze Age world on the Greek island of Thera (modern Santorini), extinguished in the fury of volcanic eruption sometime between 1520 and 1470 B.C., is being dug out of pumice and ash. One of the most difficult archeological operations afoot, the unveiling of Thera's ancient way of life is receiving top priority among Greek excavations. So far, something over 13,000 square yards have been cleared at the southern tip, in a city estimated to have been at least a mile long, with 20,000 to 30,000 inhabitants. Fine ashlar masonry facades of two- and, possibly, three-story houses are superior to the construction techniques employed by Thera's glamorous contemporary neighbors on Crete. The buildings and some of the most exquisite frescoes of the age, among other treasure, were found preserved in excellent condition, sealed against decay in a deep shroud of fine volcanic ash.

The largest intact Bronze Age fresco ever found in Greece, covering 140 square feet, is the most astonishing art find to date. Free and bold, the swiftly drawn paintings drew their inspiration from nature and human life. One section of the large fresco is a paean to spring that once covered three walls of a small sanctuary. Red Madonna lilies in clusters spring between rocks in blue, green, red and purple and, overhead, the first swallows of the new season, meeting in air, herald the event. Blue monkeys clambering over red lava rocks after ravaging a garden form another delightful piece, which also points to the possibility that such monkeys once actually inhabited the island.

Red deer and antelope were also depicted by the painters for the delectation of an art-loving clientele. The antelopes shared room space with one of the finest frescoes so far retrieved—a scene of two young boys engaged in a boxing match. Most of the frescoes, shattered when found, were pieced together and coated with preservative.

The shape and every detail of a wooden bed that had disintegrated under scalding ash was found preserved. When the ash cooled and solidified, the dimensional imprint of the bed remained intact in a vacuum. Liquid plaster, poured into the mold that resulted, enabled archeologists to obtain a replica of a totally vanished item of Theran furnishing.

SANKA KNOX
Art and Archeology Reporter
The New York Times

Welfare Island's winding Main Street (drawn by Ronald Love) will have a minitransit system, and view of the waterfront between buildings.

ARCHITECTURE

For more than half a century, architects, as part of their modern credo, have been longing to design "the total man-made environment." They are beginning to get the chance.

Philip Johnson, for instance, who built his fame mostly on rather precious individual buildings, has drawn up master plans for two entire "new-towns-in-town," as complete new communities within the city have come to be called. One, for which ground was broken in the spring of 1971, is being built on Welfare Island, a two-mile-long sliver of land in New York City's East River. It is to be an urban and urbane environment where, in a densely concentrated area and free of automobiles, 20,000 people of all races, incomes and ages will live, shop, go to school, work, play, and enjoy an abundance of medical and social services, cultural attractions, an "ecological park," and a breathtaking view of the Manhattan skyline.

Johnson's other plan is for Franklin Town, a new community that is to be built in a rundown 50-acre industrial area in Philadelphia, just a few blocks from City Hall. It is to house 12,000 people, and a far greater number will work in its offices and visit its hotels, convention hall, shops, restaurants and theaters. In contrast with Welfare Island, which is sponsored by the quasi-public, nonprofit New York State Urban Development Corporation, Franklin Town is to be built for profit by a consortium of private corporations without government help. It therefore cannot risk Welfare Island's lofty social aims and technical innovation. But for both towns Johnson and his partner John Burgee have created an architectural setting that promises a sense of place, of community, of complexity, excitement and anticipation— qualities that are devastatingly absent in most American real-estate developments of this century.

Similar comprehensively designed urban environments are on the drawing boards of numerous other architects, working in teams that include city planners, landscape architects, economists and other experts. Among them are two in New York City: Battery Park City (designed by Conklin and Rossant), which is to be built on Hudson River landfill; and a town (designed by Gruzen and Partners) that is to be constructed over the Sunnyside railroad tracks in Queens. Others include Fort Lincoln in Washington, D.C. (designed by Rogers,

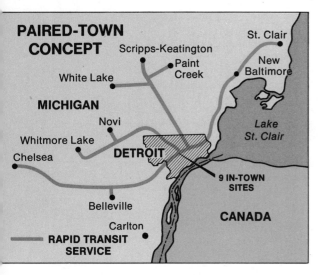

PAIRED-TOWN CONCEPT

St. Clair
Scripps-Keatington
Paint Creek
White Lake
New Baltimore

MICHIGAN

Novi
Whitmore Lake
Chelsea
DETROIT

Lake St. Clair

9 IN-TOWN SITES

Belleville

Carlton

CANADA

━━━ **RAPID TRANSIT SERVICE**

Detroit plan involves redeveloped urban areas and new towns in the country, each an entity but linked by mass-transit lines and bus services.

Taliaferro, Kostritsky and Lamb); Houston Center in Houston (designed by William L. Pereira); Mel Plaza in Pittsburgh (designed by Deeter, Richey and Sippel); Cedar-Riverside in Minneapolis (designed by Ralph Rapson); and a project for a "paired-new-town development" in and near Detroit, worked out by Skidmore, Owings and Merrill, and Howard Sims and Associates for the Metropolitan Fund.

The paired-town concept calls for the simultaneous construction of one new community within the city and another some twenty miles out in the country, the two being linked by rapid transit and complementing each other. The in-town, for example, would provide more apartment houses for young and old families and single people, as well as hospitals, schools for advanced learning, and other facilities that are best located in the city. The out-town would mostly house large families with young children and would offer playgrounds, sports fields, and parks. Being built by one developer, the out-town would supply the new housing for the families that must be displaced to build the new in-town. They would share the same municipal government and a common sense of community.

As yet none of these proposals includes any new construction technology, let alone a breakthrough, though some will finally apply industrialized building systems that have been developing in Europe for as long as 25 years. There are other innovations. Welfare Island is to introduce the country's first pneumatic refuse-collection system; it will carry wastes through underground ducts to a central collec-

tion point where they will be compacted and then carried away by trailer or barge. Cedar-Riverside plans to heat and cool all buildings and shopping arcades from one central, hydronic plant (transfer of heat by a circulating fluid in a closed pipe system).

Most of these towns will move people by built-in minirail or other new transportation devices, rather than waste too much space on automobile roads and parking. Some of this public transportation may even be free. Urban planner James B. Hodgeson, Jr., has figured out that if horizontal transportation is built into multibuilding developments, much as vertical elevators are built into multistory buildings, these "horizontallators," as he calls them, would add no more than one per cent to the construction and operating cost, and, as with elevators, the cost could be easily absorbed by the rents charged to residents, stores and offices. The benefits in greater convenience, cleaner air, and added amenity of a car-free environment are obvious.

Once the Federal New Community Development Act (Title VII of the 1970 Federal housing act) gets fully under way, Americans can expect an increasing number of such comprehensively designed towns within and near the big cities. The legislation authorizes considerable financial assistance for both privately and publicly developed new towns that will include substantial numbers of low- and moderate-income families, offer good educational, social and health services, ensure a good natural and urban environment, and advance design and technology. The legislation envisions the towns as an important means of arresting urban sprawl and pollution and of ensuring a more rational distribution of people on the land under a national urban-growth policy—an idea that architects have long favored.

The year's most widely praised individual building design was undoubtedly I. M. Pei's East Building for the National Gallery of Art in Washington, D.C. The design brilliantly solves the problem posed by a trapezoidal site on the perhaps most prominent spot on the Mall and by the need to relate the new building to John Russell Pope's stately neoclassic old one. The year's most pompous completed building no doubt was Gordon Bunshaft's Lyndon Baines Johnson Library at the University of Texas at Austin, designed "to express through monumentality the importance of its historical treasures." The monumentality appears Pharaonic. The year's gold medal of the American Institute of Architects went to Louis I. Kahn.

WOLF VON ECKARDT
Architecture Critic, *The Washington Post*

The Metropolitan acquired one of the greatest portraits, Velazquez' perceptive study of Juan de Pareja, for $5,544,000.

ARTS

Nearly every U.S. museum joined its European sister institutions in celebrating landmark anniversaries of two great artists. With the National Gallery in Washington in the lead on the west side of the Atlantic and his native city of Nuremberg as the focus of European exhibitions, publications and symposia, the 500-year anniversary of Albrecht Dürer's birth brought a spate of extraordinary displays of this great German Renaissance master's work. From Amsterdam and Boston to Princeton and Würzburg, the wide-ranging exhibitions emphasized the extraordinary combination of rationality and spirituality, of humility and pride, of medieval and Renaissance tendencies found in Dürer. He was able to impress his art upon

his own and later generations because of the focus of his personality which can easily be recognized in his expertly crafted images. His inquiring intellect, his firm beliefs and sense of his own individuality, and his mental versatility led him to develop far beyond the environment in which he was raised.

Pablo Picasso turned ninety on Oct. 25, and U.S. museums and commercial galleries were filled with the products of his protean and still very active genius. While Picasso himself shunned the occasion, France honored its adopted son by making his work the first ever by a living artist to be hung in the Louvre. In his native Spain a small exhibition of etchings from the famous Vollard suite was de-

In another historic sale, Titian's masterwork "The Death of Actaeon" was bought for $4,032,000 for the J. Paul Getty Museum, in California.

stroyed by overzealous "anti-Marxists," and an eminent art critic and historian was jailed by the Franco Government as he prepared to lecture on the most famous Spanish-born artist of our time at the University of Madrid. All this despite the recent establishment of a Picasso Museum in Barcelona, opened and publicized with official sanction.

On the contemporary scene, U.S. artists continued to work in the bewildering variety of styles noted in 1970. The development came as a relief from years of domination by one or another highly promoted vanguard group. If there were notable emphases they tended to point to the concern of young artists with social, political, economic and, above all, ecological problems. For the first time since WPA days, more and more American artists sought to in-

volve themselves with problems far beyond their immediate creative concerns. Above all, they banded together, with very few exceptions, in protests against the continuation of the war in Vietnam. When it came to particularly artistic matters, more and more of the younger generation of American artists drew away from the consideration of art as an object. Shunning the conventional environments of museums and galleries, many artists continued to involve themselves with advanced technologies. Others, pushing the ideas of concept art, turned to enormous earthworks or intangible, often nearly invisible activities.

The most ambitious project ever initiated to link contemporary art with large technological corporations was Maurice Tuchman's "Art and Technology" exhibition that opened at the Los Angeles County Museum of Art in the spring. In the works since 1968, parts of this complex undertaking were shown in the American Pavilion of EXPO'70, at Osaka, Japan, in 1970. While such notables as Roy Lichtenstein, Robert Rauschenberg, Claes Oldenburg and Andy Warhol were included in the exhibition, Rockne Krebs' mirror-laser piece, Boyd Mefferd's strobe walls and Newton Harrison's glow-discharge columns were accurately singled out by most critics as the most successful parts of the exhibition. The most intriguing aspect of the entire project came with its 386-page catalogue—a documentation that made it very clear that close collaboration between large corporations dealing with advanced technologies and individual artists seeking to use their means without much experience seems more than un-

likely in the future. From nearly every point of view the gap between the sensibilities of contemporary artists and the preoccupations of giant corporations seems unbridgeable.

"Earth, Air, Fire, Water: Elements of Art," an exhibition by some 25 artists using these media, concluded the centennial events of the Boston Museum. It included an on-site earthwork by Robert Morris; Gary Rieveschal's ice-and-fire sculpture; Otto Piene's sky event with ascending balloons; plasma-discharge objects by Newton Harrison; and Hans Haacke's water-circulating system.

While major art-auction houses continued to pile up record prices—some paid by top American collectors—U.S. art commerce was definitely depressed throughout 1971. European dealers, however, seemed to do excellent busi-

A drawing, brushed with white paint, of a girl in Dutch dress was displayed in one of the numerous exhibitions all over the world celebrating the 500th anniversary of the birth of the Nuremburg, Germany, master Albrecht Dürer.

At ninety years of age, on Oct. 25, 1971, the greatest of twentieth-century artists, Pablo Picasso, continued tirelessly creative and robustly enjoying life.

© Goksin Sipahioglu-Jocelyne Benzakin

ness until the autumn, when the international money crisis began to be felt.

The most newsworthy sale of the year came at a June 25 auction at Christie's in London where American oil billionaire J. Paul Getty—who is greatly enlarging his Malibu, Calif., museum into a fantastic Herculaneum—bid $4,032,000 for Titian's *Death of Actaeon*. Since it had been on loan for many years at London's National Gallery and public furor over masterworks leaving England has increased, the British Government refused to grant an export license for the painting for a year in order to give the National Gallery a chance to match the price bid by Getty.

Velazquez' *Portrait of Juan de Pareja* was acquired by the Metropolitan Museum (N.Y.). It had been auctioned in late 1970 at Christie's, London for $5,544,000. Collector Norton Simon, who had auctioned off part of his collection, mostly decorative works, earlier in the year, paid $775,000 for Henri Rousseau's *Paysage Exotique* at Parke-Bernet on Oct. 21, 1971, thus establishing a world record not only for the Douanier Rousseau but for any work by a twentieth-century artist. On May 5, Degas' sculpture *Petite Danseuse de Quatorze Ans* (from the Norton Simon Collection) had brought a world-record auction price for sculpture at $380,000. Women libbers were cheered by the fact that Mary Cassatt's *Summertime*, sold at Parke-Bernet for $150,000, was not only a record for that artist but for any woman artist whose work has ever been auctioned.

Cubism was the period of the immediate past most thoroughly examined. Under the direction of British art expert Douglas Cooper, the Los Angeles County Museum of Art, together with New York's Metropolitan Museum, mounted an almost overly encompassing exhibition of that era, first shown in its own galleries and then, to better advantage, at the Metropolitan. In a smaller, more personal manner, cubism came into focus as most of the collections of Gertrude, Leo, Michael and Sarah Stein were reunited by The Museum of Modern Art (N.Y.) and later shown in the Steins' hometown, San Francisco, under the title "Four Americans in Paris." In little more than a half century, a mode of vision that seemed shockingly revolutionary in the beginning had become almost traditionally conventional in these surveys of cubism.

Unveiling the large body of work bequeathed by Edward Hopper, the Whitney Museum of American Art (N.Y.) mounted an unprecedented survey of this great artist's work revealing the rich mixture of realism and romanticism that has marked so much of American art.

Later in the year, The Museum of Modern Art (N.Y.) paid tribute to the late Barnett Newman in a highly selective display of his work selected by his friend, the critic Thomas B. Hess. It included 75 paintings along with drawings and sculpture, the last medium explored increasingly by the artist toward the end of his life.

One of Newman's monumental sculptures stands over a reflecting pool of the Rothko Chapel, an impressively simple building dedicated in Houston, Texas, in February 1971. Designed by two Houston architects to hold a series of somberly monumental paintings, it

Although the medium is cement, Gordon Allen's beautiful "Windy Day" seems to be as light as down. Training as an engineer has helped his sculpture techniques.

"From the Confrontation Series: Celebration" by Ralph Arnold is crayon and pencil on paper. It appeared in the Whitney's exhibition "Contemporary Black Artists in America."

As "The Art of Maya Hieroglyphic Writing" exhibit, at the Center for Inter-American Relations, showed, the glyphs are an integral part of Maya art. Blocks of glyphs were often framed in loops of rope, feathers, tassels, rosettes and the like.

The Nigerian mask was fashioned out of ivory, iron and copper in the Benin area during the early 1500's. It represents the only ancient black African art still in existence, and was shown in the Metropolitan's exhibitions of black African sculpture.

In step with a current cause, an exhibition on women, called "Pride and Prejudice," drew mixed reactions from a wide range of visitors.

Designed by Edward Larrabee Barnes, Minneapolis' handsome new Walker Art Center building is exceptionally spacious.

is the first chapel in America built around the work of an important contemporary artist.

At summer's end, elaborate and very expensive preparations for the installation of Christo's Valley Curtain at Rifle, Colo., were nearly completed. Then gusty winds and mechanical failure on the part of the contractor involved made the curtain unfurl prematurely, and it was destroyed against the rocks. An impressive ensemble of international art critics on hand along with a great deal of the general press found the unforeseen happening as impressively beautiful as it was disappointing to the Bulgarian-born, New York-based artist.

The nineteenth-century French masters were given unprecedented exhibitions in the United States. Organized by Stanford University art historian Lorenz Eitner, a major survey of work by Théodore Géricault was mounted at the Los Angeles County Museum of Art with important loans from both private and public collections in Europe and the United States. It was also scheduled to be shown at the Detroit Institute of Arts and the Philadelphia Museum of Art. Originating at the National Gallery in Washington, "Ingres in Rome" consisted of 150 important drawings, later to be seen in Philadelphia, New York and Kansas City.

Art-minded American tourists were especially impressed by the unveiling of the Michel Monet bequest at the Musée Mammotan in Paris, the extraordinary Tiepolo exhibition at the Villa Manin, near Udine, and a marvelously revealing Morandi retrospective mounted by the British Arts Council in London.

Certainly the most significant art development of 1971 concerned the crises of finance and identity that afflicted U.S. museums. A survey by the Association of American Museums showed that 44 per cent of its members were in the red in 1970. The dismal trend was expected to continue. Ironically, museums were never more popular with the public. Attendance in 1970 at the United States' 5,900 museums was a record 700,000,000 visits.

A freeze on funds to pay guards forced the Detroit Institute of Arts to close a third of its exhibitions on a rotating basis. During the summer of 1971 the new Pasadena Art Museum (Calif.), created without adequate endowment funds and deeply in debt to banks that helped it with construction costs, was forced to reduce visiting to only four days a week. Open regularly again in the fall, its exhibition schedule was reduced by more than half, and its continued existence was in doubt. A record $1,200,-000 deficit in its 1970 fiscal year forced the Museum of Modern Art (N.Y.) to reduce staff and library services drastically, sparking first

strike ever held by professional museum staff.

The workers eventually won a two-year contract that gives the staff the right to share in the search for and selection of museum officials, a formal promotion process, and a $1,000 increase in the minimum salary to $5,750 a year.

To solve their financial problems, museums were turning to a number of sources of support. In St. Louis, voters approved a county-wide levy to support several museums. President Nixon endorsed a sizable increase in appropriations for the National Endowment for the Arts, which includes grants to museums in its program. Several congressmen sponsored a Museum Services Bill to provide $40,000,000 in Federal funds for critical needs.

In the wake of increasing union-organizing efforts by professional museum employees, Metropolitan Museum Director Thomas P. F. Hoving presented a ten-point program in November that would give his staff greater participation in museum policy making.

Meanwhile, art museums have come under increasing pressure from artists and community groups, especially minority organizations, who question the absolute power now held by trustees and staff. The most recent and extreme clash between an individual artist and a museum was the case of the Hans Haacke exhibition which did not take place at the Guggenheim Museum in April 1971. While the issues and personalities involved were somewhat complex, the problem in the end centered on the artist's insistence that he had the right to show two works that neither the museum's director nor its trustees wanted to show. After the exhibition was canceled, some three weeks before its scheduled opening, much of the world interpreted the underlying issue as one of censorship. The artist, it was said, had been unjustly deprived by the museum of his right to speak freely about certain political and social issues. Lost almost completely from sight in the controversy was another issue: the legitimacy of the museum's claim that it—and not the artist—must determine what it shows.

While U.S. art museums have always been public in one sense—by being open to the public and operated in a nonprofit manner—in another sense most of them were profoundly private at the start, private in the source of their funds, private in their control, and private even in the sense that their senior staff was drawn from a privileged social class. If they are to survive and flourish, they will have to become public institutions in a far broader sense than ever before.

HENRY J. SELDIS
Art Critic, *Los Angeles Times*

ASTRONOMY

During 1971, knowledge and understanding of various astronomical phenomena expanded steadily.

PULSARS

The first pulsar was discovered in 1967 by English radio astronomers, and by the end of 1971 about 60 had become known. They emit radio noise (and in one or two cases, light and X-ray pulses as well) at very specific intervals, ranging from 0.033 seconds for the fastest to 3.75 seconds for the slowest.

It is now suspected by most astronomers that a pulsar is a rapidly rotating neutron star with a diameter of about 5 to 10 miles and a density about 10 trillion times that of the sun. A cubic inch of material from such a star would weigh more than the combined weight of the 3,700,-000,000 people on the earth. Under such compression the protons (hydrogen nuclei) disintegrate into neutrons/positrons. A neutron star remains after a burned-out star collapses and throws off its outer layers in a supernova explosion. Supernovae in our galaxy occur at least once every century, which seems to be the rate at which new pulsars are "born." As it

collapses, the star's magnetic field also is compressed, to give a surface magnetic field of about one trillion gauss. (A gauss is an electromagnetic unit of measurement.) The earth's surface magnetic field is about one fifth of a gauss.

The elapsed time between radio bursts from a pulsar is its rotational period. From an active area on the star's surface a fan of radio noise sweeps across the earth with each rotation. At the star's surface the rotational speed is moderate, typically 300 miles per second. However, its gaseous atmosphere is held rigidly in place by the strong magnetic field. Particles far removed from the surface will then revolve around the axis at speeds nearly that of the speed of light (186,281 miles per second) and escape as extremely energetic cosmic rays. This helps to explain the production of the most energetic cosmic rays that, in part, bombard the earth. The less energetic cosmic rays come mostly from the sun.

The pulsar's period increases by only a few millionths of a second per year. Thus the shortest-period pulsars are the youngest. The pulsar at the center of the Crab nebula (resulting from the supernova of A.D. 1054) has the

Dish reflector of radio telescope in operation near Bonn, Germany, is covered with 2,352 aluminum plates and rests on a tubular-steel frame.

Yigal Paz

shortest known period and is the only one seen in visual light and by its X-ray bursts. Pulsars slow down because they lose energy by gravitational waves and by radiation of light and other rays.

However, the rate of slowing down is not always constant. Several pulsars have shown abrupt changes in period which are attributed to "starquakes," small structural changes in outer crystalline layers of the pulsars. The crystalline surfaces have odd properties, including a shear modulus (ratio of shearing stress to shearing strain) a billion billion times greater than that of steel, electrical conductivity along magnetic lines of force a hundred thousand times greater than that of copper, and a surface temperature of approximately 100,000,-000 degrees.

BLACK HOLES

Einstein's theory of relativity predicts that when light from a distant star passes close to the surface of another star, the light will bend because it is attracted by the second star's gravity (because it has energy, light has mass). This small curvature of space around our own star, the sun, has been measured near the sun's disk when the sun's light is covered by the moon during a solar eclipse. For stars with a higher gravity, the curvature is much greater. In the extreme, it is possible that some stars have so great a surface gravity that light from them could never escape, thus creating what are called "black holes." Also light and particles passing by would be pulled in and lost to view. Such objects are invisible but might be detected by their effects on surrounding stars, particularly in a double-star system. Do black holes really exist and do they cause any of the peculiarities we see among some stars? These questions are two of the most exciting ones in astronomy today. One possible case of a black hole may be the supergiant star epsilon Aurigae, which is eclipsed every 27 years by something unseen, possibly a companion star.

GIANT RADIO TELESCOPE

From 1957 the largest steerable radio telescope was the 250-foot dish at Jodrell Bank in England. That telescope is famous for its observations of satellites and astronomical objects. Now it has been exceeded by a new 100-meter (about 330 feet) dish completed by the Max Planck Institute for Radio Astronomy near Bonn, West Germany. Its 3,200 tons of moving parts can be pointed with an accuracy of 1/600 of a degree. A larger dish (the 1,000-foot-diameter telescope in Puerto Rico) exists, but it is fixed and can observe only the astronomical objects close to its zenith.

QUASARS

The record for the greatest red shift, and hence the fastest astronomical speed in vacuum ever measured, was set in observations by C. Roger Lynds, of the Kitt Peak National Observatory, and Derek Wills. They found that the spectral lines (which are displaced toward the red end as the object moves away) in the quasar 4C 05.34 are shifted by 2.877 times their normal wavelengths. After relativistic correction, this result corresponds to a receding speed amounting to 94 per cent of the speed of light. If this speed is due to expansion of the universe, the quasar's distance is so great that the light now being received on earth left the quasar just after it was "born."

At such great distances, quasars show peculiar spectral absorption lines. In the quasar PHL 957, which has the second-largest known red shift, Princeton astronomer Dr. Donald Morton found eight sets of speeds. This probably means that when the light from that quasar started toward the earth, it passed through eight or more clouds of gas that later condensed to form stars and galaxies.

X-RAY SOURCES

By using rockets to detect X rays coming toward the earth (which are totally absorbed in our atmosphere and never reach the ground), scientists have found a variety of objects that emit incredibly huge amounts of X rays. The objects include Seyfert galaxies, named for the late astronomer Carl Seyfert, who found several dozen galaxies with very bright compressed centers. The brightest X-ray source is a double star in Scorpius unlike any previously known star. The sun emits some X rays from its hot outer corona.

Rocket observations are valuable for preliminary exploration but collect information for only the five minutes they remain above the atmosphere. However, a satellite in continuous orbit around the earth could be used for months or years. The first X-ray satellite, Explorer 42, was launched by American and Italian scientists from the east coast of Kenya on Dec. 12, 1970, the seventh anniversary of Kenyan independence. In honor of the occasion, the satellite was named *Uhuru*, the Swahili word for "freedom." Among its more surprising feats was the discovery of a pulsating object in Cygnus with a period of 0.073 seconds, even though the area seems to have neither radio pulses nor supernova remnants.

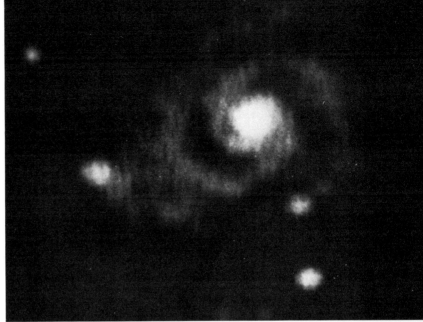

By means of the mile-long Synthesis radio telescope (in the Netherlands), astronomers obtained the first picture of a distant galaxy, the Whirlpool (top). Superimposing the radio data on a photograph taken by a Mount Palomar telescope (below) showed that the source of the strongest radio emissions was just inside the spiral arms of bright young stars. This finding lends support to the supposition that such bands indicate waves of compression that help to produce new stars.

INTERSTELLAR MOLECULES

The space between stars is extremely empty by earth standards; it is a better vacuum than can be produced in any laboratory. Nevertheless, nearly an atom per cubic centimeter exists in interstellar space, so the amount of material between the earth and a star trillions of miles away is significant. Astronomers have known for decades that the gas in interstellar space includes such elements as hydrogen, calcium, iron, titanium and so on. Also the diatomic molecules cyanogen (CN) and CH were known to exist in interstellar space, but it was suspected that polyatomic molecules could not survive the effects of ultra-violet starlight. Detectors for millimeter-wavelength radiation discovered spectral lines from other molecules. By the end of 1971, 21 different molecules, including polyatomic and organic molecules, had been found, sometimes weekly. The molecules include carbon monoxide (CO), ammonia (NH_3), formaldehyde (H_2CO), water vapor (H_2O) and such complex forms as methylacetylene (CH_3C_2H) and methyl cyanide (CH_3CN). Thus any doubt has been removed that organic molecules are widely distributed in space.

HELMUT A. ABT
Astronomer
Kitt Peak National Observatory

To an intent class in an Australian boys elementary school, Miss Gladys Fortune, of Newport News, Va., an international exchange teacher, talks of education and life in her home state.

AUSTRALIA

General economic slackness, rising prices and frequent strikes shared the spotlight with political developments. The economy was in the process of change, and while generally prosperous it was under severe strain, particularly in the wool and rural industries. Manufacturing had a lackluster year. The performance of the mining industry was spotty but successful. Nevertheless, international trade continued to run in Australia's favor and, with big investment funds from abroad, record overseas reserves exceeded U.S.$2,200,000,000.

A change in the Liberal Party's parliamentary leadership in March brought a 63-year-old self-styled technocrat, William McMahon, to the prime ministership. He succeeded John Grey Gorton, whose three years in office had been marked by frequent controversy. Although the opposition Labor Party achieved greater cohesiveness, and differences within the Liberal Party remained even after the leadership switch, the Liberal-Country Party coalition Government completed its 22nd year in office.

International relations were under review as a result of President Nixon's China initiative. Australia's combat force in South Vietnam was withdrawn at year's end.

Political Developments. The retirement on Feb. 1 of Sir John McEwen, the Country Party leader and a key member of successive coalition Cabinets since 1949, began a process of realignment of forces within the government parties. This led to Gorton's ouster as prime minister and, after five months, as minister for defense in McMahon's Cabinet. Some of the changes could be laid to personality clashes, but the overall effect was to shift the Liberal Party to a more conservative stance. In spite of the changes, criticism continued; McMahon's performance was regarded as indecisive.

Within the Labor Party, new and younger trade-union leaders came to positions of influence, and the party's base was broadened by the absorption of politically active white-collar workers and academics. At the same time the parliamentarians assumed a larger role in party-decision-making and Opposition leader Edward Gough Whitlam gained stature within the party. In July, he led an ALP delegation to Peking for discussions. Whitlam indicated that a Labor government would recognize Peking as China's sole legal government and would seek to improve Australian-Chinese trade relations. Expansion of Pacific trade is of benefit to both.

When the newspapers ran excerpts from the so-called Pentagon Papers on Vietnam, political controversy mounted over the exact nature of Australia's initial involvement in Vietnam. There were denials by McMahon and former Prime Minister Sir Robert Menzies that Australia moved other than at the behest of the South Vietnamese Government.

The Economy. Difficulties paralleled U.S. and U.K. experiences: a decline in business activity, rising prices and increasing costs. The 2 to 3 per cent inflation rate of earlier years increased

---

AUSTRALIA

Area: 2,967,909 sq. mi.
Population: 12,800,000
Capital: Canberra
Government: Sir Paul Hasluck, governor-general
—1969; William McMahon, prime minister—
1971
Gross National Product: $31,750,000,000
Monetary unit: Australian dollar (A $1 = U.S. $1.15)
Foreign trade: exports, $4,728,000,000; imports, $4,228,000,000
Armed forces: 85,000

to 5 per cent in fiscal 1971. Because of low wool prices the rural sector was in its deepest crisis in forty years. As a relief measure the Federal Government provided funds to guarantee U.S.$0.40 per pound for wool, and the Wool Commission purchased large quantities of wool when the auction price failed to reach the Government's level.

Britain's move into the European Economic Community and shifts in world-trade patterns, with the danger of resurgent protectionism, stirred concern; sugar and fruit were among industries considered threatened. McMahon visited London for discussions on the fate of Australian primary industries threatened by loss of British markets, and arranged for continuing consultations at a ministerial level on EEC matters.

With the end of the boom in mining shares, the stock exchange price index declined about 15 per cent to a five-year low. Exports rose about 6 per cent to U.S.$4,728,000,000, while imports (also up 6 per cent) amounted to U.S.-$4,228,000,000, yielding a trade surplus of U.S.$500,000,000. Japan remained the main buyer, the United States the chief supplier. For the first time, beef moved ahead of wool as the top income earner among rural products, but minerals (particularly iron ore) earned as much as beef and wool combined (about U.S.-$1,200,000,000).

Capital inflow increased by over 75 per cent to a record U.S.$1,500,000,000 in fiscal 1971. Unemployment rose slightly to about 1.5 per cent of the work force. The big immigration program was eased back for the first time.

Businessmen criticized the Government for its "tight money" policy. They pointed out that prices were rising not because of excessive demand but because of cost-push; the Government nevertheless persisted with a policy of tight credit and high interest rates. Presented in August, the budget raised the income tax and some sales taxes and postal charges. In November the first break came when the Government announced a slight easing of interest rates on its long-term loans.

The international currency crisis had only minor effect; the Australian dollar appreciated about 3 per cent in relation to that of the United States. The whole tariff structure came under scrutiny following the retirement of McEwen, who had generally favored the manufacturers' cause. Manufacturers stressed the need for a more satisfactory tariff policy to cope with industrial expansion.

Local crude-oil production (Australian wells now provide the bulk of the nation's petroleum requirements) strengthened the economy. A major new natural-gas field was discovered off the northern coast of Western Australia, in the area adjacent to the big iron-ore deposits already under active exploitation.

Foreign Affairs. Australia's continued reliance on the ANZUS pact as basic to foreign and defense policies was confirmed in November when the Prime Minister met with President Nixon in Washington. At the same time, new steps were taken to maintain a "forward defense" position in Southeast Asia. A five-power treaty involving Australia, Britain, Malaysia, New Zealand and Singapore was signed. Under ANZUK, naval, air and ground forces will remain in the Malaysia/Singapore area. Previously Britain had been responsible for these defenses, with Australia and New Zealand involved through an understanding. The new pact provides that each participating country is jointly responsible.

Even though McMahon had said in May that it was "a long-term objective" to enter normal bilateral relations with Peking, the Government was surprised by President Nixon's announcement of his intention to visit Peking. Whitlam's meeting with Premier Chou En-lai brought strong criticism from the Prime Minister but this was immediately demolished by Nixon's announcement. Australia welcomed the admission of the People's Republic to the UN but expressed disappointment at the ouster of Nationalist China.

Other Domestic Developments. Neville Bonner, 53, was chosen by the Liberal Party of Queensland to fill a short-term Senate vacancy. An expert boomerang-thrower, Bonner is the first aborigine to take a seat in Parliament.

Plans were advanced for adoption of the metric system. By 1976, the Government said, Australia would be "70 per cent metric."

The media gave considerable play to conser-

Australian Prime Minister William McMahon and his very attractive wife arrive at Kennedy Airport for a meeting with President Nixon.

vation issues. In advance of the meeting of the Australia and New Zealand Association for the Advancement of Science, an open letter, signed by eight hundred scientists, stressed the need for a new ecological approach.

See also McMahon, William; Oceania

R. M. YOUNGER
Author, *Australia and the Australians*

AUSTRIA

Austrians went to the polls twice in 1971, first to return incumbent socialist President Franz Jonas to office for another six years, and then to give socialist Chancellor Bruno Kreisky the first majority mandate in a democratic election in Austria since the end of World War I.

Jonas, 71, was reelected on Apr. 25, winning 52.8 per cent of the vote defeating the conservative People's Party candidate, Kurt Waldheim, a former foreign minister who temporarily gave up his post as Austrian ambassador to the United Nations to seek the presidency. Jonas' winning margin was more than four times greater than in 1965.

Encouraged by the swing to Jonas and discouraged by the fact that his own mandate to govern was curbed by coalition considerations, Kreisky dissolved Parliament in July and called new elections for October. Kreisky's once-divided party took 50.04 per cent of the vote in the elections. Socialists gained 93 seats in the enlarged 183-seat National Council, or lower house of Parliament, while the People's Party won 80 seats. The right-wing Freedom Party won 10 seats. Less than 2 per cent of the 4,500,000 votes went to communist candidates, and the party failed to win a single seat.

The opposition People's Party, which once dominated Austrian politics, changed leadership twice in 1971 before turning to Karl Schleinzer, 47, a gentleman farmer.

There were 165 seats in the outgoing Parliament, but the number was increased to 183 under a redistricting plan. Socialists held 81 seats in the former Parliament, but could not rule alone because the People's Party held 78 seats, and the Freedom Party, with 6 seats, held the balance of power.

Kreisky, 60, the first elected socialist chancellor in half a century and the first Jew to lead the Government, is often called a man of European stature who would command more attention and recognition if Austrian neutrality were relaxed. A red-haired pro-Westerner and former foreign minister, he fulfilled one campaign pledge by reducing compulsory military service from 9 to 6 months, but other promises remained unfulfilled. Kreisky blamed this on the shaky status of his minority Government. His electoral victory implied that Austrians, at least temporarily, rejected the once sacrosanct "red-black" formula: that is, combined socialist and conservative leadership, in control 1945–66.

Economically, the government Institute of Economic Research forecast a growth rate of 4.25 per cent in 1972 and predicted wage increases averaging 10 per cent. Prices, it forecast, would increase by 4 per cent. Record revenues and expenditures were forecast in the 1972 budget with income set at $4,500,000,000 and spending at $4,900,000,000. The deficit was slightly up from 1971. Tourist earnings again were expected to close the gap. Official reserves at the end of 1971 were about $1,900,-000,000, up about $100,000,000 from 1970.

Austria revalued the schilling on May 9, raising its value against the U.S. dollar by 5.05 per cent in the first currency adjustment of any kind since 1953.

Austria established diplomatic relations with mainland China in May, but the main emphasis in foreign affairs was its relations with Western Europe. Once the long dispute with Italy over the German-speaking province of South Tyrol (or Alto Adige, as Italians call it) was settled by treaty, Vienna's attention turned to entering some form of association with the European Common Market, which buys 41 per cent of Austria's exports.

Thirty-two years after his death, the city of Vienna at last honored Sigmund Freud, the father of psychoanalysis, by opening a tiny museum in his old apartment at 19 Berggasse. The city refused, however, to change the street's name to Sigmund-Freud-Gasse.

One of the world's best-known exiles, Jozsef Cardinal Mindszenty, 79, the primate of Hungary, arrived in Vienna in October to live. He had expressed a wish to live the rest of his life in a Hungarian priests' home in Vienna. The wish was granted.

CHARLES W. BELL
News Editor, Rome Bureau
United Press International

AUSTRIA

Area: 32,374 sq. mi.
Population: 7,500,000
Capital: Vienna
Government: Franz Jonas, president—1965; Bruno Kreisky, chancellor—1970
Gross National Product: $14,300,000,000
Foreign trade: exports, $2,857,000,000; imports, $3,549,000,000
Armed forces: 48,350

Photos General Motors

Among the innovative features of an experimental safety vehicle are: pillarless windshield and (below) a "message center" instrument panel.

AUTOMOBILES

Despite record sales, there was nothing comfortable or easy about calendar year 1971 for the U.S. auto industry. Reaching 10,200,000 domestic and import units, new-car buying in 1971 easily exceeded the strike-cut 8,300,000 in 1970, and the 9,600,000 record notched in 1968 and nearly equaled in 1969. Yet the unexpected emerged at every turn.

Regardless of perplexing economic indicators, the year opened with a buying spree fanned by demand built up by the late-1970 10-week General Motors strike. However, a booming spring market was followed by a government-ordered anti-inflation, 90-day wage-price freeze (imposed Aug. 15), and a boost in the import-car surtax from 3.5 per cent to 10.0 per cent.

Meanwhile auto makers fought for and won an extension from Aug. 15, 1973, to Aug. 15, 1975, in the government-ordered passive-restraint requirements that centered on the controversial safety air bag in cars. However, the industry still faced a bewildering array of bumper and emission-control requirements. The latter involved 1976 auto models and threatened to increase car prices by $600 to $1,000.

The unexpected surtax, plus the increased value of non-U.S. currencies in relation to the U.S. dollar, forced prices of leading cars imported into the United States upward by $100 to $300 in September–November. In several in-

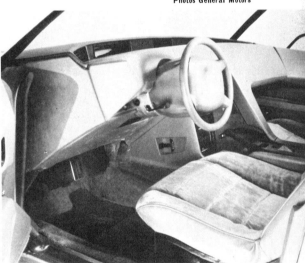

stances the cost of imports exceeded domestic-make Pinto, Gremlin and Vega for the first time. But the price boosts did not prevent another record sales year for imports. Despite stubborn East and West Coast dock strikes, the imports nudged 1,600,000 sales in the United States as compared with the record 1,230,000 posted in 1970. The imports' share of the auto market jumped from 14 per cent to nearly 16 per cent. At year's end, domestic-minicar producers were anxiously waiting to see if the import-price hikes had at least partially stemmed the sales tide.

It was against this uncertain backdrop that the auto makers reported impressive January–September dollar sales in 1971. However, sev-

In the competitive U.S.-import minicar field, Toyota offers the smart-looking Corona Mark II hardtop, 1972 model.

Toyota

eral factors, including GM's poststrike comeback, made an accurate "reading" difficult. In any event, GM's record sales (32.9 per cent above January–September 1970) and a net income that was second only to 1965 made bright headlines, as did Ford Motor Co.'s 24 per cent profit rise on a 11.2 per cent sales increase. Chrysler Corp.'s $48,400,000 profit reversed a $15,200,000 loss of 1970 and was good news, as was American Motors' $10,200,000 profit on sales of $1,200,000,000.

However, the other side of the coin "read" problems. Hefty 5.0 per cent price hikes in September were rescinded by government order. Despite permission to boost car prices 2.6 per cent in December, cost pressures persisted. The big three posted record sales for July–

September. However, GM's profits were only sixth best in its history, and the Government's wage-price regulations reduced Ford's income before taxes by $72,000,000 in the three-month period. GM and Chrysler refused to divulge their income-before-taxes figures. And for the nine months, Ford Motor Co.'s 3.9 per cent profit margin was still well below the 6.6 per cent noted in 1965. American Motors jumped into bus production to shore up its profit outlook.

By early December, Congress commenced to take action on the President's Aug. 15 proposal to repeal the 7.0 per cent excise tax on passenger cars, which would cut prices an average of $200. Meanwhile, combined domestic-import new-car sales in October topped the 1,000,000-unit

CONVERTIBLE PRODUCTION

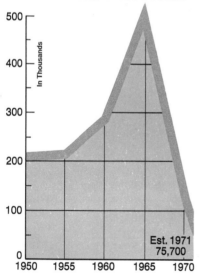

In Thousands

Est. 1971
75,700

Once a symbol of glamour, the convertible is apparently on the way out, victim of expressway speed, polluted air, perhaps fashion. The Cadillac model remains in production.

Cadillac Motor Car Div.

level for the first time ever, and sales of new trucks crashed through the 200,000-unit monthly barrier en route to the first 2,000,000 truck-sales year.

Although the 1972 models offered little that was all-new, they were selling well as the year ended. Auto makers, in effect, had embarked upon a policy of restricting style changes to conserve funds for government-ordered safety and emission features. Some 45 car models were dropped from the industry roster for 1972 as deproliferation was stepped up. Standardization of components between car lines was also accelerated, enhancing cost saving and serviceability.

At Ford the all-new Thunderbird, the Mark IV, the intermediate-size Torino and the Montego received the biggest styling changes. At Chrysler Corp. the full-size or C-body Plymouth Fury, Dodge Polara and the Chrysler car were extensively new. Giant-sized General Motors and little American Motors offered only trim and ornamentation changes. However, each unleashed a bombshell—GM with shock-absorbing front bumpers on its full-size cars (a year ahead of the government-ordered date for the feature) and American Motors with a unique buyer-protection plan. The plan guaranteed the 1972 car buyer company-paid repair and service for the first year or 12,000 miles. All-new Dodge light-duty models were the truck industry's major change.

Toyota's future was clear. Said a spokesman: "When things settle down, the U.S. small-car market—imports, U.S. minicars and U.S. compacts—will continue to grow. Such models priced between $1,800 and $3,000, now at 35 per cent of the market, will take 50 per cent by 1975, if not sooner." A pungent comment from American Motors perhaps explained why: "The big switch to imports in recent years has not been due to price alone." The import brands, it appeared, had an edge on the domestic makes in quality.

In a reverse twist the U.S. auto makers emphasized markets outside the United States, and with good reason. Auto sales in other lands continued to expand at a faster rate than in the United States. At year's end, Ford Motor Co. was in "participation" talks with Toyo Kogyo in Japan. Earlier, Chrysler Corp. bought a stake in Mitsubishi, and General Motors in Isuzu. Japan remained a holdout in permitting foreign participation in its auto market. However, in Great Britain, West Germany, France, Italy, Canada and South America, U.S. participation continued at a brisk pace. For example, production outside North America accounted for over 20 per cent of GM worldwide vehicle output,

General Motors

With the bumper removed, an energy-absorbing bumper device is revealed, developed to help meet Federal standards for 1973-model cars.

and nearly 30 per cent at Ford and Chrysler. While, in turn, there has been little plant investment in the United States by foreign auto companies, Toyota began partial assembly of minitruck production on the West Coast, and in November Nissan expressed interest in such a setup.

In the quest for cleaner air and greater safety, intensive research into alternative power plants continued. This encompassed the gas-turbine engine, stratified-charge power plants, the rotary-piston Wankel (in which GM and Ford bought a stake in 1971), and the steam engine. The nationwide air-quality standards, Washington warned, could within several years even restrict automobile use in many major cities. Meanwhile, a government-sparked drive to develop experimental safety vehicles (ESV) reached international levels and promised to influence the way cars are built in the future.

HARRY A. STARK·
Editor, *Wards Automotive Reports*

AVIATION

After a decade of investment the U.S. Congress killed off in 1971 the ambitious and costly program to develop an SST, the supersonic jet transport. Shortly thereafter, and again after much debate, the same body came through with the support required, in the form of Federal loan guarantees, to continue production on an assured basis of the Lockheed L-1011 widebody airliner with its British-built Rolls-Royce RB-211 jet engine.

Opponents of the proposal to develop an 1,800-mile-an-hour SST, after six years of little success, exploited growing public concern over the quality of the environment and in early March won a House of Representatives vote against the program. Six weeks later the House reversed itself, but only for a brief period. Similar pro and con action in the Senate led finally to the decision to end the SST venture even though almost $1,000,000,000 had already been spent, and the very process of cancellation would cost the taxpayers almost $200,000,000 more than would completion of the project.

Fairchild Industries, Inc., Germantown, Md., largest SST subcontractor to the Boeing Co. and General Electric, signed a ninety-day contract with the Department of Transportation to seek private financing. The effort was fruitless. Fairchild found that the huge sums required to revive the program and move into SST production could not be obtained from nongovernment sources.

Most of the 14,000 persons engaged in the SST program were laid off, in an industry where employment already had declined 25 per cent since 1968. Meanwhile SST development outside the U.S. moved forward under outright government subsidies, with the promise that ultimately U.S. airlines, like their counterparts in other countries, would have to buy foreign-made aircraft capable of twice the speed of U.S. subsonic aircraft. Both the Franco-British Concorde and the Soviet TU-144 made numerous supersonic-test flights, and were displayed at the Paris Aviation Exhibition in summer.

Britain's Rolls-Royce was known to be having financial problems because of its heavy investment in production of engines for the L-1011 TriStar. Nevertheless, the Feb. 4 British Government announcement that it was withdrawing support for the RB-211 engine program, and that Rolls-Royce was headed for receivership, sent a shock wave across the Atlantic and through the U.S. aerospace economy. Within days, Lockheed cut back L-1011 production at its Burbank, Calif., plant, and laid off 6,500 employees. It appeared that the $1,400,000,000 already invested in the TriStar program might be wasted.

Lockheed advised the Securities and Exchange Commission that it faced bankruptcy by the end of the year if not granted a loan guarantee. The British set up a new company, Rolls-Royce (1971) Ltd., and the United Kingdom Government formally committed $240,000,000 to finance completion of RB-211 requirements. President Nixon and Secretary of the Treasury John Connally sent the Emergency Loan Guarantee proposal to Congress in mid-May.

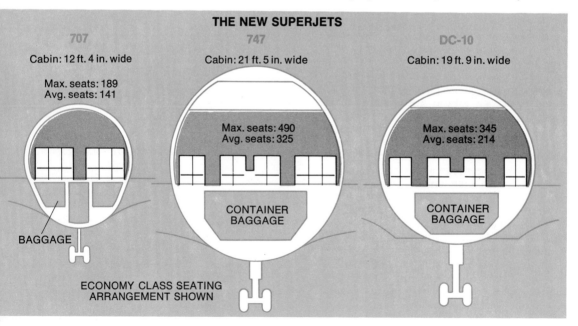

THE NEW SUPERJETS

707
Cabin: 12 ft. 4 in. wide
Max. seats: 189
Avg. seats: 141
BAGGAGE

747
Cabin: 21 ft. 5 in. wide
Max. seats: 490
Avg. seats: 325
CONTAINER BAGGAGE

DC-10
Cabin: 19 ft. 9 in. wide
Max. seats: 345
Avg. seats: 214
CONTAINER BAGGAGE

ECONOMY CLASS SEATING ARRANGEMENT SHOWN

Eastern Air Lines Chairman Floyd Hall said that the L-1011 was the preferable wide-body jet for Eastern's needs, and if the airline were forced to write off its $75,000,000 investment in the airplane, it would be the most serious financial blow ever sustained by Eastern. Trans World Airlines Chairman Charles C. Tillinghast said that competition between Lockheed and McDonnell-Douglas meant that both the L-1011 and the McDonnell-Douglas DC-10 wide-body jet would be better designed and better priced.

Early in August the Senate passed by a one-vote margin, and sent to the White House, a bill authorizing up to $250,000,000 in Federal loan guarantees for Lockheed Aircraft Corp. The 49–48 Senate vote paralleled the earlier 192-to-189 margin by which the House of Representatives had approved the measure. In September the 24-bank consortium, which had already lent Lockheed $400,000,000, approved an additional $250,000,000. Eastern, TWA and Delta Airlines signed agreements providing Lockheed with an additional $100,000,000 in TriStar prepayments. Late in the year Lockheed found itself with more than 100 firm orders and 75 second-buys or options for the L-1011.

Meanwhile the DC-10, a year ahead of its Lockheed rival, entered service with American and United in August. The DC-10 accommodates up to 345 passengers in all economy-class seating, but most of the airlines initially operated it at 250 capacity. This was some 100 less than the typical seatings in the much larger Boeing 747 jumbo jet which, at the end of its second year of service, had already become the preferred plane of a majority of air travelers for long-distance flights. Stand-up lounges installed to attract passengers to the 747 proved so popular that the traditional two-drink limit on U.S. airlines fell by the wayside. Flight attendants said that with so many places aboard the plane where a passenger could obtain a drink, it was no longer possible to police a two-drink limit. Additionally, at $1.50 or more a drink, some airlines were finding liquor service to be a considerable source of revenue.

In Europe a multinational manufacturing consortium, Airbus Industrie, pushed ahead with firm funding of the A300B in several versions, the first of which will carry 260 passengers on an 1,800-mile range. American Airlines said that it was interested in the prospect of using the A300B on high-density runs over ranges too short for economical operation of the DC-10. The French, German and Dutch governments were behind the plane and expected to have it in service ahead of the Concorde.

United Air Lines President Edward E. Carlson files for China route—on April 19, before Nixon's reversal of China policy was announced.

Having experienced a deficit of $200,000,000 in 1970, the greatest loss in aviation history, the U.S. airline industry looked for a return to profitability in 1971, thanks in part to a 6 per cent fare increase granted early in the year. The Air Transport Association of America forecast pretax earnings of $25,000,000 for the 11 trunk airlines, compared with a 1970 loss of $87,000,000. Included was a one-time item of revenue: a $24,000,000 return from SST prepayments. In an intensive belt-tightening campaign the airlines grounded many planes to reduce excess capacity, cut back flight frequency some 5 per cent, and furloughed 10,000 employees in addition to the 12,000 released in 1970. The International Air Transport Association estimated that its member airlines, accounting for more than 90 per cent of the world's scheduled air traffic, would carry about 365,000,000 persons in 1971, 10 per cent more than in 1970, and would experience a cargo-traffic increase of about 15 per cent.

Some airlines turned toward mergers as a possible solution for their fiscal woes. Trans Caribbean Airways merged with American Airlines in March. American also looked for Civil Aeronautics Board approval of its proposal to acquire Western Airlines. Northwest Airlines backed out, early in the year, of a CAB-approved merger with Northeast Airlines because the board refused to include in the transfer the authority of Northeast for its Miami–Los Angeles route. The CAB said that it wanted a further proceeding in which to consider the Florida-California issue. Thereafter Northeast and Delta entered into a merger agreement. Late in October, a CAB examiner recommended approval, again with the exclusion of the Miami–Los Angeles route for later consideration. Northwest, meanwhile, still in search of new routes, sought CAB approval of an agreement to acquire National Airlines. Two local service airlines, Allegheny and Mohawk, also proposed a merger. Eastern asked approval of an agreement to acquire Caribbean-Atlantic Airlines. Pan American and TWA discussed a possible merger but later dropped the idea. Late in 1971 Pan American and Eastern were conducting preliminary merger discussions.

The CAB resolved a long-standing dispute over air routes in the Central Pacific by giving the Trust Territory of the Pacific area largely to Continental Airlines and by granting Pan American certain island rights in the South Pacific.

Taking a firmer stand against restrictions imposed by some governments on U.S. airline operations, the CAB refused to permit Qantas Airways to inaugurate 747 jumbo-jet service to the United States until Australia eased its limitations on U.S. carrier-flight frequencies. According to an agreement reached in September, Qantas will fly four 747 flights to San Francisco, and U.S. planes will fly a total of eight jumbo jets to Australia weekly. Similarly, CAB gave Aer Lingus one-year advance notice that unless the Irish Government allowed U.S. airlines to serve Dublin rather than Shannon, the Irish airline would be denied further entry to New York.

In the early summer, Belgian Sabena Airlines announced that at the behest of its Government, it was offering reduced student fares across the Atlantic. Other airlines retaliated by offering more liberal student and youth fares.

In September international fare agreements broke down when Lufthansa German Airlines filed notice that it was reducing its 52 North Atlantic fares to 8 on Feb. 1, 1972, and would offer a New York–Germany round-trip excursion fare for as low as $210. The IATA member airlines, with Lufthansa participating, worked out a simplified fares package in Honolulu in November and met in Geneva in December to sign an agreement for the 1972 rates.

VERN HAUGLAND
Aviation Editor, The Associated Press

Dismayed Boeing Company employees listen to announcement that the Senate has rejected the SST and that 7,000 workers must be laid off.

UPI

BAHRAIN

On Aug. 14, Sheik Isa ibn Sulman al-Khalifa proclaimed his Persian Gulf island emirate an independent, sovereign nation. It comprises several islands (some uninhabited), has an area of 231 square miles and a population of about 200,000. For more than 150 years, Bahrain was a British protectorate. After Britain announced that it would withdraw its military forces from the Persian Gulf area by the end of 1971, an attempt was made to form a federation of the nine emirates there. Bahrain, the largest, finally decided, however, to act alone, although it might be more subject to the influence of Iran, Saudi Arabia or both. Bahrain became a member of the United Nations and the Arab League later in the year. Iran long laid claim to the island group but dropped the claim in 1970.

Bahrain is important economically because it lies within the fabulously rich oil fields of the Persian Gulf. Bahrain's most ambitious domestic venture is the building of a new town in the midst of the desert. Launched in 1963 and still being constructed, Isa Town will eventually provide homes for 35,000 Bahrainis, many of them from the slums of Bahrain's capital, Manama. Although the house designs are largely traditional—with flat roofs to allow sleeping there in the hot climate, high walls and screens for the seclusion of women—the houses are no longer huddled together. Instead they are divided by garages, looking to the day when every family will have a car.

BELGIUM

It was a year of dichotomy. The rebuilding of the center of Brussels emphasized the city's importance as the administrative capital of the New Europe, the supranational European Community. The troubles of the Government of Gaston Eyskens stressed the electors' concern to preserve their particular cultural identity and their local language.

The rebuilding of central Brussels was in the care of former Prime Minister Paul van den Boeynants, in 1971 the city's alderman for Public Works. Streetcars were going underground. Tower blocks were rising. Car parks were multiplying. Six thousand Common Market civil servants were in the European Building. The "NATOcrats" were housed near the airport.

Nevertheless, "the language problem," the cultural split between French-speaking Walloons in the south and Flemish-speaking Flemings in the north, intensified. In July the Government introduced a new constitutional package giving local groups considerable auton-

BELGIUM

Area: 11,781 sq. mi.
Population: 9,700,000
Capital: Brussels
Government: Baudouin I, king—1951; Gaston Eyskens, premier—1968
Gross National Product: $24,900,000,000
Foreign trade (including Luxembourg): exports, $11,609,000,000; imports, $11,344,000,000
Armed forces: 96,500

omy, and parents in bilingual Brussels the right to choose the language in which their children should primarily be taught. It was hoped that this would give Belgium a breathing space in which to tackle the very serious economic problems that had begun to loom, notably inflation. However, by November, Eyskens had resigned and a general election had been called. The result of this election, while it returned the two main coalition parties, Social Christians and Socialists, to power with their majority virtually unchanged, was that the "language parties," Walloon and Flemish, made unexpected gains at the expense of Liberals and others. This immediately put pressure on the linguistic wings within the coalition parties and exacerbated the difficulties of Eyskens, who had formed a new Cabinet. The tendency was growing to look toward a federal solution.

Another division to appear was prompted by President Nixon's economic package which forced many currencies, including the Belgian franc, to float against the dollar. Subsequently the value of the franc increased by 3 per cent.

King Baudouin and Queen Fabiola paid the first visit to Germany by Belgian royalty in sixty years when they visited Bonn for four days in April. The year 1971 was the 20th anniversary of Baudouin's accession and the 141st of the founding of the Belgian state.

Belgium established full diplomatic relations with Communist China on Oct. 26.

JOHN ALLAN MAY
Chief, London Bureau
The Christian Science Monitor

BIOLOGICAL SCIENCES

Recent developments in the biological sciences, especially in genetics and biochemistry, promise to evoke a great deal of hope—and a great deal of controversy. As Sen. Walter F. Mondale (D-Minn.) said in a speech on the floor of the U.S. Senate, "We are rapidly acquiring greater powers to modify and perhaps control the capacities and activities of men by direct intervention into and manipulation of their bodies and minds. . . . These developments raise profound and difficult questions of theory and practice, for individuals and for society."

Genetics. In his satirical novel of the future, *Brave New World,* Aldous Huxley describes how 96 identical human beings developed from a single "bokanovskified" egg. Scientists call such asexual production of large numbers of identical organisms cloning.

Cloning involves nuclear transplantation. It is a simple technique. The nucleus of an unfertilized egg is removed. It is replaced by the nucleus from a somatic cell such as a skin cell. The egg, with its transplanted nucleus, will develop as if it had been fertilized. Barring complications, it gives rise to a normal organism. The new organism is identical to the organism that provided the somatic cell; we say it has the same genotype. This is quite different from the production of an organism through the union of an egg and a sperm; such sexual reproduction produces an organism with a genotype that is not like that of either parent but, rather, is unique.

One individual could provide an unlimited number of somatic cells for nuclear transplantation. The result would be an unlimited number of identical organisms—a clone—all produced asexually from, and resembling, a single parent.

Scientists have already achieved this with several organisms that naturally reproduce only sexually: fruit flies, frogs and salamanders. Nuclear transplantation in mammals has not yet been achieved. But theoretically, clonal reproduction is possible in mammals, including man; only technical problems need to be solved.

Nobelist James D. Watson, codiscoverer of the structure of DNA, states, "If the matter proceeds in its current nondirected fashion, a human being born of clonal reproduction most likely will appear on the earth within the next twenty to fifty years, and conceivably even sooner."

A number of the technical problems are being solved by scientists working on in vitro fertilization. It is the fertilization of an egg cell by a sperm cell in a test tube, and the subsequent development of the embryo. Several laboratories have accomplished it with human cells; some of the fertilized eggs lived for seven to eight days, the age at which the embryo (now called a blastocyst) normally attaches itself to the wall of the uterus, or womb.

At this point, two paths are open to the geneticist. A human embryo could be implanted into the uterus of a woman. It has not yet been accomplished, but trials are imminent. Laboratory-grown embryos of rabbits and mice have been successfully implanted. The second possibility is to grow the embryo in vitro for the entire gestation period. In such experiments, however, growth has always ceased just after the blastocyst stage. In April 1971, Dr. Yu-Chih Hsu of Johns Hopkins University announced that he had successfully cultured mouse embryos from the blastocyst stage to a stage having a differentiated and beating heart. Development then stopped. Said Dr. Hsu, "All the embryos developed in vitro seem to be defective in one organ or the other with the present method. . . . The supply of nutrients and gases may be inadequate for further embryonic development."

Another genetic technique may soon be available, to predetermine the sex of a child. Sex is determined by the sperm cell. If it has an X chromosome, the child will be a girl; if it has a Y chromosome, a boy will develop. Thus if a method can be developed that separates X-carrying from Y-carrying sperm, it should be possible, through artificial insemination, to control, or determine, the sex of a child. In 1970–71, geneticists discovered procedures for distinguishing each of the 23 pairs of human chromosomes. Detection of the Y chromosome may serve toward successful separation of the different sperm.

Major advances have been made in genetic disease. Using a technique known as amniocentesis, doctors can sample the fluid that surrounds the unborn child in the womb. By analyzing the fluid it is possible to detect inherited diseases such as mongolism. If the fetus has such a disease, an abortion can be performed depending on the parents' views.

However, it may soon be possible to cure such inherited diseases. In October 1971, Dr. Carl R. Merril and other scientists at the National Institutes of Health reported on experiments in which human skin cells, grown in the laboratory, took up and used genetic material from the bacterium *Escherichia coli.* The cells were from a person suffering from galactosemia, in which the individual is unable to metabolize galactose (a simple sugar found in milk). The disease is fatal unless the infant is put on a milk-free diet. The material introduced into the human cells contained genetic information for making the enzyme that breaks down galactose. The human cells appeared to accept and use the enzyme; thus the cells were "cured" of galactosemia. This suggests that similar methods could be used to alter other metabolic traits.

It is obvious that these developments in genetics have numerous ethical, social, political and legal implications. In fact, said Senator Mondale: "The impact on our ideas of free will, birth, and death, and the good life is likely to be even more staggering than any actual manipulation performed with the new technologies." **Biochemistry.** The synthesis of various biological compounds and the determination of their molecular structure continues at a rapid pace. The most notable synthesis announced in 1971 was that of the human growth hormone (HGH), a complex protein produced by the pituitary gland. The hormone promotes growth, stimulates the milk glands, and apparently has important roles in repairing bone fractures and skin wounds, lowering blood cholesterol and so on. The synthesis was achieved by a research team headed by Dr. Choh Hao Li of the University of California's Homone Research Laboratory. The HGH synthesized consisted of 188 subunits (amino acids). Each one had to be identified and its proper place in the structure determined before synthesis could occur. Laboratory tests showed that the synthetic hormone had the growth-promoting and lactogenic properties of natural HGH. However, it was only about 10 per cent as active as the natural hormone.

In July 1971, Dr. Li and two associates published a modified structure for HGH that has 190 amino-acid units. At the same time, they proposed a structure for the hormone called human chorionic somatomammotropin (HCS). It is found in the human placenta; its properties are similar to those of HGH. The suggested structure for HCS consists of 190 amino acids; 160 of them occupy the same positions as they do in HGH.

The brain hormone LH-RH has been synthesized and its molecular structure determined by scientists from Tulane University and the Veterans Administration Hospital in New Orleans. The hormone regulates fertility. "This breakthrough should permit control of fertility in humans and animals and lead to the development of several new methods of birth control," said Dr. Andrew V. Schally, who headed the research team.

A current birth-control method may be improved as a result of research on pheromones, chemical sex attractants produced by females at the time of ovulation. It is not known that human females produce pheromones. But lower animals do. In June 1971, British researchers reported the isolation of such a substance from the vaginal secretions of a female monkey. It was the first proof that primates produce pheromones. If human females secrete these chemicals, it may be possible to devise a simple test for their detection, thus leading to more accurate use of the rhythm method of birth control.

In March 1971 it was announced that scientists at California's Hormone Research Laboratory had determined the molecular structure of the interstitial-cell-stimulating hormone. It stimulates and regulates ovulation, sperm maturation and the production of steroid sex hormones.

Also in March, the University of Chicago and AEC's Argonne Cancer Research Hospital announced that researchers there had isolated erythropoietin, the hormone that stimulates red blood-cell formation. Potentially, the achievement is very important to people with kidney disease, who do not produce the hormone, and thus suffer from anemia. According to Dr. Eugene Goldwasser, one of the scientists who isolated erythropoietin, treating kidney patients with the pure hormone would enable them to lead comparatively normal lives, much like diabetics who take insulin to regulate blood-sugar levels.

JENNY TESAR
Senior Editor, *The Book of Popular Science*
and *Encyclopedia Science Supplement*

UPI

Drs. Cho Hao Li (l) and Donald H. Hamashiro, of the University of California's Hormone Research Laboratory, inspect some of the equipment that helped them to synthesize a human growth hormone, an essential, complex protein that is produced by the pituitary gland.

Eastfoto

At Sofia Airport in September, arriving Soviet leader Leonid Brezhnev and Bulgarian party leader Zhivkov make usual display of amity.

BULGARIA

While Bulgaria continued its efforts to extend friendly relations with its Balkan neighbors (except Yugoslavia), internal developments had priority over foreign affairs during 1971. The Tenth Congress of the Bulgarian Communist Party reelected Todor Zhivkov as first party secretary; and the long–promised constitution, replacing the 1947 document, was adopted by referendum.

Political Affairs. The party congress, which ended April 21, effected few changes. In addition to Zhivkov, the entire Politburo was reelected. The one significant shift was the failure to reelect Lachezar Avramov, deputy prime minister and minister of foreign trade, a candidate member of the Politburo. Following the congress, Zhivkov, in accordance with the new constitution, became chairman of the State Council (a new parliamentary body), in effect becoming president while retaining his party post as well. He resigned as premier and was replaced by Stanko Todorov.

Foreign Affairs. Internationally, Bulgaria remained a faithful spokesman for the Soviet position. Bulgarian publications denounced China for inviting President Nixon to visit Peking, statements that were republished in the Soviet Union in July. As part of a joint Soviet-Bulgarian move in the Balkans, Bulgaria proposed a comprehensive eight-point program of economic cooperation with Greece, including a suggestion for a Bulgarian zone in the Greek port of Salonika. Bulgaria also continued to rail at Yugoslavia, stressing its claim to kinship with the Macedonian national minority in Yugoslavia.

In August the Bulgarian ambassador and the Soviet counselor were ordered out of Khartoum (Sudan). They were charged with aiding Sudanese Communists planning a coup against the Sudan Government.

Economic Developments. The directives for the sixth five-year plan (1971–75), adopted by the party congress, set workable targets for the economy but continued to give first priority to heavy industry.

HERMAN SINGER
Editor, *East Europe*

BURMA

Burma began to stir from its economic and political torpor in 1971. The stirring was, to be sure, very slight. Yet in a situation of total political and economic stagnation, existing for years, even the slightest movement seems dramatic. By year's end, in fact, it appeared that Burma might even be moving away from the self-imposed isolation it had endured for a decade.

Although earnings from rice exports continued to drop, and large-scale black-marketeering and the creaking inefficiency of the state-run economy did little to improve the lot of the average Burmese, there were a couple of positive aspects to the economy. Because of the troubles in East Pakistan, Burma stepped up production of jute and was expected to export 40,000 tons during fiscal 1971–72, compared with only 4,800 tons in fiscal 1970–71. The country's balance-of-payments situation would benefit thereby.

Rice, formerly Burma's most important export, still suffered under declining world-market prices. The country should nevertheless be able to export 920,000 tons of rice during the 1971–72 fiscal year, maintaining the level of income from that source.

One significant 1971 development, which might serve as a model for future deals aimed at improving Burma's basic economy, was a contract signed with the British firm John Brown Engineering. The deal involves a U.S.-

---

BULGARIA

Area: 42,823 sq. mi.
Population: 8,600,000
Capital: Sofia
Government: Todor Zhivkov, Communist Party Secretary—1954, State Council Chairman—1971; Stanko Todorov, premier—1971
Gross National Product: $8,900,000,000
Foreign trade: exports, $2,004,000,000; imports, $1,831,000,000
Armed forces: 148,000

$7,800,000 order for a 60,000,000-watt gas-turbine electric power plant for Burma's Electricity Board. Part of the cost is to be paid in rice.

Politically, Burmese Prime Minister Gen. Ne Win weathered the country's many little rebellions without any significant loss of ground. The biggest threat, from the direction of former Prime Minister U Nu, apparently petered out in 1971.

Whether moved by the threat of rebellion or by a sincere desire to give the Burmese people a greater say in their Government, Ne Win took several steps during the year to give his largely military-dominated regime a civilian look.

In June, the first Burma Socialist Program Party (BSPP) congress was held. The BSPP is the ruling party under Ne Win, who was elected chairman of the party's 150-man central committee, formed from the 1,120 delegates who attended the congress. Ne Win told the party to consolidate its position as "a people's party," to forge national unity and to draft a new constitution.

Convening the BSPP congress sparked a number of political changes. On July 9, Ne Win reshuffled his all-powerful Revolutionary Council and added four civilians to it. The new civilian members were U Ba Nyein, member of the central executive committee of the BSPP; Dr. Maung Maung, chief justice; Mahn Tha Myaing, member of the BSPP inspection committee; and U Ba Nyein II, vice-chairman of the Central People's Worker's Council.

The final 1971 political shift came a week later when Burma's Revolutionary Council, which had been ruling the nation for nine years, was converted into a cabinet of ministers. Gen. Ne Win became prime minister and defense minister. The other ten military members of the council retained their council portfolios, but as government ministers. The change in name was recommended by the Burma Socialist Program Party as a first step toward the eventual transfer of power from the military to the party. But there was no further progress in 1971 toward a true civilian regime.

Late in 1971 Burma moved to improve its relations with neighboring Thailand. At the same time, Rangoon (Burma's capital) leaked word that it would be interested in closer economic and political relations with Thailand, Malaysia, Indonesia and other Southeast Asian states.

ARTHUR C. MILLER
Senior Editor, The Asia Letter

CAMPAIGN SPENDING

Expenditures for political campaigns in the United States have been rising sharply. The estimated total in 1968 was $300,000,000, or about 60 cents per vote; this contrasts with 29 cents per vote in 1960 and 10 cents in 1944. A major reason has undoubtedly been the rapid growth in use of television and radio, the largest single item in the expenditures of the 1968 presidential campaign and undoubtedly in contests for other offices as well. It is therefore not surprising that in 1971 the subject was given renewed attention both in the press and in Congress.

Even the large sums being spent today in political campaigns are comparatively small when contrasted with the expenditures of government itself. But the political outlays loom large indeed when compared with the resources of most individuals, whether candidates or contributors. Concern has been felt that the trend is giving rise to several unfortunate political consequences: (1) Prospective candidates who lack large personal fortunes or wealthy supporters may be discouraged, regardless of their qualifications, from seeking high office. (2) Candidates dependent upon large contributions from comparatively small numbers of wealthy persons may be influenced in the conduct of their campaigns, and if elected, in their performance in office, by the wishes of these contributors. (3) Inequality in the amount of funds available to competing candidates, with resulting domination of the media of communication —especially television and radio—by one candidate, may substantially interfere with the ability of his opponent to have a fair opportunity to get his message to the voters.

Concern with these problems, although recently heightened in intensity, is not new. As far back as 1884 the United States Supreme Court expressed anxiety over "the free use of money in elections, arising from the vast growth of . . . wealth." In 1907, Congress forbade campaign contributions by corporations. This was followed by the Federal Corrupt Practices Act of 1925, which limited spending by candidates to $25,000 in senatorial elections and

$5,000 in elections for the House of Representatives, and required candidates and certain political committees to report campaign contributions and expenditures. A 1940 amendment to the Hatch Act set a limit of $5,000 for contributions by an individual to a Federal candidate or national committee, and a limitation of $3,000,000 on the amount of funds that might be received or expended by a political committee. Finally, in 1943 and again in 1947, Congress extended to labor unions the prohibitions against contributions by corporations.

Superficially, these Federal laws might appear to provide a comprehensive program for solving the problems alluded to above. In fact, however, they were characterized by President Johnson as "more loophole than law," and one congressman is reported to have said that the present law is "intentionally evaded by almost every candidate. . . . I dare say there is not a member of Congress, myself included, who has not knowingly evaded its purposes in one way or another."

The ceilings on Congressional campaign expenditures are unrealistically low. But there are really no effective controls, since there is no limit on the number of committees that may be set up in support of a candidate, or on the number of contributions of $5,000 that one person may make to each such committee. And since expenditures, as well as receipts, can be channeled through committees, limitations on donations by contributors and on expenditures by candidates are both ineffective. Despite the fact that it frequently costs more than $100,000 to conduct a campaign for the House of Representatives, and Senate campaigns have often cost in the millions, the candidates themselves have often been able to report, truthfully, that they had not spent a cent on their elections.

The intensification of interest in the subject in the last few years has resulted in many attempts at Congressional action. One suggested approach is to have the Government pay at least some of the cost of campaigns. This was recommended in 1907 by President Theodore Roosevelt, and government assumption of the entire cost was urged by the Democratic National Committee in 1971. The Presidential Election Campaign Fund Act of 1966 provided that each Federal income taxpayer could elect to earmark one dollar of his tax to be placed in a fund, from which payments would be made in the next presidential election to national party committees. The formula provided would have given the two major parties equal payments from the fund, much smaller amounts (even proportionately to the number of votes cast) to any other parties that had received

over 5,000,000 popular votes in the previous presidential election, and nothing at all to new parties or older ones that had received fewer votes. The following year, however, Congress had second thoughts about this law and, in effect, repealed it.

In 1970 a fresh effort was made, influenced in part by awareness of the disproportionate expenditures of the candidates in the 1968 presidential election. Both Houses of Congress passed a bill, applicable to the presidential and Congressional elections, that would have limited campaign expenditures for television and radio to 7 cents per vote cast for the office in the previous election (or $20,000, whichever was greater) and in certain other respects would have made access to broadcasting facilities cheaper and easier. It was vetoed by President Nixon for a number of reasons—among others, that the 7-cents-per-vote limitation was unrealistically low, that there was no limitation on expenditures other than for broadcasting, and that the problem of expenditures of committees not directly connected with a candidate was not resolved. He urged Congress, however, to draft a better statute to limit "the crushing and growing cost of political campaigning." The President's veto was sustained in the Senate.

Faced with a $9,000,000 party deficit, Democrats in both houses of Congress began to push for a campaign-funding bill again in the fall of 1971. Since it was generally felt that in a year before a presidential election, President Nixon could not afford to veto a tax bill, particularly one basically in agreement with his own recommendations, the Democratic leaders decided to tack a campaign-funding amendment onto the tax bill. On Nov. 22, the Senate passed the amendment, which resembled the funding bill passed in 1966. The amendment would have gone into effect in 1972.

Under White House pressure, Rep. Wilbur Mills, chairman of the House Ways and Means Committee, refused to accept the funding amendment and persuaded a Senate-House conference committee (the tax bill had passed in the House) to accept a compromise. Under the compromise plan, a taxpayer may designate $1.00 of his annual taxes for financing presidential candidates, after 1972 election. In addition, a taxpayer may deduct up to $50 a year ($100 for a married couple) of his campaign contributions, or can take a tax credit (i.e., an actual deduction from the amount of tax due) of up to $12.50 ($25 for a couple) for campaign contributions. Although Nixon signed the tax bill on Dec. 10, the President said that he was "confident" that with time Congress would repeal the funding plan.

In addition, a bill that would establish a ceiling on the amount of money presidential and Congressional candidates can spend for advertising during a campaign was awaiting final Congressional action as 1971 ended.

Comparable problems have also been recognized with respect to state elections, and there is a wide variety of state laws attempting to deal with them. With few exceptions, these laws are deemed just as ineffective as their Federal counterparts. British practice has been suggested as a model; expenditures for campaigns for Parliament are sharply limited, and equal broadcasting time is provided free. The British limitations apply, however, only with respect to campaigns for individual parliamentary seats and not to nationwide expenditures on behalf of political parties. Also they apply only to a very brief period of time preceding the election, which is technically regarded as the campaign, with no limits upon expenditures at earlier stages. Moreover, minor-party candidacies are discouraged through a requirement that a bond be posted, which is forfeited if the candidate receives less than one eighth of the vote.

Most proposals for campaign reform in the United States involve one or more of the following elements: (1) limitations upon the size of contributions; (2) limitations upon expenditures by or for a candidate; (3) effective requirements for reporting and disclosure of contributions and expenditures; and (4) government subsidization of part or all of the cost of the campaign. In addition, partial or total suspension or repeal of the "equal time" provisions of the Federal Communications Act has been urged on the ground that the law prevents broadcasters from arranging debates between leading candidates unless they are willing to include all minor candidates as well.

Each of these approaches involves problems, both practical and constitutional. It is contended that the right to contribute money to pay for dissemination of views in support of a candidate is itself part of the right to communicate, restriction of which would be a denial of freedom of speech and press. It is also asserted that restraints on what a candidate may spend on his own behalf similarly inhibit his expression. In addition, the problem of how to handle the expenditures of independent committees supporting a candidate is particularly difficult.

Requirements for reporting and disclosure have also been criticized on the ground that individuals might be deterred from contributing on behalf of a candidate if they feared reprisals from employers, clients, colleagues or others in

Crockett, "The Washington Star"

"No visible means of support"

the community with opposing views. If only contributors of large sums were obliged to report, however, the most likely threats of undue influence would be disclosed, while those contributors sufficiently affluent to make large contributions might be comparatively impervious to retaliation. It has been recommended that reporting be prompt and conveniently available to the press, so that even during the course of a campaign the public would know the identity of the candidates' major supporters. It has been reported that such a Florida law is extremely effective.

Subsidization by the Government may involve difficult problems, particularly with respect to primary elections and minor parties. If all candidates, no matter how unimportant, were to receive the same sums, significant amounts would not be available to anyone, and many candidates and parties more concerned with publicity than with the possibility of election might emerge in order to claim the subsidy. On the other hand, subsidies of major parties to the exclusion of minor or new parties, or greatly in excess of the sums accorded them, might be deemed unfairly discriminatory.

It seems likely that dissatisfaction with the present way in which election campaigns are financed will continue; and that with further increases in the costs of campaigning, particularly for television and radio, attempts to achieve reform through legislation will persist.

ALBERT J. ROSENTHAL
Professor of Law, Columbia University

Canadian Industry and Trade Commission delegate J. H. Warren (l), in Washington after Nixon's Aug. 15 announcement, meets with U.S. officials Paul A. Volcker, John B. Connally, Maurice Stans and Nathaniel Samuels.

CANADA

Canada gave evidence in 1971 of wanting to diversify its international relations and alter the terms of its traditionally close relationship with the United States.

Ambassadors were exchanged with Peking, following Canada's decision in 1970 to establish diplomatic relations with the People's Republic of China. Prime Minister Pierre Trudeau visited the Soviet Union in May; this was followed in

Visiting Soviet Premier Kosygin gets some tips on hockey from Canadiens star Henri Richard.

October by the Canadian tour of Soviet Premier Aleksei Kosygin. It was the first visit to Canada by a Soviet leader. Agreements were signed on both occasions to encourage trade between the two countries as well as cultural and scientific exchanges.

Concurrently there was a new appraisal in Ottawa of Canadian-American relations, particularly in the areas of trade between the two countries and of U.S. investment in Canada. The debate over "economic nationalism" intensified in 1971 and seemed likely to become one of the main issues of the general election expected in 1972. Relations between Canada and the United States became increasingly difficult in 1971.

In May, at a press conference in Moscow, Prime Minister Trudeau referred to the "overpowering presence of the United States" in Canada and said, "This is reflected in a growing consciousness amongst Canadians of the danger to our national identity from a cultural, economic and perhaps even military point of view." During a meeting with Premier Kosygin in Ottawa in October, Trudeau was reported to have said that Canada wishes to establish the same relations with the Soviet Union as it enjoys with the United States.

Official and popular attitudes toward the United States were influenced by President Nixon's imposition in August of a surcharge on U.S. imports and Washington's subsequent refusal to give Canada special dispensation. Canada sends 68 per cent of its exports to the United States and is, in turn, the United States'

The planned test of a U.S. nuclear underground device on Amchitka, in the Aleutians chain, Alaska, provokes widespread protest in Canada, here on the New York-Quebec border.

UPI

most important export customer. While automobiles and petroleum were exempted from the surcharge, and most unprocessed natural resources were little affected, the surcharge did apply to about 25 per cent of Canada's exports to the United States. Canada's total exports to the United States in 1971 amounted to more than $10,000,000,000.

Concerned about high unemployment, the Canadian Government immediately asked Washington to remove the surcharge from manufactured Canadian exports. It reminded the United States that it had no complaint against Canada about artificial exchange rates and that Canada's favorable balance of commodity trade with the United States in 1971 had to be considered in relation to the heavy flow of dollars into the United States as a result of American investment in Canada. "There is no justification for applying penalties to Canadian trade," Prime Minister Trudeau told a national television audience in August.

When it became evident that the surcharge would remain, the Government introduced an $80,000,000 program of special grants for exporting industries to prevent a predicted loss of 40,000 to 90,000 jobs. As the unemployment rate climbed to 7.1 per cent in October, Finance Minister Edgar Benson announced a 3 per cent reduction in personal income tax and a 7 per cent cut in corporate tax effective July 1, 1971, as well as a new series of employment-producing programs. Prime Minister Trudeau indicated that the Federal Government would incur a billion-dollar deficit in 1971.

At a press conference in October, the Prime Minister said: "They [the United States] don't seem to realize what they are doing to Canadians. If they do realize what they are doing

and if it becomes apparent they just want us to be sellers of natural resources . . . we will have to reassess fundamentally our relations with them. . . ."

The question of U.S. investment in Canada was a major Canadian preoccupation in 1971. Canada's international indebtedness has been increasing at an annual rate of 4 per cent during the past fifty years. At the end of 1969, Canada's net liabilities to nonresidents amounted to about $28,200,000,000, and Canada had become "one of the major debtor nations in the world," according to a government study. It showed that 57 per cent of Canadian manufacturing is foreign-controlled, mainly by Americans. Foreign interests control 65 per cent of mining and smelting in Canada and 74 per cent of the country's petroleum and natural-gas industry.

During 1971 a special task-force report was leaked to the editors of a Toronto magazine. It called for the creation of a government agency to screen foreign take-over bids. The Government had not committed itself to a policy by the time Prime Minister Trudeau visited Washington in December for discussions with President Nixon.

While the Government pondered an economic strategy for the 1970's, specific developments revealed a growing nationalist sentiment in Canada. There were official as well as public protests over President Nixon's decision to go ahead with the nuclear test on the Aleutian island of Amchitka in November. A resolution of the House of Commons was followed by a telephone call from External Affairs Minister Mitchell Sharp to U.S. Secretary of State William Rogers to express the "deep sense of disquiet" in Canada about the test. Ottawa in-

H. A. Hampson is chairman of new Canada Development Corp., to channel investments.

formed Washington that it would hold the United States responsible for any long-term effects of the test.

In January, the Liberal Government introduced legislation, first mentioned in a Liberal budget speech in 1963, to create a Canada Development Corporation as a channel for investment in industry both by the Government and individual Canadians. Initial investment by the Government will be $250,000,000 over three years. Ultimately, authorized capital of the CDC will be $2,000,000,000 with one eighth owned by the Government and the rest by private Canadian investors. The corporation's first purchases will be existing government interests in Arctic oil and natural gas, uranium mining and northern transportation and power companies. Later it will invest in "areas of critical importance in economic development:

CANADA
Area: 3,851,809 sq. mi.
Population: 21,688,000
Capital: Ottawa
Government: Roland Michener, governor-general —1967; Pierre Elliott Trudeau, prime minister—1968
Gross National Product: $90,000,000,000
Foreign trade: exports, $16,187,000,000; imports, $13,349,000,000
Armed forces: 85,000

high-technology industry, resource utilization, northern-oriented companies and industries where Canada has a special competitive advantage."

Ontario, the most populous and prosperous of the Canadian provinces, moved to protect Canadian interests in a number of fields. Premier William Davis of Ontario announced a program in July to ensure that investment firms remain "substantially Canadian" by limiting foreign control to 25 per cent. Similar legislation already applied to Ontario's loan and trust companies and had been announced earlier in the year for the province's paperback-book distributing industry to prevent a take-over by U.S. distributors. Ontario also lent about $1,-000,000 to the largest Canadian-owned book publishers, McClelland and Stewart of Toronto, when financial difficulties threatened to force a sale to U.S. interests.

These domestic policies coincided with a strong Canadian interest in diversifying international contacts, particularly with China and the Soviet Union. In May, Prime Minister Trudeau and his bride of two months spent 11 days in the Soviet Union. On his return, the Prime Minister said that he harbored "no naïve belief" that the Canadian-Soviet agreement he had signed in Moscow would suddenly create a relationship of "sweetness and tender feelings" between the two countries. But he said that it went some distance to place Canadian-Soviet consultations on the same basis as those with such countries as Britain, the United States and Japan.

During the summer, Trade Minister Jean-Luc Pepin led an economic mission to Peking. The results included a commitment by China to participate in the Canadian National Exhibition at Toronto in 1972 and by Canada to stage a trade fair in Peking in the same year. Negotiations began for a China-Canada air link. Because of the large number of U.S. subsidiaries operating in Canada, China's past policy of not buying from these subsidiaries was discussed. Pepin said after the meetings that "this should not create major difficulties." Opposition Leader Robert Stanfield visited three Chinese cities in July as part of a tour of the Far East. In the same month, Peking's first Ambassador to Canada, Huang Hua, arrived in Ottawa. He later became Communist China's first ambassador to the United Nations.

An eight-day visit to Canada by Soviet Premier Kosygin in October produced a communiqué stating that discussions between the two leaders had disclosed "a similarity of views on a number of international issues." In most cities visited by Kosygin there were protests by Jews

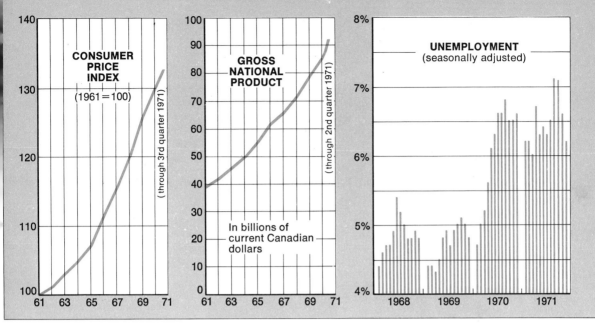

THE CANADIAN ECONOMY

CONSUMER PRICE INDEX
(1961 = 100)
(through 3rd quarter 1971)

140
130
120
110
100
61 63 65 67 69 71

GROSS NATIONAL PRODUCT
(through 2nd quarter 1971)
In billions of current Canadian dollars

100
90
80
70
60
50
40
30
20
10
0
61 63 65 67 69 71

UNEMPLOYMENT
(seasonally adjusted)

8%
7%
6%
5%
4%
1968 1969 1970 1971

and Canadians of Eastern European origin. In Ottawa on Oct. 18, during an impromptu walk with Prime Minister Trudeau on Parliament Hill, the Soviet Premier was almost pulled to the ground by a young man shouting "Long live free Hungary!"

A Defence Department White Paper in August announced a decision to get rid of two "obsolete" squadrons of Bomarc antiaircraft missiles equipped with U.S. nuclear warheads and stationed in northern Ontario and Quebec. Canadian jet interceptors in Canada will continue to use U.S. nuclear warheads. The White Paper also said that there are no plans to further reduce Canada's military contribution to NATO, cut during 1970 from 10,000 to 5,000 men.

International events and unemployment at home distracted national attention from what had become known as "the Quebec problem" in the 1960's. Following the October crisis of 1970, when a British diplomat was kidnaped and a Quebec cabinet minister was murdered, there was a lull in the activities of Quebec terrorists who want to achieve an independent French-speaking Quebec state by violence. Special legislation, suspending certain civil liberties during the crisis, was allowed to expire on Apr. 30, 1971. Justice Minister John Turner announced in Ottawa that 497 people had been arrested under the special legislation and that 435 had been released without being charged.

The Federal Government continued to expand programs of bilingualism started in the late 1960's. An advisory board under the

Official Languages Act designated 37 bilingual districts in Canada where at least 10 per cent of the population is a French-speaking or English-speaking minority and where Federal services will be offered in both languages. The Government also announced that it wants 60 per cent of its senior civil servants to be bilingual by 1975. Only 15 per cent were bilingual in 1971, despite intensive language courses for civil servants in recent years.

The Defence Department announced a target of 28 per cent French-speaking personnel for Canada's 85,000-man armed forces. In 1971, only 16.2 per cent of the servicemen and only 10.6 per cent of the officer corps were French-speaking.

In Quebec, the only province where a majority of people speak French as their mother tongue, Education Minister Guy St. Pierre announced that French will be compulsory in English-language schools and that up to 40 per cent of the curriculum in these schools eventually will be taught in French.

Unemployment remained the major weakness of an expanding Canadian economy. Despite the surcharge on U.S. imports, Canadian exports to the United States in the first nine months of 1971 were 9.2 per cent higher than in the corresponding period of 1970. In the last quarter of 1971 it was reported that expansion of the real gross national product had exceeded a 6 per cent annual rate for four consecutive quarters. Prime Minister Trudeau predicted that "our rate of growth for 1971 as a whole will likely exceed that in every major industrial country of the Western world, and even that of Japan."

Despite an intensive government program to encourage voluntary restraint by business and labor, consumer prices in September 1971 were 3.5 per cent higher than a year previously. This compared with an increase in U.S. consumer prices of 4.3 per cent over the same period, before President Nixon's wage-and-price controls had any marked effect.

Unemployment in the winter months continued to reach 7 per cent of the labor force. More than 11 per cent of workers under 25 years of age were unemployed in the winter of 1971–72, illustrating a special problem of the Canadian economy. A combination of immigration and high birthrates after World War II is giving Canada, in the years 1965–80, an increase in its labor force in absolute terms that is 20 per cent greater than the combined increases in Britain, West Germany and Italy. The combined population of these 3 countries is 8 times larger than Canada's population.

"Canadians face a formidable task of job creation in the decade ahead," warned the Government-sponsored Economic Council of Canada at the end of 1971. It said that employment will have to increase at an annual rate of 3.3 per cent to absorb the growing labor force in the first five years of the 1970's. During the first nine months of 1971, employment rose at an annual rate of only 2.2 per cent.

Discontent with the Government's economic policies was the main reason in April for the resignation of Communications Minister Eric Kierans from the Federal Cabinet. He was the second cabinet minister to resign since the Trudeau Government was elected in 1968.

Other significant events in 1971 included:

Canada's first mail-back census in 1971 produced a response rate in excess of 90 per cent, higher than the previous record of 86 per cent established by the world's first mail-back census in the United States in 1970. Final census results were still being compiled at the end of the year, but the estimated population on June 1, 1971, was 21,688,000. The fastest-growing major urban centers in Canada were Calgary (an increase of 21 per cent in 1966–71), Toronto (16.3), Edmonton (16.1) and Vancouver (14.9).

Immigration into Canada dropped by 17 per cent in 1971, but the United States moved ahead of England for the first time as Canada's leading supplier of population. In the first nine months of 1971, there were 17,270 arrivals from the United States compared with 9,060 from England. The total for the nine-month period was 94,005 immigrants.

On Oct. 30, 1971, *The Toronto Telegram* ceased publication. The 95-year-old daily was Canada's fourth-largest newspaper with a daily circulation of more than 200,000 copies. Toronto was left with two daily newspapers, the morning *Globe and Mail* and the afternoon *Toronto Star*. The *Star* paid $10,000,000 for the *Telegram*'s subscription lists, giving it a daily pressrun of more than 500,000 copies by the end of the year.

In July the Quebec legislature created the state-owned James Bay Development Corporation to develop natural resources in the James Bay watershed south of Hudson Bay, including a $6,000,000,000 hydroelectric project. The watershed contains the largest untapped hydroelectric potential remaining in Canada.

UPI

In the almost deserted newsroom, an employee reads the last, sad issue of the 95-year-old "Toronto Telegram," Oct. 30.

Prime Minister Trudeau and his bride, the former Margaret Sinclair, leave for a skiing honeymoon after their secret marriage in Vancouver, B.C.

Schiffer Photography Ltd.

A Federal subsidy of $21,000,000 and generous government credit enabled Marine Industries Ltd. of Sorel, Quebec, to land the biggest commercial shipbuilding contract in Canadian history. The shipyard will build 12 container cargo ships for 2 French companies for a total price of $123,500,000.

In May the first visitors entered Ontario Place, a $23,000,000 entertainment and cultural showplace built by the Ontario government on the Lake Ontario shoreline at Toronto.

In February, 2,100 athletes took part in the Second Canada Winter Games at Saskatoon, Saskatchewan. The prairie city got the games after building a 300-foot artificial mountain for skiing events.

David Lewis, 61, was elected in April to be leader of Canada's socialist third party, the New Democratic Party. It has 23 members in the 264-seat House of Commons. Lewis replaced T. C. Douglas, who had led the party since its inception in 1961.

A 4-day revolt by 500 prisoners at Ontario's Kingston Penitentiary ended on Apr. 18 with the release of 5 hostages unharmed. The prisoners killed one of their fellows and injured 11 others, and reduced the main cellblock to a pile of rubble.

A landslide at St. Jean Vianney in Quebec on the night of May 4 destroyed 36 homes and killed 31 persons.

The government of Ontario announced in March that it would sue Dow Chemical Company of Canada Ltd. and Dow Chemical Co. of Midland, Mich., for $25,000,000 for ecological damage to parts of the Great Lakes system and for $10,000,000 to cover depollution costs.

PETER DESBARATS
Ottawa Editor, *The Toronto Star*

The royal yacht "Britannia" bears Queen Elizabeth, Prince Philip and Princess Anne to British Columbia's 100th-birthday celebrations; opposite page, the Queen greets tour coordinator Brig. Gen. P. S. Cooper.

CANADA: Provinces and Territories

ALBERTA

In elections for the provincial legislature, the Progressive Conservative Party, which had only 10 seats in the previous legislature, won 49 of the 75 seats. Party leader Peter Lougheed, a 43-year-old Harvard-educated lawyer, became prime minister. The defeated Social Credit Party had governed Alberta for 36 years. □ In a reorganization of the various governmental departments, a new department of the environment was formed to enforce new antipollution laws. □ A law was passed placing police forces under the jurisdiction of a provincial commission and the attorney general.

BRITISH COLUMBIA

Marking the 100th anniversary of British Columbia as a province, Queen Elizabeth, Prince Philip and Princess Anne toured the province for ten days in May. □ Beginning in September, all liquor and tobacco advertising was banned. □ J. R. Chabot was appointed provincial labor minister; a month-long strike by transit workers in Vancouver and Victoria ended in February; and an unusually high unemployment rate, particularly among the young, prevailed.

MANITOBA

As a result of by-elections on Apr. 5, the government of Premier Ed Schreyer gained its first majority since coming to power in 1969. His New Democratic Party gained two legislative seats, one each from the Liberals and Progressive Conservatives. □ On Feb. 27, Sidney Spivak was elected leader of Manitoba's Progressive Conservative Party. □ Prime Minister Trudeau appointed Samuel Freedman to succeed C. Rhodes Smith as the province's chief justice, as Justice Smith reached the mandatory retirement age of 75. □ Agriculture Minister Sam Uskiw was named minister of the newly formed Department of Cooperative Development.

NEW BRUNSWICK

The premiers of New Brunswick, Nova Scotia and Prince Edward Island signed an agreement in May establishing a Maritime council of premiers. The council will coordinate policies affecting all three provinces. □ On May 31, barrister Charles E. Leger of Moncton was sworn in as the province's ombudsman. □ Former Premier Louis J. Robichaud retired as leader of the provincial Liberal Party. At a party convention in October, Robert Higgins was named Robichaud's successor.

Schiffer Photography Ltd.

McIntyre Porcupine Mines Ltd.

Grande Cache, a new town in Alberta, is literally built on coal. As good coking coal, its biggest market is the expanding steel mills of Japan.

NEWFOUNDLAND
Ignoring telephone threats against his life, Premier Joseph Smallwood presided at the opening of the 1971 legislative session. ☐ The Premier's son William R. Smallwood was suspended from the legislature for one week in May. Liberal member for Green Bay, young Smallwood had punched opposition member William Marshall, who had mentioned Mrs. Joseph Smallwood in connection with a list of persons described as slum landlords. ☐ In elections on Oct. 20, Conservatives apparently won an upset victory in the province. However, Premier Smallwood demanded a recount, and even threatened to take legal action. Issue was still undecided in 1971.

NORTHWEST TERRITORIES
Dr. Louis-Edmond Hamelin and Léo Gérard Lemieux were appointed to the Northwest Territories Council; Air Marshal Hugh Campbell and John H. Parker were reappointed to the council. ☐ An eight-month Federal study, released in January, reported that wildlife resources in the Northwest Territories and in the Yukon are threatened. A number of areas were termed critical to the maintenance and support of such wildlife as caribou, polar bears, peregrine falcons and ducks and geese.

NOVA SCOTIA
The provincial legislature enacted laws establishing day-care centers, abolishing the poll tax, setting up collective bargaining for fishermen, and lowering the age of majority from 21 to 19. ☐ John Buchanan was elected leader of Nova Scotia's Progressive Conservative Party, which had been defeated in provincial elections in October 1970. ☐ H. Russell MacEwan was sworn in as judge of the provincial magistrate's court. ☐ Oil and natural gas were discovered on Sable Island. ☐ New ministries of tourism and development were established to replace the division of trade and industry. ☐ The provincial government sponsored the first "floating trade fair," held on a ferry traveling between Yarmouth, N.S., and Portland, Me.

ONTARIO
On Mar. 1, William G. Davis, 41-year-old lawyer, was sworn in as the 18th premier of Ontario, succeeding John Robarts. On Oct. 21, in a three-way provincial election, the Premier's Progressive Conservative Party was returned

The $13,000,000 interchange in Toronto was completed before the Ontario legislature stopped work on Spadina Expressway (vertical) in 1971; it now goes nowhere.

The pool is part of a seafarming venture near Halifax, Nova Scotia. Trout and salmon are raised under controlled conditions and marketed fresh. A yearly production of 4,000,000 pounds is planned.

Photos National Health and Welfare Canada

The second Canada Winter Games open in Saskatoon, Sask., in February (above). Competing in 16 sports (swimming below), 2,100 athletes attend the 10-day event from all 12 provinces and territories.

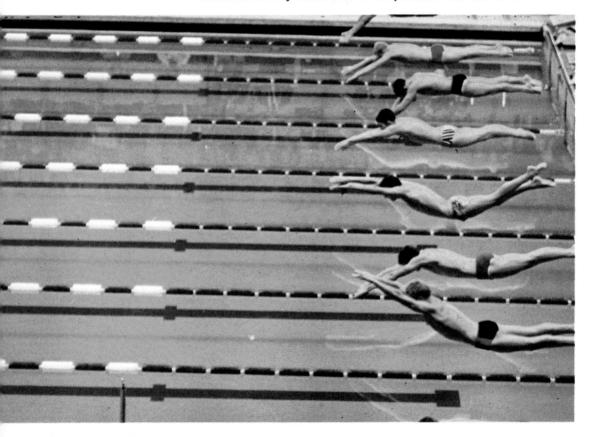

to power. □ Some 400,000 persons aged 18 to 21 were granted the right to vote and the right to drink alcoholic beverages. □ On Sept. 6 Toronto was blacked out by a major power failure. □ Ontario Place, a $23,000,000 cultural center in Toronto, opened on May 22.

PRINCE EDWARD ISLAND

Fifty-four bills, including the Public Gathering Act, were passed by the legislature during its spring session. Under the Public Gathering Act, the provincial minister of justice may ban any gathering that in his opinion might contribute to the disruption of public order or where essential services (medical services, fire prevention, police protection) are inadequate. □ To accommodate an estimated 12 per cent increase in tourism, the province added two new vessels to its Cape Tormentine, N.B.-Borden, P.E.I., ferry service.

QUEBEC

The provincial government rejected a Federally sponsored draft for a new Canadian constitution. □ Premier Robert Bourassa approved a proposed $6,000,000,000 hydroelectric project to harness the power of five rivers flowing into James Bay. □ Gabriel Loubier was elected leader of Quebec's Union Nationale Party. □ With the advent of a provincial medicare system (in late 1970), the number of people seeking medical attention rose some 20 per cent in early 1971. □ McGill University in Montreal celebrated its 150th anniversary. □ Two new all-weather ferries for service between Quebec City and Lévis on the St. Lawrence River were launched in April.

SASKATCHEWAN

In provincial elections on June 23, the New Democratic Party of Allan Blakeney scored an overwhelming victory over the ruling Liberal Party of Premier Ross Thatcher. Premier Blakeney and his cabinet took the oath of office on June 30. □ The first "odor-free" pulp mill will be built 63 miles north of Meadow Lake. To produce an estimated 1,400 tons of bleached kraft pulp daily, beginning in 1973, the mill will cost about $118,000,000.

YUKON TERRITORY

Yukon Commissioner James Smith announced a budget of about $30,000,000 for fiscal 1971–72. Not included in the total was some $5,300,-000 for police service, highway maintenance and low-cost housing loans. □ A new mine—the nickel-copper operation of the Hudson Bay Mining and Smelting Company at Quill Creek, west of Whitehorse—opened in 1971.

CANADA: Arts and Letters

Youth was the dominant figure in Canada's 1971 cultural scene. A surge of public interest in the arts, continuous since the 1967 centennial year, resulted in an almost chaotic multiplicity of cultural activities. Factors in this development were the generous grants from the public purse and the relentless growth of the electronic mass media and, most of all, the uninhibited, unsinkable participation by swarms of liberated young people. Music, theater, art, writing, dance and films popped up everywhere in Canada during 1971—in every city, town and village—in theaters, concert halls and auditoriums, in coffeehouses and on street corners, in parks and in farmers' meadows, and unremittingly on the airwaves.

While the quantity of the cultural deluge was inescapable, the quality of much of it was in dispute, largely because a young man's meat can be an old man's poison. Garish, earsplitting, eye-popping offerings appealed to crowds of university and high-school students and to the new community of restless youthful wanderers. Although some of it was slipshod, much of it was painstakingly structured in the idiom of modern youth. All of it demanded and shared top billing with the traditional cultural activities. There were literally hundreds of youth-inspired "festivals" throughout Canada. From them there sprung an infectious bit of carnival atmosphere which helped to relieve the pressure of worries about inflation and unemployment.

Although a plethora of so-called festivals marked the Canadian scene, the genuine article did take place. The prestigious Stratford Festival again provided a rich, perfectionist artistic treat. The Charlottetown (P.E.I.) Festival, with an 85 per cent season box-office take, delighted midsummer tourists with three full-scale musicals—*Mary, Jane Eyre* and *Anne of Green Gables*—along with good folk music and folk dance and a children's theater in a real circus tent.

The Orford Festival, held in the greenery of Quebec's Eastern Townships under the auspices of Jeunesses Musicales, enjoyed a prosperous season. Young music students from many parts of the world studied under renowned teachers and enjoyed an astonishing variety of theater, ballet and art presentations, while thousands of day visitors from Montreal and the summer-cottage country attended the daily concerts.

The Guelph (Ont.) Spring Festival was an impressive success with lively, professional servings of popular-classical music, theater, dance and visual arts. The Banff Festival, a new activity sponsored by the noted Banff

Ian Hogg plays Macbeth, and Kenneth Welsh, Macduff in Stratford's 19th festival season.

Stamp reproducing his "Indian Encampment on Lake Huron" commemorates 100th anniversary of death of Canada's great pioneer artist Paul Kane.

Paul Kane   painter
             peintre   Canada 7

School of Fine Arts, brought a star-studded summer week of all the arts to Alberta's picturesque Rocky Mountain resort.

The Mariposa Folk Festival, held in mid-July on Toronto's Centre Island, was an interesting experiment. The 1970 attempt to provide a serious program of night happenings of rock and folk music by noted groups and soloists had been disrupted and bedeviled by trouble-bent gate-crashers. The 1971 effort offered 3 days of "sunshine programming" in 6 areas simultaneously for 11 hours a day. There were no night performances. Thirty thousand paying visitors attended the trouble-free, successful experiment.

Festival Canada, a month-long cultural binge, gave Ottawa a rich July entertainment menu. Day and night performances at numerous locations in the capital area provided high-quality, light-textured, low-priced entertainment which booked more than 85 per cent of the potential box office. The variety of events included classical and pops concerts, jazz evenings and mornings, rock and folk happenings, full-scale opera and ballet, band music and carillon concerts, formal theater, "instant theater" in the streets and in the parks, folk dancing, choirs, fine-art exhibitions, film screenings, canoe races and lumberjacks' specialty events. You name it, Festival Canada had it. For the month of July, Ottawa was a wide-open town culturally speaking.

Among the many Canadian film festivals held in 1971, two merit special mention. An International Amateur Film Festival, in Hamilton (Ont.) in April, was a skillfully organized and well-supported show that screened prizewinning films made by amateurs in 12 countries. In Ottawa in September an International Film Week, sponsored by the Canadian Film Institute, presented the work of top-ranking professional producers in 14 countries. Each of the films shown had been a recent award winner at one or more of the world's noted film festivals.

The 1971 theater season in Canada was healthy but relatively uneventful. Box-office results were good nearly everywhere, but spiraling expenses caused a lot of balance-sheet worries. The Stratford Shakespearean company had a highly successful year (*Macbeth, Much Ado, Volpone* and *The Duchess of Malfi*), but a major financial reorganization of the undertaking was required when governmental supporters made an in-depth study of the accumulated-deficits picture.

The Shaw Festival company enjoyed its most successful (10th anniversary) season in its Court House Theatre at Niagara-on-the-Lake. In Halifax (N.S.) the bright and lively Neptune Theatre, a small house in an out-of-the-way city, drew more than 50,000 customers during its season. Citadel Theatre, in Edmonton (Alta.), reported a phenomenal box-office take for its home-based season of 7 plays. Its "on wheels" unit gave 264 performances in 94 towns, including a 3,500 air-mile side trip to 6 Eskimo villages in the Northwest Territories.

Theatre Canada, replacing the venerable Dominion Drama Festival, made its debut in May and left many theater buffs puzzled. The new organization, heavily financed by the Federal Government, aims primarily at encouraging playwriting, training stage people and upgrading theater-management skills. Once a year it will provide a week-long demonstration of what is going on in theater throughout the country. (The old DDF offered a week of adjudicated best in amateur theater in Canada.)

The starter week in Ottawa brought 24 English and French performances to the National Arts Centre and 150 informal dramalike shows at various locations throughout the capital region. It was good fun for tourist-swollen Ottawa, but it is too early to guess at the national importance of the new activity.

The comings and goings of prominent people in the arts world were, as usual, newsworthy in 1971. The appointment of Toronto-born Louis Applebaum, an experienced and admired composer and music executive, as director of the Province of Ontario Council of the Arts (POCA) was applauded throughout Canada. John Hobday, formerly with the Neptune Theatre in Halifax, became director of the Canadian Conference of the Arts (Toronto-based federation of sixty arts organizations) to replace Duncan Cameron, who moved to the Brooklyn Museum (N.Y.). An interesting surprise was the announcement that Morley Callaghan, veteran novelist and winner of many important literary awards, had joined the faculty of the University of Windsor to teach creative writing. A shrewd pairing of appointments occurred when George Davidson, president of the Canadian Broadcasting Corporation, was named a member of the National Film Board, while Sydney Newman, chairman of the NFB, was added to the board of directors of CBC. (The two agencies of the Federal Government are highly competitive.)

There was widespread regret over the deaths of three nationally admired cultural figures. Jean-Marie Beaudet, a beloved and internationally known musicologist, was music director of the National Arts Centre at the time of his death. Nathan Cohen, an interesting and controversial Toronto writer, critic and broad-

The fifty-year-old Winnipeg Philharmonic Choir was main attraction of symphony season in the city's handsome new Centennial Concert Hall.

caster, left a hard-to-fill gap. Thomas Archer, for thirty years the music and drama editor of the *Montreal Gazette,* was considered the country's preeminent music critic at the time of his death in August.

The writing, publishing, selling and buying of books were newsworthy in 1971. A spate of books about Canada's Indian and Eskimo peoples reflected a new political activism among the youth element of the so-called native population and widespread public concern about civil rights. French-Canadian writing and publishing, traditionally parochial and narcissistic, became a matter of intense interest through-

out English-speaking Canada in 1971 as a direct result of the shocking FLQ crisis of 1970.

As usual, there were minor news items relating to the Governor-General awards. (*See also* Prizes and Awards.) The Michael Ondaatje volume, *The Collected Works of Billy the Kid,* was condemned as pornographic by a high-school trustee; and winner Fernand Ouellette refused to accept his award "as a gesture of protest against the Federal Government's invocation of the War Measures Act in 1970 and its persecution of the French language." The Stephen Leacock Award for humorous writing went to Robert Thomas Allen for his *Children,*

Wives and Other Wildlife. Homegrown best sellers of the year included Mordecai Richler's *St. Urbain's Horseman,* Robertson Davies' *Fifth Business* and Pierre Berton's *The National Dream,* with James Houston's *The White Dawn* becoming a favorite after midsummer.

Canada was a musically harmonious place in 1971, with every form of music enjoying a measure of artistic and financial success. The Toronto Symphony Orchestra, the country's best-known musical organization, celebrated its 50th anniversary with a season of 36 major concerts featuring world-renowned guest conductors and soloists. Another half-century mark was reached by the Winnipeg Philharmonic Choir. It was the featured attraction of the Winnipeg Symphony's "Golden Season" in the city's spanking-new Centennial Concert Hall.

The launching of a provincially financed opera company was a natural spin-off from the opening of Quebec City's deluxe Grand Théâtre, with one of the world's largest technically sophisticated stages. At Montreal's "Man and His World," a permanent annual echo of Expo 67, more than 7,000,000 patrons enjoyed a repertoire of virtually every kind of contemporary musical event.

A February national conference of the Canadian League of Composers, in Victoria, B.C., reflected surprising vitality and professional achievement in Canada's creative music. A new national organization emerged from the first conference of Canadian symphony orchestras, held in London (Ont.) in April.

In the visual arts it was Paul Kane year. The first major exhibition of the works of the adventurous painter of North American Indian life a century ago was opened in Calgary (Alta.) in April. Sponsored jointly by the National Gallery of Canada and the Amon Carter Museum, of Fort Worth, Tex., the show was scheduled to travel for two years. A monumental study of Kane's life and works, by the authoritative scholar J. Russell Harper, was the outstanding art book in Canada in 1971. In November the Vancouver Art Gallery opened the "Sculpture of the Inuit" exhibition with 200 masterwork pieces by Canadian Eskimo carvers. The show was to move to London (U.K.), Paris, Copenhagen and Philadelphia (Pa.) in 1972.

WALTER HERBERT
Fellow of the Royal Society of Arts
Consultant on Canadian Cultural Matters

Citadel Theatre (Edmonton, Alberta) tour unit poses with its traveling home; it gave performances from the 49th parallel to the high Arctic.

CARIBBEAN ISLANDS

The growth of U.S. power in the Caribbean is one of the most significant facts in the recent history of the region. Jet airplanes, satellites and electronics have made the Caribbean archipelago a part of the East Coast of the United States.

The trading ties between the islands and the United States have multiplied. Britain was once the chief trading partner of the English-speaking islands, but today Texaco owns most of Trinidad's oil, and five American and Canadian companies are engaged in mining Jamaica's bauxite. Puerto Rico is part of the American defense system, and Antigua provides the United States with a base for tracking satellites. U.S. aid programs put American personnel and equipment into the islands, building schools and bridges, expanding health and educational services. Throughout the year, thousands of Canadians and Americans visit the islands, traveling to small remote islands or more sophisticated centers in Jamaica, Barbados and Puerto Rico.

One result has been the importation of American technology; another, the importation of American movements, values, attitudes, slogans. Together these have speeded up the pace of change which is confirmed by 1971 events. They also show the difficulties that confront small nations that must meet the costs of independence with limited resources.

Of all the English-speaking groups, Trinidad and Tobago is the most prosperous; and until the spring of 1970 it seemed to be the most tranquil. But powerful forces were at work that erupted in discontent. Workers were angry over the muzzling of their unions by an Industrialization Stabilization Act. Young unemployed regarded the Government as aloof and authoritarian. Black-power militants, strongly influenced by the U.S. black-power movement, charged that their country's economy was subject to white economic power. The Army was mutinous. The combination nearly overthrew the Government. U.S. warships appeared off the coast while students shouted American black-power slogans.

A year after the uprising, on May 24, 1971, a general election was held. It was won by the People's National Movement (PNM), led by Prime Minister Eric Williams, although both the PNM and the opposition Democratic Labor Party (DLP) claimed victory—the PNM on the grounds that it won all 35 seats, the DLP on the grounds that its boycott of the election meant that only about 41 per cent of the electorate voted. The boycott was maintained in the local-government elections in November. Thus there was no dialogue between Government and Opposition, no vent in Parliament for discontent. The racial factor aggravated matters. The DLP is almost wholly East Indian; and the PNM is largely supported by a black and brown middle and lower middle class, and a small group of Muslims. Since East Indians make up one third of Trinidad's population, the DLP boycott has, in effect, disenfranchised a large part of the country's population.

In October, Prime Minister Williams suddenly declared a state of emergency, in order to deal with a developing crisis in the oil fields, the stronghold of the country's most powerful labor union. About a score of persons were arrested under the Government's emergency powers. They included trade-union leaders and some black-power militants. As 1971 ended, it appeared that Williams' Government would remain in power because there was no alternative leadership; that the rebellious forces of 1970 would retain their strength; and that the DLP boycott and the Government's antistrike legislation would combine to increase discontent and yet drive it underground.

General elections were held in neighboring Barbados in September. The contrast with the Trinidad situation was marked. The population of Barbados is homogenous, about 95 per cent black or brown. There is a strong tradition of representative government, and a well-established two-party system. The opposition Barbados Labor Party fought a spirited election but lost to the party in power, the Democratic Labor Party, led by Prime Minister Errol Barrow. The victory was in many respects a personal one for Barrow, a powerfully built black lawyer, university trained, with a charismatic personality.

Throughout the region, the drive for economic development continued, stressing the establishment of manufacturing industries and the development of tourism. Small islands—like Tortola, in the Virgin Islands, and St. Kitts—concentrated on improving their airports and on establishing resort centers with the help of foreign investors. Dominica, St. Lucia, Grenada and St. Vincent relied on bananas and tourists. Jamaica's economy maintained a steady rate of growth, though there were ominous signs that a surplus of alumina on the world market would cut the revenue from bauxite in 1972. On the credit side, two regional organizations recently established to foster development—the Caribbean Development Bank with its center in Barbados and the Caribbean Free Trade Area (CARIFTA) with its secretariat in Guyana—began to make their influence felt in the area and elsewhere.

Events indicate that the 1970's will see a new brand of nationalism, springing from social issues. A black-power movement, influenced by the U.S. black-power movement, has come to stay. However, it differs in that blacks are in the majority in all the islands except Puerto Rico and Cuba. The elected black governments are charged by the younger nationalists with being white in attitude and white in policy. They take the line that political independence has not changed the lot of the black and brown masses of the Caribbean, who are still unemployed, underpaid and exploited. They assert that the financial decisions concerning the use of the natural resources of the Caribbean are taken not in Kingston, Port of Spain or Bridgetown, but in Washington, Ottawa and London.

The nationalists point out that up to now development has meant money for the "haves" but none for the "have-nots"; they point to the widening gap between· skilled and unskilled, literate and· illiterate, luxury suburbs and ghettos; and to the fact that the unskilled, the illiterate and the ghetto-dwellers are black; and that North American companies and investors control Caribbean insurance, banking, bauxite, petroleum, chemical industries, and the rest. They point to statistics showing that Trinidadians of European origin earn an average income of $500 a month, Afro-Trinidadians $104, and the East Indians $77. They stress that 5 out of every 100 Jamaican families have 30 per cent of the national goods and services while 60 out of every 100 share 19 per cent of the country's resources.

For the sixth consecutive year, Cuba's 1971 sugar crop (over 5,920,000 tons) failed to reach the production goal set by Premier Fidel Castro. In the fall, 22 Cubans, traveling without visas, spent ten days in the United States. The purpose of the trip was to attend an international sugar conference. The Cubans reasoned that since Cuba is the world's foremost sugar-cane producer it must be represented at such a conference. Although the Cubans claimed that they left the United States voluntarily (without attending the meeting), a U.S. spokesman said that they were expelled.

In other domestic news, the Cuban Government suspended without explanation the airlift of Cuban refugees from Havana to Miami, Fla. A "temporary resumption" of the airlift was later announced. Since it began in December 1965, the service had flown some 250,000 people to the United States.

Although Castro stated emphatically in April that he was "in no way" interested in establishing "normal relations" with the United States, the Premier chatted amicably with members of the U.S. volleyball team when it visited Cuba during the summer. (Diplomatic relations between the two nations were broken off in January 1961.) Subsequently, a U.S. State Department official testified before the Senate Foreign Relations Committee that the United States had no intentions of changing its Cuban policies. Committee Chairman Sen. W. J. Fulbright had called for steps to restore normal Cuban-U.S. relations.

Premier Castro began an extended tour of Chile in November—his first visit to South America since 1959. He was greeted at the Santiago airport by his friend and admirer Salvador Allende. Shortly after becoming president of Chile in late 1970, Allende, a Socialist, had restored relations with Cuba. Various commercial and technological agreements between the two nations were signed in 1971.

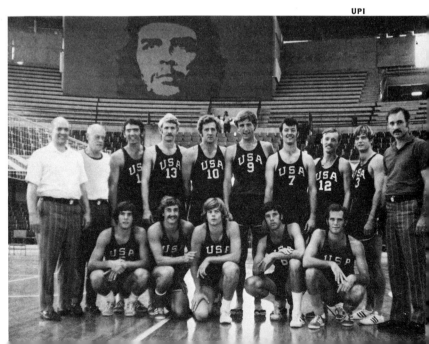

Large poster of the late guerrilla leader Che Guevara dominates gymnasium where U.S. volleyball team prepares to meet Cuban team in pre-Olympic Games match in Havana. The Cubans won the match.

Palace Guard head Gen. Gracia Jacques, well armed, listens as Haiti's new President, Jean-Claude Duvalier, speaks to the press.

Soviet Premier Kosygin spent four days in Cuba in late October. Upon concluding his visit, his first since 1967, Kosygin reaffirmed Soviet support for the Castro regime.

Haiti had a change of government through the death of Dr. François Duvalier in April. The public grief at the dictator's funeral revealed the strength of his hold on the people. An observer at the funeral, casting his mind back 14 years to the day of Duvalier's election to power, Sept. 22, 1957, and recalling the methods of his secret police, the Tontons Macoutes, and his dictatorial rule, must have found the people's sorrow surprising.

Duvalier's nomination of his twenty-year-old son, Jean-Claude, as the new president held good. Duvalier had this power because he symbolized the opposition of the middle and lower classes of the country to the bourgeois of Port-au-Prince, who for long had dominated Haitian politics. He had survived because he broke the power of the Army by creating his own army. In his early years as president he had stood up to the United States, Venezuela and the Dominican Republic and so had satisfied Haitian national pride. After his death an element in the government led by Duvalier's daughter Marie-Denise Dominique clashed with another group, led by Luckner Cambronne, a cabinet minister.

Madame Dominique lost and returned to Paris where her husband is ambassador. As the year ended, no challenger to Jean-Claude, who was relying heavily on the advice of his mother, had appeared.

The other French-speaking islands of the Caribbean, Martinique and Guadeloupe, feel themselves French "in heart, in mind, in blood." Yet a number of these islanders are influenced by West Indian nationalism. Two political parties, the Union for the Defense of the Republic (UDR) and the Socialist Party, oppose autonomy. Yet along with Aimé Cesaires' Progressive Party of Martinique (PPM), they see the necessity for changes in the present rigid system of Départements d'Outre-Mer (DOM).

SIR PHILIP SHERLOCK
Secretary-General
Association of Caribbean Universities

CEYLON

Staggering economic problems, unfulfilled election promises and disillusionment among its radical youth combined in 1971 to fire an attempt at violent revolution in Ceylon. The attempt by self-styled "Che Guevarists"—mostly young peasants, educated unemployed and university students and teachers—failed. But the real loser was Ceylon.

Ever since Prime Minister Mrs. Sirimavo Bandaranaike had regained power in Ceylon in May 1970, her three-party ruling coalition (made up of her Sri Lanka Freedom Party, the Trotskyist Lanka Sama Samaj Party and the pro-Moscow Communist Party) had been under mounting pressure. A decided leftward trend in Ceylon's politics, failure to deal with the country's near-bankrupt economy and Mrs. Bandaranaike's inability to deliver on campaign promises for lower rice prices and large free rations, lay behind the growing discontent.

Despite appeals to both the communist and noncommunist worlds, Trotskyite Finance Minister Dr. N. Martin Perera could not scrounge up the foreign loans and other assistance needed to meet pressing foreign-trade and debt-repayment obligations. At the same time, foreign investment was being scared off by Mrs. Bandaranaike's nationalization programs. Ceylon's major export products—tea and rubber—faced uncertain markets and declining prices. Prices for a number of basic commodities began rising.

On Apr. 5, a date that will mark Ceylon for many years to come, the Che Guevarist rebellion began. Furious over the Government's failure to come to grips with the country's economic problems, thousands of extreme leftist youth (75 per cent of the rebels were between 18 and 22) initiated an armed rebellion. An estimated 85,000 people were involved. A state of emergency was declared and for weeks the lush green island was a battleground.

Despite accusations that the rebels were being backed by everyone from the CIA to the North Koreans, it was painfully clear that the insurgency was wholly homegrown. In the few weeks that the rebels held the upper hand they captured schools, police stations, plantations and even big factories. They set up road and rail blocks, and at one point were apparently on the brink of overrunning the capital itself.

With help from outside, including a squadron of MiG 17's flown by Russians, the Government eventually crushed the rebellion, but not before considerable loss of life and unbearable damage to property, especially the essential rubber and tea plantations, had occurred. Mrs. Bandaranaike arrested some 16,000 people. At year's end, most were still in concentration camps awaiting trial or release. A few thousand revolutionaries fled to the hills to wage Maoist-style guerrilla warfare.

At first it appeared that the Che Guevarist insurrection would jolt the Bandaranaike Government into taking more positive steps toward solving the island's problems. Yet 1971 saw few indications that rising prices and unemployment (an estimated 500,000 out of a population of 13,000,000) were being effectively checked.

In late October, the Government announced increased gasoline and tobacco prices. Three months earlier bus and train fares had been hiked. More than ever before the country became dependent on foreign aid to make up its balance-of-payments shortfall. Most Western countries and lending institutions such as the World Bank and International Monetary Fund became exceedingly wary of putting further funds into the country. China, however, came forward quickly with a no-strings-attached, long-term, interest-free loan in June.

Regardless of the huge economic problems, Mrs. Bandaranaike pressed ahead with political reforms. Parliament was hard at work drafting a new constitution. The proposed new constitu-

tion would make Ceylon a republic and more independent of the British Commonwealth.

In a related move, Ceylon's upper house, the Senate, went out of existence on Oct. 3. Supposedly it was abolished because it was obstructing the Government's "socialist legislative measures." The opposition United National Party held a majority in the Senate. Under the new constitution there will be only one legislative body, called the National Assembly.

For Ceylon, a country steeped in the democratic tradition, perhaps the most disturbing aspects in 1971 were the tough, restrictive measures introduced to cope with the rebellion. Censorship, bans on public meetings and discussion of the rebellion and so on remained in force despite the Government's claim that the revolt had been put down.

ARTHUR C. MILLER
Senior Editor, *The Asia Letter*

Ceylon's Prime Minister Bandaranaike, whose regime barely survived a youth revolt, arrives in London for talks with British leaders.

Popperfoto

CEYLON

Area: 25,332 sq. mi.
Population: 12,900,000
Capital: Colombo
Government: Sir William Gopallawa, governor-general—1962; Sirimavo Bandaranaike, prime minister—1970
Gross National Product: $2,065,000,000
Foreign trade: exports, $339,000,000; imports, $389,000,000

CITIES

The universal urban complaints in 1971 continued to be inadequate housing, traffic congestion, air pollution, unbalanced municipal budgets, declining standards of public service, and a wave of crime, drug addiction, riots and strikes. Measures to cope with successive crises during the year introduced no basic solutions. But policies and programs were being formulated in many countries around the globe that gave rise to new hope for a more satisfactory urban future.

In the United States the population explosion was slowing down. The number of Americans increased by 13.3 per cent in the 1960's compared with 18.5 per cent during the preceding decade. In absolute terms the increase in the 1960's was 24,000,000 compared with 28,000,-000 in the 1950's. Three fourths of the growth was concentrated in the nation's metropolitan areas (areas with at least one center of 50,000 people), but the flight from central areas to suburbs resulted in an actual decline in population in some center cities. During the 1960's the drop was 4 per cent in Philadelphia, 6 per cent in Chicago, and 15 to 19 per cent in Pittsburgh, Cleveland and St. Louis. Retail business was also moving out; and in Washington and other cities there was a substantial surplus of office space. However, in the newer cities of the Southwest there were substantial increases in center-city population: Phoenix gained 30 per cent, Dallas 23 per cent, and Houston 29 per cent. The number of U.S. cities with a population of 25,000 or more, having a majority of black citizens rose from 3 to 16.

Urban growth in other parts of the world was ominous. Urbanization in Latin America, Asia and Africa was adding an awesome 90,000 persons a day to the teeming cities of each area. Places like São Paulo, Bangkok, Bombay and Caracas were becoming seriously overcrowded as the world's urban population continued to huddle together in not much more than one per cent of the earth's surface.

The frustration of the cities during 1971 was expressed in a global epidemic of strikes that idled teachers, garbage collectors, and mailmen and slowed down policemen, firemen and railway operators. New York, always unique, was snarled by a strike of bridgetenders that left 27 drawbridges locked in the open position. The disruption to traffic was closely followed by a stoppage of sewage-treatment operations that dumped millions of gallons of raw sewage in one day into the already polluted waters surrounding the city. Other parts of the urban world experienced the discomforts of power failures, brownouts, slowdowns and strikes that paralyzed public services and helped to make big-city life increasingly unpleasant and wearing.

Nearly everywhere the mounting volume of automobile travel was creating massive traffic jams, while the decline of public transit was making a nightmare of the journey to work. In the Paris region at any given time in 1971, there were 100,000 cars parked illegally, and in daylight hours 20 per cent of the cars in the city had to keep moving because there was no place to stop. Seven persons were occupying each square meter of subway space in the rush hours. According to French officials, another 10 per cent increase in peak-hour traffic would do the city in for good. Traffic in Rome was no better but only noisier. Anywhere in Europe, as in the United States, there was smog.

Cities in 1971 were also becoming poorer. In the United States the sluggish state of the economy meant that tax revenues continued to decline while inflation went on boosting the cost of government. Progress made during the year toward welfare reform and Federal revenue sharing would someday give cities more financial elbowroom, but meanwhile they were forced to curtail essential services and postpone needed public works. By midyear, according to the U.S. Department of Labor, one third of all major U.S. cities were suffering substantial unemployment. Underlying the financial problem was geography as well as economics. For along with the population, the city's wealth was also moving out to the suburbs while the city's poor, with their abnormal needs for public assistance, were left behind.

The urban picture in 1971 was not all gloomy, however. Significant gains were registered in such key areas as the environment; transportation; housing; and the creation of new cities.

The United States took positive action to reduce air, water and noise pollution. A multi-billion-dollar program for clean water will eventually have a significant effect on the many cities situated on rivers, lakefronts and the ocean. The Environmental Protection Agency announced nationwide clean-air standards, and the automobile industry began the task of meeting the 1976 deadline on the limitation of engine-exhaust pollutants. The White House announced that standards would also be set to reduce the noise created by aircraft and other transportation, and by construction work and other activities. Most of the aircraft noise occurs at the nation's 23 major commercial airports, which account for 65 per cent of the traffic. Aircraft operations have doubled in 5 years and are expected to triple in the next 10.

The decision to discontinue development of the U.S. supersonic transport (SST) plane temporarily relieved fears that sonic boom would add to the din, but both the British-French Concorde and the Soviet Union's Tupolev 144 supersonics were being test-flown to keep the prospect alive.

Americans turned their attention to the possibilities of improving deteriorated passenger railways, creating a public corporation known as Amtrak, to provide 182 trains for rail travel serving some 300 cities, a significant cutback from the 360 trains operating when 1971 started. The purpose of Amtrak is to modernize equipment and services on high-density routes so as to relieve the rails of mounting deficits and to provide a practical alternative to the airplane where big-city airports are nearing saturation.

In New York and New Jersey a milestone in transport was made when Governor Rockefeller signed the bill authorizing high-speed rail lines between Penn Station in midtown New York City and Kennedy Airport and between Newark and Newark Airport. Congress implemented its $10,000,000,000, 12-year program of transit improvements by authorizing $3,100,000,000 for the period of 1971–75. Most of the funding in the first year went for equipment: new buses, commuter railway cars and subway cars. At the same time, transit-research programs were emphasized to explore the possibilities of new high-speed ground transport, new sources of propulsion, and people-movers for local transport.

Public transit in U.S. cities in 1971 fell to the low level of 6,000,000,000 rides a year—about the same volume of patronage recorded in 1912. Nevertheless, new facilities under construction could reverse the trend. San Francisco's Bay Area Rapid Transit System was nearly completed, and Washington, D.C., began digging its 99-mile, $3,000,000,000 Metro System, one third in subways. Other subway work was proceeding in Mexico City, Munich, Frankfort, Rome, Paris, Tokyo, Milan, Buenos Aires and São Paulo. The feasibility of still more subways was being studied in Singapore, Bogota, Istanbul and Caracas.

The main thrust was on overcoming traffic congestion, yet the major problem of most cities continued to be housing. The United Nations reported that about 1,400,000,000 new houses would be needed by the year 2000, mostly in cities in developing countries. The United States was falling behind its own housing requirements at the rate of a million dwellings a year. It will be necessary to complete one housing unit every 27 seconds between now and the end of the century to overcome the backlog and keep up with new demand.

One hope for dealing effectively with housing, pollution and related community problems lies in the creation of whole new communities where a combination of housing, shops, schools, recreation and jobs in a pleasant environment can create good living conditions and avoid the congestion and misery of the accidental city. Britain was building its 27th and largest new city, Milton Keynes, for 250,000 people. It is

Striking New York municipal workers open 27 movable bridges (in the river); hundreds of thousands of motorists are caught in colossal jam.

Neal Boenzi from "The New York Times"

Daniel Dowling

"This is brought to you in living color—red"

designed to accommodate a wide range of income groups and to supply them with systems of health and education, a variety of employment opportunities, and sufficient recreation and cultural activities to overcome the new-town blues that residents of smaller and predominantly one-class new towns complain about. Other new cities were being built in Japan, France, the Soviet Union and the United States.

Columbia (Md.) and Reston (Va.) continued to be the only significant examples of thriving new-town development in the United States. The National Committee on Urban Growth has recommended, however, the construction of 110 new cities; and in 1971 David Rockefeller, chairman of the Chase Manhattan Bank, endorsed the idea, calling for a $10,000,-000,000 fund to get the work started. Meanwhile the New York State Urban Development Corporation was designing new cities for Welfare Island (in New York City) and for a planned community adjacent to the new campus of the University of New York at Buffalo. On Staten Island (New York City) a community was being planned for 450,000 people, America's largest new city.

Other countries were beyond the new-city talking and planning stage. Singapore, having created new housing for 600,000 people, one third of its population, in 10 years, was stepping up the rate of housing construction in the 1970's to create more satellite communities around the now redeveloped old city. Major work was proceeding in the new industrial city of Jurong, 12 miles out, where a deepwater port combined with industrial parks for heavy and light industry is expected to provide economic support for a city of 400,000. France was pushing forward with seven new-city solutions as the answer to the overcrowding of Paris.

The beginning of planned city building in America was reinforced by Federal housing legislation effective in 1971. Financial aid is now available to public or private agencies for land purchases, to make new cities feasible in suburbia and beyond, as well as in the form of reconstructed old cities. A Community Development Corporation in the Department of Housing and Urban Development will assist in the effort to create new satellites and intown communities where good housing and urban services, a satisfying environment, and the close proximity of homes and jobs will create a new quality of urban life. All these efforts are being strengthened by Operation Breakthrough, the program to help shift home building to an industrialized factory basis, and by the new Model Cities Program, aimed at rebuilding large areas of blighted central cities to create new cities within the old.

In 1971 the potentials of science and technology for solving city problems continued to make headlines, including electronic methods of crime detection and crime prevention; new systems of pedestrian transport, using small vehicles or people-movers; two-way community cable television and computerized information systems (demonstrated in the new town of Reston, Va.); new methods of recycling trash and garbage; tracked air-cushion vehicles for wheelless mass transit; and greater reliance on high-rise construction with computer programming of elevators.

The most significant long-run solutions to urban overcrowding and blight were the scientifically planned large-scale urban systems for the next generation of new cities, in which housing, jobs, shops, schools and recreation would all be provided as an integrated whole with maximum amenities and a minimum of the pollution and decay that typify the unplanned conventional city. The year 1971 witnessed the emergence of new city-building corporations that promise soon to create a new capability for creating entire communities with revolutionary concepts of living designed to relieve the world's hard-pressed urban population.

WILFRED OWEN
Senior Fellow, The Brookings Institution

COMPUTERS

In 1971 the computer industry continued to reel from the effects of the first recession in its relatively brief though dynamic existence. Growth-rate predictions of 15 to 20 per cent for 1971 failed to materialize. Toward year-end, it appeared that industry growth had retreated to 10 per cent annually. U.S. participation in overseas conferences, such as the one sponsored by the Association for Computing Machinery (ACM) and held in Munich, and one in Jerusalem that emphasized the impact of computers in the developing nations, indicates the growing importance of the non-U.S. market. There were few concrete signs, however, that the vitality that propelled the computer business through the 1960's as the world's fastest growing major industry had returned. According to William C. Norris, board chairman of Control Data Corporation, much of the slowdown is attributed to the Nixon administration's severe cutbacks in research-and-development funds, particularly in defense areas.

IBM, representing 70 per cent of industry sales, lowered the prices on much of its computer peripheral equipment. (Peripheral equipment is the support or "add on" hardware, such as magnetic disc and tape memories, that accounts for an appreciable percentage of the cost of the computer system.) For some time now many smaller companies, such as Potter Instrument Corporation and California Computer Products, have been offering direct replacement of peripheral equipment at costs 20 to 30 per cent below equivalent IBM hardware. IBM has adopted a favorite ploy of its competition: reducing prices for long-term contracts. According to some industry sources, IBM has taken off the gloves and will become an increasingly aggressive competitor.

For some months, RCA Corporation continued to predict around-the-corner profitability for its five-year-old computer operation. In September, however, the operation was written off, entailing a $250,000,000 charge after taxes.

Traffic Safety. General Motors Delco Electronics Division has designed a minicomputer to detect that one-for-the-road automobile driver and prevent him from operating his motor vehicle. Assuming a unique tack in automotive safety, Delco's engineers have shifted their emphasis from crash-protection devices, such as the inflatable air bag, to accident-avoidance systems. Delco's approach is called the Phystester (physiological tester). The all solid-state computer quickly analyzes four functions that are rapidly degraded by excessive amounts of alcohol, i.e., visual acuity, short-term memory, coordinated motor response, and judgment.

Delco Electronics Div., GMC

The Phystester (model in photo), programed by computer, is test of car-driver intoxication. Only a sober driver can match numbers quickly.

As the driver turns the ignition switch in his car, the dashboard-mounted computer generates and displays a random five-digit number on a miniature scoreboard. After 1½ seconds the number disappears and a push-button keyboard, located below the numeric display, lights up. The driver now has a brief moment in which to punch into the keyboard the exact number displayed. If he is successful in the allotted time, the computer will permit the ignition system to be activated. If he fails, the driver may try twice again (each time with a different display, of course). Three consecutive failures cause the computer to keep the vehicle from starting for an extended period of time.

The normal "response times" programed into the computer memory of the Phystester were determined in experiments conducted by the Department of Environmental Medicine at the Medical College of Wisconsin, in which eight volunteer medical-college students spent several hours a week under the influence of alcohol. The researchers and the Delco engineers believe that the Phystester would prevent about 50 per cent of incapable drivers from starting their autos. By "incapable" is meant a blood-alcohol concentration (BAC) of 0.1 per cent or higher (the point of legal intoxication in most states).

Japan. The Japanese securities industry has taken advantage of the massive information-handling capabilities of the digital computer to process stock transactions on the Tokyo Stock Exchange on a real-time (instantaneous) basis. Volume on the exchange reaches 500,000,000 shares on a peak business day.

Nomura Securities Co., Ltd., the largest Japanese securities firm, processing 17 per cent of the daily volume, installed large-scale Univac 1108 computers to help eliminate the backlog of paper work created by its 700,000 customers. Connected to optical mark readers at 95 offices throughout Japan, the computer system updates accounts on more than 20,000 stock transactions daily. Salesmen in branch offices mark orders on standard cards. Information is then optically scanned and transmitted to the central office. The computer immediately records this information in the customers' files and generates an order slip to the stock-exchange floor "specialist." An execution message is transmitted back to the branch office upon completion of the order.

France. The French have embarked upon an ambitious five-year growth program to enhance their position in the international computer market. According to Jean Michel Treille, executive director of the French Electronics Commission, computer installations in France will grow from 6,000 in 1971 to 15,000 at the end of the program. IBM has the largest share of the French computer market. However, Mr. Treille feels that the market will become more diverse as French firms increase their output. In addition, the French software industry, second in size only to that of the United States, will be subsidized by the Government in an effort to spur growth to 25 per cent yearly. Software constitutes the intelligence of a computer system. Composed of coded instructions stored in the computer's memory, software details the specific tasks the computer system is to perform.

The Arts. The disarray of the Hollywood film-editing room may be replaced soon by the orderliness of a computer room. The new system, conceived by Columbia Broadcasting System in conjunction with the Memorex Corporation of California, is designated RAVE (Random Access Video Editing). It is expected to save the film and television industries millions of dollars each year in the preparation, editing and collation of films and television tapes.

The heart of RAVE is its ability to collect and store all the separate scenes, or takes, of a film and then make them instantly accessible to an editor sitting at a dual-screen monitor console. The dual screen permits simultaneous viewing of the end of one scene and the beginning of the next. In order to select a particular scene for viewing, the console operator uses a sophisticated light pen to direct the computer to the proper mode of operation, e.g., playback, record, splice or edit. The light pen, a photo-electric device, is pressed against the screen of the monitor console, touching the control word of the appropriate operation. Scenes may be run forward, backward, in fast or slow motion, and may be edited on a frame-by-frame basis. Special identification codes are entered into computer memory for those scenes that are satisfactory. Furthermore, the computer remembers those scenes that have been deleted and retains them in its magnetic memory banks for possible future consideration. Utilizing RAVE a cut in videotape can be made in 2 to 3 minutes as compared with the 20 minutes currently required.

ALLAN Y. BROOKS
Communications Consultant and Project Engineer
Western Union Corporation

CMX Corp.

A computer system, RAVE, is expected soon to replace current disorderly, lengthy method of film editing. High-speed minicomputers, directed by an editor sitting before a dual screen, with a light pen, splice scenes, fix dissolves and handle overall film assembly.

CONSUMER AFFAIRS, U.S.

The newly aroused American consumer stepped up his demands in 1971, and it was clear that the politicians were listening. Paradoxically, no major consumer legislation was enacted by Congress, but at least two significant bills were poised for action in the election year that lay ahead. Meanwhile, some leading American businessmen carried on a counterattack against what they saw as ideological excesses in the name of consumerism.

Amid this heightened controversy, the weight of popular sentiment was plainly on the side of more and stricter regulation of traditional business practices. Surveys showed business prestige down and the consumer's dander up. With the movement nearing high tide, most politicians of both parties tried to appear to be riding the crest rather than erecting dams against it. "There are still a few dinosaurs thrashing around claiming that consumerism is a communist plot," said Virginia H. Knauer, President Nixon's consumer adviser. "We're encouraging voluntary action, but time is running out. If industry doesn't shape itself up soon, the Government will step in and do it for them."

Despite the near unanimity of political lip service to consumerism, however, there were sharp differences over how the principle should be applied to specific cases. The seesawing success of efforts to establish an independent Federal agency to protect consumer interests provided a striking illustration of the difference between rhetoric and reality in consumerism.

The original Consumer Protection Agency Bill, as proposed by Rep. Benjamin Rosenthal (D-N.Y.), would have established a separate agency having the power to set standards for products not governed by existing agencies. The tough intent of this bill was, in the eyes of its sponsor, changed and weakened in committee. Rosenthal resisted and voted against the final bill, which bore the name of the committee Chairman, Rep. Chet Holifield (D-Calif.), and passed by a lopsided 344–44 vote. This measure, which was in a Senate committee as 1971 ended, would divide the regulatory and enforcement powers between the new Consumer Protection Agency and a strengthened Federal Trade Commission. Official "consumer advocates" would be involved in the making and enforcing of Federal standards. Such advocates

At a news conference, Consumer Affairs Commissioner Bess Myerson accuses New York City stores of "short weight, short count [or] short measures" on 87 per cent of some 2,000 food items checked. Below are violation labels.

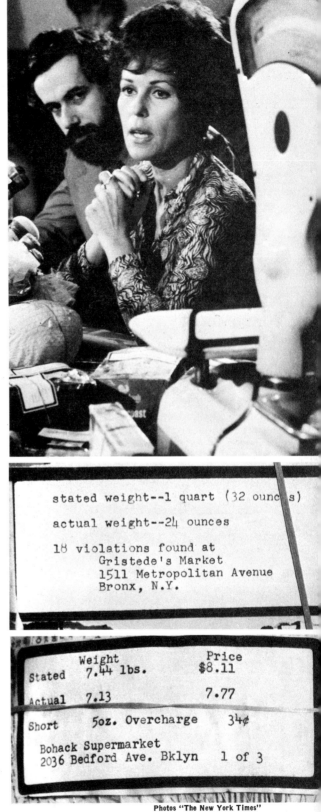

stated weight--1 quart (32 ounces)

actual weight--24 ounces

18 violations found at
Gristede's Market
1511 Metropolitan Avenue
Bronx, N.Y.

	Weight	Price
Stated	7.44 lbs.	$8.11
Actual	7.13	7.77
Short	5oz. Overcharge	34¢

Bohack Supermarket
2036 Bedford Ave. Bklyn   1 of 3

Photos "The New York Times"

Commerce Secretary Maurice H. Stans applies a lighted match to the treated fabric, which does not burn, of a child's sleepwear. Garment at left went up in flames. By 1973 all children's sleepwear that does not meet government standards will be prohibited.

would be admitted into government proceedings to argue for lower utility rates, air fares and consumer prices, and for safer foods, drugs and other products. The new agency would be empowered to take part in the formal rule-making proceedings and hearings of the Federal Trade Commission, as well as of the Food and Drug Administration and nearly three dozen other Federal agencies whose decisions affect the consumer.

Holifield worked closely with the White House in steering the final legislation through the House of Representatives, which rejected amendments from both liberals and conservatives. The result, predictably, was attacked from both sides. Rosenthal, who had consulted continually with the high priest of consumerism, Ralph Nader, termed the House version of the Consumer Protection Agency (CPA) a "sheep in wolf's clothing." Nader complained that the CPA's inability to participate in "informal," nonprocedural actions of Federal agencies meant that it would be barred from more than 90 per cent of the actions that affect consumers.

But the agency would have important powers to raise consumer interests at formal proceedings and to require other agencies to publicize and justify their actions—or lack thereof—affecting consumers. These powers seemed significant to most of the House and had won the support of the White House, which initially had rejected the concept of an independent agency. The U.S. Chamber of Commerce and other

organized business interests maintained that the legislation was not too weak but too strong; the CPA, as they saw it, would subject businessmen to invasions of privacy and unfair harassment.

If the final bill resembles the House version, independent observers regard its eventual effectiveness as dependent on two factors: the strength and ability of its director, who would be hired and fired by the President; and the decisions of the courts, which probably would have to interpret a number of uncertain provisions that have been translated differently by the opposing partisans.

Meanwhile, the Senate came up with its own major bill in the consumer-affairs area. This measure, sponsored by Sens. Warren G. Magnuson (D-Wash.) and Frank E. Moss (D-Utah), was passed, 76–2, in early November but also fell short of 1971 enactment. A House Commerce subcommittee held hearings on a companion bill by Rep. John E. Moss (D-Calif.), and it, like the Consumer Protection Agency Bill in the Senate, was expected to receive a fresh push in 1972.

The Magnuson-Moss bill was aimed at meeting frequent consumer complaints about the quality, the comprehensiveness and indeed the comprehensibility of the warranties that accompany many modern products. The bill would establish Federal standards of fairness and clarity for warranties covering consumer products. It would also give the Federal Trade Commission broad new authority to police the marketplace and would expand the FTC's capacity to combat business practices that are deemed fraudulent, unfair or deceptive. The commission would have power of injunction against companies that violate its regulations. It could also ask the Federal courts to impose fines and grant damages to complaining consumers.

The tightening of standards for warranties on products costing $5.00 or more had clear bipartisan support, but there was considerable debate over expanding the powers of the FTC. Conservative Republicans, backed by the Nixon administration and organized business, tried unsuccessfully to eliminate these provisions before the bill came to a final vote. They contended that granting statutory authority to rules promulgated by the FTC would give that administrative agency unwarranted legislative powers.

A third major piece of consumer legislation, the Product Safety Bill, had hearings in both houses of Congress but was passed by neither. There were two versions. The administration's bill would convert the Food and Drug Administration into a Consumer Safety Administration under the Department of Health, Education, and Welfare. The Democratic-sponsored bill would establish an independent regulatory agency. Products subject to regulation might include flammable fabrics and possibly hazardous household appliances. The administration version would not provide for setting standards but would require fuller disclosure of product contents that could be dangerous.

While the focus in 1971 was on proposed new legislation, there was some important action under existing laws. In July, for example, the Commerce Department set a 2-year deadline for an ênd to the sale of flammable sleepwear for children. Consumers themselves accounted for a mild resurgence of food cooperatives, which save their members money by joint buying that bypasses much of the conventional distribution system. And New York City joined Chicago, Los Angeles and Boston, among others, in requiring unit pricing—the posting of prices by the ounce, pound, pint or other appropriate unit—that lets the shopper know at a glance which brand or size is really the most economical. At the end of 1971, such unit pricing was the law in 2 states and was under consideration in 10 other states and more than 200 cities and counties.

The power of the consumer to change the conditions of the marketplace was scarcely born with Ralph Nader. The original Henry Ford, for one, learned of its existence when he tried to continue to impose the Model T

on a nation that had tired of it. But the belligerent demand for a better deal from computerized and impersonal big business was plainly a phenomenon that was waxing rather than waning. Some businessmen professed to welcome it. John M. Barnes, head of Pan American World Airways' office of consumer action, termed Nader "a modern saint." Others thought the movement had broadened into an attack on the system. James M. Roche, the outgoing chairman of General Motors, decried those who he said were "playing at the margins of product quality" and advocating "a consumerism based not on a principle of consumer sovereignty but on a conviction of consumer stupidity." The debate would continue, but in 1971 the irate customer was on the attack, and business was his target.

LOUIS RUKEYSER
Economic Editor and News Commentator
American Broadcasting Company

In Paris, sponsored by a French consumer group, U.S. advocate Ralph Nader says consumerism must "go international" because standards differ.

With thoughts of the many policemen slain on duty, officers from five states attend another's funeral.

CRIME

Crime and fear of crime both rose in 1971, but in varying degrees. The Federal Bureau of Investigation reported that serious crimes in the United States continued to grow substantially faster than the nation's population in 1970 and in the first half of 1971. But the rate of increase was slightly less. There was a 7 per cent increase in the first half of 1971, compared with an 11 per cent increase in 1970, 12 per cent in 1969, and 17 per cent in 1968.

During the first half of 1971, murder and aggravated assault were up 10 per cent compared with 7 per cent for all of 1970, and robbery rose by 14 per cent compared with 17 per cent for all of 1970. The increase in auto theft was only 2 per cent while it was 5 per cent in 1970; and forcible rape went up 7 per cent in the first half of 1971 as against an increase of only 2 per cent in 1970.

Armed robbery, which makes up about two thirds of all robbery offenses, increased 19 per cent from January through June 1971, and 20 per cent in all of 1970. Assault with firearms, which accounts for about one fourth of all serious assaults, increased 12 per cent in the first half of 1971 as compared with 10 per cent in 1970.

During the 8-month period January through August 1971, 80 law-enforcement officers were feloniously killed. During the same period in 1970, 67 officers were murdered. Ninety-six per cent of the killings in 1971 were committed through use of firearms. During the 10-year period 1961–70, 633 officers were murdered, 100 of them in 1970. In January 1971, at the end of the first 6 months of findings, a study by the International Association of Chiefs of Police concluded that unprovoked ambush attacks represented the largest single cause, 25 per cent, of police deaths.

Suburbia. Crimes in suburbia and rural areas increased faster than crimes in the cities. Cities with 250,000 or more inhabitants reported an average increase of 3 per cent in the Crime Index offenses (murder, rape, robbery, aggravated assault, burglary, larceny involving $50 or more, and auto theft) in the first half of 1971 and 6 per cent in all of 1970. Suburban areas surrounding large core cities reported an average increase of 10 per cent in the same crimes in 1971 and 15 per cent in 1970. Rural crime was up 8 per cent in 1971 and 14 per cent in 1970.

Women and Children. FBI figures showed that from 1960 through 1969, male arrests for major crimes rose 61 per cent, while for females the increase of 10 per cent in the same crimes in gained most heavily in larceny, embezzlement and narcotics violations; women also committed more robberies and assaults. Sheriff Peter Pitchess of Los Angeles County suggested one reason for this phenomenon: "As women emerge from their traditional roles as housewife and mother, entering the political and business fields previously dominated by males, there is no reason to believe that women will not also approach equality with men in the criminal activity field."

Crime committed by children also increased rapidly. Reports from school and law-enforcement officials in 13 cities indicate that the trend noted in 1969 by the National Commission on the Causes and Prevention of Violence is continuing. The commission found that in the 10-year period 1958–67, there was a 300 per cent increase in assaults by 10- to 14-year-olds and a 200 per cent increase in robberies by this age group. From 1960 through 1970, reported the FBI, police arrests for all criminal acts except traffic violations rose 31 per cent, while arrests of those under 18 more than doubled.

Fear of Crime. A June 1971 Louis Harris poll revealed that 55 per cent of Americans were "more worried about violence and safety on the streets" in their own communities than in 1970. Five per cent were "less worried" and 39 per cent were "about the same." This was the highest level ever recorded by a Harris survey in six years of polling on the subject. In 1966, 49 per cent were "more worried," 3 per cent "less," and 44 per cent "about the same."

When the results of the poll were broken down by race, a significant pattern emerged. In the case of "worry about violence and personal safety on the streets," 53 per cent of whites said this was a concern to them, but 68 per cent of blacks expressed anxiety about street violence. The higher level of black worry over personal safety on the streets, which accurately reflects the fact that crimes against blacks are more frequent than crimes against whites, led many to conclude that insecurity is far more deeply rooted in fear of street crime among all races than in racial tensions. The poll also indicated wide differences in apprehension because of sex. While just under half of all men in the country expressed a feeling of insecurity, 62 per cent of women said they were "worried about violence in the streets." Among black women that "worry-rate" went up to 80 per cent.

Crime-Control Measures. In 1971 the Federal Government established a new system of crime statistics designed to assess the level of damage and anxiety caused by crime, as well as to provide a more accurate measure of the crime rate than the FBI Uniform Crime Index. The Census Bureau will call on a carefully selected panel of 125,000 to 150,000 homes and businesses twice a year to interview persons who have been victims of crimes. Household surveys made in 1966 by the President's Commission on Law Enforcement and the Administration of Justice indicated that two or three times more serious crimes occurred than those re-

ported to the FBI by local police departments.

The large sample is necessary because only about 4 per cent of the public become crime victims each year. This means that the sample should show about 6,000 victims each year, which the Census Bureau considers statistically sound.

Using a system of detailed interviewing the Government will learn whether the level of viciousness in such crimes as robbery, rape and assault is rising or declining, as well as how much money and other valuables are stolen. The FBI Crime Index lumps crimes of varying seriousness together, equating a child's theft of his schoolmate's lunch money with a vicious mugging. The new survey will indicate both how serious crime is and how prevalent.

Crime Insurance and Victim Compensation. The Federal Government began selling crime insurance on Aug. 1, 1971 in 9 states and the District of Columbia. In these states, private insurance was not available at reasonable rates and state governments had taken no action to

Infrared aerial photography is used to find murdered farm workers in California. Decomposing bodies give off some heat and thus might show on temperature-measuring infrared photos.

provide their own insurance plans. The Federal program, under the Department of Housing and Urban Development, is operating in the following states: Connecticut, Illinois, Maryland, Massachusetts, Missouri, New York, Ohio, Pennsylvania, Rhode Island and the District of Columbia. Coverage costs the same in crime-plagued central-city areas as in the suburbs of the same city. Maximum coverage is $15,000 for a commercial policy and $5,000 for a residential policy. It covers losses resulting from burglaries, robberies, vandalism and other criminal activities. California and Michigan have state insurance that fills the same purpose.

Meanwhile, New Jersey became the sixth state in six years to provide compensation for the innocent victims of violent crime. The other states are California, New York, Massachusetts, Hawaii and Maryland. Compensation for medical costs, and in some states for loss of earnings, ranges from $5,000 in California to $45,000 in Maryland. In the six-year period 1965–71, more than $5,000,000 was paid to some 3,000 victims of crimes such as robbery, mugging and rape.

Legislation. Among the many bills introduced to meet problems of dangerous crime, the Model Criminal Justice Reform Bill was proposed by four former state attorneys general—Senators Edward W. Brooke (R-Mass.), William B. Saxbe (R-Ohio), Thomas F. Eagleton (D-Mo.) and Walter F. Mondale (D-Minn.). The bill would provide up to 90 per cent in Federal financing to any state or local government that voluntarily agreed to undertake a full-scale upgrading of its entire criminal-justice system, from police through the prison system.

The Safe Schools Bill, introduced by Rep. Jonathan Bingham (D-N.Y.), would provide Federal funds to meet the rapidly rising costs of combating crime in elementary and secondary schools. The specific decisions of how best to use the Federal funds would be left to school administrators.

Congress passed and the President signed a bill repealing the Emergency Detention Act (Title II of the Internal Security Act of 1950). This was a never-used law giving the Federal Government authority to put suspected spies or saboteurs into detention camps during time of war or insurrection. In the future, Congress voted, establishment of such camps could occur only if Congress approved. Thus a president would be prevented from setting up internment camps under an executive order, as President Franklin D. Roosevelt did in relation to Japanese Americans after Pearl Harbor.

The Nixon administration submitted legislation to Congress that would allow all Federal courts to detain certain defendants in prison before they have been tried. The Justice Department also proposed legislation that would reverse the presumption of innocence in the case of a person convicted of a felony and seeking release until the appeal of his case was heard. The proposal would allow Federal judges to imprison for sixty days defendants who constituted a "threat to the safety of the community" and who were charged with "a dangerous or organized crime act." It would be up to the individual to show that he should be freed pending appeal, rather than the Government's responsibility to show that he should not be.

Rep. John M. Murphy (D-N.Y.) submitted a bill to stop the sale of a cheap, snubnosed pistol being manufactured and sold in the United States and called the "Saturday night special." Although the 1968 gun control act bans importation of such a gun, Murphy said that some "shady entrepreneurs in the United States" are producing the pistols in "makeshift factories such as converted garages, basements and even a church." When a similar bill was submitted in the Senate by Sen. Birch Bayh (D-Ind.), Donald E. Santarelli, associate deputy attorney general, told Congress that the administration hoped to produce its own bill "in as little as 45 days from now" to outlaw the sale of "Saturday night specials," but that it was troubled by the technical problem of classifying such weapons.

Urban Violence and Terrorism. Serious urban disorders declined in the United States for the third consecutive year, but minor disorders increased and terrorism appeared to be on the rise. The Justice Department counted 11 major and 32 serious civil disorders during the first eight months of 1971. In 1970, there were 19 major and 49 serious disorders. Minor civil disorders rose to 133 through August 1971 compared with 93 in 1970.

From July 1, 1970 to June 1, 1971, the bomb-data center of the International Association of Chiefs of Police recorded 1,425 bombing incidents, resulting in 15 deaths and 155 injuries. The IACP study indicated that the ambush attacks did not show any signs of an organized campaign of terror but, rather, scattered hostility to the police.

Victimless Crime. A significant 1971 development was the start of a drive by the National Council on Crime and Delinquency to remove so-called victimless crime—"crime based on moral codes in which there is no victim apart from the person who commits the crime"—from the criminal justice system. The commonest examples of such crimes are drunkenness, drug addiction, voluntary sexual acts, loitering,

Whitman Knapp (r), prominent N.Y. attorney and head of the commission investigating alleged corruption in the city's police force, confers with an aide.

Pictorial Parade

vagrancy and gambling. Whatever harm results is to the offender himself and not to society, insists NCCD.

More than one half of all arrests are of victimless-crime offenders and one third of all arrests are for drunkenness. A representative of the National Alliance on Shaping Safer Cities, which has 57 national organizations as members, testified that nonvictim crimes cost the United States more than $20,000,000,000 from the profits of illegal gambling, narcotics and prostitution, as well as the costs of law enforcement. "Every person in the United States," said the alliance, "suffers a 'tax' of more than $100 a year—over $20,000,000,000—that is drained away into criminal hands through our efforts to 'enforce morals.' "

President Nixon told a conference on the judiciary: "We have to find ways to clear the courts of the endless streams of what are termed 'victimless crimes' that get in the way of serious consideration of serious crimes. There are more important matters for highly skilled judges and prosecutors than minor traffic offenses, loitering and drunkenness." New York City Police Commissioner Patrick V. Murphy added: "By charging our police with the responsibility to enforce the unenforceable we subject them to disrespect and corruptive influences. And we provide the organized criminal syndicates with illicit industries upon which they thrive."

Police Corruption. The Knapp Commission to Investigate Alleged Police Corruption in New York City, after 11 months of investigation, concluded on July 1, 1971, that a "substantial number" of New York policemen had been engaged in corrupt acts and that only a small group "is actively trying to do something about it." It charged that some narcotics-division officers engaged in "extortion, bribery, contradictory court testimony designed to effect the release of a narcotics criminal . . . and finally

. . . the actual sale of narcotics." It added that there was a pattern of payoffs in six other areas: gambling, prostitution, liquor, hotels, construction and tow trucking.

By Nov. 5, 1971, the commission had been credited with initiating criminal charges against 14 policemen and 9 alleged gamblers, and other agencies had investigations under way. While the Police Department had originally contended that corruption involved "only a very small percentage" of the 31,000-man force, First Deputy Commissioner William H. T. Smith later rejected the "rotten apple in the barrel" theory and said the public wants "an entirely new barrel that will never again be contaminated." Meanwhile, the U.S. Justice Department announced that 151 persons, including a Detroit police inspector and 15 other officers, had been indicted on Federal gambling charges in 37 Michigan cities.

Skyjacking. The effectiveness of the U.S. system to prevent air hijacking has not yet been proved. In the first 10 months of 1971, there were 23 attempted skyjackings, the same number as in the same 10-month period of 1970. However, the number of successful skyjackings was 10, compared with 16 in 1970, giving some hope that improved defenses were working.

The airport screening system also led to the arrest of 1,535 air passengers, most of them on charges unrelated to hijacking. Through Oct. 8, 1971, air marshals arrested 526 illegal aliens, 443 for possession of narcotics, 187 for firearms violations and 99 for possession of knives or violation of other nonfirearm laws; the balance included servicemen absent without leave; fugitives wanted by law-enforcement agencies, and 16 persons who made verbal threats on the ground of bombing or hijacking.

HARRY FLEISCHMAN
Executive Secretary
National Alliance on Shaping Safer Cities, Inc.

CZECHOSLOVAKIA

The 14th Czechoslovak Communist Party congress was held in Prague on May 25–29. The secret one at Vysocany during the Warsaw Pact invasion was declared a nonevent. General Secretary Gustav Husak officially thanked his Soviet counterpart Leonid I. Brezhnev as well as representatives from Bulgaria, East Germany, Hungary and Poland for their 1968 "timely international assistance." He expressed gratitude to these allies for answering "the requests of many unnamed party and state officials, many Communists and collectives, for help."

The 1,195 delegates elected a new Central Committee of 115 members, with only 26 carried over from the last (1966) recognized congress. Trade-union chief and Soviet collaborator Karel Hoffman replaced Evzen Erban, a Dubcek holdover, on the 11-man policy-making Presidium. Alexander Dubcek, expelled from the party in 1970, was reported working at the regional forestry administration in Bratislava.

Draft directives for the 1971–75 economic plan were adopted belatedly by the congress, with the purpose of greater efficiency. The obligatory plan involves a reversal of previous flexibility, adaptation to market needs, and the management system. The new directives thus mark an official end of the so-called market model of socialism. (A good harvest, some 200,000 tons of grain above target, apparently ensured the population enough food.)

Centralized planning represents but one step backward, as does restoration of party control over enterprises and civil service. The principle of continually purging Communists who violate or fail to comply with the political line is

The Frontier Unit Guard has patrolled Czechoslovakia's 2,000-mile boundary since 1951.

UPI

now in the party statutes. (Radio Prague on Oct. 20 discussed resistance to party policy.) Responsibility for educating youth in the spirit of communism is reflected also in the universities, where some 13,000 faculty members had their political attitudes scrutinized by party commissions.

Selection of students for admission has been transferred to loyal communist professors. This administrative intervention by the party recalls the 1950's, when political criteria and class origin also were more important than high-school records and scores on entrance examinations. The new policy may affect the national minorities, data on which appeared recently: 573,000 Hungarians; 86,000 Germans; 67,000 Poles; 59,000 Ukrainians and Ruthenians in a population that had increased only 4.5 per cent since 1960. Possible emigration of Germans waits on the results of current negotiations with the Bonn Government.

The year also witnessed the first political trials since 1968. General Vaclav Prchlik, who had revealed that the Warsaw Pact joint command consists solely of Soviet officers and that nothing in the treaty allows for the stationing of U.S.S.R. troops without an ally's consent, received a 3-year prison sentence. Sixteen young Trotskyites, held since 1969, were given up to 4 years in jail on charges of belonging to a "Revolutionary Socialist party." U.S. diplomat Samuel G. Wise, Jr., was declared *persona non grata* because of alleged testimony of an imprisoned Czechoslovak newsman who claimed to have been spying between 1968 and 1970 for the Americans. The journalist was sentenced to 10 years in prison.

National elections, held on Nov. 26–27, ended the so-called consolidation process. Some 1,800,000 young people voted for the first time. It did not affect the outcome, however, since only one candidate ran for each seat in Parliament. Nearly 200,000 deputies were elected to national committees at all levels in the country.

RICHARD F. STAAR
Associate Director
Hoover Institution on War, Revolution and Peace

Helgi Tomasson executes a brilliant entrechat in "The Goldberg Variations," to music by Bach.

DANCE

In certain of the arts—dance for one, drama for another, and probably music—the calendar year is an unnatural measure. In dance, 1971 represented the end of the 1970–71 season and the beginning of the 1971–72 season. There are times when inequality brings perspective. Looked at simply as 1971, New York City Ballet's solitary major work was Jerome Robbins' *Goldberg Variations,* a work that itself had been seen in a workshop production at Saratoga the previous summer. Yet planned for the beginning of 1972 were a new Robbins ballet and, in June, a Balanchine/Stravinsky festival. So the view of the company's creativity seen through one calendar year's work can be misleading; but simply because it does contain elements of two planned seasons it can offer insights into trends in the dance world that no seasonal roundups could give.

From the viewpoint of classic dance in the United States, 1971 probably marked the beginning of a new relationship with international ballet. Three important overseas ballet companies came to the United States: the Australian Ballet, with a predominantly classical repertory led by its guest star, Rudolf Nureyev; Maurice Béjart's controversial Ballet of the 20th Century from Brussels; and John Cranko's Stuttgart Ballet. None of these was one of the kingpin international companies—Britain's Royal Ballet, Russia's Bolshoi and Kirov ballets, or the Royal Danish Ballet—so for the first time the only major-league classic ballets to be seen in the United States were both American: New York City Ballet and the American Ballet Theater.

The New York City Ballet, American Ballet Theater and the City Center Joffrey Ballet (the last, America's third-ranking classic ballet) all enjoyed a good year. For City Ballet, 1971 was once again a great year for Jerome Robbins, with not only the structural and dynamic beauties of *Goldberg Variations* to his credit but also the hilarious revival of his old Chopin recital spoof, *The Concert.* Creatively, Ballet Theater suffered a bad year, with only the revival of Antony Tudor's *Romeo and Juliet* to sustain it, but in other directions things went better. The opening of the architecturally horrendous Kennedy Center—a building with a heart of Stone—at least has provided Ballet Theater with a part-time home for six weeks of the year. Potentially even more important was one of the year's ballet disasters, the failure of Eliot Feld's American Ballet Company, for economic reasons. Feld, probably the most important American-born choreographer since Robbins, agreed, it seems with some reluctance, to rejoin Ballet Theater on a mysteriously loose basis. But Feld is the hottest choreographic property in town, apart from Robbins, and his presence with Ballet Theater adds considerably to its future possibilities.

The Joffrey Ballet had a good year to report. A couple of ballets by its principal choreographer, Gerald Arpino, *Trinity* in the spring and *Kettentanz* in the fall, both proved successful, with the rock-ritual nature of *Trinity* contrasting happily with the pure if schmaltzy virtuoso elegances of *Kettentanz* set to com-

Judith Jamison, an "African goddess," dances the long solo "Cry," dedicated to all black women.

paratively restrained Viennese waltzes. The company gave a lift to City Center's year, as did its surprise success, the Alvin Ailey American Dance Theater.

During 1971 the Ailey company gave three two-week seasons in New York, not to mention Ailey's admittedly modestly successful *Mingus Dances* for the Joffrey Ballet. The year was one in which the modern dancer Ailey truly established himself in New York, particularly perhaps with the triumph of his solo dedicated to the black woman everywhere, *Cry,* indelibly danced by Judith Jamison, and, in the December season, *Mary Lou's Mass,* a paean to peace

and goodness, set to music by Mary Lou Williams and destined to provide an incantatory counterpart to the company's inescapable even if stirring *Revelations*.

For the Ailey company, 1971 was beautiful, but for other modern-dance companies the situation proved less happy. The Martha Graham Company—the mother of them all—not only did not appear but did not substantiate any plans for future appearances. Other companies, lesser in renown but significant in achievement, also had a bad year as far as acceptance—or at least Broadway acceptance—was concerned.

Modern dance obviously must make a new commitment to the American dance audience. Its new leaders, Merce Cunningham and Paul Taylor, have established their own rationale; and a new young generation of interesting modern-dance choreographers—Louis Falco, Manuel Alum, Lar Lubovitch, for example—has emerged toiling in moderately conventional fields. Yet there is also a new avant-garde; 1971 saw a disastrous visit to the East Coast of San Francisco's once supposedly avant-garde (they took their clothes off!) run by Ann Halprin, but also a far more interesting performance by Twyla Tharp's dancers, an all-girl troupe with more than women's liberation at heart.

It was a good year for controversy, especially the controversy over Béjart's attempts to provide a new kind of pop-ballet that is to ballet what light music is to music. It was also a good year for ballet across the United States. Notable achievements were racked up by the National Ballet of Washington and the Pittsburgh Ballet Theater; and a word is in order for the rapid advancement of Arthur Mitchell's Dance Theater of Harlem.

Overseas, perhaps the main event was the new direction of Britain's Royal Ballet by Kenneth MacMillan, who has so far proved some-

Arthur Mitchell, here teaching a class in his school, seeks to draw more young black people into ballet and has firmly established his Dance Theater of Harlem.

Dancers of the recently formed Leningrad Choreographic Miniatures Ballet Company imitate a happy-go-lucky troika, a team of three horses.

what disappointing both as a director and choreographer. His first major new work, *Anastasia* at Covent Garden, proved to be one of the artistic shipwrecks of 1971; but other events have been a little more hopeful. In Britain itself the Ballet Rambert had an interesting season; and in Holland the Netherlands Dance Theater continued to keep its position in the lead of European inventive dance.

Denmark had a moderate season. Almost its most newsworthy item was the appointment of an American, Bruce Marks, to the special position of principal *solodancer*. In Russia, Leningrad saw Konstanin Sergeyev's full-evening ballet *Hamlet* with Valeri Panov and Mikhail Barishnikov (conceivably the two greatest male dancers in the world today) alternating in the role of Hamlet. In China (to be topical) there was a fantastic ballet about Red women chasing undesirables out of China, while carrying submachine guns and indulging in the grandest of grand jetés. It has not been seen in the West, but its photographic coverage looks terrifying. But dance will survive.

CLIVE BARNES
Dance and Theater Critic
The New York Times

Bruce Marks soars; an American, he joined the Royal Danish Ballet as a principal in 1971.

NIKITA S. KHRUSHCHEV
1894–1971

On Sept. 11, Nikita S. Khrushchev, premier of the U.S.S.R. from 1958 to 1964, died of a heart attack in a Kremlin hospital in Moscow. The Soviet leaders paid little attention to his death except for a one-sentence announcement in the newspapers.

Born Apr. 17, 1894, in a mud hut, he rose to become a dominant figure in world politics. After joining the Communist Party in 1918, he fought in the Civil War, and by 1934 was a member of the Central Committee. After Stalin's death in 1953, he emerged as first secretary of the Communist Party and three years later denounced the late dictator in a speech.

While in office he concluded the Nuclear-Test-Ban Treaty, and promised peace and prosperity for Russia. It was the alienation of China and agricultural and industrial troubles that chiefly brought about his ouster.

Tass from Sovfoto

RALPH J. BUNCHE
1904–1971

In New York City, on Dec. 9, Dr. Ralph J. Bunche, a man who had devoted his life to the cause of peace, died. The 1950 Nobel Peace Prize was awarded him for his successful negotiation of the armistice between the newly formed state of Israel and the Arab states. Although Dr. Bunche was already very ill with diabetes, and heart and kidney disease, he did not resign as UN Undersecretary-General for Special Political Affairs until June of 1971.

Orphaned at the age of 13, he overcame poverty and racial prejudice to become a diplomat whose skills were legendary at the UN. He was born in Detroit, Mich., on Aug. 7, 1904, and worked his way through school. He received a doctorate in government and international relations from Harvard in 1934. During World War II he joined the War Department and later the State Department. He helped to organize the UN, which he joined in 1947.

UPI

DEAN G. ACHESON
1893–1971

On learning that Dean Acheson had died at his Sandy Springs, Md., home on Oct. 12, President Nixon said: "It is a measure of Dean Acheson's stature . . . that almost twenty years after his service as secretary of state, he continued to be recognized as one of the leading figures of his time." The tall, erect, strong-minded lawyer had been assistant secretary of state, 1941–45; undersecretary, 1945–57; and secretary, 1949–53. He later served as an adviser to Presidents Kennedy, Johnson and Nixon.

At the State Department, Acheson became convinced that only U.S. military power and political alliances could deter communism. During the Acheson years, NATO was formed, and the Korea conflict was fought.

Son of an English-born clergyman, Acheson attended Harvard Law School. His book *Present at the Creation: My Years in the State Department* won a Pulitzer Prize.

UPI

152   DEATHS

WHITNEY M. YOUNG, JR.
1921–1971

The dedicated civil-rights leader Whitney M. Young, Jr., drowned on Mar. 11 while swimming in the Atlantic Ocean at Lagos, Nigeria. He was there attending a Ford Foundation-sponsored conference on Afro-American affairs.

Born on July 31, 1921, in Lincoln Ridge, Ky., to well-educated parents, Young received an M.A. degree in social work. In 1954 he became the dean of the School of Social Work of Atlanta University, and seven years later, the executive director of the National Urban League. Through his efforts to increase job opportunities, he expanded the league into "one of the nation's primary nongovernment forces working toward the self-sufficiency of the black American poor."

At the funeral, President Nixon ended his eulogy by saying, "His dream . . . was one nation, under God, indivisible, with liberty and justice and opportunity for all."

Wide World

HUGO L. BLACK
1886–1971

Eight days after resigning as an associate justice of the U.S. Supreme Court, Hugo L. Black died in Bethesda (Md.) Naval Hospital, on Sept. 25.

During his 34 years on the bench, Black was the Court's principal supporter of the Bill of Rights. When the Court was attacked in the late 1960's for its decisions protecting the rights of criminals, and prohibiting prayer in public schools, Black replied: "The court did not do it. The Constitution did it." He believed so strongly in the Constitution that he always carried a copy of it in his pocket.

Born in Alabama cotton country, Black graduated from the University of Alabama Law School in 1906. Before being elected to the U.S. Senate in 1926, he practiced law and served as a police-court judge and as a prosecuting attorney. A New Dealer, Black was President Franklin D. Roosevelt's first appointment, in 1937, to the Supreme Court.

Wide World

JOHN M. HARLAN
1899–1971

John Marshall Harlan, who resigned as an associate justice of the U.S. Supreme Court on Sept. 23, 1971, died in George Washington Hospital in Washington, D.C., Dec. 29.

Born in Chicago, John Harlan attended Oxford as a Rhodes scholar. He studied law because it was a family tradition. In fact, his grandfather was the only member of the U.S. Supreme Court to cast a dissenting vote in the 1896 *Plessy* v. *Ferguson* (separate but equal) case.

After being admitted to the bar in 1925, Harlan practiced law. In 1954, President Eisenhower named him to the Court of Appeals and later to the Supreme Court.

Although he was considered a conservative, it was believed that Harlan might "well have played a restraining role in countering the conservative trend of the Burger court." In several cases, Harlan had voted with his liberal colleagues.

UPI

IGOR STRAVINSKY
1882–1971

Igor Stravinsky, considered to have influenced four generations of American and European composers, died in New York City on Apr. 6, of heart failure. He was 88 years old. In accordance with his wishes, his body was borne across the Venetian Lagoon to the island-cemetery of San Michele, where Sergei Diaghilev, impresario of the Ballet Russe and patron of Stravinsky's early ballet scores, is buried. Both had drawn inspiration from Venice.

Stravinsky was born on June 17, 1882, in a St. Petersburg suburb to a musical family. One of his early teachers was Rimsky-Korsakov. In 1911 his ballet *Petrouchka* was first performed. Two years later Vaslav Nijinsky choreographed another masterpiece, *Le Sacre du Printemps* (The Rite of Spring). Stravinsky became a symbol of the avant-garde through his music and composed over 100 ballets, symphonies, operas and other works.

DAVID SARNOFF
1891–1971

David Sarnoff, who had only an elementary-school education and happened to "have gone along" with radio, died in New York City on Dec. 12. Starting work as a $5.50-a-week office boy and then wireless operator, Sarnoff became chairman and chief executive officer (1930–66) of RCA. Of his career, Sarnoff said: "It's true I had some luck, the greatest the day I came to America [his family emigrated from Russia in 1901] but if I achieved anything it was mostly through hard work." He developed the "radio music box." When others saw the phonograph as a competitor of radio, he combined them in a single set. Sarnoff appeared on the first public television broadcast, and increased the sales of color TV sets by pushing all-color broadcasting.

Although the General (he was promoted brigadier general in 1944) had 27 honorary degrees, his favorite award was a diploma from a New York high school.

LOUIS ARMSTRONG
1900–1971

Louis (Satchmo) Armstrong, the celebrated jazz musician, died on July 6 in Queens, N.Y., of a heart attack at the age of 71. Thousands of fans, as well as world figures, mourned his death. The Soviet poet Yevgeny Yevtushenko wrote a poem entitled *Armstrong's Trumpet,* in which he says, ". . . With a roar [Satchmo] trumpeted to the world his love."

The man who gave command performances before royalty, made numerous worldwide tours (Africa, the Middle East, Latin America) and became known as "America's ambassador of goodwill" was born in poverty on July 4, 1900, in New Orleans. He learned to play the cornet at the Colored Waifs' Home more than 55 years ago. In the 1920's he played in bands in Chicago and at the Roseland Ballroom in New York. In 1925 he switched to the trumpet and his popularity rose. He made over 1,500 recordings.

Photos Pictorial Parade

DEATHS

Gregory Cardinal Agagianian, 75, patriarch of the Armenians 1937–71; Rome, Italy, May 16.

George W. Andrews, 65, U.S. congressman (D-Ala., 1944–71); Birmingham, Ala., Dec. 25.

Pier Angeli, 39, movie actress (*Teresa, Somebody Up There Likes Me*); Beverly Hills, Calif., Sept 10.

Lord Astor of Hever (John Jacob Astor 5th), 85, publisher *The Times* of London 1922–59; member House of Commons 1922–45; Cannes, France, July 19.

Louis E. Austin, 73, Negro publisher of *The Carolina Times* newspaper 1927–71; Durham, N.C., June 12.

Jaime Cardinal de Barros Camara, 76, archbishop of Rio de Janeiro 1943–71; São Paulo, Brazil, Feb. 18.

Ivan H. Bashev, 55, foreign minister of Bulgaria 1962–71; near Sofia, Bulgaria, Dec. 12.

J. Glenn Beall, 76, U.S. congressman (R-Md., 1943–53) and senator (1953–65); Frostburg, Md., Jan. 14.

Adolf A. Berle, Jr., 76, Liberal Party leader, member President Roosevelt's "Brain Trust"; New York City, Feb. 17.

James T. Berryman, 69, cartoonist *The Washington Evening Star* 1923–64, won 1950 Pulitzer Prize; Venice, Fla., Aug. 11.

Margaret Bourke-White, 67, photojournalist for *Life* magazine 1936–69; Stamford, Conn., Aug. 27.

Sir Lawrence Bragg, 81, physicist, won 1915 Nobel Prize for codiscovery of X-ray use to determine crystal structure; Ipswich, England, July 1.

Spring Byington, 77, actress, films and television series (*December Bride*); Hollywood, Sept. 7.

Charles Cannon, 78, industrialist, Cannon Mills; Kannapolis, N.C., Apr. 2.

Bennett Cerf, 73, publisher and cofounder of Random House, writer, television personality for 16 years on *What's My Line?*; Mount Kisco, N.Y., Aug. 27.

Paul Chavchavadze, 72, Russian translator (*Only One Year* by Svetlana Alliluyeva), novelist; Hyannis, Mass., July 9.

Walter Van Tilburg Clark, 62, writer (*The Ox-Bow Incident*), contributor to *The New Yorker*; Reno, Nev., Nov. 10.

Marie Collier, 44, Australian operatic soprano; London, Dec. 7.

Frank Conniff, 57, former national editor of Hearst newspapers, 1955 Pulitzer Prize winner for Khrushchev interview; New York City, May 25.

Lord Constantine (Learie Constantine), 69, ambassador from Trinidad/Tobago to London 1962–64, Britain's first black peer, former cricket star; London, July 1.

Gladys Cooper, 82, dramatic actress of movies, TV and stage (*My Fair Lady*); Henley-on-Thames, Eng., Nov. 17.

Robert J. Corbett, 65, U.S. congressman (R-Pa., 1939–41, 1945–71); Pittsburgh, Pa., Apr. 25.

Mike (King) Curtis, 36, saxophonist, bandleader, composer (*Soul Serenade*); New York City, Aug. 14.

Charlie Dale, 90, partner in Smith and Dale vaudeville comedy team formed in 1898; Teaneck, N.J., Nov. 16.

Bebe Daniels, 71, movie star of 1920's and 1930's in United States, England (*42nd Street*); London, Mar. 16.

Paul de Kruif, 80, bacteriologist, wrote best seller *Microbe Hunters;* Holland, Mich., Feb. 28.

August Derleth, 62, writer known for novels on fictional town, "Sac Prairie"; Sauk City, Wis., July 4.

Thomas J. Dodd, 64, U.S. senator (D-Conn., 1959–71), censured for mismanagement of funds (1967); Old Lyme, Conn., May 24.

Giuseppe Antonio Doto (Joe Adonis), 69, former underworld leader and gambling king; Ancona, Italy, Nov. 26.

Donald F. Duncan, 78, promoter of Yo-Yo toy; head, Duncan Company 1929–57; Los Angeles, May 15.

Marcel Dupré, 85, concert organist, composed symphonies, 76 chorales; Meudon, France, May 30.

Tilla Durieux, 90, German actress from 1901, "the grand old lady of the German theater"; Berlin, Feb. 21.

François "Papa Doc" Duvalier, 64, dictator-president of Haiti 1957–71; Port-au-Prince, Apr. 21.

Edgar Eisenhower, 82, lawyer, brother of late President Dwight D. Eisenhower; Tacoma, Wash., July 12.

Charles Engelhard, 54, multimillionaire, Engelhard Minerals, racehorse breeder; Boca Grande, Fla., Mar. 2.

Yuri F. Faier, 81, conductor, Bolshoi Ballet Orchestra 1924–63, virtually blind all his life; Moscow, Aug. 4.

Philo T. Farnsworth, 64, pioneer in television development; Salt Lake City, Utah, Mar. 11.

Fernandel (Fernand Contandin), 67, French comedian, star of almost 150 motion pictures; Paris, Feb. 26.

Mordche S. Friedman, 80, Hassidic leader of the Rizhiner dynasty; New York City, Mar. 2.

James G. Fulton, 68, U.S. congressman (R-Pa., 1945–71); Washington, D.C., Oct. 6.

Billy Gilbert, 77, screen and stage comedian (*Fanny*), known for his elusive sneeze; Hollywood, Sept. 23.

Harry F. Guggenheim, 80, philanthropist, cofounder (1941) of *Newsday;* Sands Point, N.Y., Jan. 22.

Sir Tyrone Guthrie, 70, director, author and producer (*House of Atreus*), founder (1963) of the Tyrone Guthrie Theatre in Minneapolis; Newbliss, Ireland, May 15.

Leland Hayward, 68, stage producer (*South Pacific, The Sound of Music*); Yorktown Heights, N.Y., Mar. 18.

Van Heflin, 60, film actor, won 1942 Oscar as best supporting actor (*Johnny Eager*); Hollywood, July 23.

A. P. (Sir Alan Patrick) Herbert, 81, member House of Commons 1935–50; humorist, wrote over 60 novels; West London, Eng., Nov. 11.

Bourke Hickenlooper, 75, U.S. senator (R-Iowa, 1945–69); Shelter Island, L.I., N.Y., Sept. 4.

Russell (Russ) Hodges, 61, broadcaster of Giants baseball games for 22 years; San Francisco, Apr. 19.

Eric Hodgins, 71, writer (*Mr. Blandings Builds His Dream House*), vice-president Time Inc. 1938–46; New York City, Jan. 7.

Spessard L. Holland, 79, U.S. senator (D-Fla., 1949–69); Bartow, Fla., Nov. 6.

Bernardo Alberto Houssay, 84, winner of 1947 Nobel Prize for research concerned with diabetes; Buenos Aires, Sept. 21.

Helen Hull, 83, wrote 20 novels (*A Tapping on the Wall*), 60 short stories; New York City, July 15.

Alvin Johnson, 96, a founder (1919) of New School for Social Research; Upper Nyack, N.Y., June 7.

Dorothy Andrews Kabis, 54, U.S. treasurer 1969–71; Sheffield, Mass., July 3.

Paul Karrer, 82, shared 1937 Nobel Prize in chemistry; Zurich, Switzerland, June 18.

Mathilde Kchessinska (Princess Krassinska-Romanovska), 99, prima ballerina assoluta, Imperial Ballet; Paris, Dec. 7.

Rockwell Kent, 88, landscape painter (*Winter*), book illustrator (*Moby Dick, Paul Bunyan*); Plattsburgh, N.Y., Mar. 13.

Dennis King, 73, stage star, musicals (*The Vagabond King*) and dramas (*A Doll's House*); New York City, May 21.

E. V. Knox, 89, editor *Punch* magazine 1932–49, contributor under pen name "Evoe"; London, Jan. 2.

Pope Kyrollos VI, 69, Coptic Orthodox patriarch 1959–71; Cairo, Egypt, Mar. 9.

Harald Lander, 66, ballet master and choreographer Royal Danish Ballet 1932–51; director Paris Opera Ballet School 1959–71; Copenhagen, Sept. 14.

Sean Lemass, 71, prime minister of the Republic of Ireland 1959–66; Dublin, May 11.

Isobel Lennart, 55, writer of novels and screenplays (*Two for the Seesaw, Funny Girl*); Hemet, Calif., Jan. 25.

Nathan Leopold, 66, convicted murderer (with Richard Loeb) of young boy killed (1924) in attempt to commit the perfect crime; San Juan, P.R., Aug. 29.

Joe E. Lewis, 69, nightclub comedian; New York City, June 4.

Ted Lewis, 80, entertainer, jazz musician, popularized song *Me and My Shadow;* New York City, Aug. 25.

Charles (Sonny) Liston, 38, world heavyweight boxing champion 1962–64; Las Vegas, Nev.; found dead Jan. 5.

György Lukacs, 86, Marxist philosopher, literary critic (*Realism in Our Time*); Budapest, Hungary, June 4.

Paul Lukas, 76, stage and screen actor, 1943 Academy Award winner (*Watch on the Rhine*); Tangier, Morocco, Aug. 15.

Diana Lynn, 45, film star of light comedies in 1940's (*Meet Me at the Fair*); Los Angeles, Dec. 18.

Reinhold Maier, 81, prime minister Baden-Württemberg 1945–53, played a leading role in establishing postwar democratic state in West Germany; Stuttgart, Aug. 18.

Robert Manry, 52, sailed the Atlantic in smallest boat ever to cross the ocean nonstop (1965); Union City, Pa., Feb. 21.

Henry (Heinie) Manush, 69, baseball star 1923–40, elected to Hall of Fame 1964; Sarasota, Fla., May 12.

Thomas E. Martin, 78, U.S. senator (R-Iowa, 1955–61), congressman (1939–55); Seattle, Wash., June 27.

Ramon Villeda Morales, 62, president of Honduras 1957–63, head of his nation's delegation to UN; New York City, Oct. 8.

Harry W. Morrison, 86, cofounder (1912) Morrison-Knudsen Co., one of world's largest builders of canals, dams, roads; Boise, Idaho, July 19.

Jim Morrison, 27, lead singer of rock group The Doors; lyricist (*Break On Through*); Paris, July 3.

Hugh N. Mulzac, 84, first Negro to command a ship in U.S. merchant marine; East Meadow, N.Y., Jan. 31.

Audie Murphy, 46, most decorated U.S. soldier of World War II, film actor (autobiographical *To Hell and Back*); near Roanoke, Va., May. 28.

Allan Nevins, 80, historian-biographer, 1933 and 1937 Pulitzer Prize winner; Menlo Park, Calif., Mar. 5.

Gerald P. Nye, 78, U.S. senator (R-N.D., 1925–45), staunch isolationist; Washington, D.C., July 17.

Lord Boyd Orr (John Boyd Orr), 90, first director Food and Agricultural Organization, winner of 1949 Nobel Peace Prize; near Brechin, Scotland, June 25.

Ann Pennington, 77, stage star in 1920's, popularized Black Bottom dance; New York City, Nov. 4.

Jan Prochazka, 42, Czechoslovak screenwriter, backed attempted reforms in Czechoslovakia; Prague, Feb. 20.

Winston L. Prouty, 65, U.S. senator (R-Vt., 1959–71); Boston, Mass., Sept. 10.

Norman Reilly Raine, 76, creator of story character "Tugboat Annie," 1937 Oscar winner for screenplay *The Life of Emile Zola;* Woodland Hills, Calif., July 19.

Clayton Rawson, 64, mystery writer (*Death from a Top Hat*), magician "The Great Merlini"; Port Chester, N.Y., Mar. 1.

Lady Reading (Stella Dowager Marchioness of Reading), 77, first woman to become member (1958) of House of Lords; London, May 22.

Dan Reeves, 58, principal owner of Los Angeles Rams football team; New York City, Apr. 15.

Michael Rennie, 62, stage, screen and television actor; Harrogate, England, June 10.

Martha Baird Rockefeller, 75, widow of John D. Rocke-

Wide World

J. C. (James Cash) Penney, 95, founded chain of 1,660 retail stores; New York City, Feb. 12.

Coco (Gabrielle) Chanel, 87, French fashion designer famous for her cardigan suits and perfume Chanel No. 5; Paris, Jan. 10.

Camera Press

Ogden Nash, 68, writer of humorous poetry, including limericks, contributed 350 poems to "The New Yorker"; Baltimore, Md., May 19.

UPI

Wide World

Reinhold Niebuhr, 78, Protestant theologian; Stockbridge, Mass., June 1.

Thomas E. Dewey, 68, New York governor 1943–54; GOP presidential nominee; Bal Harbour, Fla., Mar. 16.

Richard B. Russell, 73, U.S. senator (D-Ga., 1933–71); Washington, D.C., Jan. 21.

Bobby Jones, 69, won (1930) U.S. and British Open and Amateur tournaments; Atlanta, Ga., Dec. 18.

Harold Lloyd, 77, comedian of silent films and talkies ("The Freshman"); Hollywood, Mar. 8.

feller, Jr., former concert pianist and benefactor of music; New York City, Jan. 25.

J. I. Rodale, 72, founder (1942) of magazine *Organic Farming and Gardening;* New York City, June 7.

Michael Romanoff, 78 or 81, retired restaurateur, *bon vivant;* Hollywood, Sept. 1.

Elmo Roper, Jr., 70, public-opinion analyst, developer (1936) of political polls; Norwalk, Conn., Apr. 30.

Carl Rose, 68, cartoonist and illustrator; Rowayton, Conn., June 20.

Carl Ruggles, 95, composer of American concert music (*Sun-Treader*), founder and conductor (1912–17) Winona (Minn.) Symphony Orchestra; Bennington, Vt., Oct. 24.

Ghulam Mohammed Sadiq, 59, chief minister, Kashmir 1964–71; Chandigarh, India, Dec. 12.

Michel Saint-Denis, 73, founding director London's Old Vic Theater School, consultant-director Royal Shakespeare Theater; London, July 31.

George Seferis, 71, poet, 1963 Nobel Prize winner for literature, diplomat; Athens, Sept. 20.

Viliam Siroky, 69, premier of Czechoslovakia 1953–63, cofounder Czechoslovak Communist Party; Prague, Oct. 6.

Spyros P. Skouras, 78, retired head of 20th Century-Fox; Mamaroneck, N.Y., Aug. 16.

T. V. Soong, 77, banker, former premier Chinese Nationalist Government; San Francisco, Apr. 25.

Samuel Spewack, 72, coauthor with wife of comedies and musicals (*Kiss Me, Kate*); New York City, Oct. 14.

Arthur B. Spingarn, 93, Jewish civil-rights lawyer; president National Association for the Advancement of Colored People 1940–66; New York City, Dec. 1.

Wendell M. Stanley, 66, shared 1946 Nobel Prize in chemistry; Salamanca, Spain, June 15.

Bill Stern, 64, radio and television sportscaster 1930's–50's; Rye, N.Y., Nov. 19.

Lord Stuart (Viscount Stuart of Findhorn), 74, adviser to Sir Winston Churchill, secretary of state for Scotland 1951–57; Salisbury, England, Feb. 20.

Theodor H. E. Svedberg, 86, Swedish nuclear scientist, winner of 1926 Nobel Prize in chemistry; Stockholm, Feb. 26.

Igor Y. Tamm, 75, Russian scientist, shared 1958 Nobel Prize in physics; Moscow, Apr. 12.

Paul H. Terry, 84, pioneer in animated cartoons, Terrytoons (Mighty Mouse); New York City, Oct. 25.

W. Ross Thatcher, 54, premier of Saskatchewan 1964–71; Regina, Canada, July 23.

Dick Tiger (Richard Ihetu), 42, middleweight boxing champion 1962–63, 1965–66; Aba, Nigeria, Dec. 13.

Arne Tiselius, 69, winner of 1948 Nobel Prize in chemistry; Uppsala, Sweden, Oct. 29.

William V. S. Tubman, 75, president of Liberia 1944–71; London, Eng., July 23.

Aleksandr T. Tvardovsky, 61, Russian poet, editor of literary magazine *Novy Mir* 1950–54, 1958–70; near Moscow, Dec. 17.

Jean Vilar, 59, French actor and director, founded (1951) Théâtre National Populaire; Sète, France, May 28.

Bernard Wagenaar, 76, composer of symphonies and string quartets; Kennebunkport, Me., May 18.

John C. Watts, 69, U.S. congressman (D-Ky., 1951–71); Lexington, Ky., Sept. 24.

Sir David Webster, 67, developer of London's Royal Opera House; London, May 11.

Sir Edgar Whitehead, 66, prime minister of Southern Rhodesia 1958–62; Newbury, Eng., Sept. 23.

William Griffith Wilson, 75, cofounder (1935) of Alcoholics Anonymous; Miami Beach, Fla., Jan. 24.

Philip Wylie, 69, author of *A Generation of Vipers,* coined phrase "momism"; Miami, Fla., Oct. 25.

DEFENSE

The American military establishment, scarred by years of a frustrating war in Indochina, remained on the defensive through most of 1971. Its size and spending were reduced; and military prestige may have plummeted to a new low with disclosures of widespread drug abuse in the armed forces, post-exchange scandals and fresh charges of atrocities in Vietnam.

Publication of excerpts from a 12-volume, top-secret study of the Vietnam war—the Pentagon Papers—generated new controversy over the origin and conduct of the American involvement. Although the documents dealt with the period before President Nixon took office, he decided to seek Federal court injunctions against newspaper stories on the Pentagon study, only to be rebuffed finally by a 6–3 Supreme Court decision in favor of disclosure.

The President, often prodded by impatient members of the Senate and House, continued to "wind down" the war. He ordered a reduction in U.S. troops in Vietnam from a level of 280,000 at the start of 1971 to 139,000 or less a year later. An American-backed invasion of Laos by South Vietnamese units triggered heavy criticism of the President's Vietnam policy in February and March 1971 but he defended the attack as essential to continued U.S. withdrawal.

Nixon stirred another national debate when he stepped into the highly publicized court-martial of First Lt. William L. Calley, Jr., after a jury of six officers had found Calley guilty of premeditated murder in the village of Mylai. The President ordered the 27-year-old officer released from the Fort Benning stockade and restricted to his apartment pending the outcome of appeals of the life sentence imposed by the jurors. The President, responding to a strong outcry against the verdict, also promised to review the case personally before any sentence was carried out. Calley's term was later cut to twenty years by a three-star general under the standard reviewing procedure.

President Nixon also pursued his goal of an all-volunteer Army. Congress aided the cause by approving $2,400,000,000 for doubling the pay of recruits and privates and giving generous increases to all enlisted men and officers with the rank of captain or below. But, sensing a more critical Congressional attitude toward military spending, the Nixon administration cut back in many areas once considered sacrosanct. The President asked for $76,400,000,000 in fiscal 1971, a reduction of $3,800,000,000 from 1970 outlays. The Pentagon sliced military manpower to reach 2,500,000 by mid-1972, a cutback of 180,000 from the pre-Vietnam strength of the armed forces.

Defense Secretary Melvin R. Laird said the United States should limit its defense spending to 7 per cent of its gross national product. Laird proposed an $80,000,000,000 military-spending program in the near future, an amount several billion dollars below what top commanders have recommended.

Under Laird's "realistic deterrence" policy, the nation theoretically would be prepared to fight a major war and a minor conflict at the same time. In the Johnson and Kennedy administrations, the Pentagon strategy called for the capacity to fight two-and-a-half wars, compared with the current one-and-a-half-war plan.

Despite the note of retrenchment, the Nixon administration advocated a new manned bomber, a small fleet of new warships, a 12-site antiballistic-missile defense system, hardened Minutemen missile-launching sites and more powerful submarine-fired missiles. The military strategy was designed to undergird the "Nixon doctrine" of withdrawing American combat forces from world hot spots, such as Vietnam, but supporting other nations in resisting aggression, with military equipment and advisers.

Another cornerstone of President Nixon's global strategy was the negotiation of an agreement with the Soviet Union in the Strategic Arms Limitation Talks, known as SALT. If the United States and Russia could stop the multibillion-dollar nuclear-arms race, Nixon reasoned, both would be better off financially and equally as secure. Critics of the President, including some retired generals and admirals, said that he risked the loss of "superiority" to the Soviets by making concessions at SALT. The Soviet-American talks were conducted largely in secret but President Nixon's announcement that he would visit Moscow gave some indication of progress in the negotiations. On Feb. 11, the United States and the Soviet Union were among nations that signed a treaty prohibiting the installation of nuclear weapons on the ocean floor.

Congress increasingly tried to assert its views on the conduct of the Vietnam war. The military draft law expired June 30, 1971 because of a Senate-House stalemate on efforts by the Senate to set a deadline for withdrawal of all American troops. The draft law was passed in September without such a provision. Even in the House, however, antiwar sentiment was rising. Rep. John J. Flynt (D-Ga.), a conservative who had never voted against a military bill in his career, opposed a two-year draft extension, saying: "It is wrong to compound a six-year mistake and send young men halfway around the world to fight in a war we have not the fortitude to win or end."

During the Laos invasion, American troops generally remained outside of the country in deference to a Congressional ban on participation of U.S. ground forces in the fighting in Laos or neighboring Cambodia. The President and his supporters, however, were able to fend off a growing demand that he set a date for withdrawal of all U.S. forces in Vietnam in return for the release of American prisoners held by Hanoi.

Publication of excerpts from the Pentagon Papers in *The New York Times, Washington Post* and other major newspapers added to popular feeling against the Vietnam involvement. Documents indicated that officials of President Lyndon B. Johnson's administration had planned for five months to get a broad Congressional authorization for war in Vietnam long before the celebrated Gulf of Tonkin incident, in August 1964, led to its enactment. Many readers got the impression—denied by Johnson's top advisers—that the former President deceived the American people while gradually building up the U.S. combat role in Vietnam.

The fallout from the Indochina guerrilla war contributed to more adverse newspaper reports. The court-martial of Lt. Calley dragged out for nearly 5 months before a jury of 6 combat veterans found him guilty of murdering at least 22 unarmed civilians in a village known as Mylai 4. The verdict, coming after 13 days of deliberation, touched off an uproar in Congress and the country. Liberals and conservatives said Calley was being made a scapegoat and demanded his release. Telegrams reaching the White House favored clemency 100 to 1.

When the President acted to free Calley from the stockade and confine him to quarters, the Army prosecutor caused second thoughts for many when he wrote Nixon: "The greatest tragedy of all will be if political expediency dictates the compromise of such a fundamental moral principle as the inherent unlawfulness of the murder of innocent persons."

The criticism came from Capt. Aubrey M. Daniel III in a widely reprinted letter. Public-opinion polls indicated that 79 per cent of all Americans disapproved of the verdict and 83 per cent approved of the President's decision to release Calley from the stockade.

In other Mylai-related courts-martial, a jury quickly acquitted Calley's company commander, Capt. Ernest Medina, of charges that he was responsible for the deaths of "not less than 100 Vietnamese in the village." Capt. Eugene Kotouc, who was accused of maiming a Vietnamese prisoner by cutting off a finger, was also speedily acquitted.

Wide World

Lt. William Calley, Jr., the only officer found guilty in the Mylai case, leans in front of an antiwar poster at Fort Benning, Ga.

Maj. Gen. Samuel W. Koster, commander of the Americal division, who was charged with covering up the massacre, was cleared without a trial. He later was censured for "negligence" and demoted to one-star rank through administrative action. Koster's deputy in Vietnam, Brig. Gen. George H. Young, Jr., was disciplined with a censure but allowed to retire early. Earlier, Sgt. Charles E. Hutto, who was accused of assault with intent to murder six persons at Mylai, was acquitted after he said he was only following orders there.

Except for Calley's conviction, no one else accused of murder or assault at Mylai was found guilty in 1971. Charges against many officers and enlisted men were dropped without court-martial. Col. Oran K. Henderson was acquitted of cover-up charges at Ft. Meade, Md.

In another Vietnam atrocity case, former Green Beret Capt. Robert Marasco acknowl-

Destruction began in 1971 of the antipersonnel agents —bacteria, viruses, toxins —and the munitions to carry them, at Pine Bluff Arsenal, Ark. Operation was part of a plan to destroy total U.S. arsenal of biological and chemical weapons.

edged that he shot and killed a South Vietnamese and said he did it on orders from the Central Intelligence Agency. The victim, Thai Khac Chuyen, was described as a double agent. Marasco had been charged with the murder, along with seven other Green Berets, but the charges were dropped when the CIA refused to permit its officials to be called as witnesses.

The highest-ranking officer to be accused of atrocities was Brig. Gen. John W. Donaldson, a West Point graduate. He was accused of murdering six civilians by taking "potshots" from his helicopter. His aide, Lt. Col. William J. McCloskey, was accused of murdering two civilians. Donaldson was the first general to be charged with war crimes in seventy years.

A series of drug-abuse stories also rocked the Pentagon. Air Force Col. Gerald V. Kehrli was sentenced to three years in prison for using marijuana and giving it to enlisted men in his squadron in South Vietnam. One estimate said that 65,000 members of the armed services used drugs in some form in 1970. Other estimates said 10 per cent or more of the troops in Vietnam were addicted to heroin. President Nixon ordered new procedures to detect addicts and offer them hospitalization before discharge.

Another scandal centered on the operation of post exchanges and servicemen's clubs in Vietnam. The former Sergeant Major of the Army, highest-ranking enlisted man, was indicted on charges of conspiring to defraud noncommissioned officers' clubs in the war zone. A Senate investigation disclosed wide-scale payment of bribes to get merchandise sold in PX's and clubs. And the former Provost General of the Army, Maj. Gen. Carl Turner, was convicted of income-tax evasion and acquiring guns illegally.

The drive by minority groups for equality also had its impact on the armed forces. The Pentagon began to include race relations in all basic training courses. A new commitment was made to end housing discrimination against blacks, especially in West Germany. The Navy said it wanted to raise its black percentage from the existing 5.5 per cent in enlisted ranks to 12 per cent, the proportion of blacks in the general population. It also wants to integrate the Navy officer corps—currently 0.67 per cent black.

Counter-culture fashions received the attention of military commanders. While old-time soldiers groaned, new regulations were issued to allow longer hair, some sideburns and neatly trimmed mustaches in all services except the Marines. The Marines insisted on close-cropped crew cuts.

In a showdown with environmental action groups, the Atomic Energy Commission won a 4–3 Supreme Court go-ahead for a 5-megaton underground explosion of a nuclear bomb. The device was being tested in development of the Spartan missile, a major component of the ABM system. Citizens' groups asked for a delay of the blast to investigate further possible side effects, such as earthquakes or tidal waves. When the court refused to interfere, the explosion took place on Nov. 6 as scheduled, without any apparent harmful effects to the environment near the Aleutians' test site.

In another controversy, the Pentagon ordered a halt to military spying on civilians, as revealed in a series of newspaper stories. The Army ordered elaborate surveillance after the Detroit riots in 1967, ostensibly to help pinpoint potential troublemakers in future disorders. Finally, the House of Representatives refused to take contempt action against the Columbia Broadcasting System for its highly critical film *The Selling of the Pentagon*. CBS refused to yield the film taken but not used in the program, claiming First Amendment rights.

WILLIAM J. EATON
Washington Correspondent
Chicago Daily News

In April, the first two of several manuscripts, considered part of Iceland's cultural heritage, are presented to Iceland by Denmark. The valuable material, collected in Copenhagen about 1700, includes sagas of Vikings, gods, legendary kings and the first settlements (made from Iceland) in Greenland.

Danish Information Office

DENMARK

The nonsocialist Government headed by Hilmar Baunsgaard, and supported by the Conservative, Liberal and Radical parties, in the summer of 1971 decided to call Parliamentary elections before, under the Constitution, they would become mandatory, that is, in January 1972. The election that therefore took place on Sept. 21 resulted in a setback for the Government. The final outcome, however, remained doubtful for

DENMARK

Area: 16,629 sq. mi.
Population: 5,000,000
Capital: Copenhagen
Government: Frederik IX, king—1947; Jens Otto Krag, premier—1971
Gross National Product: $16,000,000,000
Foreign trade: exports, $3,356,000,000; imports, $4,404,000,000
Armed forces: 40,500

about two weeks because the returns in metropolitan Denmark were virtually a dead heat, and elections in the Faeroe Islands and in Greenland were not held until Oct. 5. The elections there gave the Social Democrats a one-vote edge (89 to 88) in the Folketing (Parliament). In a referendum, voters approved lowering the voting age from 21 to 20.

Unable to command a majority in the new Folketing, Prime Minister Baunsgaard's Cabinet resigned. King Frederik IX then asked Jens Otto Krag, Social Democratic leader and a former prime minister, to form a new Government. The new Cabinet proved to be the youngest in Danish history; two ministers were respectively 32 and 34 years old. Knud Boerge Andersen was appointed to head the Foreign Ministry, and the well-known politician Per Haekkerup was entrusted with the important Department of Economy.

Debate about Denmark's possible entry into

Following Sept. 21 elections, Jens Otto Krag, prime minister 1962–68, forms a new Cabinet.

the European Economic Community raged during 1971. In May the Folketing voted to continue negotiations with the EEC on eventual membership, the final decision to be made by a popular referendum. Great Britain's decision in October to seek membership made it likely that Denmark would follow suit.

The Nordic Council, the intergovernmental advisory body consisting of government and parliamentary representatives from Denmark, Finland, Iceland, Norway and Sweden, met in Copenhagen in February. The countries' differing attitudes toward membership in the EEC dominated much of the discussion.

The 1971 Nordic Literature Prize was awarded to Danish writer Thorkild Hansen for his trilogy (*The Slave Coast, The Slave Ships, The Slave Islands*) dealing with the slave trade between Africa and Denmark's former possession in the West Indies. Hansen has also written two semidocumentary books on travel and exploration, *Arabia Felix* and *The Way to Hudson Bay.*

The world's oldest daily newspaper, *Berlingske Aftenavis* of Copenhagen, ceased publication after 222 years. However, its morning edition, *Berlingske Tidende,* remains Denmark's biggest newspaper and is in good economic health. *Jyllands-Posten* and *Fyens Stiftstidende* each celebrated its 200th anniversary in 1971.

ERIK J. FRIIS
Editor, The American-Scandinavian Review

DISARMAMENT

Disarmament experts were long on resolutions and short on arms reduction in 1971. The 26-nation Conference of the Committee on Disarmament (actually a 25-member body since France consistently has refused from the start to participate) held its annual meetings in Geneva and produced a convention to outlaw the use of biological weapons. But neither the United Nations nor the world community working outside it was able to persuade the People's Republic of (Communist) China to join the Geneva talks.

The biological-weapons pact, later approved by the UN General Assembly with the hope that it would be opened for signature early in 1972, was a slight setback for the Soviet Union. It had held out for a treaty banning both biological and chemical weapons of war. A sterner setback for the Kremlin was the refusal of the UN General Assembly to go along with its demand to set up a standing world disarmament conference to meet periodically.

Instead, in a resolution engineered by Deputy Foreign Minister Nicolae Ecobescu of Rumania and Dr. Alfonso Garcia Robles, Mexico's chief delegate, the Assembly approved a substitute measure for the Soviet world-conference proposal that China had attacked and demanded be shelved. The Rumanian-Mexican version eviscerated the Soviet proposal. While approving the principle of a world disarmament conference, it left the date, place and agenda of the meeting to be fixed by the 1972 General Assembly.

Although the Assembly approved 14 resolutions dealing with disarmament, it made virtually no headway in persuading mainland China to join arms talks.

Only China and the country that for years was considered Peking's UN spokesman—Albania—voted against a resolution calling for a halt to all testing of nuclear weapons by Aug. 5, 1973. That date will mark the tenth anniversary of the treaty banning nuclear tests in the atmosphere, in space and under water. The 1963 Moscow Treaty left only underground tests with legal sanction; and massive nuclear-test blasts beneath the ground in the Soviet Union and by the United States in the Aleutian Islands brought worldwide protests in 1971.

China sought to justify its opposition with the argument that it must develop nuclear capacity as a defense against Soviet and U.S. "nuclear blackmail." It demanded that the other two "superpowers"—as the Chinese delegates derogated Moscow and Washington in UN debate—pledge, as Peking has, not to be the first to use nuclear weapons in war.

Veteran UN delegates observed that China's attitude toward nuclear disarmament was similar to that of the Soviet Union in the 1950's when its aim was to catch up with the United States in sophisticated weaponry.

China's agreement to let the Rumanian-Mexican measure on a world disarmament conference go through the Assembly without serious opposition gave rise to hope that Peking might be induced to join the Geneva talks. Thus far, the Peking authorities had shown the opposite inclination. But the Geneva delegates, due to reconvene on Feb. 29, 1972, hoped to work out sufficient flexibility to make their arms talks attractive to the Chinese and—they hoped it would follow—to the French.

The record 14 resolutions on disarmament approved by the General Assembly were:

Three on a total test ban of nuclear weapons, namely: calling for an end to all tests by Aug. 5, 1973; demanding an immediate halt to the production of nuclear weapons, and banning their deployment; a proposal, sponsored by Canada and Sweden, calling upon the United States and the Soviet Union to put forward concrete proposals to the Geneva conference in 1972 for a conclusive ban on underground nuclear tests and, meanwhile, to exercise restraint unilaterally in the number and magnitude of such tests as they might hold pending such a ban.

Three on chemical and bacteriological warfare: approving the convention against biological weapons and calling for its early opening for signature by all powers; urging the major powers to work on a ban on chemical weapons; demanding a complete moratorium on the production or use of what experts consider the most lethal of weapons, nerve gas.

Three on the overall question of "general and complete disarmament": the perennial resolution asking the Geneva disarmament conferees to resume diligently their talks on general and complete disarmament; asked the International Atomic Energy Agency, with headquarters in Vienna, to make a careful study of progress in processes of enriching uranium—a knowledge boasted of by several nonnuclear countries, and one that could lead to production of nuclear weapons—and bring it under IAEA safeguards; a demand for more scientific conferences on disarmament and more special reports on the subject by the UN secretary-general, and suggesting special disarmament seminars and studies by universities and other academic institutions on the overall problems of disarmament.

In addition, there were these resolutions: a call for publicizing the economic and social consequences of the arms race and military expenditures, calling on the UN Educational, Scientific and Cultural Organization (UNESCO) and other UN specialized agencies to assist in this; a resolution deploring the fact that the Treaty of Tlatelolco, which calls for denuclearization of Latin America, had not been signed by all nuclear powers (the United States and Britain had ratified the treaty; the Soviet Union, China and France had not even signed it); a call for the IAEA to follow up the peaceful uses of atomic energy and to give greater study to the subject; a proposal, introduced by Mrs. Sirimavo Bandaranaike, premier of Ceylon, to declare the Indian Ocean a "zone of peace" (only China voted against this); a request for the UN secretary-general to report on the effects of napalm and other incendiary weapons and all aspects of their possible use, as a matter of human rights.

BRUCE W. MUNN
Chief United Nations Correspondent
United Press International

As sixth session of SALT resumes in Geneva, Nov. 15 (from l) Austria President Jonas, U.S. Ambassador to Vienna Humes, U.S. disarmament negotiator Smith, Soviet disarmament chief Semyonov and Soviet Ambassador to Vienna Aristov join in a champagne toast to the success of the discussions.

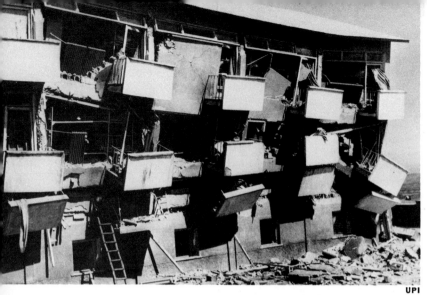

A tenement, its balconies
dangling, in Bingol illustrates the destruction
wrought by earthquakes in
eastern Turkey in May.

DISASTERS

January	2	Scotland: A steel barrier set up to channel crowds at a Glasgow soccer stadium is knocked down as fans rush for the exits; 66 persons die, 100 are injured.
	5	Malaysia: A state of emergency is declared in the western provinces following week-long floods and monsoon storms; 32 persons die, 100,000 are left homeless.
	29	Mozambique: Floods inundate the Zambezia district after 48 hours of torrential rains and cyclone winds; some 60 persons die, 20,000 are forced to flee.
February	4	Brazil: Construction workers are crushed as an incomplete government exhibit hall in Belo Horizonte collapses; 63 persons die.
	6	Italy: An earthquake destroys the center of Tuscania, an ancient Etruscan hill town, resulting in extensive damage to art treasures; 22 persons die, 120 are injured.
	9	United States: The strongest earthquake to hit Los Angeles since 1933 causes property damage estimated at $1,000,000,000. Areas of the San Fernando Valley are evacuated. The Veterans Administration hospital in the community of Sylmar is destroyed; 64 persons die, hundreds are injured.
	21	United States: An estimated 40 to 50 tornadoes sweep across northeastern Louisiana, western Mississippi and southern Tennessee. Total damage to property is over $7,500,000; 115 persons die, 500 are injured.
	26	Brazil: A flood sweeps through Rio de Janeiro with waters as deep as six feet destroying thousands of homes; over 130 people die.
March	19	Peru: An avalanche, which may have been set off by an earthquake, brings down tons of water, mud and rocks on Chungar, a mining camp in the Andes; 400 to 600 people die.
April	15	Philippine Republic: A Philippines Air Force plane crashes near Manila; 39 persons die.
	19	United States: Tornadoes rip the Texas Panhandle and cause $2,000,000 in damage; 42 persons are injured.
	26	Philippine Republic: Tropical storm Wanda strikes the central Philippines; 26 persons die, over 100 are missing.
	26–28	Brazil: Floodwaters leave damage estimated at $6,000,000 in Salvador, a city on the northeastern coast; 140 persons die, 10,000 are left homeless.
	27–28	United States: Five tornadoes hit parts of Kentucky, Illinois and Tennessee. Eight counties of Kentucky are declared a major disaster area; 11 persons die, over 100 are injured.
May	10	South Korea: A bus plunges into a reservoir near Kapyong; 77 persons die.
	12	South Africa: Floodwaters sweep a bus off a bridge near Kwa Mashu; some 50 persons drown.
	12	Turkey: An earthquake devastates town of Burdur and nearby villages; 57 persons die.
	22	Turkey: An earthquake rocks eastern Turkey, flattening town of Bingol; over 800 people die.
	23	Yugoslavia: A Yugoslav airplane crashes and burns on Krk, an island off the coast of Rijeka; 78 persons die.
	26–27	Philippine Republic: A vessel is lost at sea southeast of Manila during a typhoon; 40 persons aboard are missing.
	27	West Germany: A freight train and a passenger train collide head on, five miles southeast of Wuppertal; 47 persons, mostly children, die.
June	6	United States: An Air West DC-9 jetliner collides with an F-4 Phantom jet above the San Gabriel range in California; 50 persons die.
July	3	Japan: A Japanese TOA airplane crashes into Mount Eboshi in the north; 68 persons die.
	9	Chile: An earthquake that registers 10 on the Richter scale strikes the north-central provinces; emergency zones are declared, and an estimated 15,000 to 100,000 people are left homeless; about 90 persons die, 250 are injured.
	21	West Germany: The Switzerland Express train jumps the tracks on a curve south of Rheinweiler; 25 persons are killed, some 100 are injured.

After 11 cars of a 14-car Chicago-New Orleans train jump the tracks near St. Louis, 10 persons are left dead and 99 injured.

UPI

26–27	South Korea: Torrential rains bring floods and landslides to central and southwestern sections of the country; 64 persons die, 44 are injured.
29	Afghanistan: Floodwaters sweep away a village after a landslide near the Khinjan Pass in the Hindu Kush; over 100 people are killed.
30	Japan: An F-86 jet fighter and an All-Nippon Airways 727 jetliner collide over Iwate Prefecture in northern Japan; 162 persons are killed.
August 6	Japan: Typhoon Olive sweeps southwestern Japan and eastern Korea; 78 persons die.
11	U.S.S.R.: A Soviet Aeroflot jet airliner crashes and explodes on takeoff from Irkutsk Airport in Siberia; 97 persons die.
16–17	Hong Kong: Typhoon Rose hits the British colony with 130-mile-an-hour winds and 12 inches of rain; 130 persons die, over 200 are injured.
18	Morocco: A bus plunges into a gorge near Boulaouane; 48 persons die, 27 are injured.
22–25	East Pakistan: Floods caused by monsoon rains damage over 10,000 villages and 3,000,000 acres of crops; some 100 people die, 500,000 are left homeless.
28	Italy: A Greek ferry, the 11,232-ton *Heleanna,* catches fire in the Adriatic Sea on its bi-weekly run to Ancona, Italy, from Patras, Greece; 31 persons die, 69 are missing.
31	Japan: Typhoon Trix sweeps southern and western areas; 37 persons die, 103 are injured.
September 4	United States: An Alaska Airlines 727 crashes into the Chilkat mountains at 2,500 feet, some 20 miles west of the Juneau (Alaska) Municipal Airport; 111 persons die.
5	Persian Gulf: A motor launch with Pakistanis aboard hits a rock and sinks; 100 persons die.
7	East Pakistan: A motor launch capsizes in the flooded Padma River near Dacca; 150 persons are killed.
7	Japan: Typhoon Virginia lashes the central coastal area, leaving 22 inches of rain; 53 persons die, 27 are injured.
9	India: Week-long monsoon rains and floodwaters from the Ganges River and its tributaries in the northern states of West Bengal and Uttar Pradesh cause extensive damage; over 1,200 people die.
22	Ceylon: Monsoon storms bring floods to Ratnapura District; 5,000 people are left homeless.
23	Taiwan: Typhoon Bess destroys over 6,000 homes; 30 persons are dead, 150 injured.
October 2	Belgium: A British European Airways Vanguard crashes near Ghent after one of its four turboprop engines explodes; all 63 persons aboard die.
13	Philippine Republic: Four tropical storms hit Luzon in a week; 93 persons die.
15	Peru: The southeastern province of Aimaraes, in the foothills of the Andes Mountains, is rocked by an earthquake; 40 persons die, 6 villages are destroyed.
23–24	South Vietnam: Typhoon Hester, with 138-mile-per-hour winds, hits 5 northern provinces, destroying the town of Namhoa, and leaving thousands homeless; 88 persons die, over 100 are injured.
30	Rumania: A mining disaster at Hunedoara, a steel center, sets off a landslide; 51 persons die, 88 are injured.
29–31	India: A cyclone and 15-foot tidal wave strike the northern coast of Orissa State, on the Bay of Bengal, causing damage of $400,000,000 after sweeping inland 30 miles; 6,000 people die, according to official sources; estimates run as high as 25,000 people.
November 9	Italy: A British Royal Air Force transport plane crashes in the Ligurian Sea; 52 persons are missing.
22	Philippine Republic: A wooden cargo ship transporting passengers from the island of Leyte to the island of Cebu sinks in rough seas; 16 persons die, 90 are missing.
December 1	Taiwan: In a coal-mine explosion near Keelung, 41 persons die, 7 are missing.
24	Peru: A turboprop airliner goes down in a northern, almost inaccessible area of jungle near Pucallpa; 91 persons aboard are missing, 1 survivor found.
25	South Korea: Taeyunkak Hotel in Seoul is destroyed by a raging fire set off by a propane-gas explosion in a coffee shop; 161 persons die.

DISASTERS   165

DISTRICT OF COLUMBIA

More than 12,000 persons, mostly young men and women, were arrested in Washington in early May during a week of mass demonstrations against the Vietnam war. The Mayday demonstrators had come to the capital with the avowed purpose of bringing the Government to a standstill by blocking major traffic arteries and buildings. Their efforts were frustrated by mass arrests which totaled 7,000 on Monday, May 3, alone. There were other such arrests at the Capitol, the Justice Department and elsewhere later in the week.

Police suspended use of standard field-arrest forms during the roundups and herded the demonstrators into camps at the District of Columbia stadium, National Guard armory and other centers. Civil-rights groups charged that many persons not engaged in demonstrations were picked up and that the rights of those arrested were violated by the procedures used. But D.C. Police Chief Jerry V. Wilson and Justice Department officials defended the procedures as the only way to keep the city from being paralyzed.

President Nixon praised Wilson's role and Deputy Attorney General Richard Kleindienst said, "The truth is that the police foiled an attempt to stop the Government with a minimum exercise of authority. Any less authority would have risked letting the mob rule the national capital." The failure to use standard procedures meant that it was impossible to bring specific charges in most of the cases. The vast majority were dismissed and most of those tried were acquitted. Only a relatively small percentage were convicted of disorderly conduct or unlawful entry. The Mayday demonstrations were preceded by bitter protests against the Vietnam involvement staged by one thousand Vietnam veterans.

In September the John F. Kennedy Center for the Performing Arts opened. The $70,000,-000 structure on the Potomac River north of the Lincoln Memorial includes an opera house, a concert hall and a theater, with a small film theater to be completed later. Planning for the center began in 1958 when Congress authorized it and donated a site, but impetus for its completion came after it was named for Kennedy following his assassination in 1963. The Federal Government put up about two thirds of the cost including a $23,000,000 grant and a $20,400,000 loan. The center opened with a series of gala events: Leonard Bernstein's *Mass,* written for the occasion, was performed at the formal opening. President and Mrs. Nixon and members of the Kennedy family, but not the late President's widow, Mrs. Jacqueline Onassis, attended during the first week.

Also opening during the summer was a much praised outdoor auditorium, the Filene Center of Wolf Trap Farm, at Vienna, Va., in the Washington suburbs. Mrs. Jouett Shouse, daughter of Lincoln Filene, wealthy Boston businessman, donated 96 acres of land and $2,000,000 to build the center. Operated by the National Park Service, it attracted large crowds in its first season. A picture of the auditorium appears on page 341.

Washington lost its major-league baseball team, the Senators, after 71 years in the American League. The League voted to give the team permission to move the franchise to Arlington, Tex., between Dallas and Fort Worth.

JOSEPH W. HALL, JR.
Senate Staff, Washington Bureau
The Associated Press

UPI

The Rev. Walter E. Fauntroy wins primary in January campaign for seat in Congress—D.C.'s first (nonvoting) representative. He went on to win the election in March.

3.66 to 3.22 per US$1.00

.42 to .38 per US$1.00

5.55 to 5.12 per US$1.00

360 to 308 per US$1.00

ECONOMY

Regardless of the future course of the U.S. and world economies, there is no question that 1971 will be recorded as a landmark in economic history. In that year, the United States gave up its role as the foundation stone of the international monetary system and overturned international agreements that had existed since the end of World War II. As the year ended, the world was still uncertain of the structure that would replace the discarded Bretton Woods Agreement, which had established the system by which nations exchanged each other's currency.

American action was not confined to the international scene. A series of precedent-setting steps were taken affecting the domestic economy. The historic moves were made on the night of Aug. 15. In a nationally televised address, President Nixon announced these actions:

☐ A freeze on virtually all wages and prices for 90 days.

☐ Suspension of the 36-year-old U.S. commitment to exchange dollars for gold at the rate of $35 an ounce, which had anchored the international monetary system.

☐ Imposition of a 10 per cent surcharge on imports into the United States.

☐ A request to Congress to repeal the 7 per cent excise tax on automobiles and reinstate the tax credit for businessmen who build new plants and buy new equipment. The President asked that the investment credit be set temporarily at 10 per cent, but Congress trimmed it back to 7 per cent.

☐ A request for the advancement of some income-tax cuts, which were scheduled to take effect on Jan. 1, 1973, to Jan. 1, 1972.

The President's actions—his new economic policy (NEP)—represented a total break with previous United States policies and with his own stated conviction that wage and price controls would not solve the problem of inflation in the United States. The steps triggered howls of complaint, especially from foreign governments protesting both the suspension of gold convertibility—which in effect allowed the dollar to "float" in value in relation to other currencies—and the import surcharge. At home, labor unions caught in the midst of negotiations and businessmen planning price increases also registered dissent, although broad popular opinion seemed to back the President.

Despite the complaints, there was little doubt anywhere that bold new action by the United States had been badly needed. When he took office in 1969, President Nixon instituted a "game plan" designed to slow the country's galloping inflation by slowing business

Financial ministers of the Group of Ten—Belgium, Canada, France, W. Germany, Italy, Japan, the Netherlands, Sweden, United Kingdom and United States (International Monetary Fund)—meet in Washington.

activity. Hold-downs in government spending and a tighter money policy of the Federal Reserve Board slowed the economy to the point where, in the last quarter of 1969 and the first quarter of 1970, the country was in a recession.

Through 1970, the administration tried to stimulate an economic recovery. Administration spokesmen continually insisted that the "game plan" was working, but there were serious weaknesses. For one thing, unemployment, which climbed above 6 per cent of the work force, did not respond to the new pump priming. Business activity showed improvement through 1970 and into 1971, but at a rate much slower than had been forecast. And wages and prices kept rising despite the sluggish business activity.

Through the first part of 1971, the administration stuck to its "game plan," but pressures for change kept mounting both at home and abroad. In Washington, people as prominent as Arthur Burns, chairman of the Federal Reserve Board and a close friend of President Nixon, urged a form of "incomes policy"—another name for wage and price controls. Peter G. Peterson, former chairman of Bell & Howell Corp. who was appointed assistant to the president for international economic affairs early in the year, and John B. Connally, the former governor of Texas who became secretary of the treasury in February, later added their voices to the call for a more activist economic policy.

By midsummer the need for action was obvious even to the administration's most ardent opponents of controls. The United States' balance of trade, which has always been a bulwark of the balance of payments, suffered its third straight monthly deficit in July—more than $300,000,000—and was headed for its

first annual deficit since 1893. (The balance of trade measures the goods and services imported and exported by the United States; the balance of payments—BOP—registers the movement of money, including trade dollars, into and out of the country. The U.S. balance of payments has been in deficit, largely because of money the country has given away in military and economic aid programs, virtually since the end of World War II.)

With red ink as its strongest component, the BOP was sharply on the deficit side. By the end of September, the BOP deficit amounted to $23,400,000,000, more than the *total* of all the deficits in the previous 11 years.

In addition, the Federal budget was headed for the largest deficit since the end of World War II, even including the years of massive spending on the Vietnam war. At the end of November, the budget for the fiscal year that began in July showed a deficit of $18,110,000,-000, compared with red ink of $16,480,000,000 for the same period in fiscal 1971. Estimates of the deficit for the full fiscal year ran above $38,000,000,000.

Partly because of the budget deficit, which is always an inflationary force, prices were still rising at a rate of more than 5 per cent a year, although, despite the same deficit, unemployment was lodged at about 6 per cent.

The stronger pressures, however, came from overseas. The chronic deficits in the balance of payments had loosed a flood of dollars into the vaults of foreign central banks. The governments involved were urging the United States to devalue the dollar by increasing the price of gold. On Aug. 6, the Joint Economic Committee of Congress passed a resolution calling for the revaluation of the dollar. This had the effect of increasing the flight of dollars from the United States and adding to the speculative pressure on the dollar in foreign money markets. In one week after the resolution nearly $4,000,000,000 left the United States. About the same time, the British Government asked the United States to guarantee its holdings of $3,000,000,000 against devaluation, in effect requesting that the United States freeze that portion of its gold reserves.

The situation could not be tolerated for long. The President and his chief economic advisers met at Camp David, Md., on the weekend of Aug. 14, and the freeze was announced the next day.

The actions gave some stability to the domestic picture. A poll of consumers taken within days of the moves showed that 75 per cent of the households interviewed supported the plan; the dissenters said the action should have been taken earlier.

On Wall Street, where the uncertainties of the international situation had kept stock prices in a downtrend since early April, the response was immediate and explosive. On Aug. 16, the day after the President's shift of policy, the Dow-Jones Industrial Average scored its biggest one-day gain in history, climbing 32.93 points. The advance was 0.01 point more than that of Nov. 26, 1963, when the markets reopened following the assassination of President John F. Kennedy. Trading volume also set a record. On the New York Stock Exchange, 31,730,000 shares changed hands, the first time more than 30,000,000 shares had ever been traded in one day.

Overseas the reaction was very different. With the dollar cut loose from its ties to gold, the value of the dollar plunged in foreign money markets to its lowest levels since the exchange-rate system was begun. Countries that depend heavily on trade with the United States, especially West Germany and Japan, warned that the import surcharge might trigger an international trade war and that, because of it and the *de facto* devaluation of the dollar, a worldwide recession might result. For a while, in fact, it appeared that the Government of Japanese Premier Eisaku Sato, based on firm ties to the United States, might be forced from power.

The most dramatic domestic result of the wage-price freeze was shown in the automobile business. For one thing, car buyers seemed to feel—rightly, as it turned out—that car prices would rise when the freeze expired. For another, the proposal that the excise tax be repealed gave promise of cutting the cost of autos by an average of $200 each. (In fact,

when the excise tax was repealed in December, more than $650,000,000 was refunded to people who had bought cars since mid-August.) Auto sales boomed throughout the freeze period. In some ten-day spans, sales ran nearly half again as high as they had been in the same period a year earlier. In some cases, the increase was even higher, since General Motors had been on strike a year before. By the end of the year, the auto industry had sold 12,300,000 vehicles, including imports. As recently as August, the chairman of General Motors Corp. had forecast the year's sales at 11,100,000. Of the final total, 10,450,000 were domestic cars and trucks.

Retail sales also climbed sharply in other areas, especially the big-ticket durable items such as large appliances. Retail sales for the year were estimated at $397,500,000,000, up from $364,600,000,000 in 1970.

The confidence engendered by the wage-price freeze gave way in September and October to new uncertainties about the inflation-control program to follow. President Nixon's advisers worked on what came to be known as Phase 2 plans through the first part of the freeze. On Oct. 7, he announced that when the freeze expired on Nov. 13, it would be replaced by

Taxpayers read about the curbs announced on Aug. 15, outside the New York Stock Exchange.
UPI

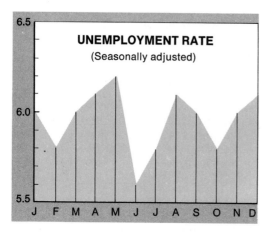

6.5

UNEMPLOYMENT RATE
(Seasonally adjusted)

6.0

5.5

J F M A M J J A S O N D

two units—the Pay Board and the Price Commission—which would be authorized to set guidelines and enforce the controls. Yet no guideposts had been set up by the time the freeze expired, and the uncertainties continued.

Internationally also confusion reigned. The United States and its major trading partners bargained over which side would institute the changes in currency-exchange rates that everybody agreed were needed. (President Nixon had said that the 10 per cent import surcharge would be lifted only when a new currency system had been arranged.) Neither side wanted to bear the onus for the changes, which were certain to work to the benefit of the United States but threatened political problems even there. Early in November, administration spokesmen, led by Treasury Secretary Connally, began to hint that the United States would be willing to increase the price of gold if other countries, in turn, would revalue their currencies upward in relation to the dollar. That reversal led to meetings in December that did realign the world's currency relationships.

The Pay Board and Price Commission began operations on Nov. 14. While they quickly came up with wage and price guidelines—5.5 per cent annual increases in wages, and 2.5 per cent boosts in prices—many hikes in both areas went beyond the guidelines and were approved. So the situation was still plagued by confusion and uncertainty.

In addition, there was great dissension within the Pay Board. The 5 members representing labor—5 others represented management, and 5 others the public—strongly opposed the board's decision not to allow payment of wage increases that had come due during the freeze. For a while, it looked as though the labor members would leave the board, but they stayed. In December, Congress passed a bill extending the

president's power to control wages and prices until Apr. 30, 1973. The bill included provisions for payment of retroactive raises, ending the controversy.

Also in December, Congress passed the tax-reduction bill requested by President Nixon in August. The bill provided for cuts of $7,990,-000,000 in calendar year 1972 and will reduce Federal government tax collections by $15,700,-000,000 over the next three years.

Meanwhile, during the first week of December, the Group of Ten met in Rome. There the representatives of the ten largest industrialized nations in the noncommunist world took preliminary steps to realign the world's currencies. On Dec. 17, they met again in Washington. Two days later they announced the first full-scale reshuffling of currency values since World War II. The United States agreed to increase the official price of gold from $35 an ounce to $38 an ounce, a devaluation of the dollar by 8.57 per cent. In turn, other countries increased the value of their currencies in relation to the dollar. In effect, the dollar was devaluated by about 12 per cent.

The end of the bargaining saw the Japanese yen, in effect, revalued upward by 16.88 per cent, considerably more than the Japanese Government had wanted. The West German mark moved up by 13.58 per cent, the Belgian franc by 11.57 per cent. The French franc and the British pound kept the same relation to gold as they had before, so their value in relation to the dollar went up 8.57 per cent, the same as the increase in the price of gold. The nations also agreed to allow currencies to fluctuate by 2.5 per cent up or down instead of by the former 1 per cent. In other words, currencies could now fluctuate within 5 per cent rather than the previous 2 per cent.

On the home front, the Pay Board and Price Commission spent the rest of the year considering applications for increases greater than the guidelines. Critics charged that the groups were not applying a firm lid to wages and prices. However, C. Jackson Grayson, Jr., former dean of the Business School of Southern Methodist University who led the Price Commission, and retired Federal Judge George Boldt, chairman of the Pay Board, insisted that their concern was with overall levels of prices and wages rather than with price tags on single items.

Supporters of the old "game plan" insisted that the President's change of signals was not necessary, that the economy was on its way to recovery, and that inflation was moderating without the drastic action taken by the administration. This was true, but the recovery was obviously proceeding too slowly, especially as a presidential election year loomed.

Economic statistics near year-end showed that recovery was in progress. Yet they also showed that official predictions made early in 1971—well before the new economic policy—had not nearly been achieved.

The gross national product, the total value of all goods and services produced in the country, rose during the year to about $1,052,-000,000,000, an increase just short of 8 per cent. Of that, some 5.2 per cent was the result of price increases, less than 3 per cent from real economic growth. In January, the Council of Economic Advisers had predicted a GNP of $1,065,000,000,000 and defended it against a multitude of critics throughout the early part of the year.

Personal income climbed to $858,000,000,-000 from $803,600,000,000, and disposable income (spendable money left after taxes) moved up to $742,000,000,000 from $687,800,000,-000. One reason for the slow rebound of the economy was the reluctance of consumers to spend much of their income. The personal-savings rate stayed about 8 per cent of disposable income through the year, more than half again above the long-term norm.

Unemployment, which had to be one of the main targets of the 1972 Nixon program—the President had often said that the chief reason he lost the 1960 election to John F. Kennedy was the high level of unemployment—refused to respond to either the old game plan or the new policy. For the year, unemployment averaged 5.9 per cent of the civilian work force, up from 4.9 per cent in 1970.

Another reason for the slow rebound was hesitation on the part of manufacturers to increase their inventories, to be expected if they thought business would improve. With the beginning of the new policies, inventory accumulation was stepped up; the total at year-end was nevertheless only $181,000,000,000, compared with $173,000,000,000 at the end of 1970.

Construction was one of the strongest areas of the economy. The total value of public and private construction rose to $109,000,000,000 from $94,300,000,000. On the other hand, capital spending by business, for new plant and equipment, edged up to only $81,000,000,-000 from $79,700,000,000.

On the positive side, interest rates slid lower most of the year. Although the decline reflected the slack business activity, and the unwillingness of businessmen to make new commitments, the cuts were hailed in Washington as a sign of a return to stability. The prime rate at the country's commercial banks, which began the year at 6¾ per cent, finished at 5¼ per cent. Some banks that abandoned the formal prime in favor of a floating "base" rate posted charges as low as 5 per cent at year-end.

The stock market went through a tumultuous year. The fear of a major collapse in the brokerage industry, which had been so real in 1970, apparently evaporated early in 1971 when Texas millionaire H. Ross Perot and a private group of investors agreed to take over F. I. du Pont Glore Forgan & Co., the last of the big firms threatened with liquidation. The Perot group invested $55,000,000 in the firm and might have to add still more in 1972.

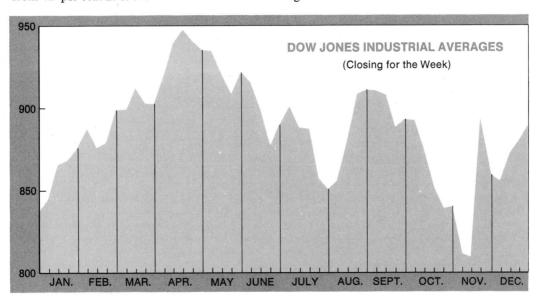

DOW JONES INDUSTRIAL AVERAGES
(Closing for the Week)

In the market itself, prices rallied through the early part of 1971, helped by what proved to be overoptimistic projections by the administration. On Apr. 23, the Dow-Jones Industrial Average reached its highest 1971 point, 947.79, representing an increase of nearly 320 points from the low registered at the bottom of its 1970 slide. At that point, though, the uncertainties of the economic picture, especially overseas, caught up with the brokers and their customers, and prices started a steady decline. That phase reached its lowest point on Aug. 13, just before President Nixon's historic speech, when the Dow Industrials fell to 839.59.

After the record-breaking rally on Aug. 16, prices started down again—this time it was the questioning about Phase 2 that was blamed—until late in November, when the Dow stood at 797.97. A rally that started on a normally quiet day, after Thanksgiving and before the weekend, anticipated the international currency agreements and kept the market on the upbeat for the rest of the year. As the year rang down the curtain, the Dow Industries stood at 890.20, a gain of 51.28 points for the year.

Thanks to a very active market early in the year—volume averaged more than 19,000,000 shares a day in April—the New York Stock Exchange set a new record for trading. According to preliminary statistics, 3,891,317,731 shares changed hands on the Big Board, up from 2,937,359,448 shares in 1970, the previous record-holder. On the American Stock Exchange, trading volume rose to 1,070,924,-002 shares from 843,116,260 shares.

The trend toward greater institutional activity in the market continued. The NYSE estimated that large-block volume—trades involving 10,000 shares or more, which are considered an indicator of activity of mutual funds, insurance companies and other large-scale investors—accounted for 18.5 per cent of total volume, compared with a 15.4 per cent share recorded by these various institutions in 1970.

There was also much activity in Wall Street aside from the stock market. On Apr. 5, commission charges on that part of large trades worth more than $500,000 were cut loose from the 179-year-old fixed-commission system. It was the first time that brokers had been free to negotiate any charges with their customers. In August, William McChesney Martin, Jr., former chairman of the Federal Reserve Board who had also been the first full-time president of the NYSE, in 1938, submitted a report calling for a reorganization of the exchange's government, to give the public a larger voice in its operation. The exchange appointed another committee to study Martin's recommendations, and, in a report submitted just before the end of the year, that group adopted several of Martin's suggestions.

Also late in December, the Securities and Exchange Commission asked Congress for new legislation giving it the authority to change rules made by the exchanges and to enforce those rules if it thinks that the exchanges are not doing their own job. Since the SEC was established in 1934, its policy has been to regulate the industry by working through the exchanges. Along with its request for new powers, the SEC submitted a 600-page report detailing "unsafe and unsound" practices of the exchanges and the brokers. The year 1972 promised to be one of great change in the way Wall Street runs its business.

The predictions that the new U.S. policy would slow business in other countries appeared to be accurate as the year wound down. West Germany and Japan, the two countries that depend most on trade with the United States, both were expected to show a downturn when the effects of inflation were eliminated.

In Germany, industrial output was down 1.5 per cent by the end of August and kept going down. Gross national product was up only 4.9 per cent, below the pace of other highly industrialized nations. After the currency realignment, the West German central bank cut its bank rate to 4 per cent from 4½ per cent, in an effort to stimulate business. In addition, the bank was considering selling off its enormous holdings in dollars, which had flowed into the country during the speculative raids on the dollar earlier in the year and in previous years.

In Japan, economic growth in 1971 came to between 5 and 6 per cent, a disappointing performance in the light of the 13 per cent and 14 per cent growth recorded so often in the 1960's.

In the United States and around the world, 1971 was a year of new directions. Steps taken by the United States and others during the year set many economies on a wholly new road and closed the books on the economic system that had allowed the Western world to emerge from the havoc of World War II.

In the new era, the accent will be on cooperation among nations, at least in adapting financial mechanisms to keep trade on an even keel. The results of the new policies were expected to become apparent fairly soon, and to govern the course of business, here and abroad, for decades to come.

PHILIP GREER
New York Financial Correspondent
The Washington Post

EDUCATION

American college and university campuses, after half a decade of internal unrest and student rebellion, in 1971 faced a different issue: the threat of unprecedented fiscal crisis. With few exceptions, the policies of confrontation had given way to gloom over budgets, tuition and jobs. Virtually no institution remained immune to the inroads of deficits, and a growing number saw the specter of bankruptcy. A few small institutions actually closed down.

The public schools also operated under austerity conditions. In Philadelphia, there was the possibility that the 1971–72 academic year would be curtailed by four weeks to save money. In many cities, including New York, supplies were so short that teachers asked pupils to provide some of their own materials. Chicago looked to an early Christmas school vacation in order to save salaries, maintenance and fuel.

The Roman Catholic parochial schools, faced not only by generally rising costs but by a shortage of priests and nuns, had to respond to salary pressures by the enlarged army of lay teachers. Parochial-school authorities, announcing that their schools were closing at the rate of one a day, were calling for Federal and state aid, but two Supreme Court rulings made it questionable whether such subsidies would be forthcoming.

However, the most compelling documentation of the fiscal crisis was provided by the Carnegie Commission on Higher Education. It disclosed in a detailed study that of all the U.S. colleges and universities, 540 were in financial difficulty and another 1,000 were heading for trouble. Harvard alone among the 8 Ivy League colleges, was still in the black, but only precariously so, despite its endowment of more than $1,000,000,000.

Inflation was the most serious cause of the crisis, and even though tuition had been rising at a rate of 7 per cent annually for some time, it could not keep pace with increasing costs. And at a time of an uncertain stock market, donations that normally close the gap had been declining for the first time in a decade, down by $20,000,000 to a total of $1,780,000,000.

After a period of maximum growth, the colleges and universities faced the recession "undercapitalized, overextended, and moving into increased areas of responsibility . . . without permanent financing," in the words of the Carnegie Commission. At the same time the Federal Government, in the process of winding down the war in Vietnam and fighting inflation at home, had reduced research spending, a major source of university income.

Emergency action was taken by many institutions, such as across-the-board budget reductions (Princeton), mandatory cutbacks by all departments (Michigan State University), three-year reductions in administrative and academic services (Columbia University) and long-term plans for major budget rollback (Stanford University). Many state-university systems were asked to hold the line on expansion and faculty-salary increases. California imposed a ban on out-of-state travel at public expense for all faculty members.

Enrollments. Total U.S. enrollments in 1971, public and private, from kindergarten through graduate school, stood at 60,240,000, thus registering an increase for the 27th consecutive year. In 1970 the total was 59,700,000, according to estimates by the U.S. Office of Education. With an increase of about one per cent, the rate of growth was, however, clearly continuing to slow down. The elementary schools (kindergarten through grade 8), which had shown their first decline by about 100,000 in 1970, were down from 36,970,000 to 36,700,000. This was a reflection of the lower birthrate of the 1960's. Of the total, 4,200,000 were enrolled in nonpublic schools, the overwhelming majority in Roman Catholic parochial schools.

The largest percentage increase, a 6 per cent gain, compared with only a 4.1 per cent rise a year earlier, was in higher-education enrollment. Apparently the trend toward easier access, particularly for less affluent students, has reversed an earlier trend toward stabilization.

In the secondary schools, grades 9 through 12, enrollment stood at 15,150,000, compared with 14,840,000 in 1970. Growth has been in the public sector, the total of 1,400,000 remaining virtually unchanged. This indicates that in the face of fiscal pressures, the parochial schools tend to eliminate elementary grades rather than cut back on secondary education.

Colleges and universities estimated that their total 1971 fall enrollment was 8,390,000, compared with 7,920,000 in 1970. The totals exclude about 600,000 undergraduates enrolled in occupational programs not eligible for credit toward degrees. Graduate enrollment was estimated at about 960,000, compared with 900,000 the year before. The proportion of students enrolled in private higher education continued to decline, with the total number at 2,160,000.

Teacher Supply. The total number of teachers was estimated at 2,981,000, approximately the same number as in 1970. Of the total slightly more than 600,000 were in higher education. The ratio of pupils per teachers stood at 22.3, the lowest on record, compared with 22.4 in 1970 and 25.8 in 1960. The teacher supply

"Shaky Position"

was ample for the second year, after a long period of scarcity. A combination of general economic recession and reduction in research grants made it difficult for Ph.D. graduates to find employment. The National Research Council reported that candidates who received doctoral degrees in the sciences in 1970 found fewer jobs than did those a year earlier. Nevertheless, unemployment rates for those with the highest academic degrees remained considerably lower than the national jobless rates for all kinds of workers.

Teachers' salaries had been rising at a rate of about 6 per cent a year during the 1960's, but during the 1970–71 school year the rate slowed to 5.5 per cent, and the result of the 1971 wage freeze was expected to bring that growth rate to an even lower level. The national average in 1971 was estimated at $9,200, compared with $9,030 the year before. In higher education, the average faculty salary was estimated at just below $13,000, compared with $11,745 in 1970. The annual bill for the teachers' salaries in the public elementary and secondary schools was estimated at about $30,-000,000,000.

Graduates, Degrees Granted. Approximately 3,100,000 students graduated from high school, the largest class in U.S. history. Approximately 77 per cent of the age group currently finish school and about 45 per cent (or more than half of the high-school graduates) enter degree programs in higher education.

In the 1971–72 academic year, the following numbers of degrees are expected to be conferred by American colleges and universities: 903,000 bachelor's and first-professional; 238,-000 master's; and 34,600 doctorates—all of them record numbers, comparing with 863,000, 224,000 and 32,000 respectively the year before. Since the beginning of the 1960's the number of bachelor's degrees conferred annually has doubled, and that of graduate degrees more than tripled.

However, for the first time, there was a relative decline, in 1971, in application to graduate schools, with the exception of law and medical schools. Approximately 100,000 applicants took the law-school entrance examinations in 1971, compared with 74,000 in 1970, in competition for only 35,000 places. About 26,000 students applied for 12,000 places in medical schools.

Expenditures and Costs. The total (fiscal 1970–71) expenditures for education at all levels, public and private, were estimated at $77,600,-000,000. They were expected to rise to $85,-100,000,000 in the 1971–72 fiscal year. The total education expenditure represented 8 per cent of the gross national product. Approximately $67,400,000,000 was for operating budgets, an increase of $3,000,000,000. Capital construction accounted for $10,200,000,000. The total expenditure for the nonpublic sector stood at $14,900,000,000. The amounts divided into $49,600,000,000 for elementary and secondary schools and $28,000,000,000 for higher education.

The Federal Government's role in the support of education continued to grow at all levels. The subsidies rose from $3,400,000,000 in 1965 to $10,100,000,000 in 1971. By the end of the fiscal year 1972, the total was expected to reach $11,400,000,000.

The per-pupil expenditure in the public schools in 1971 averaged $858, compared with $783 the year before, and more than twice what it was in 1960 but without adjustment for the decline in the dollar's purchasing power.

Parochial Schools. A national survey of the nation's Roman Catholic elementary and secondary schools ordered by the United States Office of Education showed that if the present decline in numbers continues, there may be 1,800 fewer schools in 1975. In the 1970–71 school year there were 11,351 schools; more than 400 closed. Student enrollment was estimated to have dropped by 435,000 in 1971, but consolidation of schools also accounted for some of the closings.

A study ordered by a special commission named by Gov. Nelson Rockefeller (R-N.Y.)

The 1970's one-room school (near Fort Lauderdale, Fla.) has wall-to-wall carpeting, a 16-foot-high ceiling, a library and science laboratories.

also indicated that parochial schools may be losing in enrollment for other than financial reasons: the reduction in the size of Catholic families, and what the study called "changing Catholic tastes" which motivates many Catholic families to move to the suburbs where they often send their children to the local public schools.

While supporters of Catholic education were urging increased public subsidies, two Supreme Court decisions made it dubious how such support could be offered without constitutional difficulties. In a Rhode Island case the court struck down a law that paid 250 teachers up to 15 per cent of their salaries for the teaching of secular subjects. The vote was 8 to 1, with Justice Byron R. White dissenting. In a Pennsylvania case, the court ruled that a law that set aside $20,000,000 annually from cigarette and racing revenues to nonpublic schools for teacher salaries, textbooks and instructional materials violated the Constitution. However, the court had earlier ruled as permissible the so-called textbook loan law to parochial schools which is in force in New York State.

Integration. The Supreme Court ruled in a North Carolina case that school districts are authorized to bus students to school for purposes of integration, provided the time spent on buses is not excessive. However, President Nixon ordered the Justice Department and the Department of Health, Education, and Welfare to hold busing plans to "the minimum required by law."

School Financing. In an important test case, the California State Supreme Court held on Aug. 30 that the "equal protection" clause of the Fourteenth Amendment is violated when children are offered unequal educational opportunities by virtue of their residence. At issue is the financing of the schools primarily through reliance on the property tax, with the result that wealthy communities are able to spend far more for the education of each pupil than less well-to-do districts, even when they make a greater effort.

The case involved the wealthy district of Beverly Hills and the less affluent one of Baldwin Park, but similar discrepancies can be found in districts across the country. While state equalization formulas usually try to reduce the gap, the California court found that a greater equalization effort is required. It ordered the lower courts to conduct hearings to determine whether more equitable arrangements were possible, with the implication that otherwise the state might have to take over responsibility for local school financing.

Educational Technology. The controversial technique of performance contracting entered a more advanced stage, when the school system of Gary, Ind., made a contract with an industrial producer of computerized instruction to take over a school on a trial basis. Under such contracts, teachers are either trained or hired especially for the operation. The contract with the district calls for a reduction in pay to the contracting firm for every pupil who fails to achieve according to the norm, particularly in reading and mathematics. Opponents of the approach charge that it encourages teachers to "teach for the tests" or actually to manipulate students and grades. But the Gary experiment was reported to have set up careful controls to prevent this. Initial reports, though generally encouraging, were termed by school officials to be too incomplete to allow any long-term commitments.

In another area of technology, *Sesame Street,* the daily one-hour television program for pre-school children, created and produced by the Children's Television Workshop, was generally proclaimed a proved success. In the fall of 1971, *Sesame Street* was joined by its successor program, *The Electric Company,* which aims at the elementary-school-age group and the teaching of reading. The daily half-hour show uses a regular company that includes noted television stars.

Reform Plans. In urban education, new efforts were being made to counteract the problems created by the schools' size. In New York City, for example, so-called "minischools" or schools-within-schools were set up in several of the large high schools.

In elementary schools, American adaptation of the British Open Schools, or informal classrooms, has been spreading. Under the plan, reminiscent of experimentation with progressive education, children are encouraged to explore individually or in small groups, while the teacher acts as a resource person or adviser. One version, known as the Open Corridor, groups several grades, ranging from preschool to fourth grade, around a corridor which serves as a joint meeting place in which children of different age groups may work together, sometimes under the supervision of a corridor teacher.

In higher education, the U.S. Office of Education has helped sponsor the so-called University without Walls, a cooperative venture among twenty existing colleges and universities. It permits a student to move from one campus to another or to get a substantial part of his credits in practical work in the field. The project is administered at Antioch College in Ohio.

In New York, the State University established the first "open university" at its newly created Empire State College in Saratoga.

Fashioned after the new British university, which also began operations in 1971, the aim is to service students with remote-control instruction via mailed lessons, television, tapes and books, reinforced by actual contact with instructors at occasional meetings in special learning centers.

Closely related to this experiment was the announcement by the New York State education authorities that students in selected fields would be able to get external or Regents degrees by passing examinations for work completed on their own.

The Ohio Plan. Gov. John J. Gilligan of Ohio proposed a plan that would require all students who enroll in the state's public colleges and universities to repay the state for the money it spends for their education, an estimated $3,000 for four years. Repayments would start whenever a graduate's annual income reached $7,000, beginning with a return of $50 a year. For a person with an income of over $100,000, the repayment would reach an annual maximum of $1,000. Payments would cease when the subsidy had been repaid, without interest. However, leaders of public higher education denounced the plan.

In a less drastic application, Yale University introduced a voluntary program which allows students to follow a similar deferred payment procedure to cover the year's substantial increases in tuition.

Negro Colleges. The United States' approximately 100 predominantly Negro colleges faced an even more serious crisis than the colleges at large. Few have any endowments and most of their students come from low-income backgrounds. Yet these institutions, mostly in the South, enroll 160,000 students, slightly over one third of all black students attending college in the United States. In 1971, the Ford Foundation announced that it would spend $100.000,-000 over the next 6 years to help upgrade the quality of at least 10 of the Negro colleges.

Child Development. Late in 1971, Congress passed a child-care and development bill. Intended to build on the experience with Project Head Start, the legislation provided for child–care centers for youngsters from age two, and free day care and other services for children from families with yearly incomes of less than $4,320. Calling the plan irresponsible and unworkable, President Richard Nixon vetoed it on Dec. 9.

See also Youth

FRED M. HECHINGER
Member of the Editorial Board
(Former Education Editor)
The New York Times

John Hurren

In Pontiac, Mich., where most U.S. school buses are made, resistance to school busing results in ten burnt-out buses at the city depot.

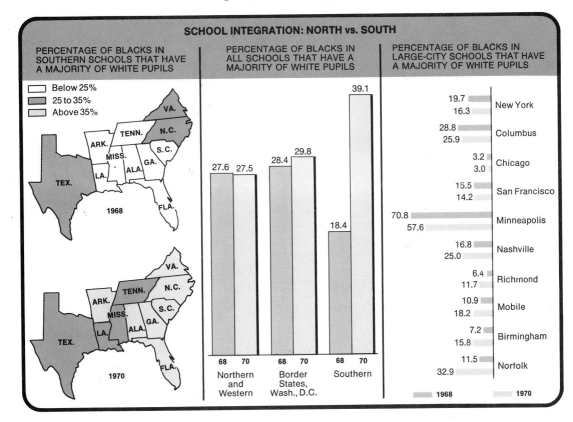

SCHOOL INTEGRATION: NORTH vs. SOUTH

PERCENTAGE OF BLACKS IN SOUTHERN SCHOOLS THAT HAVE A MAJORITY OF WHITE PUPILS

- Below 25%
- 25 to 35%
- Above 35%

1968

1970

TEX. ARK. LA. MISS. ALA. TENN. GA. VA. N.C. S.C. FLA.

PERCENTAGE OF BLACKS IN ALL SCHOOLS THAT HAVE A MAJORITY OF WHITE PUPILS

	68	70
Northern and Western	27.6	27.5
Border States, Wash., D.C.	28.4	29.8
Southern	18.4	39.1

PERCENTAGE OF BLACKS IN LARGE-CITY SCHOOLS THAT HAVE A MAJORITY OF WHITE PUPILS

	1968	1970
New York	19.7	16.3
Columbus	28.8	25.9
Chicago	3.2	3.0
San Francisco	15.5	14.2
Minneapolis	70.8	57.6
Nashville	16.8	25.0
Richmond	6.4	11.7
Mobile	10.9	18.2
Birmingham	7.2	15.8
Norfolk	11.5	32.9

The new 11.6-mile Sunshine Skyway, across Tampa Bay on Florida's Gulf Coast, seems to float between sea and sky. It is a twin-span toll bridge.

ENGINEERING, CIVIL

With construction the mainstay of civil engineering, many important projects were completed or under way in 1971, despite labor strife and the slowdown in the economy.

Bridges. In the spring, Florida's new twin-span toll bridge across Tampa Bay at St. Petersburg was opened to traffic after a 2-year delay. Work on the 2-lane, 11.6-mile Sunshine Skyway, originally scheduled to open in 1969, was delayed by discovery of a crack in one of the concrete piers supporting the structure. Dismantling and re-erecting part of the superstructure and repairing the pier added $3,000,000 to the original $22,000,000 cost of the project.

The Maryland State Roads Commission authorized $2,000,000 for the start of engineering work on a bridge to carry Interstate 695 across Baltimore's outer harbor. The 8,640-foot-long, continuous steel through-truss bridge is expected to cost about $51,300,000. The steel-truss main span will provide a 1,100-foot horizontal clearance for shipping. The decision to build the bridge rather than a tunnel across the outer harbor was made in 1970 when bids for a 2-lane, 1.2-mile tunnel were 50 per cent higher than the commission's estimate. Although much of the embankment for the tunnel approaches had been completed by the time plans were changed, the work will not be wasted. The bridge approaches will be built on the filled approaches for the tunnel.

Early in the year, construction started on Argentina's Zarate-Brazo Largo twin rail-highway bridges north of Buenos Aires. The project, consisting of 2 cable-stayed structures, is being built by an Italian-Argentine combine at a cost of $89,500,000. The identical bridges, across 2 branches of the Parana River 40 miles from the capital, will open up an isolated region between the Parana and the Uruguay River to the east. Each will be about 3 miles long with a 4-lane highway deck above a single rail track.

In Canada, plans were afoot to revive the proposed Northumberland Strait crossing between New Brunswick and Prince Edward Island. The new proposal, a project of the provincial government, calls for an 8.2-mile bridge-causeway. Private financing will be sought for the crossing, which is expected to cost $180,000,000. After spending some $16,000,000 on the original project, the Federal Government abandoned it in 1969 when the estimated cost rose to $300,000,000.

Italy's long-planned project for linking Sicily with the mainland over the Strait of Messina came a step nearer reality. Well-known American and European civil engineers have presented plans for the crossing to the Messina Bridge Group, a consortium of state enterprises and large private industrial concerns. Favored in 1971 was a 9,000-foot single-span suspension bridge, which would be more than twice the length of the Verrazano-Narrows Bridge, the present record holder. The challenging project, tentatively planned to carry 2 railroad tracks and a 6-lane highway, must be built in an area of intense earthquake activity and span the wild waters immortalized by Homer. Over 27,000 people now commute both ways by ferry between Sicily and the mainland.

In the more immediate future is another record-breaking suspension span. England will begin construction in 1972 on a bridge over the Humber River, 5 miles upstream from Hull on the northeast coast. Its 4,580-foot main span will also exceed the 4,260-foot span of the Verrazano-Narrows Bridge.

Canals. In May, President Nixon inaugurated construction of the Tennessee-Tombigbee Waterway project, planned as a 253-mile link between the Tennessee River at the lower end of the Ohio River basin and the Gulf of Mexico. First proposed in 1874 and finally authorized by Congress in 1946, the Corps of Engineers project will include a 106-mile-long canal in the Tombigbee River, a 45-mile lateral canal, and another canal cut through a high ridge that separates the two river basins. It will also involve construction of 10 locks and 5 dams. In September, however, work on the $386,600,000 project was temporarily halted by a Federal injunction ruling that the Corps of Engineers failed to comply with legal requirements for assessing the environmental aspects of the project.

Work on the $24,500,000 Venice (California) Redevelopment Project, delayed for two years by financial and legal problems, began in October. The canals, which were opened in 1905 in a former coastal resort section of Los Angeles, have been deteriorating in recent years. The restoration project will also provide 15 new side canals, arch bridges and street improvements, giving the area something of the look of its Italian counterpart.

Germany, which has some 2,100 miles of navigable rivers and canals that carry over

Canadian engineers are constructing the $130,000,000 Idiski project in India; it will include the nation's first double-curvature arch dam.

Canadian International Development Agency

110,000,000 tons of goods yearly, has under construction a new 30-mile stretch of canal. This section is part of the 105-mile-long Rhine-Main-Danube Canal, extending from the Main River near Bamberg to Regensburg on the Danube. When the $700,000,000 project is completed, it will link the Rhine and Danube and provide a shipping lane from the North Sea to the Baltic.

Engineering studies have been completed for another ambitious European canal project that will connect the Black, North and Baltic seas with a continuous inland waterway. By connecting the Danube, Oder and Elbe rivers, the 304-mile, Czechoslovakian-designed project will make it possible to travel from the Black Sea to either the North or Baltic seas. The project will cost $727,000,000 at current estimates. Hopes for connecting the 3 rivers by means of a 3-branch canal system go back to the seventeenth century. However, the international nature of the project—it will involve Czechoslovakian, Austrian, Polish and German territory —has kept them from being realized until now.

Dams. Plans for the construction of several major hydroelectric dams in the Pacific Northwest were temporarily halted in 1971 by the opposition of conservationists and the governors of Oregon, Washington and Idaho. They claim that danger to habitats supporting a great variety of wildlife will outweigh the power and irrigation benefits of the projects. At stake are Mountain Sheep and Pleasant Valley dams in the Hell's Canyon stretch of the Snake River, and the Lower Teton Project on a tributary of the Snake.

Another kind of problem is slowing work on the U.S. Bureau of Reclamation's Pueblo Dam in southern Colorado. The foundation for the dam, a 2-mile-long multipurpose phase of the $259,000,000 Fryingpan-Arkansas Project, was completed late in 1971, but award of the main construction contract has been delayed by reductions in the Federal budget.

Canadian dam builders are putting their expertise to work in various parts of the world. An important project well under way is India's $130,000,000 Idiski development. It involves construction of a 550-foot-high arch dam with a crest length of 1,100 feet. It will be the nation's first double-curvature arch dam. The project also includes a second dam, Cheruthoni, which will be a more conventional gravity structure 445 feet high. In Greece, the group of consultants and builders, together with Spanish and Portuguese consultants, is making a major study of the hydroelectric potential of several entire river basins for the government-owned Public Power Corporation. The studies may ultimately lead to the construction of 28 dams in Greece.

Tunnels. Work on the District of Columbia's portion of the long-planned 99-mile regional rail transit network, to relieve traffic congestion in the national capital area, started in February with a massive underpinning project. The first phase of the underpinning—a means of transferring building loads from existing foundations to piles extending to rock in order to prevent cave-ins during tunneling—consisted of placing over 31,000 feet of jack piling under 4 major structures along a 3,500-foot section of the planned subway route.

Another impressive and difficult subway project is under way in Amsterdam, the Netherlands, where contractors are excavating underneath city streets and canals to complete the first 11-mile section of what will ultimately be a 55-mile system. Completion of the first section, which will connect with the new satellite city of Bijlmermeer, east of Amsterdam, is planned for 1977. The cost will be $113,-000; and the cost of the entire network, involving 5 other lines, will be over $550,000,000. The work in Amsterdam is complicated by its canals and a water table only 5 feet below grade. The tunnel is being built about 38 feet below groundwater level.

In Hawaii, work has started on the 4,400-foot Trans Koolau just north of Honolulu. The first phase of the $96,000,000 project, which will carry Interstate H-3 through the rugged Koolau Range, is a pilot bore. Each of the 2 horseshoe-shaped tunnels will be 47 feet wide and will have 3 lanes of traffic. The 13- by 18-foot pilot tunnel will test construction conditions in the extremely difficult mountain terrain consisting of volcanic layers of hard basalt that absorb rains to a great depth.

Methods of tunneling through mountains with microwaves and high-pressure water jets are being studied by Japanese engineers at the Railroad Technical Research Institute in Tokyo. The new techniques are considered necessary to build roadbeds for Japan's high-speed trains, which require flat roadbeds. Conventional methods of tunneling with dynamite or boring machines are not satisfactory there because of irregular geological structures. Under microwave treatment, rock molecules or water particles in the rock collide, causing an increase of heat that makes the rock crack. The water method uses a jet that shoots water at more than 3,200 feet per second. Officials expect to complete a practical prototype machine in a few years.

MARY E. JESSUP
Former News Editor, *Civil Engineering*

Eroded land with all plant life killed off is the result of noxious fumes and fluid wastes given off by copper smelter at Copper Hill, Tenn., just outside Great Smoky Mountains Park.

Rolland R. Swain

ENVIRONMENT

In 1971 citizens began to face up to the high costs, in money and personal sacrifice, of cleaning up the environment. It was a year in which huge construction projects and weapons tests, which not long before would have received little public notice, were delayed or halted entirely to prevent environmental damage. Moreover, in 1971 there were constant reminders that even as governments debate on how to clean up pollution, environmental degradation worsens with the everyday functioning of civilization.

In the United States, business and industry critics became increasingly vocal about legislation passed in the 1970 flush of environmental enthusiasm. Auto manufacturers began complaining four years early that they could not meet the exhaust-pollution levels set for 1975 models under the provisions of the 1970 Clean Air Act. Car makers in Japan, Germany and other countries selling in the U.S. import market were voicing the same concerns.

The U.S. Council on Environmental Quality, in its second annual report, estimated that it would cost $105,000,000,000 by 1976 to meet existing U.S. pollution-control standards.

It is not only money. Solutions to some pollution problems call for changes in the way people live, their habits and schedules. The Environmental Protection Agency, in setting up national air-pollution standards, said that in addition to exhaust controls, cars might have to be banned at certain hours. Also, commuters' schedules might have to be staggered to reduce the traffic load. Despite cost and inconvenience, public support for cleaning up pollution appeared to remain high. U.S. polls on political issues continually ranked the environment among the top concerns of voters. Citizens became increasingly vocal about environmental issues in Italy, Japan and elsewhere.

Environmentalists in industrialized nations trying to keep this public support warm never had far to go to demonstrate the magnitude of the problem. Anyone breathing the air in. Los Angeles, New York or Tokyo—where Japanese cars clogging the streets belch out 700,000 tons of carbon monoxide each year—does not have to be told it may be harming his health.

Venice came in 1971 to be a symbol of the tragic ravages of pollution. A short trip on the city's canals shows all too clearly what two decades of unbridled industrial development can do to artistic and architectural beauty that had endured for centuries. Sulfur dioxide in the air converts to sulfuric acid when combined with rain. It is eating away the carving on cathedrals and palaces and despoiling statues. The canals, receptacles for uncontrolled dumping of the city's own sewage, have become so polluted that they sometimes smell foul. Although efforts at restoration have begun, some of the damage appears to be irreversible.

Ocean-minded tourists found in 1971 that water pollution had closed some beaches elsewhere in Italy; and pollution came to be a major concern at such famous strands as the French Riviera, Puerto Rico and Hawaii's Waikiki Beach. The oceans, long considered a limitless resource by man, are as subject to contamination as the rest of the earth's waters. With this realization efforts have accelerated to control dumping into the oceans of a disturbing array of pollutants.

Concern about ocean dumping was dramatized by the Dutch ship *Stella Maris*. She loaded up chemical wastes and headed into the North Sea with 600 tons of chlorinated hydrocarbons, the base for pesticides such as DDT, aboard. But protests from Norway and Sweden kept her from dumping the chemical near their shores; and Britain, Ireland and Iceland sent out armed ships to prevent any dumping in nearby waters. The *Stella Maris* eventually was forced to return home with her cargo, which was stored temporarily on land.

The British were acting under a new law empowering the Government to act against ships that pose a pollution threat, even if the ships are in international waters. Norway, Sweden and Denmark also have enacted laws to control ocean dumping. And it appeared likely that the U.S. Congress would follow suit sometime in 1972.

Tighter controls on ocean dumping could lead to critical problems of waste disposal for coastal cities, which have grown used to dumping various kinds of wastes. In New York, years of dumping sludge from industrial plants and from municipal water-treatment plants have left a "dead sea" area at the dumping ground, where almost all marine life has been killed. Tokyo dumps 55 per cent of its human waste untreated into the sea and open canals. Although Tokyo could greatly improve treatment of its sewage, disposal of sludge on land would be difficult because of lack of space. New York too, already running out of land areas to dispose of its regular trash and garbage, will find its problems compounded if it is forced to dispose of the sludge on land as well. Ocean dumping is expected to be a major topic of interest at the United Nations Conference on the Human Environment, scheduled to be held in Stockholm in June 1972.

The chairman of the conference, Canadian Maurice Strong, has continued to try to allay the fears of undeveloped nations about environmental controls. Faced with dreadful poverty and the need for economic development, these nations are anxious not to do anything that would scare industry away. Strong has seemed to be making some headway in convincing these initially skeptical underdeveloped countries that environmental degradation is a problem that eventually would affect them as well as the industrialized nations.

In the United States, 1971 was the year when environmental protection clearly joined the accepted concepts. Politicians received the message. Arguments that were once keys to the Federal treasury and government approval—national security, technological progress, economic needs—ran up against the counter environmental arguments. Congress cut off funds for the supersonic transport plane. An atomic-weapons test on Amchitka Island off Alaska was delayed and its future put in doubt. The Alaska oil pipeline was delayed for another full year. The Cross-Florida Barge Canal, which threatened a beautiful scenic river, was abandoned.

Environmentalists counted the defeat of the SST as a great symbolic victory, a halt in the momentum of technological advance for its own sake. Groups like the Sierra Club, Friends of the Earth and ad hoc committees against the plane had long contended that a full fleet of commercial SST's flying at high altitudes would seriously pollute the upper atmosphere and produce severe effects from sonic booms. In 1971, these concerns joined with the feeling of many ordinary citizens that government funds should not be spent merely to reduce flying time by a few hours for a small, affluent group of international travelers.

There has been discussion in the United States of banning all SST's from American airports. Japanese officials, in a June meeting with top American pollution-control officials in Washington, said that if the Americans did ban the SST from its airports, Japan would be likely to follow suit. "I think Japan will respect the U.S. position," said Sadanori Yamanaka, Japanese minister in charge of environmental-pollution countermeasures. Yamanaka also discussed the upcoming UN conference and the need for advances in pollution-monitoring equipment, an area in which the Japanese electronics industry is doing considerable research.

American environmental groups also acted effectively through court action against projects they believed would result in severe damage. They found a useful tool in the National Environmental Policy Act of 1969. It provides that all Federal agencies must, before taking any action, consider as fully as possible its

Confronted with numerous brands of cleaning agents, housewives have the problem of choosing the one that will be the most effective and yet be the least water polluting.

Chester Higgins

Intolerable noise: Los Angeles paid over $200,000,000 for some 2,000 new homes near airport that had to be abandoned because of jet roar.

potential impact on the environment. By charging failure to fulfill this duty, environmental lawyers delayed not only the Alaska pipeline but a wide range of dams, canals and highways.

The same law was used to delay a nuclear-weapons test on the Alaskan offshore island of Amchitka. Not only American environmentalists, but the Japanese and Canadian governments had protested that they feared the five-megation underground test would not be safe. Questions were raised about the effects on wildlife and humans of radiation escaping from the underground test, as well as the possibility that the blast would cause tidal waves. The Amchitka test eventually was detonated despite the objections.

Another Alaska project, a proposed pipeline to bring oil from the rich North Slope fields across the state to a port on the southern end, continued to be a focus of environmental controversy. Court action by environmentalists delayed the project through all of 1971, although at year's end it appeared that the project might eventually proceed with stricter environmental controls incorporated into the design. This possibility did not calm the fears of conservationists: the possibility of a pipeline break and oil spill on the frozen tundra and their adverse effects on wildlife. They also worried about oil spills at sea from the increased tanker traffic that would carry the oil from the port of Valdez to California.

An alternative possibility that continued to be discussed in 1971 was a route going from the North Slope oil fields through Canada and ending up in the American Midwest. This route was generally considered safer from an environmental viewpoint. But U.S. officials contended that it would be too costly and that the oil was needed on the West Coast, not in the Midwest. The oil industry also ran into problems elsewhere. California citizens continued to oppose further offshore drilling near Santa Barbara, site of a massive oil spill in 1969. Political pressure eventually became so great on Congress and the White House that further drilling was halted by the Federal Government. Maine further delayed and thus probably killed proposals to put large oil-tanker-unloading facilities along its beautiful coast line. Little Delaware, despite heavy lobbying from industry and the U.S. Commerce Department, passed landmark legislation that bans all oil refineries, steel mills and other heavy industry from its coastline.

The new U.S. Environmental Protection Agency got down to serious work in 1971. It has responsibility for regulating air and water pollution, solid-waste disposal, pesticides, radiation and noise, previously scattered throughout the Federal Government. Named to head the agency was William D. Ruckelshaus, a Republican lawyer from Indiana who had been an assistant U.S. attorney general. Ruckelshaus moved to establish a tough image by suing industries and cities illegally discharging pollutants into streams. "When you first get there, you've got to show people you mean business," said a Ruckelshaus aide.

It was not long before American business decided that it did not like the new look in Federal pollution-control enforcement after years of weak legislation, nonenforcement, negotiation and delay. With a presidential campaign year approaching, potential Republican contributors were soon letting the White House know that they thought EPA was being unreasonable. The friends of business in the administration pressed the argument that in a faltering economy, Ruckelshaus was taking too little account of the cost of pollution cleanup. Despite the pressure, EPA continued to sue polluters. One of its strengths was the political popularity of the pollution-control program.

It also fell to the new agency to implement a tough piece of legislation, a legacy from the 1970 public outcry about the environment, the Clean Air Act. In addition to imposing tough exhaust controls that affect all domestic and foreign autos sold in the United States, the law set up a tight system of controls for air pollution from smokestacks. EPA set standards and put the machinery in motion for achievement of the standards by 1975, as called for in the law.

Congress worked to enact a new, tougher water-pollution law. Estimates of the Federal funds needed to clean up municipal water pollution alone ran as high as $20,000,000,000 to $30,000,000,000 by 1976.

As always, Ralph Nader was there to point up deficiencies in the laws and their enforcement. Following his 1970 report on the air-pollution program, he issued a 1971 document calling water-pollution regulation totally inadequate. Nader also visited Japan and aroused considerable interest there, charging that Japan's pollution-control laws were even worse than those of the United States.

For the consumer, 1971 turned out to be a confusing year on environmental issues. One of the most direct ways that consumers had been able to show concern about the environment was to avoid buying detergents that include phosphates. They contribute to eutrophication, a speedup of vegetation growth that made such bodies of water as Lake Erie truly dead seas. Late in the year the Federal Government, whose own water-pollution specialists have long talked against phosphate detergents, announced that phosphate substitutes were considered dangerous to health and urged householders to return to phosphate detergents. The

Government made none of the expected qualifications of that stand, such as urging that phosphate content be lower in problem areas such as the Great Lakes. Many consumers were left bewildered and angry at the turnaround.

Continuing through 1971 was the controversy over the safety of pesticides, especially DDT. EPA started to cancel all remaining uses of the pesticides in the United States (chiefly for cotton and certain food crops). The agency also initiated the lengthy legal proceedings necessary to cancel use of the herbicide 2-4-5-T, which some scientists charge with causing birth defects through the defoliation program in Vietnam. Caution against a total ban on DDT was expressed, however, by international malaria-control experts. They warned that failure to control malaria-carrying mosquitoes would have consequences more serious than the environmental effects of DDT. What most alarms environmentalists about DDT is its persistence: it is passed from plants to small animals that eat foliage and then on to larger predators that eat smaller animals.

A new chemical hazard was called to world attention in 1971: polychlorinated biphenyls or PCB's. Similar in character to DDT, it is used in many industrial processes and is common in the environment. It has been shown to have serious effects on humans in isolated cases. Thousands of chickens and turkeys were ordered destroyed in the United States because it was discovered they had absorbed high levels of PCB through contaminated feed. A toxic substance previously cited as a hazard—mercury—led in 1971 to a stern warning against swordfish consumption in the United States. The U.S. Food and Drug Administration said that the levels of mercury being found in swordfish were dangerously high.

Although the world's citizens grew more aware of environmental dangers, the issue of whether strict environmental restrictions would hamper economic growth and health remained unresolved. In the more developed nations, some workers feared losing their jobs if the costs of pollution control proved too great for their employers. Governments were still trying to balance the cry for cleanup against the fear of high costs. Is public determination strong enough to support fully the stern stance against major economic interests that is needed, and will consumers be willing to pay the increased costs and accommodate themselves to the necessities of environmental protection?

JERRY C. EDGERTON
Environmental Reporter, Washington Bureau
McGraw-Hill Publications

EUROPEAN ECONOMIC COMMUNITY

After being vetoed twice by President Charles de Gaulle of France in the 1960's, Britain's application for membership in the European Economic Community (Common Market) was approved in 1971. Thus the way was cleared for enlarging the trading area into potentially the most powerful in the civilized world. Although significant steps were taken to boost Common Market membership from six to ten members (adding Britain, Ireland, Norway and Denmark), major problems touching the heart of the gigantic customs union arose to haunt such promoters of European unity as France's Jean Monnet, the "Father of United Europe."

Monnet and others sharing his vision had worked since the postwar years to knit the oft-warring Western European states together so tightly economically and politically that one doing battle with another would become as absurd as it would be technically impossible.

These major developments would certainly make the year 1971 second in historical import for the Common Market only to the 1950's when early dreams of European unity became a reality in the Treaty of Rome (creating the EEC) and the European Coal and Steel Community:

President Georges Pompidou of France and Prime Minister Edward Heath of Britain met in Paris May 20–21 in what proved to be a climactic session for the Common Market. The conference came a little more than six months after the death of De Gaulle, who had effectively barred British membership for reasons which were wearing thin with the passage of time and major economic and political evolution.

De Gaulle had written off Britain scornfully as an island that geographically and otherwise could never join the Continent. Special ties with the British Commonwealth and with the other main element in the "Anglo-Saxon" world, the United States, would make Britain a "Trojan horse" for these interests if the Common Market Six (France, West Germany, Italy, Belgium, Holland and Luxembourg) were ever unwise enough to let the bars down for the British. Besides, former Prime Minister Harold Macmillan and President John F. Kennedy had signed a nuclear pact that effectively divorced Britain from any independent Continent defense structure.

Some important factors had changed by the time Heath sat down in the Elysée palace with Pompidou in May 1971. The British Commonwealth had become less and less of a reality economically and politically, and Britain found itself more and more isolated from the remains of its once worldwide empire. A traditional marketplace, financial center and exporting nation, Britain needed to find outlets to replace the Commonwealth. Europe was obviously the answer. Britain's special relationship with the United States also seemed to have less meaning, beyond language ties, as Britain faded as a world power and the United States came to deal more directly with the Soviet Union and revised its attitude toward Communist China.

Britain could hope to recapture some of its historic influence in international affairs only through closer association with its neighbors on the Continent. Thus the question that De Gaulle often posed to Britain, "Are you really prepared to enter Europe?" with the changes in outlook that it implied, seemed to have been answered positively and convincingly for Pompidou.

The summit in Paris was a success. With France's assent, the other Common Market members hailed the prospect of British entry, which they themselves had generally backed during the days of De Gaulle snubs. Now the ball was back in the British court, where paradoxically resistance to British membership suddenly flared.

First, fears were expressed by British farmers that they would no longer receive government agricultural subsidies once Britain was in the Common Market. Prices for food products would certainly rise with British entry; and British consumers became alarmed. Outcries came from faraway New Zealand; it feared that Britain would no longer be able to accept tariff-free New Zealand dairy products.

Sensing an effective political issue, Labor Party leader Harold Wilson (as prime minister he had sought British entry into the Common Market) now dug in his heels. Prince Philip told an audience in Scotland that European farming methods were a mess and that the British would find that out to their sorrow if they entered the Common Market. Buckingham Palace succeeded in calming the storm when it said that the Queen's husband was talking about past history and not taking a stand on entry.

A month after the crucial Heath-Pompidou meeting, Common Market foreign ministers and Britain's chief negotiator, Geoffrey Rippon, met in Luxembourg to hammer out important technical details, now that political objections from the Six had been wiped away. Two major sticking points remained: the proportion of the Common Market budget Britain would pay, and the question of New Zealand's vital exports to Britain.

Press conference follows agreement on British entry; wearing glasses are Britain's Geoffrey Rippon and French Foreign Minister Maurice Schumann.

Britain entered negotiations offering to pay no more than 3 per cent of the budget. The Common Market was insisting on 15–20 per cent British participation. Britain had wanted a solid long-term transitional period for New Zealand, giving its Commonwealth partner time to diversify away from dairy products and to find other markets. The Common Market was reluctant to grant special privileges to a distant nonmember country.

As the Luxembourg talks droned on through the night—a tradition with tough Common Market discussions—a compromise developed. The French agreed to a British demand that New Zealand dairy-product exports to Britain remain at 71 per cent of their current level after a five-year period. Britain in turn agreed to raise its contribution to the Common Market budget to 8.6 per cent in 1973; it would rise to 18.9 per cent in 1978.

It was 5:30 A.M. on June 23, and champagne was ordered to celebrate the accord. "It's a historic day for Europe," a worn-out but smiling Rippon told newsmen. French Foreign Minister Maurice Schumann said he thought he could "very well stand up and justify myself" to De Gaulle had the General been present. New Zealand's Deputy Prime Minister,

John Marshall, waiting in the wings at Luxembourg where he had fought for his country's interests, said, "We have avoided disaster."

The next day in Paris, the French Government took the lion's share of the credit for easing British entry. President Georges Pompidou, conveniently making no mention of De Gaulle's vetoes, said the Luxembourg talks "showed that France by its initiatives constantly contributed positively to the negotiations" on British entry. "It is an important date in our history and in the history of Europe itself," Pompidou intoned. He added, "The completion [of the negotiation] depended on the will of Britain to turn toward Europe and to accept the disciplines of the European Community." Cabinet spokesman Leo Hamon added a sentimental note when he said that France, in accepting a modification in the Common Market rules regarding New Zealand's exports to Britain "took into account as much the close ties . . . which link Britain and New Zealand as the recollection and gratitude it retains for the children of those who fought on French soil alongside its children during two world wars."

But the heady joy of the moment was tempered with shouts of "sellout" from across the

Channel. During the following weeks there were moments when it appeared that Britain's struggle to enter the Common Market would be lost on home ground. All through the summer the debate raged. When Heath finally brought the issue to a showdown in Parliament, Wilson and other antimarketeers went down resoundingly. The Commons approved Heath's entry plans 356–244; and the Lords, 451–58.

Along with Britain, the Republic of Ireland, Denmark and Norway were expected to become members of the Common Market, although final action would not be completed until the summer of 1972. Signatures of the three countries to the accession treaty must be approved by referendums—Ireland in March or April, Denmark in June, and Norway in June or September.

Meeting in Bracciano, Italy, in November, the ten countries decided on the principle of a summit meeting to launch the enlarged European Community formally late in 1972. The overall purpose of the session would be to build a solid united front for dealing with the United States—and the problem seemed acute.

Against the euphoric European unity, a dash of cold water came from across the Atlantic in August. President Richard M. Nixon decreed measures to protect the sick U.S. dollar and to reverse a disastrous balance-of-payments deficit. Even earlier, the weakness of the dollar had begun to disturb the Common Market area. West Germany, swamped with dollars from speculators sensing a mark revaluation, finally took off some of the pressure by deciding to float the mark. It floated as high as about 8 per cent, throwing parities with other Common Market currencies seriously out of gear.

With the August measures announced by Nixon, including a 10 per cent surtax on exports entering the United States, France created a two-tier market for the franc—one a commercial exchange rate to be used for business transactions, which remained at the old parity, and the other a financial rate, which floated slightly above the old parity with the dollar.

With the two principal currencies of the Common Market moving in complex and uncertain directions, common prices for products in the Common Market—one of its basic precepts particularly in the agricultural field—became almost chaotic. France went firmly on record for a return to fixed parities, against the West German action, and called for a general realignment of Western currencies. Everyone in the Common Market saw the need for a united stand against what was considered unfair, if not illegal, action by the United States in unilaterally imposing the surcharge and re-

fusing to devalue the dollar in terms of gold.

There was no sign of real unity in Common Market ranks, except for a unanimous action by finance ministers, meeting in Versailles in November, to insist that the United States make clear its intentions, and hope that the dollar would be devalued.

It appeared to all observers that until and unless the West's monetary system is put in order that the Common Market will be seriously hampered, not only as a six-nation group but in the future as its ranks swell to ten. Nevertheless, as Monnet said in November, the movement toward European unity now seemed irreversible.

Aldo Moro, Italian foreign minister and at the time chairman of the Common Market Council of Ministers, gave the Common Market consultative assembly meeting in Strasbourg, France, a sweeping view of what the enlarged community would mean. He noted that the community would include more than 250,000,000 people. Its gross national product would be at least $632,000,000,000. In 1969 the 10 countries imported more than $102,000,000,000 worth of goods and exported about $100,000,000,000 in products. This, he said, represented triple the U.S. trade, and was 10 times higher than that of the Soviet Union.

The ten nations' productive capacity and their economic potential represent "a power comparable to the greatest industrialized ensembles of the world," Moro said. He noted that the enlarged community would be linked through a number of national and international accords with a long list of states in the Mediterranean basin and in Africa. He called for a "united approach" in dealing with these nations.

At the same time, Moro stressed "our destiny is linked with that of a great friendly nation—the United States." He said it was particularly important to realize "a climate of comprehension and mutual cooperation" with the United States.

The Common Market's relations with its immediate neighbors in Eastern and Western Europe and with underdeveloped countries in the rest of the world occupied officials in 1971 and would be of increasing concern in the years ahead. The breakup of the European Free Trade Association (EFTA), which Britain had formed in defense after it had been excluded from the Common Market, would have to forge new relations with the enlarged Common Market. Other EFTA nations may eventually join. Still others, particularly Eastern European communist regimes such as Yugoslavia and Rumania, were seeking special accords short of membership.

Farmers bring their cattle to a protest, at the Community's Council of Ministers in Brussels, against plans for basic reforms that would reduce the number of people who farm for a living. Reform advocates want to lower the vast sums—almost $1,000,000,000 in 1970 for dairy products alone—required of the Community for agricultural support.

The six Common Market nations in 1971 took the lead with a new form of aid through trade for 91 less developed nations. Tariff rates were reduced to boost the exports of the countries—in other words, the external tariff wall around the Common Market area was lifted a little.

Education ministers from the six Common Market countries made a landmark decision late in the year, to create a European University Institute in Florence, Italy. As a beginning, some 250 students would be enrolled, starting in the fall of 1973. This step, is was hoped, would help to spur a provision of the Rome Treaty that provides that university degrees in the various member countries are to be recognized generally and that members of the liberal professions may practice throughout the Common Market area.

At the end of a year filled with dramatic developments for the future of the Common Market, what appeared to lie ahead, particularly in the political sphere?

Promoters of a United States of Europe hope to see the day when all the nations of the old Continent will be members of a federation similar to that of the United States of America. This implies a virtual wiping out of frontiers, a common foreign policy, an economic and monetary union with a common currency, a common defense program, and even one day perhaps a common flag. To these dreams, most European statesmen answer "not so fast," without completely rejecting them.

Some, particularly the French, see such intimate unity as a potential disaster. The various nations of Europe, they feel, must maintain their identities—flags, uniforms, language— otherwise Europeans will be sapped of the strength and purpose that made them worthy members of the world community. France— De Gaulle and now Pompidou—sees the next logical step as a "confederation" of European nations, linked certainly in major aspects of their existence, but still maintaining their own particularisms.

British membership is expected to "reshuffle the cards" as far as leadership of the Common Market is concerned. Just how is not yet clear. Economically speaking, West Germany is the strongest of the current six members. Its political influence may grow as it shows signs of doing with Chancellor Willy Brandt's eastern policy. His initiatives in this field are troubling to some of his neighbors who feel there should be more of a team effort in seeking a *détente* with the U.S.S.R.

The prospect of a resurgent Germany recalls the disastrous days of the three past generations. To some of Germany's partners in the Common Market, the entry of Britain is to be particularly welcomed because it may provide an effective counterweight to Germany. France, especially, sees British entry in this light.

Less than a month after final parliamentary approval of British entry, France moved to reawaken the entente cordiale between Paris and London. A visit to London by French Foreign Minister Schumann was concluded with agreement on new measures to promote cooperation on a business, scientific and artistic level. Schumann and his British colleague, Sir Alec Douglas-Home, also gave a boost to the long-delayed proposal of an English Channel tunnel. Capping Schumann's visit, it was announced that Queen Elizabeth and Prince Philip would make an official visit to France in May 1972.

DAVID M. MASON
Correspondent, Paris Bureau
The Associated Press

FINLAND

In early 1971 Finland suffered one of the worst strikes in its history, as seventy thousand metalworkers walked off the job. President Urho Kekkonen had attempted to avert the strike by presenting a plan to balance prices and wages; but thanks to communist opposition it failed of adoption. After seven weeks, however, an agreement was reached, with slightly better terms for the workers than those in the President's plan. Other strikes added to the general economic malaise. A debate in Parliament on prices brought matters to a head when Prime Minister

An inviting new library in Kuopio illustrates the Finnish flair for combining respect for learning with architectural modernity.

UPI

FINLAND

Area: 130,120 sq. mi.
Population: 4,700,000
Capital: Helsinki
Government: Urho K. Kekkonen, president—1956; Teuvo Aura, premier—1971
Gross National Product: $10,300,000,000
Foreign trade: exports, $2,306,000,000; imports, $2,636,000,000
Armed forces: 39,500

Ahti Karjalainen called for the support of all the parties represented in the government coalition. The Communists refused to go along, and on Mar. 17 Dr. Karjalainen and his Cabinet resigned. After several days of negotiations, it was announced that Dr. Karjalainen would form a new Cabinet, with the same ministers except that three portfolios passed from Communists to Social Democrats.

The reconstructed Karjalainen Cabinet proved to be short-lived. It resigned on Oct. 29 because it could not settle a three-week-old dispute over prices for agricultural products. President Kekkonen had set an Oct. 29 deadline for settlement. He also had threatened to dissolve Parliament and call new elections for Jan. 2–3, 1972, if no agreement were forthcoming. After the resignations of Oct. 29, the President appointed Teuvo Aura, mayor of Helsinki, head of a caretaker Cabinet to stay in office until a new Parliament was elected.

Finland, an associate member of EFTA, made known that it does not wish membership in the European Economic Community, largely because such membership might place its neutrality in jeopardy. Expressed officially, Finland said that it wanted continued duty-free trade with EFTA countries and, concurrently, the ability to send duty-free exports to the EEC countries.

On Sept. 10 the Finnish Government surprised world statesmen by proposing a "package settlement" with both East and West Germany. Under it, Finland would recognize both governments; Finnish neutrality would be recognized by both Germanys; nonaggression pacts would be negotiated with both Germanys; and payment of some sort would be made for the destruction caused by German troops in Finland during World War II.

The Finnish press in June celebrated its 200th anniversary, with receptions and exhibitions in Helsinki and a meeting there of the International Press Institute. The first Finnish newspaper was published in Turku (Abo) in 1771.

ERIK J. FRIIS
Editor, The American-Scandinavian Review

FOREIGN AID

The United States, reacting to the high cost and frustrations of the Vietnam war, showed definite signs in 1971 of turning away from foreign aid for the first time in 25 years. The future of the multibillion-dollar program of military and economic assistance seemed dimmer than at any time since the end of World War II.

The disenchantment came at a time when President Nixon announced a New Economic Policy with America-first overtones to stem an alarming deficit in the U.S. balance of payments. The Senate stunned the nation and the world by refusing to authorize foreign-aid spending for the first time since the Marshall Plan began in 1948. A combination of conservative and liberal forces jeopardized U.S. assistance to allies and the have-not nations of Asia, Africa and Latin America. Sen. Mike Mansfield, the Democratic leader, said the aid program "very likely would die a lingering death."

President Nixon summed up some of the reasons for the change in American thinking when he told a joint session of Congress on Sept. 9 about his anti-inflation drive. "For a quarter of a century now, since the end of World War II, America has borne the principal burden of free-world defense, of foreign aid, helping old nations back onto their feet and new nations to take their first, sometimes faltering steps," the President said. "We have laid out nearly $150,000,000,000 in foreign aid, economic and military, over the past 25 years. We have fought two costly and grueling wars. We have undergone deep strains at home, as we have sought to reconcile our responsibilities abroad with our own needs here in America. . . . In the years ahead, we will remain a good and generous nation—but the time has come to give a new attention to America's own interests here at home."

A roar of approval went up from members of the Senate and House, indicating broad bipartisan support for the President's emphasis on placing American interests first. This concern was reflected in growing Congressional backing for import quotas, resisted by the Nixon administration except in the textile field, and rising criticism of the "export of American jobs" through overseas production by multinational corporations with headquarters in the United States.

Nixon had cut his foreign-aid request by 10 per cent as part of his New Economic Policy package. Later the United States agreed to devalue the dollar for the first time in nearly forty years to achieve a realignment of major

UPI

The Senate reverses a longtime trend a few days after Communist China is voted into the UN.

world currencies. A 10 per cent across-the-board import surcharge, imposed as a temporary measure to spur agreement on revaluation of the German mark and the Japanese yen, caused distress in the underdeveloped world. The surcharge tax was lifted, however, on Dec. 20.

Foreign aid was in deep trouble also with liberal members of Congress who had been its strongest supporters in the past. Speaking from this perspective, Sen. Frank Church (D-Idaho) explained why he voted against the foreign-aid authorization measure on Oct. 29 when it was defeated in the Senate by a 41–27 vote: "The experience of twenty years of aid shows that we can neither bring about fundamental reform in tradition–encrusted societies nor prevent revolution in those countries where the tide of change runs deep and strong. All we can really do is to service the status quo in countries where it is not strongly challenged anyhow."

The foreign-aid bill began its tortuous course through Congress when the House narrowly approved a two–year extension of the existing program by a vote of 200 to 192 on Aug. 3. This bill authorized the spending of $3,344,-350,000 in fiscal year 1972, and $50,000,000 more than that in the following 12-month period.

Although the figures represented a slight increase over President Nixon's request, the House spurned his elaborate reorganization plan submitted on Apr. 21. The administration's plan would have abolished the Agency for International Development (AID) and set up an International Development Corporation, an Americanized version of the World Bank, and an International Development Institute for research and training of technical experts. Military aid would have been placed under separate control, within the State Department instead of the Pentagon, and a single coordinator would have supervised the corporation and the institute. Chairman Thomas Morgan (D-Pa.) of the House Foreign Affairs Committee said the proposal was sent to Capitol Hill too late and the House supported Morgan's judgment.

In a major political surprise, the Senate refused to enact a foreign-aid authorization a few days after the United Nations voted to seat the People's Republic of China and expel the Nationalist Chinese regime loyal to Chiang Kai-shek. One factor in the Senate vote was resentment over the glee shown by some UN delegates when the United States lost its fight to preserve Nationalist China's seat.

Other Senators felt that the United States was overcommitted around the world and the aid program was a symbol of the effort to play the role of global policeman. President Nixon denounced the Senate action, claiming that it would present "unacceptable risks to the national security." AID Director John A. Hannah said the United States should not become a "world dropout." Under such pressure, the Senate approved a sharply trimmed aid authorization of $1,140,000,000 for economic and humanitarian aid and $1,500,000,000 in foreign military assistance.

The cutback was defended by Chairman J. William Fulbright (D-Ark.) of the Senate Foreign Relations Committee who said the aid program had become a "grab bag for everybody but the American people, who pay the bills." The Senate added restrictions on the use of aid funds for American troops in Cambodia or the hiring of mercenaries in Laos, North Vietnam or Thailand.

Another amendment called upon the President to end the war in South Vietnam within six months from the date of its passage, provided that U.S. prisoners of war were released by the enemy. It was this provision, sponsored by Senator Mansfield, that led to a deadlock with the House, imperiling the future of the AID agency. Although $4,700,000,000 was still available in the foreign-aid pipeline, none of the money could be used to pay the salaries or operating expenses of the program.

The aid bill became entangled in the end-of-session rush, but the Nixon administration managed to salvage Congressional approval for a resolution to permit spending at an annual rate of $2,800,000,000 until Feb. 22, 1972.

The aid program ran into other troubles. In January it was disclosed that the Food for Peace program had been used to finance $693,-000,000 worth of military equipment since 1966, including 96 per cent of the Food for Peace funds allocated to Vietnam and Korea.

While the U.S. aid effort became bogged down, the World Bank announced that it was on schedule in its drive to increase assistance to developing countries to $12,000,000,000 a year by the end of 1973. Bank President Robert S. McNamara continued to focus attention on the basic problems of overpopulation, malnutrition and inequality of wealth in the worst-off nations. "The best appraised project, with the highest rate of financial return, will be of no avail if the community as a whole dissolves into bankruptcy or civil chaos," McNamara warned.

President Nixon's import surcharge, along with the continuing uncertainties in the last months of 1971 over currency exchange rates, hit the developing countries especially hard. They export large amounts of raw commodities, such as coffee, sugar and metals, and the actions by the United States limited their markets.

The poor countries of the world, witnessing America's retreat from foreign aid, had reason to be apprehensive. As Chairman Morgan told the Congress: "Many countries in the world have come to depend on U.S. assistance. If we cut it off, the withdrawal symptoms would be severe."

WILLIAM J. EATON
Washington Correspondent
Chicago Daily News

FRANCE

President Georges Pompidou kept a steady hand on the affairs of France in 1971, riding over a few crisis peaks with the skill, if not the dramatic *éclat*, of his predecessor, Gen. Charles de Gaulle. A measure of the tone and character of the Pompidoulian regime—for the first time beyond all possible direct influence from De Gaulle—was a frequent complaint of "moroseness" among the French people. They were not really unhappy but neither were they particularly content with their direction under their rather colorless former schoolteacher leader.

De Gaulle had died in November 1970, after his retirement the previous year, and Pompidou, De Gaulle's premier, was no longer functioning with one eye on Colombey-les-deux-Eglises, where De Gaulle lived and brooded and, by his very existence after a decade of power, remained a political force. Now Pompidou was on his own, although both he and his strongly dominant party found it to their advantage to keep De Gaulle very much "alive" in the political arena and among French people in general. While Gaullist politicians from Pompidou on down pretended to be the true heirs of De Gaulle's massive political legacy, no occasion was missed to keep De Gaulle's name and image before the public.

The name of the traffic circle around the Arch of Triumph was changed from L'Etoile (The Star) to Place Charles de Gaulle. Stamps were issued marking four peaks in his career; and the first anniversary of his death on Nov. 9 was the occasion for a great outpouring of nostalgic acclaim, much of it obviously spontaneous.

If Pompidou's style of governing and dealing with France's allies were of a much less boat-rocking character, Pompidou managed to maintain three of De Gaulle's precepts or accomplishments: leadership in the European Economic Community (Common Market), monetary independence; and continuing close ties with the Soviet Union.

A May summit meeting in Paris with British Prime Minister Edward Heath—although described officially as a session to discuss bilateral

UPI

The smartly dressed Pompidous enjoy a stroll after voting in municipal elections, Mar. 14.

matters—was the occasion for formally lifting French objections to British entry into the Common Market and the other five members beckoned Britain in. Without approval from Paris it would not have been possible.

Pompidou and his politically ambitious Finance Minister, Valery Giscard d'Estaing, firmly refused to revalue the franc or let it float in relation to the dollar following President Nixon's dramatic economic measures announced in mid-August. France persisted in its demand for a formal devaluation of the dollar and sought with little immediate success to build a common front with its European partners against Washington's moves. France maintained a double market for the franc: one for commercial transactions where the franc was maintained at its former parity with the dollar (5.55); and the other for financial transactions where the franc was under the influence of supply and demand.

France, some Americans believed, was insensitive to the U.S. argument that it and other European nations should rush to the aid of their wartime ally, now in grave difficulties of its own. France's view was, in effect, that the United States should take France's medicine—devaluation of the dollar in terms of gold—and that this remedy alone would help the United States far more than Nixon's August

---

FRANCE

Area: 211,207 sq. mi.
Population: 51,500,000
Capital: Paris
Government: Georges Pompidou, president—1969; Jacques Chaban-Delmas, premier—1969
Gross National Product: $148,000,000,000
Foreign trade: exports, $17,742,000,000; imports, $18,780,000,000
Armed forces: 501,500

measures, including, particularly, the 10 per cent surcharge on imports. Pompidou told a news conference in September that France would not succumb to the "big stick" tactics of Washington.

In mid-December, at a meeting in the Azores of Presidents Pompidou and Nixon, the latter agreed to devalue the dollar by an unspecified amount (later placed at 8.57 per cent). A few days later, on Dec. 20, the U.S. 10 per cent surcharge on imports was lifted.

With Giscard d'Estaing the host, the finance ministers of the Common Market nations showed rare solidarity in November by agreeing at a meeting in Versailles that they should attempt to force the United States into a firm commitment to devalue the dollar, or at least make its monetary policy clear for the future.

De Gaulle's efforts to build a special relationship with the Soviet Union, and thus to crack both the iron curtain and the Berlin Wall, were continued with a certain success by Pompidou. The climax was the visit, delayed time and again before, of Soviet leaders to France. Communist Party General Secretary Leonid I. Brezhnev spent a week in France in late October and was received like a chief of state—residence at Versailles, and Soviet flags along the Avenue des Champs Elysées.

During the visit, marked by sporadic demonstrations of hostility by Jewish militants and little popular enthusiasm by the French public, France and the Soviet Union signed an agreement giving the French state-owned Renault auto works a share in a rich contract for a truck plant on Russia's Kama River.

The French and Russians also signed a lengthy declaration of principles governing their future relations and spelling out their attitudes to world problems, in the Middle East, India-Pakistan and Southeast Asia. Paris and Moscow have long had similar views on them. Close contacts are to continue and commercial and cultural relations to be developed, the declaration said. However, the document fell short technically of a formal friendship treaty, which Brezhnev wanted. For France that would be pushing relations with the Soviet bloc a little too far and would imply a breakaway from the North Atlantic Treaty Organization of which France has remained a member.

France was aware too that the Brezhnev visit was part of a Soviet diplomatic offensive, noted in many parts of the world, following the announcement of Nixon's coming visit to Peking and Communist China's gradual move onto the world stage after decades of isolation. By signing a friendship treaty with Russia at this particular juncture, Paris would seem to be playing the Russians' game at the expense of the Chinese. France, in recognizing Peking in 1964, had long encouraged China to forge an opening to the West.

Brezhnev's visit followed one by China's Minister of Foreign Trade Pai Hsiang-kuo. Pai was the highest ranking Peking official to visit

Catherine Ursillo

In spite of protests, Les Halles, the famous nineteenth-century Paris market, is being torn down. Its 12 huge pavilions, airy structures of iron and glass, were city landmarks that sheltered restaurants (serving onion soup in the early morning) as well as stalls.

the West since the Communists took over mainland China in 1949, and much was made of this fact by the French in stressing their special ties with China. But Pai, unknown in the West and a lower-rank official than the French had expected, made very little impression, particularly in a political sense, as he traveled throughout France. He extended invitations to French officials, including Pompidou and Giscard d'Estaing, to visit China. There were indications that all or some of the bids would be accepted.

Another visitor of stature, although largely symbolic, was Emperor Hirohito of Japan, who charmed his French hosts and the public and built further goodwill between Paris and Tokyo, although nagging problems persisted. Japan would like France to let more Japanese goods onto the French market and is disturbed that France persists in nuclear tests in the Pacific.

But it was not Japan that forced the French at least to suspend the tests, but Peru. France announced in September that tests scheduled that month would not take place "because there was no further need." In fact, it was clear that protests by Peru, which had threatened to break relations with France if the tests continued, led to scrapping of the September blasts. France is attempting to develop markets, particularly for its arms industry, in South America, and a break with Peru would not have eased this operation.

In relations with other countries, France came close to a bitter split with its former North African colony of Algeria over the issue of oil and natural gas which had been discovered by the French before Algeria became independent. In February, Paris was shaken by an Algerian announcement nationalizing most French oil and gas interests and the means for transporting their products out of Algeria. In April, talks were broken off as France pressed without success demands for compensation and for what it considered reasonable prices for Algerian oil on which it is largely dependent. Later the breach narrowed, and commercial ties between Algiers and Paris were put on a new basis. It was forced by the fact that France and Algeria are interdependent as far as petroleum products and their exploitation are concerned.

At home, labor and student discontent was held to a manageable level by the Pompidou Government, although there were periods when the potential for disaster seemed to be nearing the explosion point of May–June 1968. In February, a Paris *lycée* (high school) student accused of hitting a policeman during a riot was freed by the courts as thousands of students

UPI

On his first Western tour, Soviet party chairman Brezhnev waves to crowd at Paris' City Hall.

staged a sitdown strike on the Left Bank. Thus a crisis that in the eyes of many observers could have set student forces aflame was defused, although a certain ill feeling remained.

In April and May, Renault auto workers struck over pay demands for a small category of employees. The strike and resulting lockout ended in 26 days, although not before France's efforts to hold wages in line had suffered, but not seriously. In October, metro (subway) conductors struck for wage-preference continuation, but after ten days the Government—with a dramatic television and radio appeal by Premier Jacques Chaban-Delmas—faced the conductors down, and they went back to their trains just as Paris commuters were getting dangerously fed up with walking.

Pompidou did what he could to boost the fortunes of the French-British Concorde supersonic transport plane. He became a flying salesman in May as he traveled to Toulouse to promote the plane, which many believe will never be a profitable commercial craft. The Concorde's only competitor, the Soviet Tupolev 144, made its first appearance in the West at the Paris air salon in May.

DAVID M. MASON
Correspondent, Paris Bureau
The Associated Press

FUELS AND ENERGY

In 1971 the corporate giants that pump oil, produce electricity, and mine coal were buffeted by powerful international trends that kept them in a constant state of crisis—and their customers in continuous suspense. No major blackouts occurred in the United States, and no cities went without fuel. But the situation was touch and go, and it will continue tense in the years ahead.

Fuel companies were in the center of controversy after controversy, usually battles fought on criteria far different from the supply-price questions that had been at the center of most traditional debates over how well energy producers were living up to their public obligations. Now conservationists were declaring that protection of the environment has first priority even if it means curbing consumers' propensity to buy still newer gadgets that use still more power. A recent surge of economic nationalism brought new strains to decades-old relationships. A new populist power behind antitrust enforcement so focused on energy matters that by the year's end the Federal Trade Commission had more staff professionals working on related questions than on any other single subject. All these currents produced overlapping crises, giving corporate brass a distinct sense of being singled out for harassment. "We find ourselves operating in what I would describe as an atmosphere of regulatory overkill," Texaco, Inc., Senior Vice-President Kerryn King complained to a New York meeting of the American Bar Association. "In trying to get on with the job, we are faced with shifting ground rules and criteria, duplication of laws and regulations, a multitude of licensing requirements, and multiple enforcement agencies at the state and local levels. This situation has created chaotic conditions in an industry that to operate effectively and efficiently must be able to plan in an orderly fashion and on a long-range basis."

In truth, the troubles began in the mid-1960's, when suddenly U.S. energy demands began outpacing the growth in gross national product—after more than a half century of growing less fast than the general economy. Utilities and producers of fuels found their careful economic projections suddenly inadequate. And since there is not yet any general agreement on why demand suddenly accelerated, there is no good way to get a fix on the future. Talking about just one important part of the situation, Philip H. Trezise, assistant secretary of state for economic affairs, said, "Wrong guesses have been as common about petroleum as they are about the roll of the dice in Las Vegas."

One measure of the size of the mistakes: Predictions of energy demands for the year 1970, published in 1968, turned out to have set the estimate too low by 4,000,000,000,000,000 BTU's (British thermal units). That figure translates into a requirement for 32,000,000 tons of coal plus 1,200,000,000 cubic feet of gas plus more than 250,000,000 barrels of oil.

If there are no firm definitions of what energy consumers expect of the suppliers, it is nonetheless clear that a prodigious job is involved. A 1971 report from the Senate Committee on Public Works projected an annual increase of about 2 per cent a year in the per capita consumption of energy, producing an overall increase of more than 75 per cent by the end of the century. And, of course, most analysts see a significant population increase compounding that demand. For oil (the biggest single U.S. source of energy) that means, in order to keep reserves at present levels, finding 500,000,000,000 barrels of new oil sources in the next 20 years, an amount just about equal to the total discoveries in the past 100 years.

In the new definitions of how the energy companies should meet their responsibilities, the question is not one of merely supplying enough fuel to head off a crisis, but of supplying the right kind of fuel, produced and transported in the right way. Fuels with high sulfur content, for instance, no longer will serve.

The Environmental Protection Agency in 1971 decreed that by 1975, seven major cities in Eastern and Midwestern United States must have levels of air purity that can be achieved only by using substantially less coal and oil, for both are high in sulfur content. There are no commercially feasible methods of removing the sulfur from coal, and the petroleum desulfurization plants operating and under construction in the Caribbean will not be able to come near meeting the demand. Carl Bagge, former member of the Federal Power Commission and now president of the National Coal Association, complains that EPA moved too quickly: "In the desire to obtain clean air as fast as possible, restrictions on sulfur content of fuel have been imposed in advance of the arrival of technology. Many people, some of them in high government posts, labor under the delusion that energy consumers such as power plants can simply switch to low-sulfur fuels. This is not a realistic option."

The Court of Appeals in the District of Columbia halted construction of the big Calvert Cliffs nuclear power plant and told the Atomic Energy Commission to overhaul all its rules on assessing the environmental impact of such

Gas and condensate have been brought up in test drills on Sable Island, some 175 miles east of Nova Scotia, in what may be a rich Atlantic field.

plants. Judge J. Skelly Wright told the commission that not even the "specter of a national power crisis" could let the commission proceed with construction permits until its own studies showed that new nuclear operations would not degrade their natural setting. Similar environmental questions kept the fate of a trans-Alaskan oil pipeline in controversial limbo all year. The same concerns kept Washington from offering oil companies new leases to explore offshore areas of Alaska and the eastern coast.

Antitrusters exercised control over energy affairs most dramatically with a Federal Trade Commission order to Kennecott Copper Company to rid itself of Peabody Coal, one of the two biggest U.S. coal companies. Commission staffers were also working up a case against the acquisition of Consolidation Coal Company—by a few carloads a year bigger than Peabody —by Continental Oil. The oil-coal combines were suspected of reducing possible competition between the fuels, perhaps even leading to coal reserves being left undeveloped. Yet the oil companies say they expressly moved into coal, as C. Howard Hardesty, Jr., a senior vice-president of Continental Oil (Conoco), put it, "better to adapt to an expanding, changing and surprisingly unpredictable market. . . ." The antitrust forces in the Senate Judiciary Committee were worried about links between electric and gas distributors, and held hearings in 1971 on legislation to force the breakup of such ties.

Middle Eastern oil-producing countries banded together on stiff requirements for continued access to their rich stores of crude petroleum. Their North African ally, Libya, actually stopped the oil flowing for months. As a result, the international oil companies agreed to substantially higher prices for oil, giving the producing nations a bigger share of the profits. Estimates of the cost of the package settlement ran to more than $10,000,000,000 over the five years of the agreement. Also in 1971, Algeria acquired the controlling interest in French oil companies operating there; and Venezuela said it would take back all oil concessions when current contracts ran out in 1983.

Throughout this buffeting, there has been virtually no coordinated investigation of the various problems facing energy companies, or of the impact of decisions in one realm on the availability of energy elsewhere. Much of the debate during 1971 was over how the Government could best see the energy picture as a totality. Sen. Jennings Randolph (D-W.Va.) warned in 1971 that until "a national fuels and energy policy is clearly enunciated and effectively instituted, this nation will continue to proceed from mild crisis to crisis until irreparable damage is done by a crisis of major proportions." The Office of Emergency Planning spent almost six months studying the situation, but came up with an essentially disappointing report. It said what people had already realized: that foreign fuel supplies are essential to the security of the United States.

The House of Representatives defeated—by a 128–218 vote—a resolution to set up a special committee to study the entire problem. It would have considered the reserve situation, reasons for delays in new power-plant construction, pricing policies, transportation problems, and environmental impact. Chairmen of existing committees fought the measure. Many of them had some responsibility in at least one of the study areas and argued that a new group would undercut existing powers and perquisites.

President Nixon focused attention specifically on energy problems, especially as they are affected by the drive for a cleaner environment, in a package of proposals sent to Congress with a special message in June. "The assumption that sufficient energy will always be readily available has been brought sharply into question with the last year," he said. "The brownouts that have affected some areas of our country, the possible shortages of fuel that were threatened last fall, the sharp increases in certain fuel prices and our growing awareness of the environmental consequences of energy production have all demonstrated that we cannot take our energy supply for granted any longer."

The White House proposals included greatly increased imports of oil from Canada, and more Federal money for research into new and better ways of producing energy. At the same time, Nixon made it clear that he expected private industry to step up its own spending on new processes and techniques. One proposal on how this could be done came from Charles F. Luce, chairman of Consolidated Edison Company of New York. He suggested that utilities be allowed to increase their bills by one hundredth of a penny per kilowatt hour, producing some $150,000,000 a year specifically earmarked for research.

The main thrust of the President's new fuels-research effort is to spur the achievement of a commercially feasible "fast-breeder" reactor for nuclear-powered electric generating plants. Calling it "our best hope today for meeting the nation's growing demand for economical clean energy," Nixon promised to have a demonstration plant in the 300 to 500 megawatt range ready for utilities to copy by 1980. Because such reactors literally create new fuel as they operate, they greatly expand the potential for significant amounts of power from limited uranium resources. One member of the Atomic Energy Commission estimated that known uranium reserves would run conventional atomic plants for 40 years, but with breeder reactors would last 1,000 years.

The administration power program also calls for stepped-up research on the conversion of coal into a gaseous fuel. One of the main arguments raised by the antitrusters to the take-over of coal reserves by oil companies is that it has slowed down investigation of how the solid fuel could be turned into a head-on competitor of the companies' traditional money-makers: oil and natural gas. The FTC notes that ten years ago it was predicted that liquefaction and gasification of coal would be a reality by today, but that was before the research leader in the field, Consolidation Coal, was taken over by Conoco. Under such Washington pressure, though, work on coal conversion stepped up during 1971.

Other technologies were being considered as ways out of the energy crisis. The Government hopes to begin commercial exploitation soon of geothermal steam locked underground in the western states. Since the main supplies of this resource are far from the population centers where energy consumption is highest and the situation most critical, the role that geothermal energy can play appears to be limited.

An even more distant hope, although it was getting more attention in 1971, is atomic fusion, the basis of the hydrogen bomb, as a means of producing electric power. The fuel would be deuterium (heavy hydrogen), which is abundant in seawater and recoverable at low cost. The Federal Government invested about $30,-

000,000 in research projects on the concept, and private utilities put more than $1,000,000 into related research at the universities of Texas, Princeton, Cornell and Wisconsin, the latter three all begun in 1971. Thus far it is only a theoretical possibility. The biggest problem is how to control heat that would hit hundreds of millions of degrees.

To satisfy more immediate needs, the fuel companies devoted a bigger chunk of their resources to finding new sources of established energy materials, to be used in conventional ways. Canada's Quebec Province, for instance, was developing a $6,000,000,000 hydroelectric project on James Bay, which would ship power as far south as New York City.

The international oil companies explored the North Sea intensively in 1971. It is an attractive site geologically (especially since the Phillips Petroleum Company discovery of the Ekofisk field southwest of Norway in 1970) that has the special virtue of being near the big Western Europe markets. U.S. investors were especially interested in the possibilities of oil finds offshore in Canada, both in the Arctic and off Nova Scotia. Optimism drew American dollars into the Canadian stock exchanges. Mobil Oil was test drilling in the north, and Katy Industries was exploring off Newfoundland. Other companies were test drilling along the west coast of Africa and in the East China and South China seas.

The possibility of oil in offshore concessions from Vietnam was much in the news during 1971, at least as much because of U.S. involvement in the war raging there as because of the geology of the region. Standard Oil of New Jersey was reported to have made a significant find in a Malaysian offshore grant adjacent to the ocean segments that Saigon could open for exploration. The company fanned speculation higher by opening, in February, a large refinery in Singapore. Although more than a dozen petroleum giants were bidding for search rights on such concessions, the U.S. State Department tried to minimize the likelihood of an oil race there.

The only part of the energy picture that was not full of uncertainty in 1971 was the actual production statistics. They kept rising steadily. The final figures are likely to show that U.S. utilities produced 1,600,000,000,000 kilowatt hours of electric power, up about 100,-000,000,000 from 1970. The new supplies of all oils, including domestic and imports, amounted to about 5,540,000,000,000 barrels, compared with 5,370,000,000,000 in 1970. Bituminous coal miners, before a strike in the fall, had been headed for a production total of almost 650,000,000 short tons, 7.5 per cent above the 1970 output.

DANIEL B. MOSKOWITZ
Correspondent, Washington Bureau
McGraw-Hill World News

Model of proposed plan for building floating nuclear-power plants; they would be prefabricated and pretested before delivery to site.

"The New York Times"

"La Nacion"

Bobby Fischer defeats Tigran Petrosian and wins right to play Boris Spassky for world title.

GAMES: Bridge

The United States once again won the world title at the championships held in Taipei, Taiwan. The professional team known as the "Aces" successfully defended its title. The famous Blue Team of Italy once again did not play but indicated that it would represent Italy at the World Bridge Olympiad to be held in Miami Beach in June 1972. The Blue Team beat the Aces in a challenge prize money match in Las Vegas, Nev., possibly presaging things to come at the Olympiad.

A team of "Goren Stars," selected by Charles Goren from former teammates who had won national championships with him, beat the Aces in the semifinals of a special invitational event at Las Vegas that drew the strongest teams in the world to compete. The Goren Stars then went on to lose to the Blue Team in the finals. The Goren team consisted of Harold Ogust, Boris Koytchou, Howard Schenken, Peter Leventritt, William Root and William Seamon.

Winners of the 1971 U.S. National Championships were:

Vanderbilt Teams: The Aces (William Eisenberg, Robert Goldman, Robert Hamman, James Jacoby, Michael Lawrence, Robert Wolf).

Spingold Teams: Steve Altman, Gene Neiger, Joel Stuart, Peter Weichsel, Tom Smith.

Blue Ribbon Pairs: John Grantham, Roger Bates.

Life Master Pairs: Alvin Roth, Barbara Rappaport.

Life Master Men's Pairs: Peter Weichsel, Alan Sontag.

Life Master Women's Pairs: Ruth Bloomfield, Delle Levinson.

Mixed Teams: Ronald Andersen, Sue Picus, John Anderson, Marilyn McCrairy.

Reisinger Teams: George Rapee, William Grieve, Edgar Kaplan, Norman Kay, Lew Mathe, Don Krauss.

CHARLES H. GOREN
Bridge Authority

Chess

For the first time in history the United States produced a contender for the world championship when Bobby Fischer thoroughly defeated former titleholder Tigran Petrosian (U.S.S.R.) 6½–2½ in Buenos Aires. It was the climax of an unprecedented 12-game winning streak in preliminary matches against Mark Taimanov (U.S.S.R.) and Bent Larsen (Denmark). Fischer is favored to wrest the world title in a 24-game match against Boris Spassky (U.S.S.R.) in 1972.

The biennial World Junior Championship in Athens attracted representatives from 44 nations. It was won by Werner Hug (Switzerland) followed by Zoltan Ribli (Hungary) and Kenneth Rogoff (U.S.A.). The 18th Students Team Championship in Puerto Rico was captured by Russia in a field of 16 nations. The defending U.S. team finished second.

The U.S. Open in Ventura, Calif., was captured by Walter Browne and Larry Evans in a record field of 400. The National Open in Reno was won by Evans, who also went on to triumph in a major new event in Lone Pine, the Statham Masters' Open. The U.S. Junior title was shared by Kenneth Rogoff and Gregory DeFotis.

Other 1971 Tournament Winners:
Costa del Sol: Arturo Pomar, Spain
Goteborg: Vlastimil Hort, Czechoslovakia;
Ulf Anderson, Sweden
Havana: Vlastimil Hort
IBM: Vassily Smyslov, U.S.S.R.
Lidums Open: Lajos Portisch, Hungary
Mar del Plata: Lev Polugaievsky, U.S.S.R.
Soviet Championship: Vladimir Savon,
U.S.S.R.
Tallinn: Paul Keres, U.S.S.R.; Mikhail Tal,
U.S.S.R.
Wilk Aan Zee: Viktor Korchnoi, U.S.S.R.

LARRY EVANS
Chess Grand Master

GEOLOGY

In 1971 the earth sciences continued to progress rapidly, with exciting discoveries. The chief spurs to this evolution of fresh ideas were the realization of the fundamental role of the earth sciences in studies of the environment; the results obtained by fresh landings on the moon; and continued discoveries on the ocean floors.

PREDICTION AND CONTROL OF EARTHQUAKES

The earth has never been a static body, and has always been subject to earthquakes great and small. Many devastating ones occur every year killing tens of thousands of people. A single one in China in A.D. 1556 was responsible for the death of 820,000 people, mostly killed by the collapse of buildings. Another,

which was followed by a great tsunami, or wave, destroyed Lisbon in A.D. 1755 and killed 60,000.

Yet prediction of and possibly some control over such disasters have only recently even been contemplated. Until this century the cause of earthquakes was unknown, and prediction was limited to the general observation that some regions, like Japan, experience many severe earthquakes while other regions, like the western plains of North America, have only minor ones at long intervals. The ancient Chinese and some countries in the Middle East kept the first systematic records, which show that the pattern of distribution of earthquakes has changed considerably over the centuries; some areas that formerly had many shocks now have few.

Rescuers probe ruins of a veterans hospital after a major earthquake on Feb. 9 in the Los Angeles, Calif., area, which bestrides a fault.

Wide World

Peter Lake from Black Star

The great Lisbon earthquake led Europeans to begin systematic studies of the intensity of major shocks and the size of areas damaged, but sensitive instruments to record distant earthquakes were developed only at the end of the nineteenth century. At that time John Milne, working first in Japan and later in England, established the first worldwide network of observatories. The work of such Europeans laid the basis for a proper understanding of the nature of earthquakes, which was greatly advanced by the study that H. F. Reid made of the great California earthquake of 1906. He showed that earthquakes are not due to explosions or the collapse of cavities, as had been thought, but to the slip of one large region of the earth's crust past another along a fracture, or fault. Such large moving regions are now called lithospheric plates. He suggested that although the motion between the two may be steady, the slipping at the boundaries is not, for local friction can lock the two sides of a fault together and in those sections block any motion for years or even centuries. Meanwhile the ground nearby becomes compressed and thus stores up energy until ultimately it is released in a sudden large slip.

It is now known that the floor of the Pacific Ocean is moving northward past North America at a steady rate of about two inches a year. The San Andreas fault, which bisects California, forms part of the boundary between these huge plates. However, the section of the fault near San Francisco was locked without slipping and

hence without large earthquakes for years before 1906, when the western side suddenly jumped northward relative to the eastern side. The maximum extent of this sudden slip was about twenty feet. Because ground is compressible the same movement did not extend all along the San Andreas fault but died away within a few scores of miles of the maximum displacement near San Francisco. In Southern California there was no motion and no earthquake then.

By plotting all recorded earthquakes, B. Gutenberg and C. F. Richter showed that all major earthquakes occur along narrow belts which encircle the globe and mark the boundaries between plates.

In 1957 it was realized that more extensive networks of observatories with better instruments were required for monitoring underground nuclear explosions adequately. These installations have led to much improved observations from which geophysicists have deduced a new theory of the earth's behavior, called plate tectonics. It is that slow upwellings or convection currents in the hot and somewhat malleable interior of the earth break the cold and brittle lithosphere or crust into plates and move them about. At present six large and a dozen small plates constitute the whole earth's surface. Jerks in the motion of plates past one another give rise to earthquakes. The plates move steadily, but the edges may catch, now at one place, then at another place somewhere else along an active fault.

The Southern California disaster left other perils in its wake, especially in the San Fernando Valley. A main highway (l) buckled and blocked traffic completely. After the concrete wall of a dam (below) collapsed, the reservoir waters behind it began to gnaw at the remaining earth retaining wall. Although the threat of flooding did not materialize, some 80,000 people were evacuated from below the dam before the danger passed.

The modern network of instruments pinpoints the sites of earthquakes, and in many places geological mapping on land and geophysical studies at sea can connect these earthquake focuses to particular faults. Thus in California and in northern Turkey active faults that are apt to move have been distinguished. The next problem is to predict where an active fault will move. Formerly it was considered most likely to expect an earthquake where others had been recorded, but the concept of plate tectonics has modified that view. Earthquakes are now expected in those sections of active faults that have been locked for some time.

Modern research into earthquake prediction first started in Japan a few years ago and now is under way in California and in the Middle East. The first endeavor has been to determine which faults are active. Along active faults accurate surveys are made to determine which sections are locked and which are moving. This determines the sections in which earthquakes are to be expected. Instruments show any unusual movements occurring before an earthquake. With experience it may be possible to forecast a coming shock.

In Japan unusual accelerations have been observed before earthquakes occurred, and some of the latter have been predicted. In the United States, work is still in the preliminary stages. Progress is necessarily slow because prediction depends upon having noted the local behavior immediately before a large earthquake, which does not happen very often.

The San Fernando (Calif.) earthquake of Feb. 9, 1971, was the best documented of any earthquake in United States history. Incidentally it provided the first really comprehensive practical test of building codes in an area close to an earthquake's origin. A preliminary report was particularly critical of the risk imposed by the Van Norman Dam, which was so severely damaged that eighty thousand people living below it had to be evacuated. The fifty-mile bend in the San Andreas fault north of the San Gabriel Mountains was blamed for causing the blockage that led to the earthquake.

There is some hope that scientists can exert a measure of control over the occurrence of earthquakes. The first indication that human activity can spark the onset of earthquakes arose from the observation that creation of large artificial lakes has in many cases resulted in nearby earthquakes. A second, more significant possibility was observed in 1966 near Denver, Col. There the pumping of waste fluids into deep wells was followed by many small and medium-sized earthquakes where there had previously been none. The pumping was stopped and after some months so did the earthquakes, but pumping was not resumed for fear of earthquake damage to Denver.

Three years later a similar phenomenon was noted in the Rangely oil field in Colorado where pumping, as part of a process for extracting oil, initiated a spate of small earthquakes. The area is now the scene of an experimental program. After a year the flow was reversed by pumping water out for six months. This brought about a dramatic drop in the number of earthquakes. Pumping has been started again to see whether it causes more earthquakes. The experiments suggest that increasing the hydrostatic pressure by pumping water into the ground reduces the fracture strength of the rock and promotes movement along faults, while pumping water out tends to strengthen the rock and to block movement on faults.

There is no suggestion that any techniques can stop the motions of global plates, but there is the possibility of controls to dissipate the movement in small, relatively harmless earthquakes and to keep them from building up into devastating ones. Thus the floor of the Pacific Ocean will continue to move north along the San Andreas fault.

The scientists' efforts aim to promote steady motion and avoid prolonged blockages whose release would cause major shocks. Suppose that at each of two places several miles apart on an active fault the two sides can be temporarily locked together by pumping out water at those places. An earthquake might then be induced in the intervening section by pumping water into it. Such an earthquake would be confined to the section between the blockages. Because the length of rupture as well as the extent of movement determines the severity of an earthquake, the technique may provide a means of releasing small controlled shocks. It could be repeated in many places to encourage the release of energy regularly in small packets.

All the foregoing is still speculative. At present the best warnings possible are statements, based upon previous records, of the statistical probability of an occurrence and its strength. Such predictions can at least indicate that precautions should be taken in construction.

More than anything else, the studies of the ocean floors have brought about a revolution so that we now think of the earth as a mobile rather than a static body. We now appreciate the true cause of earthquakes and have hope of improved earthquake prediction and even of easing these disasters. One can foresee other practical consequences including improvements in prospecting for petroleum and minerals.

GEOLOGY OF THE MOON

The year 1971 saw a much better understanding of the nature of the moon. The new findings support the validity of speculations about the nature of the interior of the earth and about the universe. The moon landings have given men a second, if smaller, planetary observatory, without an obstructive atmosphere.

The "man in the moon" is a connected series of dark patches called mare (plural, maria), most of which are roughly circular. Telescopes reveal that the surfaces of the maria are smooth with few craters and that their dark filling seems to have flooded the intervening brighter highlands which are pockmarked with craters. The most popular theory to account for this has been that the circular maria are giant craters filled with basaltic lava that has overflowed, and that the highlands are older debris that had been thrown out and heaped up by the impact of the asteroids that formed the craters. Information from the 1971 moon exploration strongly supports this concept.

The first extensive data by satellite began coming in 1966 from the five Orbiter observatories that photographed the whole surface of the moon and revealed the existence of mascons. "Mascons" is an abbreviation for concentrations of mass; that is, they indicate denser material beneath each circular mare. Their precise nature remains a puzzle.

Between June 2, 1966, and Jan. 9, 1968, five unmanned Surveyor spacecraft made successful soft landings on the moon. The information gained thereby enabled astronauts to land in July and November 1969, respectively in Apollo 11 on the Sea of Tranquillity, a circular mare, and in Apollo 12 on the Ocean of Storms, an irregular one. In February and July 1971, Apollo missions 14 and 15 landed in the highlands, respectively in the foothills of Fra Mauro and beside Hadley Rille at the base of the Apennine Mountains. In 1971 only preliminary results were yet available from Apollo 15. Additional information was provided by the unmanned Soviet Luna missions.

Villagers and tourists survey a flow of molten rock, menacing vineyards, from Mt. Etna (Sicily) erupting in April-June. No lives were lost.

Bunte from Pictorial Parade

Regarding the better-known maria, it is clear that they are generally similar and are filled with basalt. These rocks are fine-grained lavas, largely silicates of iron, magnesium, aluminum and calcium. Half the rocks from Apollo 11 and most of those from Apollo 12 are basaltic rocks.

The compositions do not match any terrestrial rocks, being richer in iron and poorer in sodium than any terrestrial, volcanic basalts. They also differ between the two main sites. The rocks from Tranquillity Base have noticeably more titanium than any elsewhere. The surface of the mare there is covered with a lunar soil upon which the astronauts could walk without difficulty. It has much the same composition as the rocks and has apparently been created by the impact of many meteorites. Shock waves from the impacts have altered many minerals. Heat has generated tiny glass spherules, which make up part of the soil. The heat of impact has packed some of the loose material into breccias (sharp rock fragments imbedded in fine-grained matrix). The exposed surfaces of rocks have many tiny glass-lined pits, presumably the result of bombardment by micrometeorites arriving from outer space at enormous speeds.

Pools of water may lie beneath the arid surface. All the mare rocks are between 3,200,000,000 and 3,900,000,000 years old, and all tested have been at least feebly magnetized. This probably means that all those billions of years ago the moon had a magnetic field and hence a small liquid iron core to generate it.

The lunar soil, or moon dust, contains large quantities of the inert gases helium, neon, argon, krypton and xenon, almost certainly derived from the solar wind of tenuous gas emitted by the sun. Surface effects suggest that the rocks collected on missions 11 and 12 had not been disturbed for hundreds of millions of years.

The highlands have been less well studied, and landings have been made only in the foothills. That of Apollo 14 near Fra Mauro was on a blanket of loose material thought to have been ejected from Mare Imbrium by a major impact shortly before the mare lavas formed.

Nearly all of the samples collected are breccias, many probably transported by the impact that caused the small Cone Crater, apparently formed only about 10,000,000 years ago. These rocks have less iron and titanium and more aluminum and trace elements than the mare basalts have. Some fragments, usually older, rich in potassium (K), rare-earth elements and phosphorus have accordingly been named KREEP. The general conclusion is that the Apollo 14 rocks could have been derived by ejection from the Mare Imbrium crater which deposited them in a thick, hot blanket in which they were subsequently slowly annealed.

Many of the Apollo 15 rocks are anorthosite (a light feldspar), and some are green glass. The largest rock is a coarse-grained anorthosite, nicknamed "Genesis rock." It has been found to be at least 4,100,000,000 years old, the oldest yet recorded. All the rocks collected were loose, but photographs show that the walls of Hadley Rille are flat lava flows. The rille may be the collapsed course in which a stream of lava once flowed. Photographs of the Apennine Mountains reveal even more striking structures dipping in places at 20° to 30°.

The moon probably formed with the solar system about 4,550,000,000 years ago. It is likely that at first it had a heavy infall of meteoritic material which has since died away. Geochemists think that the surface to a depth of a hundred or more kilometers soon melted and then cooled again to produce coarse igneous rocks like anorthosites by 4,100,000,000 years ago. Over long ages different kinds of rocks developed: the highland rocks could not produce the basalts by partial melting, and the basalts could not produce the Fra Mauro rocks. Between 3,900,000,000 and 3,200,000,000 years ago, further cratering generated the circular maria and produced local melting to form the mare basalts. One of the last major events was the creation of Copernicus crater perhaps 2,000,000,000 years ago. However, the Apollo finding of unexpectedly high heat flowing from below may alter some long-held theories.

Seismologists have found that the moon is very transparent to earthquake waves and entirely solid, shown by the recorded impact of the discarded LEM from Apollo 15 at a distance of 700 miles from their instruments. They also believe that moonquakes are regularly triggered at depths of about 200 miles by tidal forces. Their magnitude is less than 1 on the Richter scale, too small to be recorded on earth because of noise from traffic and wind. The existence of mascons indicates that the moon can hold up large masses permanently and suggests great rigidity.

These conclusions puzzle magneticians. For the old mare rocks to be magnetized they think that at least the central part of the moon must have melted so that a core could form and generate a magnetic field. The problem is that once the center had melted, it would have been hard to extract enough heat from such depths to enable the interior to solidify again. Yet the lack of a field at present suggests that there is now no liquid core.

Photos NASA

Astronaut James Irwin, of Apollo 15, adds to the load of rocks on the lunar vehicle Rover. It allowed Irwin and David Scott to explore more of the moon and to carry out their geological goal of study-ing the terrain and gathering as wide a variety of rocks as possible. The largest and most famous, the "Genesis rock" (r), is now known to be at least 4,100,-000,000 years old, the most ancient rock that has thus far been recorded.

OTHER DEVELOPMENTS

The Deep Sea Drilling Project being carried out by the ship *Glomar Challenger* continued to give support to the theory of continental drift and to reveal unexpected complexities in the geology of ocean floors. Results of drilling in the autumn of 1970 indicated that the Mediterranean Sea is being closed by compression, but that in the process large east and west motions of some parts relative to others are opening local basins such as the Tyrrhenian between Corsica and Italy. Drilling has recovered cores containing rock salt about 5,000,000 years old. That long ago it appears that the whole Mediterranean evaporated either by being raised above sea level or by being cut off from the main oceans.

The first cruise of 1971, in the Caribbean area, successfully tested a recent technique: it enables a drill to be withdrawn from a hole started in the sea floor, the cutting bit replaced and the drill put back into the old hole to deepen it. Important sedimentary sections were thus cored.

The *Glomar Challenger* then passed through the Panama Canal to investigate the complex region off its western end, and continued to Hawaii. Drilling showed that before 5,000,000 years ago, sea-floor spreading, at a rate of 6½ inches a year, had been faster than any recorded since then, and that the Central Pacific plate has moved 1,800 miles north in the last 100,000,000 years. Much of the period was one of great volcanic activity in the region also. The ship then turned north to Alaska to investigate, in the Aleutian Trench and the Bering Sea, the effects of the northward movement which presumably has carried the Pacific floor down and back into the earth's interior beneath the Aleutian Islands.

In recent years the expanding use of, and increasing dependence upon, oil and gas for power have focused attention upon the dwindling reserves of these products in conventional petroleum fields and upon the hazards they create by pollution. During 1971 the American Association of Petroleum Geologists published an important summary of the geology of giant petroleum fields. It shows that although the demand is greatest in North America, the resources are much larger in Eurasia. The difficulty of finding fields in convenient locations has stimulated successful search offshore on coasts all around North America and in remote regions on the north coast of Alaska and in the Canadian Arctic islands. Drilling on the sea floor is more hazardous and more likely to lead to pollution than drilling on land as blowouts off Santa Barbara and the Gulf Coast have illustrated all too well.

Great efforts are being made to develop less conventional sources. In June 1971 the United States Government described a plan that may develop the oil-shale resources that underlie about 11,000,000 acres of Colorado, Utah and Wyoming. While expensive to mine and process, the shales contain a vast reserve of petroleum. Mining of the somewhat richer and extensive tar sands of northern Alberta is already under way.

Another power source of considerable geological interest is the use of volcanic steam or hot water. Large power plants using steam released from volcanic regions by drilling have been in operation in Italy and New Zealand for many years. An extensive operation is under way at The Geysers, Calif.; and smaller plants are operating in Iceland, Japan, Mexico and the Soviet Union. Altogether the production of over 1,500,000 kw is contemplated.

The great concern of earth scientists in the preservation and where necessary the restoration of a healthy environment was evident in 1971. The United States Geological Survey produced a guide for evaluating the environmental impact of proposed works of man. At a conference in Virginia, over fifty geologists and planners discussed the problems of creating the environment of a new town. An awareness has developed of the need to consider environmental factors in all major plans for cities and in the extraction industries.

The Appalachian Mountains were one of the first regions ever to be examined geologically, and for over two centuries they have been a classic font of many fundamental geological ideas, including geosynclines, structural geology and geomorphology. John Rodgers made the accumulated knowledge about the Appalachians readily accessible for the first time, in 1971.

In August 1971 about 3,000 geophysicists met in Moscow for their 15th reunion, the 2 previous meetings having been in Zurich and Berkeley. Perhaps the major feature was a week-long symposium reviewing the results of the decade-long Upper Mantle Project. The theories of sea-floor spreading and of plate tectonics, the modern versions of continental drift, received almost universal acceptance from Soviet as well as Western scientists. A new International Geodynamics Program was launched, primarily to investigate the details and causes of these motions. In 1972 the world's geologists will meet in Montreal with field trips planned throughout Canada.

J. TUZO WILSON
Professor of Geophysics
University of Toronto

In West Berlin Town Hall, Dec. 11, Ulrich Müller (r) of West Berlin and Günther Kohrt of East Germany initial Berlin treaty.

GERMANY

Without doubt the major event in Germany during 1971 was the completion of an agreement on Berlin by the four powers that had conquered the Third Reich 26 years before.

Berlin. The accord signed on Sept. 3 by the ambassadors of the United States, Britain, France and the Soviet Union provided not only for an easing of the tensions that had beset the divided city for so many years, but also for material improvement in the lives of the 2,130,-000 West Berliners. Chief among these improvements was a Russian guarantee that movement of persons and goods on the land routes between West Berlin and West Germany would henceforth be "unimpeded." This signaled an end to the annoying and costly harassments of traffic on the highways, railroads and waterways perpetrated by the East German communist authorities for over two decades. It also meant that West Berlin's isolation, 110 miles inside East Germany, would be less precarious.

The accord, reached after 17 months of wearying negotiations, included much more for the West Berliners. It opens the way for them to visit relatives and friends in East Germany for the first time in almost six years. It provides them with West German consular protection in East Europe. It secures West Berlin's economic and cultural connections with West Germany. It authorizes exchanges of parcels of land between West Berlin and East Germany, easing access for several hundred citizens stuck in tiny enclaves virtually surrounded by East Germany's walls and death strips.

The Big Four agreement on the status of West Berlin was filled in further by two accords initialed on Dec. 11 by the governments of West Germany, East Germany, West Berlin and East Berlin.

East-West Relations. There was meaning enough in the first substantial and detailed East-West agreement on the perennial postwar trouble spot that Berlin had been. Yet the significance of the Berlin accord went much further, for it lay at the roots of a whole series of East-West efforts at *détente* in Central Europe.

For one thing, the United States and its partners in the North Atlantic Treaty Organization had made it clear to the Soviet Union that the Western Alliance was not interested in discussing such pressing matters as mutual troop cuts and reductions of strategic arms until a Berlin settlement was reached. For another, West German Chancellor Willy Brandt had made it equally clear to the Russians that he could not proceed with parliamentary ratification of West Germany's 1970 goodwill treaty with the Soviet Union until agreement on Berlin was complete. Finally, the Western allies told the Russians that they could not consider the Soviet proposal for a general European security conference until the Berlin issue had been settled. It was this series of connections that made the agreement imperative to the Russians and led them to make last-minute concessions which none of the Western negotiators had expected.

In the Western view of the Berlin negotiations, the conclusion was unanimous that the final four-power accord could not have been reached so soon without two major changes within divided Germany. The first breakthrough came as a result of Chancellor Brandt's decision, in August 1970, to sign Bonn's goodwill

**GERMAN DEMOCRATIC REPUBLIC
(EAST)**

Area: 41,610 sq. mi.
Population: 16,200,000
Capital: East Berlin
Government: Erich Honecker, communist party secretary—1971; Willi Stoph, premier—1964; Walter Ulbricht, chairman council of state—1960
Gross National Product: $34,000,000,000
Foreign trade: exports, $4,581,000,000; imports, $4,847,000,000
Armed forces: 126,000

treaty with Moscow. The second great prod was the ouster in May 1971 of Walter Ulbricht as leader of East Germany's ruling Socialist Unity (communist) Party. The 78-year-old Ulbricht, who prided himself on his Leninist orthodoxy, had dug himself in as the chief obstacle to a Berlin settlement, declaring to his Soviet allies that concessions would ultimately weaken his German Democratic Republic.

East Germany. Ulbricht's obstinacy on this point and, as well, his increasingly high-handed way of dealing with his Russian allies in ideological matters contributed to his downfall. With the U.S.S.R. backing him, Erich Honecker (Ulbricht's disciple and the number two man in the East German party) made the run to unseat Ulbricht. After a false start in the summer of 1970, Honecker finally succeeded in May 1971 and was confirmed as the new first

secretary at the eighth party congress a month later. Honecker moved quickly to strip away the special "apparatus" that Ulbricht had built up to run East Germany. In the following months he dismissed people and policies associated with his onetime mentor. The old man hung on in the ceremonial post of head of state. But that was about all.

The effect of Honecker's assumption of power was not only beneficial to the Berlin negotiations but also served to scale East Germany down to size in relation to the rest of the Soviet bloc. Under Ulbricht, East Germany had tended to act as schoolmaster for the rest of East Europe, including the Soviet Union. Under Honecker, it appeared, East Germany would no longer stand out as extraordinary or eccentric on the European communist scene. The rewards for Honecker's obeisance to Moscow were expected to be acceptance of East Germany in the United Nations and, in time, diplomatic recognition of the East German Government by the Western states that had steadfastly denied that acknowledgement in the past. Finally, the changing of the guard in East Germany and the Berlin agreement made possible a gingerly *rapprochement* between the two German states, although it had yet to be negotiated by the end of 1971. At least the path was at last open, and it seemed that in time Bonn and East Germany would take up formal ties.

The first of 88 RF-4E Phantom reconnaissance jets, promised by the United States, arrive at Bremgarten Air Base, southwest Germany, Jan. 20.
UPI

Erich Honecker (r) succeeds 77-year-old Walter Ulbricht as first secretary of East German Communist Party.

Camera Press

West Germany. The Berlin agreement put a seal of approval on Willy Brandt's *Ostpolitik*—his policy of seeking normal relations with the governments and peoples of Eastern (communist) Europe. Crowded against the iron curtain since the end of World War II, the Federal Republic had been the last Western bastion of cold-war thinking until Brandt became chancellor in 1969. Soviet party chief Leonid Brezhnev paid tribute to the change personified by Brandt, inviting him to his Black Sea vacation retreat at Oreanda in the same month that the Berlin agreement was signed. It was a unique honor for a Western statesman in 1971, although to some it smacked of untoward intimacy. Brandt and Brezhnev agreed to consult more or less regularly on mutual problems and on their joint efforts toward securing peace in Central Europe. The Oreanda meetings seemed to have a positive influence on general East-West efforts toward understanding and cooperation. For West Germany the prospects of normal ties with Czechoslovakia, Hungary and Bulgaria were distinctly improved.

Brandt gained another mark of distinction in October with the announcement that the Norwegian Parliament had awarded him the 1971 Nobel Peace Prize. (See Nobel Prizes.) Coming from a country that had been invaded and occupied by the Nazis in World War II, the Nobel Prize signified a national emergence from the international doghouse for many Germans. A further sign of a kind of return to normalcy for the West Germans was the visit of Queen Juliana of the Netherlands to Germany in the autumn of 1971. The Dutch had long clung to anti-German sentiments. Another "normalization" event was the state visit of Emperor Hirohito of Japan, the wartime ally of Germany, which had also returned to international respectability.

Ordinary Germans in both the West and East parts seemed to feel that these events, in sum, meant the end of the postwar period and the beginning of a new era of international relations. The pain of Germany's national division hardly diminished, however. East Germans attempting to escape across the high, wide barriers to the West were still being shot down by communist border guards, and thousands of families remained split.

The miseries of division provided fuel for arguments by the parliamentary opposition in Bonn. Early in October the conservative Christian Democratic Union picked Rainer Barzel, who had consistently criticized Chancellor Brandt's *Ostpolitik*, as its party chairman and putative candidate for the chancellorship in 1973. Once chosen, Barzel modified his opposition to Brandt's still unratified treaties with the Soviet Union and Poland, and in December he journeyed to Moscow to hear the Russian side of things. By the end of 1971 it was still uncertain whether Barzel and the Christian Democratic deputies would vote against ratifying Brandt's treaties in the Bundestag, that is,

FEDERAL REPUBLIC OF GERMANY (WEST)

Area: 95,743 sq. mi.
Population: 58,900,000
Capital: Bonn
Government: Gustav Heinemann, president—1969; Willy Brandt, chancellor—1969
Gross National Product: $185,000,000,000
Foreign trade: exports, $34,189,000,000; imports, $29,814,000,000
Armed forces: 467,000

An automotive company's 330-foot-high, $31,-000,000 office building goes up in Munich.

the lower house of the West German Parliament.

On Dec. 10, at a meeting of the NATO ministerial council in Brussels, it was announced that West Germany had agreed to pay more of the costs of maintaining U.S. troops in West Germany.

The Economy. The conservative opposition, which has kept Brandt's parliamentary majority down to about six votes, also campaigned strongly against the Government's economic policies. During the first three quarters of 1971, West Germany was beset by inflationary tendencies. Prices went up about 6 per cent.

The Government's troubles were compounded by chaos on the international currency markets. "Hot money" flowed into the land of the ever stable Deutschmark. Bonn's Economics Minister Karl Schiller made a lonely decision in May 1971 when he ordered that the German mark be "floated" indefinitely. The effect was to revalue the mark upward by almost 10 per cent in relation to the U.S. dollar. The American Government welcomed the step, but the French and some other industrial nations deplored it. The mark continued to float through the summer and late fall pending a realignment of parities among the leading Western industrial powers.

Professor Schiller was having difficulties on other fronts as well. In May, Bonn Finance Minister Alex Möller quit his job, objecting to attempts by his fellow cabinet ministers to increase the Federal budget. Chancellor Brandt immediately handed the Finance Ministry to Professor Schiller, making him a kind of "superminister." In November his state secretary, Philip Rosenthal, resigned, complaining that Minister Schiller had ignored his ideas on tax reform.

Topping this off the Metal Workers Union called a strike in November that soon put 600,000 laborers off the job. The unionists, worried by rising prices, demanded an 11 per cent wage increase. The employers offered 4.5 per cent. A mediation offer of 7.5 per cent was accepted by the unions and rejected by the employers, who evidently saw the strike and accompanying lockouts as a means of putting new pressure on the Social Democratic-Liberal coalition led by Chancellor Brandt. However, the strike ended on Dec. 16 when management accepted the 7.5 per cent offer.

The effects of inflation, however mild when compared with other national rates, were also felt by several renowned German concerns. Volkswagen, which had made an international success with its "beetle" model, could not meet the rising competition from Japan combined with new American tariffs. The company replaced its chairman, Kurt Lotz, with a new man, Rudolf Leiding, and cut down its new-model program. The Voigtlander camera company, unable to produce new models that would increase sales, collapsed.

For Germans themselves the year's notable events included other matters scarcely noticed abroad: a drought that left the Rhine River at its lowest in more than a century and also created one of the century's best wine vintages; a huge bribery scandal in the national soccer league; a national debate over whether to abolish legislation barring abortions; and the statistical report that German women were getting taller and curvier.

DAVID BINDER
Chief Correspondent, Germany
The New York Times

On stopover in Greece, Vice-President Agnew visits home of his great-grandfather in Gargalianoí.

GREECE

Premier George Papadopoulos eased martial law in Greece during the year, but refused to set a date for a return to democracy even under pressure from Washington. U.S. Vice-President Spiro T. Agnew highlighted the year for many Greeks with an official visit to the land of his ancestors.

Economically, the country continued to struggle with growing indebtedness and trade deficits and failed again to attract the foreign investments it has sought since the military coup in 1967 overturned civilian leadership. A major setback came on Nov. 8 when the Government and shipowner Aristotle Onassis agreed to drop a $600,000,000 deal, the biggest investment package in Greek history, because of differences over finances.

Papadopoulos dismissed his entire 30-man Cabinet on Aug. 24 and two days later formed a 37-member Government, the fifth shakeup since the coup. Papadopoulos retained three main portfolios and downgraded two key colleagues, one of them Deputy Premier Stylianos Pattakos, in a move observers said increased Papadopoulos' power.

The 52-year-old former tank commander partially lifted martial law Apr. 17 as a gesture to mark the Greek Orthodox Easter and the fourth anniversary of his coming to power. The music and songs of two prominent Greeks, composer Mikos (*Zorba the Greek*) Theodorakis and actress Melina (*Never on Sunday*) Mercouri were banned. However, Papadopoulos' move relaxed the military grip on civilians, especially in the courts.

The Government announced on Oct. 9 that it would hold limited elections before the end of 1971 for 60 members (15 others are appointed) of a Consultative Committee, a "mini-parliament" to advise Papadopoulos but with no lawmaking powers. About 11,000 persons, chiefly leaders of professional organizations and labor unions, voted on Dec. 12.

In a ninety–minute speech to the nation on Dec. 18, Premier Papadopoulos announced that after Jan. 1, 1972, martial law would be limited to the Attica area, which includes Athens and Piraeus, and to the city of Salonika. The Premier also said that political prisoners would be released, income taxes would be cut, and special family allowances would be paid in effort to reverse the declining birth rate.

But Papadopoulos refused to set a date for national elections. He said on July 16 that he would not order elections under pressure from anyone or as a way of winning more foreign aid from the United States, adding: "We may hold elections tomorrow, in 20 months or 20 years." The statement came after a U.S. House of Representatives committee voted to suspend military aid to Greece, set at $118,000,000 in 1971, as a way of applying pressure on Athens to restore democracy.

Agnew arrived on Oct. 16 for an eight–day official and private visit, his first to the country his father left in 1897 to go to the United States. When the Vice-President left, he said he thought Papadopoulos intended to restore democracy. A government spokesman said Agnew was correct, but refused to set a date although Papadopoulos said he was working "ceaselessly" to build a democracy.

Agnew received a warm welcome despite a threatened Left-wing campaign to disrupt or curtail his visit. Security was so strict that Agnew never heard even a boo. Two days after Agnew left, the Government said it had rounded up 36 persons on the eve of the vice–presidential visit, one of them Dimitrios Partsalidis, one–time "premier" of a 1940's communist guerrilla movement.

Antigovernment violence dropped sharply in 1971 although an explosion on May 14 at a statue of former President Harry S. Truman killed a policeman. The bombing was blamed on an organization that said it would destroy American property and symbols as a sign of displeasure at alleged Washington support of Papadopoulos.

The number of trials involving antigovernment activities also fell sharply. In the most publicized trial, Lady Amalia Fleming, 62, widow of the Nobel Prize winner who discovered penicillin, was sentenced to 16 months imprisonment on charges of conspiring to free a man convicted in a 1968 assassination plot against Papadopoulos. The Government stripped Lady Fleming of her Greek citizenship on Nov. 14 and deported her to Britain. Civilian courts, rather than military tribunals, took over jurisdiction in sedition cases. In the major case of this kind, 7 of 25 defendants were found guilty on Aug. 6.

On the international front, Greece established diplomatic relations on May 6 with Albania in a move signaling an era of closer ties among Balkan states. Albania and Greece were technically still at war when they agreed to exchange ambassadors. Pattakos left on Feb. 10 for official visits to Cairo and Addis Ababa (Ethiopia), the first such visits by any Greek official since the military takeover.

On Feb. 1, about a hundred construction workers staged the first strike since the coup in support of demands for unpaid wages. Three months later, the Government said it would revise existing labor laws and permit some strikes under certain conditions.

Poet George Seferis, 71, who won the Nobel Prize for Literature in 1963, died on Sept. 20. His body was escorted to an Athens cemetery by thousands of Greeks chanting "freedom." He was one of the Government's sternest critics.

Tourism was the brightest note in the economy, despite embarrassment to government offi-cials at the peak of the summer season when the Greek Orthodox Church prayed for divine protection against tourists, "invaders from the West." A record 1,600,000 foreigners came in 1970, spending a record $192,700,000; and in the first eight months of 1971 tourists spent $187,000,000. Otherwise economically the balances of trade and payments, foreign-reserve holdings and budget deficit were unfavorable.

Exports through Aug. 31 totaled $363,000,-000, down from 1970; imports totaled $1,229,-000,000, up from 1970 when Greece reported an overall trade deficit of $1,315,000,000. "Invisible," or nontrade, revenues reduced the deficit through Aug. 31 to $278,000,000, which was almost exactly the total of the country's holdings in U.S. dollars and gold.

Per capita income was $892 at the end of the year, and the Government predicted an annual growth rate of 7.6 per cent for the 1970's. Prices went up only 3 per cent while industrial production increased by 10.9 per cent. Officials reported an increase of 7.1 per cent in the gross national product. The budget deficit for 1971 was $283,000,000 but officials said it would be covered by domestic and foreign loans.

The collapse of the Onassis deal was the biggest disappointment of the year for the Government. The agreement had been signed in 1970. By its terms, the Government had granted Onassis a concession to supply Greece with 64,000,000 tons of crude oil in exchange for investments worth $600,000,000 in industrial projects, including an oil refinery, a power plant and an aluminum factory. Onassis sought a revision in the terms after oil and freight costs soared early in 1971. After a dispute, which included threats by Onassis to sue, the Government voided the deal and returned a $7,000,000 guarantee posted by Onassis, who in turn dropped his demands for compensation payments totaling $20,000,000.

CHARLES W. BELL
News Editor, Rome Bureau
United Press International

GREECE

Area: 50,944 sq. mi.
Population: 9,000,000
Capital: Athens
Government: Constantine II, king—1964; George Papadopoulos, premier—1967
Gross National Product: $9,200,000
Foreign trade: exports, $643,000,000; imports, $1,958,000,000
Armed forces: 159,000

HIGHWAYS

The rapid pace of road building set in 1970 continued in 1971. Despite growing interest in mass-transit systems of transportation, the noncommunist world again spent over $41,000,000,000 on its highways. With the aid of World Bank loans, highways were being built or improved around the world, from the emerging nations of Africa to the wilds of Malaysia.

South America. The concentration on roads was particularly marked in South America where, until recent decades, there had been little interest in highway transport. In 1971, $1,650,000,000 was spent on highways there.

The Argentine Highway Department contracted for the construction of 1,678 miles of new highways. The work, to cost $250,000,000, will include stretches of the Rosario–San Nicolas expressway, the Buenos Aires–San Nicolas expressway, and the international road to Chile. To the north, progress was reported on two ambitious projects. The 4,800-mile Marginal Forest Road, planned for completion in 1985, will integrate the highway systems of six countries and open cultivable land on the isolated east slope of the Andes. Brazil's $500,000,000 trans-Amazon road project, begun in 1970, will open a vast wilderness area to settlement and eventually cross the Andes to the Pacific. The first stage of the project, a 4,000-mile largely two-lane highway, will extend to the Peruvian border.

An unusual road is being built by Guyana volunteers. Called the National Self Help Road, the project is a 123-mile section of a 400-mile highway that will connect Georgetown, the capital city on the Atlantic coast, with Lethem on the Brazilian border. Built in difficult jungle terrain, the road is scheduled for completion in late 1972.

Closing the Darien Gap. In May, U.S. Secretary of Transportation John Volpe and public works ministers of Panama and Colombia signed the long-awaited agreement to close the 250-mile Darien Gap. It is the missing link in the 14,000-mile Pan American Highway extending from Fairbanks, Alaska, to Tierra del Fuego, near the tip of South America. Congress authorized $100,000,000 for the project, and Panama and Colombia will pay $50,000,000. Until recently, engineers believed that the gap could not be closed because the highway must traverse thick jungles and deep swamps.

Europe. France, which until the 1960's lagged behind other European countries in road building, launched the second phase of an ambitious program. The $270,000,000 project will include over 180 miles of expressways in the Alps and link Lyons, Grenoble, Bourguoin, Chambery and Geneva. The initial stretch of highway, connecting Lyons and Bourguoin, will open in 1974. As England completed its first 1,000 miles of four-lane expressways, Parliament granted $1,200,000,000 for another 1,000 miles. The ultimate aim of the program is to connect every major British city (with populations of at least 250,000) and to serve all ports and airports.

United States. The United States remained the world's major highway builder, expending

Mass is said for workers building road through the remote wilds of Amazonia in Brazil. Eventually the road will cross the Andes to the Pacific.

over $18,000,000,000 on highway construction and improvement in 1971. Projects and plans ranged widely, from completion of a $500,000,000 project for widening the northern 30 miles of the New Jersey Turnpike to a 2,200-mile highway network to spur industrial development in northern Michigan, Minnesota and Wisconsin at a cost of $2,100,000,000.

Though ecological and community groups succeeded in blocking planned highway projects in Boston, Baltimore, San Francisco and other urban areas, over 32,000 miles of the 42,000-mile Interstate Highway System were open to traffic by midyear. The system will be the nation's key highway network, connecting more than 90 per cent of its cities with populations of 50,000 or more and carrying 20 per cent of all its traffic. Sections of the Interstate opened to traffic during 1971 included a difficult 18-mile stretch across a Louisiana cypress swamp.

MARY E. JESSUP
Former News Editor, *Civil Engineering*

HOBBIES

Although sales of many leisure products declined during 1971, a tight economic period, hobby sales prospered. Estimated retail sales of hobby products totaled $910,000,000 in 1971, up from $850,000,000 in 1970. In fact, since 1965, sales of hobby products (kits, accessories, articles for handicrafts, and supplies for making and collecting models) have increased 10 to 15 per cent a year.

Two factors have helped sales. As a number of drugstores and supermarkets began carrying hobby products for the first time, people who might never have known about a specific hobby became aware of its existence. In addition, improved packaging enabled hobby manufacturers to enhance the self-selling characteristics of their products.

Coin collecting continued to come under attack in the Soviet Union. Early in the year, as in 1970, several coin collectors were brought to trial accused of violating the Soviet law against speculation—the sale of valuables for profit. In addition, the Soviet Society of Philatelists has dropped its separate numismatic branch. The society considers coin collecting harmful to "communist education." In behalf of coin collecting, a leading Soviet archeologist said: "The significance of numismatics for his-

A macramé bib (knotted work) is created out of blue beads and matching blue and red rug yarn.

torical science is great and does not require special evidence. The material assembled by collectors is a basic source for the creation and enlarging of the state's numismatic wealth. Hence it is understood that coin collecting is positive."

For the stamp collector, two interesting events occurred in July. On July 1, the U.S. Post Office Department officially became the U.S. Postal Service. On July 26, in London, stamps from Bangla Desh (East Pakistan, which had earlier declared its independence of Pakistan) appeared. Since the region's independence had not been recognized officially, the stamps were not generally accepted as postage. They were, however, a means by which stamp collectors sympathetic to the East Pakistani cause could contribute to it financially.

General Trends. Excluding stamps and coins, hobby items that sold best in 1971 include model planes, trains, rockets and ships. These hobbies are meant for the avid fan who is past youth, usually male and has money to spend. In model building the trend was toward greater realism in color and design. A growing number of modelers mix various kits, using two or more to form designs of their own.

Newer categories of hobby products also did well, especially those with an educational appeal. However, the year's biggest hobby success was in crafts. Sales increased from an estimated $150,000,000 in 1970 to an estimated $210,000,000 in 1971. There were many new companies in the field. More important, more crafts were offered in kit form. Macramé (knotting cord to create decorative designs), batik fabric dyeing, candlemaking, staining glass, jewelry making, needlework, decoupage (the art of applying prints to a wood surface and then treating the surface so that it resembles a painting), making holiday decorations, Indian crafts, creating artificial flowers and leather articles were most successful. Although the emphasis was on crafts for home décor, many women—the bulk of the crafts market—made their own clothes and accessories during 1971. Particularly popular were homemade macramé belts, ponchos and vests.

Coin Collecting. On July 27, 1971, President Nixon presented Mrs. Dwight D. Eisenhower with the first Eisenhower dollar, the first dollar coin produced in the United States since 1935. Containing 40 per cent silver, the coin bears the likeness of President Eisenhower on one side and the insignia of the Apollo 11 moon mission on the other. A highly polished proof set of the dollar cost $10.00, and an uncirculated coin sold for $3.00. The Bureau of the Mint put an undetermined number of copper-nickel versions of the new dollar into general circulation late in the year. The copper-nickel U.S. half-dollar, which was released in April, met with mixed opinions from both collectors and the general public.

Silver coinage also made news in Canada. To mark the 100th anniversary of British Columbia's entry into the Confederation, the Government issued its first silver dollar since 1967. Costing Can$3.00, the coin became available to the collector through the numismatic section of the Royal Canadian Mint.

During 1971, several other countries minted new coins of interest to the numismatist. To mark the 479th anniversary of its discovery by Columbus, Haiti issued a pure silver coin, measuring 30 millimeters. As a bonus to collectors it was minted in frosted proof condition. Independent since 1968, the Indian Ocean island nation of Mauritius issued its first gold coin in October. The Republic of Liberia also minted frosted proof sets. A proof set, which cost the collector $15.00, consisted of 6 pieces in denominations of 1, 5, 10, 25, 50 cents and $1.00.

National Coin Week was observed in the United States, Canada, Mexico and elsewhere, Apr. 18–24. Sponsored by the American Numismatic Association, the occasion was marked by special exhibits. A record crowd of 10,571 persons attended the association's annual convention in Washington in August. John Jay Pittman, a chemical engineer, was inducted as the association's new president.

Stamp Collecting. To mark the establishment of the new U.S. Postal Service, collectors were offered a souvenir envelope with the insignias of the new and old offices. Gordon C. Morrison, a lifetime stamp collector, was named director of the Service's Philatelic Affairs Division.

On July 4, the Government released the first of a series of stamps marking the 200th anniversary of the United States. The last stamp of the series will come out in 1976, the bicentennial year.

From the moon, Aug. 2, Apollo 15 commander Col. David Scott held first-day-cover ceremonies for a pair of stamps honoring U.S. space achievements. Immediately after the ceremonies on the moon, first-day sales opened at Cape Kennedy, Fla.; Houston, Tex.; and Huntsville, Ala. Other 1971 U.S. commemoratives honored the 450th anniversary of the founding of San Juan, Puerto Rico; the 25th anniversary of the CARE program; the sport of bowling; and the 10th anniversary of the Antarctica Treaty. To coincide with Drug Prevention Week in the United States, Oct. 3–9, a multicolored vertical stamp, designed by Miggs Burroughs of Westport, Conn., was released.

U.S. Postal Service

Copying a daguerreotype, the only picture ever taken of the poet, stamp shows her in her teens.

The second of the American Poets series bears a portrait of Emily Dickinson holding a nosegay.

The Canadian Government released a Maple Leaf in Autumn commemorative, produced in 5-color lithography; a 7 cent, larger than usual, commemorative honoring Paul Kane's painting *Indian Encampment on Lake Huron;* and a British Columbia centennial stamp. The UN General Assembly named 1971 "International Year for Action to Combat Racism and Racial Discrimination." A number of nations issued stamps on the theme. Great Britain's 1971 anniversary stamps honored the 1,900-year-old city of York, the sport of rugby, and the British Legion—men and women who served in the nation's armed services, including military nurses.

Taiwan's 1971 Folk Tale series defined the "primary virtues of life." The stamps were adapted from 24 *Folk Tales of Kuo Chu-yeh* (Yuan dynasty, 1279–1368). The Government of Uruguay released a 9 cent commemorative for Dan Mitrione, a U.S. official killed by guerrillas in Uruguay in 1970. For the 60th birthday of Prince Bernhard of the Netherlands, husband of Queen Juliana, June 29, 4 new Dutch airmail stamps were issued.

GEOFFREY WHEELER
Editor, Hobby Publications, Inc.

HONECKER, ERICH

As the son of a hard-line communist worker, Erich Honecker, the new first secretary of East Germany's ruling Socialist Unity Party, rates as a "noble Communist"—still a rather rare distinction in the land. He was born Aug. 25, 1912, in Neunkirchen, a small Saar industrial town and, at age 10, was enrolled in the Young Pioneers, a communist youth organization. He has been an unswervingly dedicated party zealot ever since. Full party membership came in 1929 at age 17, when he was learning the roofer's trade. In 1931 he attended a seminar for young party workers in the Soviet Union. On his return to Germany, he was assigned the post of agitation-propaganda secretary in the party's Saarland youth association.

When the Nazis came to power in Germany two years later, Honecker assumed an alias and went on underground missions for the Communists. He was captured by the Gestapo in Berlin in 1935 and sentenced to ten years' imprisonment for "treason." He served most of these years in the large penitentiary at Brandenburg-Görden, escaping in March 1945 while on a work detail. Two months later, as the nazi forces were surrendering, he made contact with the group of emigré Communists from Moscow led by Walter Ulbricht. Honecker was given the job of building up a new communist organization, Free German Youth, which was to provide cadres for the party.

After further schooling in Moscow in 1956–57, he was elected a full Politburo member and secretary of the Central Committee with the key responsibility for organization and security affairs. All this time he was considered a loyal disciple of Ulbricht and his logical successor.

After a false start in 1970, he won Soviet support for pushing the stubborn and aged Ulbricht out of the party chieftainship in the spring of 1971. Since then he has shown himself to be more flexible than Ulbricht in responding to Soviet demands, particularly on easing the tension over divided Berlin. At the same time, he has forged ahead with his own special policy of "fencing off" East Germany from West Germany by breaking off remaining cultural and technical contacts wherever he can.

A natty dresser, the short and slender Honecker has been married twice, first to an older former Social Democrat, Edith Baumann, and then to a younger Communist, the former Margot Feist, who is currently minister for education. He has a daughter from each marriage.

DAVID BINDER
Chief Correspondent, Germany
The New York Times

HONG KONG

Only 400 square miles on Communist China's underbelly, the British crown colony was reminded in 1971 that neither nature nor the world's most powerful nations consider Hong Kong insignificant. Typhoon Rose struck on Aug. 16–17, killing 130 people and prompting Peking to counter the Hong Kong government's U.S.$165,016 relief plan with an offer of U.S. $1,300,000 to its "compatriots." Then, on Washington's Oct. 15 deadline, Hong Kong agreed, after months of pressure, to limit U.S.-bound synthetic and wool textiles to a 7.5 per cent annual growth rate. For export-or-die Hong Kong, this clamp on its biggest market overshadowed even President Nixon's Aug. 15 ditching of the dollar's gold convertibility and his imposition of a 10 per cent import surcharge. (The surcharge was removed as 1971 ended.)

In February the European Economic Community had conceded that Hong Kong was a "developing country" as far as UNCTAD's (UN Conference on Trade and Development) generalized preferences scheme was concerned. But protectionism abroad was the biggest problem confronting Sir Crawford Murray MacLehose, the Scottish-born career diplomat who became governor on Nov. 19 at the end of Sir David Trench's thrice-extended tenure of 7½ years. On the heels of a highly publicized strike by 154 blind workers demanding pay raises, the new Governor's first-day speech pledged new social-welfare efforts for the colony's 4,000,000 people (98 per cent of them Chinese). Near the end of 1971, estimated per capita annual income was U.S.$800. Although the consumer price index showed a rise of only one per cent in the year ending in September, it omitted massive increases in residential rents, a source of growing social unrest.

A British ballistics expert was maimed in a March bomb blast, and street crime was increasing. The murder count by October 1971 had exceeded 1970's total of 72, the highest since the communist-inspired riots in 1967. To counter obvious social dissatisfaction the government in 1971 introduced free (and compulsory) primary education and moved to give the Chinese language equal status with English in governmental and judicial affairs. Communists in the colony's minuscule labor movement were docile and took no part in the year's only "political" activities: demonstrations favoring language reforms, and violent student protests against Japan's claim to the Senkaku Islands which, they claimed, belong to China.

DEREK DAVIES
Editor, *Far Eastern Economic Review*

HOUSING

Home building in the United States in 1971 represented a booming business in a sluggish economy. During much of the year, home construction ran at the annual rate of nearly 2,000,000 conventional units, plus 500,000 mobile homes, those units that are mobile only while being towed from building site to homesite. Thus home building during the year showed its best results in almost two decades.

The cost of financing a house purchase came down a little during the year. At their peak, home mortgage rates averaged slightly more than 8 per cent, a record for the country. But the average was lowered to about 7.5 per cent, or even a bit more in some sections of the nation, before rising to an average of about 7.7 per cent. Then came President Nixon's freeze on wages, prices and rents. Although interest rates were not covered they remained stable during late 1971 and even declined in a few cities. Because more money was available for home building, the ratio of single housing units vs. multi-units (meaning apartments, for the most part) increased during the year. For every 100 units started in 1971, about 60 were single-family homes and 40 were multi-unit; in 1970, the ratio was 55 to 45.

The change in mortgage rates from their peak to the lower yearly averages does not sound like much. Yet it is estimated that for a typical home buyer a decline of 0.5 per cent in the mortgage rate represents a $9 lower monthly mortgage payment. That is a total of $2,160 for a 20-year mortgage.

In midyear, builders and would-be home buyers got another incentive when the Federal Home Loan Bank Board (the agency that supervises savings and loan associations) authorized Federal savings associations to make conventional home loans with down payments as low as 5 per cent. About the same time, the Nixon administration acted to keep mortgage rates at 7 per cent on Federal Housing Administration and Veterans Administration-guaranteed home loans. Secretary George Romney of the Department of Housing and Urban Development (HUD) cited as plus factors in the home-building picture the administration's efforts to remove building-code restraints in many cities, to gain cooperation from construction unions and builders in eliminating restrictive labor practices (and thus hold down costs) and to encourage factory-built housing. The latter Federally assisted effort is called Operation Breakthrough. It began in 1969 and during 1971 showed its first concrete results. A number of mass-housing assembly plants were opened, and tangible results appeared in such places as Kalamazoo, Mich.; Macon, Ga.; Sacramento, Calif.; Indianapolis, Ind.; and Seattle, Wash.

All this is not to say that the housing picture remained totally bright and spotless in 1971. On the other side, the overall cost of housing continued to climb. In a special message, President Nixon said that despite sharp increases in housing output during the year, "housing costs continue to rise, pricing many families out of the market for adequate homes. . . . In 1965, an average newly constructed home purchased with an FHA-insured mortgage cost a little more than $16,800. At interest rates then prevailing, total expenses for mortgage expenses, taxes, insurance, utilities, and maintenance and repair to operate that house came

Modular units are used in construction of an apartment house designed to meet demand for second homes, near Sugarbush, Vt., ski slopes.

"The New York Times"

The cozy interior with the country air is part of a dwelling built out of prefabricated units of selected white cedar, treated so that it never requires either paint or stain, inside or out. The standard models can be tailored to meet individual requirements.

American Timber Homes, Inc.

to approximately $147 a month. To build a similar-sized house on a similar-sized lot [today] probably would cost $24,500, and with financing at present rates plus all the operating expenses, total monthly payments on such a house would be nearly $265." In August, the United States Savings and Loan League said "the typical new home today, with three bedrooms, two baths and 1,400 square feet of living space, costs $32,000, compared with $25,000 as recently as 1966. Some estimates say that in another 10 years, a new home with those specifications will be priced in the $50,-000–$60,000 range."

The league said "the cost of buying a home is being pushed upward by spiraling land prices, increases in building material prices, high interest-rate levels and skyrocketing construction labor costs." Rising property taxes also have made the cost of owning a home more expensive. In 1966 the typical property tax on a house and lot with a sale value of $25,000 was $495; in early 1971, the tax totaled almost $625. The latest available property-tax data on such a house and lot show the following: Alexandria, Va., $447; Anaheim, Calif., $569; Boston, $1,130; Cedar Rapids, Ia., $837; Chicago, $550; Detroit, $590; Duluth, Minn., $590; Greensboro, N.C., $484; Kansas City, Mo., $539; Little Rock, Ark., $349; Niagara Falls, N.Y., $974; Racine, Wis., $1,004; St. Petersburg, Fla., $457; South Bend, Ind., $916; Utica, N.Y., $1,195; and Waterbury, Conn., $787.

While many Americans were struggling to save to buy a house, or were hunting an apartment, the nation heard a continuing plea for more low-cost housing—the kind occupied by the poor and often by members of minority groups. The Republican administration and the Democratically controlled Congress struggled for most of the year over a variety of proposals to pump more funds into low-cost housing and to redirect Federal moneys into the Model Cities program, designed to permit cities to put up not only government-assisted housing but to embark on a variety of other projects. There existed in 1971 a patchwork of thirty Federally-subsidized public and private housing programs.

But of all the housing issues debated during the year the one that received the sharpest attention and hottest debate revolved around erecting low-cost (hence, Federally-assisted) projects in the suburbs. The issue involved not only housing but race, for the fact is that many low-cost housing projects in and near big cities are peopled by blacks, and the suburbs by whites.

Blacks and other minority groups, supported by civil-rights organizations and even the U.S. Civil Rights Commission, argued that since job opportunities were rising in suburbia, so should low-cost housing. Also, these groups contended, it was morally and legally wrong to put up more mass housing in the ghettos. This housing issue was the subject of numerous court tests and brought a major statement by President Nixon. He said the Federal Government would use its power to bar racial or religious discrimination but would "not seek to impose economic integration upon an existing local jurisdiction."

ROBERT W. DIETSCH
Business-Economics Editor
Scripps-Howard Newspapers

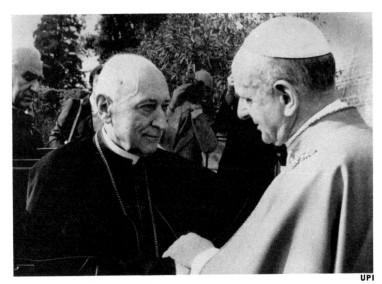

Pope Paul VI welcomes Jozsef Cardinal Mindszenty to the Vatican. The Roman Catholic Primate of Hungary had been sentenced by the Communists to life imprisonment in 1949 and had been in self-imposed exile in the U.S. Embassy in Budapest since 1956.

UPI

HUNGARY

Hungary continued its slow progress toward political and economic reform. Election reforms were implemented in the voting for the National Assembly and the local councils. The New Economic Mechanism (NEM) gave additional responsibility to middle-level managers. A 15-year-old problem was solved when Jozsef Cardinal Mindszenty, Roman Catholic primate of Hungary, who had taken refuge in the U.S. Embassy in Budapest following the 1956 revolution, settled in Vienna after agreeing to give up his self-imposed confinement.

Election Returns. The electoral reform permitted multiple candidacies, but all of them had to accept the program of the communist-dominated Patriotic People's Front. When the elections were held on Apr. 25, 49 constituencies had more than one candidate, representing 14 per cent of the National Assembly's 352 contests. In some 70,000 local council elections, only 4.3 per cent were contested.

Trade Unions. The 22nd National Congress of Trade Unions, held in Budapest May 4–8, gave evidence of a further degree of limited independence of action by the body representing the country's workers. Some aspects of the economic-reform program, particularly in regard to wages and prices, were criticized. The trade-union organization insisted that it must be heard before the program was changed. Premier Jeno Fock promised that such cooperation would be forthcoming.

The NEM. On the economic-reform program, in its third year in 1971, Fock asserted that the NEM had proved itself in practice as it had avoided two potential problems, unemployment and inflation. Still to be solved, however, were

the problems of unprofitable state investments, unnecessary construction projects, stockpiling, high labor costs, and the balance-of-payments deficit. To deal with the investment problem, enterprise managers were given authority to draw up investment plans for their factories, releasing the state from involvement in overambitious projects.

Intrabloc Relations. In a gesture obviously inspired by the Soviet Union, Hungary took the lead in condemning Rumania for its posture of independence vis-à-vis the Soviet Union, and for its outspoken support of the People's Republic of China. On June 24, Zoltan Komocsin, Politburo member, speaking before the National Assembly, condemned "small country separatism" and pointed to the danger of any Chinese intervention in the Balkans. Komocsin's remarks were rejected sharply by his Rumanian counterpart, Paul Niculescu-Mizil. Despite the flurry of recriminations, normal governmental relations were not broken between them.

International Affairs. Hungary became the first communist country to obtain a Eurobond loan, a 10-year, $25,000,000 bond issue at 8.75 per cent interest. The loan was underwritten by Morgan Grenfell and the National Westminster

---

HUNGARY

Area: 35,919 sq. mi.
Population: 10,300,000
Capital: Budapest
Government: Janos Kadar, Communist Party Secretary—1956; Jeno Fock, premier—1967
Gross National Product: $14,400,000,000
Foreign trade: exports, $2,317,000,000; imports, $2,506,000,000
Armed forces: 103,000

Bank of Great Britain and the Soviet Union's Narodny Bank, with headquarters in London. The money will be used for imports.

The Mindszenty Case. The decision of Cardinal Mindszenty to leave Hungary on Sept. 28 followed years of discussion among Vatican representatives, the Hungarian regime and the Cardinal. He had insisted on full legal dismissal of the charge that he was a "conspirator and traitor" for having supported the 1956 revolution. Before taking up a new assignment in Vienna, the Cardinal visited the Pope at the Vatican.

HERMAN SINGER
Editor, *East Europe*

ICELAND

The parliamentary elections on June 13 were a kind of watershed in Icelandic politics. The Government coalition parties, conservative Independence and Social Democrat, lost their parliamentary majority, as a result of which the Government resigned, after 12 years in office. No single Icelandic government has had a longer tenure. On July 14 a new left-wing Government took office, consisting of the three former opposition parties. It was the first time since 1927 that an entirely new Government had come to power, i.e., without a party from the outgoing Government participating.

Election results showed a marked swing to the left. The Independence Party lost 1 seat and obtained 36.2 per cent of the total vote compared with 37.5 per cent in 1967. The Social Democrats lost 3 seats, obtaining only 10.45 per cent of the total vote compared with 15.7 per cent in 1967. The Progressive Party (mostly agrarian), the largest opposition party, also lost 1 seat, dropping from 28.1 per cent in 1967 to 25.25 per cent of the total vote.

Even though the People's Alliance (left-wing socialist) received the same number (10) of seats as in 1967, this represented a considerable victory, as during the last electoral period 3 of the party's members of Parliament defected. One joined the Social Democrats, and the other 2 formed the new Liberals and Leftists Party. The latter, campaigning for the first time,

emerged as the chief victor of the elections with 3 new seats in addition to the 2 defectors. The party polled nearly 9 per cent of the total vote. Thus the left-wing members in the 60-member *Althing* (Parliament) increased from 10 to 15.

A sixth party, consisting mainly of dissatisfied young students who satirized Icelandic politics generally and called themselves the Candidates' Party, succeeded in attracting 2 per cent of the total vote. This party became immensely popular during the election campaign. Its spokesmen were quite unorthodox in their behavior, even though they were forbidden to use songs, signs or posters in their television appearances, and managed to keep up the same witty and sarcastic tone to the very end. The party, its program and candidates were one of the most successful political jokes Iceland has ever seen.

The head of the new left-wing Government is the chairman of the (Center) Progressive Party, Olafur Johannesson, who is also minister of justice and church affairs. His party is in charge of foreign affairs, finance and agriculture. People's Alliance ministers are in charge of fisheries, commerce, industry and health, while Liberals and Leftists control education, social affairs and communications. The three government parties have a majority of 4 in the *Althing,* with 32 seats against the two opposition parteis' total of 28 seats. The new Government aims to end the 1961 agreements on fishery limits with Britain and West Germany, and to extend the present fishery limits from 12 to 50 miles not later than Sept. 1972; have the United States gradually evacuate the NATO base at Keflavik Airport by 1975; continue membership in NATO (though the parties are not in agreement on this). Iceland supported the admission of the Chinese People's Republic to the UN and would support the admission of both West and East Germany. At home, the new Government retained a price freeze and strict price controls; shortened the workweek to 40 hours, and increased, by 20 per cent in two years, the purchasing power of the lowest paid workers; established a State Planning Board for control of investment and planning of industry; authorized construction of 15 to 20 additional stern-trawlers; increased old-age and disability pensions.

Extension of fishery limits has priority, and the Foreign Minister went to London and Bonn to prepare the ground. He also addressed the United Nations General Assembly. However, the question of the American military base will not be dealt with until sometime in 1972.

SIGURDUR A. MAGNUSSON
Editor, *Samvinnan*

ICELAND

Area: 39,768 sq. mi.
Population: 203,000
Capital: Reykiavik
Government: Kristjan Eldjarn, president—1968; Olafur Johannesson, prime minister—1971
Gross National Product: $400,000,000
Foreign trade: exports, $147,000,000; imports, $157,000,000

Photoreporters Inc.

An Indian Army tank waits at the side of the road to Jessore, East Pakistan town not far from border, which quickly fell to the Indians.

INDIA

In no other year since its independence in 1947 has India witnessed as many dramatic developments as in 1971. The year opened with Mrs. Gandhi's ruling Congress Party fighting for its political life, and India's economy beginning to exhibit solid and broadly based economic growth. But that economic growth was accompanied by a sharp public debate on increasing unemployment, great wealth amidst greater poverty, and the privilege of former princely rulers in a democratic republic. Millions of destitute refugees from East Pakistan strained India's resources. Then, in December, came the bitter armed clash in which India decisively defeated Pakistan.

Politics. Mrs. Gandhi, both to strengthen her Government's position in the country and to save herself from a possible parliamentary defeat, called a general parliamentary election for the late winter. For the first time in Indian history, the national elections did not coincide with elections in the Indian states, and the voters therefore could not consider local and national issues jointly. By this shrewd move, Mrs. Gandhi weakened provincialist opposi-

Photoreporters Inc.

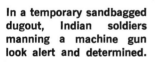

In a temporary sandbagged dugout, Indian soldiers manning a machine gun look alert and determined.

ployment and a "socialist pattern of society" set Mrs. Gandhi against the conservative parties which were her principal adversaries.

The results of the election in March were unexpected. Mrs. Gandhi's ruling Congress Party won 350 of 521 seats in Parliament, a majority so large that it needed no partners for amending the constitution. The conservative wing of the Congress Party, which had broken with Mrs. Gandhi, lost badly and witnessed its decline from 65 to 16 seats. The religious-Right party, the Jan Sangh, lost 11 seats, declining from 33 to 22. The economically conservative Swatantra Party lost even more dramatically, from 35 seats to only 8. While the popular vote for the Congress increased only marginally, it was the beneficiary of many contests in which independents and many parties contested the seats, leaving the ruling Congress the largest single organization.

While Mrs. Gandhi had championed so-called socialist issues, her party had in fact "moved Right" during the campaign. On the highly visible issues of the banks and princes, there was a national consensus that Mrs. Gandhi was pursuing a reasonable policy. But few sophisticated voters imagined that any Indian Government could make dramatic inroads on the unemployment policy. On the other hand, it was clear to all that the problem had to be attacked with vigor, and, politically, only Mrs. Gandhi seemed to recognize that fact. The decisive fact, however, was that the election pitted Mrs. Gandhi against no one. The ranks of the opposition parties were filled either with unknowns or with very old, tried-and-rejected politicians.

The 1971 elections accomplished the unforeseen. They restored an effective one party dominant system to India and immeasurably strengthened Mrs. Gandhi within the Government, and the Government within the country. From that position, she saw to the nationalization of private banks and the elimination of the privy purses of princes, and she attempted to galvanize the administration into labor-intensive development plans to attack unemployment.

Foreign Affairs. In the winter of 1970–71, India's neighboring state Pakistan held elections after 12 years of army-presidential rule under Field Marshal Mohammad Ayub Khan. The result of the elections was a landslide victory for a secessionist party in East Pakistan (Bengal), the Awami League. In the wake of elections, Pakistan's politicians and military leaders attempted to draft a constitution that would preserve national unity while allowing Bengal maximum autonomy. In late March,

Campaigning before the elections, Prime Minister Gandhi speaks on rostrum above lifelike symbol, a cow and nursing calf, of her Congress Party.

tion and ensured that the campaign would be fought on national issues alone.

The issues that the Prime Minister chose to dramatize for the election were nationalization of private banks, the elimination of the financial allowances of the former princes, and the need for extraordinary efforts to eliminate or reduce unemployment. On the first two issues, Mrs. Gandhi had been frustrated by the courts and weakened by her small majority in Parliament which did not allow for the constitutional amendments necessary for accomplishing these acts. The concern with unem-

In support of the East Pakistanis' desire for greater self-government, Indians demonstrate in front of the Communist Chinese Embassy in New Delhi. (China backed the Pakistan Government.)

UPI

efforts to arrange this understanding broke down, and civil war broke out in East Pakistan. Almost immediately, thousands of Bengali leaders fled Army suppression, and were given asylum in India.

India protested the steps of the Pakistan Army, and allowed Bengali refugees to organize both a government-in-exile and some guerrilla forces in Indian areas bordering East Pakistan. Pakistan responded by sending more troops to East Pakistan and by arming local forces in East Pakistan that remained loyal to the central Government. These forces began attacking groups thought to be loyal to what was being called "Bangladesh," and Bengali guerrillas supported by Indian regular forces made all frontier districts unsafe. These developments led to a massive refugee flow into India, principally of Bengali Hindu peasants living near the Indian frontier. By December the number of refugees that had fled to India was estimated to be between 7,000,000 and 10,000,000.

As tensions had developed earlier in the year, and as the United States had begun to cultivate better relations with China, India had signed a treaty of peace, friendship and cooperation with the U.S.S.R. This defense treaty, coupled with increased Soviet supplies to India's armed forces, was part of a diplomatic maneuver to isolate Pakistan and prepare for a military showdown. While protesting West Pakistani suppression of East Pakistan secessionists, India also appealed for international assistance in meeting the heavy financial burdens imposed on it by the millions of refugees. In November, Mrs. Gandhi traveled to West Germany, France, Britain and the United States looking for assistance, a settlement of the Pakistan civil war that would allow the return of the refugees, or Western forbearance should India take military steps to free Bangladesh. In the first week of December, India took such steps, and war broke out between the two countries. India's victories in the East compelled surrender there less than two weeks later; and on Dec. 16 India ordered a cease-fire on both East and West fronts. It was only a question of time before a Government of Bangladesh would be recognized, and a treaty of close cooperation signed between it and India.

The refugees and the war cost India its development budget for 1971, and immeasurably increased the difficulties of the eastern Indian provinces. But the war's victories left Pakistan a shattered state, and as a consequence permanently foreclosed Pakistan's ability to compromise India's flanks, at least in the east. Moreover, the bold steps and sophisticated diplomacy of Mrs. Gandhi and their reflection in India's military victory fur-

INDIA

Area: 1,261,813 sq. mi.
Population: 547,000,000
Capital: New Delhi
Government: V. V. Giri, president—1969; Indira Gandhi, prime minister—1966
Gross National Product: $50,000,000,000
Foreign trade: exports, $2,026,000,000; imports, $2,095,000,000
Armed forces: 980,000

ther strengthened the Prime Minister's popularity in the country. By the end of the year, Mrs. Gandhi's strength in the country had been completely reversed from its weak beginnings, and India's strength as a political system and as a power had been convincingly demonstrated.

Economy. Thanks to good rains, increased use of fertilizers, hybrid seeds and better storage and marketing arrangements, India's agriculture continued to grow in 1971, and the near-famine years of the late 1960's appeared to be well behind the increasingly successful "green revolution." Indian industry continued to exhibit problems; in some fields, such as textiles, there was surplus capacity. In other areas, steady expansion of exports and increasing domestic markets led to broad-based expansion. The urban-industrial economy was not growing fast enough to create jobs for the millions of new members of the labor force or for peasants "freed" from the land by more scientific agriculture, however. And Indian planners continued to have much more modest aims for their efforts, especially as foreign-aid amounts declined and debt repayments for past development loans consumed an ever larger percentage of exports.

On balance, however, before the war with Pakistan, most Indian economists were modestly optimistic about the near future. In some areas, such as defense production, India was making great strides, and increasing agricultural production gave the country some breathing spell in the race against population growth. But the arrival of 10,000,000 refugees, new measures of taxation to support them, a major reduction in the U.S. economic-assistance program, and the war costs seem to have once again brought the economic performance of the society into doubt. The burdens that Bangladesh will put on India are also likely to be heavy in the future, and it seems most unlikely that more than a few of the refugees will be willing to return to the Muslim-majority villages in Bangladesh where their lands have already been expropriated in a desperately overcrowded area. The replacement of war materials lost in battle will mortgage the Indian economy further to the U.S.S.R., and reduce amount of exports available for convertible-currency earnings.

Neo-Nationalism. The year 1971 found India in the midst of nationalist revival. Strengthened by economic performance, cordial and close ties with the U.S.S.R., and military prowess, India's national self-confidence was restored. Mrs. Gandhi's domestic policies shifted attention from growth to more equitable distribution, and the knitting together of classes that had not shared in economic growth.

Whether such confidence is sufficient to overcome the problems of the Indo-Pakistan war, the disintegration of urban services in cities like Calcutta and Bombay, the extraordinary pressure of a population that grows by 13,000,000 to 14,000,000 people a year, 10,000,000 refugees, and high defense expenditures is still to be seen. In spite of the magnitude of the problems, most Indians probably felt surer of their nation's future at the end of 1971 than they did at its beginning.

WAYNE WILCOX
Professor and Chairman (on leave)
Department of Political Science
Columbia University

Photoreporters Inc.

Officials hand-count the votes by which Mrs. Gandhi won an overwhelming and unexpected triumph at the polls in March.

South Vietnamese troops, in a camouflaged tank, move into Laos. With U.S. withdrawal continuing, ground fighting passes largely to South Vietnamese.

INDOCHINA

In the Indochina war, it was a year of steady withdrawal of U.S. troops from Vietnam. As 1972 began, the United States armed forces, which had peaked three years before at more than 500,000 men, were down to 139,000. Except for U.S. air support, the combatant role had passed largely to the South Vietnamese armed forces. What had been an international conflict, since U.S. entry into the conflict in 1965, reverted to essentially a civil war between the communist North and the Saigon Government of President Nguyen Van Thieu. Yet the big powers still were providing the money and weapons: the Soviet Union and the People's Republic of China to Hanoi, and the United States to Saigon.

While there was progress from the U.S. military viewpoint in Vietnam, the related struggles in adjoining Cambodia and Laos worsened. Moreover, despite Congressional limitations on financial aid, U.S. participation and employment of mercenaries in these side conflicts, and the best intentions of U.S. diplomats and military planners of keeping within prescribed limits, U.S. involvement was more noticeable, particularly in Cambodia.

The relentless drift stopped short of putting U.S. ground troops into Laos and Cambodia, and no level-headed observer was predicting that "another Vietnam" was in the making in either satellite war.

The best hope for peace in Indochina still appeared to be through negotiations. Nevertheless, the Paris peace talks remained stalemated, even after a new U.S. negotiator, William J. Porter, took over.

For the American side, the most pressing 1971 issue was the release of some 460 American prisoners: 378 believed held in North Vietnam, and the remainder thought to be captives in Laos or enemy-occupied areas of South Vietnam and Cambodia. (*See also* Prisoners of War)

In Vietnam, 1971 was only a month old when the Army of the Republic of Vietnam (ARVN) made a daring, large-scale foray into Laos. The objective was to reach Tchepone, or Sepone (preferred spelling by the National Geographic Society), 25 miles inside Laos on Route 9, and fan out on both sides of the old French colonial highway to cut the enemy's Ho Chi Minh Trail, a network of roads, paths and rivers running north-south through eastern Laos. Over these transport arteries, using trucks, sampans and backpackers, the North Vietnamese Army (NVA) has continued to supply its war fronts in South Vietnam, Cambodia and Laos itself, in spite of the heaviest and most concentrated U.S. bombing of any war.

For 44 days early in 1971, South Vietnamese troops (l) invade Laos to crush North Vietnamese supply lines along Ho Chi Minh Trail. United States provides air, artillery and logistical support (above, U.S. helicopters carry South Vietnamese paratroopers from Khesanh to advance positions in Laos) but, by Congressional order, no ground troops.

The ARVN operation, called Lam Som 719 by the Saigon high command, had the approval of the U.S. commander, Gen. Creighton Abrams, and was supported by U.S. troops of the Fifth Mechanized Division and 101st Airborne Division as far as the Laos border.

About 19,000 ARVN troops crossed the border, most of them flown in by U.S. helicopters whose pilots braved some of the heaviest antiaircraft fire of the Vietnam war. The invaders soon ran into stiff North Vietnamese resistance. It was home ground for the enemy, and they fought tenaciously although pounded by U.S. bombers.

The lead units of rangers, airborne and troopers of the First ARVN division reached some trails and destroyed stockpiles, but withdrawal from Laos was ordered several weeks

ahead of plan. There were heroic acts by rearguard ground troops, and courageous helicopter evacuations of cutoff troops. There also were instances of panic and rout. Both U.S. and Saigon commands put the best possible face on the 44-day operation, but hardheaded appraisal marked Lam Som 719 a failure.

In losses it may have been a standoff. The ARVN suffered some 5,000 dead, wounded and missing, and the NVA troops were believed to have been hit even harder by the bombing. Yet the supply flow down the Ho Chi Minh network had barely been touched.

The performance of the U.S. helicopter armada rated both plaudits and chills. The U.S. Army definition of downed choppers was complicated (if recovered by a heavy-lift-crane helicopter, a crashed whirlybird was not con-

UPI

Correspondent Kate Webb writes story of her capture and release by Vietcong. It had been reported that the 28-year-old Australian was dead.

came the day of glory when a chartered airliner or a ship took them "back to the world," the United States.

Many professional officers regretted that the armed forces were leaving without "having done the job." Others, veterans of two or three tours in Vietnam, were convinced that victory in the traditional sense had never been possible, and that by passing the job on to a well equipped and trained Saigon Army, Navy and Air Force, the United States had fulfilled its obligation. Seldom troubled by a sense of inferiority, the average ARVN officer appeared glad to see his U.S. counterpart departing. ARVN officers reasoned that without American pressure, combat might be slowed to an Asian pace, if the NVA were willing.

Except for heavy U.S. bombing of the North during the Christmas weekend, the Vietnam conflict seemed at year's end to be in a lull. The Hanoi Defense Minister, Gen. Vo Nguyen Giap, concentrated his forces in Cambodia and Laos as a new dry season began in those regions.

The low level of combat postponed a significant test of Vietnamization. Lam Som 719 had been too ambitious an undertaking. But could Saigon's 1,000,000 men under arms (476,000 regulars, the remainder militia) do well without U.S. support in defending the Southland against mixed bands of NVA regulars and Vietcong guerrillas? Insurgents remained in large areas of South Vietnam, although the Saigon Government claimed that 70 per cent of the countryside was under its control and 90 per cent of the people were loyal.

UPI

sidered "shot down"). By commonsense tally, more than 50 troop-carrying choppers, gunships and observation birds were downed in Laos, and some 100 crewmen killed.

The losses raised anew the contention that the helicopter, while a spectacular success in giving mobility to American troops fighting a guerrilla war, may be too vulnerable in conventional battle.

The rollback of the U.S. presence in Vietnam had, by late 1971, reduced the number of Americans killed in combat to about twenty a month. Remaining units eagerly awaited the order to "stand down"—turn over weapons and equipment to Vietnamese, and prepare other gear for "retrograde" shipment to home storage bases. Then, after GI's had passed tests showing them free of drug addiction,

Cambodian soldier keeps automatic weapon ready as his task force moves down the strategic Highway 4.

Nguyen Van Tien, Vietcong deputy negotiator at Paris peace talks, and William Porter, U.S. negotiator from Sept. 9, attend initial 1972 session.

Northern provinces below the demilitarized zone were already looking run-down as the last full U.S. division in Vietnam—the 101st Airborne—began to pack up. Central coastal provinces, around Quinhon and Danang, also were considered no longer secure—if they ever had been. The departure of the 50,000-man South Korean contingent—last of the Allies to phase out—left large gaps in the defense of such infamous provinces as Binh Dinh, where the Vietcong had hung on even during the era of energetic American search-and-destroy operations.

Except for three American infantry brigades of about 5,000 men each, almost complete responsibility was handed over to the ARVN. The Vietnamese Navy had acquired all the inland-waterway boats of the U.S. Navy. Only the American effort to build a viable Vietnamese Air Force (VNAF) continued; helicopters and planes were being turned over as pilots and ground crews became available. VNAF had 900 aircraft, 400 of them helicopters and the rest simple jet fighter-bombers and old but reliable prop planes.

There were no plans to give the VNAF more sophisticated American jets. It became obvious that from bases in Thailand and from the decks of carriers in the Gulf of Tonkin, the Americans would continue to perform the major role in the assault on the Ho Chi Minh Trail. The U.S. Navy and the Seventh/Thirteenth Air Forces in Thailand would also be available to provide an aerial umbrella for ARVN should

it become hard pressed. Only a satisfactory Indochina peace treaty would allow a pullout of the 450 American bombers and fighters that were aloft daily as 1971 closed.

Within Vietnam itself, the U.S. Air Force was down to 4 jet-fighter squadrons, and the Army helicopter fleet had been reduced from 3,000 to 1,900 birds. Nevertheless, the Indochina air war, in which triple the tons of bombs dropped in World War II had already been dumped, began a new and menacing phase.

In what appeared to be counteraction to the punishing bomber blows, the North Vietnamese Air Force began sneak raids over northern Laos.

Soviet-made MiG fighters were aloft, and radar-directed antiaircraft guns and missiles began to take a toll of U.S. fighter-bombers, although they had yet to knock down one of the high-flying, super-bombing B-52's.

The Seventh Air Force in Saigon, directing the Indochina air battles, escalated—with President Nixon's approval. On Dec. 26 a 200-plane strike force hit airfields and missile sites in North Vietnam, and similar attacks followed during the next several days. It was the biggest assault on the North since the formal halt in 1968 of the campaign to bomb North Vietnam into submission.

From a military standpoint, two critical uncertainties confronted South Vietnam's President Nguyen Van Thieu. First, were the South Vietnamese troops, after more than a decade of war and the continuing prospect of 20,000 dead each year, too war-weary to fight? For himself, Thieu remained dogmatically opposed to an end to the war except on Saigon's terms. His platform, as he campaigned for a second four-year presidential term, consisted of four noes. No neutrality, no coalition government, no concession of territory to the enemy, no surrender.

As a general, Thieu also was said to be concerned about continuing ARVN involvement in the Cambodia war, with 10,000 troops permanently committed, and another 10,000 making periodic cross-border forays.

This commitment to a "fireman" role in Cambodia to relieve pressure on Cambodia's own forces when under attack by the NVA was at the urging of the United States. At least the permanently stationed troops were paid a bonus by the United States Government. Their absence from normal positions in the Delta and around Saigon added to the worries of defend-

UPI

Reelected—he was the only candidate—Vietnamese President Thieu proposes economic reforms.

South Vietnamese girl sells lottery tickets showing photo of Thieu instead of war scene.

UPI

ing the Vietnam homeland. The VNAF seemed almost entirely committed to the Cambodian war, and its aircraft made no meaningful contribution in other regions, leaving the job to American forces.

The steady U.S. pullout compounded President Thieu's economic problems. American aid in various direct and indirect forms would be needed to keep the Saigon Government solvent. The amount required might be more than Congress would be willing to provide, unless Thieu were willing and able to effect and enforce some austerity measures proposed by his economic brain trusters in November 1971.

The end of American military construction and the closing of bases resulted in the firing of some fifty thousand direct-hire Vietnamese employees during 1971. Hard times hit several hundred thousand Vietnamese profiting from the free-spending GI who was going, going, gone.

In Cambodia, 1971 was remarkable for the fact that the Government of Gen. Lon Nol survived. His Army continued to be mauled when it came to grips with the North Vietnamese, and he suffered a stroke that left him partially incapacitated. During the latter part of 1971, he shared power with an astute politician, Lt. Gen. Sirik Matak. As deputy premier, Matak ran the Government. Lon Nol provided the inspiration and controlled the Army.

Military setbacks occurred steadily throughout 1971, with only a small "victory" claimed occasionally when the North Vietnamese and

Lt. Gen. Sisowath (l) greets Lon Nol as the partially incapacitated Cambodian leader returns to Pnompenh after undergoing treatment in Hawaii.

their Khmer Rouge collaborators chose to fall back rather than fight. The NVA battle strategy seemed similar to that practiced in Vietnam and Laos: Cut government roads; harass the capital, Pnompenh, for prestige and propaganda gain but do not burden the cause by taking it; avoid massing and thus becoming a target for U.S. aircraft; and fall back when confronted by superior forces or faltering supply lines.

Such tactics left refugee-swollen Pnompenh periodically cut off from its main supply port, Kompong Som on the Gulf of Siam. When it suited the enemy, other highways leading out of town were cut, sometimes as close to the city as ten miles. The Government became primarily dependent at times on gunboat-escorted convoys up the Mekong River from Saigon, although heavily armed convoys could get through by highway from Thailand.

Once a beautiful French colonial city like Saigon, Pnompenh was beginning to look embattled and battered—in the manner of Saigon during the "bad years" of the mid-1960's. Boulevards were blocked off; sandbagged gun positions guarded government buildings and the homes of prominent officials.

There were terrorist acts, mostly directed against the staff of U.S. Ambassador Emory C. Swank (he himself was a target, but the explosive charge did not ignite) and the 60-man U.S. Military Equipment Delivery Team. MEDT members are soldiers in mufti, who doubled in number during 1971 and were in-

creasingly seen in the field with Cambodian troops, despite a ban on advisers.

The hastily expanded Cambodian Army grew in 21 months from a parade-ground 35,000 to a chart-listed 220,000. At training camps in Vietnam and in neighboring Thailand, recruits were learning how to be soldiers, and bright young Cambodians were being turned into officers. But the Army had not yet jelled, although patriotism and nationalism were not the missing ingredients, as they had been during the early years of the ARVN expansion.

While direct U.S. involvement in Cambodia and Laos was blurred, U.S. military men appeared to be steadily assuming a supervisory role in the Cambodian war. This was always true in Laos, and the only new U.S. ground-combat involvement there was the hiring of Thai Army soldiers to fight alongside the feeble Laos Government Army.

It became known in 1971 that some four thousand Thai Army troops were in Laos, with their own unit commanders. As with the Thai contribution to the Allies in Vietnam, these Thai troops were called volunteers and drew their pay directly from U.S. funds.

So again the question was raised as to whether in Laos, and with the intention of doing the same in Cambodia, the Nixon administration was not fighting the war with mercenaries when it was not politically possible to use U.S. ground troops. Congress has passed legislation banning the use of mercenaries. The argument over whether the ban was being circumvented degenerated into semantics over the meaning of "volunteer" and "mercenary."

Employment of U.S. fighter planes for close support of embattled Cambodian and Laotian troops also escalated. Once limited to an "interdiction role," U.S. aircraft now flew low over all the Indochina war fronts. The only limit to their effectiveness was the lack of English-speaking spotters with the Indochinese infantry on the ground. Helicopters were increasingly being used to deploy both Cambodian and Laotian troops.

"Once you start helping a friend, and he starts depending on you, how can you turn him down when he needs more help?" an American officer in Pnompenh argued plaintively.

In Laos the dry-season advance of the NVA and its Pathet Lao auxiliary went deeper into Laotian Government territory and stayed longer. But they retreated or were driven back partway during the rainy season.

As the dry season began again at year's end, the NVA had already regained complete control of the strategic Boloven Plateau in southern Laos, and was knocking at the outer guard of the key U.S.-Laotian base of Long Cheng in the north.

If the NVA suffered a setback in Laos, it was the documented revolt of Pathet Lao units against their North Vietnamese masters. It occurred in the Boloven where, for several months, Pathet Lao units walked into the government town of Pakse to volunteer to fight against NVA leaders who, as one junior Pathet Lao officer explained, "have treated us badly."

Politically, it was a slightly embarrassing year for U.S. defenders of the Vietnamese and Cambodian "democracies."

President Thieu was reelected to a new term, but in a manner that just about destroyed the carefully constructed "free elections" introduced in previous years to please the Americans. Thieu outmaneuvered one candidate, forced the other prominent contender to the sidelines through a court proceeding, and so ran without opposition. Thieu turned the vote into a plebiscite and got a more than 90 per cent endorsement.

In Cambodia, Lon Nol and Sirik Matak eliminated the National Assembly as an obstruction. This, coupled with the dissolution of the Thai Parliament and the voiding of a short-lived Thai constitution by the ruling military junta, made it a bad year for rule by the people in three Southeast Asian countries given strong American support.

Another unsettling development was the devaluation, in quick succession, of the beleaguered currencies of Cambodia, Laos and South Vietnam. In all three, the causes were the same: rampant inflation and loss of production arising from debilitating wars.

JACK FOISIE
Southeast Asia Correspondent
Los Angeles Times

In Danang harbor, a part of the U.S. Third Marine Amphibious Force prepares to return home.
Wide World

INDONESIA

The 1971 political scene in Indonesia continued to reflect the pragmatic personality of President Suharto. General elections were held on July 3, for the first time since 1955, with the government-backed Sekber Golkar (Functional Groups) landsliding to victory over the 9 political parties permitted to take part. Although the campaign was sometimes stormy, election day was quiet. In Western terms, Golkar's win gave the Suharto administration a two thirds majority among the 360 candidates elected to the House of Representatives. With an additional 100 legislators (75 from the armed forces, 25 from civic-military groups) appointed by the President, the 460-seat house was sworn in on Oct. 28.

The shifting of the Government toward a civilian administration continued in 1971, leaving only 4 generals (including the President) and an air vice-marshal among 18 cabinet-rank ministers and 6 ministers of state. Although cells of the banned Peking-orientated Indonesian Communist Party survived, internal security improved.

In Indonesian foreign affairs, the debts incurred by the Sukarno regime were rescheduled: terms taking repayments up to the year 2000 were signed with East Germany, Czechoslovakia and Poland. Other rescheduling had been agreed to in 1970.

Foreign Minister Adam Malik was elected president of the UN General Assembly on Sept. 21. In August, Queen Juliana and Prince Bernhard of the Netherlands visited Indonesia, an event viewed as an act of reconciliation between former colonist and colonized.

Jakarta was quick to feel the impact of 1971's international monetary crisis, and the rupiah was devalued on Aug. 23 by 10 per cent. Agriculture continued to contribute half of the gross national product whose average annual growth rate, according to 1971 figures, was 7.5 per cent in 1970, 6.3 per cent in 1969. Behind the economy's rapidly increasing strength was a fast rise in development expenditures (and foreign investments; by June 1971 capital commitments totaled U.S.$1,563,000,000). With more technocrats in government, the second five-year plan, starting Apr. 1, 1974, was expected to switch the emphasis from agriculture to industry.

Distributing the population remained a major problem. The Transmigration Ministry continued its efforts to move families from overcrowded Java and Madura to outer islands. Still one of the world's least privileged peoples (with an average annual income of less than U.S.-$100), Indonesians were showing some re-

sponse to governmental family-planning programs. Meanwhile the massive Civil Service was being examined following the Sept. 9 appointment of Dr. Emil Salim. He was charged with making the structure efficient after years of time-wasting bureaucracy, corruption and expensive mismanagement.

Developments in the oil industry brightened the trade picture: in January-June 1971 exports totaled U.S.$622,500,000, an increase of 7.4 per cent over the same period of 1970. After oil, the greatest increases were in timber, coffee, palm oil, and pepper. Imports in January-June 1971 totaled U.S.$659,800,000. Throughout, Indonesian official phraseology described the country as "active and independent." Relations with the United States were good, and in August a team of Soviet experts arrived to restart work on two big Soviet development projects (steel and superphosphate).

DEREK DAVIES
Editor, *Far Eastern Economic Review*

INDUSTRY

The year 1971 may be remembered as one in which industry became productive again. It was also a year when many industries faced difficult internal adjustment. The U.S. business slowdown was contagious. Although Japanese industry continued to pace much of the world, it grew more slowly. In West Germany, the floating deutsche mark slowed down export sales. Industry in almost every nation was affected by the mid-August U.S. dollar crisis and the 10 per cent surcharge placed on U.S. imports.

Multinational U.S. companies, which had been transferring production overseas from high-cost U.S. plants, reconsidered moving in the light of changing costs. Not only did the Nixon economic program make overseas investment more expensive but the higher duties made it more costly to bring the product back into the United States. Within the United States, recovery was sluggish. Renewed buying of nondurable goods, as well as automobiles and houses, aided consumer-oriented industries.

However, defense-related industries—including aerospace, electronic components, metals and capital goods—spent most of the year trying to find their way out of the recession. Overall, U.S. industry operated at 73 per cent of capacity. Stress was laid most heavily on boosting productivity. Companies removed excess "fat" by cutting payrolls, closing inefficient facilities, eliminating unprofitable products and reducing such "frills" as travel and entertainment and executive-development programs.

Building. Construction was the bright spot of the economy. U.S. housing starts reached close to 2,000,000 units, a new record. Expenditure on new residential housing was up some 32 per cent over 1970. Builders looked for the pickup in housing to continue throughout 1972. It would help not only the construction industry but also appliance manufacturers and several other major industries.

Chemicals and Plastics. Chemical companies recovered slowly in 1971. Nevertheless, sales of most chemicals were up, and as a result of stringent cost-reduction programs many chemical concerns increased their earnings. The increase in profitability was far from universal. For example, final figures for Bayer, Hoechst and BASF—Germany's "big three"—were expected to show earnings down 15 to 20 per cent, despite slightly higher sales. The main cause was the high cost of amortizing the big expansion programs planned when the economic outlook was rosier.

U.S. chemical companies cut their work force by over 5 per cent. An estimated 33,000 jobs were eliminated. Chemical companies concentrated production in high-capacity, low-unit-cost plants. Unprofitable product lines, such as Du Pont's Corfam, were discontinued. All this helped to improve productivity and boost profits.

The high level of housing starts helped sales as did the growth in retail sales, the increased use of synthetic fibers—particularly for carpeting—and an end-of-year surge in automotive buying. For example, the average 1971 Detroit-made car contained 110 pounds of plastics, compared with 100 pounds in the 1970 model. Total U.S. sales of plastic resins were up some 6 per cent, far less than the 12 per cent annual increase that plastic producers had come to expect.

Large-volume plastics—such as polyvinyl chloride, phenolics, polypropylene and polystyrene—either declined or showed only slight growth. However, specialty plastics—such as ABS, urethanes, polyesters, polyacetyls, fluorocarbons, polycarbonates and nylons—made big gains. As a result, resin makers stepped up development of these engineering-type plastics, which have unusual properties.

Food Processing. World food production established new records in 1971. The U.S. harvest was the largest in the country's history. Output was up some 12 per cent over 1970. Processed-food prices increased so little that Americans continued to spend a smaller proportion (16.4 per cent) of their disposable income on food than do people anywhere else in the world.

Iron and Steel. Steel production rose in the developing countries, but slumped in the industrialized nations. The less developed nations of Asia, Latin America and Africa have been building steel mills in order to save hard-to-come-by foreign exchange. The new capacity has cut into the lucrative export markets of Japan and the traditional steelmaking nations of Western Europe and North America. Overall world steel production was about 5 per cent under the 594,600,000 metric tons produced in 1970. Western Europe, Japan and the United States all produced less steel than in 1970.

In the United States, steel mills did well early in 1971 as car manufacturers built up inventories in anticipation of a possible steel strike. An agreement was reached on Aug. 1 without a strike. According to U.S. Steel, the settlement would increase labor costs by 15 per cent during the first year. On Aug. 2 the company announced price increases averaging 8 per cent. This was in addition to a 7 per cent increase announced in January.

The inflationary nature of the steel wage-and-price increases was among the major factors that led President Nixon to announce a wage-and-price freeze on Aug. 15. When the freeze went into effect, the price increases had affected only about 45 per cent of the steel industry's products. The inability to keep up with higher wages was an element in the fact that most U.S. steelmakers operated at a loss in the last five months of 1971. The other major problem was the sharp decline in orders because steel buyers were working off the inventories built up in anticipation of a strike.

For the year as a whole, U.S. steel production reached some 120,000,000 tons, an 8 per cent decline from 1970. Shipments came to about 86,000,000 tons, with 2,500,000 tons exported. This was a 64 per cent decline. On the other hand, imports soared to 18,000,000 tons. Total U.S. steel consumption was close to 102,000,000 tons.

On the technological side, keen interest continued in new direct-reduction processes, ore pelletizing, continuous casting, and computer control of rolling mills. Researchers were par-

A 26-foot grinding mill has a vital part in the expansion program of a copper complex in northeastern Turkey. Three such mills, valued at an estimated $1,500,000, will increase the capacity of the Black Sea Copper Works, near Murgul, by some 40,000 tons yearly.

Allis-Chalmers

ticularly interested in new pollution-control systems.

Machinery. With much of industry operating far below capacity, little new capital equipment was purchased. Thus, with few exceptions, manufacturers of industrial equipment had a very poor year. Over 25 per cent of the U.S. manufacturing capacity was idle. Expenditures for new plant and equipment totaled some $82,000,-000,000. Taking into account the increase in prices, this represented a decline from 1970 capital expenditures.

Some multinational companies expanded more rapidly overseas than in the United States, as they found it possible to build and produce far more cheaply in Europe or Japan. The trend was strengthened by the boost in productivity that during the 1960's had increased output per man-hour 11 per cent a year in Japan, 8.3 per cent in the Netherlands, 6 per cent in West Germany and 4.7 per cent

in France. The U.S. productivity gain had only been 3.3 per cent a year. The rush to build overseas slowed after President Nixon announced his new economic program on Aug. 15.

Among the industries hurt most by the economic slump was machine tools. Despite the development of numerically and computer-controlled tools, the industry's big customers in the auto, aircraft and appliance industries were not buying. Where new tools were needed, old machines were retrofitted to do the job. As a result, final figures were expected to show that total 1971 new orders for U.S. machine tools were not much over $840,000,000. In comparison, in 1969 new orders had amounted to $1,728,000,000.

Not all parts of the machinery industry were in the doldrums. Tighter pollution-control standards aided makers of filters, classifiers, scrubbers, electrostatic precipitators, and water-treating-equipment suppliers. In addition, the demand for boilers, turbines, generators, transformers and other equipment to help overcome the electric-power shortage also was high. Overall, at the end of 1971, U.S. machinery makers were hoping for legislation approving new-investment tax credit which might stimulate capital spending.

Nonferrous Metals. The slowdown in industrial activity in Western Europe, Japan and the United States created a surplus of nonferrous metals. The excess capacity resulted from new facilities coming into production that had begun in the more expansionary mood of the late 1960's. With metal-using industries cutting back production, primary producers faced overcapacity, weak prices and falling profits.

Hard hit was aluminum. Between 1960 and 1970, world aluminum production had expanded from 4,543,000 tons to 10,042,000 tons. The average annual percentage growth rate was 8.3 per cent, far higher than that of any other metal. Aluminum-company executives had become so accustomed to being in a market-oriented growth industry that in 1971 they had a hard time adjusting to new conditions.

The excess capacity came about because new reduction plants, planned three to five years earlier, were completed when demand was sluggish. In addition, fabricators of sheet, plate and wire diversified by building their own reduction plants and oversizing them in order to have ingots to sell to others. Thus in the United States, the number of primary producers expanded from 3 in 1948 to 13 in 1971. Add new plants in such former import markets as the United Kingdom, New Zealand, Mexico and Argentina to this, and it is clear why U.S. aluminum exports in 1971 were only about half of those of 1970.

Total U.S. aluminum production for 1971 was estimated at slightly below 1970's 3,976,000 tons. At the end of 1971, reduction plants were operating at some 82 per cent of installed capacity. With increased use of aluminum predicted, industry executives were looking for a substantial upswing. Yet it may be two or three years before the new demand will catch up with capacity.

The copper industry started 1971 with a heavy surplus. But as a result of a month-long strike against U.S. copper companies in July, the expropriation of U.S. mines in Chile and the earthquake there, the industry ended 1971 with consumption more nearly balanced by supply. Prices, which had fallen in 1970 after a ten-year rise, continued to fall.

U.S. exports of copper were down but imports up. Final figures were expected to show total U.S. production of primary and secondary copper in 1971 some 10 per cent below the 1,684,000 tons produced in 1970.

Of vital concern to copper producers were the new air-quality control standards. The largest U.S. producer, Kennecott Copper Co.,

A video-voice system links New York and Tokyo: Black-and-white TV pictures are transmitted on the same circuits as the voice communications.

said that the additional equipment required by its 12 smelters to meet these standards would cost in excess of $250,000,000. This is on top of the nearly $300,000,000 the U.S. copper industry has spent on pollution-control devices during the past 20 years.

Nickel sales nosedived in 1971. Total worldwide 1971 production was expected to be about half of the 575,000 tons produced in 1970. The slackened demand was primarily the result of overstocked customer inventories. In spite of the decline, nickel producers maintained their long-range optimistic forecasts. International Nickel, the top producer, continued its ambitious growth program and spent close to $250,-000,000 in expanding its Canadian facilities.

Increased use of galvanized steel in housing and the demand for zinc die castings for cars helped boost U.S. zinc consumption about 7 per cent above the 1,180,000 tons used in 1970. But U.S. production was off as a result of four smelter closings. This was partially offset by the opening of a new $30,000,000 zinc mine and mill in New York State's Adirondack Mountains.

Lead sales declined in 1971 because of increased use of leadless gasoline. At the end of the year, however, the sharp boost in automotive output, as well as a swing away from unleaded gasoline, helped firm the lead market.

Textiles. Apparel sales made substantial gains over 1970. The big change was toward greater variety in women's wear and the emergence of a specialty high-risk, high-profit men's wear retailing industry, similar to women's wear stores. The big-selling items were double-knits. As a result of explosive growth, in men's wear they may capture half the market by 1975. Double-knits already have 35 per cent of the women's and children's wear market.

STEPHEN W. KANN
Editor and Publisher, *Industrial World*

To help offset sagging U.S. zinc production (four smelters closed), a $30,000,000 mine and mill opens in Balmat, upper New York State.

St. Joe Minerals Corp.

INSURANCE, AUTOMOBILE

By far the most significant development in the U.S. automobile-insurance industry in 1971 was the enactment by several states and the consideration by a growing number of others of "no-fault" insurance legislation. No-fault insurance provides for timely reimbursement by an individual's own insurance company ("first party") for loss sustained in consequence of an automobile accident, without regard to the question of who was at fault.

Proponents of no-fault contend that the existing U.S. tort liability automobile-insurance system, based on the "fault" concept, is excessively costly, unnecessarily protracted, frequently unjust and increasingly unworkable. A variety of "limited" and so-called "pure" no-fault programs have been proposed.

"Limited" no-fault insurance provides automatic compensation for certain classes of loss—most commonly medical expenses, although in some instances loss of income and damage to property—up to a prescribed dollar ceiling. Under most "limited" programs, the damaged individual retains the right to bring tort liability action against the other party to an accident if loss claimed exceeds the level compensated by his no-fault coverage. "Pure" no-fault insurance provides for automatic first-party compensation of all measurable loss sustained, generally without regard to a ceiling. The right to secure further redress in the courts is denied, and compensation for "pain and suffering" is generally limited to medical expenses incurred.

As early as 1946, the Canadian province of Saskatchewan adopted a joint government-industry first-party no-fault system covering both medical and property-damage losses, retaining the right of lawsuit. Voluntary, limited accident-benefits programs, covering personal injury, have been in effect in eight other provinces for some years; and the Commonwealth of Puerto Rico—first entity under U.S. jurisdiction to adopt no-fault—has adopted a government-administered first-party no-fault system compensating personal-injury losses.

In addition to the states that enacted "limited" no fault-laws, others either gave consideration to specific no-fault proposals or authorized studies of the subject. Pioneer in the field was Massachusetts, whose no-fault law became effective Jan. 1, 1971. A "limited" plan, administered through private companies and compensating for medical expenses (up to a ceiling of $2,000) and up to 75 per cent of wages and salaries, the Massachusetts program experienced a reported 53 per cent drop in the statewide number of accident claims during its first six months of operation. The program also resulted in a 15 per cent reduction in premium rates and the average claim amount dropped from about $370 to $169.

At the Federal level, two important approaches to no-fault received Congressional attention in 1971. Following a major study, the Department of Transportation issued recommendations calling for the states themselves to move toward no-fault insurance systems. In the Senate, a national no-fault insurance law was proposed by Senators Philip Hart (D-Mich.) and Warren Magnuson (D-Wash.). During public hearings before the Commerce Committee, a number of consumer-oriented groups and significant segments of the insurance industry itself expressed support for no-fault. Opposition was voiced by several national organizations of trial lawyers, whose income from accident-claim suits would be drastically affected by adoption of the no-fault principle. Milder opposition was presented by others within the insurance industry, which remained divided over the question.

As it stood at the end of 1971, the Hart-Magnuson proposal provided for: (1) mandatory, noncancelable no-fault automobile insurance for all U.S. car owners; (2) premium rates based on an individual's driving record, income level, and amount and type of safety equipment in his vehicle; (3) payment within 30 days by his own insurer, without regard to the question of fault, of an individual's total hospital and rehabilitation expenses, lost wages up to $1,000 a month, property damage (except to his own car), required household help, and funeral expenses; (4) availability of optional coverage for damage to an individual's own automobile and for "pain and suffering" associated with an accident; (5) arbitration of disputes between an insured and his insurer at the latter's expense, and provision for "pain and suffering" court proceedings with lawyers' contingency fees limited to 25 per cent of gross amount recovered. A compromise between the Hart-Magnuson and DOT approaches was also pending at year's end.

In other developments, several states considered statutory revisions designed to make the existing tort liability system more equitable. Most notable of these would affect the present practice in most states of denying a plaintiff accident damages if he is found to have been negligent in any way himself. The practice of Wisconsin and several other jurisdictions of allowing recovery of damages after relative degrees of negligence of the two parties are weighed received attention in several states.

JOHN E. SHIELDS
Editor, *Congressional Digest*

Representatives of British and U.S. oil companies meet in Tehran in January for price negotiations with Persian Gulf producers.

IRAN

Glittering ceremonies to mark the 2,500th anniversary of the Iranian monarchy focused international attention on Iran in October. Shah Mohammad Reza Pahlavi presided over a gathering of some fifty crowned monarchs and uncrowned heads of state for the celebrations, which were held in a tent city at the site of Persepolis, ancient capital of Cyrus the Great, the monarchy's founder. The cost of the event, said to be $16,600,000, was criticized abroad as being an inappropriate expenditure for a developing nation. But the Shah was determined to build an international image of Iran as a state with the oldest unbroken traditions of nationalism and sovereignty in the world.

The Shah announced at the ceremonies that he would abdicate when his first son, now 11, completes his studies. Barring accident this would make the Shah's reign, already 31 years, one of the longest in history. Extraordinary security precautions during the celebrations underscored his absolute rule. Several hundred "political undesirables" were held under detention; schools and government offices were closed; and soldiers ringed the tent city. Protest was not entirely damped down, however. The Iranian Consulate in San Francisco was bombed by anti-Shah students.

IRAN

Area: 636,294 sq. mi.
Population: 29,200,000
Capital: Tehran
Government: Mohammad Reza Pahlavi, shah—1941; Amir Abbas Hoveida, premier—1965
Gross National Product: $10,900,000,000
Foreign trade: exports, $2,355,000,000; imports, $1,658,000,000
Armed forces: 181,000

During 1971 the Shah conducted foreign affairs vigorously, particularly in regard to the Persian Gulf. With British military withdrawal from the Gulf scheduled for the end of 1971, he took no chances on the formation of an Arab coalition against Iran, or the replacement of British by Soviet or other influences in the region. In December, Iranian forces occupied three islands in the Persian Gulf. The Government also began a program of military expansion for the 181,000-man armed forces, including $750,000,000 in arms purchases.

In July, elections for the Majlis (Parliament) gave an absolute majority of its 258 seats to the Shah's Iran Novin Party, formed in 1963 to replace the multiparty system by a broad national front. Voting was light because of security measures and lack of interest. Mardom, the only party that contested the elections, won 39 seats.

The Tehran Agreement between the major oil companies and the six Gulf oil-producing states assured Iran of greatly increased oil revenues. Production almost doubled, to 111,000,000 tons, the world's highest, in the first half of 1971. With more than $1,000,000,000 in royalties available, the future for continued economic growth was bright. Joint government-private industrial and agricultural ventures were allocated $160,000,000 as Iran sought energetically to diversify its development and reduce its dependence on oil.

WILLIAM SPENCER
Professor of History
The Florida State University

The Iranian monarchy's 2,500th anniversary is celebrated among the equally ancient ruins of Persepolis. Soldiers march in long-ago uniforms; and guests enjoy a sumptuous banquet in a tent.

IRELAND, REPUBLIC OF

A troubled year drew to a close with the Fianna Fail Party Government of John M. Lynch clinging precariously to the power it had held for 14 years. Prime Minister Lynch won a confidence vote in the Dail (Parliament) on Nov. 10 by 72 votes to 69. A decisive vote on this occasion was that of former Finance Minister Charles Haughey, dismissed from the Cabinet in May 1970 for suspected complicity in attempts to import illegal arms into Ireland. Haughey voted for the Government under protest, but also in the realization that the alternative would be a critical state of political instability.

Public attention was focused on the troubles of the six counties of Northern Ireland. There the "provisional wing" of the Irish Republican Army (IRA), supported at least tacitly by the North's Roman Catholic minority, has been waging guerrilla warfare against the British Army, the Royal Ulster Constabulary and the local government at Stormont Castle, controlled by the Protestant majority for fifty years.

The aim of the IRA is reunification of the whole island. It was originally partitioned in 1920, following first a rebellion against British rule and then a civil war. The Protestant majority in the 6 northeastern counties wanted to stay united with Great Britain and voted to do so. The Catholic majority in the other 26 counties, however, voted to form the Irish Free State. In 1949 this state assumed full independence and became the Republic of Ireland. The same year, the North, commonly called Ulster, was given to understand that no change would be made in its status as a self-governing province of the United Kingdom without the consent of the Stormont parliament. Such is the genesis of the present conflict.

Today the unity of Ireland is a plank in the platform of every political party in the south. But both the governing party, Fianna Fail, and the Labor Party condemn achieving it by violence. Thus the campaign of violence in Ulster increasingly threatens the political stability of the Republic as well. The IRA, the military wing of the Sinn Fein Party, is illegal. Sinn Fein, of course, is legal. The situation is inherently unstable. However strongly reunification is supported, success for the IRA in the North might trigger a political explosion in the south.

Prime Minister Lynch visited England twice, in September and October, to talk personally with British Prime Minister Edward Heath. There were also tripartite talks that included Prime Minister Brian Faulkner of Ulster. Lynch sought to persuade the others to agree on a timetable for the withdrawal of British troops and the phasing out of British subsidies to the North's economy. His hope was that Ulstermen would then "turn their eyes south" and that the reunification of Ireland could be achieved by peaceful means. Heath and Faulkner insisted that the IRA campaign must first be brought to an end, but Faulkner was in no mood even to consider reunification. His "Unionist" Government draws its support from Protestants who are determined to maintain the union with Britain.

In December, Prime Minister Lynch criticized the IRA severely and gave warning that his Government was preparing to curb its activities within the Republic's borders. He told the Dail that the IRA has "no mandate from anyone."

The other main concerns of the Republic were entry into the European Economic Community (Common Market), inflation, and the question of legalizing contraception (opposed by the Catholic Church).

Ireland's application to join the Common Market moved parallel with that of Great Britain. Acceptable terms for Britain were reached at the meeting in Luxembourg that ended on June 24. For both Ireland and Britain one critical problem remained unsolved as 1971 drew to a close: fisheries policy. The EEC, a net fish importer, had adopted a common policy on fisheries before negotiations opened with Britain, Ireland, Denmark and Norway, all big fish exporters. The main question at issue between community and applicants has been the requirement that unrestricted access to national fishing grounds must be offered to the fishermen of all other member countries.

Ireland is anxious to join the EEC if possible, mainly so that its heavy economic dependence on the British market can be reduced; it took two thirds of Ireland's 1970 exports. The effect of the Common Agricultural Policy also is expected to double the income of Ireland's farmers, increase the output of beef, lamb and milk, and relieve the Government of a $250,000,000 bill for subsidies.

JOHN ALLAN MAY
London Bureau, *The Christian Science Monitor*

IRELAND, REPUBLIC OF

Area: 27,136 sq. mi.
Population: 3,000,000
Capital: Dublin
Government: Eamon de Valera, president—1959; John M. Lynch, prime minister—1966
Gross National Product: $3,500,000,000
Foreign trade: exports, $1,040,000,000; imports, $1,573,000,000

An Israeli girl soldier searches the load a youngster is toting. As explosions and other forms of violence continue, alertness remains the order of the day.

M. Gorkin

ISRAEL

The problem of relations with its Arab neighbors dominated Israel's external affairs during 1971; no positive steps were taken toward an Arab-Israeli settlement. The Government held fast to its basic position of no withdrawal from occupied Arab territories, held since the June 1967 war, without face-to-face negotiations and a peace treaty that would recognize Israeli independence within secure and defensible borders. These borders, in the Israeli view, should include the Golan Heights, Sharm el-Sheikh and a demilitarized Sinai Peninsula as the minimum guarantees required for an overall peace settlement.

Aside from the strain on the economy imposed by the continued military stalemate and the need for preparedness, Israel's intransigence regarding its basic terms for a peace settlement subjected the country to increasing criticism abroad. U.S. eagerness to secure either a temporary agreement that would permit the reopening of the Suez Canal in return for a partial

Israeli troop withdrawal from the canal's east bank, or at least the start of serious negotiations, opened a breach between Israel and its principal ally. Although a group of U.S. senators introduced a resolution urging expanded military aid and Congress at one point authorized $85,000,000 in aid, the general attitude of the Nixon administration was that Israel's refusal to make concessions was undermining both the Israeli position and U.S. interests. In November the sale of Phantom jets was definitely halted as the United States rejected Israeli claims of a military imbalance in the Middle East because of increased Soviet arms deliveries to Egypt. Although the Senate subsequently voted $500,000,000 in military aid, State Department spokesmen stressed the restraint in Soviet Egyptian–aid policy, and the evident desire of the U.S.S.R. for an Israeli-Arab settlement, in refusing to lift the ban on further shipments.

In December, Premier Golda Meir met with President Nixon who apparently promised con-

Teddy Kollek, the ebullient, dedicated mayor of Jerusalem, calls attention to city sights as he takes newsmen on a personally conducted tour.

tinued U.S. financial and military support, but no immediate sale of Phantom jets.

Jerusalem was another issue on which Israel's stand was criticized. A resolution in the Knesset (Parliament) declared that the city would remain the nation's "historic, irrevocable capital." Subsequently, in September, Jordan complained to the UN Security Council about steps taken by Israeli authorities to change Jerusalem's status as an international city sacred to three religious faiths. The council voted 14–0 to order Israel to abstain from changes in the UN-approved Jerusalem statute. However, like all other UN resolutions on the Middle East, its provisions could not be enforced.

The Israeli economy continued to boom although defense expenditures amounted to $850,000,000 out of a total $1,500,000,000 budget. Israeli munitions industries contributed to the economic growth with exports of $15,-000,000, a 50 per cent increase, mainly in ammunition and the effective Uzzi submachine gun, popular in African countries. But continued growth was offset by inflationary pressures. The foreign-trade deficit reached $700,-000,000, while tax and retail-price increases matched wage raises in industry. In August the Israeli pound was devalued, and a wave of strikes followed that crippled essential services until they were halted by government action.

Relaxation of the ban on emigration of Soviet Jews resulted in the unprecedented number of 9,000 people, including many highly skilled technicians, leaving for Israel. Their arrival imposed further strains on Israeli society because Oriental and North African Jews, mostly unskilled, were displaced in order to integrate the newcomers.

WILLIAM SPENCER
Professor of History
The Florida State University

ISRAEL

Area: 7,992 sq. mi.
Population: 3,000,000
Capital: Jerusalem
Government: Schneor Zalman Shazar, president —1963; Golda Meir, prime minister—1969
Gross National Product: $5,400,000,000
Foreign trade: exports $731,000,000; imports $1,410,000,000
Armed forces: 75,000 (plus 225,000 reservists)

ITALY

Italians described 1971 as chiaroscuro, meaning there was more light than dark in the nation's economic and political pictures. There still was enough uncertainty and unrest to cause Premier Emilio Colombo some anxious moments. He survived several wrangles, some of them incomprehensible to outsiders, among the parties making up the center-Left coalition he led in 1971, including the withdrawal in February of the small but influential Republican Party from his Cabinet. He also survived a rare vote of confidence in the Chamber of Deputies in the spring, after a quarrel over whether Communists should join or collaborate in the Government. He said no and made it stick.

The most serious political strains showed in November as Parliament began considering the election of a successor to President Giuseppe Saragat. Electoral jockeying among several candidates spread to bickering over possible revision of the controversial divorce law passed in 1970. Colombo found himself caught between his own antidivorce Christian Democrat colleagues and prodivorce coalition partners.

On Dec. 24, after balloting had been prolonged for 16 days, the 1,008-member electoral college elected Giovanni Leone, a moderate Christian Democrat, as Italy's sixth president. The 63-year-old professor of law and former premier received 518 votes (only 13 more than necessary), while socialist leader Pietro Nenni obtained 408 votes. In accordance with parliamentary tradition, Premier Colombo immediately submitted his Government's resignation to the new President. Later Leone asked the Colombo Cabinet to remain in office.

About 7,000,000 voters went to the polls on June 10 to elect a Sicilian government, and 693 local councils, ranging in size from Rome to hillside villages. The Christian Democrats took 31 per cent of the vote. The biggest surprise was the strength shown by the neofascist Italian Social Movement (MSI), which took almost 14 per cent of the vote and became the third largest party in Italy. Political observers called the MSI advance a backlash reaction to both the drifting and wrangling Government and the Italian Communist Party, which usually gains most protest votes. Both the Christian Democrats and Communists slipped slightly at the polls, but the alignment of power remained almost unchanged.

Both the political and labor fronts were unusually quiet, except for noisy quarrels, but the economic situation remained a disturbing factor for bankers and businessmen. They said Italy was caught up in an era of "stagflation," that is, a combination of inflationary trends and stagnating industrial production. A feared full-blown recession failed to develop, although several key economic indicators reflected a sluggish mood. Industrial production for the first six months of 1971 was down 5 per cent from 1970. Unemployment exceeded 1,000,000.

Parliament approved a major overhaul of the tax system on Oct. 7. Some politicians called it the most important single act of legislation since World War II. The new law shifted the emphasis from indirect taxation, which had accounted for 70 of every 100 lire in tax revenues in 1970, and was designed to end tax evasion, which Italians often describe as the nation's favorite sport. Among the taxes dropped was one on salt, dating back to the days of the Caesars.

The 1972 budget, with a record $5,823,400,-000 deficit, including the heavy indebtedness of several state agencies, received cabinet approval at midyear. The deficit was up 27 per cent from 1971, chiefly because of increased expenditures for education, housing, health services, and the backward deep south.

Italy ended 1970 with a trade deficit of $1,740,000,000, the biggest since 1963, compared with a 1969 deficit of $737,600,000. However, "invisible" non-trade earnings such as tourism, shipping and money sent home by Italians working abroad more than covered the deficits. The country's overall balance of payments through Sept. 30 showed a surplus of $1,148,000,000 compared with a deficit of $426,900,000 for the same period in 1970. Another $1,000,000,000 year for tourism was recorded despite a series of strikes that discouraged many foreigners and sent others home earlier than they had planned.

The lira escaped much of the monetary turmoil that involved most European currencies. The stock market floundered and hit a six-year low in July; but because of its limited size and low turnover it did not make much difference in the overall economic picture.

Business reported a so-so year. Montedison, the mining-chemical complex that controls 970 large and small companies, had a particularly troublesome year. Eugenio Cefis, previously president of the state oil agency ENI, was elected Montedison president in May, the fourth man to hold the post in little over a year.

President Nixon's economic moves, especially imposing a 10 per cent surcharge on foreign imports, removed the rosy glow from Italian trade with the United States, but did not harm business as much as was feared at first. The United States was Italy's third largest export market in 1970 with $1,350,000,000 in sales. Although that total was reduced somewhat in 1971, the Italian Government offset most losses with rebates and tax credits to industries concerned.

An element disturbing businessmen was the slump in consumer demand at home, especially for new cars and home appliances. By the end

Pears are plowed under, near Ferrara, in an effort to maintain market prices, reduced because of extremely high yields.

Photoreporters Inc.

of 1971, warehouses were estimated to be bulging with about $2,000,000,000 worth of unsold goods.

Salaries were up by as much as 12 per cent, one key factor in the sharp drop in the number of man-hours lost through strikes. Another factor was the worry among labor leaders about the state of the economy and fears of large-scale layoffs. The nation's three major labor unions pressed ahead with plans for a single giant union and set mid-1972 as a tentative date for it.

Regional jealousies, which had erupted in rioting in 1970, declined during 1971. There were fresh outbreaks of trouble in Reggio Calabria, however, scene of months of disorders earlier, and in L'Aquila. Hundreds of riot police restored order, but it took days of intense fighting in Reggio Calabria to end the rebellion there sparked by the choice of rival Catanzaro as regional capital.

It was one of the worst years on record for art thefts. Officials announced the loss of more than 3,000 paintings and sculptures during the first 10 months of 1971, including 15 masterpieces stolen on Feb. 19 from the home in Venice of American expatriate heiress Peggy Guggenheim. Many of the paintings stolen were later recovered by police.

ITALY
Area: 116,303 sq. mi.
Population: 54,100,000
Capital: Rome
Government: Giovanni Leone, president—1971; Emilio Colombo, premier—1970
Gross National Product: $93,200,000,000
Foreign trade: exports, $13,210,000,000; imports, $14,939,000,000
Armed forces: 414,000

Mt. Etna, the loftiest and most active volcano in Europe, rumbled and bubbled lava for more than 60 days at midyear, washing away more than 200 buildings and engulfing forests and farmland in a display that attracted thousands of tourists anxious to see the most fiery and noisy eruptions in 43 years. No one was killed, and only one person was injured.

Gunmen ambushed and killed the chief public prosecutor of Palermo on May 5 in the first high-level assassination in Italy since the immediate post-World War II period. The crime was still not solved at year's end, but police cracked down on reputed Mafia bosses in Sicily, banishing dozens of them to two remote Mediterranean islands on the grounds that they were dangerous to society.

A 35-year-old Rome housewife made medical history July 22 when doctors removed 15 perfectly formed fetuses from her womb. Doctors called it the largest multiple pregnancy ever reported.

Raffaele Minichiello, a former U.S. marine from Seattle who carried out the longest aerial hijacking in the world, from near Los Angeles to Rome in 1969, was freed on May 1 after serving an 18-month jail term. He decided to remain in Italy and accepted a job as a waiter in a Rome restaurant.

In a key legal decision, the Constitutional Court, equivalent to the U.S. Supreme Court, ruled on Mar. 17 that it is no crime to distribute birth-control information. The decision annoyed the Vatican, but pleased many politicians and civil-rights groups. Two separate bills to allow abortion had been introduced in Parliament by year's end, but no action was taken on either.

CHARLES W. BELL
News Editor, Rome Bureau
United Press International

JAPAN

The events of 1971 for Japan were of enormous momentousness and gravity. So stunning was their impact that the Japanese were quick to dub 1971 the year of "shock."

The year started out calmly enough, with Prime Minister Sato and his ruling conservative coalition of Liberal Democrats firmly in the driver's seat. In December 1970, the *Asahi*, Japan's most widely circulated daily newspaper, reported that the Sato Cabinet had reached a new peak of popularity. On Jan. 5, 1971, Premier Eisaku Sato set a new record as the prime minister with the longest period of continuous service in Japanese modern political history.

By the end of the summer, Sato's popularity had declined dramatically. Unusual motions of no confidence against the Sato Government and a couple of its most prestigious ministers were raised in the national Diet (Parliament) on several occasions. These motions were without success, but their appearance clearly indicated that Sato's days were numbered.

What had happened was an increasingly grave series of events, primarily sparked by the United States, which—at least in Japanese eyes —rocked the very foundations of hitherto sacrosanct government policy. From the dairy farms of Hokkaido to the hothouse economy of Okinawa to the smoke-filled Ginza pubs, all felt the "Nixon shock."

Most Americans have no idea of the impact of U.S. policy on Japan. Regardless of Japan's increasing economic strength, most Japanese continue to believe that their country cannot hope to stand up to the United States, let alone surpass or become economically independent of "the champion of the twentieth century," as the United States has been called in some Japanese statements. As the old saying goes, "When the United States sneezes, Japan catches pneumonia."

Prime Minister Sato's conservative Liberal Democratic Party, in power almost without interruption since the end of World War II, had always believed that close relations with the United States were crucial to Japan's welfare, stability and security. In the minds of a majority of Japan's elected leadership in the mid-1960's, what the United States said was in its interest in Southeast Asia was also—almost *ipso facto*—in Japan's.

On the domestic battleground, close alignment with American foreign policy often was translated as an important part of a "special" relationship with the United States. After all, Americans purchased about 30 per cent of Japan's annual export production; they seemed to be inexhaustibly rich; and they threatened any would-be aggressor with nuclear retaliation for any attack on Japanese territory. A special relationship with the United States appeared normal and vital. Sato's Government

Gigantic sign is designed to show ski records at 1972 Winter Olympic Games in Sapporo, Japan.

On the first trip abroad of a reigning Japanese monarch, Emperor Hirohito and Empress Nagako are entertained royally. Above: At Brussels, Belgium, airport, he is escorted by King Baudouin; below: The Emperor and Empress sit on either side of the Lord Mayor of London at a banquet.

based its foreign policy upon that assumption and boasted at home that it alone had the intimate contacts with the American Government and political leadership that Japan needed to maintain its special partnership. According to the Sato party line, therefore, it followed that a government formed by one of the opposition parties, which were said not to have the requisite special contacts with the Americans, would head Japan in an extraordinarily perilous new direction.

In July 1971, President Richard Nixon sharply reversed American policy by announcing that he intended to visit the communist People's Republic of China sometime before May 1972. Despite their self-proclaimed special relationship with the United States, Prime Minister Sato and his Government were not consulted before the stunning announcement. Sato, who on almost all issues had thrown his Government's support behind traditional American policy toward mainland China and Taiwan, was caught short. His earlier proposal of offering Japan as a bridge to better relations between the United States and China was left waiting at the church. This was "Nixon shock" number one.

In August 1971, President Nixon, in another sharp reversal of American policy, announced that he was implementing a "temporary" import surcharge of 10 per cent, as well as "temporarily" suspending the convertibility of the dollar into gold. No advance warning had been given to the Japanese Government. Coming on the heels of domestic predictions of an economic slowdown, the Nixon economic announcements, which the local press estimated would cost the Japanese economy about $1,200,000,000 annually in lost sales, sent the Tokyo stock market into a tailspin. By the end of the year, however, the market was well on its way to a spectacular recovery.

An important purpose of the Nixon economic pronouncements was to force an increase in the value of the Japanese yen, which had remained at 360 to the dollar from 1949, in spite of tremendous changes in the productive capacity of the Japanese economy. Speculators were already well prepared. During the first two weeks of August, they poured billions of dollars through the windows of the Bank of Japan. In a desperate attempt to support the old parity, the bank continued to buy dollars, but, by the end of August, with $12,000,000,-000 in foreign-currency reserves (almost all in United States dollars), the Japanese Government finally capitulated. Finance Minister Mikio Mizuta announced that Japan would float the yen instead of trying to maintain the 360 rate. Such American economic pronouncements and their consequent aftermath in Japan were "Nixon shock" number two.

That shock was felt even more severely later when the United States, on Dec. 18, agreed to raise the price of gold from $35 to $38 per troy ounce, in effect devaluing the dollar by 8.57 per cent. (Gold convertibility remained suspended.) In combination with the corresponding upvaluation of other major currencies (except the Canadian dollar), the actual dollar devaluation spread amounted to 11 per cent. Most affected was the yen, which leaped from an exchange rate of 360 to the dollar to 308. As the new rate could fluctuate within a "band" of 2.5 per cent—that is, within 314 to 301—the yen's revaluation could reach almost 20 per cent. The Japanese called it *kiri–age* (the upward cut). Japanese exports would thereby become more expensive abroad, and its export industries slowed. In the anxiety aroused by all this, the removal of the United States' 10 per cent import surcharge on Dec. 20 was almost overlooked by the general public.

In September 1971, President Nixon, in still another stunning message for Japan, announced that the United States would impose quotas on textile imports on Oct. 15 unless Japan agreed to submit to earlier American demands for "voluntary" restrictions on Japanese textile sales to the United States. The fact that presidential authority for threatening to take such strong action was said to be grounded in an old law, the Trading with the Enemy Act, was hardly calculated to improve relations.

American specialists on Japan, as well as several of the nation's leading newspapers, were surprised not only by the severity of the Nixon ultimatum regarding Japan but also by the abrupt manner in which it was presented. Other Americans, when they discovered that the Japanese share of the total American textile market was less than 3 per cent of all sales, were puzzled by what appeared to be an unnecessarily curt series of actions against Japan by President Nixon. In searching for reasons for the Nixon ultimatum, political analysts frequently saw American domestic presidential politics and the South's small but powerful textile lobby as two of the most important factors. In an attempt to prevent a further worsening of relations, the Japanese Government, which seemed to have no alternative, again capitulated to American demands and agreed to limit textile exports to the United States. The U.S. action taken against Japanese textile interests was "Nixon shock" number three.

Since the mid-1960's, when the balance of their joint trade swung in Japan's favor, U.S.

business—including textiles—has been increasingly hard put to deal competitively with Japan on equal terms. Much of the pinch on American industry has been caused by inflation outpacing industrial productivity. Although Japanese industry has faced similar problems, unlike their American counterparts, the Japanese have been able to increase productivity. The decreasing ability of the United States to remain on a competitive basis, plus Japan's traditional reserve in tolerating a reasonable amount of foreign investment and direct participation in its domestic marketplace, combined in 1971 to raise the tempers of American businessmen, especially when they discovered that Japan was discriminating against the import of some American goods, or that a few Japanese industries were not above dumping products on the American market. In more-traditional times, when the United States maintained a competitive edge over Japan, these relatively minor problems received a minimum of fanfare; but in the heated, hard-pressed days of 1971, American businessmen complained loudly. Their cries fell on sympathetic ears in Washington.

Many Americans felt that 1971 was indeed a time for readjustments between the Japanese and U.S. economies. What worried some at year's end was that the passions generated by the "Nixon shocks" might endanger the substance of the U.S.-Japanese alliance, which remained a mutually beneficial agreement that without doubt had helped to provide peace and stability in East Asia since the Korean conflict. Although the Japanese did increase the pace of their economic "liberalization" dramatically in 1971, making it somewhat easier for American business to penetrate the lucrative Japanese consumer market, it was clear that many more conciliatory actions needed to be initiated by the Japanese Government before American business—and Washington—would be placated.

The series of "Nixon shocks" ends here for 1971. By no means were American-Japanese relations hopelessly on the rocks, although the seriousness of the economic confrontation between these two productive giants was beyond doubt. Gloom was not all-pervading. President Nixon, perhaps in the realization that his policies had pushed the Japanese into eating a lot of humble pie, made a special symbolic effort to assuage rumpled feelings in September when he and Mrs. Nixon journeyed all the way to Anchorage, Alaska, to greet the Japanese Emperor and Empress on the occasion of the first imperial visit to non-Japanese territory. The Emperor, who was on his way to Europe, holds no political authority (being only a symbol of the state according to the Japanese Constitution), and he could not engage in substantive talks with President Nixon. Nevertheless, given the tenor of the times, the historic imperial visit appeared to be a step in the right direction. Much more crucial to good American-Japanese relations was the fulfillment of the American promise to return Okinawa to Japanese control, from which it had been taken by the United States as a prize of war in 1945. No doubt reflecting the delicacy of the issue and the severity of the strains in American relations with Japan, the U.S. Senate in November voted —with an amazing lack of opposition—to ratify the treaty returning Okinawa to Japan.

Unfortunately for Sato, the "Nixon shocks" were not the only ones felt by the Japanese Government in 1971. Elections to the House

Japanese Ambassador to the United States Nobuhiko Ushiba looks on with a smile as Secretary of State William Rogers displays signed treaty by which Okinawa will return to Japanese control in 1972. Standing are Joint Chiefs of Staff Chairman Admiral Thomas Moorer, Undersecretary of State U. Alexis Johnson and Defense Secretary Melvin Laird.

The lovely Yasukuni Shrine in Tokyo, dedicated to the souls of all those who died fighting for Japan in the past hundred years, was a center of controversy in 1971. A bill to place the shrine's upkeep and management in the hands of the Government was opposed as an attempt to reestablish Shinto as a state religion.

Consulate General of Japan, N.Y.

of Councillors (upper house of the national Diet) took place on June 27. The results were disappointing for Sato's Liberal Democrats. The Japan Socialist Party, largest of the four opposition parties, reversing a recent trend, gained 5 seats while the Liberal Democrats lost 1. The Japan Communist Party picked up 3 seats to give it a total of 10, a number that allows it new influence through participation in the organization and membership of upper–house committees. The increase in left-wing strength on the national level must have been an especially bitter pill for the Liberal Democrats, who were still aching from the April local elections, which saw the Socialist-Communist-backed "independent" Ryokichi Minobe win another four-year term as governor of Tokyo.

Part of the Liberal Democrats' problems stemmed from the slow erosion of their position in traditional conservative strongholds in agricultural areas. Faced with an inflation rate that has outstripped their government subsidies, Japanese farmers have not been unwilling to bite the conservative hand that has helped to sustain them. Opposition parties on the Left have been quick to try to capitalize on agricultural dissatisfactions.

JAPAN

Area: 142,811 sq. mi.
Population: 104,700,000
Capital: Tokyo
Government: Hirohito, emperor—1926; Eisaku Sato, prime minister—1964
Gross National Product: $195,000,000,000
Foreign trade: exports, $19,318,000,000; imports, 18,811,000,000
Armed forces, 259,000

A symptomatic source of urban unhappiness with the conservative majority was revealed in late June when an appalling incidence of photochemical smog poisoning was reported in several urban areas. A record number of 8,500 cases of eye irritation, sore throats, and headaches caused by photochemical smog occurred in Tokyo on June 28. The conservative Government could not offer convincing evidence to many urban dwellers of the sincerity of its pledges to strive for improvement of their beleaguered condition. Again it was demonstrated that unless the Liberal Democrats showed an ability to reduce the plethora of urban ills, their days of urban power were numbered.

On the international scene, Japan and the Liberal Democrats received several other shocks. The communist regime of mainland China continued its barrage of propaganda against Sato, accusing him of leading Japan toward a policy of military expansionism. The Japanese, however, who contribute a considerably smaller proportion of their gross national product to the military than do the Chinese Communists, continued to support their Constitution, which uniquely and unequivocally forbids their military to take aggressive action. When Emperor Hirohito met with forceful displays of contempt during several of his public appearances in Europe in the autumn of 1971, all Japan was disturbed by the intensity of anti-Japanese feelings. Apparently the Chinese Communists were not the only ones who harbored feelings of contempt, envy and distrust of a newly rich and increasingly vigorous Japan.

F. ROY LOCKHEIMER
Associate Executive Director
Japan Society, Inc.

KOREA

A surge of hope for a genuine reduction of tension followed the start of talks between the North and South Korean Red Cross Delegations at Panmunjom in August, the first such discussions in 23 years. But year-end developments—renewed South Korean charges of an imminent attack by North Korea, the declaration of a state of national emergency by President Park Chung Hee and the enactment of legislation controlling all aspects of life in the South—threw chances for an accommodation into jeopardy.

Power shifts in Asia, particularly the improvement in U.S.-China relations, meant new uncertainties and greater dangers in Korea. A solution to the political division of Korea remained an enigma in a powder keg.

SOUTH KOREA, REPUBLIC OF (R.O.K.)

Politics. President Park and his ruling Democratic Republican Party (DRP) swept to victory in the Apr. 27 presidential election. Park won a third term (a 1969 revision of the constitution enabled him to run) with 6,342,828 votes to 5,435,900 for Kim Dae Jung, of the opposition New Democratic Party (NDP). A blend of creditable administration performance, a powerful, well-financed party organization and authoritarian use of police and the R.O.K. Central Intelligence Agency (CIA) to harass and intimidate the opposition accounted for the Park victory. The younger Kim Dae Jung, 45, ran a vigorous campaign, attracted huge crowds and used his candidacy to advocate new policies on North Korea, on security and on the Vietnam conflict.

National Assembly elections on May 25 contradicted forecasts and brought happier results to the Opposition. The NDP won 89 seats to President Park's DRP total of 113 (2 seats went to minor parties). Kim Dae Jung retained his Assembly seat as his party dominated the urban areas, winning 13 seats to 1 in Seoul. The NDP success will force the Government to deal with the Opposition in the National Assembly, requiring for the first time in Park's rule cooperation between the executive and legislature. Most significant, the NDP success will prevent the Government from amending the constitution to make President Park "generalissimo for life."

Fears that the Park administration would not tolerate a revived political opposition or demands for greater social justice in economic matters were borne out in October by the Government's use of troops and terror against student protests directed at official corruption. Army troops occupied campuses, deploying machine guns and tanks, conscripted dissident students, and harassed faculty members.

December brought a total curtailment of civil liberties, and extraordinary controls over all aspects of life. On Dec. 6, President Park declared a "state of national emergency," citing the threat of imminent invasion by North Korea. The U.S. State Department immediately disputed the allegation; opposition leaders termed it an excuse for repression; and North Korea categorically denied the charge. Nevertheless, on Dec. 23, President Park's DRP introduced a 12-article bill, the Special Measures Law for National Security and Defense, in the National Assembly. On Dec. 27, in a predawn session, from which protesting opposition assemblymen were excluded, the extraordinary-powers bill was passed. Total elapsed time for passage was reported as three minutes.

The new law gives President Park power to control the economy, the press, labor unions and all political activity, including outdoor meetings and demonstrations. Penalties of up to ten years imprisonment were stipulated. Reports from South Korea indicated increased surveillance of intellectuals and deepening fear of greater intimidation and arrests.

Security. The reduction of U.S. ground forces was effected by March, after long acrimonious public disagreement between South Korea and the United States. One infantry division was withdrawn, and the remaining division was placed in reserve away from the DMZ area. R.O.K. forces assumed responsibility for the entire DMZ for the first time.

Some U.S. Air Force units were shifted to Korea from Japan, and the United States announced a military-modernization program, pending Congressional approval, of $1,000,000,000 to $1,500,000,000 over 1971–75. The United States also announced that there would be no further troop withdrawals, in a move to reduce South Korean anxieties. At the same time, U.S. officials insisted that U.S. ground forces were not essential to R.O.K. security and hinted at additional, perhaps total, withdrawals in 1973.

South Korean policy on Vietnam was unchanged despite the alleged invasion threat from North Korea and heightened U.S. Congressional and public attention to atrocities by R.O.K. troops in Vietnam and the strategic role of South Korean troops in U.S. Vietnam policy in the 1970's. South Korea began a token withdrawal of 12,000 troops but apparently would keep about 38,000 in Vietnam indefinitely as part of the U.S. residual force.

Economy. The economy continued to show impressive gains in 1971, the final year of the second five-year plan, 1966–71, but serious problems loomed.

Commodity exports in 1970 of $834,000,000 fell short of the overambitious official goal of $1,000,000,000. A 1971 export goal of $1,140,-000,000 appeared attainable as exports rose in June by 41 per cent over the preceding 12-month period. The GNP rose by 8.7 per cent in 1970, and at least a similar increase appeared certain with a reported second quarter 1971 GNP increase of 13.3 per cent. Foreign-exchange holdings were $531,000,000 in October, down from $590,000,000 in 1970.

Three major problem areas attracted attention: the trade deficit, U.S. restrictions on textile exports, and Japanese economic penetration. The trade deficit reached $1,149,000 in 1970. An 11 per cent official depreciation of the *won* in 1971 and import controls were expected to narrow the gap. Inflation continued to be a critical factor at an annual rate of 13 to 15 per cent.

The U.S.-R.O.K. textile agreement, effective Oct. 1, limits exports of synthetic fibers. R.O.K. estimates of a $1,000,000,000 loss over the next five years were accompanied by bitter criticism of the U.S. act and appeals for special consideration.

Japanese economic activity in South Korea steadily expanded. An August Japan-R.O.K. ministerial meeting removed the ceiling on public loans by Japan. As a result, Japanese loans and credits were expected to average $200,000,000 a year during the third five-year plan, 1972–76. Japan had already reached a dominant position in the South Korean import market with sales of $809,000,000 in 1970 compared with U.S. sales of $584,800,000.

KOREA, REPUBLIC OF (SOUTH)

Area: 38,922 sq. mi.
Population: 32,900,000
Capital: Seoul
Government: Chung Hee Park, president—1963; Kim Chong Pil, premier—1971
Gross National Product: $8,300,000,000
Foreign trade: exports, $834,000,000; imports, $1,984,000,000
Armed forces: 634,250

KOREA, DEMOCRATIC PEOPLE'S REPUBLIC (NORTH)

Area: 46,540 sq. mi.
Population: 14,300,000
Capital: Pyongyang
Government: Kim Il Sung, premier—1948
Gross National Product: $4,000,000,000
Armed forces: 401,000

NORTH KOREA (D.P.R.K.)

Diplomacy. North Korea responded to the shift in U.S.-China relations with cautious approval and continued to advocate political negotiations between the two Korean governments to settle outstanding issues.

In April the D.P.R.K. Foreign Minister proposed a meeting of representatives of North and South Korean political parties and social organizations. On Aug. 14, Premier Kim Il Sung declared the North's willingness to discuss unification with any parties or organizations in the South, dropping a long-standing opposition to negotiating with the Park administration or DRP. North Korea agreed immediately to Red Cross delegation talks and urged the extension of discussions beyond the humane issue of divided families to basic political problems. North Korea promptly denied President Park's December charges of aggressive intent and urged continued contacts. Moreover, it was noticeable that North Korea had stopped denouncing Park as a "lackey of the imperialist aggressors."

Other North Korean diplomatic activities included a state visit by Rumania's President Nicolae Ceausescu and the attendance of representatives from 34 countries at the 6th Congress of the League of Socialist Working Youth of Korea. Japanese economic interest in South Korea and Japan's defense plans were termed aggressive. The D.P.R.K. called for the complete withdrawal of all U.S. troops and the termination of UN involvement in Korea.

Economy. North Korea began a new six-year plan (1971–76) and announced that 1971 targets had been achieved. Although absolute figures were not provided, North Korea claimed a 2.6-fold increase in machine-tool production, a 1.4-fold increase in steel and a 1.3-fold increase in cement production. Accelerated achievements in 1971 were aimed at completing the first two years of the plan by Apr. 15, 1972, the birthday of Premier Kim Il Sung. North Korean spokesmen suggested that the plan might be accomplished by 1974.

North Korea already claims the highest degree of industrialization in Asia, after Japan. The new plan's emphasis upon development of heavy industry, decentralized management and a self-help ideology, which eschews foreign aid and loans, will strengthen that claim. Impressed foreign observers have noted that the D.P.R.K. is rapidly becoming a model for third-world economic development.

FRANK BALDWIN
Assistant Professor of Korean
Department of East Asian Languages and Cultures
Columbia University

Freighters lie idle in their East River (New York) berths as the dock-workers' strike on the East and Gulf coasts (except Texas) continues.

LABOR

For labor, as for other elements in society, 1971 was the year of the battle against "stag-flation"—that is, economic stagnation combined with price inflation. It was a battle waged not only in the United States but in most other advanced nations of the world. The struggle continued into 1972, with signs of improvement as 1971 moved to a close.

United States. Perhaps the year's most spectacular economic development was President

Mayor Kenneth Gibson (center), union President Mrs. Carole Graves and board President Jesse Jacob stand together as teachers' walkout ends.

Nixon's abandonment of his former "game plan," under which he relied largely on fiscal and monetary measures to cool off inflation and overcome stagnation. As these measures failed, the President acted under a Congressionally enacted stabilization law that he had previously refused to use, and initiated a ninety-day wage-price freeze, effective from Aug. 15 through Nov. 14. This was coupled with moves to curb America's rising trade deficit, and requests to Congress, later approved, to repeal the auto excise tax, reinstate a tax credit to industry for investment in new plant and equipment, and increase the personal income-tax exemption.

The effectiveness of the freeze was widely debated, with the administration terming it a success and labor assailing it as discriminatory. It was followed by Phase 2, a partial thaw under which guidelines were established with the goal of holding wage increases to an average of 5.5 per cent a year and price rises to 2.5 per cent. The guidelines, however, were not rigid. On the wage front they were administered by a tripartite (labor-industry-public) Pay Board, on the price side by an all-public Price Commission.

Before the freeze was imposed, labor settlements, usually for three-year periods, had been reached in most major industries, some after lengthy strikes. In general, these agreements provided for about 30 per cent in pay increases over three years, though front-loaded to provide a greater share of the raise in the first year. Some of the settlements, particularly in construction and on the railroads, exceeded the 30 per cent pattern.

In construction, negotiated wage increases escalated to as high as 15 to 20 per cent a year. There the administration acted before the freeze, securing voluntary establishment of a tripartite Construction Industry Stabilization Committee to pass on wage settlements. The committee succeeded in slowing down the pace of pay increases to about 10 to 11 per cent.

Among the major settlements of the year were those in steel, copper, aluminum, can manufacturing, the railroads, communications, aerospace and coal mining. Some of them were reached during or after the freeze; but because of their tandem relationships with earlier agreements, they won Pay Board approval, sometimes by split votes, even though they far exceeded the guidelines. A few were pared down.

Many of the strikes that preceded the settlements were long-drawn-out. At Western Union Telegraph the stoppage lasted 8 weeks; in the copper mines, 24 days or more; in coal mining, 6 weeks; in the telephone industry, only 6 days, except in New York state, where the telephone strike was prolonged.

In steel, an exception to the rule, an agreement was reached on Aug. 1 without a strike. The railroads were shut down by a national 2-day strike called by the Brotherhood of Railroad Signalmen in May (and halted by an act of Congress). Also, in the summer, selected railroads were struck for up to 17 days by the United Transportation Union, representing crafts in train, engine and yard service. These selective strikes ended with the negotiation of a tentative national rail settlement. This dispute was more difficult to resolve than others on the railroads because, in addition to wages, it involved carrier demands for sweeping changes in long-established work rules, some of which managements termed featherbedding. In the settlement, a compromise was reached on the rules issue. The wage portion followed the pattern set by other rail unions—of 42 to 45 per cent in increases over a 42-month period, dating back to Jan. 1, 1970.

The Department of Labor reported that pay increases agreed upon in collective bargaining during the first nine months of 1971 averaged 8 per cent a year over the life of the contracts, down from 8.7 per cent in 1970. In manufacturing, the average was 7.1 per cent; in construction, 11.7 per cent. For all private nonagricultural workers, union and nonunion, gross

UPI

Picket line forms at Ravenna, Ohio, hospital after 19 kitchen workers are fired for sick-call strike.

average weekly earnings rose 6.6 per cent in 1971, the Labor Department reported.

The rise in unit labor costs slowed down in 1971 as productivity mounted. By the third quarter of 1971 they were rising at only a one per cent annual rate, compared with 6.3 per cent in 1970. At the same time, the Consumer Price Index de-escalated, rising by 3.4 per cent, much less than the 6 per cent rate of 1970.

Among the longest strikes that jolted the economy in 1971 were those of longshoremen on U.S. coasts, and they remained unsettled at year's end. The Pacific Coast strike by 15,000 members of the International Longshoremen's and Warehousemen's Union began July 1 and lasted for 98 days before being suspended by an 80-day Taft-Hartley Act injunction on Oct. 6, issued by the courts at administration request. A complicating factor in this dispute, outside of wages, was that the union's leader, Harry Bridges, once a symbol of labor radicalism, found himself under fire from a militant minority. This internal struggle was exacerbated by a sharp decline in longshore jobs under the previous agreement negotiated by Bridges.

On the East and Gulf Coasts over 40,000 members of the International Longshoremen's Association walked out Oct. 1 at the expiration of a three-year agreement. One major issue here was a demand by shipping companies in the New York area for modifying a clause in the old agreement guaranteeing dockers in the area 2,080 hours of work or pay per year. The companies claimed that the clause had cost them three times what they had anticipated and that it was "bankrupting" them.

New York shipping firms opposed invocation of Taft-Hartley injunction procedures because these would restore the *status quo,* including the annual wage guarantee. However, after 57 days of this strike, the administration finally turned to the courts and got 80-day Taft-Hartley injunctions halting the strikes until Feb. 16, 1972, and restoring the prestrike *status quo.*

A highlight of 1971 was a trend toward the four-day week on an experimental basis. The initiative for this change came mainly from managements and generally from nonunion establishments. Predominantly, the change was to four 10-hour days. Some of the plans, however, called for less than 40 hours a week. Most companies inaugurating the plan said it resulted in less absenteeism and turnover, greater productivity, and longer hours of service to the public, particularly where shifts were arranged to provide 6 or 7 days of service a week.

The trend was given impetus by a book entitled *4 Days, 40 Hours,* written by Mrs. Riva Poor, editor of the monthly *Poor's Work-Week Letter.* She estimated that 700 firms had converted to the 4-day week by mid-1971, with the number increasing every week. The Department of Labor put the total at 600. Mrs. Poor estimated the number of workers covered at 130,000, while the Labor Department put the figure at 75,000. The AFL-CIO said both figures were inflated. Mrs. Poor claimed that the trend would escalate; the Labor Department said it was too early to judge. The department's study cited some 12 firms that had tried the 4-day, 40-hour week, then discontinued it. While some local unions agreed to the 4-day experiments, the AFL-CIO officially opposed lengthening of the 8-hour day at straight-time pay and contended that the longer day would be nonproductive in the long run.

Unemployment was the dark spot underscoring the year's stagnation. It hovered around the 5,000,000 mark, or 6 per cent, most of the year. However, as the labor force grew, the number of persons employed also rose, passing the 80,000,000 mark for the first time in July.

Union membership continued to rise slowly. In a study published in 1971 the Labor Department placed the total at 19,400,000, plus 1,900,000 members in professional associations that engage in employee representation. This was up 500,000 from 1968 for the unions, and 100,000 for other employee associations.

Conflict steadily sharpened during the year between the AFL-CIO and the Nixon administration as inflation and unemployment continued. During the freeze, the AFL-CIO charged that while wages were tightly controlled, prices, profits, dividends, interest and executive compensation were not similarly restrained. The conflict carried over into Phase 2, with labor agreeing to serve on the Pay Board only after it received signed assurance from President Nixon that the administration's Cost of Living Council would not veto specific board decisions.

The gulf widened further at the AFL-CIO convention in November. There, President George Meany denounced "failures" of the administration in handling the nation's economy. Also, the convention adopted a resolution providing that AFL-CIO representatives would stay on the Pay Board only as long as "a reasonable hope" remained that the board, among other conditions, would fully honor all valid union-management contracts. In addition the resolution specified that union representatives would not "cooperate" with objectionable board policies.

President Nixon appeared personally at the convention after the delegates adopted the policy of noncooperation with the board. Among other things, he made it clear that the stabilization program would continue whether or not labor cooperated. He got a cool but

Ending the threat of a nationwide strike only three hours before the deadline, United States Steel Workers President I. W. Abel (l) and U.S. Steel Vice-President R. Heath Larry announce agreement on a three-year contract, on Aug. 1.

correct reception, which was publicized as "rudeness," a charge that Meany angrily denied. On the heels of the convention, relations between organized labor and the administration grew steadily more frigid.

Canada. Rising unemployment increased tensions in 1971. The seasonally adjusted jobless rate reached a 10-year high of 7.1 per cent in September, then dropped back to 6.2 per cent in December.

Adding to the job problem was the U.S.-imposed temporary surcharge of 10 per cent on imports (revoked on Dec. 20), which had an adverse impact on employment in some Canadian industries. The Government sought to meet the economic setbacks with an added $500,000,000 in public-works spending, with corporate and individual income-tax cuts, and with $80,000,000 in "employment-support" funds for industries hurt by the U.S. surcharge. Also, another $500,000,000 was allotted for winter works projects. The Canadian Labor Congress held that these steps fell short of what was needed and called for an expanded program of job creation, plus greater tax relief for low-income individuals.

Inflation, however, was a relatively moderate problem in Canada. The Consumer Price Index rose by less than 4 per cent, while wage increases negotiated by unions in major industries averaged 7 to 8 per cent, mostly without strikes.

Some strikes occurred in public service. City firemen in Montreal struck for wage parity with Toronto firemen, but an injunction halted this walkout after seven days. Later, members of the firemen's union, by a narrow margin, accepted a 7.1 per cent pay increase, failing to win parity with Toronto.

As in the United States, there was a limited trend toward experimental 4-day, 40-hour weeks, and some employers reported conspicuous success with the change. An oil refinery in Winnipeg went further and tried out a weekly work schedule changeable between three 12-hour days and four 10-hour days, for a year-round average of 38.8 hours per week.

An unusual development on the labor front was action by the Quebec Federation of Labor in reversing past positions and endorsing Quebec's right to self-determination and even independence.

Japan. A minirecession agitated labor and the nation during 1971, but what Japan regarded as a slump would look like a boom in the United States or elsewhere. The jobless rate edged up over the one per cent mark. Many companies sharply reduced the mass hiring of high-school and college graduates, and some

even laid off employees, though with payment of 80 to 100 per cent of basic wages during the layoff period. The Government announced higher spending to ease the economic downturn and to help offset the impact of U.S. trade restrictions.

Earlier in the year, the annual *shunto,* or spring wage offensive staged by Japan's unions, yielded pay increases averaging 16.6 per cent in the private sector, down from 18 per cent in 1970. In government services the increases were somewhat less. Traditional summer and winter bonuses, also a subject of struggle between unions and management, likewise showed a smaller rate of increase. The Consumer Price Index, meantime, rose approximately 7 per cent.

A growing trend from 5½- or 6-day working weeks to the 5-day week was reported by the Japan Institute of Labor. Another trend, spurred by union pressure, is toward raising the compulsory retirement age above 55, which is customary in most industry. Traditionally, workers get lump severance upon retirement at 55 but are often rehired on a temporary basis at lower pay. Government pensions start at age 60. The age-55 retirement has been linked to a system of "lifetime employment," up to that age, which has prevailed in Japan.

Europe. Economic downturns, accompanied by inflation, occurred in most Western European countries during 1971.

Britain was particularly hard-hit. Production slumped and unemployment passed the million mark at year's end, with a jobless rate exceeding 4 per cent, described as the highest in over 25 years. In trouble-wracked Northern Ireland, the rate of unemployment approached 15 per cent.

Britain's Conservative Party Government responded with a billion-dollar program of public works and tax cuts in efforts to spur the economy. The Trades Union Congress and the Labor Party clamored for accelerated action to combat joblessness, and stormy unemployment demonstrations broke out in London. Strikes were widespread, mostly to secure wage increases that would keep earnings ahead of price rises, which reached as high as 10 per cent above 1970. In the first half of 1971, man-days lost from strikes were double the 1970 rate. Negotiated wage settlements generally exceeded the 10 per cent level.

One of the year's most troublesome disputes broke out in August at Glasgow's Upper Clyde where unionists seized the shipyards in protest against the Government's decision to close some of the yards and to cut down drastically on shipbuilding employment.

Despite labor protests, Parliament enacted broad industrial-relations controls designed to curb strikes, particularly the wildcat kind, and to regulate unions in other ways. The legislation was likened to the Taft-Hartley Act in the United States. Failing to stop it, the Trades Union Congress adopted a boycott policy, which called for nonregistration under the new law and noncooperation with it wherever possible.

West Germany, after thriving economically in recent years, faced the double whammy of a production slowdown and inflationary pressures during 1971. Unemployment rose, but was low by Western standards—slightly over one per cent—and the problem was met partly by paring down the importation of foreign workers, the number of whom had passed the 2,000,000 mark in 1971.

Record wage gains by unions in 1971—an average of 16.5 per cent—led to rising unit labor costs in 1971 as productivity increases fell far short of matching the wage escalation. In consequence, the cost of living advanced 6 per cent in 1971. Both the Government and industry sought to hold down the pace of wage demands in 1971 and this produced a series of strikes. The biggest of these broke out in the auto industry in November. West Germany's largest union, the Metal Workers, sought wage increases of 11 per cent, while employers held out for no more than a 4.5 per cent raise. This strike led to a widespread lockout by auto companies and supplier firms, and also to many plant shutdowns for lack of parts produced by strikebound factories. At the peak of the dispute about 600 plants closed, idling 600,000 workers and paralyzing much of West Germany's industry. The dispute was settled in mid-December with a 7.5 per cent pay increase plus a year-end bonus.

Italy, as in 1970, was beset by strikes in private industry and government services during 1971. Most were short—24 hours or so—but were often repeated. Some were called to press demands for wage increases and improved working conditions. Some aimed at pressuring the Government to institute social and economic reforms. The turmoil occurred as production slumped about 7 per cent below 1970 and prices rose 6 per cent or more.

Also, about 1,000,000 workers were estimated to be unemployed or underemployed, 400,000 more than in 1970. Amid the turbulence, Italy's three main labor confederations—one under communist control, a second under democratic socialist influence, and a third, predominantly Catholic—reached agreement in principle to merge.

France emerged with a better economic showing than most of West Europe. It had an economic growth rate of over 5 per cent, and fewer strikes than neighboring lands. However, railway strikes in June snarled passenger travel and freight traffic for over 10 days. Also, a subway motormen's strike in Paris paralyzed the capital for 9 days. The rail strike was settled by a wage compromise, but the subway motormen lost their fight for wage parity with locomotive engineers.

Among *Scandinavian countries,* Sweden reported the worst situation. Its economy slipped and unemployment approached 3 per cent, double that of a year earlier. Many strikes occurred both in private industry and public service, including the government-owned railroads. In March, Parliament imposed a 6-week ban on strikes and lockouts, and stepped up mediation efforts to settle disputes. Living costs soared about 8 per cent above 1970, and wage agreements carried increases in the 9 to 10 per cent range.

Other, *smaller European countries* suffered a combination of production slippages, rising prices, higher unemployment and industrial strife. Even some of the totalitarian lands—notably Spain and Yugoslavia—experienced a series of strikes, although they are prohibited by law.

Latin America. *Chile,* ruled by the Marxist regime of Salvador Allende—which instituted widespread nationalization of industries—had a honeymoon with organized labor for a time. However, economic problems mounted during the year, and unrest spread on the industrial and agricultural fronts as workers sought to keep wages ahead of inflationary price advances and as consumers demonstrated against food shortages.

Argentina, ruled by a military junta, was hit by many strikes as labor fought to maintain wage standards in a period of runaway price increases, as high as 5 per cent a month. Meantime, the economy stagnated and unemployment soared. Some strikes were also called over political issues.

Peru, likewise under the reign of a military junta, was buffeted with strikes, the biggest of them at the mining and processing complex of the Cerro Corporation. Some of the strikes were pressure tactics aimed at spurring nationalization of the mines and other basic resources.

Other South American nations, whether ruled by dictators or parliamentary regimes, were affected by economic strife and struggled to surmount "stagflation."

RUBEN LEVIN
Editor and Manager, *Labor*

In Rancagua, in the copper-mining district, Chilean President Allende explains the nationalization of U.S. copper-company interests to a crowd that includes many copper miners.

David Mangurian

LATIN AMERICA

With the triumph of the Allende regime in Chile and the leftward moves of the governments of Bolivia and Peru, there was a real danger that South America would be split, like Europe, into two halves: a pro-U.S. sector, with Brazil as its strong point; and a pro-Soviet sector, inspired by Chile. Since the idea of private property has never been strong among the Indians, it was feared that communism might have an especial appeal for the underprivileged Indians and mestizos of the Andean countries.

Another danger was that of confrontation between the opposing ideological blocs. The Chilean Government feared being overthrown from Argentina; and in January, President Salvador Allende Gossens announced that he had proof that right-wing landowners were smuggling arms in from Argentina. The Argentine military Government was acutely afraid that the Allende Government would propagandize the Chilean minority in Patagonia and thus subvert the Argentine state. This mutual fear led to a strange pact, the Declaration of Salta, issued in the northern Argentine city in July by Gen. Alejandro A. Lanusse, president of Argentina, and President Allende. Lanusse visited Peru and Chile in October and made statements that sounded strange coming from one regarded as an anticommunist "gorilla" (reactionary army officer).

The military governments of Brazil and Paraguay, feeling surer of themselves than the Argentine junta, showed no inclination to placate the Marxists, and, to say the least, they welcomed the overthrow of the leftist Bolivian Government of Gen. Juan Jose Torres in August. Uruguay survived, thanks mostly to the rivalry between Brazil and Argentina for control of the area. It was partly this that dissuaded the Brazilian military from intervening in Uruguay to eradicate the Leftist Tupamaros,

who had kidnaped Brazilian Consul Aloysio Dias Gomide and held him for ransom. It was paid. The Brazilian press angrily rejected Argentine charges that Brazil had imperialist intentions.

The Latin American Free Trade Association (LAFTA) was in almost as much disarray as the Central American Common Market (see below) because of Argentina's growing trade deficit with Brazil. A special Argentine-Brazilian Coordination Commission was created, but its meetings displayed marked bitterness. A positive development was the June signing of the Act of Asuncion, aimed at coordinating the economies of the River Plate countries (Argentina, Bolivia, Brazil, Paraguay and Uruguay).

Following Allende's recognition of the Castro Government, the Leftist governments of Latin America moved toward resuming relations with Cuba, a trend that could aggravate the continental split. Another divisive factor was created when Allende opened the doors of Chile to Leftist refugees, including many charged with terrorism, from all over Latin America.

The announcement of President Nixon's trip to Peking and the admission of Communist China to the United Nations led to a reassessment of the anticommunist policies imposed by the United States on Latin America. There was a general move to recognize Communist China.

Terrorism became a problem. The Organization of American States (OAS) met to discuss it, but the meeting broke up as six nations, led by Argentina and Brazil, walked out in protest against the weak measures adopted. The first regular session of the OAS General Assembly met in San Jose, Costa Rica, in April, giving the Latin Americans a forum to air their grievances against the United States. Despite an increasingly favorable trade balance ($917,-000,000 in 1970) with Latin America, and despite the recommendation for tariff prefer-

NATION	POPULATION (in millions)	CAPITAL	AREA (in sq. mi.)	HEAD OF STATE AND/OR GOVERNMENT DATE INSTALLED (as of Jan. 1, 1972)
Argentina	24.7	Buenos Aires	1,072,158	Alejandro Agustin Lanusse, president—1971
Barbados	0.3	Bridgetown	166	Sir Winston Scott, governor-general—1967
				Errol W. Barrow, prime minister—1961
Bolivia	4.8	La Paz	424,163	Hugo Banzer Suarez, president—1971
Brazil	95.7	Brasilia	3,286,478	Emilio Garrastazu Medici, president—1969
Chile	10.0	Santiago	292,259	Salvador Allende Gossens, president—1970
Colombia	22.1	Bogota	439,736	Misael Pastrana Borrero, president—1970
Costa Rica	1.9	San Jose	19,575	Jose Figueres Ferrer, president—1970
Cuba	8.6	Havana	44,218	Osvaldo Dorticos Torrado, president—1959
				Fidel Castro, prime minister—1959
Dominican Republic	4.4	Santo Domingo	18,816	Joaquin Balaguer, president—1966
Ecuador	6.3	Quito	109,483	Jose Maria Velasco Ibarra, president—1968
El Salvador	3.6	San Salvador	8,260	Fidel Sanchez Hernandez, president—1967
Guatemala	5.3	Guatemala City	42,042	Carlos Arana Osorio, president—1970
Guyana	0.8	Georgetown	83,000	Arthur Chung, president—1970
				Forbes Burnham, prime minister—1964
Haiti	5.4	Port-au-Prince	10,714	Jean-Claude Duvalier, president—1971
Honduras	2.8	Tegucigalpa	43,277	Ramon Ernesto Cruz, president—1971
Jamaica	2.0	Kingston	4,232	Sir Clifford Campbell, governor-general—1962
				Hugh Shearer, prime minister—1967
Mexico	52.5	Mexico City	761,602	Luis Echeverria Alvarez, president—1970
Nicaragua	2.1	Managua	50,193	Anastasio Somoza Debayle, Jr., president—1967
Panama	1.5	Panama	29,205	Omar Torrijos Herrera, head of state—1968
Paraguay	2.5	Asuncion	157,047	Alfredo Stroessner, president—1954
Peru	14.0	Lima	496,223	Juan Velasco Alvarado, president—1968
Trinidad and Tobago	1.1	Port of Spain	1,980	Sir Solomon Hochoy, governor-general—1962
				Eric Williams, prime minister—1961
Uruguay	2.9	Montevideo	68,536	Juan Maria Bordaberry, president—1971
Venezuela	11.1	Caracas	352,143	Rafael Caldera Rodriguez, president—1969

ences in the 1969 Rockefeller report, Secretary of State William P. Rogers' statement that the Nixon administration would propose legislation to grant tariff preferences to developing countries, was viewed as belated and unconvincing. The European Economic Community and Japan had already taken action in the matter. The OAS has been drawing closer to Western Europe. Secretary General Galo Plaza moved the OAS European office from Geneva to Brussels, Common Market headquarters. Chile led a violent protest, apparently regarding the Common Market with Soviet-line dislike.

In view of the anti-Americanism spreading through Latin America, the United States showed less inclination to provide financial help. The Senate placed restrictions on U.S. contributions to the Inter-American Development Bank. In Lima, Peru, the Andean Pact countries issued a statement on the control of foreign (chiefly U.S.) investments, a statement that alienated many U.S. investors. The so-called Andean Code calls for the fade-out of foreign investments, insisting that they be sold to local interests within twenty years.

Nevertheless, the United States took no strong action in the face of such provocation as the expropriation of U.S.-owned copper mines by the Chilean Government. Instead, the United States chose to keep a low profile hoping to avert further anti-U.S. demagoguery. It did not push the sale of arms in Latin America, which looked more and more to France, Italy,

Britain and Sweden for supplies. It protested but did not act effectively against the attacks on U.S. fishing vessels resulting from the claims of Argentina, Brazil, Chile, Ecuador, El Salvador, Nicaragua, Panama, Peru and Uruguay to sovereignty over a 200-mile-wide strip of territorial waters. A proposal to discuss the issue was abandoned because Ecuador, the most aggressive in seizing U.S. boats, refused. In 1971, Ecuador alone seized about fifty private U.S. fishing vessels and fined them $2,500,000 in exchange for their freedom. The U.S. Congress retaliated by delaying an extension of the International Coffee Agreement. The U.S. Sugar Act, up for renewal, was the subject of amendments that, while favoring Western Hemisphere countries in general, would penalize countries that expropriate U.S. property without adequate compensation.

Through its Southern Command (Southcom) headquarters in Panama, the United States had focused its continental military presence in the heart of Latin America; Southcom was abolished in 1971 and its responsibilities moved to the continental United States.

Argentina. Unlike Brazil, where the Army was in firm control, the Argentine junta was faced with an alliance of political parties: Peronistas, Radicals, Progressive Democrats, Socialists and Popular Conservatives. Moreover, the General Confederation of Labor (CGT) openly opposed the Government, and there were violent riots in Cordoba. President Roberto M. Levingston tried nationalism to win support by announcing an "Argentinization of the economy" program drafted by Minister of Economy Aldo Ferrer. It was denounced by Alvaro Alsogaray, former minister of economy and ambassador to the United States. The plan failed, and Ferrer was dismissed.

The main issue was the return to constitutional government. Levingston wanted to put this off for four or five years, but Gen. Alejandro Lanusse, the strong man of the Government, demanded faster action. In March, Lanusse simply deposed Levingston and assumed the presidency. He named Arturo Mor Roig, member of the Radicals of the People (one of two branches of the Radical Party), minister of the interior in an obvious effort to revitalize party life. A frantic realignment of political groups followed. As the Peronistas controlled a large mass of voters, the struggle was primarily to see who could make a deal with them. Jorge Paladino, secretary-general of the Peronista party and Peron's personal representative, went to Madrid to discuss with the former dictator a platform he had drawn up with the Radicals of the People, the Social Democrats and various minor groups. However, the CGT, the hard core of the Peronista movement, opposed the deal. Paladino was replaced by Hector Jose Campora.

Living well in Madrid, Peron showed no intention of returning to Argentina. President Lanusse said that if he did, he would face trial on an old charge of seducing a 14-year-old girl (a charge that was quietly shelved later). Other political groups began to form, including the moderate, semiofficial "Hour of the People" and the "Argentine People's Encounter." Former President (1958–62) Arturo Frondizi emerged with plans to form his own military-backed coalition. After being suspended for five years, political parties were allowed to function again as of July 1. About seventy parties registered, most of them insignificant. Presidential elections were scheduled for March 1973.

Several plots were aimed against the Lanusse Government. In May, Gen. Eduardo Rafael Lablanca tried, from Tucuman, to establish a Leftist and nationalistic government, in vain. In all, seven officers were dismissed from the Army. In October, the garrison at Azul, south of Buenos Aires, revolted unsuccessfully to establish a conservative, Catholic regime; Levingston and Col. Manuel Alejandro Garcia, a leader of the plot, were arrested for complicity.

A rather ghoulish episode concerned the body of Eva Peron, which disappeared after the fall of Peron. Its whereabouts had stirred widespread speculation and passionate interest, at

Sphere more than sixty feet high is part of a nuclear-power plant being erected in Argentina, near Parana River, to provide more electricity.

least on the part of Peronistas. Following secret negotiations, it was returned to Peron in September. Apparently, it had been buried in Italy under a false name, but how the body was shipped to Spain remained a mystery.

Bolivia. The Government of Gen. Juan Jose Torres, who had seized power in October 1970, began 1971 by strengthening its position and by moving decisively to the left. It established a Popular Assembly; meetings began in May under the chairmanship of Juan Lechin, with

Col. Hugo Banzer becomes Bolivian president after overthrow of another military Government.

the motto "Power for the People." Both communist parties participated, but the Nationalist Revolutionary Movement (MNR) was excluded on the grounds that it was conservative. However, conditions soon became chaotic, with university students attacking the Leftist Government from the left. The Bolivian University Confederation (CUB) held an anti-imperialist week; its climax was the burning of a U.S. flag. The tin industry, Bolivia's economic key, had been in a state of confusion since nationalization of the large mines in 1952. The Popular Assembly demanded that COMIBOL (the government mining corporation) be turned over to the tin workers, controlled by Lechin. President Torres refused.

In August, conservative army elements, based in Santa Cruz, revolted against the Torres Government. After bloody fighting in which well over a hundred people were killed and seven hundred wounded, the Government was defeated. Torres fled to Peru and former President and MNR leader Victor Paz Estenssoro returned from exile there. Col. Hugo Banzer Suarez assumed the presidency, heading a Government consisting of the military, the MNR and the Bolivian Socialist Falange. Paz Estenssoro proclaimed himself the "caudillo of Bolivia," hoping that he and the MNR would make a comeback.

Brazil. The Brazilian junta was in firm control and running the country with technical efficiency. After Swiss Ambassador Giovanni Enrico Bucher, who had been kidnaped, was released in January, the Government refused to make any further deals with terrorists. Foreign embassies were told to speed the move from Rio de Janeiro to Brasilia (the inland capital) where diplomats could be better protected. Terrorists killed a Danish-born businessman who had organized a progovernment, antiter-

Sidewalk tax consultants thrive as income-tax deadline nears in Brazil. Translated, the sign says "Fill in tax forms here."

UPI

rorist group called Ultra. Within two days the police had killed several people, alleged to be the assassins. The Death Squad, supposedly drawn from the police, continued to carry out vigilante justice toward criminals.

Political life remained dormant, as the Government's National Renovating Alliance (ARENA) heavily outnumbered the opposition Brazilian Democratic Movement (MDB). Plans to create other parties and thus revive the old multiparty system were effectively discouraged. Two former presidents, Jânio Quadros and João Goulart, were charged with using the Graduate Institute of Brazilian Studies to spread subversive propaganda. Over a thousand people, including former presidents, members of Congress and governors as well as intellectuals, were sentenced to the loss of political rights for ten years; the Government made it clear that they must stay out of politics.

Despite the efforts of SUDENE, a partly U.S.-financed government corporation created to develop the arid Northeast, where some 30,-000,000 people live in poverty, the region suffered an acute crisis because of an unusually severe drought. The Government hoped that the 3,350-mile highway, under construction across the Amazon basin, would encourage Northeasterners to migrate west to the empty jungle lands. The Government took a number of steps to develop Amazonia and the west, including sending groups of university faculty members and students to launch pilot projects.

Central America and Panama. The integration of Central America suffered a serious setback with the withdrawal of Honduras from the Central American Common Market. The Honduran Government claimed that technically it had not withdrawn. After Costa Rica broke its trade ties with the other Central American countries (see below), an emergency meeting was held in June to salvage the organization.

New Central American organizations were nevertheless formally established. In September the Central American Parliament officially opened its headquarters in Guatemala City. It created an Executive Council in Guatemala City; and a Court of Justice, in San Jose, Costa Rica. The Parliament itself will rotate its meetings among member countries, moving each year.

The attempts of the U.S.S.R. to gain a diplomatic foothold in Central America, in Costa Rica, coincided with the discovery of an alleged Soviet-inspired plot to overthrow the Mexican Government. The upshot was closer relations between Mexico and Central America. Mexican President Luis Echeverria Alvarez conferred with Central American government leaders although plans for a Middle American bloc were hindered by violent student riots in Mexico in June (*See also* Mexico).

In Guatemala, President Carlos Arana Osorio was elected in 1970 as a tough man who would suppress terrorism, but his efforts failed. However, he seemed to have the confidence of other governments, and West Germany agreed to name a new ambassador; the post had been vacant since Ambassador Karl von Spreti was assassinated in 1970. Despite a sharp reduction in trade with Honduras and trade difficulties with the United States, trade with Japan and Germany boomed. A mission to the U.S.S.R. and six other East European countries returned with forecasts that Guatemalan exports to that area, especially coffee, would increase substantially. The Central Bank reported that its international reserves were the highest in history.

Political tension increased in El Salvador as the 1972 elections neared. President Fidel Sanchez Hernandez ruled with the support of the National Coalition Party (PCN), which had 34 seats in Congress. The opposition Christian Democratic Party, with 15 seats, created an antigovernment broad front, the National Opposition Union. The government candidate was Col. Arturo Armando Molina; the opposition candidate, Jose Napoleon Duarte, former mayor of San Salvador. The PCN Government has been stressing social development and modest land reform in a conservative country traditionally controlled by "14 families." The conservatives formed two Right-wing opposition parties to oppose these policies. In the political spectrum the PCN occupied a strong central position.

The military Government of Honduras decided to allow presidential elections to take place in March. The contenders were Jorge Bueso Arias for the Liberal Party and Ramon E. Cruz for the National Party. The latter won and was inaugurated in June; he promised to continue the policies of outgoing President Oswaldo Lopez Arellano.

On a Latin American trip for President Nixon, Robert H. Finch signed an agreement on Nov. 22 by which the United States gave Honduras the tiny Swan Islands. Under the U.S. flag from 1863, they had long been claimed by Honduras (they are only 97 miles off its coast), not because they have any great value but as a matter of prestige.

President Anastasio Somoza Debayle of Nicaragua made a deal with Fernando Aguero, president of the Conservative Party, by which the constitution would be amended to permit Somoza to continue in the presidency after an interim period during which a three-man junta, including one Conservative, would rule. Four other opposition parties joined forces to fight this deal, as did many Liberals. They protested that it was simply a means for Somoza to perpetuate his rule at the expense of the Liberal Party, which the Somoza family has headed for decades. Nicaraguan foreign trade boomed, thanks largely to high cotton prices.

Like Honduras, but for different reasons, Costa Rica had unpleasant relations with the Central American Common Market. With higher living standards and higher costs, Costa Rica complained that its markets were being flooded with products from Guatemala and El Salvador. In June it virtually barred the import of goods from other Central American countries, thus provoking reprisals. It quickly dropped the ban. The big issue in foreign affairs was the proposal to resume diplomatic relations with the Soviet Union. President Jose Figueres had fought a resolute civil war against communist infiltration, but he justified the proposal on the grounds that Costa Rica must sell coffee. The country's balance of payments was unfavorable, and the outlook for the colon remained uncertain. Because of evidence of communist subversion, a deal involving Soviet machinery and Costa Rican coffee was several times reported on and off. The proposal to open a Soviet embassy in San José aroused so much opposition that it was postponed.

Panamanian politics were overshadowed throughout 1971 by the Canal Zone issue. Negotiations with the United States continued virtually paralyzed. In October strong man Gen. Omar Torrijos staged a mass meeting in a large square next to the Canal Zone to voice support for his intransigent position. However, substantial progress was made on the plan to complete the Pan American Highway, which requires building the missing 250-mile Darien section to the Colombian border. The United States agreed to pay two thirds of the cost, with Panama and Colombia paying the remaining third. Although tense, Panama, whose balboa is interchangeable with the dollar, boomed financially. Money fleeing from other Latin American countries has found a haven in a country imitating Swiss banking practices and offering depositors secrecy and numbered accounts.

Chile. The Allende Government continued to introduce measures allegedly devised to help the people. Rents were frozen. Private banks, including some foreign ones such as the Bank of America, were nationalized. Interest rates were sharply reduced. Agriculture Minister Jacques Chonchol, who was living in Cuba

LATIN
AMERICA

was forced to respect the constitution. He was also compelled to postpone his plan to overcome congressional opposition by changing the constitution and replacing Congress with a single People's Assembly. He attacked the Supreme Court but took no action against it. He established neighborhood courts to mete out people's justice in the case of minor crimes. His supporters conducted a malicious campaign against the conservative *El Mercurio* but did not dare to close it down. However, the Government's acquisition of Zig-Zag, the country's largest magazine publisher, showed that it would use every legal device to control the book and magazine business. (Zig-Zag publishes some twenty magazines.) Its plan to control newsprint would effectively muzzle the press.

The election in February of Carlos Altamirano as secretary-general of the Socialist Party was regarded as a victory for the elements in the Allende Government that wanted to contain the totalitarian Communists. The nationwide municipal elections in April were regarded as a test of Allende's strength; the government coalition won a victory, but the Christian Democrats remained the country's largest party. Former President Eduardo Frei Montalva criticized the Allende Government for veering toward totalitarianism, and in return a virulent campaign was loosed against Frei. Even Allende was shocked when Frei's close colleague in the Christian Democratic Party, Edmundo Perez Zukovic, was assassinated in June. Two members of the extreme left-wing Organized People's Vanguard (VOP), suspected of being the murderers, died in shoot-outs with the police. Allende was blamed because he had pardoned "political prisoners," including the alleged VOP assassins.

The United States avoided an open fight with Chile, which would have provided Allende with a pretext for whipping up nationalist sentiment, but Washington showed a marked coolness. Claiming schedule difficulties, the Navy canceled a visit to Valparaiso by the U.S. nuclear aircraft carrier *Enterprise*. The Export-Import Bank refused to grant credits for the purchase of jet passenger planes for the new Santiago-Havana-Madrid run.

Allende cultivated the U.S.S.R., which advised him to maintain correct relations with the United States. He also opened diplomatic relations with Communist China. He visited Peru, Ecuador and Colombia in August, with the aim of making his regime more popular in other Andean countries. In November, Fidel Castro paid a visit to Chile.

Early in December, more than 150 people were injured in Santiago when riots followed

during the early days of the Castro dictatorship, pushed through a land-reform program expropriating farms of more than 176 acres. The Government seemed to be aiming ultimately at a take-over of all private lands. Nationalization of mining continued; having nationalized the major U.S.-owned copper mines, including El Teniente, the world's largest underground copper mine, Allende moved to nationalize the Bethlehem Chile Iron Mines. He attempted to win the favor of the Chilean armed forces by offering them participation in the state agencies handling copper and iron. Foreign-owned industrial plants such as Ford were taken over.

As its price for helping Allende win the presidency, the Christian Democratic Party forced him to make the Statute of Democratic Guarantees a part of the Chilean constitution. Throughout the year, the Government was inclined to disregard these guarantees but, despite pressure from his Marxist followers, Allende

a protest by women against the Government, who called for "democracy." As a result, Allende decreed a state of emergency in the city and the Army took over control of public order.

Colombia. Elected in 1970 as the last of the four presidents under the 16-year truce between the two major political parties, known as the National Front, Conservative President Misael Pastrana Borrero faced the violence of Leftist students and rural guerrillas. He reorganized his Cabinet in June to give it a more progressive complexion. Leftists attempted to disrupt the Pan-American Games held in Cali in July–August. Although the Liberal Party remained the largest in the country, at its annual convention it broke into two rival factions, one supporting former Vice-President Julio Cesar Turbay Ayala, and the other former President Carlos Lleras Restrepo and former Foreign Minister Alfonso Lopez Michelsen. The latter wanted to adopt a socialist (but not communist) policy. The National Popular Alliance (ANAPO) of former dictator Gen. Gustavo Rojas Pinilla rejoiced, saying that, as in other Latin American countries, the traditional political parties were disintegrating. ANAPO formally became a third party, no longer a group of disgruntled Liberals and Conservatives, and began to prepare for the 1974 elections. Rojas Pinilla himself was 71 and in poor health. An obvious candidate for the leadership was his daughter, Maria Eugenia Rojas de Moreno Diaz, a 37-year-old senator who aspires to a role similar to that of Eva Peron in Argentina. Accusations that ANAPO is a fascist organization led to violence in the Congress in August. The Roman Catholic Church, which traditionally has supported the Conservative Party, declared itself politically neutral.

Colombia's most severe economic problem was the drastic drop in agricultural production. The Government expropriated many large estates, dividing them into less productive five-acre lots. Landowners feared that, as in Chile and Peru, the estates might be expropriated completely.

Armed clashes with Venezuela occurred over potentially oil-rich border areas. As a result, Venezuela showed even less inclination to join the Andean Pact, although at year's end the Andean countries were having some success in overcoming this difficulty.

Ecuador. The four universities of Ecuador (Quito, Guayaquil, Cuenca and Loja), which had been closed because of their opposition to the regime of President Jose Maria Velasco Ibarra, reopened in January. Velasco Ibarra was forced to dismiss his nephew Jorge Acosta Velasco as minister of defense but named him ambassador to Spain. It was clear that the military would thwart any attempt to keep the presidency in the family. Velasco Ibarra's imposition of a poll tax on Ecuadorians crossing the Colombian border caused a riot in the border town of Tulcan. Troops charged the rioters, and 350 fugitives, including Tulcan's mayor, fled to neighboring Ipiales, in Colombia. Since closing Congress in 1970, Velasco Ibarra had been widely denounced as a dictator. Trying to counteract this view, he first said he would hold a constitutional plebiscite. But then he promised to revive the 1946 constitution and hold elections at the end of his term in 1972.

U.S. fishing vessel is one of a number captured by Ecuador in nearby waters; Ecuador claims jurisdiction over them up to 200 miles from shore.

Although numerous political leaders were in jail or in exile, several announced their candidacy for the presidency, including former Guayas Provincial Governor Assad Bucaram, exiled in Panama. In July, Velasco Ibarra expelled three Soviet diplomats accused of financing a strike by the Confederation of Ecuadorian Workers (CTE) aimed at overthrowing his Government.

Guianas and Trinidad-Tobago. After establishing diplomatic relations with the U.S.S.R. in 1970, Guyana sent its first ambassador to Moscow in 1971. Black power became influential in Guyanese politics with the organization of the African Society for Cultural Relations with Independent Africa (ASCRIA). To win its support in his running battle with the East Indian majority led by Marxist Cheddi Jagan, the Government nationalized the big Canadian-owned Alcan bauxite mines, expelled the Peace Corps for "imposing white culture," and reduced the role of AID.

The Trinidad Government of Prime Minister Eric Williams was threatened by black power, even though it had jailed the leaders of the destructive April 1970 revolt. Williams' People's National Movement swept the island elections, winning all 36 seats in the House of Representatives when most of the opposition abstained. High unemployment among young blacks was the main cause of unrest.

The government of Surinam (Dutch Guiana) survived violent riots in September. French Guiana has become a center for launching satellites going into equatorial orbit; but the unsuccessful launching in November of the Europa II rocket (manufactured jointly by France, Britain and West Germany) and Britain's withdrawal from the Europa II program clouded the future of European rocketry.

Paraguay. The Roman Catholic Church continued to be the most vocal critic of the dictatorship of Alfredo Stroessner. In January, the Paraguayan Episcopal Conference, whose publication *Communidad* had been banned, issued a denunciation that was read at all services. Catholic Archbishop Ismael Rolon Silvero of Asuncion excommunicated several government officials, whereupon the Government gave the Church a stern warning. Paraguay maintained cordial relations with Brazil, and greeted the overthrow of the Leftist Government of Bolivia with satisfaction.

Peru. The Government attempted to win popular support by releasing a number of political prisoners, including Hugo Blanco, in jail from 1964 on charges of leading a peasant uprising in the Cuzco area. It continued to break up large estates and developed plans for large-scale irrigation of the Piura Valley of northern Peru. It harassed the opposition press, provoking a denunciation by the Inter-American Press Association. A squabble with the Roman Catholic Church broke out when Interior Minister Gen. Armando Artola detained Auxiliary Bishop Luis Bambaren on charges of inciting squatters. President Juan Velasco Alvarado sided with the Church, and Artola resigned.

The state-owned corporation Mineroperu was given control of mineral production and sales.

Religious-civil ceremony launches celebration of 150 years of independence in Peru, where religion, cooperatives and capitalism are blending.

Cerro de Pasco's refinery was closed for weeks on end; in November, unions shut down its mines also. Anaconda abandoned its Cerro Verde and Arequipa concessions, the Southern Peru Copper Corporation its Michiquillay concession. Relations with the United States had been cold since the expropriation in October 1968 of the properties of the International Petroleum Company (a subsidiary of the Standard Oil Company of New Jersey). Early in 1971, however, the U.S. Government adopted a conciliatory attitude, and the Peruvian Government again welcomed certain kinds of U.S. investment. A few oil companies, such as Occidental Petroleum, Shell and Phillips, began operations in the Oriente. However, in a speech at the 12th annual meeting of the Board of Governors of the Inter-American Development Bank, Velasco Alvarado defied the international financial community.

Velasco Alvarado represents what used to be called "Nasserism," i.e., the doctrine that only the army can bring about a social revolution. His example has encouraged other Latin American armies to abandon their traditionally conservative role although not always with success.

Uruguay. President Jorge Pacheco Areco refused to make any deals with the Tupamaro terrorists, and the struggle continued. In January they kidnaped British Ambassador Geoffrey Jackson and held him prisoner until September. The Government subjected the traditionally free press to prior censorship in order not to give the Tupamaros publicity. Pacheco Areco unsuccessfully demanded that Congress renew the suspension of civil liberties. In September, 106 Tupamaro terrorists made a mass escape from a Montevideo jail. Pacheco Areco thereupon turned maintenance of public order from the police over to the Army.

Leftist opponents of the Pacheco Areco regime banded together in the political struggle leading up to the November elections. A movement known as FIDEL and controlled by Communists and Christian Democrats expanded into the Broad Front with the addition of young members of both Colorado and the Nationals (Blanco) parties. Tupamaros supported the Broad Front. Pacheco Areco closed down the newspaper *Ya,* which also supported the Broad Front. Its candidate for president was former Gen. Liber Seregni. Nationals and Colorados were, as usual, divided. In July, Pacheco Areco stated that he would submit a constitutional amendment permitting reelection, in the hope of being reelected himself. Opponents of this constitutional change named a rival candidate, Jorge Batlle, thus dividing the Colorado Party, in the majority, which finally offered six candidates. A former National Party member, Juan Maria Bordaberry, became a candidate with the support of Pacheco Areco, who lost hope of reelection. In a record voter turnout on Nov. 28, and after a long, slow count, the strong Leftist coalition was found to run a poor third to the Colorados and Nationals. In the close vote between the last two, Bordaberry had a lead but doubt remained as year ended.

Because of the Tupamaros, the Uruguayan economy was badly hit. Tourists, primarily Argentinian, stayed away and the international resort of Punta del Este had a very poor season in spite of special low rates to tourists. However, industrial and agricultural production were good.

Venezuela. Long touted as a paradise for U.S. investors, especially in the oil business, Venezuela felt the nationalism sweeping Latin America. It led the Government to make threats against foreign-owned oil properties. It established higher posted rates for crude oil, which would yield an additional $440,000,000 annually in taxes. Congress approved an extreme law that, among other things, would require all oil installations be turned over to the Government when the forty-year concessions expire, mostly in 1983–84, or even immediately if the Ministry of Mines and Hydrocarbons decides that production is inadequate. The principal oil producers, Creole (a division of Esso) and Royal Dutch Shell, appealed to the Supreme Court. The same nationalistic forces were trying to push Venezuela into the Andean Pact, which it had refused to join in 1969. Venezuela businessmen objected that Venezuela was bound to lose from an association with the poorer countries of the West Coast of South America.

Despite the efforts of the Christian Social (COPEI) Government of President Rafael Caldera to stimulate popular support, former dictator Marcos Perez Jimenez evidently thought he had regained enough popularity to run in 1973 presidential elections with the help of his National Civic Crusade. Yet he remained in exile in Lima, Peru, believing that he would be jailed if he returned to Venezuela to occupy his seat in the Senate. The Communists split over subservience to Moscow. A young Communist, Teodoro Petkoff, well known as the author of a book criticizing the Soviet invasion of Czechoslovakia, had led the unorthodox out of the party to form the Movement for Socialism (MAS) in late 1970. Pompeyo Marquez became the party's secretary general in 1971.

RONALD HILTON
Professor, Stanford University
Executive Director
California Institute of International Studies

LAW

The year 1971 is likely to be remembered by Supreme Court historians as the year when the "Nixon Court" was born—with considerable birth pangs. When he ran for president in 1968, Richard Nixon campaigned on a pledge to reverse the liberal judicial philosophy of the Warren Court by appointing "strict constructionists": justices who would "interpret" the law, not "make" it. In September, he was given an opportunity to change the direction of the court when Justices Hugo L. Black and John M. Harlan retired.

Justice Black, the 85-year-old disciple of literal adherence to the Bill of Rights, had been the moving intellect behind many of the activist moves of the Warren Court. He retired on Sept. 17 and died on Sept. 25 of inflammation of the arteries. Justice Harlan had been widely considered the court's most accomplished legal technician, a conservative judge who stressed consistency and respect for precedent. He retired on Sept. 23 after a back ailment was diagnosed as cancer.

Under any circumstances, the departure of the Supreme Court's most strong-willed activist and its most scholarly conservative would have had a substantial impact upon its course. But

"Needless to say, gentlemen, I highly approve of the changing face of this great institution."

the impact was magnified because Nixon had already named Chief Justice Warren E. Burger and Justice Harry A. Blackmun to the court, and this gave the President an opportunity that few presidents have had, the chance to appoint four justices in one four-year presidential term.

During October, President Nixon moved to name two Supreme Court nominees to cement the "Nixon" brand of conservative judicial philosophy upon the court, resulting in the kind of appointive crisis that had become almost a trademark of the Nixon presidency. Thwarted in his earlier efforts to place a Southerner on the court when the Senate denied confirmation to Clement F. Haynsworth, Jr., and G. Harrold Carswell, Nixon made no secret of his intention to name a person from the South to fill the "Southern seat" vacated by Hugo Black of Alabama.

It was no secret in Washington that the person at the top of Nixon's list was Rep. Richard H. Poff, a conservative Republican from Virginia who shared the President's law-and-order philosophy. However, opposition to him developed among civil-rights groups and labor-union leaders, who pointed out that he had voted against every major civil-rights bill and had signed the "Southern Manifesto" that denounced the Supreme Court's school-desegregation decision of 1954. Others noted that he had almost no legal experience, having been elected to Congress four years after he had passed his bar exams. With criticism rising but with Senate confirmation still likely, Representative Poff abruptly took himself out of consideration on Oct. 2, saying he wished to spare the nation and his family a "protracted and controversial" Senate confirmation struggle.

A few days later, President Nixon declared at a press conference that not only would he name the nominees for both seats together, he would do so within a week. This would have been quick work under any circumstances, but it was complicated for Nixon because his administration had pledged not to nominate anyone to the Supreme Court without first giving the American Bar Association's Committee on the Federal Judiciary an opportunity to rate the judicial qualifications of the potential nominees. A few days later, six names were sent to the ABA. Word quickly leaked out that four of the names were only a "smoke screen," that the President was interested only in the top two names on the list. One was Herschel L. Friday, a Little Rock, Ark., corporate lawyer who was virtually unknown outside his state, but who had a reputation there as an effective defender of school boards against desegregation suits. The second was Judge Mildred L. Lillie of the

California Court of Appeal in Los Angeles, who was known in California as a tough-on-criminals jurist but not as a particularly distinguished one.

The disclosure of the names brought a wave of criticism from editorial writers, lawyers and Democrats, and even some cool words from some Republicans. It was said that Nixon was attempting to score political points with segregationist elements in the South and with women, at the expense of the overall quality of the Supreme Court justices. The ABA committee had been evaluating nominees since the days of the Eisenhower administration without ever finding one unqualified, but it voted to give "not qualified" ratings to both Friday and Mrs. Lillie. President Nixon responded by asking for television time on the evening of Oct. 21, when he surprised almost everyone by naming two widely respected lawyers, Lewis F. Powell, Jr., of Richmond, Va., and Assistant Attorney General William H. Rehnquist.

In making the nominations, the President stressed that the two men shared his conservative philosophy, and there was no doubt that both did. Lewis Powell was a 64-year-old former president of the ABA who was known as a racial moderate but who had made strong speeches against the "heresy" of civil disobedience and had complained that some Supreme Court decisions had served to protect criminals and hobble law enforcement. William Rehnquist, 47, was a former Phoenix, Ariz., lawyer who professed an unabashed conservatism that included support for wiretapping of radicals without court authority, mass arrests of antiwar demonstrators, and dismissals of any government employees who protested the Government's policies.

Although liberals criticized the conservative records of both men, neither was vulnerable to the ethical or mediocrity attacks that had defeated earlier Nixon nominees. Their critics were never able to build up a groundswell of opposition against them. After confirmation hearings, Rehnquist was confirmed on Dec. 10 and Powell on Nov. 6.

President Nixon was still one justice short of having named a majority of the Supreme Court, but there was little doubt that the era of the "Nixon Court" had begun. Some observers had started calling it that even before

Two distinguished lawyers step up to the Supreme Court: Lewis F. Powell, Jr. (l) and William H. Rehnquist, who are shown testifying before they were confirmed. Powell is a Virginian, and Rehnquist an Arizonan.

Justices Black and Harlan retired, because the addition of Chief Justice Burger and Justice Blackmun had already turned the court in a decisively conservative direction.

Some presidents have been disappointed after naming men to the Supreme Court only to see them strike out in unexpected directions after they donned the lifetime robes of a justice. This did not happen with Burger and Blackmun, who came to be called the "Minnesota Twins" by the news media because both are from that state and they almost always voted together—and usually on the conservative side. Of the 102 cases decided by written opinions during the court term that ended in June 1971, they were on the same side on all but four. In the others, they frequently voted to narrow or reverse liberal doctrines that had been laid down while Earl Warren was chief justice.

This often aligned them with three other justices—Potter Stewart, Byron R. White and Harlan—so that for the first time in more than a decade, the conservative view of the law more often than not had precedence in the Supreme Court's rulings. The American Jewish Congress, which has been evaluating the Supreme Court's record on civil-liberties issues annually since 1957, concluded in its 1971 study that for the first time the court was rejecting civil-liberties claims more often than it was granting them. With Burger and Blackmun rejecting asserted claims of individual rights almost two thirds of the time, the court as a whole denied slightly more than half the civil-liberties claims brought before the Supreme Court.

The new "Burger majority" did not directly overturn any of the rulings of the Warren era, but it clearly demonstrated that the Supreme Court was no longer moved by the spirit of the liberal Warren Court.

The Warren Court had said that unless persons were warned of their rights, confessions could not be used as evidence; the Burger majority held that such confessions can, however, be used to impeach the defendant's testimony (*Harris v. New York*). The Warren Court had held that illegitimates have equal rights with legitimate offspring to sue for their parents' wrongful death; the court ruled in 1971 that illegitimates do not have equal rights to inherit from their parents (*Labine v. Vincent*). The Warren Court had decided that Congress could not pass laws by which citizens could lose their citizenship; the Burger majority held that it can if it established the standard for citizenship in the first place (*Rogers v. Bellei*). The Warren Court had said that a public referendum could not be used to deny

housing to Negroes; the Burger Court decided that a referendum could be used to deny public housing to the poor (*James v. Valtierra*). The Warren Court had said that search warrants are required before officials can inspect a businessman's premises; the Burger majority declared that no search warrants are required for welfare workers who wish to inspect welfare clients' homes (*Wyman v. James*). The Warren Court had declared that juvenile courts must grant children the same due-process safeguards as are accorded adult defendants; the Burger Court held that juveniles nevertheless are not entitled to jury trials in juvenile court (*McKeiver v. Pennsylvania*).

In each instance, the new decision left intact the doctrine that the Warren Court had so recently laid down. But it was clear that a legal watershed had been reached in 1971 and that the basic course of the Supreme Court would thereafter follow a different and more conservative direction.

Not all of the decisions fit this pattern, and one that came as 1970 ended was so bizarre as to defy any pattern at all. It concerned Congress' effort to lower the voting age to 18 years by means of a statute, although constitutional amendments had been used to grant the vote to women and to abolish poll taxes. Congress reasoned that denying the vote to people who are old enough to be drafted violated the Fourteenth Amendment's prohibition against denying anyone equal protection of the laws. Because the Fourteenth Amendment gives Congress the authority to pass laws to enforce this antidiscrimination provision, Congress reasoned that it had the power to pass one granting 18-year-olds the right to vote in every state.

The issue split the Supreme Court down the middle, with four justices saying such a change requires a constitutional amendment, and four others saying a statute is sufficient. The fifth justice, Hugo Black, neatly split the difference. He declared that in Federal elections the 18-year-old-vote law is valid, thus upholding it by a 5 to 4 vote. However, he said also that the law is invalid for state elections, thus creating a 5 to 4 majority in favor of leaving state laws intact (*Oregon v. Mitchell*). With 18-year-olds authorized to vote for national but not state offices, chaos threatened. The 26th Amendment was quickly approved, lowering the voting age to 18 for all elections.

In another offbeat action, the Supreme Court agreed to hear the draft-evasion case of former heavyweight champion Muhammad Ali (Cassius Clay) just in time to keep him out of jail for his attempted comeback against champion Joe Frazier. On Mar. 8 Frazier won the fight,

MAJOR SUPREME COURT DECISIONS[1]

CHIEF JUSTICE: Warren E. Burger (1969)

ASSOCIATE JUSTICES

HUGO L. BLACK (1937)[2]
WILLIAM O. DOUGLAS (1939)
JOHN M. HARLAN (1955)[2]
WILLIAM J. BRENNAN, JR. (1956)
POTTER STEWART (1958)

BYRON WHITE (1962)
THURGOOD MARSHALL (1967)
HARRY A. BLACKMUN (1970)
LEWIS F. POWELL, JR.[3]
WILLIAM H. REHNQUIST[3]

CASE	DATE	DECISION
MAYBERRY V. PENNSYLVANIA	JAN. 20	Rules that a judge, when insulted in court by an offender, may immediately impose a contempt sentence. However, if he waits until the end of the trial, another judge must impose punishment. Vote 9–0.
MONITOR PATRIOT COMPANY V. ROY; OCALA STAR-BANNER COMPANY V. DAMRON	FEB. 24	Declares that the press has the right to publish alleged charges of criminal behavior by public officials or candidates even if the accusations are untrue. Vote 9–0.
BODDIE V. CONNECTICUT	MAR. 2	Finds that the state must pay the filing fees and court expenses for indigent people who want a divorce but cannot meet these costs. Vote 8–1 (Black).
TATE V. SHORT	MAR. 2	Rules that a person cannot be sent to jail solely because he is too poor to pay the fine levied on him. Vote 9–0.
GILLETTE V. UNITED STATES; NEGRE V. LARSEN	MAR. 8	Declares that a man who wishes to be classified a conscientious objector by the military must oppose all wars and not just the Vietnam war. Vote 8–1 (Douglas).
UNITED STATES V. FREED	APR. 5	Upholds the Federal Firearms Law of 1968, making it a crime to possess unregistered sawed-off shotguns, automatic weapons and such devices as grenades and bombs. Vote 9–0.
UNITED STATES V. VUITCH	APR. 21	Upholds the District of Columbia's abortion law, allowing abortions to be performed only to protect the life and health of the mother. Vote 5–2 (Potter, Stewart; Brennan, Marshall not voting).
LEE V. NEW YORK	MAY 3	New York State's antibusing law is declared unconstitutional. Vote 9–0.
McGAUTHA V. CALIFORNIA; CRAMPTON V. OHIO	MAY 3	Holds that the death penalty does not violate the Constitution and can be imposed by juries. Vote 6–3 (Douglas, Brennan, Marshall).
COATES V. CINCINNATI	JUNE 1	Finds that cities cannot make it a crime for small groups of people to loiter in an "annoying" manner in public places. Vote 5–4 (White, Burger, Blackmun, Black).
ROSENBLOOM V. METROMEDIA, INC.	JUNE 7	Rules that private individuals involved in public affairs cannot sue for libelous news accounts unless malice can be proved. Vote 5–3 (Marshall, Harlan, Stewart; Douglas not voting).
WHITCOMB V. CHAVIS	JUNE 7	Declares that states are not required to carve out separate legislative districts for urban Negroes (or other minority groups) who may get little representation in the election of legislators "at large." Vote 5–3 (Brennan, Douglas, Marshall; Harlan files separate concurring and dissenting opinions).
GRIFFIN V. BRECKENRIDGE	JUNE 7	Holds that persons can sue in Federal court anyone who conspires to deprive them of their civil rights. Vote 9–0.
PALMER V. THOMPSON	JUNE 14	Rules that a community can close its recreational facilities rather than obey court orders to desegregate them. Vote 5–4 (Brennan, Douglas, Marshall, White).
UNITED FEDERATION OF POSTAL CLERKS V. BLOUNT	OCT. 12	Upholds a Federal law forbidding strikes by government employees. Vote 6–1 (Douglas).
ORLANDO V. LAIRD	OCT. 12	Upholds a lower court's ruling that the Vietnam war is constitutional; thus servicemen cannot refuse to be sent to Vietnam on the grounds that the war is illegal. Vote 5–2 (Douglas, Brennan).
REED V. REED, ADMINISTRATOR	NOV. 22	Declares unconstitutional an Idaho statute that gives men preference over women in administering deceased persons' estates. This marked the first time the court had invalidated a state law on sex-discrimination grounds. Vote 7–0.

1 Not discussed in Law article   2 Resigned in September 1971   3 Appointed in 1971

but three months later Ali won his case. The court ruled that draft officials should have given more weight to a Justice Department hearing officer's finding that Ali's conscientious objections to participation in the Vietnam war were sincere (*Clay v. United States*).

Perhaps the most far-reaching Supreme Court ruling of the year was the decision declaring it unconstitutional for states to supplement the salaries of teachers in parochial schools. Rising costs have been threatening many Roman Catholic schools with extinction, and ten states had responded by giving substantial subsidies to them. Other states gave indirect aid, and the trend appeared to be toward more state assistance. The Supreme Court drew the line at schemes that were tried in Pennsylvania and Rhode Island, where the state treasuries paid a percentage of parochial teachers' pay in order to keep it on a par with salaries in the public schools. The court held that this violated the principle of separation of church and state (*Earley v. Dicenso*). It upheld, however, the Federal law that grants U.S. funds for constructing buildings for nonreligious purposes on the campus of church-related colleges (*Tilton v. Richardson*).

In the field of civil rights, the Supreme Court's path remained unchanged. It expanded the rights of Negroes against job discrimination, holding that companies may not use aptitude tests that tend to weed out minority-group job applicants, unless the skills necessary for scoring well on the test are also helpful in performing the job (*Griggs v. Duke Power Company*). The justices also ruled on the job rights of women for the first time, declaring that companies cannot bar employment to the mothers of small children unless they also bar fathers of young families (*Phillips v. Martin Marietta Corp.*).

The civil-rights issue made its greatest impact in the Supreme Court's first major ruling on the busing of students to achieve racial balance in the public schools. Ruling only with regard to Southern communities that had all-black schools left over from the official segregation that was declared unconstitutional in 1954, the justices declared unanimously that massive busing must be used, if necessary, to erase the old patterns (*Swann v. Charlotte-Mecklenburg Board of Education*).

Before 1971 most of the school-desegregation cases in the South had involved rural areas where black and white children who lived in salt-and-pepper neighborhoods had been sorted out and sent to "Negro" and "white" schools. But in April 1971 the court dealt with two Southern cities—Charlotte, N.C., and Mobile,

Ala.—that were much like cities in the North where segregation was largely a result of housing patterns. Thus when the court held that busing might be required to break up the all-black schools that had survived despite the desegregation ruling of 1954, the decision implied that similar busing might also be required in the North. Busing was quickly ordered by Federal judges in Pontiac (Mich.), Detroit, Denver, San Francisco, San Diego and other cities where segregation had not been decreed by law but where it was found to have been abetted by school officials.

It became obvious that similar court orders might be imposed in almost every major city with large black populations, and political pressure began to build up for a constitutional amendment to outlaw school assignments on the basis of race. This made it likely that in 1972 the Supreme Court will have to rule on the sensitive question of school integration in the major cities of the North.

Elsewhere, lower courts were continuing the activist trend made respectable by the Warren Court, and in the process generating new issues that in time the Supreme Court would have to resolve.

One was the question of the right of newsmen to protect their confidential sources. Previously, courts had said that unless state legislatures had granted newsmen a privilege of not revealing their sources, they must obey subpoenas to testify. But when the Justice Department sought in 1970 to subpoena Earl Caldwell, a *New York Times* reporter, to tell a grand jury what he knew about the Black Panther Party, lower Federal courts said he could refuse to appear. The reasoning was that Caldwell would probably get no more news from the Panthers if he testified, and the Government had not shown that it needed his testimony. The Government appealed to the Supreme Court.

In a somewhat analogous vein, the lower Federal courts declared unconstitutional Attorney General John N. Mitchell's claim that the Federal Government has the authority to use wiretapping without court approval against "dangerous" domestic radical groups that are suspected of disloyalty or subversion. The lower courts held that the Government could no more wiretap without warrants than it could make searches or arrests without warrants. The Government, asserting that the president has the constitutional power to act on his own to combat threats to the national security, appealed to the Supreme Court.

In another far-reaching lower-court decision, the Supreme Court of California declared unconstitutional the state's system of financing public education, which is typical of the method used in most states. The court held that school revenues cannot be raised on a county-by-county or district-by-district basis, when the result is that poor districts cannot afford educational opportunities equal to those of the schools in wealthy districts. If upheld and applied to other states, this would probably require that school taxes be collected everywhere by the states and spent equally in poor and rich communities.

This question, too, was destined for final resolution by the United States Supreme Court, which continued to be confronted with issues that had the potential to work vast changes in American life.

FRED P. GRAHAM
Supreme Court Correspondent
The New York Times

The Pentagon Papers Case

By far the most dramatically publicized case of the 1970–71 U.S. Supreme Court term involved the celebrated Pentagon Papers, the "top secret" 7,000-page, 47-volume *History of U.S. Decision Making Process on Vietnam Policy*. Commissioned by former Secretary of Defense Robert S. McNamara in 1967, the secret study surveyed the development of American policy in Southeast Asia from the end of World War II to the beginning of 1968.

The New York Times, through the efforts of reporter Neil Sheehan, obtained a copy of the secret study and printed the first of a series on Sunday, June 13. Attorney General John N. Mitchell requested the *Times* to cease further publication of the study of Vietnam policy but the *Times* refused.

The Department of Justice then filed an action in the U.S. District Court in New York City seeking to enjoin the *Times* from further publication of the study on the grounds that information contained in the study was classified as "top secret" and that its disclosure would pose an "irreparable injury" to the "national security" interests of the United States. The District Court granted a temporary four-day injunction which was later dissolved on the grounds that the Justice Department—during a secret in-chambers trial before the judge—had not proved its case of injury to the national security. The U.S. Court of Appeals reversed, reimposed the censorship ban and the *Times* appealed to the Supreme Court.

Six days after the original publication by the *Times, The Washington Post* started its own series based on a copy of the Pentagon Papers it had obtained. The Justice Department filed a similar complaint against the *Post,* but both the U.S. District Court and the U.S. Court of Appeals in Washington refused to enjoin publication. Thus, the Justice Department appealed the *Post* case to the Supreme Court. The Supreme

Queue forms to attend special Supreme Court session on Pentagon Papers case, which involved subtle interpretations of constitutional law.

Court held an unusual Saturday session to hear both cases. It was apparently the first time in American history that any Federal court had issued a prepublication censorship ban against an established news publication.

The Department of Justice relied basically on two arguments: 1. The Constitution gives the president the "inherent" and "exclusive" power to control foreign affairs and protect the "national security." Therefore, the Federal courts did not have the right to "second-guess" the President on whether or not publication of the study would "severely damage" the national security. 2. Even if the Federal courts did have jurisdiction to hear the case, the Justice Department had presented enough evidence—in secret trials before two U.S. District Courts and Courts of Appeal—to justify a finding of fact that further publication would pose a "clear, immediate and irreparable" injury to the national security.

The *Times* and the *Post* took the position that the Federal courts must have the power to hear the case because the executive branch requested an injunction that infringed on the First Amendment guarantee of freedom of the press. The newspapers then argued that the Justice Department had not presented enough facts in the secret trials to warrant a finding of a "grave and immediate" danger to the national security.

Four days later, the Supreme Court, by a 6–3 vote, dissolved its own temporary injunction against both newspapers and ruled that the study could be published. The four-paragraph decision said only that "any system of prior restraints comes to this Court bearing a heavy presumption against its constitutional validity" and that the Government "had not met that burden" of proving that publication would seriously damage the national security. The six majority decisions were written by:

Justice William O. Douglas and the late Justice Hugo L. Black, who restated their "absolutionist" position that the First Amendment bars prepublication censorship in any form.

Justices William J. Brennan, Jr., and Thurgood Marshall, who argued that the Government had not presented enough evidence to justify even the original June 15 restraining order against the *Times*.

Justices Byron White and Potter Stewart—the so-called "swing-vote" justices—said that publication of the study would pose "substantial damage to public interests" but did not pose a "grave and immediate danger to the national security."

The three dissenters were Chief Justice Warren E. Burger, Associate Justice Harry Black-

mun and former Associate Justice John M. Harlan. They complained that the "frenetic haste" of the litigation deprived the Supreme Court of sufficient time to carefully weigh the issues. They would have continued the censorship bans against both newspapers and sent the cases back to lower courts for further hearings.

While the *Times* greeted the decision with "complete joy and delight" as a "ringing victory for freedom under law," many other publications—including the *Post*—saw the decision as a minimal victory for the freedom of the press.

In terms of legal precedent, there was no disapproval by the majority of the original restraining order against the *Times;* no criticism of the secret trials from which the public and the press were excluded; no constitutional guideline for what the "burden" of proof should have been; no discussion of the facts in the case—and thus no standards for editors, judges and lawyers who may be faced with similar problems in the future. Or as the *Post* said in its editorial: "There is not much comfort, let alone clear-cut law, to be found in yesterday's outcome."

Indeed, there were many experts among constitutional liberals, including the American Civil Liberties Union, who thought that the press was probably weakened by the whole affair. After all, the Nixon administration had succeeded in an endeavor that no prior Government—since the Alien and Sedition laws of the Adams administration, in 1798, which themselves had provoked wide controversy—had even dared to suggest.

It had silenced four of the most respected newspapers in the nation by court injunctions: the *Times* for 15 days, the *Post* for 11 days, *The Boston Globe* for 8 days and *St. Louis Post-Dispatch* for 4 days. (The *Globe* and the *Post-Dispatch* had subsequently obtained portions of the Pentagon Papers and been served with Justice Department complaints.) It had convinced three Supreme Court justices and a majority of the U.S. Court of Appeals in New York City that the bans should have been extended even longer. Or as Solicitor General Erwin Griswold said after he heard the decision: "Maybe the newspapers will show a little restraint in the future."

On June 28, the Justice Department indicted a former Defense Department employee, Dr. Daniel Ellsberg, for giving the study to the *Times* in alleged violation of the Espionage Act.

JACK C. LANDAU
Supreme Court Correspondent
Newhouse News Service

LIBRARIES

Annually since 1956 the U.S. Government has shown its interest in strengthening the nation's libraries, and in the past decade its appropriations for school, academic and public libraries and for library training and research have not been negligible. With the tightening of budgets in 1971 many programs faced the prospect of curtailment. Nevertheless, Congress approved $90,000,000 for school-library resources ($10,-000,000 more than the preceding year's appropriation); $46,568,000 for public-library services, substantially more than anticipated; and $9,500,000 for public-library construction. The Education Appropriations Act earmarked $11,000,000 for college-library resources, down from $15,325,000 for 1971.

The National Commission on Libraries and Information Science was activated with President Nixon's nomination of 14 members, the 15th member being the Librarian of Congress. The commission was established in 1970, but its activities await Congressional appropriations.

Limited financial resources of states and cities left many libraries with reduced income though costs were rising. The New York Public Library was seriously affected, with a loss of $1,000,000 which had been received from the City University of New York. The impact was felt most acutely in the research division of the library, forcing a curtailment of its service from 78 to 40 hours a week. Furthermore, President Richard W. Couper of the li-

brary saw the prospect of further reductions in 1972, with its collections in science and technology, music, dance and theater, and the Rodgers and Hammerstein Archives of Recorded Sound closed to the public.

How confidential are library circulation records? This issue arose out of the request from the Internal Revenue Service to the Milwaukee Public Library for information on the use of materials on explosives. A similar request went to the Atlanta Public Library. Discussions between representatives of the library profession and Internal Revenue officials led to agreement that the individual's right to privacy in library use would be respected, though an attempt would be made to identify situations where inquiry might be justified.

At least three libraries in California suffered from the earthquake on Feb. 9. The library of San Fernando State College suffered considerable damage, and over 250,000 volumes fell from the shelves. At California State College Library over 2,000 volumes tumbled, and the Los Angeles Public Library estimated damage to its buildings of about $1,200,000.

A number of significant changes in personnel occurred. Edward G. Freehafer, director of the New York Public Library for 16 years, retired and was succeeded by John M. Cory, formerly deputy director. The Chicago Public Library, hard on the heels of a sweeping survey, appointed five new administrators: Leonard H. Freiser, deputy chief librarian; Henry E. Bates,

Across the United States, libraries have been suffering a mounting wave of book thefts. One (expensive) means of coping with the situation is an electronic detector, Checkpoint. Each library volume has a laminated strip pasted in it: the turnstile locks at once when such a book passes through.

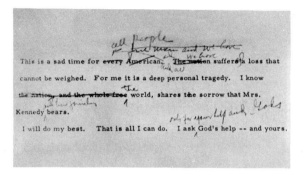

The thousands of documents in the L. B. Johnson Library include his speech (with his corrections) when he became president in 1963.

Eliza A. Gleason and Richard O. Pautzsch, assistant chief librarians; and John F. Galvin, personnel manager. At the University of Chicago, Herman H. Fussler, after supervising the construction of and the move to the magnificent Regenstein Library, resigned to become full-time professor at that institution's Graduate Library School. Richard DeGennaro moved from Harvard to become director of libraries at the University of Pennsylvania, replacing Warren J. Haas, who returned to Columbia University as library director. Miss Ann Marie Murphy, associated with Fordham University for 16 years, became its director of libraries. John P. McGowan was appointed librarian of Northwestern University, succeeding Thomas R. Buckman, who resigned to become president of the Foundation Center in New York. Eugene P. Kennedy was named to administer the new Elmer Holmes Bobst Library and Study Center of New York University, a 12-story structure on the Washington Square campus.

Among new library-school deans or directors were Patrick Wilson (California), Perry D. Morrison (Oregon), Morris Gelfand (Queens), William Goffman (Case Western Reserve), Ivan Kaldor (Geneseo, New York), Edward G. Holley (North Carolina), and Donald Foos (Louisiana State).

The Lyndon Baines Johnson Library was dedicated in May. On the campus of the University of Texas in Austin, it contains manuscripts, documents, state papers, and memorabilia to serve scholarship and to interest the casual visitor. One feature is a reproduction of the Oval Office as it was when occupied by President Johnson in the White House.

Oberlin College received $2,750,000 to help defray the cost of the new Seeley G. Mudd Learning Center, designed to accommodate 800,000 volumes, at an estimated cost of $11,-000,000. Georgetown University acquired an

extensive collection bearing on Sen. Eugene J. McCarthy's campaign for the presidency in 1968. An August Strindberg collection of rare and first editions came to New York University's Fales Library from Arvid Paulson. Col. Richard Gimbel's aeronautical collection of 20,000 items was presented to the Air Force Academy. The University of California (Los Angeles) acquired a copy of Ptolemy's *Liber Geographiae,* printed in Venice in 1511, as well as a collection of Sean O'Casey manuscripts, Gertrude Stein materials, and a library on mountaineering. Syracuse received $100,000 for its Von Ranke collection of rarities and manuscripts; Tulane got $500,000 from the Mellon Foundation; and Yale received $17,-000,000 from Edwin J. Beinecke, almost half of it to be used for acquisitions by the Beinecke Library.

LIBRARY ASSOCIATIONS

The American Library Association held two conferences, in Los Angeles in January and in Dallas in June. Both considered changing the organization to permit greater member participation and to establish more effective agencies. A somber undercurrent was the conflict between limited financial resources (caused in part by declining membership) and costly new programs.

The theme of the Dallas meeting was "Response to a Restive World." The incoming President, Keith Doms, librarian of Philadelphia, in his inaugural address emphasized the interrelatedness of all media, print and nonprint; he proposed that the 1972 conference, to be held in Chicago, focus on "Media: Man, Material, Machines."

UNESCO sponsored a conference in Paris in October to consider the feasibility of a world science-information system, and a meeting of experts in Uganda to plan documentation and library service in Africa.

The International Federation of Library Associations held its meeting in Liverpool, England, Aug. 27–Sept. 4, to discuss the organization of the library profession. It will meet in Budapest in 1972, designated International Book Year by UNESCO.

The International Association of Orientalist Librarians met in Canberra, Australia, in January to discuss international cooperation. It was the first conference of the association since its formation in 1967. The Library Association of Australia held its 16th biennial conference in Sydney, with invited guests from abroad.

LEON CARNOVSKY
Professor, Graduate Library School
University of Chicago

LITERATURE IN ENGLISH

Ghosts, political and literary, haunted the publishing scene in 1971. *The New York Times'* publication of the classified *Pentagon Papers,* commissioned in 1967 by then Secretary of Defense McNamara, exposed the sordid background of American involvement in Vietnam and elicited a historic Supreme Court decision in favor of the *Times.* With amazing rapidity the papers found their way into book form. Then former President Johnson published *his* version of the controversial Vietnam decisions in *The Vantage Point,* a disappointingly unrevealing memoir of his years in the White House.

On the literary front, a similarly disappointing ghost from the past was E. M. Forster's much-heralded novel *Maurice,* written in 1913 but suppressed until after the author's death because of its now tame homosexual theme.

Yet the most notable poetry volume of the year was T. S. Eliot's half-century-old *The Waste Land,* issued for the first time in a handsome facsimile of the original drafts and showing how much of the poem's immense impact on the twentieth century came from rigorous editing by Eliot's friend Ezra Pound. The two best collections of short stories were by Flannery O'Connor and Carson McCullers, gifted Southern ladies of Gothic imagination who died in 1964 and 1967 respectively. Appropriately then, the best literary biography—by the English scholar-translator Michael Meyer—was of Henrik Ibsen, the cranky Norwegian dramatist who wrote *Ghosts.*

Otherwise, book prices continued to soar despite President Nixon's wage-price freeze, giving additional point to one of the few publicity sensations of the year that had nothing to do with "sensuality"—Abbie Hoffman's high-spirited yippie guide to rip-offs, *Steal This Book.*

Jack Clayton

From Canadian novelist Mordecai Richler came the wide-ranging "St. Urbain's Horseman."

Fiction. No one novel outdistanced all others in 1971, but some fairly old hands produced some of their best work in years. Bernard Malamud's *The Tenants* gives bleak, powerful insight into the troubled relations between blacks and Jews against a festering urban background reminiscent of his early success, *The Assistant.* In *The Tenants,* Harry Lesser, an experienced Jewish writer who is having trouble finishing his latest novel, tries at first to encourage Willie Spearmint, an angry young black writer who has moved into the slum building of which Lesser is the last, tenacious, tenant. Before long the two writers are at each other's throats. Malamud makes their mortal combat both believable in human terms and ideologically significant, because he treats both with corrosive yet compassionate irony.

Much lighter in tone but equally serious as art was Canadian novelist Mordecai Richler's

Anniversaries—American writers Theodore Dreiser and James Weldon Johnson were born in 1871.

Photos Culver Pictures

fourth novel, *St. Urbain's Horseman.* Here the scene shifts from the Jewish quarter of Montreal ("the Paris of North America") to the London of the Profumo scandals. The hero, Jake Hersh, is a sort of Canadian brother to Alexander Portnoy. His sexual feats as a rich television director in swinging London are the source not only of unflagging comedy but of a serious examination of the complicated success-ethic of our time.

The despair of *The Tenants* and the febrile gaiety of *St. Urbain's Horseman* both suggested that despite temperamental and national differences, novelists in 1971 had a distinct sense of whistling on the brink of a precipice.

America has already fallen over the edge in Walker Percy's *Love in the Ruins,* a nihilistic vision of what we may expect life to be like in twenty years. Subtitled "The Adventures of a Bad Catholic at a Time Near the End of the World," *Love in the Ruins* concerns the picaresque experiences of Dr. Thomas More, a descendant of the great philosopher-theologian, now living in a world about ten minutes from Armageddon. Race riots are a constant: a distracted hedonistic populace seeks comfort in Masters-and-Johnson-type sex clinics. Howard Johnson motels have been put to the torch; Jesus Christ is proclaimed "the greatest pro of them all"; and a sodium cloud hovers ominously overhead. Dr. More's adventures in a thoroughly demoralized America are funny, terrifying and, above all, accurate. Although it recalled Huxley, Orwell and Evelyn Waugh, *Love in the Ruins* was the most distinguished—and oddly original—satiric novel of the year.

Biography and Autobiography. It took three volumes in England and one hefty one in the United States to contain all Michael Meyer knows of the life and works of *Ibsen,* a giant of modern literature curiously neglected by English biographers. Success was a long time coming to the quirky genius of the north. Yet the tale of his early struggles with the backward theaters of his time is made no less exciting than Meyer's knowledgeable account of Ibsen's years of fame, in which he practically invented modern drama as well as the Women's Lib view of women. This is a biography with warts and all—the warts involving stinginess, cowardice and just plain orneriness—all redeemed by a fiery theatrical imagination.

The greater the figure, seemingly, the better the biography in 1971. Another titan of our times, Albert Einstein, received full treatment by the English biographer Ronald W. Clark. For all Einstein's surface simplicity of manner, Clark showed the man to be no less complex than the theories that revolutionized twentieth-century physics and resulted in the creation of the atom bomb. Devoted to humanity at large, Einstein was no better a husband and father than misanthropic Ibsen. The most unpolitical of beings, he found his later years engulfed in political causes: first anti-Nazism, then a Zionism that kept landing him in controversy and disturbing the peace of his Princeton sanctuary. In addition to showing what made Einstein the man tick, Clark actually manages to make his notoriously abstruse relativity theory comprehensible to anyone who has passed high-school physics.

Lucid essayist E. B. White won National Medal for Literature, published "Points of My Compass."

Barbara Tuchman offered "Stilwell and the American Experience in China, 1911–45."

The man who gave Einstein the green light to continue research on the atom bomb was Franklin D. Roosevelt, whose relationship with his wife, the indefatigable Eleanor, is thoroughly—almost ruthlessly—explored by Joseph P. Lash in *Eleanor and Franklin*. It is a haunting narrative, largely drawn from Eleanor's papers, of the unhappy marriage between the handsome, gregarious politician who led his country through two of its most severe crises, and· his shy, "ugly-duckling" wife who stood loyally by him long after she knew of his disloyalty to her. Lash's revelations of the Roosevelt marriage could have been prurient, scandalous or one-sided. That they are fascinating and deeply moving instead made this rather unorthodox dual-biography one of the triumphs of the year.

History and General Nonfiction. The admission of Communist China to the United Nations and the possibility of more normal relations between China and the United States gave heightened interest to Barbara Tuchman's *Stilwell and the American Experience in China 1911–1945*. The expert historian of *The Guns of August* trained her sights not just on the irascible figure of old "Vinegar Joe" Stilwell but on the entire history of modern Sino-American relations. From his vantage point in Burma, Stilwell was able to send salty appraisals of the Kuomintang and communist leaders back to Washington, and he had a unique observation point from which to see the internecine squabbling that nearly lost the war to Japan and ultimately resulted in the Red take-over.

Equally complex a subject was the ancient Egyptian civilization that built the Great Pyramid of Cheops some six thousand years ago. It was explored by Peter Tompkins in *Secrets of the Great Pyramid*, a lavishly illustrated compendium of all the facts and speculations that monument has elicited over the years. Recent scholars tend to see the pyramid—like Stonehenge in England—as possibly being related to highly sophisticated mathematical and astronomical research, rather than as a vainglorious monument to an egoistic dictator. Tompkins is most fascinating as he clearly expounds these modern scientific theories.

No year's historical writing is complete without a contribution from Admiral Samuel Eliot Morison, and 1971 saw one of his finest, most idiosyncratic productions, *The European Discovery of America: The Northern Voyages, A.D. 500–1600*. As he did in his classic biography of Columbus, Morison combined the research skills of a trained historian with the practical savvy of an old naval hand in charting the course of such doughty voyagers as Cartier,

Jill Krementz

John Updike's "Rabbit Redux" surpassed even his "Rabbit, Run," acclaimed ten years before.

Davis and Frobisher in leaky ships across the broad Atlantic. Along the way, all the legends from the Norse explorations to Raleigh's "lost colony" in Virginia are given careful scrutiny and personal appraisal, making this an entertaining as well as a vastly informative book.

Poetry. Aside from the facsimile edition of Eliot's first thoughts on *The Waste Land*, serious poetry-lovers were most excited by Ramon Guthrie's long poem *Maximum Security Ward*. These free-flowing meditations from a hospital bed oddly resemble Eliot's masterpiece in their tendency to range backward in time to a mystical medieval past, and in their bitterness about the present. Clearly, the division between serious poetry and sentimental kitsch come to a head in 1971, with *Maximum Security Ward* and Ted Hughes' *Crow* of the previous year reflecting a "contemporary" despair that goes back at least as far as the 1922 *Waste Land*, while most readers found easy comfort in the slick bathos of Rod McKuen and Leonard Cohen.

RICHARD FREEDMAN
Associate Professor of English
Simmons College

FICTION

Anthony Burgess, *MF,* idiosyncratic novel of incest, filled with Joycean word games

Ivy Compton-Burnett, *The Last and the First,* last word on nasty family intrigues by the late Dame Ivy

L. J. Davis, *A Meaningful Life,* a poor *nebbish* tries to rehabilitate a Brooklyn tenement only slightly more decrepit than himself

John Gardner, *Grendel,* the epic of *Beowulf* as seen through the eyes of its much-maligned monster, poor Grendel

Shirley Ann Grau, *The Condor Passes,* the rise of an unethical Southern businessman, by a Pulitzer Prize winner

Mary McCarthy, *Birds of America,* young American innocent caught in the Paris of the 1968 revolution

Sylvia Plath, *The Bell Jar,* autobiographical novel by the talented young American poet who killed herself in 1963

Thomas Tryon, *The Other,* ghost story of two haunted New England brothers

BIOGRAPHY

Graham Greene, *A Sort of Life,* the tormented first 27 years of one of England's finest living novelists

Ralph Ketcham, *James Madison,* best one-volume treatment of our little-known but highly important fourth president

Hildegard Knef, *The Gift Horse,* acerbic memoirs of the German actress who has little use for Hollywood or marriage

Aaron Latham, *Crazy Sundays,* F. Scott Fitzgerald's tragically frustrated last years in the Hollywood Dream Machine

Charles Mingus, *Beneath the Underdog,* lusty memoirs of the jazz bass player and composer

Arthur Mizener, *The Saddest Story,* huge biography of Ford Madox Ford: prolific novelist, great editor, and star-crossed lover

A. W. Raitt, *Prosper Mérimée,* best known for the story that inspired *Carmen,* Mérimée was a man of many other talents as well

Joanna Richardson, *Verlaine,* an English appraisal of a human disaster but a great and significant lyric poet

Jasper Ridley, *Lord Palmerston,* the 19th-century British prime minister who bullied most of Europe

Robert Sencourt, *T. S. Eliot,* a rare, intimate glimpse into the troubled marriage and religious conversion of the great poet

Stanley Weintraub, *Journey to Heartbreak,* Bernard Shaw's unpopular pacifist participation in World War I

HISTORY

Stephen Birmingham, *The Grandees,* the Spanish-Portuguese Jews, or Sephardim, and their influence on American social history

B. H. Liddell Hart, *History of the Second World War,* military history of England's late expert in the field

Alistair Horne, *The Terrible Year,* centenary tribute to the Paris Commune, which took over after the Franco-Prussian War

E. Tangye Lean, *The Napoleonists,* fascinating study of English sympathizers with England's great enemy

James A. Michener, *Kent State,* sober analysis of what lay behind the shooting of four students at Kent State in 1970

Hugh Thomas, *Cuba,* an immense history of the troubled island by the author of the much-acclaimed *Spanish Civil War*

GENERAL NONFICTION

Turner Catledge, *My Life and The Times, Times* bigwig's response to Gay Talese's irreverent *The Kingdom and the Power*

Albert Goldman, *Freakshow,* exciting collection of pieces on rock, pop, black humor, and other cultural phenomena of our time

Germaine, Greer, *The Female Eunuch,* the most literate entry yet in the Women's Lib sweepstakes, by a real charmer

Lester Grinspoon, M.D., *Marihuana Reconsidered,* a thorough, medically responsible examination of pot, suggesting that we'll survive it

Norman Mailer, *The Prisoner of Sex,* Big Norm takes on Kate Millett and the Women's Libbers generally in a highly personal statement

Mike Royko, *Boss,* a blistering look at Mayor Daley of Chicago, by an old-pro newspaperman of that town

B. F. Skinner, *Beyond Freedom & Dignity,* the world's ranking behavioral psychologist questions our fetish for individualism

Gay Talese, *Honor Thy Father,* a typical Mafia war, by a reporter deeply involved in the family that fought it

POETRY

A. R. Ammons, *Briefings* and *Uplands,* fairly traditional nature-poetry with an underlying Frostian sense of evil

Jim Harrison, *Outlyers and Ghazals,* folksy but tough-minded poetry, very much in the American grain

Samuel Menashe, *No Jerusalem but This,* lyrics steeped in Jewish tradition

Charles Olson, *Archaeologist of Morning,* collected poems of a major American poet, recently deceased

James Wright, *Collected Poems,* academic, but deeply-felt lyrics, occasionally influenced by Spanish traditions

RELIGION

Eliot Elisofon and Alan Watts, *Erotic Spirituality,* picture-book about the Sun Temple of Konarak and the place of eroticism in Hinduism

Hans Kung, *Infallible?,* a young German theologian's inquiry into the dogma of papal infallibility

George Riemer, *The New Jesuits,* statements by American Jesuits about how they interpret their religious commitment in the modern age

Ignazio Silone, *The Story of a Humble Christian,* play about a medieval pope by the author of the leftist novel *Bread and Wine*

LITERATURE, NON-ENGLISH

The annual October Book Fair in Frankfurt not only exhibited 241,000 titles, among them 19,000 new works, but also provided publishers and authors from 58 countries with an opportunity to discuss the latest literary trends. Most participants in this international debate agreed that books on science, technology, the humanities and the arts were prevailing over fiction; that experimental prose and poetry as well as sex and pornography were on the decline; that documentary and factual narratives were finding ever-growing audiences; that tales of fantasy and imagination had gained as much popularity as science fiction; that nationally

Some 19,000 new works from writers all over the world were shown at the October Book Fair in Frankfurt, West Germany.

based literatures were becoming more subject to foreign influences; and that an increasing number of translations from Asian and African languages were being offered. The international spirit, stimulated probably by the mass communication media, led to an explosion of travelogues (mostly on China) and had a strong impact on plot and location in many recent narratives.

In France this was particularly evident in novels of such leading avant-garde writers as Alain Robbe-Grillet in his half-parodistic, half-oneiric *Projet d'une revolution à New York,* and J. M. Clezio whose *Hai* is an enthusiastic picture of a primitive, happy African tribe. The much-talked-of 600-page *Le sac du palais d'été* (*The Sacking of the Summer Palace*) by J. P. Remy follows the same current. The protean hero of this cosmopolitan fantasy, a young Belgian, wanders from China to Paris, from Algiers to Munich, and from Singapore to the Afghanistan mountains. Closely related to this trend is *Abraham de Brooklyn* by Didier Decoin. The author mixes imaginative fiction with documentary description of New York in the 1880's, when the Brooklyn Bridge was built, and blends biblical symbols with modern poetic techniques.

The prestigious Goncourt Prize was awarded in 1971 to Jacques Laurent for *Les bêtises,* referring to the novel within the novel *Les bêtises de Cambrai* (*The Stupidities of Cambrai*), the name of a French candy. The book is considered an autobiography in disguise. A prolific writer, Laurent uses 11 pseudonyms. The noted Prix Femina was awarded to *La maison des Atlantes* (*The House of the Atlantes*), a novel by Corsican writer Angelo Rinaldi. Pascal Laine's *L'Irrevolution* (*Nonrevolution*) won the Prix Medicis.

The best sellers of the year, however, were in a more traditional vein: *Elle, Adrienne* by Edmonde Charles Roux, a former Goncourt Prize winner, is a broad, ambitious chronicle of French life in the 1930's and 1940's, in which the heroine becomes the mistress of a nazi officer. *Un assassin est mon maître* (*A Murderer Is My Master*), by the septuagenarian Henry de Montherlant, offers a psychological study of a paranoiac intellectual; and *La mort heureuse* (*A Happy Death*), a posthumous novel by Albert Camus on the search for identity, is actually the first draft of his well-known *The Stranger.*

Greatly appreciated by critics and general readers were J. P. Sartre's *L'Idiot de la famille* (*The Family Idiot*), the first one-thousand-page volume of a monumental biography of Flaubert; and the two-volume *Matisse* by Louis Aragon. Both works fall between imaginative narrative and critical monograph. Even more popular was *Les chênes qu'on abat* (*The Felled Oaks*), by Andre Malraux, a biographical and political report of the author's conversations with General de Gaulle. The second volume of the General's *Memoires d'espoir* (*Memoirs of Hope*) sold half a million copies right after publication.

In Germany, *Gruppenbild mit Dame* (*A Group Photograph with a Lady*), by Heinrich Böll, the popular novelist and recently elected international president of the Pen Club, was hailed as his highest literary achievement and became the most widely read and discussed German book of the year. Its heroine, Leni Gruyten, born in 1922, experiences wealth and poverty, three marriages, various love affairs, overcomes trials and misfortunes, and ends up as a sort of apotheosis of all these events, surrounded by freaks and bizarre non-conformists. Her life story, projected against a background of nazi Germany, is written with insight, humor and brio. More politically oriented is the second volume of Uwe Johnson's

© Royal Danish Ministry

Winner of the Nordic Council prize, Torkild Hansen's subject is Danish colonial policy.

Jahrestage aus dem Leben von Gesine Cresspahl (*Anniversaries from the Life of G. C.*), which contrasts the New York of 1967–68, where the heroine and her daughter live, and nazi Germany in 1936–45. One of the biggest successes of the year was the 1,300-page *Wallenstein* by Golo Mann (son of Thomas), a romanticized tale of the adventurous, brilliant and tragic destiny of the eighteenth-century captain in the Thirty Years' War. Another best seller was the vivid *Memoirs* by Countess Marion Denhoff, a Prussian aristocrat. As a young girl she had escaped on horseback from the family manor. She became a writer and a liberal politician and today runs *Die Zeit*, one of the largest and most important of German weeklies.

Io e lui (*He and I*), Alberto Moravia's first novel in five years, made a big stir in Italy. Some of the critics accused the author of indecency although his book is actually a parable similar to the French eighteenth-century libertine philosophical tales. Its hero, a movie scenarist aspiring to great creative work, is blocked by his physical drives. The grotesque theme is combined with a mischievous satire on Italian customs and politics.

Completely different were the novels awarded the prestigious Strega Prize: *La Spiaggia d'oro* (*The Golden Beach*), by Raffaello Brignetti; and *Paura e Tristezza* (*Fear and Sorrow*), by Carlo Cassola. Brignetti's protagonists, a professor and a little girl, are sailing a sloop to a dream island, and embody man's longing for innocence, happiness and communion with nature. In his usual dry, sober, understated style, Cassola tells the dull, miserable fate of a simple, quite ordinary Tuscan girl. The poetic, experimental *Vogliamo Tutto* (*We Want Every-*

thing) by Nanni Balestrini seems to have interested critics more than readers.

Spanish-language books occupy third place in world production but the output is confined to Spain and Latin America. A number of such works are written by expatriates who, for political reasons, must publish outside their native countries. Ramon Sender's latest half-macabre, half-ironical *A Gracious Henchman* came out in Paris. In Spain, one of the best novels of the year was *Torre Vigia* (*Watch Tower*), by Ana Maria Matute. She uses the legends of medieval knights to evoke her childhood in her usual blend of mystery, magic and sensuality.

The influential Nadal Prize sought by 112 candidates was awarded to Jesus Fernandez Santos for his *Libro de las Memorias de las Cosas* (*The Book of Recollections of Things*), a rather curious novel about Protestant communities in aggressively Catholic Spain. The 1971 Nobel Prize conferred on Pablo Neruda, the 67-year-old Chilean poet of communist persuasion, was interpreted also as a tribute to Latin American literature.

A creative renewal was evident in Portugal. *Esteiros*, a novel by Joaquin Pereira Gomez, and a historical work by Antonio Saraiva, *Inquisicao e Cristaos novos* (*Inquisition and New Christians*) led the Lisbon best-sellers list. In Brazil the humorous, realistic novels of Jorge Amado continue to be highly popular, his last being about the inhabitants of Bahia: *Gabriella, Cinnamon and Cloves*.

The prize of the Nordic Council, representing Norway, Sweden, Denmark and Finland, was awarded to Torkild Hansen, author of several books on Danish colonial policy in Africa and the Caribbean. Many Swedish novelists prefer psychological exploration to political commitment, as does Lars Gustaffson in his caustic, ironical and autobiographical *Mr. G. Himself*, and Lars Morin in *Apiculturists*, a novel on drug addicts. An unexpected blending of the two tendencies was offered by Steffan Seeberg in *Walking through Vasa Park*, where a couple interrupt their love making to converse about socialism and capitalism.

The Blown-Away Cities by A. Tsirkos won success in Greece; but *The Diary of Resistance* by Mikis Theodorakis, banned at home, had to be published in France.

Political restrictions continued to hamper literary life in eastern and central Europe. The Russian novel *August 1914* by Aleksandr Solzhenitsyn, Nobel laureate, banned in the U.S.S.R., was published abroad. The first volume of an epic trilogy, it mainly depicts the rout of the Russian army in Prussia caused by the blunders of czarist General Headquarters and the inefficiency of courtiers. Vladimir Maximov, author of *Seven Days of Creation,* succeeded in publishing part of this impressive family chronicle in Moscow. The censored chapters, however, mainly on the detention of dissenters in mental institutions, were printed only in the West.

Two outstanding Czech works received similar treatment: *The Case of Adam Juracek* by Pavel Kohout, and *The Porpoise* by Ludvik Vaculic were both published in German in Switzerland. In Rumania, the recent tightening of controls over art and literature resulted in the removal of more than a hundred titles from the book shops, among them *The Absent Ones* by Augustin Buzuru, awarded the National Prize of the Novel. The exhibition at the Frankfurt Book Fair of the German translation of *Ostinato* by Paul Gnoma, a remarkable narrative about camp and prison inmates, aroused such wrath among Rumanian officials that they closed their stand and left the fair.

In Japan the success of the novels *The Cloud over the Hill* by Rjotoro Sciba, and *I Can't Hear the Swan Song* by Kaozu Scjagi seem to have been overshadowed by *The Jews and the Japanese,* a sharp analysis of Nipponese psychology and customs by Isaiah Bendasan, which sold over a million copies.

MARC SLONIM
Professor Emeritus of Comparative Literature
Sarah Lawrence College

LITERATURE, JUVENILE

During 1971, U.S. juvenile publishers announced 2,271 new children's books for publication, thus nearly maintaining the average number published each year (2,400) since 1966 despite a serious drop in sales. The sales drop began in 1969 with the Nixon administration's slash of the appropriations supporting programs to purchase books for school libraries, and worsened after the announcement in mid-August of Phase 1 of the economic "freeze."

Both actions are destined to have long-term effects on the new book budgets of the schools and public libraries that account for approximately 90 per cent of the sales of children's books each year. Sales in the bookstores were also down as the episodic book buyers resisted the impulse purchase of children's books. The cumulative effect of nearly three full years of falling sales on juvenile book publishing was already apparent. During 1971 four established houses announced that they were closing their children's book departments. Most of the juvenile publishers reduced staff and promotion budgets. The fact that their lists remained almost as big as ever reflects the optimism of 1969–70 when these books were contracted for, as well as the momentum of publishing, which usually takes two years to reflect the economy whether it is rising or falling.

Because the public and school libraries represent the profit in children's book publishing, the expressed needs and wants of the librarians involved are heavily influential on both the quality and the subject matter of the children's books published. Among the growing concerns of librarians over the last decade have been the quality and quantity of children's books reflecting the black experience in the United States, both past and present, and improved representation of black African folklore to more closely balance collections hitherto weighted toward the European heritage of white American children. Each year has seen a growing number of picture books, novels and nonfiction at every reading level published in these areas. Largely through the continuing efforts of the Council on Interracial Books for Children, more black writers and illustrators are involved in providing these books.

Realism and fantasy take turns in a gripping story about a black school dropout.

Macmillan

The Planet of Junior Brown
VIRGINIA HAMILTON

Political satire in the main, Neufeld's book also touches on once-taboo aspects of the teens.

In 1971 the highest critical praise for a juvenile novel examining contemporary black experience went to Virginia Hamilton's *The Planet of Junior Brown*. It centers on a school dropout, his companions and his feelings in a blend of realism and fantasy that fulfills the storytelling promise displayed in this talented writer's previous children's books, *Zeely* and *The House of Dies Drear*.

The problem of portraying contemporary realities in novels for older children has focused the critical attention of publishers, librarians, teachers and children's-book specialists. Librarians, always careful to observe their young readers' reactions to new books offered, have observed a relatively new sophistication and cynicism among 7th, 8th and 9th graders about fiction that paints too rosy a picture of family

and community life as it is lived today. The rah-rah high-school novels that once characterized this level of juvenile publishing have given way to such books as John Neufeld's *Sleep, Two, Three, Four*, which satirizes political action, describes sexual awakening, and employs some of the casual cursing that can be overheard anywhere among young teens but has heretofore seldom appeared in the fiction published for them.

Organized parent, political and religious groups have made themselves heard against this trend in school and public-library districts across the United States, often demanding the removal of such books from established library collections and curriculum reading lists. The librarians, the teachers and the children's-book critics are thus left in the quandary of deciding how much reality can constitute literary realism in a juvenile novel and how much can reduce a claim to literary excellence in this genre. The concentration of specialists' attention on these questions accounts for the dearth of critical attention being paid to the fiction and nonfiction published for readers in the middle grades, where the reading appetite and the time to satisfy it have always been appreciably greater.

Publishing patterns for the middle-grade readers (4th, 5th and 6th) have been traceably affected since 1969 by the steady demands of librarians and classroom teachers for more and more various books to support a broadened curriculum in the sciences and the social sciences for these grade levels. Nonfiction about current social problems, Vietnam, and books more critical of the methods of American expansion, particularly as it affected American Indians, have been the result.

The nonfiction for this reading level most clearly affected by these demands for more accuracy and more thorough critical discussion is juvenile biography, where the once heavy annual production has slowed to a trickle. The juvenile biographies published in 1971 lacked the once-accepted mode of fictionalization of fact or completely adulatory inflations of the biographees. Another factor in the slowdown in publication and purchase of juvenile biographies is the spate of confessional autobiographies from athletes writing for adults. The younger readers who used to swallow whole the perfect-hero images of current sports figures in juvenile biographies are not as willing to do so today, nor are the adults responsible for buying their books and guiding their reading time so willing to offer them such fatuous noninformation.

Perhaps the most startling of developments in the children's book field in 1971 surrounded the organized efforts of various groups across the United States to remove from library collections two picture books intended for the youngest children: William Steig's animal fantasy *Sylvester and the Magic Pebble,* which had won the prestigious Caldecott Medal for the best-illustrated children's book of 1969; and *In the Night Kitchen,* a dream fantasy depicted by Maurice Sendak, who has been honored both in the United States and in other countries as one of the greatest of children's book illustrators. Action by protesting citizen and police groups in various parts of the country against *Sylvester* was motivated by the depiction on one page of pigs dressed as policemen. This led to the unprecedented step of the American Library Association's issuing guidelines to members on the threat to intellectual freedom posed by demands to remove a children's picture book from school and public library collections. *In the Night Kitchen* portrays a small, nude boy in his dream of what goes on in his kitchen during his sleep. The fact of the boy's nudity, not the quality of the story or of the illustrations, evoked this controversy. Many commentators consider that it symbolizes the schizophrenia of our time, in which an observable general relaxation of adult taboos is yet withheld from the next generation.

LILLIAN N. GERHARDT
Editor in Chief
School Library Journal

NEWBERY MEDAL
Betsy Byars, *Summer of the Swans*

CALDECOTT MEDAL
Gail E. Haley, *A Story, A Story*

NATIONAL BOOK AWARD
Lloyd Alexander, *The Marvelous Misadventures of Sebastian*

FOR OLDER READERS
Olivia Coolidge, *Gandhi*
Leon Garfield, *The Strange Affair of Adelaide Harris*
Virginia Hamilton, *The Planet of Junior Brown*
June Jordan, *His Own Where*
John Neufeld, *Sleep, Two, Three, Four*
Florence Engel Randall, *The Almost Year*

FOR INTERMEDIATE READERS
Abayomi Fuja, compiler, *Fourteen Hundred Cowries*
Ernest J. Gaines, *A Long Day in November*
Erik Christian Haugaard, *The Untold Tale*
Hettie Jones, compiler, *The Trees Stand Shining: Poetry of the North American Indians*
E. L. Konigsberg, *Altogether, One at a Time*
Robert C. O'Brien, *Mrs. Frisby and the Rats of Nimh*
Ellen Raskin, *The Mysterious Disappearance of Leon (I Mean Noel)*
Reiner Zimnik, *The Bear and the People*

FOR YOUNGEST READERS
Arnold Adoff, illustrated by Emily Arnold McCully, *MA nDA LA*
Lloyd Alexander, illustrated by Ezra Jack Keats, *The King's Fountain*
John Burningham, illustrated by the author, *Mr. Gumpy's Outing*
Betsy Byars, illustrated by Emily Arnold McCully, *Go and Hush the Baby*
Janina Domanska, illustrated by the reteller, *If All the Seas Were One Sea*
Russell Hoban, illustrated by Lillian Hoban, *Emmet Otter's Jug-Band Christmas*
Clyde Watson, illustrated by Wendy Watson, *Father Fox's Pennyrhymes*
Harve Zemach, illustrated by Margot Zemach, *A Penny a Look*

The National Book Award winner lived up to its title with a droll, imaginative story.

E. P. Dutton Co.

LUXEMBOURG

There were two particularly important dates in the Grand Duchy of Luxembourg's year. On Feb. 9 the Council of Ministers of the European Economic Community (Common Market) decided to create as far as practicable a monetary and economic union by the end of the 1970's. The plan was originally prepared by a group of experts under the chairmanship of Luxembourg Prime Minister Pierre Werner. As the Werner Plan it now bears his name.

The U.S. dollar crisis and the subsequent floating of a number of European currencies, even within the Belgium-Netherlands-Luxembourg Economic Union, shook the foundation of the plan, though it was not toppled over. The first stage, aimed only at harmonizing monetary and economic policies and intended to be strictly experimental, was scheduled to run until the end of 1973.

The second date, June 23, marked the successful end of the EEC's negotiations with Great Britain, preparing the way for British entry.

The negotiations took place in Luxembourg. Appropriately they were concluded on the eve of Grand Duke Jean of Luxembourg's official birthday. The whole Duchy was *en fête*, and Luxembourg city was ablaze with fireworks. The last period was put to the agreements reached between the minister of the Six (the six EEC countries) and Britain's chief negotiator Geoffrey Rippon at 4:15 A.M., as dawn was breaking.

Membership in the community is extremely important to the Duchy. The European Coal and Steel Community had its headquarters in Luxembourg from 1951 until it merged in 1967 with the Atomic and Economic communities, providing a valuable "growth point" for the economy. The Council of Ministers of the combined community meets in Luxembourg three times a year, and the city has become the seat of the European Investment Bank, the Court of Justice, the secretariat of the European Parliament, and the Publications Department of the European Commission.

LUXEMBOURG

Area: 999 sq. mi.
Population: 400,000
Capital: Luxembourg
Government: Jean, grand duke—1964; Pierre Werner, premier—1959
Gross National Product: $900,000,000
GNP growth rate: 5.2 per cent
Foreign trade: incorporated with Belgium's
Armed forces: 550

Although steel output in the community as a whole reached a record level in 1970—109,-200,000 metric tons—Luxembourg's production declined slightly to 5,460,000 tons. Eleven per cent of the population is still employed in agriculture. The farm population is declining at about 3 per cent a year, the lowest rate in the community.

Although by no means insulated from the worldwide problems of inflation and unemployment, Luxembourg remains one of the most stable as well as one of the richest countries in Europe. In 10 years the real wages of its people have risen 50 per cent. It has the highest proportion of cars in Europe—250 per 1,000 people (Germany, 215).

JOHN ALLAN MAY
Chief, London News Bureau
The Christian Science Monitor

McMAHON, WILLIAM

William McMahon, 63, became the twentieth prime minister of Australia on Mar. 10, 1971, following a change in the leadership of the Liberal Party. The party has been the principal partner in the progressive-conservative Liberal-Country party coalition, in power in Australia since 1949. In spite of a great wave of support from newspapers and other opinion makers, a leading commentator claimed that McMahon had been chosen prime minister "reluctantly and by default."

Deputy leader of the Liberal Party from 1966, McMahon attained the leadership after Prime Minister John Grey Gorton clashed with his senior ministers. Following a three-hour Liberal Party caucus, Gorton's parliamentary colleagues were deadlocked at 33–33 in a vote to depose Gorton as party leader and consequently as prime minister. As chairman of the meeting, Gorton cast the deciding vote against himself.

Immediately after being sworn in, the new Prime Minister stressed that he would return to a strictly cabinet system of government. McMahon promised firm leadership but also said that his administration would share responsibility more broadly than under Gorton's so-called presidential system.

Short, dapper, and balding, McMahon had served in Australian governments for twenty years. This included three years (1966–69) as an outstanding treasurer. In 1969, Gorton transferred McMahon to the less important Ministry of External Affairs. McMahon completely restructured the department, and his title was changed to foreign minister.

Born in Sydney, Feb. 23, 1908, McMahon

attended Sydney Grammar School and graduated from Sydney University with degrees in law and economics. After serving in the military during World War II, he entered Parliament in the big Liberal swing of 1949. Two years later he was given his first portfolio, Ministry for Navy and Air. McMahon was minister for social services, 1954–56; for primary industry, 1956–58; and for labor and national service, 1958–66.

A bachelor until 1965, the Prime Minister is married to the former Sonia Hopkins. They have a son and a daughter.

R. M. YOUNGER
Author, *Australia and the Australians*

MALAYSIA

Malaysia's multiracial population of 11,100,000 will remember 1971 as the year in which the 128,430-square-mile federation returned to parliamentary rule, suspended after May 1969 race riots left more than 200 people dead. The reconvened Parliament's first session was held Feb. 22, two days after Tun Abdul Halim Muazzam, sultan of Kedah and nephew of Tun Abdul Rahman (premier from 1957 to Sept. 22, 1970), was installed as head of state.

The strict National Operations Council, which had ruled since the 1969 disturbances, was replaced by a National Security Council. Predictably, the new Parliament quickly amended the Sedition Act and effectively stifled criticism of the Government's economic and language (Bahasa Malaysia or Malay) policies. Organized political opposition declined in 1971 and the main pillars of the ruling Alliance coalition—the United Malays National Organization and the Malaysian Chinese Association—became stronger. The coalition's third partner, the Malaysian Indian Congress, meantime was preoccupied with an internal leadership struggle.

A Chinese Unity Movement was started in February by English-educated attorney Alex Lee. Aimed at providing a peaceful counterweight to Malay political dominance the CUM gained support from Tun Tan Siew Sin, president of the MCA, who saw a chance to draw young blood into the association's unpopular old-guard ranks. The CUM collapsed seven months later, but Lee and two other members gained positions on the MCA's 15-man executive at its Aug. 21–22 congress.

In February a Communist Chinese dance troupe from Hong Kong visited Kuala Lumpur to raise funds for victims of January floods which killed 32 people and left thousands homeless. Thereafter Sino-Malaysian relations

warmed, and in May an official trade mission visited Peking. An agreement, by which Malaysia will sell rubber, timber, palm oil, and plywood to China, was signed with a Chinese mission in Kuala Lumpur in August, cutting out Singapore and Hong Kong as middlemen.

Five-power defense arrangements (with Singapore, Britain, Australia and New Zealand) came into force in 1971 with the ending of the Anglo-Malaysian Defense Agreement.

Kuala Lumpur's regional activities during the year were directed mainly at securing cooperation to stop the decline in rubber prices. In July 1971 the Second Malaysia Plan (under the New Economic Policy aimed at ending racial economic imbalance) was introduced: to cost U.S.$4,705,880,000 over the five-year period, it called for a 6.5 per cent annual increase in GNP. Per capita yearly income was estimated at U.S.$353 in December 1970. While the Malaysian dollar held its own, inflationary trends indicated that the usual annual increase of one per cent in the cost of living index would be exceeded.

Malaysia's internal security situation deteriorated slightly, and a White Paper on the resurgence of a "new armed communism" was published in October.

DEREK DAVIES
Editor, *Far Eastern Economic Review*

MALTA

The independent nation of Malta consists of several rocky islands with a total area of less than 125 square miles, and a population of about 320,000. Much the largest island is also called Malta; and the chief town and port, Valletta, is there. Strategically located, where the Mediterranean narrows between Sicily and North Africa, Malta has been called the "plug" of the vast sea.

Under British control from the early 1800's, Malta became independent within the Commonwealth in 1964. In return for a defense pact, permitting the British Navy to use Grand Harbor and British battalions to garrison the

MALTA

Area: 122 sq. mi.
Population: 320,000
Capital: Valletta
Government: Sir Anthony Mamo, governor–general—1971; Dom Mintoff, prime minister—1971
Gross National Product: $185,200,000
Foreign trade: exports, $38,296,800; imports, $147,638,400

island of Malta, Britain agreed to pay Malta about $12,000,000 a year, half in loans and half in grants. Britain changed the ratio to 75 per cent loans, 25 per cent grants, in 1969, arousing resentment in Malta. In addition, an unofficial NATO headquarters was established on Malta although Malta has never been a NATO member.

Malta's economy has been declining. The rate of unemployment is high—some 5 per cent of an estimated 106,000 workers. It carries a national debt of $103,000,000 and has an annual balance-of-payments deficit of some $100,-000,000.

This was the situation on June 16 when, in general elections, the island Labor Party won a one-seat majority in the legislature, ending nine years of Nationalist Party administration. The Nationalist leader, George Borg Olivier (who supported closer ties with Britain and NATO), was replaced by Labor leader Dom Mintoff (who is a Socialist) as prime minister.

Almost at once British Governor-General Sir Maurice Dorman resigned, and the NATO Naval Commander, Italian Admiral Gino Birindelli, was asked to leave. On the advice of Mintoff's Government, Queen Elizabeth appointed a Maltese, Sir Anthony Mamo, governor-general on July 3.

Mintoff's chief aims were pretty obvious: to restore Malta to economic health and to keep it unaligned internationally. He would open its military facilities to any country willing to pay the price. He asked $72,000,000 a year.

Although Malta's bases are really no longer very important to NATO and its members, the situation was critical because of the Soviet Union's growing naval might in the Mediterranean. It has long been seeking use of Malta's facilities. Another factor was control of airspace between the Mediterranean and Sudan. In addition, Libya would like to use Malta as a base for a large new fleet of Arab oil tankers.

NATO headquarters began leaving Malta, and the island Government broke formally with NATO on Aug. 16.

A compromise agreement was reached in September: Britain and NATO will pay an annual rent of $22,800,000 (Britain half) for the use of Malta's naval facilities. Other NATO countries also promised to consider how they can help the islands' economic development.

NATO vessels assemble in the harbor of Valetta, capital of Malta. In the future, Malta may refuse such use to NATO and to Britain.

UPI

Young people wait outside the Los Angeles Free Clinic for attention to a variety of ailments. However, more than 25 per cent prove to have a venereal disease.

MEDICINE AND HEALTH

There was hardly a field of medicine that was uneventful in 1971, but perhaps one of the most significant happenings was an experiment that, while probably meaning little to the man in the street now, could have considerable therapeutic weight later. Research by three Americans appeared to show that they had "repaired" a genetic defect in a human cell by introducing a substitute gene from a bacterium, using a virus as the "messenger."

Doctors Carl C. Merril, Mark R. Geier and John C. Petricciani of the (U.S.) National Institutes of Health experimented with cells from a patient with a hereditary disease known as galactosemia. The disease is caused by a defective gene which normally directs the production of a particular enzyme: GPU-transferase. When a virus infects a cell it may capture and incorporate into its own genetic makeup one or more of that cell's genes. The Americans took a virus that had so acted on a GPU-transferase gene from a bacterium. The virus was then used to infect the human cells, which "repaired" their deficiency and acquired a wholeness lasting through several cell generations.

As biological concepts expanded, the world continued to shrink, increasing the risk and speed of disease transmission. Gonorrhea maintained pandemic proportions. Although

venereologists (venereal-disease specialists) worked with health authorities in trying to remove the disease's stigma, U.S. servicemen brought home some strains of the gonococcus highly resistant to antibiotic treatment. In Britain, the same old story appeared in the post-European holiday graphs showing the incidence of the disease. As young Europhiles flew home, attendance at the clinics rose sharply, but not sharply enough. Not all infected people were seeking treatment. There were the additional problems of maintaining treatment and selling the idea of the condom as an effective preventive measure. In the absence of a long-hoped-for vaccine, the Scandinavians tackled the problem in novel form: using advertisements with the sex appeal normally employed in selling automobiles, bath soaps, and candies.

An excellent regimen was devised in Philadelphia, Pa., by Dr. H. L. Shapiro and his colleagues, who call it the one-day treatment. Patients with gonorrhea were given three capsules of 500 milligrams each of anhydrous ampicillin. The first was taken at the clinic under qualified supervision, and the patients took the other two capsules at home during the following 24 hours.

All patients were asked to return to the clinic five days later and, meanwhile, to abstain from intercourse. The setup seemed near-per-

Vaccine is labeled and packed for shipment to such areas as southern Texas, infected in the summer by Venezuelan equine encephalomyelitis (VEE). The virus disease attacked some human beings—fatally in at least a few cases —and left hundreds of horses sick or dead.

fect. No moralizing, no stigmas, just a day and night of capsule swallowing. Yet the results only served to illustrate the difficulty of applying any type of treatment for venereal disease, no matter how simple the procedure. Many patients did not reappear. Of the 454 men and 198 women who returned for checkups, more than 90 per cent were considered cured. No adverse reactions were reported by any patient, so it appears that this kind of intensive treatment may, at the very least, be a partial answer to the problem.

Other diseases on the move by land, air and sea included cholera and rabies, the former highlighted by the tragic events of the Pakistan conflict. The suddenness of the situation, the refugees, the first diagnoses of the disease alerted the world to the need for quickly supplying vaccination equipment, disinfectants, diagnostic media and sera. India's efforts to check the disease were nothing short of magnificent.

The World Health Organization reported in June 1971 that cholera had been more widespread during 1970 than in any other year since the start of the seventh pandemic in 1961. It appeared in some countries of North, East and West Africa for the first time in this century. In all, emergency cholera teams visited 21 countries in response to an appeal from WHO, and several nations donated equipment and medicine at short notice. Behind all this was a steady continuation of research on immunity, spurred by the fact that cholera vaccines thus far give only limited and short-lived immunity.

On the rabies front was the world's most unusual fox hunt. Not, as Oscar Wilde put it, the unspeakable after the uneatable, but biologists keeping tabs on the migratory habits of the fox and helping WHO in its efforts to unravel the mystery of how the virus is transmitted. They caught several foxes (one of the main carrier culprits) and put collars on them containing radios that gave out signals for the biologists to follow. Since 1939, when the disease was found among badgers and foxes in Poland, the virus has spread westward at a rate of 40 kilometers (about 25 miles) a year. It has pervaded both Germanys as well as parts of Czechoslovakia and Hungary. The frontiers of Belgium, Luxembourg and Austria, Switzerland and France have also been breached. The behavioral data gathered from the fox may one day lead to effective control or possibly eradication of what to man is a painful and often fatal disease.

If the plane is implicated in the spread of organic disease, it has also produced a psychological phenomenon that can affect the happiness and careers of many young business and professional men throughout the world. Called flight phobia, an inordinate fear of flying, it is receiving a considerable amount of medical attention.

A major contribution to the treatment of the condition was revealed in Britain. There Dr. Patrick O'Connor prescribes that the patient fly in a light aircraft next to the pilot and be allowed to take the controls. Dr. O'Connor is an air vice-marshal in the Royal Air Force and is based at their Central Medical Establishment in London. The aim of his treatment is to relieve the patient of his symptoms rather than forage in the psyche for the causes. In flying there is a close relationship between the psychological and physiological systems. Homeostasis (the body's internal environment) is affected by altitude, g-tolerance and the rotations or acceleration of an aircraft. Although an airborne human's systems may be truly disturbed, it is difficult for doctors to say which comes first, the fear or the disturbance.

His patients were asked to make a list of memories about flying, starting with the first moment they felt fear about an impending flight: for instance, a senior telling a junior executive he must fly out to a meeting. Also, it has been discovered that there is often a feeling of insecurity as the aircraft flattens into level flight. For such a patient, Dr. O'Connor gave a short course in aerodynamics and the logic of flying that lurks in wing angles and air currents. The patient was taken through each item on his list of memories, all the time learning to relax every muscle.

The combination of education and reassurance may seem a lot of trouble merely to make a person sit in a flying machine, but it is worth considering that in 1970 more than half the passengers flown by one major airline were on business trips—and that airline carried 8,400,000 passengers.

In cancer research, fresh impetus, if it were needed, was given to research by an expression of political determination and a tragedy. President Nixon announced an all-out drive to find effective treatment. On a more personal level the public saw the harrowing finale to the life of Lillian Board, the beautiful British athlete. They responded with money to a fund named after her in an atmosphere of considerable gloom.

In the laboratories and clinics, however, there were glints of hope on three fronts: treatment, pharmacology and biochemistry. An unusual children's party was given at the Royal Marsden Hospital in London. Every child there was being successfully treated for acute lymphoblastic leukemia. Doctors once hoped for a single drug that would treat this disease, but a whole battery of them was found necessary. For the treatment of lymphoblastic leukemia, the possible permutations of drugs and doses add up to over a thousand. Thus the doctor is often faced with a bewildering choice.

To establish some order and prevent clinical chaos, a working party of the Medical Research Council helped organize trials throughout Britain. Results have been encouraging. Further trials are under way, as they are in the United States where results have been steadily improving for the last ten years. Fifty per cent of one group in whom the disease was diagnosed in 1966 survived for more than two years, and 35 per cent survived for three years.

The day of the lone researcher is far from over, as was shown by some good results among terminal cancer patients being treated by a single physician in the north of England. Against the run of gloomy prognoses, he achieved a 28 per cent remission rate, using a combination of cell-killing drugs and biological compounds.

At the Imperial Cancer Research Fund headquarters in London, there was considerable optimism over a compound known as ICRF 159. After mixed fortunes as an antileukemic drug, it was found to inhibit the spread of secondary tumors in mice. Late in 1971 that optimism was still maintained.

In the meantime, a previously unknown infective agent, even smaller than the smallest virus, was described by workers in Beltsville, Md. It was thought that it might be linked with the genesis of cancer. It was given the name viroid and thought of as a possible "missing link" between viruses and genes. Viroidlike

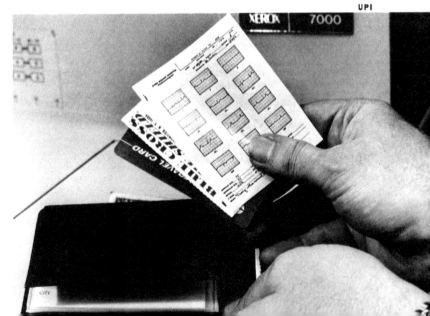

UPI

What looks at first glance like a credit card is a miniature electrocardiogram of holder's heart. Greatly reduced, and reproduced on a wallet-sized card, the information would help to speed treatment in case of an emergency.

Soft hydrophilic contact lenses are made of a flexible plastic that absorbs liquids, and feels comfortable in the eye right away.

particles, permanently present in human cells, may play a part in the processes of heredity. They may also be involved in the transformation of cells from normal to a cancerous state.

At the same time, a hunt for the link between virus and cancer was going on in Kampala (Uganda, Africa) on a massive scale involving some 55,000 children between the ages of 5 and 10. The study will last 5 years. Uganda was chosen because it has many cases of Burkitt's lymphoma, in which viruses are highly suspect.

On a more specific level, a surgeon in Sydney, Australia, advocated local rather than radical surgery for selected patients with cancer of the rectum. Success was reported with a series of 30 patients. Twelve had survived for 10 years or more; in another 6, survival exceeded 5 years. There were deaths from other causes, but the surgeon reported that in no case was there any appearance of distant or local secondaries.

Criticism of eating habits continued to give the impression that many people are in danger of digging early graves with their teeth. A possible link between bad nutrition and cardiovascular disease was suggested by workers at the Nuffield Institute of Comparative Medicine in London where food fats have been under study. It appears that because we have rearranged our ecosystems (the whole physical environment) more than a little, the diets of domestic animals such as pigs and cattle have suffered, and consequently our own. We appear to be taking in more high-energy fats than we need and not the right proportion of structural fats required by the cells for growth and repair.

Inevitably in the news were babies: the wanted and the unwanted, and there appeared to be a much greater tolerance in the West toward girls with unwanted pregnancies. Family-planning doctors in Britain demanded more National Health Service terminations or at least some form of outpatient basis for the newly pregnant at fees small enough to hit private clinics. There were some disturbing multiple births throughout Europe following treatment with the so-called fertility drugs. Although the more expert doctors could avoid "littering," none was prepared to say that single pregnancies could be guaranteed within the foreseeable future.

Success in the treatment of male sterility was reported from Tel Aviv, Israel, with the use of an essential amino acid, arginine. Of 80 such patients at the university medical school who received four grams of the drug daily, 49 had a considerable increase in sperm count and motility, with 8 wives becoming pregnant shortly after their husbands' treatment. Sixteen of the patients had a moderate increase in sperm count and motility, and 15 showed no improvement.

While Russian scientists at the Estonian Institute of Experimental and Clinical Medicine were concerning themselves with protecting local miners from industrial noises, doctors farther west were taking another look at the effects of teen-age noise—the driving, throbbing pop music in discotheques—to see if there is any real danger of hearing damage. The *Journal* of the Canadian Medical Association reviewed and commented on some aspects of the noise that is peculiarly young and defined "older people" as those over the age of 25. In a survey made in Copenhagen, a doctor reported that among 80,000 people investigated at hearing centers throughout the city over the preceding 19 years, not a single case of deafness could be attributed to beat music. There was supportive evidence from Swedish and American studies.

The *Journal* gave the year in medicine a philosophical, faintly envious touch: "Just as march music quickens the step of the tired soldier, so does loud beat music induce an ecstatic state manifested by powerful and agreeable body movements." It presumed that the lack of hearing defect at noise levels above those tolerated in industry meant that the noise was discontinuous and thus provided intervals for the ear to recover. "For us older citizens, lesser noise levels will usually generate more pleasure even if we no longer can point to the harmful effects on our juniors."

PETER BROCK
News Editor, *World Medicine;*
Medical Columnist, *London Evening News*

DRUG ABUSE

From early in 1971, American public concern over drug abuse began changing its major focus from marijuana to heroin—"junk" or "horse," in the street lingo for that dangerously addictive drug. For, indeed, "horse" was riding out of the ghetto into the suburbs, into industry, and riding home from war in Vietnam.

For years, heroin had been taking a terrible toll of human life and health mainly in city ghettos. It was one tragic motive for the commission of crimes large and small—to support a habit that could cost $20 to $50 to $100 per day. That price in crime now is increasing.

In the mid-1960's, Federal officials usually estimated that there were only 60,000 or so heroin addicts in the entire country, but admitted they were not sure. Whatever the number, it was enough to support a highly lucrative international trafficking of heroin into the United States. Heroin is derived from morphine, which is derived from the opium harvested from poppies.

Today various officials estimate that 200,000 to 500,000 Americans are addicted to heroin, and that somewhere between 5 and 10 per cent of servicemen in Vietnam and other areas of Southeast Asia are addicted or potentially addicted to heroin. This could mean that some 30,000 returning veterans will each need daily doses of a drug that in Vietnam cost them only $3.00 to $4.00, for 96 per cent pure heroin. The price of heroin of the same potency at home would be astronomical. And U.S. troops serving in Germany were reported widely abusing opium and hashish, the potent relative of marijuana.

Surveys indicated that there are at least 100,000 heroin addicts in New York City alone, and at least 17,000 in Washington, D.C. Many are young blacks seeking surcease from the social-economic-psychological despair of slum life. A small army of young people, including even some grade-school children, in middle- and upper-class white suburbs are becoming the "new-style junkies," partly because heroin was "the in-group drug to take in 1971," says Dr. David E. Smith, founder and medical director of the Haight-Asbury Medical Clinic in San Francisco. He thinks some 500,000 addicts are being seen and treated in drug clinics springing up around the country.

Heroin use is spreading, say some authorities, partly because young people are ignorant about its dangerous qualities and do not believe warnings about it because they "distrust their elders who had once oversold them on the dangers of marijuana."

As for industry, the National Industrial Conference Board of New York reported that 53 per cent of 222 companies surveyed across the United States said they found abuse of heroin, marijuana, cocaine and other drugs current among employees during working hours.

In Vietnam the military began giving urine tests to all returning men to detect those using heroin. Addicts then could be detoxified before going home, freed of their physical dependence on the drug at least for a time, but there was no assurance that they might not return to the habit. The Department of Defense also made it mandatory for all the armed services to offer "amnesty" programs for servicemen who turned themselves in for rehabilitation. Earlier, admission of addiction to drugs brought down on the serviceman a dishonorable discharge.

The Veterans Administration set up specialized drug-abuse treatment centers, and by late 1971 had established sixty such units, including neuropsychiatric wards able to receive drug-dependent veterans.

UPI

The attractive boy and girl, both only 15 years old, tell the Senate Government Operations Subcommittee about their experiences when they were heroin addicts. They were brought to the hearing by New York City's Addiction Services Agency Commissioner Graham S. Finney (l).

Crockett in "The Washington Star"

"Under the Gun"

Expanded help was coming for veterans and civilians young and old from other Federal and state and city sources. President Nixon established a Special Action Office for Drug Abuse Prevention, headed by an expert in the field, Dr. Jerome Jaffe, Chicago psychiatrist, to coordinate the work of at least nine Federal agencies responsible for education, treatment, rehabilitation, research, prevention and law enforcement. The President requested $150,000,-000 for the new program, on top of $201,000,-000 already in the fiscal-1972 budget for drug-control activities.

Voluntary groups joined states and cities in setting up an expanding network of clinics, and therapeutic communities where psychological aid is provided addicts wanting to kick the habit. Many of the clinics employ the controversial drug methadone, which blocks the euphoric physical effect of taking heroin. A drawback is that it must be taken daily, but proponents say it is permitting many former addicts to live normal lives. Opponents say that since methadone itself is a narcotic, its use simply means substituting one addicting drug for another.

Two other drugs attracting interest are cyclazocine and naloxone, which are antagonists that block the psychological effects of heroin. Research was intensified to develop new drugs that could wean the addict from dependence on heroin.

Cooperating in the international struggle to control the drug trade, Turkey announced on July 1 its decision to stop growing opium poppies. The U.S. Federal Bureau of Narcotics had estimated that Turkish farmers in recent years were supplying 80 per cent of the world's illicit supply of opium. Still open and more difficult to control were the trade lanes through which opium flowed from northeastern Burma, northern Thailand and northwestern Laos.

Mexico, concerned about drug abuse at home, joined with the United States in Operation Cooperation, which included search by Mexican soldiers to find and destroy fields of marijuana and of opium poppies.

Yet in overall numbers the main source of drug abuse continued to be marijuana ("pot"), amphetamines or pep pills, barbiturates and other sedatives (not to mention alcohol) employed occasionally or chronically by literally millions of Americans, including housewives and businessmen. A survey by the Columbia University School of Public Health indicated that 1 in 7 American youths aged 12 to 17 had smoked marijuana, although many simply experimented once or twice.

Research continued to seek an answer on whether chronic use of pot produces deleterious effects, and if so what they are. Some of the hysteria over marijuana waned. From the mid-1930's, marijuana had been officially presented as a highly dangerous drug resulting in loss of control and even crime. By law, possession of pot was a felony, and conviction meant a permanent blot on one's record and a loss of voting rights. Yet possession of LSD (lysergic acid diethylamide) was only a misdemeanor, though medically and physiologically it is hundreds of times more potent than marijuana as a "mind-expanding" drug. Marijuana is a mild hallucinogen. Many youths saw the discrepancy in official law as foolish or as a temptation to defy unreasonable law.

As of May 1, 1971, Federal law was changed to make simple possession of marijuana for personal use a misdemeanor, not a felony, with the possibility that a first offender could be placed on probation without jail sentence or blotch on his record.

Since 1968, 27 of the states have revised their laws on marijuana, generally to reduce the penalty for a first conviction of possession, and giving judges more latitude in dealing with first offenders. Other states are considering changes, but some retain strong laws. In Texas, possession of marijuana could bring a sentence of two years to life.

However, in 1971 it was heroin, not marijuana, on center stage.

ALTON BLAKESLEE
Science Editor, The Associated Press
New York

METEOROLOGY

During 1971 the Sixth World Meteorological Congress met in Geneva, Switzerland, on Apr. 5–30. Attended by delegates from 123 member nations, the meeting developed plans for a wide range of programs in meteorology for the quadrennial period 1972–75.

International Meteorology. Since its inception in 1967, the World Weather Watch has improved considerably the weather-observing and forecasting aspects of international meteorology. During the congress, it was decided to continue the program and to implement further technological advances. In research, a number of projects under the general heading of a Global Atmospheric Research Program were proposed. They included a plan for observing the global atmosphere up to a height of 30 kilometers (about 20 miles), and a study of the effects that tropical weather systems, e.g., hurricanes, have on the larger-scale storms and circulations of middle latitudes. The education of meteorologists, particularly in developing countries, is to have increased attention.

Interactions between man and his atmospheric environment were discussed. Stressed were not only the effect of climate on man's physical and cultural development but also his influence on the climate itself. The carbon dioxide from the burning of coal and oil has increased almost twice as much since 1969 as in any previous biennium, a factor that could lead to significant increases in temperature within the lower atmosphere. Other man-caused influences on the climate include industrial and domestic dust, which may reduce appreciably solar heating over local areas; urban space heating and industrial-energy production that, in large cities, may amount to one third of the heat received from the sun; and the indirect effects of air pollution, which may influence the distribution of rainfall around areas of population concentration.

Weather Modification. In contrast to these inadvertent and generally undesirable effects of man's activities, there were attempts in 1971 to modify some of nature's destructive atmospheric phenomena. With the cooperation of the National Oceanic and Atmospheric Administration and the U.S. Air Force and Navy, a task force including some 15 aircraft attempted to reduce the power of hurricanes. As Project Stormfury, the annual program began in 1969 when the winds of hurricane Debbie appeared to show a 30 per cent decrease as a result of two days of seeding the clouds with silver iodide. In 1971, hurricane Ginger was seeded on Sept. 26 and 28. Subsequent analyses showed that primary cloud systems appeared to expand outward, a change that would tend to disperse the storm's energy and decrease the maximum winds near the storm center.

Efforts to increase the rainfall in drought-stricken areas were also made. One project aimed at relieving the worst drought in Florida's history was carried out in April and May, when aircraft seeded clouds over central Florida. On 10 of the 14 days of seeding, heavy rainfall occurred over the parched Everglades, and substantial rain also occurred in Miami. The moisture eased significantly the drought conditions. Similar cloud-seeding attempts were made over drought areas in the Southwest, with inconclusive results.

In January and February, scientists of the National Oceanic and Atmospheric Administration and New York research organizations carried out experiments aimed at reducing the heavy snowstorms that blanket western New York state each winter. The technique involves seeding the storm clouds with an overabundance of silver-iodide crystals, so that snowflakes tend to be smaller than normal. The flakes then fall more slowly and are dispersed by the winds over wider areas, thus preventing the accumulation of heavy drifts.

Ocean-Atmosphere Advisory Committee. Appointed by President Nixon on Apr. 15, a new National Advisory Committee on Oceans and Atmosphere is to conduct a continuing review of the progress of United States marine and atmospheric science and service programs. Dr.

Door of a house in Ottawa is completely blocked after worst series of snowstorms to blanket the Canadian capital and other cities since 1915.

UPI

What was once the bottom of a Texas lake is left baked and cracked by Southwest's long drought.

William A. Nierenberg, director of the Scripps Institution of Oceanography, was named chairman, and 24 other leaders in the fields of oceanography and meteorology were appointed members. The committee is to submit a comprehensive report every June.

Weather Highlights. The year 1971 opened with a gigantic storm that covered the United States from the Rocky Mountains to the eastern seaboard. Snow, sleet and strong winds crippled plane and highway travel, and caused cancellation of such major events as Philadelphia's Mummers' Parade on Jan. 2. The storm was followed by a cold wave that invaded Florida, damaging the citrus crop severely. A new all-time Alaskan (and United States) low temperature record of −79.8° F. was set at Prospect Creek Camp, Alaska, on Jan. 23. In Canada, a snowfall of 48 inches in Vancouver was the greatest monthly depth ever reported there, while drifting snow and strong winds paralyzed traffic in southern Ontario around the middle of the month. A severe snow and ice storm covered much of Europe early in January. Monsoon rains devastated Kuala Lumpur, Malaysia, during the same period. A tornado struck the Kona coast of Hawaii on Jan. 28. A major storm caused severe flooding and considerable loss of life near Lourenço Marques, Mozambique, on Jan. 29.

Snow and cold weather continued into February over central and northern United States. Five deaths were reported in Minnesota as a result of heavy snow during the first week. Temperatures dropped as low as −40° F. in Wisconsin on Feb. 8. Shortly after midmonth, a severe snowstorm moved across the central plains, disrupting traffic and damaging telephone lines over Kansas and Nebraska. Associated with this storm a series of tornadoes ravaged Tennessee, Louisiana and Mississippi on Feb. 21. The twisters killed 113 persons, injured more than 1,200, and caused $10,000,-000 in property damage. In Canada, February was generally mild, although heavy snows occurred in the upper St. Lawrence Valley, and

DROUGHT SEVERITY

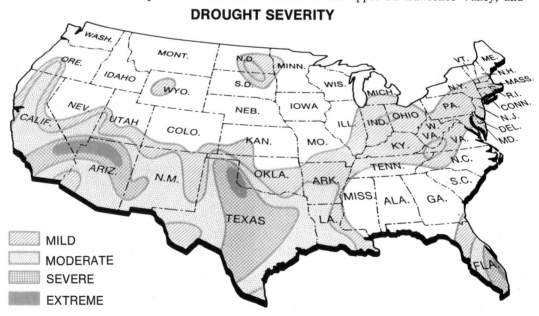

- ▨ MILD
- ▦ MODERATE
- ▦ SEVERE
- ■ EXTREME

a monthly total of 63 inches of snow at Ottawa marked an all-time record for that city.

March began with a cold wave that penetrated as far south as the Gulf of Mexico. At Tallahassee, Fla., a temperature of 23° F. on Mar. 5 was the lowest temperature for the month ever recorded there. Accompanying the cold weather, a storm moved northeast along the Atlantic coast bringing snow and freezing rain from the Ohio Valley to New England. By Mar. 12, the winter's snowfall at Portland, Me., had reached 126 inches, a new record. Wind and dust storms, reminiscent of the 1930's, occurred in the great plains during the last half of the month. In Canada, snow and cold weather prevailed over the central provinces; the seasonal total of 148 inches at Montreal exceeded all previous accumulations of snow in that city.

April weather in the United States ranged from cold, snowy conditions in the Ohio Valley to sunny skies and temperatures of over 100° F. in the southwest. A severe drought afflicted Florida, Oklahoma and Texas. On Apr. 22 a tornado struck near Ideal, Ga., killing one person, injuring 15 and causing considerable property damage. On Apr. 27–28 a series of tornadoes lashed Kentucky, Illinois and Tennessee, resulting in 11 deaths and severe property damage. Canadian weather was cool and dry, except in Manitoba and northwest Ontario where twice the normal precipitation occurred.

Generally warm spring weather prevailed over the United States in May. However, late snows in the Pacific Northwest brought the seasonal total at Paradise Ranger Station in the Washington Cascades to 1,017 inches (about 85 feet), the heaviest snowfall ever recorded in the United States during one season. Rains during the month—some due to artificial cloud seeding—relieved drought conditions in Florida and the Southwest. Continued sunny weather prevailed in Canada, but heavy rains and snow runoff resulted in a massive cave-in at St. Jean Vianney, Que.; 35 homes were destroyed and a number of persons were killed.

Summer weather in the United States brought record-breaking heat to the Southwest. A temperature of 109° F. on July 13 at Winslow, Ariz., broke an 83-year record there. Heavy rains fell in Alaska, and heavy floods closed roads around Anchorage and Fairbanks. Tropical storm Doria moved north along the Atlantic coast during the last week in August, bringing rains of 4 to 6 inches and winds of up to 74 miles per hour from the Virginia capes to New England. In Canada, a violent thunderstorm near Toronto on June 28 was accompanied by golf-ball-sized hailstones. Monsoon rains in Korea brought death to more than 100 persons near Seoul. Typhoon Olive killed 78 people in Japan and Korea on Aug. 6; and typhoon Rose caused over 50 deaths in Hong Kong on Aug. 17.

September was "hurricane month" in the United States. On Sept. 10, thousands of persons were evacuated along the Texas-Louisiana coast as hurricane Fern moved inland near Galveston. Hurricane Edith claimed scores of lives in Nicaragua and Honduras, and then slammed into the Louisiana coast on Sept. 17. On Sept. 14–15, hurricane Heidi brought heavy rains and floods to Pennsylvania and New Jersey, leaving 15 persons dead and more than 1,000 homeless. As the month closed, hurricane Ginger moved inland over the North Carolina coast, and more than 2,000 people were evacuated to escape the storm's 75-mile-per-hour winds. The first snows moved into western Canada and spread as far south as the Sierra Nevada of California.

October weather was near normal over most of the United States, although a record-breaking 90° heat wave persisted over southern California for the first 2 weeks. Adding to the discomfort, severe smog conditions blanketed the Los Angeles area. The season's first blizzard closed schools and marooned thousands of motorists in Wyoming, the Dakotas, Colorado and Arizona. In Vietnam, typhoon Hester swept across the northern and central provinces on Oct. 25, causing over 100 deaths and millions of dollars in damage. Over 100 American aircraft and a number of military bases were damaged or destroyed by the storm. An Indian Ocean cyclone (hurricane) struck India's east coast on Oct. 29, causing hundreds of millions of dollars in property damage.

Winter weather prevailed over most of the United States during November. A three-day air-pollution crisis in Birmingham, Ala., ended on Nov. 19 when welcome rains washed the smog from the air. The Thanksgiving holiday was marred by a major snowstorm that tied up highway traffic and curtailed many traditional outdoor activities over the northeastern part of the country. Laura, a late-season tropical storm, lashed Cuba's west coast on Nov. 18, but decreased in intensity as it moved onshore in Central America. In Europe, the first major winter storm brought traffic-stalling snows to the Alps and flooding as far south as Venice, Italy.

JACK C. THOMPSON
Professor of Meteorology
San Jose State College, Calif.

METRIC SYSTEM

Sooner or later most people in the United States are going to stop thinking in terms of inches, pounds and degrees Fahrenheit. Instead they are going to use the metric system of measurement. The sooner this change is made, the better it will be for the United States. Within a few years, virtually every other major nation on earth will be using only the metric system. North Americans must join them promptly, or the United States' foreign trade will be hampered and its people isolated culturally from the rest of the world.

These are the basic conclusions of a three-year study authorized by Congress and completed in the summer of 1971 by the National Bureau of Standards. Secretary of Commerce Maurice Stans accepted the findings and urged that the United States begin immediately to plan a ten-year program for changing measurement systems.

In one way or another, conversion to metric would affect almost everyone in the United States, although many people would continue to use the old measurements in casual conversation, much as they spice their speech with slang. But when conversion was complete, milk would be sold by the liter instead of by the quart. Meat would be sold by the kilogram instead of by the pound. The collars of men's shirts would be measured in centimeters instead of in inches. Highway signs would be posted in kilometers instead of in miles. And television announcers would report the temperature in degrees Celsius instead of in degrees Fahrenheit. (See conversion table on page 299.)

The change seems inevitable. Indeed, use of the metric system in the United States has been gradually increasing for years. Scientists and many engineers use metric measurements almost exclusively in their work. A growing number of schools are teaching the metric system in the first and second grades. More than ten years ago the pharmaceutical industry started making prescription drugs in metric doses. With the growing popularity of foreign cars, made with metric parts, almost every garage mechanic has had to get metric-sized wrenches and other tools.

In the long run, the United States would benefit greatly from a deliberate, nationwide change to metric over a period of ten years. At the rate things are now drifting, it might take another fifty years for the U.S. measurement language to become mostly metric. Meanwhile the people are paying a high price for speaking two measurement languages and being out of step with the other countries. It is expensive to keep on hand both metric and nonmetric bolts, nuts and other parts and tools. Schoolchildren are burdened and confused by having to learn two measurement systems. The U.S. role in world trade and foreign aid is already being made difficult because North Americans cling to a peculiar measurement system. Other nations, for example, are sometimes reluctant to buy U.S. machinery because nonmetric spare parts are available only in the United States.

A conversion program would involve quite a lot of trouble and expense. Various industries and businesses would have to get together and decide when to make changes from one system

COMMON EQUIVALENTS AND CONVERSIONS

Approximate Common Equivalents

1 inch	= 25 millimeters
1 foot	= 0.3 meter
1 yard	= 0.9 meter
1 mile	= 1.6 kilometers
1 square inch	= 6.5 sq. centimeters
1 square foot	= 0.09 sq. meter
1 square yard	= 0.8 sq. meter
1 acre	= 0.4 hectare
1 cubic inch	= 16 cu. centimeters
1 cubic foot	= 0.03 cu. meter
1 cubic yard	= 0.8 cu. meter
1 quart (liq.)	= 1.0 liter
1 gallon	= 0.004 cu. meter
1 ounce (avdp.)	= 28 grams
1 pound (avdp.)	= 0.45 kilogram
1 horsepower	= 0.75 kilowatt

Conversions

inches × 25.4	= millimeters
feet × 0.3048	= meters
yards × 0.9144	= meters
miles × 1.60934	= kilometers
sq. inches × 6.4516	= sq. centimeters
sq. feet × 0.092903	= sq. meters
sq. yards × 0.836127	= sq. meters
acres × 0.404686	= hectares
cu. inches × 16.3871	= cu. centimeters
cu. feet × 0.028316	= cu. meters
cu. yards × 0.764555	= cu. meters
quarts (liq.) × 0.946353	= liters
gallons × 0.003785	= cu. meters
ounces (avdp.) × 28.3495	= grams
pounds (avdp.) × 0.453592	= kilograms
horsepower × 0.7457	= kilowatts

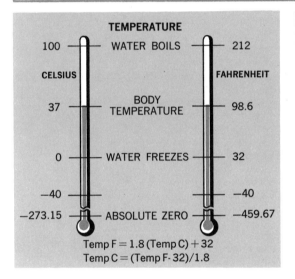

TEMPERATURE

CELSIUS — FAHRENHEIT

Celsius		Fahrenheit
100	WATER BOILS	212
37	BODY TEMPERATURE	98.6
0	WATER FREEZES	32
−40		−40
−273.15	ABSOLUTE ZERO	−459.67

$$\text{Temp F} = 1.8\,(\text{Temp C}) + 32$$
$$\text{Temp C} = (\text{Temp F} - 32)/1.8$$

NAMES AND SYMBOLS FOR METRIC PREFIXES

Prefix	Means
tera (10^{12})	One trillion times
giga (10^{9})	One billion times
mega (10^{6})	One million times
kilo (10^{3})	One thousand times
hecto (10^{2})	One hundred times
deca (10)	Ten times
deci (10^{-1})	One tenth of
centi (10^{-2})	One hundredth of
milli (10^{-3})	One thousandth of
micro (10^{-6})	One millionth of
nano (10^{-9})	One billionth of
pico (10^{-12})	One trillionth of

to the other. Supermarkets, for example, would not be able to sell vegetables by the kilogram until their scales were converted from the old pound-ounce system. Nevertheless, a deliberate conversion program would soon pay for itself. Following ten years of adjustment, the whole nation would thereafter collect the benefits of having one simple measurement system.

Few people realize what a Tower of Babel the old measurement system has become. Growing haphazardly for hundreds of years, it is now so complicated that probably no one person really knows more than half the measurement terms that are commonly used.

First of all, there are two more or less "pure" languages: the International Metric System and the customary pound-inch-Fahrenheit system. Also, there are literally hundreds of ancient terms that are still used in special circumstances. Logs are bought and sold by the cord, while finished lumber comes in board feet. Printers measure type in points, picas, ems and ens. The furlong, an old term for an eighth of a mile, is still used in horse racing. The National Bureau of Standards has established an official size for the bushel; but in actual practice peaches, corn, wheat and other products are marketed in bushels that are either a little larger or a little smaller than the official measure. Even scientists and engineers speak special measurement dialects. For different purposes they use more than twenty units to describe energy, including: British thermal units, ergs, horsepower-hours, kilowatt-hours, therms, frigories, electron volts, tons of TNT, and six kinds of calories.

Whether the United States should adopt the metric system is a controversy that is almost as old as the nation itself. The Constitution gave Congress the authority to fix standards for weights and measures. In his first term as president, George Washington asked his Secretary of State, Thomas Jefferson, for suggestions. Jefferson, one of the most imaginative inventors of his day, worked out an original measurement system. It was based largely on a "foot" measure derived from the length of a pendulum that swung once per second, and each foot was divided into ten inches. This, he pointed out, would simplify doing arithmetic, since the number system was already decimal.

The advantage of using measurement units related by fractions or powers of ten was recognized also by the French scientists who first developed the metric system. (See table of prefixes on page 299.) Instead of determining length with a pendulum, however, they based the meter on what today would seem a crude measurement of the earth's circumference.

In the first years of the nineteenth century, the metric system began to spread through most of Europe and South America as well. There were many in the United States who were convinced that adopting metric was the only logical course for their country. In 1821, John Quincy Adams, then secretary of state and later president, reported to Congress that the metric system was inherently better than the inch-pound-Fahrenheit system. Still he was reluctant to abandon the old system since it was used in Great Britain.

From that point on, proponents and opponents of the metric system were deadlocked in an argument that has waxed and waned. Congress never fixed a national system of weights and measures. Nevertheless, the United States did become a metric nation officially. In 1876 it joined with all the other major nations in signing the Treaty of the Meter, which modernized the metric system for international use. Since that time the yard, the pound and other units commonly used in the United States have been defined as fractions of standard metric units.

In the spring of 1965 the metric question suddenly took on a new importance and urgency. It was then that Great Britain announced its intention of converting to the metric system over a period of ten years in a coordinated program that was launched by British industry. Other nations of the British Commonwealth that had not already converted to metric soon announced plans to follow Britain's lead. It was thus clear that the United States would soon be speaking a measurement language no one else in the world understood.

The proposal that the United States adopt a conversion program similar to Great Britain's worries some people. Most of the objections have come from those who do not clearly understand what would and would not be required for conversion. Some are frightened by the thought that use of the inch, the pound and other familiar measurements would abruptly become illegal, that they would have to change their ways of thinking and buying and manufacturing in a few hectic years.

But a crash program of conversion was never seriously considered in the National Bureau of Standards' study. Thousands of people in all walks of life filled out questionnaires, took part in interviews or made studies of their own. The consensus was that a coordinated conversion program would proceed smoothly, as it has been doing in Great Britain, and that in ten years almost everyone who had to use the metric system would be able to make the adjustment.

People who have thought seriously about the problems of changing the measurement system are confident that with careful planning there will be a minimum of confusion during the changeover. Some things would be changed rapidly, some slowly and some never. It would be ludicrous to tear down homes and factories just because they were not built to metric dimensions. Clothing, plumbing fixtures, construction units of all kinds and most other things that we use would be replaced with metric versions only when they wore out.

Nor would it be disgraceful to continue to use nonmetric language. Even in countries that have been metric for many years, scientists continue to use convenient nonmetric terms. Astronomers, for example, persist in talking of distances in light-years or parsecs instead of trillions of kilometers. And even in France, the birthplace of the metric system, a few housewives still ask the grocer for *une livre de beurre* (one pound of butter). They get a half-kilogram package, which is roughly the same weight as the old French pound.

Will the United States begin deliberately to modernize its measurement system within the next few years? Most of industry wants to see the change made. Educators are eager to move ahead. There is, in fact, no organized opposition to the metric system. Nevertheless, few congressmen are as yet convinced that the matter is urgent, and so a national program is not likely to get under way until the late 1970's.

GEORGE A. W. BOEHM
Special Assistant
U.S. Metric Study Group
Department of Commerce

Attorneys General Julio Sanchez Vargas (Mexico) and John Mitchell (U.S.) sign agreement to increase co-operation between their two countries to combat traffic in narcotics, marijuana and other dangerous drugs.

UPI

MEXICO

President Luis Echeverria Alvarez took office in December 1970 for a six-year term. He is a member of the Partido Revolucional Institucional (PRI), the dominant party that has elected every president, senator and governor from the time of its founding over forty years ago. The party's elements range from wealthy industrialists to organized labor, from peasants who have received land under the Government's agrarian reform program to dwellers in urban shantytowns. As the Mexican Establishment, the party has kept itself in power through four techniques: cultivation of its mystique as the embodiment of the glorious Mexican Revolution of 1910; a policy of "balance," which tries to cater to all interests and neglect none; a high and sustained rate of economic growth; and occasional small-scale repressive measures against obstreperous opposition elements. The crisis of 1971 developed over the use of the last.

"Balance" dictated that Echeverria pursue a policy to the left of his predecessor, Gustavo

MEXICO

Area: 761,602 sq. mi.
Population: 52,500,000
Capital: Mexico City
Government: Luis Echeverria Alvarez—1970
Gross National Product: $31,580,000
Foreign trade: exports, $1,373,000,000; imports, $2,461,000,000
Armed forces: 68,500

Diaz Ordaz, who had unnecessarily and brutally repressed peaceful student demonstrations in 1968, ending with the "Massacre of Tlatelolco," which had made Diaz one of the most hated presidents in Mexican history.

In the style of Mexico's great Leftist president of the 1930's, Lazaro Cardenas, Echeverria made unannounced weekend visits to the provinces to listen to local complaints. His speeches stressed the need for social justice, and his economic policies de-emphasized sheer economic growth and stressed instead more equal distribution of wealth, as in the 10 per cent tax he imposed on luxury goods. He also ordered the gradual release of the prisoners still held in jail without trial in the aftermath of the 1968 disturbances. Prisoners were released in small groups, because a general amnesty was opposed by powerful hard-line Rightists within the regime. These elements also organized and financed Right-wing gangs, or *porras*, which attempted to intimidate student liberals in the universities.

However, during the first part of 1971, disturbances occurred at the universities of Nuevo Leon, Jalisco and Puebla, and in May students occupied the buildings of the medicine and economic faculties at the National University in Mexico City, to protest against the *porras* and to demand the release of the remaining prisoners. Finally, on June 10, Corpus Christi Day, students from the National University began a march of protest to the main plaza. According to unofficial reports, the President planned to tell the students he agreed with their views but needed their support against reactionary elements within the regime. Nevertheless, en route to the presidential palace, the students were fired on by a hooligan gang known as *Los Halcones* (the Hawks). At least 13 students were killed and many more injured, as police stood by without intervening.

Stunned and shaken by what had taken place, Echeverria seems to have realized that influential members of the Government would pursue a repressive policy regardless of who was president, either making him their prisoner or forcing his resignation. However, he was able to secure a unanimous pledge of support from senior army commanders. He was thus able to force Mexico City's Mayor Alfonso Martinez Dominguez (once considered a likely future president), the attorney general and the Mexico City police chief to resign. The commander of the Federal District "special forces" was arrested. The President thus seemed to be gaining the upper hand in the battle against conservatives within the regime but only slowly and with difficulty.

Leading Leftists declared their support of the President. In September the internationally famous writers Carlos Fuentes and Octavio Paz called for founding a new democratic socialist party, to be known initially as the Movement of Popular Consultation. It was expected to rally followers of the 1968 student movement and others, presumably behind Echeverria.

However, the far-Left Movimiento de Accion Revolucionaria (Revolutionary Action Movement) began to attack the Echeverria Government with bank robberies and planned kidnapings. Many MAR members were arrested. The Government expelled diplomats from North Korea, where MAR members had received training; and from the Soviet Union, including the chargé d'affaires, for allegedly facilitating travel between Mexico and North Korea. MAR guerrillas under former teacher Genaro Vazquez Rojas were rumored to be in the state of Guerrero, others in Tabasco and Chiapas. MAR members kidnaped, among others, Julio Hirschfeld, director general of airports, releasing him when a ransom of 3,000,-000 pesos ($250,000) was paid.

On the economic front, the boom that Mexico has sustained for many years continued, although with reduced force and with some minor disturbing signs, one a 6 per cent rate of inflation. However, President Echeverria promised that the stability and international convertibility of the peso would be maintained. The recession in the United States had an ad-verse effect on tourism, Mexico's largest earner of foreign exchange. In 1970 a trade deficit of over $1,000,000,000 was registered. The situation worsened with President Nixon's imposition of a 10 per cent surcharge, which affected 40 per cent of Mexico's exports to the United States. In addition, Mexico's foreign indebtedness reached a high of $3,500,000,000, as a result of Diaz Ordaz's policy of borrowing abroad. Echeverria embarked on a program to increase foreign-exchange earnings by expanding exports and reducing imports. The President modified existing law to allow foreign ownership of seacoast land, hitherto forbidden on security grounds. It resulted in a real-estate boom as U.S. land developers rushed to buy up sites suitable for tourist resorts.

Efforts were made to attain self-sufficiency in petrochemical products and, by further irrigation projects in the north of the country, which suffered severe drought in 1971, to reduce the need for wheat imports. Similarly, plans were made to increase copper production to a level that would satisfy domestic demand and leave a surplus for export. As part of this program, in August the Government paid $40,-000,000 for 51 per cent of the stock of the Cananea Mining Company, a subsidiary of Anaconda. It plans to resell the stock to private investors, workers in the industry, and the national bank. Tuna fishing also expanded.

Outside of the political and economic fields, perhaps the most interesting item of news in 1971 was the rock festival held early in September at Avendaro, a small town 150 miles southeast of Mexico City. To the astonishment of the festival's promoters, over 200,000 young people flooded into the area, creating monstrous traffic jams. The good time enjoyed by many of the participants, who got high on marijuana, bathed nude in a lake, and listened to 12 Mexican rock bands play all night, was mitigated by the unhappiness of others who could find nothing to eat, who could not get to the festival because of the traffic jams, or who were involved in accidents. Five deaths were reported in traffic and drowning incidents.

After considerable arm-twisting by the Nixon administration, the Mexican Government agreed to cooperate in cracking down on drug traffic. Marijuana crops were destroyed and customs inspections became more severe.

Equine encephalomyelitis, introduced into Mexico with the importation of diseased horses from Venezuela, was wiped out by a mass inoculation campaign.

MARTIN C. NEEDLER
Director, Division of Inter-American Affairs
University of New Mexico

MIGRATION

In discussing recent trends in migration, it is important to keep in mind that some people emigrate from their homes, towns, cities and at times even their countries of their own free will, while others are forced to move because of circumstances beyond their control: natural disasters (earthquakes, floods) and man-made disasters (war, persecution, oppression). People who migrate because of circumstances beyond their control are called refugees.

REFUGEES

In March 1971 a devastating civil war broke out in Pakistan over the status of its eastern region. As the result of December 1970 national elections, Pakistan's first since independence in 1947, the Bengalis of East Pakistan (led by Sheikh Mujibur Rahman) gained an absolute majority in the National Assembly. However, instead of convening the legislature, Pakistan President Yahya Khan, who was severely shaken by the election results, doubled the number of Federal forces in the East and staged a ruthless attack against the area. This forced as many as 50,000 Bengalis to flee into nearby India daily, adding to the country's already overcrowded population. (The dominant religion of India is Hinduism, while Pakistan is a Muslim nation. Consequently the two nations have been historic adversaries. However, the proportion of Hindus living in East Pakistan is much greater

than in the West, and this is one reason why the Bengali refugees were welcomed in India.)

Before 1971 ended, India had overwhelmingly crushed Pakistan in a two-week war (*see also* India; Pakistan), and a new nation, Bangladesh (East Pakistan), was being born. However, the problems of the refugees remained. As of Dec. 31, only a small portion of some 10,000,000 Bengali refugees had returned to their homeland. Cholera and malnutrition had claimed the lives of thousands, and the number of children, aged 1 to 8, dying daily in the refugee camps continued in the hundreds.

The World Bank estimated that India would have spent $750,000,000 by March 1972 on its Operation Lifeline program in trying to care for the refugees. The United Nations High Commission for Refugees was the focal point of the relief-aid effort. As a result of a special appeal from UN Secretary-General U Thant, $99,400,000 had been designated for the refugees by mid-July. Final action on the 1971 U.S. foreign-aid appropriations bill was expected early in 1972. The legislation earmarked approximately $250,000,000 for South Asia, primarily the Bengali refugees.

Although the Bengali refugees were the "largest group of displaced persons in the world" in 1971, millions of victims of the Indochina war continued to wander as refugees from one region to another. One fourth of the 28,000,000 people living in South Vietnam,

IMMIGRANTS TO THE UNITED STATES
(by country of birth)

	Fiscal 1971		Fiscal 1970
Total from all countries	370,478[1]		373,326
From Europe	96,506		118,106
Led by			
Italy	22,137	Italy	24,973
Greece	15,939	Greece	16,464
Portugal	11,692	United Kingdom	14,158
United Kingdom	10,787	Portugal	13,195
From Asia	103,461		92,816
Led by			
Philippine Rep.	28,471	Philippine Rep.	31,203
China (both)	14,417	China (both)	14,093
India	14,310	India	10,114
Korea	14,297	Korea	9,314
From North America	140,114		129,114
Led by			
West Indies	68,176	West Indies	61,403
Cuba	21,611	Cuba	16,334
Jamaica	14,571	Jamaica	15,033
Dominican Republic	12,624	Dominican Republic	10,807
Mexico	50,103	Mexico	44,469
Canada	13,128	Canada	13,804
From South America	20,700		21,973
From Africa	6,772		8,115
From Oceania	2,923		3,202

[1]Two immigrants born en route to the United States.

Source: Immigration and Naturalization Service, U.S. Department of Justice.

Laos and Cambodia have been uprooted at least once. In South Vietnam alone, there are at least 5,000,000 displaced persons out of a total population of 18,000,000. In addition, an estimated 20,000 Chinese, escaping from mainland China, crossed the Canton estuary of the South China Sea to the British colony of Hong Kong in 1971. Many of them swam.

IMMIGRATION AND EMIGRATION

United States. During the 1971 fiscal year a total of 370,478 immigrants arrived in the United States. The influx represented about 20 per cent of the nation's population growth in the same period. During the 1950's, immigration had accounted for only about 10 per cent of the annual population growth.

Since 1965, when Congress rewrote the immigration laws, abolishing the quota system, people from Asia, southern and Eastern Europe and the Caribbean islands have been entering the United States in increasing numbers. Previously, immigrants from Canada, England and the northern European countries had predominated. Some officials feel that the drop in immigration from northern Europe is due to increased availability of jobs and the lower cost of living (compared with the United States) in northern Europe. However, through an industrial-recruitment plan, officials of the New England states were luring European companies to their region in 1971. As a result of the program, some forty European companies were expected to open offices in six New England states.

Immigration from the Latin American countries continued high. Cubans, averaging about 2,000 per month, formed the largest group of Latins to enter the United States. Since 1959, when Fidel Castro became Cuba's premier, a total of 600,000 Cubans have migrated to the United States. In August 1971 Cuba advised the U.S. Department of State of its desire to terminate the airlift to Miami, Fla., which had flown 250,000 people to the United States since 1965. However, later in the year the airlift was temporarily resumed.

Migration from Puerto Rico declined in 1971. At the end of June 1970, there were 44,-082 more Puerto Ricans entering the United States than going back to their homeland; as of June 30, 1971, the total had dropped to 1,800. The decline was attributed to the economic slowdown on the U.S. mainland.

Between 1960 and 1970 some 500,000 blacks migrated from the southern states to the industrial cities of the North. In 1971 this trend began to slacken. According to Robert Atkins, associate manager of the Chamber of Commerce in Memphis, Tenn., "the opportunities are in the South for the college-educated black people." Also opportunities for the unskilled southern laborer were increasing as more companies moved to the South. Civil-rights leader James Meredith claims that many black people between the ages of 30 and 45 are moving south for economic and social reasons. In the South, living costs are cheaper, and the people are "friendlier."

Approximately 40,000 Americans left the United States in 1970 to settle in other English-speaking countries. Canada received most of these emigrants (24,424 in 1970). Many leave the United States to escape the fast pace and tension, high cost of living, racial strife and high crime rates. Still others leave to retire to the place of their birth. These people live on their savings and social-security benefits. Every month the U.S. Government mails 215,000 social-security checks abroad.

Canada. In 1971 some 120,000 immigrants entered Canada. The largest group, almost 50 per cent, came from Europe. It is interesting to note that during the fourth quarter of 1970, 7,294 Americans as compared with 5,850 English and Irish citizens arrived in Canada. This was the first time that the U.S. total exceeded the United Kingdom's.

During the summer months of 1970, the number of U.S. males, aged 20–24, entering Canada daily to escape the U.S. military draft averaged between 40 and 50. As U.S. forces continued to be withdrawn from Vietnam, the number dropped in 1971 to between 10 and 15 daily.

U.S.S.R. and Israel. According to the 1970 Soviet census, there were 2,150,000 Jews living in the Soviet Union. Emigration policies eased somewhat in 1971, enabling between 7,500 and 10,000 Jews to leave the U.S.S.R. Most of the Jews went to Israel, which received an estimated 40,000 immigrants from all countries in 1971.

GYPSIES

After years of harassment, gypsies began pressing for international recognition in 1971. Gratton Puxon, secretary of the British Gypsy Council, presses for respect for the gypsies' unique life-style. He protests that "In Eastern Europe there are laws against nomads, except in Yugoslavia. They've tried to settle gypsies and prevent people from traveling."

On Apr. 12, the first international congress of gypsies in 36 years ended. Several gypsy leaders prepared reports for the UN Commission on Human Rights and the Council of Europe.

LYDIA COHEN
Staff Writer

Rep. Wilbur Mills explains his views to a "Meet the Press" television audience. Supporters of the Arkansas Democrat frequently suggested him as a possible 1972 presidential nominee.

MILLS, WILBUR DAIGH

Wilbur Daigh Mills, the soft-spoken Arkansan long considered a top power in the House of Representatives, blossomed during 1971 into a national political figure. With the 1972 Democratic presidential nomination up for grabs among a dozen or more contenders, some of his House friends from both North and South suddenly demanded "Why not Mills?" and launched a campaign to try to put him in the White House. They pointed out that most of the other candidates were senators, and declared that Mills had regularly bested the Senate in conferences to shape major legislation during the preceding 12 years. Mills himself did not endorse these efforts publicly, but he did not discourage them either. He accepted an unprecedented number of speaking engagements over the nation, several to state legislatures. To these audiences, he stressed his differences with the Nixon administration on economic policy and revenue sharing.

It was not the first time that the stocky, urbane Congressman had been mentioned for high office. At times he had been considered a strong possibility for Speaker of the House; and there were rumors during the Johnson administration that he might be named to the Supreme Court.

Despite this talk, Mills' power and prestige in the House are grounded solidly in the job he has filled since 1958: chairman of the Ways and Means Committee. Clearly the most important legislative group in the House, the committee has jurisdiction over tax, social security, welfare and trade legislation. Mills has made himself a master of all these fields and has played the major role in shaping all of the bills dealing with these subjects during his chairmanship. He has been particularly adept at achieving a consensus in his committee on what should be done, and in persuading the Rules Committee to require that his bills be considered by the House under a procedure barring amendments. Then, with a strong House vote to back him up, he has been in a position to resist successfully Senate changes in his measures with which he did not agree.

The 1971 session offered a good example of his pivotal role in the Congress; and he was not always in opposition to President Nixon. He piloted the President's welfare-reform plan through the House but bottled up Nixon's revenue-sharing proposal. He was strongly critical of the administration's go-slow economic policies, but pledged swift and favorable action on the President's tax recommendations once Nixon switched economic course in mid-August.

In the past Mills has often been an enigma to his colleagues, to reporters and even to presidents. He helped to block Medicare in the Kennedy administration, yet, once the 1964 election had clearly established a majority for it in Congress, he smoothly switched course and had a big part in drafting the plan that became law in 1965.

Mills was born May 24, 1909, in the small town of Kensett, Ark., still his home. He graduated from Hendrix College and attended Harvard University Law School, then worked in family businesses and was elected to Congress in 1938. He and his wife live quietly in a Washington apartment, shunning the social circuit and never going on junkets. His favorite pastimes are playing with his four grandchildren and going to baseball games.

JOSEPH W. HALL, JR.
Senate Staff, Washington Bureau
The Associated Press

MINE SAFETY

Much of the U.S. mining industry turned its attention to improving the health and safety of its workers in 1971 as controversy arose over Federal efforts to better conditions in underground coal mines. Critics and safety advocates charged that the Interior Department's Bureau of Mines had failed to enforce the Coal Mine Health and Safety Act of 1969, in effect since April 1970. At the same time, the Social Security Administration drew criticism for its handling of a program under the act's health provisions to pay benefits to coal miners disabled by black lung, or pneumoconiosis, caused by the inhalation of microscopic coal-dust particles.

Almost unnoticed as these disputes wore on were new Federal standards for uranium, stripcoal and other mining operations. The uranium industry was forced to cut back the time that miners could be exposed to radiation emitted by ore. Surface coal mines were required to tighten safety procedures.

The new health and safety laws brought complaints from the coal industry that productivity was suffering. Mine operators said that the presence of Federal inspectors, especially in underground mines, and the extra safety precautions consumed the miners' time and reduced individual efficiency as much as 20 per cent. To compensate, the operators said, they were obliged to hire more men, increasing the total coal work force to 148,400 men in July compared with an average of 123,267 during 1969. Industry spokesmen said further that individual productivity had declined from a high of 19.90 tons per day in 1969 to less than 18 tons a day in 1971. Costs, meanwhile, were increasing. The situation still left American miners far ahead of their European counterparts whose productivity averaged about 4 or 5 tons daily.

The Bureau of Mines responded that it had no evidence that the health and safety law had impeded individual output. Whether or not the law affected production, it did cause problems for the mining industry generally and the Bureau of Mines.

Mine operators faced the threat of fines of up to $10,000 for serious hazards in underground mines. Criminal prosecution also was a possibility. The first such case came up on June 23 when Charles Finley and the Finley Coal Co., of Hyden, Ky., were indicted by a Federal grand jury on charges stemming from a Dec. 30, 1970, mine explosion that killed 38 miners. The indictment accused Finley and the company of 24 violations of the health and safety law, including the illegal use of high-powered dynamite, which triggered the blast in the company's Number 15 and 16 mines. The Hyden disaster brought mine fatalities for 1970 to 260, a mark the Bureau of Mines set out to reduce in 1971.

As months passed, however, the fatality rate paralleled that of the preceding year, and critics began to complain that the bureau was not doing its job. Further doubts were raised when the bureau was charged with having moved slow to build the 1,000-man inspection force required to enforce the underground law; then having delayed collection of some $1,400,000 in overdue fines.

Still more controversy arose when the bureau attempted to award a contract for a safety campaign, aimed principally at miners, to the public-relations firm of Allison, Treleaven and Rietz, which had managed President Richard M. Nixon's successful 1968 election campaign. This brought accusations that the bureau was attempting to put the blame for coal-mine accidents on the miners instead of on management. Bureau officials denied this and said the campaign would have supplemented law-enforcement efforts to make the mines safer. Whatever the case, the contract was never awarded and the idea finally was dropped.

In spite of such attacks, the bureau could point to some achievements. It stepped up its funding of safety-research programs and increased the number of mine inspections. It also continued a crash program to hire and train more inspectors.

In September, bureau director Dr. Elburt F. Osborn removed Henry P. Wheeler, Jr., from his post as deputy director for health and safety. Osborn said that Wheeler, the bureau's number two man, had been demoted because of mounting criticism. Most complaints, however, had been directed at Edward D. Failor, an assistant to Osborn and the man who had asked the public-relations firm to draw up the abortive safety-campaign proposal. Failor, an Iowa lawyer and Republican Party fund raiser, had been appointed in January on the recommendation of the White House. His lack of mining experience and his confident statements, along with those of other officials, that conditions were improving in the coal mines soon made him a target for criticism, some of it from members of Congress.

Donald P. Schlick, a mining engineer and head of the coal-mine health and safety activities of the bureau, was named as Wheeler's successor. Wheeler was appointed bureau liaison officer in Jackson, Miss.

LAWRENCE E. TAYLOR
Washington Correspondent
St. Louis Post-Dispatch

MINORITIES, AMERICAN ETHNIC

Comparison of the status—political, economic, legal, educational, and so on—of different groups in the United States is a highly political issue, as well as a scientific one. While there is little controversy over many facts, controversy does arise over their interpretation. Thus census figures on the income of black families in the United States are generally accepted, but great controversy arises over the reasons for the deficiency in income of black families when compared with white (discrimination? poor education? concentration in the South? concentration in poor-paying occupations and industries? etc., etc.).

The question of which "ethnic minorities" are properly the subject of social concern and record-keeping and investigation is itself no simple matter. The blacks are by far the largest American racial minority (1970: 22,600,000, 11 per cent of the population). Their status as slaves was written into the Constitution. The body of law affecting them, by name or indirectly, is enormous. There is no question that one must begin any discussion of the status of minorities in the United States with blacks. American Indians form a group closely connected with the origins of American society, a group with a complicated legal status. However, their number is much smaller. In 1970 (preliminary census figures) there were only 792,000 American Indians, 0.4 per cent of the population.

The legal status of the two groups is entirely different. The recent direction of U.S. law has been to strike down any attempt to legally define or refer to Negroes for any purpose, since generally the purpose of such definition is discriminatory. On the other hand, the American Indians are defined by law, since certain rights and benefits inhere in the status of being an Indian. Among these benefits are access to special health and education programs, and rights to reservation lands. Ironically, racial definitions (what "per cent Indian" must one be to get Indian benefits, participate in reservation elections, divisions of land and property?) still persist.

A third group that is a subject of concern —the Mexican–Americans—has never had a legal definition in the United States. Just as the term "black" has come to replace "Negro" among more militant and younger blacks, so has "Chicano" come to replace "Mexican–American." In 1930 the Census Bureau listed "Mexicans" as a race. In 1950 and 1960 it made special tabulations for the "Spanish-surname" population of five southwestern states (sidestepping the question of whether they were

Pat Fulton

Dr. David Risling, Jr., a Hupa, waves title to land/buildings of first university, at Davis, Calif., to be run by Indians and Chicanos.

"Mexican," "Mexican–American" or what have you), and also made tabulations for the Puerto Rican-born and their children. In 1969 it made a special tabulation of "persons of Spanish origin," recognizing that Mexican–Americans may now be conceived of as part of a larger deprived minority group.

But what is this larger group? The special tabulation showed that of 9,200,000 persons of "Spanish origin" in the United States (5 per cent of the population), 55 per cent were of Mexican origin, 16 per cent of Puerto Rican origin, 6 per cent of Cuban origin, 6 per cent of Central or South American origin, and 17 per cent of "other Spanish origin." The census report does not list "Spanish origin"—that is, originating in Spain itself—separately. If it did, the question could well be asked: Why a special tabulation for the Spanish-origin population while none for Greek, Italian, Lebanese, or other derivation?

Part of the answer, however, is clear enough. Mexicans are not only immigrants, for some are the descendants of a conquered population, and many who are immigrants still feel like the descendants of a conquered population and are treated that way by "Anglos." Puerto Ricans come to the mainland from an island that is a possession of the United States. They are citizens but at the same time feel that their personal status is in some way affected by the special status of their homeland. Immigrants from the free countries of Central and South America and from Spain are closely akin to other immigrants. Yet we are aware that most of those of "Spanish origin"—principally Chicanos and Puerto Ricans—have suffered from a discriminatory status, and it is incumbent upon Americans to recognize and act on that reality. And they do. In 1969 President Nixon signed a bill elevating the "Inter-Agency Committee on Mexican-American Affairs," established in 1967, to the higher status of "Cabinet Committee on Opportunities for Spanish-speaking People." Institutions of higher education now regularly count their Mexican–American and Puerto Rican students. The U.S. Civil Service counts their number in Federal employment.

Unfortunately there is no way of systematically defining which groups are proper subjects of concern as ethnic minorities. It is not true that all "racially different" groups are or should be subjects of concern. Some, by certain measures, are better off than whites. History determines which group becomes both subject to discrimination and prejudice and a problem. Some groups that are or have been subject to drastic discrimination and prejudice are no longer "problem" groups. There is no public concern over their status—e.g., Chinese, Japanese and Jews. Other groups have met relatively modest degrees of prejudice and discrimination and yet do become a "problem" because their condition is a deprived one. As already indicated, the three groups in the forefront of public concern in the United States in 1971 were: Negroes, Spanish-origin and American Indians.

BLACKS

Legally, blacks have the same rights all other Americans do. They may not be segregated by public authorities, and many private institutions as well, for any purpose. They may not be discriminated against in voting rights, in legal rights, in employment, in housing, in education, in public facilities. These rights are now written into the many civil-rights laws passed during the 1960's and into a vast array of legal decisions by the courts at many levels. These laws and decisions were occasioned by a vast body of law, generally in the Southern states, that segregated Negroes in public institutions and that limited their capacity to vote. Both the older discriminatory legislation and the new antidiscriminatory legislation rarely refer to Negroes or blacks by name. As a result, other groups besides blacks are protected by the new legislation and the judicial rulings. Nevertheless, the laws and judicial rulings were occasioned generally by the massive system of discrimination against blacks, built up before and after slavery. The many governmental agencies and thousands of employees now devoted to enforcing nondiscrimination have blacks as their primary clients.

While the first aim of such historic rulings as the Supreme Court's 1954 ban on segregation in public education was to overcome discriminatory law, the aim of subsequent civil-rights legislation—dealing with employment, housing, and voting rights—was to overcome discrimination that was enforced in practice but not based generally on law. Thus the main index of the status of blacks shifted in the 1960's from a concern with their formal legal status (could they eat in lunchrooms?, take unsegregated transportation?, attend unsegregated schools?) to their actual status (were they really in majority white schools?, were they really voting?, were they actually getting better jobs?, better housing?).

Education. During the 1960's there was a great increase in the number of blacks completing high school and attending college. In 1960, 36 per cent of male Negroes aged 25–29 and 63 per cent of male whites of the same ages had completed high school. In 1970, 54 per cent of Negro males and 79 per cent of white males had graduated. Negroes completing college in the 25–34-year-old group rose from 4.3 to 6.1 per cent; whites from 11.7 to 16.6 per cent. College enrollment rose to 16 per cent of Negroes 18–24 in 1970 (27 per cent of whites). In 1964, 51 per cent of Negro college enrollment was in predominantly Negro schools, in 1970 28 per cent.

While higher education of blacks became largely desegregated, the situation for elementary and secondary schooling was confused. In the South, the formal separation of the public schools into two systems was largely overcome, but separation because of different residential areas became the major problem there just as it had been all along in the North. And while the Federal Government and courts wielded powerful legal instruments to overcome separation in the South, the instruments were weaker in the North, where there was little history of public action to segregate. In the very large cities in which most Northern Negroes were concentrated, it was enormously difficult, practically and politically, to overcome segregation. In 1971 the largest Northern city attempting a complete desegregation by busing was San Francisco. But this was not universally accepted by blacks, was strongly opposed by many whites, and was also strongly opposed by another racial minority, the Chinese.

Housing. The failure to overcome school desegregation in the North and West was largely a result of the failure to overcome residential segregation. Studies showed that this pattern did not change at all during the 1960's. As to whether it was based on discrimination or on economic incapacity to move into newer suburban areas by blacks or on taste—and how much on each—this was in dispute. Discrimination in most housing was banned by law; but it still continued massively. Aside from segregation and discrimination, however, the housing conditions of blacks showed improvement in the 1960's. In 1960, only 59 per cent of blacks occupied housing with all plumbing facilities; by 1970 it had risen to 83 per cent (95 per cent in central cities of metropolitan areas, where blacks are concentrated, against a white figure of 97 per cent).

Income, Jobs, Family. The median income of Negro families in 1970 was $6,279; of white, $10,236. The Negro median was 61 per cent of the white median; in 1965 it was 54 per cent of the white median. Outside the South, Negro family income was closer to white family income, and among young families even closer. Husband-wife families with the head under 35 years old, in North and West, earned median incomes that were 91 per cent of those earned by whites. There were great changes in occupational distribution. Between 1960 and 1969, the number of Negroes in professional and technical occupations increased 109 per cent (white, 41 per cent). Negroes in clerical occupations rose 114 per cent (whites, 33 per cent). Other economic indexes were less positive. In July 1971 the general unemployment rate was 5.8 per cent; among nonwhites, 10.1 per cent. Among nonwhite teen-agers it had been 29.1 per cent in 1970; among white teen-agers, 13.5. In addition, there was substantial underemployment (part-time, at poor jobs), and many

Some members of the Congressional Black Caucus hold a hearing; they symbolize the growing influence of blacks in U.S. political life.

UPI

Negroes had dropped out of the labor force and were listed as neither looking for work, employed nor in school.

Between 1950 and 1971, nonwhite families with female heads rose from 17.6 per cent to 28.9. The white figure remained stable at about 9 per cent.

Politics. There was an enormous change in the number of elected Negro officials. In 1962, four Negroes were elected to the House of Representatives; in 1970 13 Negroes won House seats. In addition, the number of Negroes in state legislatures rose from 52 to 198. A number of large cities have Negro mayors (Gary, Ind.; Newark, N.J.). In other cities, Negroes came close to winning. The number of black voters increased greatly in the South. Nationally, however, a smaller proportion of Negroes voted than of whites, and consequently black political power was less than it might be.

Any overall assessment of the status of blacks is open to dispute. Some students point to the statistics as signs of progress; others point to the gaps as signs of failure. Most blacks look forward to an increasing measure of well-being and integration; but others demand separation. They insist that blacks are a colonial people and only freedom—not fully defined—is the proper objective, not integration and prosperity.

SPANISH ORIGIN

We have pointed out that a number of groups are included under this rubric. Some seem to suffer no more from prejudice, discrimination and deprivations than do European-white immigrants. Immigrants from South and Central America are generally voluntary immigrants, often of middle-class background, often coming for educational opportunities. Cubans who have concentrated in Miami are generally of middle-class background. They open businesses, gain higher education, enter the professions and are not seen as a particular "problem." Many were already well educated before they came.

The two elements of the Spanish-origin population over whom there has been the most concern and among whom, following the black pattern, many of the youth are now involved in militant movements, are the Mexican-Americans (the Chicanos) and the Puerto Ricans. The Puerto Ricans—1,500,000—are concentrated in New York City. There are smaller communities in other large and smaller industrial northeastern cities. There is also a migratory-labor component among them. New York City statistics show that they earn less than Negroes, have higher unemployment and are in occupations inferior to those of Negroes. On all indicators, except family stability, they score lower than Negroes. A higher proportion is on welfare. It was estimated that as much as two fifths of New York City's Puerto Rican population was on welfare in 1971.

There are some positive signs. The second generation generally shows a rapid advance. Legally Puerto Ricans are citizens and may vote. In 1970, Herman Badillo of New York City became the first person of Puerto Rican background to be elected to Congress.

UPI

Norman Mineta, the first Japanese-American mayor of a major U.S. city—San Jose, Calif.—plays baseball with his son. Today the Japanese-Americans are a highly respected minority.

Mexican-Americans are far more numerous, some 5,000,000 concentrated largely in two states, California and Texas, and in smaller numbers in three other states, New Mexico, Arizona and Colorado. Most Mexican-Americans are immigrants and must, as other immigrants do, take formal steps to gain citizenship and establish citizenship rights. In 1969 the median income of Mexican-Americans was $5,641 (lower than black but higher than Puerto Rican). The educational attainment of Mexican-Americans is lower than that of blacks. In 1960, 12.8 per cent of Southwest Spanish-surname persons had completed 12 years or more of schooling, as compared with 17.4 per cent of Southwest blacks. They meet more discrimination and prejudice in Texas than in California.

Education is an area of great difficulty. Mexican-Americans usually do poorly and seldom advance. Many experts believe it is because non-Mexican teachers show contempt and disdain for both the children and their culture, and because Southwest schools have failed to adapt themselves to pupils from Spanish-speaking homes and of different cultural background. In recent years Federal legislation has supported programs of bilingual education, and many such programs have been started. The weak educational background means that few Mexican-Americans attain professional and white-collar status.

AMERICAN INDIANS

If one uses the kinds of measures that we have applied to blacks and Spanish-origin groups, the American Indians score still lower—in educational achievement, in income and in occupation. Yet it is doubtful whether these are fully suitable measures of status for American Indians. They do have a distinctive legal position. The majority live on reservations where the Federal Government, through the Bureau of Indian Affairs, is responsible for education, health, public works and the like. In 1968 there were 452,000 Indians on or near reservations and over 300,000 off reservations. Whereas blacks and Spanish-origin groups are largely urban, Indians are still largely rural.

If Indian traditional cultures, adapted to the areas in which they lived, were still intact, then the traditional measures of educational achievement, income and occupational achievement would hardly be relevant. But while still largely rural and on or near reservations, Indian traditional cultures are almost everywhere in decay. More and more Indians are congregating in cities, and increasingly Indians must live like everyone else in a market society. In these

UPI

Indians clash with Bureau of Indian Affairs guards, and claim that efforts to give them a greater voice in their concerns are being stifled.

respects they are very badly off. Statistics on American Indians are very limited, but a few figures are known: 28 per cent of rural Indian families earned less than $1,000 in 1960, as against only 10 per cent of the whole population. Few were in the professions or worked as managers, clerks, salesmen or craftsmen; many are unskilled laborers and service workers. Only 9 per cent of rural male Indians had completed high school (against 22 per cent of all rural males); less than 1 per cent of rural male Indians had completed college (against 4.4 per cent of all rural males). Among reservation Indians, unemployment is on a vast scale; about two fifths of reservation Indians were unemployed during the 1960's.

Although the Federal Government spends about $500,000,000 a year on Indian programs, dispute and disagreement are rife over the effectiveness and direction of the funds. The principal issue is whether the traditional legal position of the Indians, as members of tribes holding property in common, should be maintained or whether the tribes and reservations should be dissolved. The issue affects views on every matter affecting Indians, including educational and economic programs.

NATHAN GLAZER
Professor, Graduate School of Education
Harvard University

A tremendous hit with romance-starved audiences, if not critics, "Love Story" starred Ali McGraw and Ryan O'Neal, here in a happy moment.

MOTION PICTURES

What can be said about cinema in 1971, except that its story of a 25-year-old girl who dies made $70,000,000? That was Hollywood's *Love Story*, a rocketing box-office success that seemed to be the long-awaited reaction to months of screen violence, nudity, motorcycles and drugs. By the end of 1971 the picture was on the way to a record as one of movies' all-time box-office successes. To the credit of the film makers, however, Erich Segal's novel-made-film did not immediately spawn a host of imitations, as *Easy Rider* and *The Graduate* had done in previous years.

Trade sources said more people went to movies in 1971 than in the best of earlier years. The films were going in every direction. Diametric opposites like the gentle *Summer of '42* and *Willard*, a movie about rats, pulled in moviegoers across the United States. American Westerns revived—John Wayne, predictably, in three of them: *Rio Lobo*, *Big Jake* and *The Cowboys*. Horror films, a staple of the industry from its beginnings, were released widely and wildly attended by a youth audience that the Motion Picture Association of America estimated at 74 per cent of the whole. Three out of four moviegoers were under the age of thirty.

Commonplace movie ingredients abounded to be sure. Exploitation of youth as in *Two-Lane Blacktop;* of sex (sexploitation films, as the trade papers loved to call them) increased as the movie rating systems were applied less strictly. A shoestring cheapie called *The Stewardesses*, for instance, featuring unknown performers and filmed in 3-D, made $10,000,-000. Science fiction had its day in *The Hellstrom Chronicle*, in which insects bid to take over the earth. The redoubtable Walt Disney studios gave children some funny moments in such films as *Bedknobs and Broomsticks* and *The $1,000,000 Duck*.

But no one could ignore *Love Story*, which turned a slender Yale classics professor's slender novel into a monolith. Ali McGraw and Ryan O'Neal starred in the story of a Harvard blueblood and his Italian-Catholic girl from Radcliffe who dies of leukemia while the sound-track orchestra sobs away and the patrons do no less.

Burned once with *Easy Rider* and a line of flop carbon copies about traveling youth on Hondas, the industry looked beyond *Love Story* for material. Herman Raucher's novel about three adolescent boys coming of age in the war years yielded *Summer of '42*. The boys were charming and human, the way middle-aged viewers today like to remember themselves as 15-year-olds. A new actress named Jennifer O'Neill, like Ali McGraw a former model, was luminescent as an "older woman" of 22. The film was an immediate hit.

Maybe it was merely nostalgia that swept the United States in 1971, but the old days looked good to the moviemakers as well as to theater professionals, clothes designers, and publishers of paperbacks. Perhaps the definitive picture in this genre was *The Last Picture Show,* the work of a young writer-critic, Peter Bogdanovich, who directed it. The cast included some young actors and a gentlemanly veteran of dozens of Westerns, Ben Johnson, as the owner of the last movie house in a dying Southwestern small town. The picture looked back on American small town life, which anthropologists are beginning to find interesting.

Mike Nichols rebounded from his flop *Catch-22* to film a look at the 1950's in *Carnal Knowledge.* A big commercial winner, the film traced the sexual and emotional hang-ups of two college friends, played by Jack Nicholson and singer Art Garfunkel, from campus days to the present. The result was not pleasant, but it quickly made a dramatic star of thirty-year-old singer-actress Ann-Margret and kept Jack Nicholson in the forefront of pop-screen stars. Nicholson directed a film himself, his first, called *Drive, He Said.* It was booed when introduced at the Cannes Film Festival and many American critics disliked it; it sank in appeal at the same rate that *Carnal Knowledge* rose.

Film makers shunned violence, with the exception of horror films and some gory Westerns like *Valdez Is Coming.* No major pictures appeared about war, though many tackled the drug problem—most of them poor. Some emotional films were made about conserving life, of humans or lower animals—Stanley Kramer's oafish *Bless the Beasts and the Children* (about buffalos), Dalton Trumbo's heavy *Johnny Got His Gun* (about a World War I quadruple amputee).

A film with a title similar to that of Bogdanovich's excellent film was Dennis Hopper's lamentable one, *The Last Movie.* It is of interest, however, because it was the year's lone heir to the *Easy Rider* legacy. Two years after the fact, Dennis Hopper, one of *Easy Rider's* costars, went to Peru and made a movie about a group of Hollywood actors and dope-culturists going to Peru and making a movie. Critics said mainly that they hoped the title indicated Hopper's film future. The other *Easy Rider* star, Peter Fonda, also directed a film, *The Hired Hand,* and it too flopped.

Nevertheless, over the months, the number of genuinely expert films increased. Critics wore themselves out seeking suitable adjectives for a film made in London, *Sunday, Bloody Sunday.* "Civilized" was most often used to describe the story of a three-way love affair involving a fashionable career woman and a homosexual, middle-aged doctor both in love with the same young man. Glenda Jackson and Peter Finch were the older sharers and, directed by John Schlesinger, gave acutely sensitive performances.

Although the caliber of films was rising, all the old-fashioned profit seekers had not left Hollywood. To them, art is giving the public what they think it wants. Some of the public evidently wanted to see the latest Jacqueline Susann novel made into a film, and they got it in *The Love Machine,* a tacky melodrama about a greedy television executive. The same school of producers came up with *Doctors' Wives,* this a 1940's pop glop. It made a great deal of noise at the box office in spite of an inexpressibly gory sequence showing an open-heart operation, amid all the country-club adultery.

As films are maturing, black film makers are getting their first real opportunities. One, Melvin Van Peebles, wrote, produced, directed and starred in *Sweet Sweetback's Baadasssss Song,* a vehement antiwhite statement about a Negro hustler. The picture made a fortune. Although most critics deplored its blatant amateurishness,

Coming of emotional and sexual age in the "Summer of '42" involved Jennifer O'Neill as an "older woman" and Gary Grimes as a 15-year-old.

the growing black audience took to it immediately, making *Sweet Sweetback* one of the year's screen landmarks. The talented Gordon Parks, the first black man to direct a major American film (*The Learning Tree*) made *Shaft* in 1971. It tells of a black New York detective who finds interracial supporters. Parks' more durable film was on its way to as great a success as *Sweet Sweetback.*

The decline of Hollywood as the U.S. filmmaking center continued. More and more pictures were being made in New York and on location elsewhere in the country. Some of the outstanding films, as always, came to the United States from abroad. Director Joseph Losey won the Cannes (France) Film Festival grand prize with his elegaic *The Go-Between,* a bittersweet story about an interclass love affair in pre-World War I England, with Julie Christie, Alan Bates and a Harold Pinter screenplay. Sweden's Bo Widerberg produced a film about a Swedish labor organizer who immigrates to the United States, *Joe Hill.* Luchino Visconti took on the Thomas Mann novella, *Death in Venice,* but the Mann story of an aging writer's (a composer in the film) unrequited love for a beautiful boy was lost in a welter of gorgeous costumes, Venetian palazzos, canals and Technicolor. Costa-Gavras, the Greek director who sat the Greek Government back on its heels in 1969 with the emo-

Tom Courtenay played title role in "One Day in the Life of Ivan Denisovich," based on novel by Russian Nobelist Aleksandr Solzhenitsyn.

Cinerama Releasing

tionally propagandistic *Z,* employed that film's star Yves Montand again in *The Confession.* It was based on the Stalinist political trials in Hungary in 1956 and Montand was pluperfect as the tortured defendant and victim.

England's middle-aged enfant terrible Ken Russell plumbed deeper and deeper into sensationalism with two films: *The Music Lovers* and *The Devils.* Neither was an artistic triumph. But after *The Devils,* with its naked nuns in religious frenzy, bloodletting, torture and the burning of a priest at the stake (in close-up), many U.S. filmgoers wished Ken Russell would try another tack. Claude Lelouch, a trend-setter of 1966 with *A Man and a Woman,* came up with a gangster souffle, *The Crook,* with Jean-Louis Trintignant as a likable kidnaper. Trintignant in *The Conformist* took on different coloring altogether, in Bertolucci's visually hypnotizing story of a 1930's Italian fascist. The film features chic costumes, a tango orchestra and the atmosphere of a very nasty period. The cerebral and charming Eric Rohmer of France wrote and directed *Claire's Knee* and *La Collectionneuse.* Of all the pictures made outside of the United States, probably the standout was *One Day in the Life of Ivan Denisovich,* with Tom Courtenay starring in the film version of the Aleksandr Solzhenitsyn novel. Filmed in sub-zero weather in Norway, the movie captured the invincible humanity of a political prisoner and writer in Siberia as well as the killing conditions he describes.

Films made in other countries are almost always produced on smaller budgets than U.S. ones. What costs less to make costs less to buy for the U.S. market. Interestingly, the three leading countries—India, Japan and Nationalist China (Taiwan)—in feature-film production seldom see their products that are shown in the United States. Mexico in recent years has surpassed the United States. Indian films, as well as other Oriental ones, have rarely been successful in the United States, perhaps because of the extreme difference in cultures with which average American audiences have little empathy. Satayjit Ray has much the greatest international reputation of any director in India. He had no film in circulation in the United States in 1971. Japan sends a packet of pictures to the West every year. Of the five best in 1971, four starred the remarkable Toshiro Mifune, an Oriental combination of John Wayne and Paul Newman, in the Samurai vein. In *Machibuse,* Mifune confronts 8 bad guys, wipes out all 8 and strides off into the mist. For the first time, Nigeria showed a film in the United States, *Kongi's Harvest. Paix sur les Champs (Peace Over the Fields)* was sent by Belgium. The Dutch re-

Menelaus (Patrick Magee) keeps Helen (Irene Papas) from killing herself, as Hecuba (Katharine Hepburn) and the other "Trojan Women" watch, blaming the Greek Helen for Troy's suffering.

Under the white thatch is Walter Matthau. As Mr. Joseph P. Kotcher—"Kotch"—he is a talkative old man whom children find irresistible.

leased *Rubia's Jungle*. Belgians and Dutch produced *Mira*.

It was doubtful that Americans would see two of 1971's most tantalizing films, at least from their descriptions. Peter Brook filmed *King Lear* in Denmark with Paul Scofield in the title role; and a film version of Dylan Thomas's stage-poem *Under Milk Wood* was seen only in Europe—with Elizabeth Taylor, Richard Burton and Peter O'Toole.

An official Peking delegation appeared at the Venice Film Festival with a Maoist work having the nonlyrical title *Women's Section of the Army*. It was described as a "polemic, ideological ballet film," and featured ballerinas dancing in Red Guard uniforms.

The major international directors continued to contribute. Ingmar Bergman made his first film in English, *The Touch*, with American actor Elliott Gould. Consensus was that Bergman was better in Swedish, let alone without

A perilous real-life adventure was filmed in "Blue Water, White Death." Using special elevators, four divers searched the sea for the great white shark, called the deadliest of cold-blooded predators.

Gould. France's François Truffaut added another section to the autobiographical series *Bed and Board.* The highly regarded Czech Milos Forman made a picture in English too, about disaffected American youth and their parents, *Taking Off.* Federico Fellini directed a quasi-documentary, and appeared in *The Clowns.* Michael Cacoyannis made a disappointing (to some) film *The Trojan Women,* about the terrible aftermath of the Trojan War, with a galaxy of female stars: Katharine Hepburn, Irene Papas, Genevieve Bujold and Vanessa Redgrave. Italy's Pier Paolo Pasolini persuaded opera singer Maria Callas to act *Medea* for him.

Robert Altman, one of the best directing talents to emerge in the United States in recent years, made an 180-degree turn from *M*A*S*H* and *Brewster McCloud* to *McCabe and Mrs. Miller.* Warren Beatty and Julie Christie starred in the story of a gambler and a sporting lady on the Northwest frontier. Altman's picture captured with incredible realism, color and feeling the brawling, sweating and scratching for territory. Another talented young director, William Friedkin (*The Boys in the Band*) took the story of a $32,000,000 heroin case and created a detective story of headlong speed and excitement in *The French Connection.*

Willard was not the best but it was the most bizarre. It stunned everybody with any sensitivity, and drew horror fans by the millions. Chiefly to do with rats attacking people, *Willard* was a barometer of one segment of public taste. The monsters were all back: vampires, werewolves, diabolical mad scientists. Count Dracula returned, played by Dr. Fu Manchu himself, Christopher Lee. There were *Lust for a Vampire, The Velvet Vampires* and the indefatigable Vincent Price as *The Abominable Dr. Phibes.*

Not everybody was off cringing at horror films, however. Some people wanted to laugh a little. *Kotch* starred Walter Matthau as a 72-year-old retiree who wants to be useful. The film was directed by novice director Jack Lemmon and the whole enterprise was wonderful. Matthau was less successful in *Plaza Suite* but it was the Neil Simon play on screen and as such gave pleasure. Barbra Streisand's only 1971 film was *The Owl and the Pussycat.* At year's end, another Simon comedy was forthcoming, *Star Spangled Girl,* with Sandy Duncan.

Just when everybody said the big-budget musical had had its day in Hollywood, director Norman Jewison hired the Israeli actor Topol and made a film out of history's longest-running Broadway musical, *Fiddler on the Roof.* Before it was even released, theater owners were scrambling for options. There were no other musicals to compare with *Fiddler,* however. Money was spent heavily on *Nicholas and Alexandra,* the story of the last Czar. *Mary, Queen of Scots* was a costly film, starring Glenda Jackson.

Notably absent from the activity were a great many of Hollywood's most publicized personalities. For reasons of their own, some went into television series: Jimmy Stewart, Henry Fonda, Anthony Quinn, Shirley Mac-Laine. George C. Scott won an Oscar (which he refused) for his role in *Patton* and then made two not-so-popular films, *The Long Run* and *They Might Be Giants.* Glenda Jackson won an Oscar for her role in *Women in Love.* She did not turn up at the ceremonies either but accepted her Oscar by proxy.

LAWRENCE DEVINE
Entertainment Editor and Drama Critic
The Detroit Free Press

MUSIC, CLASSICAL

Thirteen years after it was first authorized by the U.S. Congress, and seven years after the ground was broken, the John F. Kennedy Center for the Performing Arts finally opened its doors on the bank of the Potomac. Washington's need for new musical facilities has never been in doubt—not at least to anyone who has endured the acoustic and esthetic deficiencies of the city's only previous concert auditorium, Constitution Hall. Yet Kennedy Center was never thought of as merely a cultural meeting place for the city of Washington; it was conceived from the start as the cultural showplace of the nation.

Thus the barrage of criticism, both pro and con, that greeted the opening of the operatic and symphonic auditoriums in the center in September 1971 was also nationwide. Criticism of the building itself, designed by Edward Durell Stone, was almost unanimously negative; only the acoustics of the two halls won favor. The building itself was condemned as too vast, too austere, too unfriendly to the arts, while the interior of the opera house was variously described as garish and stifling.

Mixed too was the reception accorded the work commissioned to open the center, a vast, eclectic work by Leonard Bernstein, choreographed by Alvin Ailey, titled *Mass* but hardly the sort to find much favor in church. The text, which in part follows the Catholic liturgy, written by Bernstein himself and Stephen Schwartz, tended toward a cynical, doubting attack on the survival of faith in a world racked by war and hypocrisy; the final plea for peace seemed, under the circumstances set forth by the text, both tearful and hopeless. Bernstein's music drew upon his familiar theatrical style, unashamedly reminiscent of

Leonard Bernstein's "Mass," composed for the opening of the John F. Kennedy Center for the Performing Arts, in Washington, included dancing and such elements as bongo drums, religious chants, and rock.

Fletcher Drake

many other composers of past and present, embracing such dissimilar elements as religious chant and rock. The theatrical effectiveness of the piece, especially as performed by a talented and mostly youthful assemblage, was hardly in question, but it was generally agreed that Bernstein had written more distinguished music in his career.

The other new work for the center's inaugural was Alberto Ginastera's *Beatrix Cenci*, an opera based on Shelley's violent and tortured account of evil in a medieval Italian family. Ginastera, who might be described as a conservative-atonal composer, explored no new paths in the work beyond his now famous earlier operas. But the terse, powerful score won cheers, as did the performance by the Opera Society of Washington, conducted by Julius Rudel with the brilliant American soprano Arlene Saunders in the title role. A later performance, also conducted by Rudel, concluded the festivities: Handel's *Ariodante* in its first American staging, with the brilliant Beverly Sills leading a splendid cast. The concert hall was inaugurated by what will be its principal tenant, the National Symphony Orchestra under

its new conductor, Antal Dorati, with a solid but safely conventional concert that was attended by President Richard M. Nixon and his family.

If Washington was, for the festive opening of Kennedy Center, the nation's temporary musical capital, there was still plenty of news in the permanent capital, New York. Shortly before the year began, the Metropolitan Opera announced, with pride and relief, that it had finally ended its long search for a successor to Rudolf Bing, in the person of Goeran Gentele. Goeran *who?* was the question widely voiced, since the director of the Stockholm Opera was hardly a known quantity in American musical circles. Gentele had come to his Swedish post after long experience as a stage director, both for theater and opera. His appointment was taken to mean, at very least, that the Met will reconsider under his leadership some of its antiquated ideas about staging. Gentele's first American appearances impressed most observers with his charm, wit and diplomacy, all of them qualities that will be much needed when he assumes command in the fall of 1972. Gentele also won high marks with his an-

Goeran Gentele (l), director of the Stockholm Opera, takes command of the Metropolitan Opera in the fall of 1972; retiring manager Sir Rudolf Bing bows in acknowledgment of a spontaneous, standing ovation.

Metropolitan Opera Assn., Inc.

Wide World

SOME MAJOR 1971 CLASSICAL RECORDINGS

Bach, *Keyboard Concertos,* complete, Igor Kipnis (Columbia)

Bach, *A Musical Offering,* Concentus Musicus (Telefunken)

Bach, *Art of the Fugue,* Lionel Rogg (Angel)

Beethoven, *Quartets, Opus 18,* Guarneri Quartet (RCA)

Bellini, *Il Pirata,* Gavazzeni (Angel)

Berlioz, *Les Nuits d'Eté,* Davis (Philips)

Berlioz, *Requiem,* Davis (Philips)

Bizet, *Carmen,* Frühbeck de Burgos (Angel)

Borodin, *Prince Igor,* Ermler (Angel)

Britten, *Rape of Lucretia,* Britten (London)

Bruckner, *Symphony No. 9,* Bernstein (Columbia)

Byrd, *Keyboard Musick,* Gould (Columbia)

Charpentier, *La Peste de Milan,* Waldman (Decca)

Crumb, *Ancient Voices of Children,* DeGaetani, Dash, Weisberg (Nonesuch)

Donizetti, *Anna Bolena,* Varviso (London)

Dvorak, *Concerto in B for Cello,* Du Pré (Angel)

Handel, *Ariodante,* Simon (RCA)

Handel, *Julius Caesar,* Richter (DGG)

Haydn, *Symphonies, Nos. 57–72,* 3 vols., Dorati (London)

Mahler, *Symphony No. 6,* Solti (London)

Mahler, *Das Klagende Lied,* Boulez (Columbia)

Massenet, *Manon,* Rudel (ABC-Paramount)

Mozart, *Last Symphonies,* Karajan (Angel)

Mozart, *Die Zauberflöte,* Solti (London)

Partch, *Delusion of the Fury,* Mitchell (Columbia)

Penderecki, *Devils of Loudun,* Janowski (Philips)

Ruggles, *The Sun-Treader,* Thomas (DGG)

Schubert, *Collected Lieder,* 2 vols., Fischer-Dieskau (DGG)

Schumann, Four Symphonies, Solti (London)

Scriabin, *Etudes,* Merzhanov (Angel)

Smetana, *Ma Vlast,* Kubelik (DGG)

Strauss, *Also sprach Zarathustra,* Bernstein (Columbia)

Tchaikovsky, *Eugene Onegin,* Rostropovich (Angel)

Tippett, *Midsummer Marriage,* Davis (Philips)

Verdi, *Don Carlo,* Giulini (Angel)

Wagner, *Die Meistersinger,* Karajan (Angel)

Wagner, *Parsifal,* Boulez (DGG)

Weber, *Oberon,* Kubelik (DGG)

---

nouncement that the distinguished conductor Rafael Kubelik would be engaged by the company as music director, a post that had never existed before.

Among the new Metropolitan Opera productions in 1971 were two operas that had been absent from the company's repertory for several decades: Massenet's *Werther* and Weber's *Der Freischütz.* The consensus was that the operas

At only 26, Michael Tilson Thomas is Boston Philharmonic's associate conductor (rehearsing here) and Buffalo Philharmonic's music director.

Ted Polumbaum

The great cellist-composer Pablo Casals, 95 years old in December 1971, plays his arrangement of a Spanish folk song at the end of a United Nations Day concert, which included his beautiful "Hymn to the United Nations."

had been worth waiting for, but not the productions. Higher marks were awarded the new stagings at the "rival" New York City Opera: a bright, imaginative *Carmen* and a sparkling first-time-in-New-York staging of Benjamin Britten's racy comic opera, *Albert Herring.* Another City Opera novelty was a new work by the prolific Gian Carlo Menotti, *The Most Important Man.* The work was in Menotti's familiar, attractively melodic vein, although there were some hands raised against the naivety of the composer's own libretto, a rather romantic view of racial tensions in an African city. Other operatic news was made around the country by the premiere, at the Santa Fe Opera, of *Yerma,* a posthumous work by the late Brazilian composer Heitor Villa-Lobos; and, in San Francisco, the first American staging of Donizetti's *Maria Stuarda.* The battle of the red-haired prima donnas continued; Joan Sutherland sang *Maria Stuarda* in San Francisco, whereupon it was announced that Beverly Sills would appear in the same work in 1972 at the New York City Opera.

Pierre Boulez began his tenure as conductor of the New York Philharmonic with programs that promised an exciting if somewhat grating era for the orchestra. In his first season Boulez announced that the complete orchestral *oeuvre* of Alban Berg would be performed, along with a huge festival of music by Franz Liszt. The familiar masterworks of the Beethoven-Brahms orbit, meanwhile, were in relatively short supply. Among Boulez' other innovations was a series of concerts performed in an informal atmosphere in a Greenwich Village theater, consisting entirely of hardcore new music and aimed at attracting a young audience who would be encouraged to ask questions at the concerts. The series was an immediate sellout, much to the encouragement of Philharmonic officials who have, naturally, been somewhat concerned as to where their next generation of subscribers might be keeping itself.

Michael Tilson Thomas' star continued to rise when the 26-year-old prodigy was appointed music director of the Buffalo Philharmonic, dividing this position with his post as associate conductor of the Boston Symphony. Another young American joined the firmament when the 41-year-old Lorin Maazel was appointed conductor of the Cleveland Orchestra as successor to the late George Szell. Maazel, a strong-willed and powerful figure on the podium who has been pursuing his career in Europe for the most part, was not exactly welcomed by the orchestra itself, which voted 77–2 against his appointment. But cooler —or, at least, other—heads prevailed.

ALAN RICH
Music Critic, *New York* Magazine

MUSIC, POPULAR

The one overpowering, inescapable element in popular music in 1971 was the complex of operations that made up *Jesus Christ Superstar*. It all began with a song, *Superstar*, that was written in 1969 by two Englishmen: Andrew Lloyd Webber, a composer, who was then 21; and Tim Rice, a lyricist, who was 24. Released as a single disc, it soon sold a million copies which is nothing spectacular in the pop-music world.

But this acceptance encouraged Webber and Rice to write what they called an opera, dealing with the last seven days of Christ's life, in which *Superstar* was the climactic number. The opera, *Jesus Christ Superstar*, was recorded as a two-disc album, released in the United States by Decca. It got off to an uncertain start during the last two months of 1970 but then began bubbling close to the top of the hit charts early in 1971. Before midyear, it had become a sensational seller. Before the year was out, sales registered over $40,000,000.

Meanwhile, concert productions of *Jesus Christ Superstar* began spreading through the country during the summer of 1971 with tremendously lucrative results, providing a torrential publicity buildup for the opening of a Broadway production lavishly staged by Tom O'Horgan (who had staged *Hair*) in October. Neither the fact that Broadway critics tended

SOME MAJOR 1971 POPULAR RECORDINGS

Lynn Anderson, *Rose Garden* (Columbia)
Joan Baez, *The Night They Drove Old Dixie Down* (Vanguard)
Bee Gees, *How Can You Mend a Broken Heart* (Atco)
Carpenters, *For All We Know* (A & M)
Carpenters, *Rainy Days and Mondays* (A & M)
Cher, *Gypsies, Tramps and Thieves* (Kapp)
Perry Como, *It's Impossible* (RCA)
Dawn, *Knock Three Times* (Bell)
John Denver, *Take Me Home, Country Roads* (RCA)
Fifth Dimension, *One Less Bell to Answer* (Bell)
Aretha Franklin, *Bridge over Troubled Water* (Atlantic)
Aretha Franklin, *Spanish Harlem* (Atlantic)
George Harrison, *My Sweet Lord/Isn't It a Pity* (Apple)
Isaac Hayes, *Theme from "Shaft"* (Stax/Volt)
Honey Cone, *Want Ads* (Buddah)
Jackson Five, *Never Can Say Goodbye* (Motown)
Elton John, *Your Song* (Uni)
Janis Joplin, *Me and Bobby Mchee* (Columbia)
Carole King, *It's Too Late/I Feel the Earth Move* (Ode '70)
Jean Knight, *Mr. Big Stuff* (Stax)
Gordon Lightfoot, *If You Could Read My Mind* (Reprise)
Lobo, *Me and You and a Dog Named Boo* (Ampex)
Paul and Linda McCartney, *Uncle Albert/Admiral Halsey* (Apple)
Ocean, *Put Your Hand in the Hand* (Kama)
Osmonds, *One Bad Apple* (MGM)
Osmonds, *Yo-Yo* (MGM)
Donny Osmond, *Go Away Little Girl* (MGM)
Partridge Family, *Doesn't Somebody Want to Be Wanted* (Bell)
Raiders, *Indian Reservation* (Columbia)
Carly Simon, *That's the Way I Always Heard It Should Be* (Elektra)
Sammi Smith, *Help Me Make It Through the Night* (Mega)
Ringo Starr, *It Don't Come Easy* (Apple)
Rod Stewart, *Maggie May/Reason to Believe* (Mercury)
Barbra Streisand, *Stoney End* (Columbia)
James Taylor, *You've Got a Friend* (Warner Brothers)
The Temptations, *Just My Imagination* (Motown)
Three Dog Night, *Joy to the World* (Dunhill)
Andy Williams, *Love Story* (Columbia)
Bill Withers, *Ain't No Sunshine* (Buddah)

With such hits as "Rainy Days and Mondays," "Close to You" and "It's Only Just Begun," The Carpenters dominate the top-ten charts.

A & M Records

to be distressed by O'Horgan's staging (although they felt the music held up) nor a storm of religious controversy that blew up in the wake of the Broadway presentation did anything to stem the overall success of what Rice and Webber had wrought.

With so much attention being lavished on *Jesus Christ Superstar,* the other musical superstars of the year rose and shone with less notice than they might otherwise have received from the general public. However, the inner core of pop music fans, many of them tiring of the *Jesus Christ Superstar* fanfare, were quite aware of who was coming and who was going. Going, at the moment, was James Taylor, the superstar of 1970 who simmered down from the peak adulation aroused by his album *Sweet Baby James* (Warner Brothers) in 1970 to a more normal but still enthusiastic reception for his next album, *Mud Slide Slim and the Blue Horizon* (Warner Brothers), which appeared after a lapse of more than a year.

The new superstar in 1971 was Elton John, an English pianist, singer and composer, who wrote his songs with lyricist Bernie Taupin. John proved to be a somewhat equivocal star in that he was much more effective in personal performance than on records. He used lyrics—the cutting edge of today's songs—that were not his but Bernie Taupin's. He was, in effect, primarily a visual act and his initial impact in the United States began to wear off toward the end of 1971 as another English singer, Cat Stevens, was giving evidence that he might be the next in the pop line of superstars.

There were others who found it a good year. Carole King, a successful songwriter for more than ten years, usually in collaboration with Gerry Goffin, played (she is a pianist) and sang an album of her own songs, *Tapestry* (Ode '70), which clung to the top of the best-selling lists through most of the year.

The Partridge Family has successfully followed the trail blazed a few years earlier by the Monkees, using a television series as the basis for success on records. The Monkees worked as a group, à la the Beatles, but the focal vocal point of the Partridge Family is David Cassidy, the 21-year-old son of Broadway singing star Jack Cassidy, and the stepson of Shirley Jones, the film and stage singer who plays his mother in the TV series. Another follow-up operation was successfully performed by the Osmonds, a

As a member of the Partridge Family, David Cassidy (top) succeeded first on television. English pianist-singer-composer Elton John (below, r) was most persuasive in person; his songs' lyrics were written by Bernie Taupin (l).

top: Bell; bottom: Uni Records

In a benefit for East Pakistani refugees, two of the Beatles were reunited: Ringo Starr (l) and George Harrison (r). Their guest was Bob Dylan (center). Some 40,000 fans cheered them in Madison Square Garden.

group of young singers who won a following comparable to that of another young set of brothers, the Jackson Five, the year before.

Janis Joplin, who died in 1970, had a posthumous success with her album, *Pearl* (Columbia) in 1971; and two other voices from the past —Paul McCartney and George Harrison, former Beatles—made individual imprints on the year's music, Harrison with *All Things Must Pass* (Apple), McCartney joined by his wife, Linda, with *Ram* (Apple).

The year's new star in country music was Lynne Anderson, daughter of the veteran country singer Liz Anderson. Lynne's recording of *Rose Garden* lifted the song from a country hit to a national pop favorite. Charley Pride, a phenomenon in country music for several years as the only successful black singer in a field that has been consistently white down through the years, rose another notch when he was chosen male vocalist of the year by the Country Music Association.

Folk music, which has been overshadowed for years by the somewhat folklike approach of much contemporary pop music, had an unexpected hit in 1971 in Joan Baez's recording of *The Night They Drove Old Dixie Down* (Vanguard). Jazz, however, had to be content with acclaim for two groups that played what was essentially a mixture of jazz and rock: Chicago, which produced rock with a jazz surface in the manner of Blood, Sweat and Tears; and Chase, a group led by Bill Chase, an experienced jazz trumpeter, which aimed directly at the rock audience.

The year 1971 was rather disastrous for jazz in that the Newport Jazz Festival, founded in 1954 and a focus of the wide popularity of jazz in the 1950's, was closed by the city of Newport as the result of an invasion of the park—not, ironically, by overwrought jazz fans but by a small element of rock followers who, along with thousands of other rock fans, had arrived at Newport because there were no rock festivals to go to on the East Coast.

Theater and film scores aroused little interest during the year. The most successful Broadway-cast album was the recording of the revival of the 47-year-old musical *No, No, Nanette* (Columbia). The soundtracks most in demand were *Woodstock* (Cotillion), a holdover from 1970; *Love Story* (Paramount), the big pop film of the year; and *Shaft* (Enterprise), a black-oriented private-eye film that had special appeal for black audiences.

JOHN S. WILSON
Popular-Music Critic
Contributor, *The New York Times*

NETHERLANDS, THE

By April 1971 the Netherlands economy was in an explosive state. There was a balance-of-payments surplus of $500,000,000. Investment in factory buildings was down by 2 per cent. Nevertheless, capital from abroad was flooding in, and in spite of wage controls the money supply appeared excessive.

No fewer than 28 parties contested the general election called in April, which saw the coalition Government of Piet de Jong lose its overall majority. After 63 days of negotiations a new coalition was formed under the premiership of Barend W. Biesheuvel, head of the Anti-Revolutionary Party. To the four parties of the preceding coalition—Catholics, Liberals, the ARP and the Christian Historical Union—was added the Democratic Socialist Party, a completely new force in Dutch politics.

The DSP under Dr. Willem Drees, Jr., broke away from the main Labor Party, whose policies it considered too Leftist. It won 8 seats. The election was noteworthy in a number of other ways. The Kabouters, or Gnomes, a youthful protest party, contested an election for the first time. The party had earlier had successes in municipal elections in Amsterdam, campaigning against pollution, high-rise building and the use of cars in cities. Now it polled fewer than 23,000 votes and failed to gain national representation. At the same time, the Farmers' Party, a right-wing group, which had won 7 seats in 1967, lost all but one of its seats in Parliament.

The new Cabinet, considered somewhat right of center, included 6 Catholics, 3 Liberals, 3 ARP, 2 Calvinists and 2 Democratic Socialists. One of its first acts was to lift the wage-and-price controls imposed by the preceding Government. A new voluntary wages policy was being worked out.

The first budget provided for increased taxes on incomes in the highest brackets, but predicted a record deficit of $926,000,000. Government spending was up by rather more than this, but mostly to pay higher wages. Overall Dutch earnings rose 14 per cent. GNP was expected to rise 5 per cent in 1971, but only 3 per cent in 1972. Some pressure was taken off the economy by the floating of the guilder. The Netherlands prime interest rate, which stood at 6 per cent at the start of 1971, was reduced to 5½ in April and then to 5 per cent.

After 19 years as Dutch foreign minister, Dr. Joseph Luns retired to take over from Manlio Brosio as secretary-general of NATO. On June 18, Queen Elizabeth II of Great Britain made Dr. Luns an Honorary Member of the Order of Companions of Honour, one of Britain's highest awards. Dr. Luns had been a consistent supporter of the British case in the councils of Europe.

Queen Juliana and Prince Bernhard of the Netherlands visited Indonesia from Aug. 25 to Sept. 5, returning a visit paid to Holland in 1970 by President Suharto. That visit had been cut short by violent demonstrations against Indonesia by Amboinese residents of the Netherlands, claiming the right to establish an independent Republic of the South Moluccas, the easternmost islands of the Indonesian Archipelago. Prison sentences of up to three years had been passed on a number of those taking part. An agreement was reached to give help to any Amboinese wishing to return from Holland to Indonesia but to place no difficulties in the way of those who wished to remain in the Netherlands. The Dutch will invest in development projects in which returning Amboinese can be employed. But the Moluccas will not be granted separate status.

The Netherlands joined the project to build a European Airbus, the A-300B. Fokker will have a 6.5 per cent interest; its main job will be to produce the aircraft's flaps. The airbus is planned to seat 250 passengers and to have a range of 3,000 kilometers (1,860 miles) at 600 miles per hour. France and West Germany are each paying 43 per cent of the costs. Although the British Government opted out, Hawker Siddeley of Britain has a 7.5 per cent share in the project.

JOHN ALLAN MAY
Chief, London News Bureau
The Christian Science Monitor

THE NETHERLANDS

Area: 15,766
Population: 13,100,000
Capital: Amsterdam
Government: Juliana, queen—1948; Barend W. Bieleuvel, premier—1971
Gross National Product: $31,300,000,000
Foreign trade: exports, $11,766,000,000; imports, $13,393,000,000
Armed forces: 116,500

NEW ZEALAND

Economic issues, primarily inflation, dominated New Zealand affairs. Apart from measures to halt price and wage rises it was a wait-and-see year. Political leaders were unwilling to introduce new policy lines, pending the outcome of Britain's EEC negotiations.

The economy absorbed the effects of big costs increases carried over from 1970 and the countermeasures applied in the opening months of 1971. By midyear the immediate problem of severe inflationary pressures had been brought under control. Overseas reserves were at record levels, and the economic picture was officially viewed as warranting "cautious optimism." Yet this confidence was scarcely reflected in the stock exchange. Stock prices were down about 15 per cent to a four-year low.

In foreign affairs, new initiatives were evident in regional cooperation, and there was the usual close rapport with U.S. policies. Vietnam faded as an issue after the Government announced complete withdrawal of the New Zealand combat force by year's end.

The year began with temporary price restraints in effect as a means of halting the severe wage-price spiral that in 1970 lifted average weekly earnings 14 per cent and prices about 10 per cent. As other deflationary measures had proven ineffectual, in February Parliament passed a stabilization act to hold all prices and wages. From then on, problems in the business sector (brought about through lending restrictions) and in the farm sector, coupled with uncertainties about the future of the economy, were deterrents to expansion and to further price rises. The inflation rate came down to about 2 per cent in the second quarter of the year. In July, the watchdog authority on wages permitted a 4.8 per cent rise for workers whose wages had been pegged. In addition, a temporary 10 per cent surcharge on income tax (imposed in October 1970) was dropped on schedule.

Manufacturing showed solid gains and expanded export sales. Forest products won additional markets. Tourism receipts were up about 25 per cent. Meanwhile, farm incomes were adversely affected by higher costs coupled with low wool prices and slow growth in overall production. The Government promised a comprehensive review of the farm position following the outcome of Britain's EEC negotiations. Sharp deterioration in New Zealand's balance of trade—the price index of imports rose 10 per cent in the year to Mar. 31—brought general acknowledgement that an annual 4.5 per cent growth rate in the gross national product, which was set by the National Development Conference in 1969, could no longer be achieved.

Notable expansion occurred in industrial capacity and power resources. The Kapuni natural-gas field met much of the industrial and domestic demand, and the new offshore Maui field was investigated as a possible further source. Using Australian alumina, the U.S.-$93,000,000 smelter at Bluff began producing aluminum ingots. An important new outlet for

NEW ZEALAND

Area: 103,736 sq. mi.
Population: 2,862,631
Capital: Wellington
Government: Sir Arthur Poritt, governor-general —1967; Keith J. Holyoake, prime minister— 1960
Gross National Product: $5,300,000,000
Foreign trade: exports, $1,225,000,000; imports, $1,245,000,000
Armed forces: 13,135

export trade opened with the first shipment of ironsands to Japan.

In international affairs, Prime Minister Sir Keith Holyoake reaffirmed the ANZUS treaty as the cornerstone of foreign policy and defense. He welcomed the decision to admit the People's Republic of China to the UN while deploring the expulsion of the Republic of China (Taiwan).

A significant new defense pact (ANZUK), signed in November, joined New Zealand with Australia, Britain, Malaysia and Singapore. ANZUK provides that Australia, New Zealand and the United Kingdom will continue to maintain naval, air and ground forces in the Malaysia/Singapore area.

A bill, introduced in July, making it an offense to discriminate on grounds of color, race or ethnic origin in matters such as employment, housing or provision of goods and services, reaffirmed the Government's commitment to racial equality. The proposed legislation was a routine endorsement of an accepted principle.

Environmental issues received greater attention than ever before. Conservation groups scored a victory when the Government decided not to raise the level of Lake Manapouri by 27 feet (which had been proposed as part of a plan to develop additional hydroelectric power for metals smelting).

R. M. YOUNGER
Australian Free-Lance Writer

NIXON, RICHARD MILHOUS

In 1971, Richard Milhous Nixon exercised the powers of the presidency as never before in his three years in office. Critics who had written of his frustrations were confounded by the dramatic moves that gave him a posture as an action president. He could face an election year with new confidence reflected in the headlines and on the television screens.

The most dramatic surprise was his announcement on July 15 that he would visit Peking for a meeting with Premier Chou En-lai and Mao Tsetung. The White House had

President Nixon meets with President Georges Pompidou of France in a lovely Azores setting, where Nixon finally agrees to devalue the dollar.

managed to keep the preliminary negotiations carried out by the President's adviser on national security affairs, Henry A. Kissinger, in Peking so quiet that the announcement came as a shock. This was particularly true in Japan and elsewhere in Asia, and the President was accused of failing to inform his allies. But the reaction in the United States to the reversal of a twenty-year policy of isolating mainland China seemed on the whole favorable.

The second shock came with the President's televised statement on Aug. 15 of far-reaching

Another meeting is with German Chancellor Willy Brandt, at the Biscayne Bay White House.

changes in the nation's finance and economic policies. The dollar would no longer be convertible in gold, and to right the balance of payments a 10 per cent surcharge on all imports would be imposed. The President called on America's trading partners to revalue their currency so that the dollar would not be at a disadvantage.

The result was an intense controversy with Western European nations, Japan and Canada that continued through the closing months of the year. Despite repeated statements by Secretary of the Treasury John B. Connally that the dollar would not be devalued, Nixon did agree, in a meeting with President Georges Pompidou of France, in the Azores, to devalue the dollar. A subsequent session just before the year's end of the ten nations most directly involved in the financial tangle resulted in a detailed agreement whereby the price of gold was raised from $35 to $38 an ounce, in effect a devaluation of the dollar by 12 per cent when the changes in other currencies are taken into account.

The President called it the greatest financial transaction in the history of the world. From the administration came claims that seemed extravagant to some critics, notably that it would mean 500,000 new jobs. Skeptics believed that the beneficial effects of the agreement would be felt more slowly and that unemployment, running roughly at 6 per cent of the work force, would continue to trouble the administration in a political year.

On domestic issues, the President had less success. Welfare reform, and revenue sharing with the states and the cities, two of his important proposals, met with a lagging and a doubting Congress. Similarly, the promises the President had made in the campaign of 1968 to curb crime and reform the judicial system were frustrated as crime rates continued to climb, although at a slower rate than in the past. But with a White House staff of record size, spokesmen made generous claims for a triumphant year.

On his pledge to remake the Supreme Court of the United States, the President had good fortune in contrast with the Senate's refusal to confirm two previous nominees. Lewis F. Powell, Jr., a former president of the American Bar Association, was confirmed with only one dissenting vote. William H. Rehnquist, an assistant attorney general, encountered stiff opposition but was confirmed with 26 Senators voting in the negative. With four strict constructionists, in the President's definition, on the court, it seemed likely that before the end of his fourth year he would give the highest tribunal a new conservative direction.

As he flew from summit to summit in late December, Nixon promised in the new year to dominate the news media as few presidents in the television era have done. Yet his problems with the economy, in particular the enforcement of wage and price controls, highly unpopular with conservatives, remained the big question mark. Events had shaped the President's course and he had made decisions, as in the control of wages and prices, directly contrary to previous pronouncements. Nevertheless, as an activist President, he was also shaping events.

MARQUIS CHILDS
Contributing Editor
St. Louis Post-Dispatch
UPI

In still another 1971 "little summit," discussion is with British Prime Minister Edward Heath, in Bermuda.

Central Press

PEACE: WILLY BRANDT

West German Chancellor Brandt, 57, received the award for his efforts to bridge the gap between Western and Eastern Europe, extending "his hand to reconciliation between countries that have long been enemies." Forced into exile in Scandinavia by the Hitler regime, Brandt resumed German citizenship in 1947, distinguished himself as mayor of West Berlin 1957–66, and was elected chancellor of West Germany in 1969. Acting on his Ostpolitik (Eastern policy), he has negotiated a number of friendship pacts with East European nations, and signed the international treaty banning the spread of nuclear weapons.

UPI

PHYSICS: DENNIS GABOR

Hungarian-born Dr. Gabor (also forced to flee by Hitler), 71, received the award for his discovery of the basic principles of holography, a giant advance in optical science. In this process, by means of coherent light beams (laser light) and without a lens, an object can be recorded in its entirety—that is, in three dimensions, not merely the flat two dimensions of ordinary photographs. Engineer and inventor as well as physicist, Dr. Gabor is professor emeritus of applied electronic physics at the Imperial College of Science and Technology, London; and a staff scientist at CBS Laboratories in Stamford, Conn.

UPI

CHEMISTRY: GERHARD HERZBERG

Another of Hitler's gifts to the free world, German-born Canadian Dr. Herzberg, 66, of the National Research Council of Canada, earned the award "for his contributions to the knowledge of electronic structure and geometry of molecules, particularly free radicals." Free radicals are bits of molecules that react and combine easily with other molecules. Under his direction, his laboratory has become the world's foremost center for molecular spectroscopy; and his definitive three-volume *Molecular Spectra and Molecular Structure* is honored by chemists all over the world.

LITERATURE: PABLO NERUDA

Chilean diplomat (Ambassador to France from January 1971) and communist leader, Pablo Neruda, 67, was cited "for poetry that, with the action of an elemental force, brings alive a continent's destiny and dreams." Often compared to Walt Whitman, Neruda has long been considered Latin America's outstanding—and certainly most prolific—poetic genius. A railroad man's son, Neruda has had his work published since the age of 17. Many critics consider his three-volume *Residence on Earth* the greatest surrealist poetry in any language. Although many of his poems are political, his lyrical gift has been expressed in gentle love poems as well.

PHYSIOLOGY AND MEDICINE: EARL W. SUTHERLAND, JR.

Vanderbilt University (Nashville, Tenn.) Physiology Professor Sutherland, 55, was recognized "for his discoveries concerning the mechanisms of the action of hormones." For 25 years he has been conducting experiments that have opened up promising new research areas on how hormones influence the activities of cells. In 1956 he isolated cyclic AMP, or c-AMP (adenosine 3′, 5′-monophosphate); later research showed that it is the master molecule in the control of cellular metabolism. Today some 2,000 scientists are thought to be working on cyclic (meaning that it has a ring structure) AMP, which is implicated in various diseases, above all cancer.

MEMORIAL (ECONOMICS): SIMON S. KUZNETS

In awarding Russian-born Professor Emeritus Kuznets, 70, of Harvard University, the memorial prize, the Swedish Academy cited the economist for his "empirically founded interpretation of economic growth which has led to new and deepened insight into the economic and social structure and process of development." He is called the father of the concept of gross national product, a way of taking a country's economic pulse. The wide use of the method is attributed to his work, most of all to his massive two-volume *National Income and Its Composition, 1919 to 1938*.

NORTH ATLANTIC TREATY ORGANIZATION

The 22-year-old NATO, created in 1949 to stem the threat of a Soviet march across Western Europe and beyond, moved cautiously in late 1971 toward agreeing to cut back its forces if Moscow and its allies would do the same. The move toward "mutual and balanced force reductions" (MBFR) and related preparations for a European Security Conference (ESC) brought to the optimistic eye a vision of a new era of guaranteed peace with sharply trimmed defense budgets. More realistic observers saw much frustrating bargaining ahead, while admitting that significant first steps had been taken.

With evident signs of a *détente* in central Europe—the 1968 invasion of Czechoslovakia by the Russians was a fading consideration—Soviet and Western officials seemed for the first time seriously prepared respectively to consider reducing the 3,159,900 NATO troops, and cutting back the 2,090,500 men under arms in the Warsaw Pact countries, under Soviet control.

Two important considerations have dominated force-reduction thinking. The U.S.S.R. wanted to keep its front line with NATO cool and thinned out to leave more strength for its Eastern frontier area, where a Communist Chinese threat has been taking precedence over any possible trouble from the Washington-led NATO area. At the same time, such voices as that of Sen. Mike Mansfield (D-Mont.), Senate Democratic leader, were demanding sharp cutbacks in the 300,000 U.S. troops committed to NATO. The demand intensified with the Aug. 15 economic and monetary measures the United States took to improve its disastrous balance-of-payments position. Mansfield argued in September that "the trends in Europe are toward *détente*" and said the United States should cut back from its present four divisions in Europe to two, reduce its participation in the NATO command structure and withdraw some of its ships from the Sixth Fleet in the Mediterranean. Mansfield had earlier sought unsuccessfully to get a 50 per cent cutback in U.S. forces in European NATO countries.

With these considerations in the background, in October NATO decided to test in a practical way Soviet leader Leonid I. Brezhnev's May statement challenging the allies to "taste the wine" and start talks on force cutbacks. The NATO countries, with France in a familiar dissenting role, decided to dispatch freshly retired NATO Secretary General Manlio Brosio to Moscow. Brosio's mandate was to feel out the Russians on the possibilities of mutual force cutbacks on a step-by-step basis, first in central Europe.

To those who looked beyond the heady surface appearance of force reductions, the problem's complexities seemed enormous. The United States could well agree to withdraw to home base one man or one tank for every man or tank the Russians pulled back on Soviet soil. However, in the first case the distance covered would be some 3,000 miles, mostly over the Atlantic Ocean, while the Russian withdrawal would be only 200 or 300 miles, on land all the way. Soviet forces withdrawn from Eastern Europe would be in position for a quick return, while American forces pulled out would take days to return to Europe.

Thus the key word in force reduction discussion was "balanced" but what did it mean precisely: ten Russian soldiers for one American, for instance? Such problems might occupy Brosio and NATO ministers for months.

The veteran Italian diplomat gave up his job as secretary general of NATO on Oct. 2 after seven years in the post. He was succeeded by Joseph Luns, longtime Dutch foreign minister, who was expected to give the job a more dynamic style.

France, which remained a member of NATO's political structure after De Gaulle withdrew its forces from the integrated command, stood aside from the MBFR discussions and the decision to send Brosio to Moscow. The French argument was that bloc-to-bloc (NATO and Warsaw Pact) discussions were undesirable because they would tend to fix the existence of the two opposing forces and infringe on French sovereignty. More than anything, however, the French did not trust the Russians, in any eventual agreement, to reduce their forces effectively in Europe. The French continued to insist that the presence of U.S. forces in Europe was the best guarantee for *détente,* this despite the fact that De Gaulle had ordered American troops out of France and the NATO military command.

On the other hand, the French were pushing with the Russians on the idea—still in a formative stage—of a European Security Conference. They hoped it would bury the hatchet between East and West for good. With varying degrees of enthusiasm, France's allies appeared willing to go along with the idea of a conference. It would bring together thirty or more countries, including the United States, Canada and other NATO members, to discuss military security and further exchanges of persons, goods and ideas across the East-West barriers in place since the end of World War II.

UPI

NATO foreign ministers who met in June included (l to r): Joseph Luns (Netherlands), Andreas Cappelen (Norway), Rui Patricio (Portugal), Osman Olcay (Turkey), Sir Alec Douglas-Home (U.K.) and William Rogers.

France and the Soviet Union hoped that preparations for ESC could be completed by early 1972, with the conference itself held in Helsinki, Finland, at the end of that year. In the French view, a summit meeting of all participating countries could "crown the enterprise." The Western nations favoring ESC felt that the September 1971 Big Four agreement on Berlin-access problems would first have to be ratified by the two Germanys.

The alliance faced a minor crisis in the summer with the election of Dom Mintoff as premier of the fortress island country of Malta. Left-leaning Mintoff quickly made clear to NATO that it was no longer welcome. Mintoff ousted Italian Admiral Gino Birindelli, NATO's naval commander stationed on Malta, and NATO wrote off the island as an alliance base. Secretary General Brosio used the occasion to point out that NATO, unlike the Warsaw Pact, moved forces into countries only by invitation; when the welcome was no longer warm, out they went. In September, however, an agreement appeared to pave the way for continuing Western defense facilities on the longtime bastion, now particularly important because of the buildup of the Russian fleet in the Mediterranean.

At the opposite end of the NATO area, Iceland disturbed alliance officials in midyear when a coalition government, with two communist ministers, took over. At the end of 1971, Iceland remained in NATO.

Another, familiar theme was heard in the United States: Europeans must pay more of the bill for mutual defense. The United States has always believed that NATO's European members, particularly in periods of *détente,* have never faced up to their NATO commitments. The U.S. Senate Armed Services Committee noted in a report that the United States spends 8.6 per cent of its gross national product on military programs, compared with only 4.1 per cent by other NATO members.

The United States tried to maintain its commitment to NATO, reiterated at the December 1970 ministerial meeting in a message from President Nixon. He said there would be no cutback of U.S. forces "unless there is reciprocal action from our adversaries." One plan for attempting to do this, while still reducing the American balance-of-payments deficit, was the so-called "dual-basing" concept; that is, certain U.S. army and air force units committed to NATO would be rotated to Europe for periodic maneuvers. The plan received only lukewarm approval from military strategists who believe that there is no substitute for troops on the spot.

NATO's Supreme Allied Commander in Europe, Gen. Andrew J. Goodpaster, warned that Soviet military might was still growing despite the easing of strains between the Western and Eastern groups.

DAVID M. MASON
Correspondent, Paris Bureau
The Associated Press

NORWAY

The Cabinet changed in March, after Prime Minister Per Borten's Government resigned. It had included representatives of the Center Party, the Conservatives, the Liberals and the Christian People's Party. The crisis leading to the Borten Cabinet's downfall began on Feb. 26 when the Prime Minister admitted, after first denying it officially, that he had shown confidential papers concerning Norway's possible entry into the European Economic Community to a representative of an organization opposed to such entry.

The nonsocialist parties tried to form another coalition, to no avail. On Mar. 16, Trygve Bratteli, chairman of the Labor Party, was entrusted with forming an all-Labor minority Cabinet, based on Labor's 74 seats in the 150-member Storting (Parliament). The important post of foreign minister was given to Andreas Cappelen.

Local elections, for seats on the many councils that govern cities, towns and rural communities, were held on Sept. 19–20. The Center Party (formerly the Agrarians) and the Christian People's Party, a minor party, made some gains. The other four parties, Conservative, Labor, Liberal and Socialist People's, suffered setbacks in many local councils.

A daughter, their first child, was born on Sept. 22 to Crown Prince Harald and Crown Princess Sonja, and was baptized Märtha Louise. Since its adoption in 1814 the Norwegian constitution has specified that only males may succeed to the throne of Norway. Today, however, some sentiment is growing

UPI

Labor Party head Trygve Bratteli waves after being asked to form new Government Mar. 10.

for an amendment that would allow Norway, like Great Britain, Denmark and the Netherlands, to have a female monarch.

Possible entry into the European Economic Community (Common Market) was widely dis-

UPI

A new Norwegian princess makes her first public appearance: Princess Martha Louise, born Sept. 22, is held by her beaming parents, Crown Prince Harald and Crown Princess Sonja.

cussed. Norwegian voters, even within the Labor Party as well as the Center Party, which had taken the initiative in opening negotiations with the EEC, were deeply divided. On June 17 the Storting decided by a 113–37 vote to continue such negotiations. Since the Opposition (in 1971 at least) commanded only one vote less than the number needed to bar Norwegian membership, it is likely that the final decision will be made not only by the Storting but also by a consultative popular referendum. However, Norway's special need to protect its fisheries and agriculture from severe foreign competition created a snag. Great Britain's decision in October to seek membership in the EEC had buoyed the hopes of those who believe that EEC membership will benefit the Norwegian economy. But on Dec. 12, Norway refused to accept the market's fisheries policy, which guarantees free access by all EEC members to the EEC'c coastal waters, for ten years.

Tonsberg, Norway's oldest city, celebrated its 1,100th anniversary in 1971. On the Oslo Fjord, Tonsberg was founded a year before King Harald the Fairhair, in A.D. 872, became the first king of a united Norwegian realm. The city's population today is about 12,000.

Among the social advances adopted during 1971 was a law that gives two-week vacations to all farmers owning at least 2.5 acres of cultivated land. Each farmer and his wife will receive 1,000 kroner for vacation purposes, but only if the vacation is actually taken.

ERIK J. FRIIS
Editor, *The American-Scandinavian Review*

NUTRITION

The importance of a proper diet for good health and physical, perhaps even mental, development is only now beginning to be understood by those in the health sciences. This is true because only in recent years have most people on earth begun to live long enough to suffer from nutritional disorders. As a result of the lifesaving chemotherapeutic drugs, antibiotics and the vaccines, many more people reach adulthood and live to old age. Since the effects of poor nutrition on the human body develop very slowly, unless they are the result of acute deprivation, the sequelae of poor nutrition are rarely apparent until adulthood. Of course, the effects of acute malnutrition are readily apparent at any age.

There are few better examples of acute malnutrition in the world today than the blindness one can observe in four- and five-year-old children in the Middle East. It is caused by the nearly total absence of vitamin A in their diet. Poor nutrition is now regarded as the reason for the fact that in the developing countries most blind persons are children. In the developed countries, blindness occurs most frequently after age 45; whether it is associated with nutrition then we do not know. This, however, clearly illustrates the first principle of nutrition that more and more physicians accepted in 1971: the greater the body's need for a foodstuff, the more consequential will be the results of its lack.

Although the National Nutrition Survey was halted before it was completed in 1971, enough was done to show that most malnutrition suffered in the United States works subtly, with consequences that will probably be made manifest only in years to come.

In 1971, medical scientists made several important discoveries that represent advances in scientific nutrition. Foremost among them were the results of research on the important role that tiny, trace amounts of minerals are now believed to play in the nutritive quality of food. There is evidence that unless the diet includes small amounts of zinc, amounts measured in one hundredths or one thousandths of a gram, growth in youth can be stunted. There is new evidence that too much selenium causes nervous diseases, but no selenium at all slows recovery from disease. There is evidence that chrome, never considered of dietary importance before, may indeed be very necessary for good nutritional health. Since these trace minerals are not found in all foods, the first essential element for good nutrition is variety.

Statistics show that overweight people are more vulnerable to high blood pressure, diabetes, heart disease. Yet it is not easy for many people to keep their weight down. Although fad diets come and go, no one has yet designed a dietary regimen guaranteed to keep a person slender. In 1971, medical scientists gained new knowledge about the way the cells develop in fat people. According to these discoveries, each of us seems to have been born with a different number of cells that store fat. Some people have more of these cells than others, and they are almost certain to become fat. Such individuals must exert strong control over the amount of food they eat. Others may eat as much as they like and never gain weight. If the new concept of fat-storing cells proves true, we will have made real progress in the battle against obesity.

The Epidemiological Investigation of Cardiovascular Disease, the Framingham Study, was completed in 1971. The National Institutes of Health began the study in 1949 in Framingham, Mass. It is considered the most thorough study of the causes of heart disease ever undertaken. The Framingham scientists found five factors to be equally important in causing mankind's greatest killer disease, hardening of the arteries (atherosclerosis). The factors were too many calories and saturated fats, too high blood pressure, too little exercise, too much sugar and too many cigarettes. Any one of the factors would make it more likely for a person to develop atherosclerosis, which leads to heart disease, but it is the combination of these factors that is most important.

The study's major conclusions, however, did not satisfy many scientists. Some still maintained that other studies had proved that faulty diet (too much animal fat) is either the sole or the primary cause of hardening of the arteries. It is obvious that the average Western man's food habits, his lack of exercise and liking for sweetstuffs and cigarettes all play important roles in his physical health. Although he may be aware that his habits may lead to disease, it can prove extremely difficult to throw off ingrained ones.

Even as the Framingham Study was being published, confirmatory reports for its findings came from the South Pacific and the Arctic. They showed that both the Maori (the Polynesians of New Zealand) and the Eskimos of the far north are beginning to suffer from arthritis, heart trouble, diabetes, obesity and high blood pressure as they take on the eating habits of modern man. As a result, the U.S. Government has become more concerned than ever before with the quality of human food.

The Food and Drug Administration has begun studies that may lead to the labeling of the nutritional content of all foods. The regulatory authorities are giving closer attention to nutritional adequacy. To make certain that schoolchildren would get all the food they need, the School Lunch Program was launched in 1946, under the Department of Agriculture. On the twenty-fifth anniversary of the program, it was announced that over 7,400,000 children were receiving part or all of their luncheons without charge. This was a dramatic increase

over the 5,200,000 and the 3,000,000 children who received such lunches in 1970 and 1969 respectively. Nevertheless, all schools do not yet have a lunch program, and a concerted campaign is under way to launch a program so that lunches will be available to all children. Nutrition experts say that a good lunch at school is essential.

CORTEZ F. ENLOE, JR., M.D.
Editor and Publisher, *Nutrition Today*

OCEANIA

For the island peoples of the South Pacific, the pace of self-expression continued to quicken, and the islanders showed a clear determination to strengthen existing institutions and to buttress recent economic and social gains. A contentious issue was the French Government's decision to proceed with nuclear tests at Mururoa, in French Polynesia, in 1971.

A forum of island leaders was held (in Wellington, New Zealand) in August when the prime ministers of the four independent states —Fiji, Nauru, Western Samoa and Tonga—and the self-governing Cook Islands met, together with New Zealand's Prime Minister and the Australian Minister for External Territories, to discuss trade, shipping, tourism and education. Fiji undertook to seek ways to "represent" the other three island-states in world counsels.

Economic and Social Progress. Significant overall improvement was indicated by the growing number of trained and skilled islanders in such fields as education, social sciences, health education, social welfare needs and planning, beekeeping, care of agricultural machinery, and the use of coconut-plantation pastures for raising cattle. Common interests included protection of the environment, development of tourism, prospects for attracting capital from abroad, development of mineral resources and ocean resources, and finding employment for young people as they complete school.

At the South Pacific Conference, held in Noumea in September, Chairman Oala Oala-Rarua, a member of the PNG House of Assembly, summing up prevailing views, said the island states look to the South Pacific Commission to play a significant role in helping development at a time when the Pacific peoples are progressing very rapidly toward modernization; it nevertheless is important to preserve worthwhile values rather than to replace them with what the island peoples find "strange and totally foreign." Frederick Betham, of Western Samoa, was elected the commission's secretary-general. A U.S.$1,300,000 program for the year was approved by the commission.

Moving toward self-government, Papua New Guinea adopts a flag: the Southern Cross in white on a black ground, and a bird of paradise in gold on a scarlet ground—the four colors most often used in the art of the area.

"The Sydney Morning Herald," Australia

Fiji. Inflationary pressures aroused concern. Following a strike, dockers' wages rose 30 per cent. Sharply expanded receipts from tourism, however, dampened fears of a recession (especially in the sugar industry); negotiations were begun on how the sale of Fiji's sugar will be handled after Britain enters the Common Market.

A new spirit of conciliation between Fijians and Indians was evident. Reflecting tougher attitudes among Fijians on wage issues, the dock strike spurred discussion about the political future of all low-wage groups. A sense of interracial harmony has been nurtured by Prime Minister Ratu Sir Kamisese Mara. In Parliament, the (largely Indian) Opposition members showed less bitterness and more confidence.

Papua New Guinea. A change of title from the Territory of Papua-New Guinea to Papua New Guinea and the adoption of a flag and coat of arms at midyear heralded a new stage toward national status. In July the assembly passed a Bill of Rights and called for the complete unification of Papua and New Guinea, abolishing the "border." It was recommended that PNG prepare for self-government during the 1972–76 Parliament (to be elected in February/March 1972). The Australian Government accepted that target date.

Meanwhile, PNG's economic base was steadily widening. The inflow of private investment capital, including the Bougainville copper project, was running at over $100,000,000 a year. Exports rose about 10 per cent during the year. Australia secured EEC approval for preferential tariffs on manufactured products from PNG but there was no comparable concession on the more significant matter of agricultural exports. At Cape Hoskins, on New Britain, a $14,000,000 oil-palm project (backed by the administration and an English company) was opened. It was the most important agricultural development since the first coffee plantings of 25 years before, since oil-palm exports are expected to earn substantial income within 5 years.

New Hebrides. The Anglo-French Condominium took definite steps to expand the tourist inflow, and with New Caledonia and Papua New Guinea set up a Melanesian Tourist Federation. To benefit from the Condominium's "tax haven" status, more international companies registered in Vila (New Hebrides capital), and a second Australian bank and other financial institutions opened offices. During 1971 the total of such "foreign" registrations passed the 500 mark.

Niue. One of the South Pacific's last remaining islands-in-isolation joined the air age when the first commercial flight was made from Suva (Fiji) into Niue, a 100-square-mile coral atoll 300 miles east of Tonga, inaugurating a weekly service. It is hoped that the weekly prop-jet service will attract tourists.

R. M. YOUNGER
Australian Free-Lance Writer

OCEANOGRAPHY

Attempts to explore, to study, to exploit and to protect the oceans are making us increasingly aware of their importance.

The Ocean Surface. Winds, as they move over the oceans, set the upper layers of water in motion. The water circulates vertically in units called convection, or Langmuir, cells. Such cells were thought to be some 20 feet in depth. Then, in May 1971, Columbia University scientists reported that they are up to 900 feet deep.

This indicates that the mixture of surface water with deep water occurs much more rapidly than had been supposed. "We find that surface layer turbulence of ocean water is not as random as previously believed," reported Dr. Arnold L. Gordon. "This is relevant to pollution studies. The surface level of the ocean bears the brunt of man-made pollution, either intentional or inadvertent. We should know how pollution spreads and how fast it might be diluted."

Winds of only six miles per hour are strong enough to set up convection cells. The life of a cell depends on the wind. "The cells decay quickly when the wind dies, and appear quickly when the wind picks up," said Dr. Gordon.

The Ocean Floor. New evidence continues to indicate the comparatively young age of the ocean floor and to support the theories of sea-floor spreading and plate tectonics. Much of this evidence, and other important information about the sediment, is being gathered by researchers aboard the Deep Sea Drilling Project's ship, the *Glomar Challenger.*

Scientists on the 15th segment, or leg, of the project found that the Caribbean is not as old as geologists had believed. The oldest sediments contained fossils of plants and animals that lived 75,000,000 to 85,000,000 years ago. (In comparison, the oldest part of the North Atlantic is about 180,000,000 years old; the oldest continental area is about 3,500,000,000 years old.)

Leg 16 findings supported a recent hypothesis on the formation of the Isthmus of Panama. At one time a deep trench existed near the western edge of what is today the isthmus. It was an extension of the trench that presently extends along the western coast of North and Central America. The hypothesis, developed by scientists at Oregon State and Columbia universities, suggests that some 10,000,000 to 15,-000,000 years ago an ocean ridge extended eastward from the present site of the Galapagos Islands. The ridge split lengthwise; the northern piece broke into several smaller pieces that slowly moved northward in response to thermal currents deep within the earth. When they reached the deep trench, they filled it. This cramming of materials into the trench caused the crustal plate on the eastern side of the trench to rise above sea level. The elevated ocean floor became the Isthmus of Panama and the southeastern part of Costa Rica. The process continues today; parts of Costa Rica are still rising and in another 10,000,000 years Acapulco, Mexico, now at sea level, may have an elevation of 1,000 feet.

Extensive crustal movement was also noted by Leg 17 scientists. Evidence indicates that the Central Pacific floor has moved 1,800 miles northward during the last 100,000,000 years.

Deep-sea trenches are places where one crustal plate is moving against and under another plate. The convergence and underthrusting cause deformation of the sediment layers that cover the ocean floor. This was proved by Leg 18 scientists along the continental margin from Oregon to Alaska, where the Pacific Ocean crust is moving under the North American continent. Core samples contained sediments that are compact, hard and very deformed.

The first drilling and coring of the Bering Sea floor was done during Leg 19. Investigators hoped to learn how the origin and history of such marginal seas differs from that of the open oceans.

Funded by the National Science Foundation, the project was originally to last 18 months. In October 1969 it was extended through June 1973. Now chances are excellent that another extension will be granted. This would enable extensive coring in the Arctic and Antarctic.

Man and the Sea. "The real value of the new impetus for ocean exploration is that we are striving to make major use of the oceans beyond their traditional functions as a highway for commerce, as a military-defense advantage, and for fishing," said Dr. Paul F. Frye, Woods Hole Oceanographic Institution president. Many nations are turning to the oceans for the rich mineral resources they know, or suspect, are there. There is a growing awareness of the need to direct and regulate the development of oceanic resources in a manner that is fair to all nations. Realizing this need, the UN General Assembly decided "to convene in 1973 . . . a Conference on the Law of the Sea."

In February 1971, 67 nations signed the Treaty on the Prohibition of the Emplacement of Nuclear Weapons and Other Weapons of Mass Destruction on the Seabed and the Ocean Floor and in the Subsoil Thereof.

JENNY TESAR
Senior Editor, *The Book of Popular Science*
and *Encyclopedia Science Supplement*

PAKISTAN

The year 1971 was one of tragedy for Pakistan. Already divided geographically, the nation was split politically and a new nation, Bangladesh, was born.

The fateful year began with East Pakistan, a place of perpetual tragedy separated from West Pakistan by more than 1,000 miles of Indian territory, recovering from one of history's most devastating natural disasters. In November 1970 a cyclone-spawned tidal wave had swept over the low-lying and heavily populated coastal plain on the Bay of Bengal, destroying thousands of homes and killing an estimated 300,000 people or more.

In spite of the disaster, the Pakistani Government went ahead with elections (after postponing them once in October) in December 1970, and thus set the stage for the tragic developments of 1971. East Pakistan's Awami League, under the leadership of Sheikh Mujibur Rahman, won 167 seats in the 313-seat National Assembly, campaigning on a platform of autonomy for the East. The stunning victory of the Awami League, which would give it a majority in the National Assembly, caused deep concern in West Pakistan. The central Government was located there, and its leaders had controlled Pakistan since the nation's birth in the 1947 partition of British India.

The Pakistan People's Party, led by former Foreign Minister Zulfikar Ali Bhutto, won the bulk of the seats in the Western wing, creating a situation in which the two major parties had purely regional representation. President Yahya Khan, a military man who had promised to restore constitutional government when he took office in 1969, urged Bhutto and Rahman to work out a suitable compromise on framing a new constitution that would provide stable government for the entire nation. Bhutto and Rahman could not agree.

On Feb. 13, Yahya announced that the National Assembly would meet in Dacca, capital of East Pakistan, on Mar. 3. Two days later, however, Bhutto said his party would not attend the scheduled Assembly session unless there was some assurance of "some amount of reciprocity from the majority party." A week later, Rahman replied that his Awami League majority would "go it alone and frame the constitution" if the West Pakistan politicians refused to participate in the session.

On Mar. 1, Yahya postponed the convening of the Assembly until an indefinite later date to give the civilian politicians time to come to an understanding. In doing so, Yahya pledged that his intention of transferring power to civilian rule remained firm. On Mar. 3, he invited 12 leaders of parliamentary groups in the National Assembly to meet in Dacca on Mar. 10 in an effort to resolve the crisis. Rahman rejected the invitation.

Yahya announced on Mar. 5 that the inaugural session of the National Assembly would be held on Mar. 25 and warned that his patience was wearing thin. On Mar. 7, Rahman put forth four demands to be met before his Awami League would agree to attend the Mar. 25 session. The demands included immediate lifting of martial law and immediate transfer of power to the elected representatives before the Assembly session.

On Mar. 15, Yahya flew to Dacca for talks with Rahman. At the same time, the Awami League and its supporters were moving to assert their power, virtually taking control of East Pakistan. There was some violence as anti-West Pakistan fever spread throughout the East wing. A week later, Bhutto arrived in Dacca to join the meetings at Yahya's request.

At the end of the meeting, Yahya rescinded his order for the Mar. 25 convening of the National Assembly and suggested that it be convened on Apr. 2. Rahman rejected this. Subsequent meetings produced no progress; and on Mar. 25, Yahya suddenly left East Pakistan.

Asserting that the Awami League was planning an armed uprising to secede from and break up the country, the Army moved against the Awami League and its Bangladesh supporters in the early morning hours of Mar. 26. The Army also accused India of fanning the flames of dis-

	WEST PAKISTAN	EAST PAKISTAN (BANGLADESH)
AREA	310,403 square miles	55,126 square miles
POPULATION	55,000,000	77,000,000 (incl. est. 10,000,000 who fled)
GROSS NATIONAL PRODUCT	$12,000,000,000	$6,000,000,000
PER CAPITA INCOME	$130 (est.)	$77 (est.)
RELIGION	99 per cent Muslim	89 per cent Muslim
CAPITAL	Islamabad	Dacca

Pakistani refugees are air-lifted by a Russian plane from densely crowded Calcutta to a refugee camp farther away from India's border.

Sheik Mujibur Rahman enjoys his pipe a few days before his arrest. Popularly called "Mujib," he tried to win greater self-government for East Pakistan.

content in East Pakistan. Consisting primarily of West Pakistanis, the Army moved swiftly, and ruthlessly. Rahman was arrested and taken to West Pakistan. Thousands died in the fighting that followed. This touched off a massive flow of refugees—mainly Bengali Hindus—to India.

Indian political leaders, ranging from Prime Minister Mrs. Indira Gandhi down, expressed sympathy and support for the Bangladesh elements, and on Apr. 13 a rebel Bangladesh government was formally proclaimed in Calcutta by rebel leaders who had fled to that Indian city. India, strongly supported by the Soviet Union, helped arm and train the Bangladesh rebel forces and gave covert military help in raids along the East Pakistan border during the ensuing months. The size and scope of these Indian-supported guerrilla-type operations increased gradually.

After the crushing move by the Army in East Pakistan, Yahya tried to move ahead on the political front. On June 28, he outlined a plan for a new draft constitution and to hold by-elections for the seats of the Awami League, which had been outlawed. He renewed his promise of "transfer of power to the people" but said martial law would continue.

The clouds of war grew darker with the increasing flow of refugees from East Pakistan, the serious economic drain on India's scarce resources, and the stepped-up activities of the Bangladesh rebel forces along the India-East Pakistan border. On Aug. 9 India and the Soviet Union signed a friendship and cooperation treaty including clauses that gave it the appearance of a military pact as well. From then on, India's support of the Bangladesh rebels movement became more overt and stronger.

In West Pakistan, Rahman went on trial for treason. At the same time, the Government announced that 88 members of the outlawed Awami League in East Pakistan would be permitted to retain their seats in the National Assembly and others would be given an opportunity to clear themselves of criminal charges.

On Sept. 1, Yahya appointed Dr. Abdul Motaleb Malik, a veteran civil servant, as gov-

The very young, the old and the ill huddle in a camp. As the refugee flood rose to 10,000,000, thousands a week died of malnutrition, exposure or disease (mainly cholera).

Peter Carmichael, Transworld Feature Syndicate Inc.

ernor of East Pakistan, replacing Army Lt. Gen. Tikka Khan, who had taken over as acting governor and martial-law administrator after the fighting broke out in the East in March. Replacing Tikka Khan as martial-law administrator in the East was Lt. Gen. Amir Abdullah Khan Niazi.

In early August, the Pakistani Government issued a 125-page white paper on the events in East Pakistan that had led up to the Army crackdown in March. The white paper accused the Awami League and Rahman of plotting an "armed rebellion" and a "secessionist bid to break up the country."

On Sept. 19, the Calcutta-based rebel Bangladesh government announced formation of a multiparty National Liberation Front and said this was aimed at expanding "the struggle for independence" in East Pakistan. Included in the National Front were representatives of the Awami League, the pro-Russian Communist Party of Pakistan, two factions of the National Awami Party, and the Pakistan Congress Party.

During the first two weeks of October, both India and Pakistan strengthened their defenses along both the East and West Pakistan borders.

On Oct. 12, Yahya announced that the reorganized National Assembly would meet on Dec. 27 following promulgation of a new constitution to be drafted under his direction. But he severely limited its powers in advance.

On Sept. 18, a new cabinet was sworn in under Malik in East Pakistan in the first step toward the return of civilian government in the East since the March civil war had broken out.

By the end of October it was clear that if the by-elections Yahya had scheduled for East Pakistan were held, they would be little more than a farce.

In mid-November, seven minor right-wing parties joined to form a United Party under the leadership of Nurul Amin an East Pakistani politician and head of the Pakistan Democratic Party. He insisted that an East Pakistani should be made prime minister of the country.

While the political jockeying was continuing in Pakistan, Indian military activity along the East Pakistan border became bolder. On Nov. 23, Pakistan declared a state of emergency, accusing India of launching major attacks inside East Pakistan.

Full-scale war came on the night of Dec. 3. Indian troops drove into East Pakistan in strength, and an Indian Government spokesman declared, "no holds are barred in East Pakistan." Pakistan responded with a series of air strikes against Indian air bases, and fighting then flared along the border of India and West Pakistan as well. Pakistan found itself in the impossible posi-

tion of trying to defend its Western wing and still hold the Eastern half of the country more than 1,000 miles away, supply routes to which were more than 3,000 miles long.

Once the fighting escalated into open warfare, the end came quickly for Pakistan. India ignored a United Nations resolution calling for a cease-fire and drove quickly toward Dacca. The UN resolution was adopted overwhelmingly by the General Assembly after the Soviet Union had vetoed similar resolutions in the Security Council. Pakistan accepted the UN General Assembly resolution, but India made it clear that it would not do so until East Pakistan was under its control. Indian troops took Dacca on Dec. 16 and accepted the unconditional surrender of West Pakistani forces, a total of 93,000 troops, at a racetrack.

With a military victory, and the Bangladesh government, now formally recognized by India, installed in East Pakistan, India agreed to a cease-fire on the West Pakistan border. An uneasy truce prevailed at year's end.

Following on the truce there were dramatic political developments in West Pakistan. Bhutto, who had presented Pakistan's case at the United Nations, was summoned home to take over the presidency from Yahya, who resigned. Bhutto also became martial-law administrator. He was the first civilian ruler the country had had in more than 13 years.

Feeling ran high against Yahya for the humiliating defeat suffered in the 14-day war, and demonstrations began against him in many cities. The demonstrators also attacked Soviet buildings because of Russian support of India. Bhutto moved swiftly, surely and dramatically. He retired many other generals along with Yahya, put some under arrest and talked of bringing some of them to trial for the tragedy they had brought to the nation.

With the nation's economy severely damaged by the war and the loss of East Pakistan's jute earnings as well as other dollar-producing products, Bhutto also moved on the economic front. He tightened foreign-exchange controls and ordered the nation's rich families to bring back money they had banked abroad. He fired military men from important economic posts and nationalized almost a dozen basic industries as well as banks.

He released Rahman from prison and held a series of talks with the East Pakistani leader before permitting him to leave the West and return, by way of London, to Dacca. There the Sheikh received a tumultuous hero's welcome as the new year, 1972, dawned.

ARTHUR C. MILLER
Senior Editor, *The Asia Letter*

PARKS

A significant change in philosophy and policy in the administration of the U.S. National Park Service became apparent during 1971. Concern for the needs of people has finally been established as an accepted goal of the service, along with its traditional role as conservator of natural resources and historic sites.

The change in philosophy, first called for by President Nixon in 1969, was implemented by then Secretary of the Interior Walter J. Hickel. He added two more principal goals: a "Parks to People" program to be carried out "by means of new and existing parks, recreation areas, and projects near urban centers"; and a program that would emphasize "the educational and inspirational values that make parks an effective instrument for promoting social cohesion and community understanding."

Secretary of the Interior Rogers C. B. Morton has advanced this thrust even further in his "Guidelines for a Second Century of National Parks." Among other things, he calls for more parks where people need them—in and near large urban complexes; study of transportation and accommodation costs with the aim of greater use of the parks by all economic groups; development of cultural parks; expansion of the "Parks for All Seasons" program launched in Washington, D.C.; special emphasis on recruiting and training rangers to cope with the problems visitors create in the parks.

People and national parks are not necessarily compatible. As George B. Hartzog, Jr., director of the National Park Service, points out, there is a built-in contradiction in the mandate to his agency to provide for both "use" and "preservation."

The 202,000,000 visitors to U.S. national parks in 1971 represent over 6 times as many people in the parks as there were 20 years before. This resulted in serious overuse of park areas, and aggravated traffic congestion, safety hazards, crime, vandalism and destruction of the natural resources that make the parks attractive in the first place.

Through changes in both regulations and traditional practices, some solutions to these

The red-cedar auditorium of Wolf Trap Farm Park, in the Virginia countryside near Washington, D.C., glows in the light of the setting sun.

Kluane Game Sanctuary in Yukon's majestic St. Elias Mountains (North America's highest range) is slated to become part of a new Canadian park.

Dept. of the Interior, Australia

Some 11,500 acres 25 miles southwest of Canberra are being developed as Tidbinbilla Nature Reserve, to protect Australia's remarkable fauna.

Foaming surf etches the forested shore of Canada's Pacific Rim National Park recently created on the west coast of Vancouver Island, B.C.

British Columbia Govt.

Visitors pause before ruins of old mansions on wild, lush Cumberland Island, off Georgia's coast, most of which is to become a National Seashore.

problems are being effected. The Park Service continues to acquire sites suitable for national parks near large urban centers. One example is Gateway National Park, which may soon be serving the needs of metropolitan New York. Planning includes provision for mass public transportation to ensure easy accessibility.

The first cultural park in the U.S. National Park System, Wolf Trap Farm Park, near Washington, D.C., was dedicated in July 1971. It is unique both as the first national park for the performing arts and because the 100-acre farm and the money ($2,000,000) for building the auditorium, Filene Center, were a gift of a private art patron, Mrs. Jouett Shouse. The park will also help to develop new talent; some 800 high-school and college students, on scholarships, attended the first 8-week summer workshop in 1971.

Another new program came into its own in 1971 with the expansion to urban units of the National Park Service in Richmond, Va., and St. Louis, Mo., of the "Summer in the Parks" activity in the national capital. The "laughing tree" symbol, representing recreation programs, could be seen everywhere in the Washington, D.C., area from Wolf Trap Farm to the parks in the Virginia and Maryland countryside. The symbol drew attention to art exhibits and folk festivals on the Ellipse, to noontime programs in the city's plazas, to the *Wood Duck,* a converted Army riverboat that daily plied the

Potomac with a cargo of inner-city youngsters on their first boating excursion. Designed as a model for use in other urban areas, "Summer in the Parks" was a long step upward from traditional concepts, and its success led to the establishment of the "Parks for All Seasons" program.

A Panel on National Parks, with delegates from Japan and the United States, held its fifth meeting in 1971. The director of the National Parks of Canada attends these meetings as an unofficial observer.

The problems of traffic congestion and overuse are not unique to U.S. parks. Populous nations like Japan, England, Germany and France are faced with the same issues, and their solutions are similar. They also have certain trends in common, such as the establishment of marine parks. John Pennekamps Coral Reef Preserve in Florida for underwater exploration is being copied by many nations.

It is appropriate that in 1972, the centennial of the world's first national park, Yellowstone, the Second World Conference on National Parks will be held there and in the Grand Tetons. Of 126 nations reporting on 1,204 national parks or equivalent reserves, nearly 90 will be represented at the conference, an indication of the great interest in national-park development everywhere.

SIDNEY G. LUTZIN
Editor, *Parks & Recreation* Magazine

A restored "African Queen" plies the Deschutes River, Oregon; the doughty little boat carried Katharine Hepburn and Humphrey Bogart on a perilous journey in the great 1951 motion picture of the same name.

PEOPLE, PLACES AND THINGS

Bishop Senuda, an Egyptian priest, becomes 117th pope of the Coptic Church, which embraces the largest Christian minority in the Arab world.

Trixie received the 1971 Ken-L Ration gold medal as the dog of the year for rescuing her two-year-old master, Ricky Sherry, from a pond.

The first black admiral in the history of the U.S. Navy, Samuel L. Gravely, Jr., stepped up from the rank of captain, in command of the missile frigate USS "Jouett," here in Fremantle, Australia.

"London Daily Express"

Carousel for your backyard? After Palisades Amusement Park land is sold, the glittering, 62-horse, 43-year-old merry-go-round is put on the block.

Palisades Amusement Park

Morton Broffman

Paul N. McCloskey, Jr., California Republican and congressman, muses below a map of Indochina. He had announced his candidacy for president, thereby challenging President Nixon.

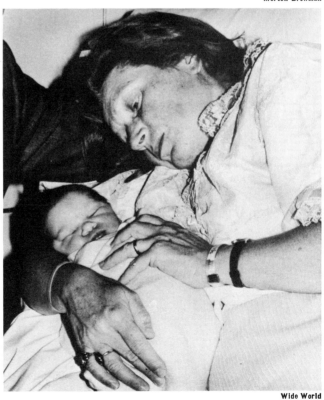

A grandchild, Olga, of Stalin's is born an American citizen, on May 21, near San Francisco. The baby's parents are Stalin's daughter, Svetlana, and her American husband, Wesley Peters.

Wide World

Ralph E. Collins, senior career diplomat and Canada's first ambassador to the Peking Government, was born in China, the son of missionaries, and learned to speak Chinese during his childhood there.

A Choctaw Indian, Wilma L. Victor, is chosen special assistant for Indian affairs to U.S. Secretary of the Interior Rogers C. B. Morton.

Black lawyer Patricia R. Harris achieves 1971 distinction as Credentials Committee head for 1972 Democratic convention, and a director of IBM.

Dr. Leon Sullivan, Baptist clergyman, is first black man to be elected to board of directors of the General Motors Corporation.

349

PHILIPPINE REPUBLIC

The political grip of President Ferdinand Marcos was substantially challenged in 1971, amid repeated charges that he sought to perpetuate himself in office unconstitutionally.

Politics. Off-year elections were unusually violent. A record 200 persons died in incidents related to the November senatorial and local balloting. Nine deaths occurred in August at the opening Manila rally of the opposition Liberal Party when a grenade attack also wounded 96 persons (including all 8 Liberal Senate candidates). President Marcos subsequently suspended habeas corpus and authorized the police to hold suspects without being charged, provoking demonstrations and further violence.

The November voting was a rejection of the President's leadership, the Liberals winning six of eight contested seats. Liberals also scored strong victories in such major cities as Manila, Cebu and Quezon City.

The Nacionalista defeat clouded the issue of whether Marcos would seek to serve beyond his current second term (the constitution prohibiting a third term). A sitting constitutional convention could change the basic law, however, and the President publicly speculated that his wife, Imelda, might run to succeed him.

Insurrections. Marcos stated in January that the

PHILIPPINE REPUBLIC
Area: 11,830 sq. mi.
Population: 39,400,000
Capital: Quezon City
Government: Ferdinand E. Marcos, president—1965
Gross National Product: $8,545,000,000
Foreign Trade: exports, $1,067,000,000; imports, $1,210,000,000
Armed forces: 33,000

Government had broken the back of the communist insurgency. But before the year ended, he was confronted by new violence instigated by communal as well as communist elements. Marcos blamed the Maoist "New People's Army" for the August attack at the Manila Liberal Party rally.

No more than four hundred armed communist insurgents roamed the country, most of these (in the "New People's Army") in the northern Luzon province of Isabella. Some remnants of the Huk rebels of the 1950's were still active near Angeles City (near U.S. Clark Air Force Base). Communist-inspired incidents increased during the year, but clashes with government forces were infrequent.

More deadly was the fighting in the southern provinces of Cotabato and Lanao del Norte on the island of Mindanao, where Muslims fought both Christians and government troops. More than 1,200 persons were killed during the year, and another 100,000 fled from the countryside to the cities.

Foreign Affairs. U.S. moves to moderate differences with Communist China surprised the Philippines and increased official and public questioning of the value of U.S.-Filipino defense and other ties. Talks between the two governments on U.S. bases in the country were begun and were expected to decrease the American military presence in the islands.

President Marcos announced on Dec. 15 that the Government had decided to establish formal diplomatic and trade relations with some (unnamed) Eastern European countries, broken for 25 years.

Economy. The economy continued to make limited progress, about 5 per cent in terms of the national growth rate in 1971, as restrictions on spending and borrowing, inaugurated the previous year, remained in effect. Unemployment was about 8 per cent (with another 25 per cent of the working-age population underemployed). Exports were strong.

RICHARD BUTWELL
Chairman, Department of Political Science
State University of New York College
at Brockport

Claiming that the rifle had been given to the Communists, President Marcos invokes emergency security measures to combat threatened terrorism.

UPI

PHOTOGRAPHY

Judging by the number of cameras hanging from the necks of people from 7 to 70 plus in parks, at resorts and in public generally, and by the crowds in camera stores, it is safe to assume that photography is at a peak as today's personal, mass folk art. In fact, the use of a camera is becoming the sign of a new sort of literacy. In spite of this, the year 1971 saw no auspicious advances in the understanding of photography, either artistic or technical, or in new and exciting equipment.

Although the number of photography shows and exclusively photographic galleries increased during the year, no new insights about the medium were revealed. New trends are generally instantly recognizable, but it takes time, discernment and judgment to pinpoint the features that will prove most valid and lasting. What is more important, however, is that a new critical language about photography is needed. In judging photography one cannot depend exclusively on the criteria that apply to the older forms of art, although, of course, there are overlapping esthetic areas.

Of the few important shows held in 1971, the most ambitious was the W. Eugene Smith Show at the Jewish Museum in New York City, Feb. 3–May 9. It consisted of over five hundred prints, the work of one man. It revealed what most of us already knew: that photography is a craft requiring great technical competence. More important, it is a craft that can reveal the compassion and sympathy inherent in humane human beings in a way that no other medium has ever attempted. At The Museum of Modern Art in New York City, the old and well-tried shows of Walker Evans' work and an exhibit of the photography of Clarence H. White were the outstanding events of the year. The latter show revived a style associated with photography at the turn of the century. It is a style rather closely attuned to the sentimental painting of that era. Nevertheless, in keeping with the taste of that time, the pictures exhibited a pleasant charm. A feature of the prints is that the image is in platinum rather than silver, which is used in conventional photographic paper. Platinum images are said to be more fade-proof. In addition, it is believed that the brownish image encompasses a greater and more subtle tonal range than the best silver-image photographic paper. Another feature was the ability to coat "artistic" drawing paper, or even on silk, with the sensitive material.

In other quarters too, platinum and some of the older pictorial processes sparked new interest. A course in platinum printing was taught

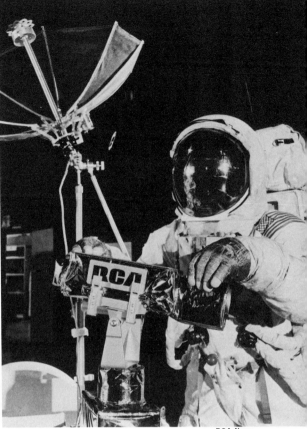

RCA News

Mounted on Apollo 15's Lunar Rover, the special color TV camera was controlled from earth by radio. Even light control could be adjusted.

at the New School for Social Research in New York City. Workers such as Scott Hyde and Fred Burrell continue to explore the older processes as well as graphic uses of new ones. The value of historical platinum and other prints as collectors' items has risen, partly due to the enthusiastic response to auctions of photographs from the collections of Ralph Greenhill (Don Mills, Ontario) at the Parke-Bernet Galleries in New York City, and from the sale of Sidney Strober's collection of photos in 1970. Such galleries as Witkin and Neikrug in New York City, Carl Siembab in Boston and the Focus Gallery in San Francisco have also been instrumental in calling public attention to the value of photographs. At the Witkin Gallery, platinum prints by the English master Frederick H. Evans as well as shows by Edward and Brett Weston and other workers were featured.

Powerful as photography may be as an art medium, it is even more powerful as a tool for science and exploration. Without photography and its ally, television, missions to the moon, such as Apollo 15 (July 26–Aug. 7, 1921), would have had no feeling of immediacy and relevance except for those involved. The spec-

"Death of Gus-Gus," a study of childhood grief, was among the hundreds of prints in the one-man show of humanist W. Eugene Smith's work.

Considered the father of the "concerned photographers" of the documentary school, Lewis Hine took his "Newsboys in St. Louis" about 1910.

Its massiveness stressed by the tiny human figures below, Fort Peck Dam, Montana, appeared on the first issue of "Life" in a photograph by Margaret Bourke-White. She won her first reputation for her studies of industry.

Margaret Bourke-White, "Life" magazine © Time Inc.

With Agfacontour Professional film, which has both scientific and artistic uses, a scene can be reduced from many tones to a single density level.

Agfa-Gevaert, Inc.

Home-movie possibilities are expanded with the Kodak XL55 movie camera, which can take pictures in low light. It is gripped as binoculars are.

tacular photos of U.S. astronauts walking on the moon are important as records as well as sources of pride and inspiration. The pictures made for scientific reasons are expected to give us clues about the makeup and origin of our solitary natural satellite. In fact, without photography, modern scientific and medical research would be severely handicapped.

A unique film, Agfacontour Professional, received the Interkamera Medal at the International Interkamera Conference in Prague, Czechoslovakia. This film has the unique capability of being able to isolate a specific density. Thus, for example, a specified heat zone, a specific depth in an X ray, or a specific color may be expressed as a specific or "equidensity" line in a scene or photograph. Besides scientific applications, Contour film has a number of creative pictorial applications.

Products of interest, announced in 1971, included two new 35mm single lens reflexes, the Canon F 1 system and the Nikon F 2. Although new in overall construction, both are essentially refinements of earlier ideas. A new Leica M5 was announced. It is the world's first coupled range-finder camera to have behind-the-lens exposure metering. From Nikon came a prototype of a 80mm AF-Nikkor $f/4.5$ auto focusing lens. No delivery date was promised.

In the movie field, Kodak announced two Super 8 Cine Kodaks that usually do not require auxiliary lights. This is accomplished by use of a fast, $f/1.2$ lens and a new, higher speed Ektachrome movie film.

Photo Expo 71, a trade show, was held at McCormick Place exhibition hall in Chicago, Ill. Overshadowed by Photokina, held in Germany in October 1970, it drew a relatively small crowd. Photo Expo's new products were mostly those already seen at Photokina. There was also an exhibition of photographs. Although much larger and more extensive than previous photo exhibitions at U.S. trade shows, it was received with only mild praise and moderate attendance.

The year saw the death of several important persons in the world of photography, above all former magazine photographer Margaret Bourke-White. The cover on the first issue of *Life* (Nov. 23, 1936) was a Bourke-White photo. Although especially gifted in the portrayal of industry, she became equally proficient with human situations. Another *Life* photographer, Larry Burrows, perished in a helicopter in Laos. Burrows, sensitive and compassionate, was known mainly for his war photographs.

NORMAN ROTHSCHILD
Senior Editor, *Popular Photography*

Dubbed a "nuclear scalpel," a new electron-positron linear accelerator (Lawrence Radiation Laboratory) delicately probes unknown nuclear areas.

PHYSICAL SCIENCES

Physicists, chemists and other scientists are responding vigorously to the widespread concern about man's environment. The year 1971 was conspicuous for the large number of ingenious new ideas that focused on pollution of water, air and land and suggested ways of preventing the insidious damage or cleaning it up. Significantly, a good many of the reports came from scientists who had previously devoted most of their careers to theoretical work.

Typical was a paper delivered at a national meeting of the American Chemical Society by Manfred Ehrhardt and Max Blumer of the Woods Hole Oceanographic Institution on the "fingerprinting" of oil slicks at sea. Five to ten million tons of oil are spilled into the ocean each year, and the total is increasing because more oil is being produced and transported. Rarely has it been possible to put the blame for an oil slick on the guilty party. Except when a tanker runs aground or comes apart at the seams, oil is usually dumped into the sea accidentally and in relatively small amounts—e.g., from small leaks in submarine pipelines, from the cleaning out of ballast or from the disposal of used lubricating oil.

Dr. Ehrhardt, who read the paper, said that it is now possible through sensitive chemical analysis to match an oil slick with its source. This kind of detective ability is necessary to ensure the effectiveness of laws and regulations

that have been considered for reducing this particular kind of pollution. "The composition of crude oil is so complex that . . . no two are identical," he explained. "Every oil has its own compositional features which are as typical and persistent as a fingerprint."

As a demonstration, he described the analysis of a floating ball of tar recovered near Bermuda. Using spectrometers and a technique known as gas chromatography, chemists studied the tar. Although it had changed greatly in the weeks since it had been dumped into the sea, they were able to identify it as the remains of some crude oil that had been taken from wells in west Texas—a feat of which Sherlock Holmes would have been proud.

A new way of soaking up oil slicks and converting them into useful material was patented by Joseph Winkler, an engineering consultant at Hazleton, Pa. Shredded rubber and polystyrene plastic absorb oil to make a jellylike mass that can easily be converted into asphaltlike materials for roads, roofing, floor tiles and other products. The process, soon to be tested on a large scale, could help clean up the sea while also disposing of worn-out tires and other unsightly scrap that litters the land.

Analytic chemists can now detect most air pollutants, and possibly the vapors from drugs, many miles away from their sources, according to a report from the U.S. Army's Edgewood Arsenal in Maryland. In addition to helping trace the spread of ordinary pollutants, the Army scientists believe they can even locate a field of marijuana or an illicit drug factory perhaps several miles away.

A group of men and women who formerly worked on rockets has diverted its efforts to a novel way of disposing of domestic and industrial solid wastes. Since organizing The Combustion Power Co. in Menlo Park, Calif., the group has designed a disposal unit with a capacity of 400 tons per day of solid wastes, which is roughly the amount produced by 160,-000 people. The unit first sorts out useful parts of the waste, such as metal and glass, then dries the rest and burns it in an extremely hot gas stream (about 1,700° F.). The gas that emerges is suitable for generating considerable amounts of electricity. If the process lives up to its promise, it will reduce the cost of waste disposal to $1.20 per ton. At present it costs $2.00 per ton to use solid wastes for filling in land, and $7.00 per ton to incinerate them, so the savings could be huge.

Many of the objections to insecticides and weed killers may be met by a new way of applying them, which was announced in 1971 by Professor N. F. Cardarelli, of the University of Akron, and the Creative Biology Laboratory at Barbarton, Ohio. Environmentalists are especially disturbed when such chemicals are sprayed in huge doses at infrequent intervals, because of the harm that may be done to plant and animal life. In the new method the insecticide or weed killer is incorporated in a kind of rubber that releases it so slowly that the level of the chemical in the environment is never high. This should enable a farmer to get the protection he wants with only about one per cent of the chemicals he now uses.

For several years some noted scientists have been working on an alternative to ordinary insecticides. Called juvenile hormone, in nature it controls the metamorphosis of insects from the crawling larva to the flying adult. In laboratory experiments, infinitesimal amounts of juvenile hormone have kept larvae from maturing. They grow bigger and bigger, but they never change to the flying form or reproduce. So far as is known, a specific kind of juvenile hormone is utterly harmless to man or even to other insects, and thus it could be used selectively to wipe out an insect pest over a wide area. Only it has been impossible to get juvenile hormones in useful amounts—even an ounce or two. In 1971 two Harvard professors, E. J. Corey and Hisashi Yamamoto, reported a new and easier way of synthesizing considerable quantities of two such hormones that are specific for certain moths.

Chemistry on an almost microscopic scale scored another success in a test reported by a group of Nebraska scientists. They have developed a way to analyze urine that will reveal whether a "safe" drug addict is taking methadone, a chemical that satisfies the craving for dangerous narcotics, or whether he has relapsed into his heroin habit. The technique takes just an hour and is simple enough for use by private physicians and small clinics.

The promise of cheap, clean and virtually limitless power has never appeared brighter than it did in 1971. For the last two decades, physicists in most advanced nations have been wrestling with the problem of making hydrogen atoms combine so as to release enormous amounts of energy. In effect, they have been striving to control the hydrogen-bomb reaction so that it releases its energy gradually instead of in a destructive explosion. The aim is to make a thin gas of hydrogen hot enough and dense enough and to keep it confined long enough so that the atoms will fuse, the process that releases the energy.

Exciting results are coming from a new generation of fusion machines modeled after some large doughnut-shaped containers that Russian physicists call Tokamaks. The first encouraging Soviet results have been duplicated at Princeton, and similar machines are being built in the United States at Oak Ridge National Laboratory, the University of Texas, Massachusetts Institute of Technology, and the Gulf General Atomic Company in San Diego. The Princeton scientists are so confident that in 1971 they suggested that only minor improvements are needed to make a machine, perhaps by 1980, demonstrating finally that controlled fusion is feasible.

Science's mightiest machine, a new "atom smasher" near Batavia, Ill., underwent its first trials during the summer. Occupying almost 7,000 acres of prairie near Chicago, it accelerates atoms and pieces of atoms through a circular tunnel four miles long. About 1,000 powerful magnets are needed to keep the particles flying around the track until they reach 99.999 per cent of the speed of light. The enormous energy of these atomic bullets will be used to probe into details of atomic structure so fine that physicists have never yet been able to examine them. Recently some noted theorists have been speculating that the neutron and the proton, which are supposedly basic and indivisible constituents of matter, are really made up of several pieces, tentatively called "partons." When the Batavia machine is fully tuned and brought up to full power, it may be able to show whether partons actually exist.

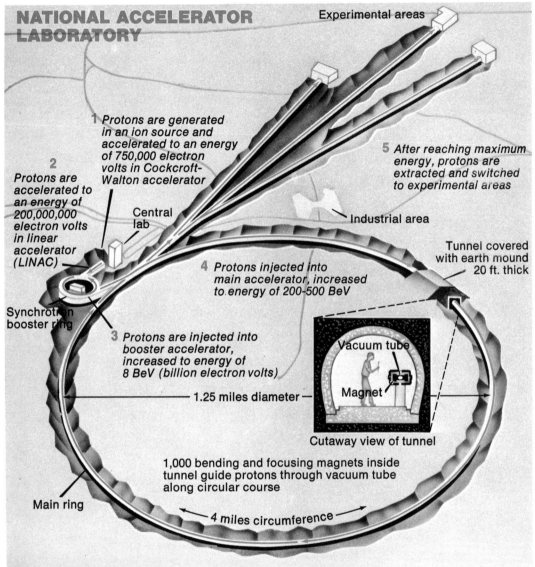

Experimental areas

1 Protons are generated
in an ion source and
accelerated to an energy
of 750,000 electron
volts in Cockcroft-
Walton accelerator

2
Protons are
accelerated to
an energy of
200,000,000
electron volts
in linear
accelerator
(LINAC)

Central
lab

Synchrotron
booster ring

5 After reaching maximum
energy, protons are
extracted and switched
to experimental areas

Industrial area

4 Protons injected into
main accelerator, increased
to energy of 200-500 BeV

Tunnel covered
with earth mound
20 ft. thick

3 Protons are injected into
booster accelerator,
increased to energy of
8 BeV (billion electron volts)

Vacuum tube

Magnet

1.25 miles diameter

Cutaway view of tunnel

1,000 bending and focusing magnets inside
tunnel guide protons through vacuum tube
along circular course

Main ring

4 miles circumference

Diagram by V. Puglisi © 1971, Time Inc.

The mapping of the planet Mars began even before the most recent Mariner space vehicles radioed back their first closeup photographs. Physicists at the Massachusetts Institute of Technology began using their Haystack radar telescope—a dish 125 feet in diameter—to measure surface features of a 100-mile belt south of the Martian equator. The radar probes provided remarkably detailed information about mountains, valleys, gorges and other features, with an uncertainty of 100 yards or less. The information is being combined with Mariner photographs to get better pictures of our red neighbor. The radar, for example, showed that a certain large crater is nearly half a mile deep and has a flat bottom. Earlier Mariner photographs had revealed the same crater but had provided few clues in regard to its depth and shape.

For the last several years an instrument called the laser has been called "a solution looking for a problem." Lasers convert energy into an extraordinarily well-controlled form of light. A laser beam is made up of light waves that are all of one color and are closely in step with each other. The beam travels in a thin straight line, unlike a flashlight or headlight beam, which spreads rapidly within a few feet. These strange features of the laser continued to be exploited by physicists in 1971.

produce a bright picture of a dimly lit object while retaining all the natural coloring.

Still another laser has been used to make the world's fastest optical shutter in experiments at Bell Telephone Laboratories in Murray Hill, N.J., and International Business Machines Laboratories at San Jose, Calif. This laser, developed several years ago, emits a burst of light that lasts only one trillionth of a second (a picosecond, physicists say). The light opens a "shutter," a small block of cadmium sulfide, that is transparent only when struck by a laser beam. It is hoped that the new instrument will enable chemists to study many ultrarapid chemical reactions that cannot be visualized in any other way.

GEORGE A. W. BOEHM
Free-Lance Science Writer

A pulse of laser light—fastest moving object on earth—is caught in a stop-motion photo as it travels right to left through water.

Operating like a machine gun and using carbon-dioxide gas, a new laser yields its energy in more than 2,000 bursts (the star) per second.

A laser that operates like a machine gun was demonstrated by staff members of the Battelle Memorial Institute at Richland, Wash. Filled with carbon-dioxide gas (which is made to emit the light) the new instrument dispenses its energy in more than 2,000 bursts per second. It promises to be useful for cutting a great variety of materials. It can be used for drilling holes in almost any material, trimming plywood veneer, or punching holes in ceramics and glass. At full power of 1,500 watts, it will slice through quarter-inch steel plates at the rate of more than 10 feet per minute.

Another kind of laser that may solve problems as yet unthought of is filled with a liquid dye. In 1971, three Stanford University scientists used it to make a light amplifier that will

POLAND

As an aftermath of the December 1970 riots of dock workers along the Baltic coast, the Government announced on New Year's Day 1971 an allocation of 7,000,000,000 zlotys (about $440,000,000) to raise the lowest wage rates and old-age pensions. The new communist leader, Edward Gierek, followed up with a statement to a Central Committee plenum. He revealed that 2,000,000 tons of grain would come from the U.S.S.R. during the year (a total of 3,000,000 had to be imported) and promised a scientific-technological revolution, i.e., modernization, during the 1970's.

However, in mid-February a strike by women textile workers shut down seven plants in Lodz. It took the presence of the Premier, two party secretaries, and the new trade-union chief to persuade the strikers to return to work. A few days later, increases in food prices, which had triggered the riots, were annulled "thanks to credits obtained from the Soviet Union." Purchasing power was thus increased by about 11,000,000,000 zlotys (about $690,000,000). A new labor code and trade-union law were being prepared during the year, and a new constitution was promised for 1972.

Help to farmers (85 per cent private entrepreneurs) included elimination of compulsory grain, potato and livestock deliveries from Jan. 1, 1972; promises of adequate farm machinery, transport, fuel and building materials; a one third reduction of taxes on middle-sized and large farms.

The peasants remain overwhelmingly Roman Catholic, and the regime made concessions here also. On June 23, Parliament passed a law transferring 4,700 former German churches

POLAND
Area: 120,724 sq. mi.
Population: 33,300,000
Capital: Warsaw
Government: Edward Gierek—Communist Party secretary—1970; Jozef Cyrankiewicz, president—1970; Piotr Jaroszewicz, premier—1970
Gross National Product: $42,500,000,000
Foreign trade: exports $3,548,000,000; imports $3,608,000,000
Armed forces: 265,000

and 2,200 related buildings and lands to the Polish episcopate, exempt from taxation. The areas (40,000 square miles) belonged to Germany before World War II. Stefan Cardinal Wyszynski again asked Pope Paul VI to redraw diocesan boundaries that would reflect *de facto* borders.

Only one day after the above legislation was enacted, Mieczyslaw Moczar lost his Secretariat post in which he had controlled the military and security forces. Long considered a potential party leader, he remained chairman of the Supreme Control Chamber, a post of little power. In this new position Moczar replaced another hard-liner, Zenon Nowak, who became ambassador to Moscow.

Late in the year, the ruling Politburo and the Secretariat of the Central Committee of Poland's Communist Party were realigned. In addition, the 23-member Council of Ministers was reshuffled: Stefan Olszowski was appointed foreign minister, and former Foreign Minister Stefan Jedrychowski became finance minister. It was generally believed that the changes were

Eastfoto

Premier Jaroszewicz and party leader Gierek (hand raised) are surrounded at a party congress in Cracow Province.

The modern traffic circle in the lively center of Warsaw has an underground pass (in foreground).

intended to increase support for Gierek's reform program.

At midyear the new five-year plan became public. It promised a shift from heavy industry to the manufacture of consumer goods, and called for a 25 per cent increase in housing. By 1975, real income is supposed to rise by 17 to 18 per cent, including social benefits. Investments in food industries are to total the equivalent of $2,000,000,000. Coal output is expected to reach 170,000,000 tons per year at the end of the planning period.

The five-year plan; a program for the 1970's; and the prospects of the 1980's were discussed at the sixth Polish United Workers' (communist) Party congress, Dec. 6–11 in Warsaw. It had been preceded by a "talk campaign" or purge of members. The 1,800 delegates unanimously reelected Gierek as leader and approved the economic program. The regime faces a choice between higher living standards and full employment, the latter to include 3,500,000 youths who enter the labor force in 1971–75. An average 40 per cent increase in salaries was promised 40,000 teachers over the next five years, to begin in May 1972.

It is difficult to say whether these measures will bring stability. The mere fact that they are introduced administratively may prove counterproductive. A population that is alienated from the regime and excluded from participation in the decision-making process may again choose the only means available to express its opposition, violence. Reports of trouble

in the Gdansk shipyards during the fall of 1971 indicate that many unsolved problems and dissatisfaction with party organizations remain.

In foreign affairs, a political dialogue continued throughout the year with the Nordic countries as well as with members of Benelux and other West European states. The purpose is to get their support for a security conference that would ratify the *status quo* in Europe. Plans for an American-built memorial to Casimir Pulaski (Polish soldier who fought in the American Revolution) were revealed. The $9,000,000 cost would come from $333,000,000 in "frozen" counterpart funds, in the form of zlotys at the Warsaw Bank that had been deposited there in return for U.S. grain deliveries. Former Foreign Trade Minister Witold Trampczynski was named ambassador to Washington.

Before the 30th anniversary observance of the Workers' Party to be held on Jan. 5, 1972, an official government press release in the English language was circulated. It recalled that the party had been "set up at the initiative of the Polish Communists during the nazi occupation." Postwar achievements were allegedly thanks to "the patriotism and social consciousness of the working class." They were attained "in spite of the bitter resistance of the reactionary forces, supported by United States imperialism."

RICHARD F. STAAR
Associate Director
Hoover Institution on War, Revolution and Peace

POLITICAL PRISONERS

A political prisoner is one who is detained or imprisoned for holding political or religious beliefs unacceptable to the government. In late 1971 an estimated 500,000 men and women were serving time in the jails and prisons around the world under conditions often unfit for the most wretched of animals. Some of the more publicized prisoners are in the work camps of the Soviet Union, the People's Republic of China and other communist countries, as well as of such so-called "free world" nations as Greece, Brazil, Rhodesia, Portugal, Nigeria, Iran, Pakistan, Kenya, Mexico, Argentina, Algeria, South Africa, Turkey, Egypt, Taiwan, India, Haiti, South Korea, Bolivia, Spain and South Vietnam.

In no instances, either communist or non-communist, are the political prisoners held because they have been violent or advocated violence. Their imprisonment is traceable solely to their having ideas or plans the government considers criminal, such as: practicing a minority religion, either through public worship or dissemination of religious literature; advocating cultural or national autonomy; attempting to organize a political party in opposition to the one in power; acting in ways the government or armed forces consider insulting; organizing independent labor unions for the purpose of bargaining or striking; refusing military service for reasons of conscience.

Many political prisoners are rounded up in mass arrests, often following public rallies. Others are tracked down by the secret police. Either way, the capturing governments rarely overconcern themselves with legal refinements. The prisoners may be tortured, either as a form of "instant justice" or as "persuasion" to extract information. Prisoners are routinely denied the help of lawyers. Often a person may languish behind bars for years before any charges are brought against him. A few governments—such as those of Brazil and Greece, where economic and social ties to the United States are strong—work hard both to justify and cover up their tactics. They also deny that much terror goes on. Press reports constantly verify the injustices, not only in these countries but in others also.

In the United States, little is known about political prisoners. Yet the prisoners are not entirely forgotten. An organization called Amnesty International, in operation since 1961, works to free political prisoners around the world. Amnesty International headquarters is in London, and has an active office in New York City. Members write letters to authorities, requesting that such and such a prisoner be released; picket embassies; make speeches; stage informal visits to the offending country for the purpose of publicity or news stories. These forms of persuasion may appear tame—compared with freeing the prisoners by force—but Amnesty International officials report success in a large number of cases. Most world governments are prepared to deal directly with Amnesty officials. The organization has consultative status with the United Nations. In 1971 nearly 1,000 membership groups existed in 36 countries. A group is formed when interest has been aroused among people in the fate of a prisoner in another country. For example, a group at Hesston College, Kansas, is seeking freedom for Tobias Manyonga of Rhodesia. Arrested in 1962, he was released in 1967 and immediately rearrested. He has been held in prison since then. The college group has been collecting funds for his defense.

Amnesty International in New York has a file cabinet weighing nearly 300 pounds and containing the folders of over 6,000 cases. Some of the prisoners concerned have been locked away for ten years. They include: Chrysoula Gogoglou, under house arrest in Greece for his political views, and Ping-Mei Kung, a Roman Catholic bishop who is serving a life sentence in China for counterrevolutionary activity. Julio Rojas is in prison in Paraguay, accused of "communist activities." Yevgenia Forminichna Kislyachuck is in a Russian labor camp because she belonged to Jehovah's Witnesses, the religious denomination banned in the U.S.S.R. Cuba has put away Huber Matos for "counterrevolutionary treason."

A debate exists on whether the United States has political prisoners. If the standards of Amnesty International are accepted, the answer is yes. In 1971, hundreds of young men were in prison because they refused—for reasons of conscience—to be drafted into the armed forces. No violence or aggression was committed by these young men; their offense was peacefully refusing to obey a law—the Selective Service Act—they considered in conscience to be unjust.

A pattern emerges in the lists of world political prisoners: many of the countries that jail people for unorthodox ideas or beliefs are run by military men. A onetime political prisoner, Miguel de Unamuno, the Spanish philosopher, wrote in 1936: "There is no culture that can come to life and flourish under a military regime. . . . It is impossible, impossible. Under militarism, nothing can prosper; they're just blustering fools."

COLMAN MCCARTHY
Editorial-Page Staff, *The Washington Post*

PORTUGAL

The first major reforms of the post-Salazar period were promulgated by an extraordinary session of the Portuguese National Assembly in the summer of 1971. Constitutional amendments promised, among other things, greater autonomy for Portugal's troubled colonial possessions; while special laws guaranteed the rights of the non-Catholic minority and would bring an end to press censorship, except under certain conditions.

The impact of these reforms will depend largely on how they are carried out. They could be neutralized by regulatory decrees, as has happened before. Or they could bring about substantial change, particularly in Lisbon's relations with its Overseas Territories.

An immediate effect of this rare outpouring of legislation, which has been called "a parliamentary hemorrhage," was to secure Premier Marcello Caetano's position. Hard-line right-wingers had charged that his proposal to convert the Overseas "provinces" into "autonomous regions" was the first step toward their abandonment. Regime liberals, on the other hand, had insisted that the most urgent reforms needed were in the domain of public liberties, hardly touched by the Government's bills. Caetano's followers, however, successfully engineered his moderate reform program through Parliament, virtually intact.

Outside the Palace of São Bento, where the National Assembly meets, life continued in its slow and narrow way much as it had under the late dictator Antonio de Oliveira Salazar. The process of liberalization, set in motion when Caetano succeeded the ailing Salazar in September 1968, seemed to retreat. Press controls, eased in the first months of Caetano's rule, were reinforced. The political police, whose name was changed from PIDE (International Police for the Defense of the State) to DGS (General Department of Security), resumed its repressive activities after a brief interlude of reorganization.

There was a sharp new crackdown on students, who were beginning to protest timidly against the colonial wars in Portuguese Africa and military service, which had been extended up to four years. The authorities clamped down on the more militant *sindicatos* (labor unions), after briefly allowing them to hold their own free elections. Peaceful demonstrations by Lisbon shopworkers and bank employees were brutally dispersed. Several union leaders were arrested and the bank employees' *sindicato* closed down.

After a short period of debate during the national elections, the Government again barred all criticism of its colonial policy. Two priests were brought to trial for opposing the wars in Portuguese Africa. The Rev. Joaquim Pinto de Andrade, an Angolan, was condemned to three years in prison plus security measures that could mean indefinite detention. The Rev. Mario Pais de Oliveira was acquitted but forced to flee the country. Socialist leader Mario Soares also forced into exile for advocating peace talks on the basis of self-determination.

The National Commission for Aid to Political Prisoners reported that the number of political prisoners had doubled over the first seven months of 1971 in a "brutal wave" of arrests. The commission, which is made up of 64 prominent citizens, said that the number of political prisoners had risen from 79 to 160 in Metropolitan Portugal, while the number in Portuguese Africa was believed to be in the thousands.

Most of those arrested in Portugal were said to be either labor unionists or communist suspects, allegedly linked to a new secret organization called ARA (Armed Revolutionary Action). ARA has claimed responsibility for a series of acts of sabotage aimed at "destroying Portugal's colonial war machine." Bombs have exploded in ships of Portugal's African line; in Lisbon's main communications center during the North Atlantic Treaty Organization's ministerial council in June 1971; and at the Portuguese military air base at Tancos, destroying some twenty aircraft.

The main bar to easing the authoritarian regime, however, was the colonial wars. The Portuguese were holding their own militarily against nationalists in Angola, Mozambique and Portuguese Guinea, but there was no end in sight to the guerrilla warfare, which was pinning down some 140,000 Portuguese troops.

Lisbon has been pouring about 50 per cent of the national budget into defense and security, which means that most economic and social reforms have remained on paper. Caetano's team of pragmatic economists have drafted development plans to bring Portugal in line with the

---

PORTUGAL

Area: 35,553 sq. mi.
Population: 8,700,000
Capital: Lisbon
Government: Americo Thomaz, president—1958; Marcello Caetano, premier—1968
Gross National Product: $6,100,000,000
Monetary unit: escudo (25 escudos = U.S. $1.00, as of Sept. 8, 1971)
Foreign trade: exports, $950,000,000; imports, $1,582,000,000
Armed forces: 185,500

rest of Europe, but to little avail because first priority goes to the defense effort.

Notwithstanding protests from the hard-line colonialists, the Caetano Government declared that Portugal's future was with Europe and opened negotiations for entry into the Common Market. For the democratic opposition, new hope was born that Europe would pose conditions of democratic and social reform before admitting Portugal into the club.

MARVINE HOWE
Special Correspondent
The New York Times

POSTAL SERVICE, U.S.

Winton M. Blount, who had served as U.S. postmaster general from January 1969, resigned in October 1971. Two months later the Board of Governors of the new Postal Service, which had formally replaced the old Post Office Department in July 1971, appointed Elmer T. Klassen as postmaster general.

As a result of new management techniques, postal productivity increased 3.5 per cent in the 1971 fiscal year. While Postmaster General Blount acknowledged that the increase was minimal, he noted that in the previous 14 years the rate averaged less than 0.5 per cent annually. Blount also pointed out that increased efficiency enabled the new Postal Service to reduce the total number of employees by 12,000 at the same time that the amount of mail was increasing dramatically.

A new express-mail service began in 1971. Blount said that the service would provide overnight mail delivery between 33 of the largest U.S. cities. For $1.50 a letter may be sent before 5 P.M. from New York City and arrive at a San Francisco post office by 10 A.M. the next day. If the schedule is not met, customers will be entitled to a refund. If preliminary tests are successful, the service will be enlarged.

In 21 plants under construction, and in 12 auxiliary facilities, bulk mail will be processed independently of letter mail. The bulk-mail system, planned for full operation by 1975, will cost about $1,000,000,000, a savings of more than $300,000,000 in operating expenses.

Postmaster General Blount was responsible for reorganizing the postal service, which involved improving the reporting system so that top management will have up–to–the–minute information on the multibillion–dollar concern's efficiency, and local postmasters (postal managers) will have more independence. Postal managers may now purchase equipment and make changes in their routes that would have required approval previously.

UPI

Elmer T. Klassen became postmaster general of the new Postal Service toward the end of 1971.

To make the postal system more businesslike, computers are being used increasingly, and labor–management relations are being reconstituted. Computers are used, for example, to advise the bulk–mail network of new facilities. Consultants are hired to introduce new efficient operating methods and to eliminate excess permanent staff. The latter practice has incurred some Congressional criticism. Some Congressmen charged that executive politics entered into the employment of consultants.

The most significant innovation, according to postal officials, is the fact that the service itself, not Congress, controls its finances. "The main difference between the old operation and the present operation from a business standpoint is that we have the right to get the revenue we need to operate the system," Hargrove said. He added that this financial independence gives the Postal Service greater flexibility in acting.

As of November the rate commission had not yet approved permanent higher postal rates. Without a permanent rate structure to reassure potential investors, the Postal Service was compelled to postpone the $250,000,000 bond offering announced for the fall. The Postal Service finally settled on January 1972 to make the first public offering, an issue of $250,000,000 in 25-year bonds. The bonds will give the service new and indispensable capital. In a preliminary prospectus for the bonds, the service revealed a net loss of $2,347,000,000 in the 1971 fiscal year, compared with a 1970 fiscal loss of $1,500,000,000. Of the total net loss in 1971, $1,400,000,000 resulted from deficient rates and fees.

Through higher rates, amounting to $1,600,000,000, and a government subsidy of $1,200,000,000, the Postal Service canceled the old Post Office Department's deficit. As the government subsidy is decreasing and will be eliminated by 1984, the service must resort to additional rate increases or more efficient service or both to remain solvent.

Meanwhile the number of private mail–delivery services is increasing. By law these companies cannot deliver first–class mail but only third–class, advertising and bulk mail. More and more customers are making use of their efficient and low–cost services.

In May the postal rates for magazines and newspapers increased by some 30 per cent. Publishers can expect the remainder of a 145 per cent increase by 1975. Some 30 to 40 publishing companies indicated that they were investigating the possibiilty of using private delivery companies.

Government postal officials claim that they are not concerned about the private delivery of third–class mail. They are worried, however, about the success of the United Parcel Service in gaining a considerable share of the parcel–post business. The Postal Service is trying to win this business back.

Some 500,000 people acted on a new Federal law and reported to the Postal Service that they did not wish to receive "sexually oriented" mail. Under the new law, their names go on a list that is available to smut dealers for $5,000 a year. If a dealer persists in sending such mail to a person on the list, the dealer can be fined or imprisoned.

EDWARD NEILAN
Washington Bureau, Copley News Service

PRISON REFORM

It was a year of turmoil in American prisons. A few promising developments combined with a series of disturbing riots and allegations of racial discrimination and brutality to put prisons, as never before, in the spotlight of public interest. Whether the increased public awareness would lead to greater social and political concern and to the investment of sufficient funds to achieve a reordering of correctional priori-

ties and the gradual elimination of the excessively large maximum-security prisons that dominate state correctional systems, remained at issue.

Despite an increase in numbers and rates of serious crimes over the decade, the prison population in 1971 was substantially less than that in 1961. The daily average of men and women in U.S. state and Federal prisons (not including jails) in 1971 was approximately 200,000. This represents a reduction of 40,000 from the high point of the middle 1960's and of 14,000 from 1961. The reduction reflects the lower clearance rates of serious crimes by the police, which declined from 31 per 100 in 1961 to 20 per 100 in 1970; the increased pressure on the courts, prosecutors and public defenders leading to more extensive "plea bargaining" and a consequent reduction of prison terms imposed; and an increasing dissatisfaction with imprisonment as a rational response to crime, particularly for less serious offenses. In the result, though the prison population declined, the proportion of more confirmed criminals and

difficult-to-handle prisoners in the total prison population increased, with a consequent increase in tension.

The unrest within prisons that led in late 1970 to riots in four New York City jails and in the Holmesburg Penitentiary in Pennsylvania spread widely in 1971 throughout many state prisons and local jails. The most notorious outbursts were at San Quentin in California and at the Attica prison in upstate New York. At Attica, 11 guards and civilian prison employees, who had been taken hostage, and 32 prisoners were killed. More than 80 other prisoners required hospitalization. With few exceptions, the loss of life and bodily injury were the product of the massive force that was used by the prison authorities to regain control. The wisdom and timing of this paramilitary operation, which terminated the prisoners' resistance, were under investigation by several commissions of inquiry as 1971 ended.

The events at Attica dominated the press and other news media throughout America for over a week. Predominantly black activist pris-oners seized 38 guards and civilian employees as hostages, threatened them with knives and other prison-made weapons, and then sought to negotiate an extensive list of "demands" for prison reform. Most of these were readily agreed to by the prison authorities of New York; but some, particularly a total amnesty in respect to the taking of hostages and the loss of one hostage's life prior to the negotiations, proved intractable within the period of negotiation.

Immediately following the events at Attica, turbulence, unrest, attacks on guards, prisoner work and food strikes, widely publicized allegations of brutality and racial discrimination, and a sense of imminent violence became widespread in American prisons. Two kinds of minority imbalance fed the latent violence of prison life. Racial minorities, particularly blacks, are grossly overrepresented in the prison population. The inner-city areas that have long been the most fertile soil for crime now hold increasing numbers of ill-educated, insufficiently employed, rootless black youths who

Breaking with old grim designs, the New Jersey State prison, at Leesburg, has a dining pavilion "raised for the view" (opposite); cells open on a glass-walled corridor facing a landscaped court.
Photos George Cserna

disproportionately find their way to prison—and with an increasing sense of racial injustice. There they discover that all but a few guards are white.

Increasing black political activism in society generally is greatly magnified in prisons, and the black prisoner tends to wrap around himself the cloak of political activism and to turn his first attention to his immediate environment, the prison, where ample signs of political and economic neglect abound. At the time of the uprising in Attica, over 75 per cent of the 2,245 prisoners held there were black or Puerto Rican. All but one of the guards were white. In September in Illinois there was a riot at the Pontiac prison; it held 993 prisoners, 75 per cent of whom were black; there were 7 black guards and 1 black deputy warden.

In late November at the Rahway (N.J.) State Prison, rebellious prisoners held the prison's warden and 5 guards hostage for 24 hours. After Gov. William T. Cahill promised to consider the prisoners' grievances—which included inadequate medical care, poor food, unfair disciplinary action and "racism" by the guards—the hostages were released. In contrast to Attica, there were no deaths and only minor injuries at Rahway.

Prisons magnify problems of race relations; they blend the technology and antisocial attitudes of the criminal with the ideology of the political and racial activist. The mixture is rendered more volatile by repeated political promises of prison reform which have not, so far, been fulfilled.

Some prison reforms did get under way or were intensified in 1971. Twenty states were using work-release or educational-release programs, with prisoners going out from prison to work or school each day. Furlough programs expanded. Self-government systems of a limited or more extensive character, such as at the Walla Walla prison in the state of Washington, were developed. Methadone-maintenance programs as an alternative to or follow-up of the imprisonment of heroin addicts were extended. Many former-prisoner groups were formed to provide support for prisoners on parole and, thereafter, to provide an informed pressure group for reform of the criminal-justice system. Several new prisons were built for smaller populations and with an environment more fitted to rehabilitative efforts than the traditional extend-stacks of steel and concrete cages. In some of the newer prisons for less dangerous offenders—for example, the prison at Vienna in Illinois—the inmate keeps a key to his own cell to assure privacy for himself and his prison property. His mail is uncensored, he may tele-phone his family regularly, and his educational, vocational and self-development opportunities are substantial. But such prison reforms are isolated instances in the continuing protracted caging in idleness, squalor and occasional brutality of the still "unreformed" prison system.

The courts continued in 1971 to receive a flow of habeas corpus applications protesting a wide range of prison conditions, particularly disciplinary processes and practices. This "outside" enquiry, though seen as uninformed interference by many prison administrators, seems to have built up effective pressure toward desirable prison reforms.

In fiscal year 1971 the Law Enforcement Assistance Administration of the U.S. Department of Justice spent $529,000,000, allocated under the Omnibus Crime Control and Safe Streets Act of 1968, on improving the criminal-justice system of the states. Of this, $178,000,000 was reserved for developments in prison and other correctional practice; a substantial increment from the $2,000,000 so allocated in 1969. It is hard to assess the impact of these funds. They give a measure of freedom to the more innovative prison and jail administrators to initiate new programs, but they form only a small part of total state and local expenditures on corrections—about 3 per cent—and the tax base that supports state and local prisons and jails is declining. Prison reform, like many other state and local activities, is bedeviled by the imbalance between Federal and other taxing capacities. It is a politically challenging task to find sufficient funds for what is a doubtfully popular cause, prison reform.

The lessons of reform, unrest and violence in prisons in 1971 were discussed at a three-day National Conference on Corrections held in Williamsburg, Va., in December, which was addressed by Attorney General John N. Mitchell. Correctional leaders attending the conference laid plans for a yet increased investment of resources in an effort to modernize America's correctional system, to reduce racial tensions within prisons, and to provide training for leadership in prison reform. The justifications for such efforts are not merely humanitarian and certainly are not sentimental. It is now realized that in the absence of a more effective correctional system there can be no significant improvement in the criminal-justice system as a whole. Only through integrated and far-reaching police, court and correctional reform can we provide effective and humane social protection from crime and criminals.

NORVAL MORRIS
Director, Center for Studies in Criminal Justice
University of Chicago

PRISONERS OF WAR

The Vietnam war has set many records for frustration, and one of the most painful is that in no previous conflict have American prisoners of war been held so long. Nor has there ever before been such sparse word of their well-being, or even an enemy's acknowledgment that they are alive or dead.

Under such circumstances, the release of the prisoners of war (POW's) became one of President Nixon's fundamental goals in any Vietnam war settlement. Hanoi made release conditional on complete American withdrawal and abandonment of the Saigon Government. It was a cruel choice and, for the time being at least, it was rejected. But at year's end there were faint signs that a solution might be in the offing. The U.S. Army was preparing reception centers in Thailand, and treatment facilities back home.

As a result of North Vietnamese intransigence, the Hanoi authorities identified only 343 Americans—mostly fliers—as captives in North Vietnam. Another 80 Americans were believed to be in camps in Laos, or were "roving captives" held by insurgent bands in South Vietnam and Cambodia.

A few men were imprisoned as early as 1962. A few had begun POW life after being shot down in the December 1971 flare-up of the air war in the north. The majority were "Red River rats"—crews who had flown north of the Red River during the height of the bombing attacks of 1966–68 and been downed by intense antiaircraft fire. In addition, another 1,200 Americans were listed as missing in Indochina. How many of these were alive and incarcerated no one knew.

For wives, children, parents and other kin, waiting for the release of their men was agonizing. The emotional strain they all suffered brought wives and mothers together. They formed organizations and traveled to the world capitals where Hanoi has representatives or intermediaries. The women appealed, if not for the release of their men, "just for information" about them. The entreaties usually were politely received but seldom answered.

Well-meaning but sometimes ill-advised efforts to shame Hanoi into humanitarian access to the confined men were made by computer millionaire Ross Perot and others. At Christmas in 1971, while on his annual tour of military bases in Asia, comedian Bob Hope flew to Vientiane, Laos, hoping to obtain from the North Vietnamese Embassy there a visa to Hanoi. He suggested ransom for the prisoners in the form of assistance to North Vietnamese victims of the war.

All the appeals appeared to fall on deaf ears. The Communists said they had made their own new proposal at peace talks in Paris in July and were waiting for it to be accepted.

The new approach was offered by Madame Nguyen Thi Binh, the Vietcong delegate. As the key point in a seven-item proposal, Madame Binh declared that if President Nixon would agree to withdraw all U.S. forces from Vietnam by the end of 1971, the liberation of prisoners could begin immediately and continue at a rate proportionate to the speed of the American pullout. It was an improvement. Previously Hanoi had promised only to discuss the prisoners' release after the United States had set a date for complete withdrawal from Vietnam. However, the new offer was part of a package that contained all the old unacceptable demands.

The White House turned the offer down as lopsided. The decision shattered the solid support that POW wives had previously given the President. The organizers of a new group, POW-MIA (Missing in Action) Families for

Former POW, Navy Lt. Robert Frishman helps brothers of other POW's load letters and petitions to N. Vietnam Mission in Paris.

UPI

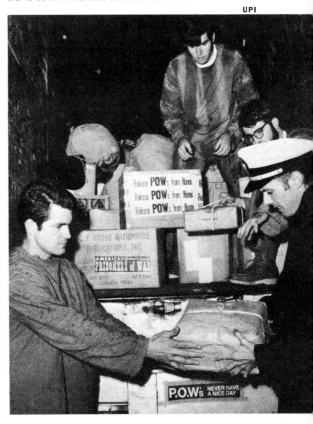

Immediate Release, indicated that it wanted the administration to set a total withdrawal date. The established National League of Families of POWs-MIA opposed any agreement with Hanoi that would not ensure the release of the prisoners and an accounting of those listed as missing. To some observers the administration at best was being less than candid on the issue.

Speaking for the large group of moderates among POW relatives, Mrs. Richard Bodden of Downers Grove, Ill., declared: "We have one President. He is head of the country and has access to most of the knowledge. I have faith."

At the urging of the U.S. Ambassador in Saigon, President Thieu released a sizable number of NVA prisoners held in South Vietnam. It was hoped that the gesture would start a reciprocal exchange. But it did not.

There was, however, a one-for-one exchange in October of an American soldier for a North Vietnam officer. Freed was Sergeant John C. Sexton, Jr., who limped out of the Cambodian jungle to become the 24th American released by the Vietcong. He carried a note requesting that two Vietcong prisoners be released. The U.S. command settled for the NVA officer and flew him to freedom in a helicopter.

Nothing further came of that gesture. Joy reigned in the Sexton home in Warren, Mich., however, and some hope was restored among the kin of all the men held in the Indochina war zone.

George Bush (l), U.S. ambassador to UN, talks with Mrs. John Wendell, wife of a POW, as National League of Families petitions the UN.

JACK FOISIE
Southeast Asia Correspondent
Los Angeles Times

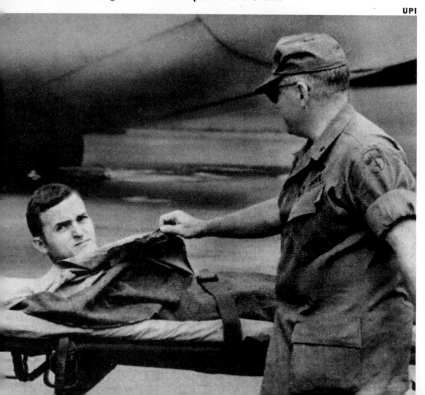

Staff Sgt. John C. Sexton, of Warren, Mich., starting long trip home, is 24th American POW to be released by the enemy in Indochina. He had been held captive for two years.

PRIZES AND AWARDS

ART, ARCHITECTURE, DANCE AND MUSIC

American Institute of Architects Awards

Critics' Medal: SIBYL MOHOLY-NAGY, critic and teacher (died Jan. 8, 1971)

Gold Medal: LOUIS I. KAHN

American Institute of Graphic Arts Medal: WILL BURTIN, designer

National Academy of Recording Arts and Sciences Awards (Grammy Awards)

Album: BRIDGE OVER TROUBLED WATER, Simon & Garfunkel

Classical album: BERLIOZ: LES TROYENS, Colin Davis conducting Royal Opera House Orchestra and Chorus

Contemporary vocal performance—group: CLOSE TO YOU, The Carpenters

Contemporary vocal performance—female: I'LL NEVER FALL IN LOVE AGAIN, Dionne Warwick

Contemporary vocal performance—male: EVERYTHING IS BEAUTIFUL, Ray Stevens

Jazz performance—small group or soloist with small group: ALONE, Bill Evans

Jazz performance—large group or soloist with large group: BITCHES BREW, Miles Davis

New artist: THE CARPENTERS

Record of the year: BRIDGE OVER TROUBLED WATER, Simon & Garfunkel

Recording for children: SESAME STREET, Joan Cooney

National Institute of Arts and Letters Awards

Awards in Art ($3,000 each): ILYA BOLOTOWSKY, ROBERT GOODNOUGH, ALFRED LESLIE, NORMAN LEWIS, LUDWIG SANDER, HEDDA STERNE, HAROLD TOVISH

Awards in Music ($3,000 each): SYDNEY P. HODKINSON, FRED LERDAHL, ROGER REYNOLDS, LOREN RUSH

Arnold W. Brunner Memorial Prize in Architecture ($1,000): JOHN ANDREWS

Charles E. Ives Award ($5,000): VIVIAN PERLIS

Charles E. Ives Scholarship ($5,000): LOUIS SMITH WEINGARDEN

Marjorie Peabody Waite Award ($1,500): BEN BENN, painter

Richard and Hinda Rosenthal Foundation Award for painting ($2,000): DONALD PERLIS

JOURNALISM

Claude Bernard Science Journalism Awards for "responsible science reporting which has made a significant contribution to public understanding of basic research in the life sciences, including medicine" ($1,000 each)

Magazines: MORTON HUNT, *Playboy Magazine,* for "Man and Beast"

Newspapers with circulations over 10,000: LAWRENCE K. ALTMAN, *The New York Times,* for "Twelve Dogs Develop Lung Cancer in Group of 86 Taught to Smoke"

Newspapers with circulations under 10,000: LAWRENCE H. BUSH, *Ann Arbor* (Mich.) *News* for "Lab Animals' Roles Important"

Drew Pearson Prize for "excellence in investigative reporting ($5,000): NEIL SHEEHAN, *The New York Times,* for his articles on the Pentagon Papers

National Magazine Awards

Fiction: ESQUIRE, for "maintaining consistently high literary standards while reaching out to present fiction which is highly experimental in both form and substance"

Public Service: THE NATION, for "demonstrating that enterprising reporting of matters of public concern can be done by a magazine of limited resources and that a venerable journal of opinion can still be venturesome"

Reporting Excellence: THE ATLANTIC, magazine, WARD JUST, writer, for "the two-part article 'Soldiers' in the October and November 1970 issues"

Specialized Journalism: ROLLING STONE, magazine, for "freshness of presentation and effective formula-free group journalism as reflected in its exhaustive reports on the Charles Manson case and the tragedy of the Altamount rock festival"

Visual Excellence: VOGUE, December 1970 issue, for "the imaginative choice and interpretation of artistic, poetic and scientific subject matter either well known or unexpectedly new"

Overseas Press Club Awards

Asia award for best article or report on Asia in any medium: HARVEY MEYERSON, *Vinh Long,* a book on South Vietnam

Bache award for best business-news reporting from abroad in any medium: THE NEW YORK TIMES, for "outstanding coverage of economic developments overseas," by such reporters as Clyde Farnsworth, Hy Maidenberg, Brendan Jones, Edward Cowan and Takashi Oka

Book on foreign affairs: JOHN TOLAND, *The Rising Sun: The Decline and Fall of the Japanese Empire, 1936–1945*

Cartoon on foreign affairs: TOM DARCY, *Newsday,* for cartoon *Withdrawal,* about Vietnam

Daily-newspaper or wire-service interpretation of foreign affairs: HARRISON E. SALISBURY, *The New York Times,* for his editing of the Op-Ed Page

Daily-newspaper or wire-service photographic reporting from abroad: DENNIS COOK, United Press International, for his picture of an East Pakistani flood survivor

Daily-newspaper or wire-service reporting from abroad: JOHN HUGHES, *The Christian Science Monitor,* for series "The Junk Merchants: International Drug Traffic"

George Polk Memorial Award for the best reporting in any medium requiring exceptional courage and enterprise abroad: JOHN LAURENCE, correspondent, KEITH KAY, cameraman, JAMES CLEVENGER, soundman, RUSS BENSLEY, producer, ERNEST LEISER, executive producer, CBS News, for "The World of Charlie Company"

Latin America award for best article or report on that area in any medium: DAVID BELNAP, *Los Angeles Times,* for reports on Chile

Magazine interpretation of foreign affairs: AN-THONY LEWIS, *The New York Times,* London bureau, for the magazine-section article "Biafra—How Pointless It All Seems Now"

Magazine reporting from abroad: ROBERT SHAPLEN, *The New Yorker,* for articles on Southeast Asia

Photographic reporting or interpretation from abroad in a magazine or book: LARRY BURROWS, *Life* magazine, for coverage of the East Pakistan disaster

Radio interpretation of foreign affairs: NBC RADIO NEWS, "Vietnam: The Way Out," Peter Burns, Kenley Jones, Bob Green, Phil Bradley, Lou Davis and Robert Goralski

Radio reporting from abroad: LOU CIOFFI, ABC Radio News, for reports on the East Pakistan tidal wave; CBS RADIO NEWS, for broadcasts from Cambodia and other areas

Robert Capa Award for superlative photography requiring exceptional courage and enterprise abroad: KYOICHI SAWADA, United Press International, for photos taken during six months in Cambodia

Television interpretation of foreign affairs: TED KOPPEL, ABC News, for series "Vietnam: Topic A"

Television reporting from abroad: KENLEY JONES, NBC News, for Vietnam battlefront reports

LITERATURE

American Library Association Awards

Grolier Award for "her great contribution to library service for young adults" ($1,000) SARA L. SIEBERT, coordinator of Young Adult Services, Enoch Pratt Free Library, Baltimore

John Newbery Medal for the "most distinguished contribution to American literature for children": BETSY BYARS, *Summer of the Swans*

Randolph J. Caldecott Medal for the "most distinguished American picture book for children": GAIL E. HALEY, *A Story—A Story*

Bancroft Prizes for "books of exceptional merit and distinction in American history (including biography), American diplomacy, and the international relations of the United States" ($4,000 each): ERIK BARNOUW, *The Image Empire;* DAVID M. KENNEDY, *Birth Control in America: The Career of Margaret Sanger;* JOSEPH FRAZIER WALL, *Andrew Carnegie*

Bollingen Prize in Poetry ($5,000 shared): MONA VAN DUYN, *To See, To Take;* RICHARD P. WILBUR, *Walking to Sleep*

Britain's Booker Prize ($12,000): **V. S. Naipaul,** *In a Free State* (novel)

Canada Council's Governor General's Literary Awards ($2,500 each): MONIQUE BOSCO, *La femme de Loth,* novel; JACQUES BRAULT, *Quand nous serons heureux,* play; DAVE GODFREY, *The New Ancestors,* novel; B. P. NICHOL, *Beach Head, Still Water, The True Eventual Story of Billy the Kid,* poetry, *the cosmic chef: an evening of concrete,* anthology; MICHAEL ONDAATJE, *The Collected Works of Billy the Kid,* prose and poetry;

FERNAND OUELLETTE, *Les actes retrouvés,* essays

Canada Council's Molson Prizes to "recognize and encourage outstanding contribution to the arts, humanities or social sciences, or to national unity" ($15,000 each): NORTHROP FRYE, literary scholar; DUNCAN MACPHERSON, Toronto *Star* cartoonist; YVES THÉRIAULT, writer

Council on Interracial Books for Children Awards ($500 each): RAY ANTHONY SHEPARD, *Warball;* VIRGINIA DRIVING HAWK SNEVE, *Jimmy Yellow Hawk;* JUAN VALENZUELA, *I Am Magic*

Mystery Writers of America Awards (Edgars)

Fact crime book: MILDRED SAVAGE, *A Great Fall*

First mystery novel: LAWRENCE SANDERS, *The Anderson Tapes*

Juvenile mystery: JOHN ROWE TOWNSEND, *The Intruder*

Mystery novel: MAJ SJOWALL and PER WAHLOO, *The Laughing Policeman*

Mystery short story: MARGERY FINN BROWN, *In the Forests of Riga the Beasts Are Very Wild Indeed*

National Book Awards ($1,000 each)

Arts and letters: FRANCIS STEEGMULLER, *Cocteau*

Children's book: LLOYD ALEXANDER, *The Marvelous Misadventures of Sebastian*

Fiction: SAUL BELLOW, *Mr. Sammler's Planet*

History and biography: JAMES MacGREGOR BURNS, *Roosevelt: The Soldier of Freedom*

Poetry: MONA VAN DUYN, *To See, To Take*

Science: RAYMOND PHINEAS STEARNS, *Science in the British Colonies of America*

Translation: FRANK JONES, *Saint Joan of the Stockyards;* EDWARD G. SEIDENSTICKER, *The Sound of the Mountain*

National Medal for Literature "for the excellence of his total contribution to the world of letters" ($5,000): E. B. WHITE

National Institute of Arts and Letters Awards

Awards in Literature ($3,000 each): WENDELL BERRY, poet and novelist; STANLEY BURNSHAW, critic; MARTIN DUBERMAN, essayist and playwright; RONALD FAIR, novelist; CHARLES GORDONE, playwright; BARBARA HOWES, poet; ARTHUR KOPIT, playwright; LEONARD MICHAELS, novelist; LEONARD NATHAN, poet; REYNOLDS PRICE, novelist; WILFRID SHEED, novelist

Morton Dauwen Zabel Award ($2,500): CHARLES REZNIKOFF, poet

Richard and Hinda Rosenthal Foundation Award ($2,000): CHRISTOPHER BROOKHOUSE, novelist

MOTION PICTURES

Academy of Motion Picture Arts and Sciences Awards (Oscars)

Actor: GEORGE C. SCOTT, *Patton*

Actor (supporting role): JOHN MILLS, *Ryan's Daughter*

Actress: GLENDA JACKSON, *Women in Love*

Actress (supporting role): HELEN HAYES, *Airport*

Direction: FRANKLIN J. SCHAFFNER, *Patton*

Foreign-language film: INVESTIGATION OF A CITIZEN ABOVE SUSPICION, Elio Petri, Italy

Picture: PATTON

Song: FOR ALL WE KNOW by Fred Karlin, Robb Wilson and Arthur James, from *Lovers and Other Strangers*

Writing (screenplay—based on material from another medium): M*A*S*H, Ring Lardner, Jr.

Writing (story and screenplay—written directly for the screen): PATTON, Francis Ford Coppola and Edmund North

Jean Hersholt Humanitarian Award: FRANK SINATRA, for charitable activities

Special award for contributions to the film industry: ORSON WELLES

Cannes International Film Festival Awards

Actor: RICARDO CUCCIOLLA, *Sacco and Vanzetti*, Italy

Actress: KITTY WINN, *Panic in Needle Park*, United States

Film (Golden Palm award): THE GO-BETWEEN, Joseph Losey, England

First film: PER GRAZIA RECEVUTA, Nino Manfredi, Italy

Jury Prizes: JOE HILL, Bo Widerberg, Sweden, LOVE, Karoly Makk, Hungary

Special Jury Prizes: JOHNNY GOT HIS GUN, Dalton Trumbo, United States, TAKING OFF, Milos Forman, United States

Special Super Festival Prize (25th anniversary): LUCHINO VISCONTI, *Death in Venice*, Italy

International Film Critics' Award

Film: JOHNNY GOT HIS GUN

National Society of Film Critics Awards

Actor: GEORGE C. SCOTT, *Patton*

Actor (supporting role): CHIEF DAN GEORGE, *Little Big Man*

Actress: GLENDA JACKSON, *Women in Love*

Actress (supporting role): LOIS SMITH, *Five Easy Pieces*

Direction: INGMAR BERGMAN, *The Passion of Anna*

Film: M*A*S*H, Robert Altman

Screenplay: ERIC ROHMER, *My Night at Maud's*

PULITZER PRIZES

Journalism ($1,000 each except for public-service gold medal)

Cartoons: PAUL CONRAD, *Los Angeles Times*

Commentary: WILLIAM A. CALDWELL, *The Record* (Hackensack, N.J.)

Criticism: HAROLD C. SCHONBERG, music critic, *The New York Times*

Editorial writing: HORANCE G. DAVIS, JR., *Gainesville Sun* (Florida), for editorials supporting peaceful desegregation of state's schools

Feature photography: JACK DYKINGA, *Chicago Sun-Times*, for illustrating overcrowding and other poor conditions, Lincoln and Dixon State Schools for the Retarded

International reporting: JIMMIE LEE HOAGLAND, *The Washington Post*, for coverage of the struggle against apartheid in the Republic of South Africa, Apr. 12–May 25, 1970

Local reporting (general): AKRON BEACON JOURNAL STAFF (Ohio), for coverage of the Kent State University tragedy, May 4, 1970

Local reporting (special): WILLIAM HUGH JONES, *Chicago Tribune*, for exposing collusion between police and some private ambulance companies to restrict service in low-income area; reports led to major reforms

Meritorious public service: JOURNAL, TWIN CITY SENTINEL (Winston-Salem, N.C.), for coverage of environmental problems, such as a strip-mining operation which would have damaged much scenic country; both newspapers led a campaign that blocked operation

National reporting: LUCINDA FRANKS, THOMAS POWERS, United Press International, for documentary on life and death of Diana Oughton, a 28-year-old revolutionary, "The Story of Diana: The Making of a Terrorist"

Spot-news photography: JOHN PAUL FILO, a photography student, for pictorial coverage of Kent State University tragedy, May 4, 1970

Letters and music ($1,000 each)

Biography: ROBERT FROST: THE YEARS OF TRIUMPH, 1915–1938 by Lawrance Roger Thompson

Drama: THE EFFECT OF GAMMA RAYS ON MAN-IN-THE-MOON MARIGOLDS by Paul Zindel

Fiction: No award

History: ROOSEVELT: THE SOLDIER OF FREEDOM by James MacGregor Burns

Music: SYNCHRONISMS NO. 6 FOR PIANO AND ELECTRONIC SOUND by Mario Davidovsky

Nonfiction (general): THE RISING SUN by John Toland

Poetry: THE CARRIER OF LADDERS by William S. Merwin

SCIENCE

Albert Lasker Medical Research Awards ($10,000 each)

Basic Medical Research: SEYMOUR BENZER, California Institute of Technology; SYDNEY BRENNER, Cambridge University; CHARLES YANOFSKY, Stanford University

Clinical Medical Research: EDWARD D. FREIS, Veterans Administration Hospital, Washington, D.C.

American Cancer Society's Alfred P. Sloan Jr. Memorial Award: MARY LASKER for "dedication to the cause of cancer control"

American Heart Association Awards

Louis N. Katz Basic Science Research Prize for Young Investigators ($1,500): CRISTOBAL G. dos REMEDIOS, University of California, Berkeley

Research Achievement Award ($1,000): EARL W. SUTHERLAND, JR., Vanderbilt University School of Medicine

Louisa Gross Horowitz Prize for "outstanding research in biology" ($25,000): HUGH E. HUXLEY, Cambridge University

U.S. National Medal of Science: RICHARD D. BRAUER, Harvard University; ROBERT H. DICKE, Princeton University; BARBARA MCCLINTOCK, Carnegie Institution of Washington; GEORGE E. MUELLER, Systems Development Corporation; ALBERT B. SABIN, Weizmann Institute of Science; ALLAN R.

SANDAGE, Hale Observatories; JOHN C. SLATER, University of Florida; JOHN A. WHEELER, Princeton University; SAUL WINSTEIN (posthumous), University of California, Los Angeles

Vetlesen Prize for Geophysics ($25,000); S. KEITH RUNCORN, University of Newcastle-upon-Tyne (received half the prize money); ALLAN V. COX, Stanford University, and RICHARD R. DOELL, U.S. Geological Survey (shared the remaining half)

TELEVISION AND RADIO
George Foster Peabody Awards
Radio education: THE DANGER WITHIN: A STUDY OF DISUNITY IN AMERICA, NBC

Radio news: DOUGLAS KIKER, *Jordan Reports,* NBC

Radio promotion of international understanding: GARRY MOORE, *New York, New York,* Voice of America (Washington, D.C.)

Radio public service: MEDICAL VIEWPOINT and PEARL HARBOR, LEST WE FORGET, WAHT (Lebanon, Pa.)

Radio youth or children's programs: LISTENING/4, WFBE-FM (Flint, Mich.)

Television education: THE EYE OF THE STORM, ABC

Television entertainment: EVENING AT POPS, Public Broadcasting Service (PBS); THE FLIP WILSON SHOW, NBC; THE ANDERSONVILLE TRIAL, PBS, KCET (Los Angeles)

Television news: POLITITHON '70, WPBT (Miami); 60 MINUTES, CBS

Television promotion of international understanding: CIVILISATION, BBC (New York); THIS NEW FRONTIER, WWL (New Orleans)

Television public service: MIGRANT: AN NBC WHITE PAPER, NBC; PEACE . . . ON OUR TIME: KMEX-TV AND THE DEATH OF RUBEN SALAZAR, KMEX (Los Angeles)

Television special award: THE SELLING OF THE PENTAGON, CBS

Television youth or children's programs: HOT DOG, NBC; THE DR. SEUSS PROGRAMS, CBS

Special Individual Award: JOHN E. DREWRY, for his role in founding and administering the Peabody Awards

National Academy of Television Arts and Sciences Awards (Emmy Awards)
Actor-comedy series: JACK KLUGMAN, *The Odd Couple,* ABC

Actor-dramatic series: HAL HOLBROOK, "The Senator," *The Bold Ones,* NBC

Actor-single performance: GEORGE C. SCOTT, *The Price,* NBC

Actor-supporting performance in comedy: EDWARD ASNER, *The Mary Tyler Moore Show,* CBS

Actor-supporting performance in drama: DAVID BURNS, *The Price,* NBC

Actress-comedy series: JEAN STAPLETON, *All in the Family,* CBS

Actress-dramatic series: SUSAN HAMPSHIRE, *The First Churchills,* PBS

Actress-single performance: LEE GRANT, *The Neon Ceiling,* NBC

Actress-supporting performance in comedy: VALERIE HARPER, *The Mary Tyler Moore Show,* CBS

Actress-supporting performance in drama: MARGARET LEIGHTON, *Hamlet,* NBC

Children's programing: BURR TILLSTROM, performer, *Kukla, Fran and Ollie,* series, PBS; SESAME STREET, series, PBS

Comedy series: ALL IN THE FAMILY, CBS

Cultural documentary programing:
Programs: ARTHUR PENN, 1922– : THEMES AND VARIANTS, PBS; THE EVERGLADES, NBC; "THE MAKING OF BUTCH CASSIDY AND THE SUNDANCE KID," NBC

Individuals: NANA MAHOMO, narrator, *A Black View of South Africa,* CBS; ROBERT GUENETTE and THEODORE H. STRAUSS, writers, *They've Killed President Lincoln!,* NBC; ROBERT YOUNG, director, *The Eskimo: Fight for Life,* CBS

Director-comedy, variety or musical special: STERLING JOHNSON, *Timex Presents Peggy Fleming at Sun Valley,* NBC

Director-drama special: FIELDER COOK, *The Price,* NBC

Dramatic series: THE SENATOR, *The Bold Ones,* NBC

Magazine-type programing:
Programs: GULF OF TONKIN SEGMENT, *60 Minutes,* CBS; THE GREAT AMERICAN DREAM MACHINE, series, PBS

Individuals: MIKE WALLACE, correspondent, *60 Minutes,* CBS

New series: ALL IN THE FAMILY, CBS

News documentary programing:
Programs: NBC WHITE PAPER: POLLUTION IS A MATTER OF CHOICE, NBC; THE SELLING OF THE PENTAGON, CBS; THE WORLD OF CHARLIE COMPANY, CBS

Individuals: FRED FREED, writer, *NBC White Paper: Pollution Is a Matter of Choice,* NBC; JOHN LAURENCE, correspondent, *The World of Charlie Company,* CBS

News-programing specials within regular shows:
Programs: FIVE-PART INVESTIGATION OF WELFARE, *NBC Nightly News,* NBC

Individuals: BRUCE MORTON, correspondent, "Reports from the Lt. Calley Trial," *CBS Evening News with Walter Cronkite,* CBS

Special-events coverage:
Programs: CBS NEWS SPACE COVERAGE FOR 1970–71: *Aquarius on the Moon: The Flight of Apollo 13* and *Ten Years Later: The Flight of Apollo 14,* CBS

Individuals: WALTER CRONKITE, correspondent, *CBS News Space Coverage for 1970–71*

Special program-drama or comedy: THE ANDERSONVILLE TRIAL, PBS

Special program-variety or musical:
Classical music: LEOPOLD STOKOWSKI: NET FESTIVAL, PBS

Variety and popular music: THE BURT BACHARACH SPECIAL, CBS

Trustees award: ED SULLIVAN, for "pioneering in the variety format," CBS

The televised Tony Awards program brought joy to winners (l to r) Rae Allen, Hal Linden, Helen Gallagher, Patsy Kelly, Maureen Stapleton, Brian Bedford; it included selections from 25 years of Tony-Award musicals.

Calling up some of the musical theater's most enchanted evenings were excerpts from "The King and I," with Yul Brynner, the original "King"; and "The Music Man" with its first one, Robert Preston.

Variety series-musical: THE FLIP WILSON SHOW, NBC

Variety series-talk show: THE DAVID FROST SHOW, syndicated

Writer-comedy, variety or music special: BOB ELLISON, MARTY FARRELL, *The Burt Bacharach Special,* CBS

Writer-drama special:
Adaptation: SAUL LEVITT, *The Andersonville Trial,* PBS
Original teleplay: MARVIN SCHWARTZ, TRACY KEENAN WYNN, *Tribes,* ABC

THEATER

Antoinette Perry Awards of the American Theater Wing (Tony Awards)
Actor (dramatic): BRIAN BEDFORD, *The School for Wives*
Actor (dramatic featured or supporting): PAUL SAND, *Story Theatre*
Actor (musical): HAL LINDEN, *The Rothschilds*
Actor (musical featured or supporting): KEENE CURTIS, *The Rothschilds*
Actress (dramatic): MAUREEN STAPLETON, *Gingerbread Lady*
Actress (dramatic featured or supporting): RAE ALLEN, *And Miss Reardon Drinks a Little*
Actress (musical): HELEN GALLAGHER, *No, No, Nanette*
Actress (musical featured or supporting): PATSY KELLY, *No, No, Nanette*
Director (play): PETER BROOK, *A Midsummer Night's Dream*
Director (musical): HAROLD PRINCE, *Company*
Lyrics: COMPANY by Stephen Sondheim
Music: COMPANY by Stephen Sondheim
Musical: COMPANY produced by Harold Prince
Musical book: COMPANY by George Furth
Play: SLEUTH by Anthony Shaffer
Scenic designer: Boris Aronson, *Company*

New York Drama Critics Circle Awards
American play: THE HOUSE OF BLUE LEAVES by John Guare
Musical: FOLLIES by James Goldman and Stephen Sondheim
Play: HOME by David Storey

Outer Critics Circle Awards
Achievements: JOSEPH PAPP, producer, New York Shakespeare Festival; PAUL SILLS, producer, *Story Theatre;* THE PHOENIX THEATRE
Productions: A MIDSUMMER NIGHT'S DREAM, FOLLIES, NO, NO, NANETTE

Village Voice Off-Broadway Awards (Obies)
Actor: JACK MacGOWRAN, *MacGowran in the Works of Beckett*
Actress: RUBY DEE, *Boesman and Lena*
Foreign plays: AC/DC by Heathcote Williams; BOESMAN AND LENA by Athol Fugard; THE DREAM ON MONKEY MOUNTAIN by Derek Walcott
Play: THE HOUSE OF BLUE LEAVES by John Guare

UNITED STATES AND WORLD SCENE

Europe Prize for Statesmanship ($85,000): EDWARD HEATH, prime minister of Great Britain

Four Freedoms Foundation Award for distinguished service in behalf of the four freedoms: EDMUND S. MUSKIE, U.S. senator from Maine

Max Berg Award for a "major achievement in prolonging or improving the quality of human life" ($10,000): RALPH NADER, founder, Center for the Study of Responsive Law

National Civil Service League Career Service Awards ($1,000 each): CHARLES M. BAILEY, director of Defense Division, U.S. General Accounting Office; JAMES BRUCE CARDWELL, assistant secretary, Department of Health, Education, and Welfare; ALAN M. LOVELACE, director, Air Force Materials Laboratory; DAVID DUNLOP NEWSOM, assistant secretary of state for African affairs; JOHN E. REINHARDT, assistant director, U.S. Information Agency; WILFRED H. ROMMEL, assistant director for legislative reference, Office of Management and Budget; WILLIS H. SHAPLEY, associate deputy administrator, National Aeronautics and Space Administration; R. J. SMITH, deputy director for intelligence, Central Intelligence Agency; LOUIS W. TORDELLA, deputy director, National Security Agency; MAURICE J. WILLIAMS, deputy administrator, Agency for International Development

Rockefeller Public Service Awards for "outstanding service to the Government of the United States and to the American people" ($10,000 each)
Administration (shared): SAMUEL M. COHN, assistant director for budget review, U.S. Office of Management and Budget; ROBERT C. MOOT, assistant secretary, Department of Defense
Human Resource Development and Protection: MARY LEE MILLS, nurse-consultant, Community Health Service, Department of Health, Education, and Welfare
Intergovernmental Operations: JOSEPH J. SISCO, assistant secretary of state for Near Eastern and South Asian affairs
Physical Source Development and Protection: LUNA B. LEOPOLD, senior research hydrologist, U.S. Geological Survey, Department of the Interior
Professional Accomplishment and Leadership: ROBERT SOLOMON, director, Division of International Finance, Federal Reserve System

U.S. Presidential Awards for Distinguished Federal Civilian Service: SAMUEL M. COHN, assistant director for budget review, Office of Management and Budget; U. ALEXIS JOHNSON, undersecretary of state for political affairs; EDWARD F. KNIPLING, director of entomology research division, Department of Agriculture; FRED LEONARD, scientific director of medical biomechanical research laboratory, Department of the Army; GEORGE H. WILLIS, deputy to the assistant secretary of the treasury for international affairs

U.S. Presidential Medals of Freedom: MANLIO BROSIO, secretary-general, North Atlantic Treaty Organization (1964–71); SAMUEL GOLDWYN, motion-picture producer, founder, Goldwyn Pictures Corporation; WILLIAM J. HOPKINS, executive assistant to six U.S. presidents (1931–71)

PUBLISHING

During 1971, book, magazine and newspaper publishers in the United States and Canada recorded some new highs, experienced some severe losses, and suffered from the effects of higher postal rates and other cost hikes.

While the U.S. economy was somewhat gloomy, booksellers prospered as many new titles appeared. The magazine industry was shocked, though not too surprised, at the death of *Look*. The newspaper industry engaged in a long, bitter struggle with Federal authorities over the Pentagon Papers (classified material on the Vietnam war, published by several newspapers).

Books. Book-publishing receipts nearing the $3,000,000,000 figure were predicted for 1971, reflecting a continuous growth. Much of this, however, came from higher prices of books rather than increased sales. The American book-title output increased over 1970. In 1970, new books had jumped from 21,787 to 24,288, while new editions climbed from 7,792 to 11,783, for a combined total of 36,071 titles. *Publishers' Weekly*, which compiles these annual reports, noted a "strong growth in the output of hardcover facsimile reprint publishing" as well as the "continuing proliferation of paperback reprints and new editions, especially non-mass-market paperbacks and trade paperback nonfiction."

In late 1971 the fiction best sellers included *The Exorcist, Passions of the Mind, The Other* and *The Day of the Jackal*. In the nonfiction listing, *The Female Eunuch* was a leader. Biographies were popular, with *Boss* (Chicago Mayor Richard Daley) and *Capone*. Even Chief Red Fox was in the act. *The Sensuous Man* replaced *The Sensuous Woman*. *Future Shock* and *The Greening of America*, which first appeared in part in *The New Yorker*, were widely read. Dr. David Reuben hit the comeback trail with *Any Woman Can*.

Some fears were expressed over the gains reported by the Government Printing Office in its competition with private firms. Publishers were quick to benefit from current events, with *The Pentagon Papers, Khrushchev Remembers*, and the views of Daniel Ellsberg, an associate at MIT who released the Pentagon Papers to the press. Former President L. B. Johnson's memoirs came out late in the year, with syndication through *The New York Times*. The death of *Look* deprived a number of authors of condensations of their books.

Canadians voiced "increased concern with their role in world affairs" and resented the influx of so many American publications. Schoolbooks should tell more about Canadian folk heroes and pioneers, according to Canadian wholesalers and publishers. Others urged government subsidies to Canadian publishers.

Charles Scribner's Sons celebrated its 125th anniversary in 1971; while the book industry mourned the death of Bennett Cerf, cofounder of Random House, on Aug. 27.

Political leaders debated a "two-China" policy while American publishers voiced more concern over the increase in pirating books in Taiwan. In recent years more than six thousand titles have been pirated, with Taiwan publishers by far the worst offenders.

The Supreme Court decision supporting newspapers in the controversial Pentagon Papers case rates a streamer headline in the "Times."

UPI

Gardner Cowles announces the suspension of "Look" magazine, reporting that his heart said "Keep it going" but his head said "Suspend it."

Magazines. *Look* died with the last issue on Oct. 19, 1971. Gardner Cowles blamed "ridiculously high" postal-rate increases as well as the price hike for coated paper. Its advertising income dropped 19 per cent in 1970; it was down 12 per cent in the first half of 1971. Losses had reached $5,000,000 annually. Some 1,000 employees were affected.

Cowles suspended *Venture* in July, after seven years. Earlier the company disposed of *Family Circle,* the Modern Medicine group of professional magazines, three Florida newspapers and a book company to The New York Times Company.

Magazine historian Theodore B. Peterson, dean of the College of Communications of the University of Illinois, urged the publications "to adapt to changing social conditions and technology" to survive. He stressed the expanding emphasis on specialization, and said the weekly magazine was anachronistic in these days of competition with television and radio. *Good Housekeeping* editor Wade Nichols, Jr., had another view. "The death of every established magazine I've known in over thirty years has had precisely the same cause—the incapacity, lack of commitment or just plain

stupidity and greed of top management." The Postal Service objected to the heavy blame placed on its rates, noting that in 1969–70 *"Look"*'s circulation dropped 15 per cent; its ad pages dropped 15 per cent and its ad revenue for all editions 19 per cent." Obviously, this debate will continue for years.

Some old-timers reappeared in 1971 as quarterlies. *Liberty,* the first to return, was followed by *The Saturday Evening Post.* Featuring Norman Rockwell's drawings, and familiar typography, subjects and authors, *SEP* sought to recapture readers who made it number one for years.

The Publishers Information Bureau noted that advertising revenues were up 3 per cent for the first half of 1971, to $620,611,709. A better second half would place total revenues near the $1,300,000,000 mark, up slightly from 1970. Seeking to save paper and postage costs, *Esquire, Holiday* and *McCall's* cut their page sizes to about that of *Time* magazine.

Saturday Review continued to grow, and acquired new owners, John Veronis and Nicholas Charney, formerly of *Psychology Today.* Norman Cousins, who has brought the magazine from a circulation of 20,000 to 660,000 in three decades, resigned as editor.

Robert Shnayerson, a former senior editor at *Time,* became editor in chief of *Harper's Magazine.* He succeeded Willie Morris, who resigned because of "severe disagreements" between the "literary men" and the "business management over the purpose, the existence and the survival of *Harper's Magazine* as a vital institution in American life." John Cowles, Jr., is chairman of the board of *Harper's.*

The reputation of William Buckley's *National Review* was challenged by what *Time* called "an elaborate schoolboy prank" when the *Review* published 14 pages of purported Pentagon secret papers that were "composed out of nothing." Some newspapers canceled Buckley's column.

Time Inc. earned $20,100,000 on revenues of $632,600,000 in 1970, down slightly from 1969. Its chief product, *Life,* dropped 14 per cent, to $132,000,000, in ad revenue. *Life*'s decline continued well into 1971; it was challenged for top position by a sister publication, *Time. TV Guide, Sports Illustrated, Woman's Day* and other specialized magazines reported gains in ad pages and in circulation.

Continuing a trend evident for several years, newcomers were specialized. *New Woman* publicized a new feminine philosophy, while *You* was directed at women in the 18–35 category. *Easygoing* was for younger, 14–21, student travelers; and *Vintage* obviously was designed for wine buffs. *Black Sports* had its special-interest group, as did *Sexual Behavior* and others. Communications/Research/Machines, Inc., publishers of *Psychology Today*, introduced *Intellectual Digest*, with sections on the arts, politics and the sciences.

Circulation leaders were well-known publications, with *Reader's Digest* (18,200,000) still tops. It was being challenged by *TV Guide*, which passed the 16,200,000 figure. Among other leaders with circulations of 5,000,000 or more were *Better Homes and Gardens*, 7,900,000; *Woman's Day*, 7,600,000; *McCall's*, 7,500,000; *Family Circle*, 7,400,000; *Life*, 7,200,000; *National Geographic*, 7,200,000; and *Ladies' Home Journal*, 7,000,000. *Look* had 6,600,000 at the end. Getting into the 6,000,000 category was *Playboy*.

Sports Illustrated, advertising itself as "The Third Newsweekly," passed the 2,150,000 mark. A recent arrival, *Psychology Today*, had approached the 600,000 group by late 1971. *New York* went from red to black ink during its third year.

Newspapers. With debate over publication of the Pentagon Papers continuing as 1971 ended, some publications reported a "victory for the press"; others were not so sure. The University of Missouri Freedom of Information Center, which went to court to seek publication of all the classified material, noted that "public reaction to the government-press clash has shown once again that many Americans are not aware of, or do not believe in, the vital role of the press in our society." Pointing out the traditional role the press takes as the "fourth branch of government," the center thought the basic question is an imponderable: Whether people will demand access to that information enabling them to exercise their responsibilities as citizens in a democracy, and whether they can, or will, give up the easy peace of letting the president and his cabinet make the decisions. (*See also* Law: Pentagon Papers Case)

In Canada, the Senate was concerned with press mergers. Some political leaders urged government control to halt future combinations. The largest Canadian chain, The F. P. Publications, Ltd., has eight dailies and some 855,000 combined circulation. Other leaders are the Southam and Thomson groups. Of $1,100,000,000 in ad revenue for Canadian publications in 1970, dailies had the biggest share, $290,000,000. The 95-year-old Toronto *Telegram* announced plans to fold.

Although President Nixon and Vice-President Agnew continued to have problems with the press, Nixon said that he benefited from their probing. Other debates centered on the televised press conference. Former presidential Press Secretary George Reedy, Jr., called it "a setup too easily dominated by the President." Newsmen complained of too few conferences. Agnew complained of "inaccurate reporting" of his summer global tour.

Newspaper economist Dr. Jon G. Udell predicted that the 1970's would be the decade of greatest circulation growth, with 77,000,000 seen for 1980. *Editor & Publisher Year Book* reported 1,748 dailies in the United States in 1971, down 10. Their total circulation climbed some 50,000 to 62,107,527 daily; Sunday editions neared 50,000,000. The tabloid New York *Daily News* continued to lead with 2,130,000 daily sales, while the *Los Angeles Times* passed the 1,000,000 mark and took over second place. *The New York Times* (850,000) was in third place. Many newspaper groups reported higher profits. Gains were noted by Knight, Los Angeles Times Mirror, Gannett, Ridder and others. *The New York Times* sought to pare its $85,000,000 payroll to counteract a decline in profits.

The Gannett Company added more papers, owning 51 in 1971. On the basis of combined circulations, the Chicago Tribune Company was the leader with papers in Chicago, New York and Florida. The American Newspaper Publishers Association began a campaign for a $10,000,000 endowment fund. The three major goals of the fund are: to develop competent staffs better qualified to tell the public about the changing world; to strengthen public understanding of a free press; and to cultivate thinking and informed newspaper readers.

Many papers expanded facilities, remodeled plants and added equipment. Offset printing gained new toeholds. The Atlanta *Journal* and *Constitution* planned a nine-story news and office building, while the New York *Daily News* allotted $29,000,000 to expanding its manufacturing facilities. Knight set out to upgrade its Philadelphia *Inquirer* and *News* plant with $15,000,000. To help celebrate its centennial in 1973, *The Detroit News* mapped plans for a new satellite plant.

Although the suburban press continued to expand, journalism graduates found the going rougher in the metropolitan areas. One group totaling 1,250 papers in 32 markets joined forces to get greater ad revenues. Strikes were not so noticeable, although Pittsburgh readers went months without their *Post-Gazette* and *Press*. Veterans of World War II were pleased to see the Postal Service recognize newsman Ernie Pyle with a special stamp.

WILLIAM H. TAFT
Professor of Journalism, University of Missouri

PUERTO RICO

The debate over whether Puerto Rico should remain a commonwealth, apply for statehood or seek independence continued in 1971. A special commission, appointed by President Nixon and Gov. Luis A. Ferre, recommended that Puerto Rico ask Congress to pass a constitutional amendment that would give Puerto Ricans the right to vote in U.S. presidential elections. A referendum on the issue was planned.

A new industrial–development plan, continuing on the lines of the successful Operation Bootstrap, got under way in 1971. (As Puerto Rico's unemployment rate has continued high, 11.5 per cent in mid-1971, industrial development is of prime importance.) In an interview, Manuel A. Casiano, director of Puerto Rico's Economic Development Administration since early 1971, pointed out that during the twenty–year period 1950–70 the gross national product increased from $755,000,000 to more than $4,600,000,000, while Puerto Rico's population rose from 2,000,000 to nearly 3,000,000. "The $2,000,000,000 of investment in that time created about 150,000 jobs, and if in the next ten years, population grows at the same rate, we will have to create at least 300,000 new jobs, and for this we will need a minimum of $4,000,-000,000 if not $6,000,000,000," Casiano said.

Despite the new industrial–development plan, Puerto Rico's principal industries, tourism and garment and shoe manufacturing, declined. Factors responsible for the decrease in tourism included: the economic slowdown on the U.S. mainland; low–cost European–travel packages; violence among the various statehood–independence factions, which caused many visitors to cut short their island stays; Puerto Rico's high prices (in peak season a single room without meals costs as much as $60 per day) and generally poor, indifferent service. Many hotels were forced to close, permanently or temporarily. Others made an effort to combat the decline, offering special package plans, or reducing their rates. In addition, the island legislature increased the travel advertising budget to $750,000. Almost immediately, full-page ads, extolling the advantages of a Puerto Rican vacation, began appearing in mainland newspapers.

Under an agreement reached in January 1971, the U.S. Navy will yield almost all control over the 6,000-acre island of Culebra, 20 miles east of Puerto Rico. The Navy agreed to leave the island in a "reasonable time," once an alternative gunnery-range site is found. In April, Secretary of Defense Melvin R. Laird said that he would "make the final decision" regarding an alternative site by the end of 1972.

In February, Ruben Berrios, president of the Puerto Rican Independence Party, and 13 others had been sentenced to three months in jail for disobeying a Federal court order prohibiting sit-in demonstrations near the naval training areas on Culebra.

Two policemen and a student were killed during riots at the University of Puerto Rico in March. The riots followed a fight between members of the university's Reserve Officers' Training Corps (ROTC) and two groups that contend that the ROTC program must be terminated if Puerto Ricans "are to be truly independent" of the United States.

Other developments included a three-day strike by 660 of the island's firemen which ended in early February; the expelling of six Roman Catholic priests, some of whom were reported to be involved in the independence movement, from their rural parishes.

QATAR

The tiny, oil-rich sheikdom of Qatar announced its independence from Britain on Sept. 1. It occupies a peninsula on the western side of the Persian Gulf, with an area of about 4,000 square miles and a population of about 110,000. Sheik Ahmad decided that his country should stand alone rather than join a federation, after being a British protectorate from 1916. Qatar joined the United Nations later in the year.

RADIO

The tiny, oil-rich sheikdom of Qatar announced network financed by the Corporation for Public Broadcasting, began operations in May 1971. With headquarters in Washington, D.C., the network was inaugurated with the program *All Things Considered*, a 90-minute "magazine formulated show with a current-affairs emphasis." By the end of the year, the network had 98 members with 115 stations in 34 states, the District of Columbia and Puerto Rico.

The Upper Midwestern Conference on Broadcasting and the People was held in the spring in Sioux Falls, S.D. The conference stressed that local networks are' responsible to and must serve the local communities, and showed how local groups or individuals can bring effective pressure to bear on local stations or even the Federal Communications Commission. Strong protests have resulted, in numerous cases, in improved programing or service or both.

RCA developed the Audio Center radio, an AM/FM radio that also transmits sound from UHF and VHF television. Introduced following a two-year product-feasibility and marketing study, the radio has characters in braille on the dial, so that blind or near-blind people can operate it.

Classical-music broadcasting, extremely popular from 1967 in New York City, declined there. It was never particularly successful elsewhere in the United States. . . . FM radio had a financially profitable year. . . . Arthur Godfrey, a fixture on radio for some 40 years, announced that he would give up his regular CBS radio program in April 1972.

RAILROADS

Railroads moved ahead in 1971 to improve their position as a basic mode of ground transportation for both freight and passengers.

In the United States the year was marked by the advent of a system of long-distance passenger routes, Amtrak, under government sponsorship; a landmark labor agreement; wage and freight-rate increase; and new passenger-train technology. At the same time, a depressed economy and rising costs kept railroad traffic and earnings close to the restricted levels of 1970.

Amtrak, created by the National Railroad Passenger Corporation, went into operation on May 1 with a score of carriers providing service by 182 trains to more than 300 cities. The system dropped 178 trains from the previous network. This represented a cut of 47 per cent in passenger-route miles. Several routes were later restored. The system soon found itself in need of additional capitalization beyond the original Congressional outlay of $40,000,000, guarantees of $100,000,000 in Federal loans for improvements, and $197,000,000 in guaranteed Federal loans to railroads for contributions to the corporation.

The labor agreement, reached by management and the United Transportation Union after an 18-day selective strike on 10 railroads, cleared the way for the elimination of costly work rules, by binding arbitration if necessary. Labor won a 42 per cent wage increase over 42 months. Elimination of many featherbedding practices should lessen the impact of the big wage hike, which also is to be met in part by higher freight rates approved and in prospect.

Regarding rail mergers the year's principal developments were the acquisition of the Monon by the Louisville & Nashville, and abandonment of the proposed merger of Norfolk & Western with Chesapeake & Ohio railways. Reorganization efforts continued for a number of bankrupt railroads, including the Boston & Maine and the Central of New Jersey. In addition, the monumental task of restoring Penn Central to solvency remained. Prospects for the latter were nebulous at year's end, raising the specter of government take-over as a last resort.

Dramatic developments came to the fore. The Interstate Commerce Commission approved the start of service between Alexandria, Va., and Sanford, Fla., of trains carrying passengers in conventional cars and their automobiles on bilevel flatcars in the same train. Each of 13 enclosed flatcars carries 8 automobiles; passengers are accommodated in 8 coaches with sightseeing domes. Time for the trip has been set at 13 to 14 hours, compared with more than 20 hours by road and 19 hours by usual rail service. If accepted by the public, service may later include Los Angeles-San Francisco and Chicago-Denver.

The U.S. Department of Transportation (DOT) continued to promote the development of high-speed ground transportation. The nation's first passenger-carrying air-cushion vehicles are to start operations in 1972 on a 13.5-mile line between suburban (McLean, Va.) Washington, D.C., and Dulles International Airport. This is considered the forerunner of services that may reach speeds of 300 miles an hour in the 1980's.

Of more immediate importance were the performance of and plans for improved rail service in the Northeast Corridor—the Boston-New York and New York-Washington routes. Turbo Train, a turbine-powered operation on the N.Y.-Boston segment since 1969, is to continue until at least 1974. The two trains will be renovated and two cars added to each. Schedules of Turbo Train and the high-speed Metroliner on the N.Y.-Washington run were adjusted so that the two meet in Pennsylvania Station, New York City. This provides through service in the corridor. The Department of Transportation also took Turbo Train on a 12,600-mile tour of 31 states to evaluate the equipment for possible use elsewhere. Such routes include Los Angeles-San Diego; Portland-Seattle; Chicago-St. Louis; Cincinnati-Chicago; and Buffalo-New York City.

Getting people back on the rails and off the highways is being promoted as a means of combating air pollution and environmental damage from highway construction. The Metroliner has been doing its share. Twelve daily round trips carry upward of 35,000 passengers a week, half of whom have switched from other transport modes. Linked with Turbo Train in a cross-platform change at New York, Metroliner provides a through trip,

The auto train was a 1971 railroad innovation. Passengers ride in coaches with sightseeing domes; their cars travel in bilevel flatcars.

Washington-Boston, in 7 hours and 4 minutes for the 459 miles, against a conventional train schedule of 8 hours and 55 minutes. The DOT says that with an investment of about $360,-000,000 by local, state and Federal authorities in new equipment and improvement of track, the Boston-Washington time could be cut to less than 5 hours within 3 years.

Outside the United States, faster schedules, new types of equipment, extended electrification, elimination of unprofitable lines and creation of new routes are playing a part in improved ground transportation.

In Great Britain, extension of electrified lines has cut London-Glasgow time to 6 hours, a run of more than 400 miles. On completion of the project in 1974, the time is expected to be down to 5 hours. Similar improvements have been made on lines between other British cities.

France continues to stress the use of turbotrains. Also the government-owned railroad is moving ahead with installation of an air-cushioned train on a 15-mile route between two airports in the Paris vicinity, to be completed in two or three years. Designers are also at work on a linear-motor, elevated monorail for suburban use. Some more powerful and more comfortable turbotrains are slated for service in 1972.

The German Federal Railway continues to improve its lines for high-speed service. In 1972, at least 72 cities are expected to be linked by trains capable of speeds of 100-125 miles an hour. West Germany is also testing, near Munich, the prototype of an electromagnetic train designed for speeds of up to 350 miles an hour. Its sponsors say it requires less power for greater loads than air-cushion vehicles.

The Soviet Union continues to project a Moscow-Leningrad service one hour faster than the present one, but severe winter operating conditions have hampered the proposal.

Italy has been moving ahead in passenger-train speeds, both internally and on international routes. Between Rome and Milan, the world's longest nonstop route, the 389 miles is covered in 5½ hours. Other fast schedules are Rome-Naples and Milan-Naples. The Rome-Paris trip now moves at 60 miles an hour over-all for the 905 miles. Italy plans to link Rome with Frankfort and Cologne, in West Germany.

Japan's Tokaido Line between Tokyo and Osaka continues to receive world attention. Frequency of service has been stepped up to 62 trains a day. A 100-mile extension of the line, from Osaka through Kobe to Okayama, is expected to be in service in 1972. Top speed will be about 155 miles an hour. Otherwise, Japanese railroads continue to suffer from heavy labor costs and uneconomic or obsolete lines.

Argentina ordered 250 U.S. diesel locomotives at a cost of $100,000,000; and Brazil ordered 80 U.S. diesels, costing $34,000,000. The Argentine power, which will receive 80 new units in 1972, is scheduled to upgrade the nation's rail plant, replacing wood-, coal- and oil-fired engines.

FRED B. STAUFFER
Transportation Specialist

RELIGION

In 1971 religion was involved in controversies or conflicts touching almost every area of man's national and community life—spiritual, social and political. While no major new religious movements were launched, certain trends of recent years intensified. The spread of the Pentecostal movement in the United States, Africa and South America indicated a drive to restore the freshness and spontaneity that, many say, Christianity lost after Emperor Constantine made it the state religion of Rome in the fourth century.

Growth was reported by some fundamentalist bodies—one conspicuous example was the Southern Baptist Convention—and by a number of churches outside the traditional framework of organized religion, including Latter-Day Saints (Mormons), Seventh-Day Adventists and Jehovah's Witnesses. Meanwhile traditional, mainstream churches reported minor declines in membership and financial support. These bodies included Protestant Episcopal, United Presbyterian, Roman Catholic, United Methodist, United Church of Christ and several Lutheran denominations.

In the United States, interest increased in Eastern religions such as Zen Buddhism and Krishna consciousness, and in transcendental meditation. Witchcraft (a form of paganism) and Satanism were also popular in some quarters. Sharp rises were reported in the sales of Ouija boards and tarot cards. Astrologers were doing a thriving business.

There was nothing strange in the simultaneous vogue of so many different nontraditional approaches to the supernatural. It appeared to reflect widespread disillusion with a civilization that can put man on the moon but has not been able to control violence, eradicate want and bring security. Viewing organized religion as "a tool of the Establishment," many persons have turned to systems not subject to rational laws, logic or the niceties of theology. They seem to be motivated by the·common conviction that "there must be a better way."

Aside from its own internal life and conflicts, religion was an important element though not necessarily the main issue, in several major world crises. In Northern Ireland, Protestant and Catholic were pitted against one another; in Pakistan, Hindu against Muslim. In South Africa, churches were almost the only active opponents of harsh racial discrimination practiced under the apartheid system. In South Vietnam, the powerful An Quang Buddhists, a key influence in the downfall of the Diem regime in 1963, called for a boycott of the one-man presidential election.

ROMAN CATHOLICISM

The major event in Roman Catholicism was the third World Synod of Bishops, convened in Rome by Pope Paul VI to consult with him on two issues: the ministerial priesthood and justice in the world. Documents on each subject were prepared for the Pope's use by this body of 211 bishops and members of the religious orders (with priests and lay auditors present). The Synod was in session Sept. 30–Nov. 6.

Since the Synod functions in a purely advisory capacity to the pope, the documents have no legislative effect. However, the work of the body cannot help but have a wide influence as it expresses the views of a worldwide representation of Catholic authority. It was generally agreed, however, that the Synod tried to do too much in too short a time.

While 107 bishops voted in favor of a resolution "to retain intact" an unmarried clergy, 87 bishops supported a declaration urging the Pope to permit the ordination of mature married men "in particular cases on account of pastoral ·necessity."

Meanwhile the Catholic Church faced disturbing statistics. According to a Vatican study, priests have been leaving the active ministry at an increasing rate not likely to subside. In the first three months of 1969, 1,141 departed, by comparison with 563 between 1939 and 1963.

In the Synod's justice document were two proposals that could have far-reaching effects. One called for the establishment of a mixed commission to study profoundly the role of women in the Church. The other recommended a revision of all Catholic education to train people to recognize social disorders and to assume personal responsibility for correcting injustices.

On Dec. 30, leaders of the Anglican (Church of England) and Roman Catholic churches announced agreement on the "essential" teaching regarding Holy Communion. The agreement was described as "the most important statement since the Reformation for Anglicans and Roman Catholics."

UNITED STATES

The Jesus revival or neo-Pentecostal movement, which surfaced on the West Coast about 1967, burst upon the national consciousness in 1971 by virtue of publicity in mass magazines. Its appeal lies in its promise that anyone who yields himself fully to the Lord, accepting Jesus Christ wholeheartedly as personal Savior, will find peace, fufillment and a balanced answer to life's problems. Participants in Pentecostal services speak or sing as they feel moved to do, sometimes "talking in tongues," a form of expression that sounds like gibberish

In 1971 *Newsweek* magazine commissioned The Gallup Organization to conduct a nation-wide survey of U.S. Catholics above the age of 17. Some of the questions asked and major findings follow:

	Sundays and holy days	Less frequently	More frequently
How often do you attend Mass?	52%	38%	10%

	Never	Once	More than once
How often have you gone to confession in the past 8 weeks? (Don't knows omitted)	63	24	12

	Yes	No	Don't Know
Can a good Catholic ignore the Pope's condemnation of artificial birth control?	58	31	11
Is a divorced Catholic who remarries living in sin?	28	60	12
If your child decided to leave the church, do you think he could still be saved?	78	8	14
If no government funds were allowed parochial schools, would you be willing to spend more to keep them going?	49	38	13
Should sex education be taught in parochial junior high schools?	73	16	11
Should priests be permitted to marry?	53	36	11
Do you think Catholics who raid draft boards to protest the war in Vietnam are acting as responsible Christians?	16	69	15
Do you know who the Berrigans are?	38	62	

but that is held to be a language of divine origin. The movement is inspired by the day of pentecost (a word of Greek origin meaning fiftieth) as described in the Biblical account of the descent of the Holy Spirit upon the Apostles on the fiftieth day after the resurrection of Jesus.

Among those who have taken it up are:

Young so-called hippies, known as "Jesus Freaks," who generally reject organized religion, including many who formerly "turned on" to drugs and now "turn on" to Jesus.

College students who are involved in evangelistic programs sponsored by several organizations, such as the Campus Crusade for Christ, that encourage church affiliation.

Roman Catholics who are seeking a "charismatic renewal" within their church. They regard the Pentecostal approach not as a substitute for the Mass but as an enrichment of it by making the presence of Jesus in their daily lives more vivid and complete.

The numbers involved in the Jesus revival seem to constitute only a small minority of the nation's Christians. Enthusiasts believe the movement will develop into a large-scale "awakening" to Jesus. Others foresee its abatement when it has lost its emotional charge.

The Berrigans. In many nationwide controversies, religious figures were prominent. Protesting U.S. involvement in Vietnam, the Berrigan brothers were able to keep their position before the public though confined in a Federal prison for draft-file destruction. The Rev. Philip Berrigan, S.S.J. (Society of St. Joseph), was indicted, along with two other priests, a former priest, a nun, a Muslim and a Protestant, on charges of conspiring to kidnap Henry Kissinger, presidential aide, and blow up heating plants in Washington, D.C., buildings. Arraigned in a Federal court in Harrisburg, Pa., the eight were scheduled to go on trial there in 1972. The Rev. Daniel Berrigan, S.J. (Society of Jesus) was named a coconspirator. However, he was not indicted and later his name was dropped altogether.

Black Christians continued to protest racism which they charged still exists in major denominations. The United Presbyterian Church in the U.S.A. was rocked by the announcement that one of its agencies had contributed $10,000 to the Angela Davis defense fund. A number of black Presbyterians made up the $10,000 out of their pockets, but the issue remained a source of bitterness among many white members.

Two women were elected to head churches: Mrs. Marcus Rohlfs of the American Baptist Convention, and Mrs. Lois H. Stair of the United Presbyterian Church.

During the year, religion invaded the theater and the popular arts as never before. Some of the top song hits were rock tunes in which Jesus Christ was the theme. Leonard Bernstein created a sensation with his *Mass,* presented at the inaugural of the John F. Kennedy Center for the Performing Arts in Washington. *The Trial of the Catonsville Nine,* as dramatized by one of the defendants in that case, the Rev. Daniel Berrigan, was presented on and off Broadway. *Jesus Christ Superstar,* a rock opera, reached Broadway after fantastic recording sales.

ECUMENISM

The ecumenical movement, so brightly promising in the 1960's, appeared to be waning. The nine member bodies of the Consultation on Church Union have found common ground regarding the sacraments, and there appear to be no important theological barriers where one church touches another. But some church leaders fear that a united body would turn into a superchurch, complicating the bureaucracy that many Christians deplore in the separate institutional churches. Furthermore, there are sharp differences in concepts of structure, the system of church government. It is on such issues that enthusiasm for union has cooled.

In regard to unity talks between Roman Catholics and others, some progress on a world scale was noted; but while a kind of rapport on the Eucharist (Communion) was said to have been reached with Anglicans—just as a similar accord had been attained with Lutherans in 1970—Protestant bodies seemed as far as they ever were from accepting the Catholic dogmas of papal primacy and infallibility, and the hierarchical structure of the Roman Catholic Church.

JUDAISM

Arab-Israeli political antagonisms heightened during the year, but there were no big new religious developments in the Middle East. The Vatican newspaper *L'osservatore Romano* stirred up a dispute by charging that Israel was expelling Christians and Muslims from the former Jordanian sector (the Old City) of Jerusalem. But other Catholic sources, as well as some Protestants, denied it and sided with Jews in defending Israel and commending its avowed policy of maintaining open access to all holy places.

The position of Jews in the Soviet Union was a matter of international concern. Stirred by evidence of the repression of Jewish culture in Russia and the Government's harsh treatment of Jews seeking to emigrate, a world conference was called in Brussels. It demanded that the Soviet Government allow the Jews to

Western followers of Hare Krishna, a branch of Hinduism, worship in a one-room "temple."

live as Jews and to move to Israel if they so desired.

ASIA, AFRICA, LATIN AMERICA

Japan. Heated debate was set off by the Government's efforts to nationalize the Yasukuni Shrine in Tokyo, where Shinto ceremonies honor the spirits of men who died fighting for Japan during the past century. Shinto, a form of nature and ancestor worship, is the only major religion in Japan that is of native origin. Nineteenth-century leaders used Shinto to foster nationalism, promoting it not as a religion but as a state cult. Shinto was disestablished by U.S. occupation authorities after World War II, and the Japanese constitution of 1947 separated church and state, forbidding the Government to sponsor religious activities or use public money for religious institutions. Shinto shrines have continued to be active but without state funds.

A bill introduced in the Diet in 1971 by Premier Eisaku Sato was designed to place the management and upkeep of the Yasukuni Shrine in the hands of the Government. The move was defended on the basis that the shrine is not a religious center in the Western sense but dedicated to all soldiers, regardless of belief, who died for the nation. Opponents viewed the bill as an indirect attempt to reestablish Shinto as the state religion.

Lively discussion in Japan also concerned the political intentions of Soka Gakkai, the militant society of lay members of the Buddhist Nichiren Sho sect. A politico-religious movement founded in 1930, Soka Gakkai has grown like wildfire since World War II. Its present membership is estimated at 17,000,000, about half of the 30 per cent of the Japanese people who reportedly are aligned in some manner with religious organizations. One reason for its fast growth has been the use of aggressive conversion tactics to which critics have expressed sharp aversion. The sect is dedicated to the "absolute happiness" of each person and seeks practical answers to life's daily problems, disregarding the philosophical and mystical.

In 1970, Daisaku Ikeda, its president, announced the separation of Soka Gakkai from its political arm, Komeito (Clean Government Party). Nevertheless, there is evidence of continued strong ties in practice. Party officials belong to Soka Gakkai, and members of the sect faithfully vote for Komeito candidates. One controversial move was the sending by Komeito of a team to Communist China to investigate the possibility of future relationships.

Africa. Africa experienced its own form of the "Jesus movement," as its independent Christian churches continued to multiply. These bodies combine elements of native tribal religions with Western Christianity, something that missionary-founded churches in Africa never sought.

Since World War II, the independent churches have proliferated to become the "fourth force" in African Christianity. There are 45,000,000 Roman Catholics in Africa; 29,000,000 Protestants; and 14,000,000 Orthodox and Coptic adherents; while the estimated 5,000 independent churches have a membership believed to total 9,000,000. In comparison, non-Christians number 249,000,000 out of a total African population of 346,000,000. While beliefs and practices differ among the independent churches, spontaneity of expression is common to all. In this they resemble American pentecostalism, but in a different context.

Latin America. In Latin America, churchmen were coming forward as never before to align themselves against oppressive policies and to seek a better life for impoverished masses.

The ruling oligarchies of Brazil and Paraguay, long uncontested by religious circles, were under increasing fire from church officials. The hierarchy of Paraguay attacked the regime of Gen. Alfredo Stroessner on grounds of "abuses and physical assaults on priests" and "systematic persecution of the laity." A church-state struggle in that country led to the excommunication of thirty government officials.

In Chile, reactions to the Marxist Government may prove to be the key to Christian-Socialist collaboration and coexistence in South America. Clergy and other church leaders took a "wait and see" attitude toward the Chilean regime.

A hopeful sign in Latin America was the opinion of Gary MacEoin, a leading Catholic writer and Latin-American expert, that liberal Catholics and Protestants have joined forces to "remake society in Christ."

ACTIVIST, LIKE IT OR NOT

The continuing argument of many churches over whether their major endeavors should concentrate on individual soul-saving or on social-action ventures appeared purely academic when viewed against the perspective of a world in which, whether it consciously chose to be there or not, religion was in the middle of the daily life of people everywhere. Religion as a force in human affairs is flourishing as never before.

WELDON WALLACE
Religion Editor, *The* (Baltimore) *Sun*

RUMANIA

Soviet-Rumanian differences in 1971 provoked sharp words and the implied threat of invasion by the Soviet Union. The Soviets were particularly annoyed by Rumania's friendship with Communist China.

Independence Declarations. Party leader and President Nicolae Ceausescu made clear that Rumania would defend its right to act independently of the Soviet Union and other members of the Warsaw Pact. This view was stressed in a speech to the 24th congress of the Soviet Union's Communist Party on Apr. 1 in Moscow. On May 7, 50th anniversary of the founding of the Rumanian Communist Party, Ceausescu was even more emphatic. He asserted that "respect for the right of each people to decide its own destinies independently, that is the cornerstone of international cooperation." The war of nerves became somewhat ominous in July, when Warsaw Pact maneuvers were conducted on Hungarian soil by Soviet, Czechoslovak and Hungarian forces. On Aug. 2, at a conference held in the Crimea of Warsaw Pact leaders, all the first secretaries of the Soviet-bloc countries appeared except Ceausescu. His absence led to rumors that the possibility of an invasion of Rumania, similar to what happened in Czechoslovakia in 1968, was being discussed at the conference. Soviet Ambassador Drozdenko met with Ceausescu in Bucharest and, according to reports, the Soviet diplomat complained about Rumania's attitude. Following the meeting, an emergency session of party and government leaders endorsed President Ceausescu's stand that Rumania would not yield to outside pressure.

The China Issue. Soviet displeasure with the Rumanians derived in part from Ceausescu's active support of Communist China. (Reports were aired that the Rumanian leader had played a role in arranging the *rapprochement* between the United States and China.) Ceausescu visited China in June and received a warm welcome from the Chinese leaders. They also repeated their promise of support, apparently against a Russian threat. Rumanian and Chinese military delegations exchanged visits, and plans were made for the employment of Chinese experts in projects included in the $250,000,000 loan made to Rumania by China. Apparently at Soviet instigation, Hungarian, East German and Czechoslovak commentators all attacked Rumania's pro-China stance after Ceausescu returned from Peking. The Rumanians were particularly sharp in responding to the Hungarian criticism, since the attack included a reference to the Hungarian minority in the Transylvania region of Rumania.

RUMANIA

Area: 91,699 sq. mi.
Population: 20,600,000
Capital: Bucharest
Government: Nicolae Ceausescu, Communist Party secretary—1965, head of state—1967; Ion Maurer, premier—1961
Gross National Product: $21,400,000,000
Foreign trade: exports, $1,851,000,000; imports, $1,960,000,000
Armed forces: 160,000

Comecon Cooperation. In spite of the differences with its Warsaw Pact colleagues, Rumania played host to the Comecon Council, held in Bucharest in July. The group, which consists of the premiers of all the member countries, approved a long-term program of economic integration within the East European mutual economic cooperation organization.

Domestic Unity. Apparently in response to pressure from the Soviet-bloc countries, Ceausescu launched a program designed to stress Rumania's unity. The trade-union congress was assured that its views would be received more sympathetically. Touring Transylvania, Ceausescu promised greater cultural freedom to the region's Hungarians. He also sparked a drive for greater ideological orthodoxy among the country's intellectuals, which did not sit very well with the young and liberal writers opposed to reimposition of stringent party control.

International Ties. Rumania continued to strengthen its diplomatic and trade ties with East and West. Yugoslavia was favored among the communist countries. In the West, the United States, West Germany and Greece expanded their economic agreements with Rumania. A new law permits foreign firms to own 49 per cent of joint companies organized in Rumania.

Economic Development. A bumper agricultural crop helped overcome the shortage caused by the 1970 floods. On the industrial front, however, problems arose out of failures in transportation and supply.

HERMAN SINGER
Editor, *East Europe*

SHIPPING

Though the number of American flag ships has dwindled to about 690, and they carry only about 5 per cent of U.S. cargo moving in foreign trade, the U.S. maritime industry was honored with the National Safety Council's 1971 award of first place for safety. It was the first time the shipping industry had captured the coveted award.

LASH *Italia*. Competition is fierce in shipping, and engineers and architects are constantly working on technological developments geared toward creating greater efficiency in the transportation and handling of cargoes. One of the latest concepts became a reality on Jan. 28, 1971, when the LASH *Italia* arrived in New York on her maiden voyage. LASH (Lighter Aboard Ship) *Italia* features a giant 500-ton gantry crane that lifts 61-foot-by-31-foot lighters aboard or off the ship. The crane is mounted on rails that run the full cargo working length of the ship, enabling it to place the lighters into, or retrieve them from, the ship's hold. Since the barges can be towed to and from the ship, the operation eliminates pierside docking. Thus port time is cut considerably, and smaller ports can now receive cargo from ships too large to enter. LASH *Italia* was the first American-flag commercial vessel to enter the U.S. merchant-marine service since President Nixon signed the Merchant Marine Act of 1970 (designed to revitalize the dwindling U.S. fleet). She was the first of five LASH sister ships to be placed into service by Prudential-Grace Lines.

The complexion of the merchant-marine fleets of the world is changing. To meet these challenges, Seatrain International, S.A., char-tered *Euroliner,* the world's largest and fastest container carrier and the first privately owned commercial ship to use gas turbines. The new ship made her debut in April with an impressive passage that saw her reach a speed of 28 knots.

Containers. An ambitious plan to operate the fastest container-freight service between the U.S. Pacific seaboard and Southeast Asia was inaugurated by the Japanese "K" (Kawasaki Kisen Kaisha) Line. The service will feature specially built container vessels, each equipped with a set of two mobile gantry cranes to load and unload containers at ports lacking modern container-terminal facilities. The line plans a thrice-monthly service through five U.S. and Far Eastern ports: Hong Kong; Kaohsiung and Keelung (Taiwan); Pusan (South Korea); Seattle (Wash. State) and Long Beach (Calif.). The Seattle-Hong Kong run will take only 15 days, 5 days less than previously because the projected route skips Japanese ports. The "K" Line has a fleet of 97 vessels aggregating 3,340,-000 deadweight tons, which ranks it third in Japan and third in the world.

Though U.S. containerships handle about 60 per cent of all container cargo crossing the North Atlantic, container trade in non-U.S.

The "Euroliner," the world's largest container carrier and first privately owned commercial ship to use gas turbines, is brought into service.

vessels has increased tremendously. There is a noteworthy trend toward cooperation between companies. Typical of this new cooperation are the working agreements of Australia Europe Container Service, consisting of Overseas Containers Ltd., Associated Container Transportation (Australia) Ltd., Australia National Line, Messageries Maritimes and Lloyd Triestino. The thirteenth ship to join this service, the *Abel Tasman,* can carry 862 standard 20-foot containers in 6 holds and (on deck) 728 units. Another ship is projected for the future with an underdeck capacity of 2,000 standard 20-foot containers.

Still another example of the new cooperation is the Scanstar service between Europe and the West Coast of the United States and Canada. Scanstar is the container company formed by Blue Star Line of London and the East Asiatic Co. of Copenhagen. Each company contributes two ships to the service.

Tankers. Following the closing of the Suez Canal in 1967, tankers sailing between the Persian Gulf and Western Europe, around the Cape of Good Hope, have had a trip of more than 11,000 miles one way. It was obvious that it would be necessary to have either twice as many tankers or twice the tanker capacity to carry the same amount of oil as before from the Middle East. Though the trend toward larger tankers had already started, the canal's closing spurred the age of the supertanker. The giants of some 250,000 deadweight tons and more are over 1,000 feet long and mainly ply the run between the Persian Gulf and Europe, as few ports can accommodate them. Most U.S. ports can handle tankers of only 38,000 to 50,000 deadweight tons, which illustrates the need for tankers of all sizes to meet the requirements of each geographic area.

In 1971 a British company delivered a 372,-400-dwt tanker to Nisseki Maru, a Tokyo tanker company. It was the world's largest tanker then but was unlikely to hold that distinction long. Tankers of 477,000 dwt were under construction as the year ended.

Seaborne oil transportation has increased tenfold in recent years and makes up some 60 per cent of the world's ocean commerce. About 32,500,000 barrels of oil are moved each day by noncommunist tankers, with the U.S. fleet amounting to 6 per cent of the world fleet. Of the total world tanker fleet, 31 per cent are owned by oil companies, 65 per cent by independents, 1 per cent by the military and 3 per cent by Soviet-bloc countries.

Passenger Ships. Although transatlantic crossings are almost a dying luxury, cruises are on the upswing generally. In fact they are so

Esso

The "Esso Northumbria" (253,000 deadweight tons) is an example of the new breed of supertankers, spurred by closing of the Suez Canal.

popular that over a dozen new or newly renovated cruise ships are due to be delivered in the next few years. New York, although still an important port of embarkation, is facing direct competition with the modern facilities of Port Everglades and Miami, Fla. In addition there are numerous cruises sailing from other East and West Coast ports besides Mediterranean and Scandinavian ports.

Typical of the new interest in cruises is the fact that the Holland-America Line is building an 8,700-ton ship to sail out of Singapore through the Indonesian archipelago. The line hopes to attract vacationers from China, Japan and Europe.

Among the new ships commissioned in 1971 were Flagship Cruises' *Sea Venture* (to be joined early in 1972 by her twin, *Island Venture*), Royal Caribbean Cruises' *Nordic Prince* and Cunard Line's *Cunard Adventurer.* Among older ships being reconditioned was Holland-America's *Statendam.*

Though the large passenger ships, such as the *Oceanic* (Home Lines) and the *Rotterdam* (Holland-America), are favorites, smaller cruise vessels, in the 20,000-ton range, are being built and operated, aimed at the middle-class market.

The East and West coasts of the United States suffered a major dockworkers' strike. For more information on the strike see the article Labor.

DIANE DURYEA
Yachting Magazine

SINGAPORE

For the first time since the 224-square-mile island severed its link with the Malaysian Federation in 1965, Singapore Prime Minister Lee Kuan Yew in 1971 was confronted with a domestic political crisis, based on press freedom. On May 2 four executives of the Chinese-language daily *Nanyang Siang Pau* were detained without trial for "glamorizing Chinese communism." The English-language *Eastern Sun* closed on May 16 after the Government claimed that it was communist-financed. Next, the ten-month-old *Singapore Herald* was accused of subversive journalism and dubious financial backing; it died in June when a protracted struggle ended with cancellation of its printing license.

The crisis spotlighted Premier Lee's growing autocracy, but if his popularity diminished among the intelligentsia, it remained high with local and foreign businessmen. Industry and exports expanded. Politically, stirrings of dissent were apparent. A People's Front Party joined a dozen ineffectual opposition groups in March 1971 but sank into confusion after Lee identified one of its leaders as a government agent. The year saw crackdowns on environmental pollution, drugs and hippies; family-planning programs were tightened to help stabilize the 2,000,000 population. Tobacco advertising was banned.

In January, Singapore played host to the British Commonwealth Prime Ministers' Conference. Later, however, foreign affairs were marked by apprehension over Communist China's diplomatic forays. Trade offensives were mounted as neighboring Malaysia signed a trade agreement with Communist China, cutting out the British colony of Hong Kong and Singapore as middlemen.

In fiscal 1971, government revenue totaled U.S.$340,500,000, exceeding estimated spending by a few hundred dollars. Meanwhile the Oriental version of the Eurodollar, Singapore's Asiadollar market, grew slowly but steadily and holdings in late 1971 were put at U.S.$500,000,000. Mindful of the expected Southeast Asian oil bonanza, Singapore welcomed a U.S.$50,000,000 shipyard investment by Japan's Mitsubishi.

In November the British military establishment ended a 150-year tradition and handed Malaysia-Singapore defense responsibilities to a five-power treaty force, including Australian, New Zealand and British commitments. Singapore's relations with Malaysia in 1971 were cordial although a row developed when Australia balked at a U.S.$4,500,000 annual rent demand for the use of Singapore barracks.

In August 1971 Singapore's per capita annual income was put at U.S.$840. The consumer price index by July was 113.7, two points higher than in 1970, but it was based on 1960 weightings that no longer reflected consumer preferences. Benjamin Henry Sheares became Singapore's president in 1971, succeeding President Yusof who died in 1970.

DEREK DAVIES
Editor, *Far Eastern Economic Review*

UPI

Arnold Smith (l), secretary-general of the Commonwealth, and S. Rajaratnam (r), Singapore's foreign minister, listens as Prime Minister Lee Kuan Yew gives welcoming address to 31-nation Commonwealth Conference meeting in January.

SOUTH AFRICA, REPUBLIC OF

South Africa was afflicted with a record post-World War II level of inflation during 1971. It was one of the chief brakes on the rate of economic growth. After achieving a healthy 6.1 per cent a year from 1964 onward, the rate fell below the 1971 target of 5.5 per cent to between 4 and 3.5 per cent.

For wool producers, 1970–71 was the worst season in years. The sale of automobiles sagged. While sales taxes were increased, payrolls were cut. Diamond cutters and polishers were particularly hard hit by unemployment. Reserves of gold declined; and in December the rand was devalued by 12.28 per cent in terms of gold, following on the world monetary crisis.

Paradoxically, in spite of severe unemployment in some fields, the other big reason for the slowed economy was an acute shortage of manpower—above all, of skilled labor.

It was on the labor front that cracks became most visible in the policy of apartheid—racial separation. In the crippled construction industry, the rules were eased to allow Coloreds (Africans of mixed ancestry) to take jobs that had been reserved for white workers, such as bricklaying and plastering, in spite of strong resentment on the part of right-wing white building workers. In another area, the serious shortage of nurses resulted in permission for nonwhite nurses to take duty in white wards.

Further, nonwhite workers were slowly beginning to receive the same wages as white workers. South Africa's two largest banks (Standard Bank of South Africa; Barclays, South Africa) announced in August that they would pay nonwhite clerks (who had been getting about $112 a month) the same rates as white clerks (about $500 a month).

A long-simmering conflict sharpened between the Government and the "English" churches; that is, all those except the Afrikaners' mother church, the Dutch Reformed. The aspect of the struggle that received the widest international attention involved the Anglican Dean of Johannesburg, the Very Rev. Gonville Aubrey ffrench-Beytagh. Openly critical of apartheid, he was arrested in January and held for eight

Photoreporters

Anglican Dean ffrench-Beytagh is sentenced to five years imprisonment under Terrorism Act.

days in Pretoria, under the Terrorism Act. The act permits the security police to detain indefinitely any person suspected of being connected with terrorist activities. Moreover, the accused is presumed guilty until he proves himself innocent. At his trial, which started on Aug. 2, the Dean pleaded "not guilty" to charges of plotting to overthrow the Government. When he took the stand, he called the charges against him "absolute fantasy" and said "I do not believe in violence." Nevertheless, he was convicted on 4 of 10 charges against him and was sentenced to 5 years imprisonment on Nov. 1. His fate and government moves against other opponents of apartheid sparked the strongest protest in ten years.

Spending for defense rose to a record level. A test of the first South African-designed air-to-air missile was successful. Early in the year, Britain agreed to sell helicopters and spare parts to the South African Navy for maritime defense.

South Africa is the world's only industrialized country without television. In 1971 the Government approved the introduction of TV service, probably to go into operation after 1975.

Although the Government took some highly qualified steps toward racially integrated sports, Australia canceled the Springbok cricket tour because South Africa would not allow blacks or Coloreds on the team to tour Australia.

SOUTH AFRICA

Area: 471,444 sq. mi.
Population: 20,600,000
Capitals: Cape Town; Pretoria
Government: J. J. Fouche, president—1968; Balthazar J. Vorster, prime minister—1966
Gross National Product: $17,600,000,000
Foreign trade: exports, $2,148,000,000; imports, $3,556,000,000
Armed forces: 44,250

SPACE

Space activity in 1971 was highlighted by two more manned landings on the moon, the first visits to a prototype space station, and the start of the most comprehensive unmanned exploration of the planet Mars.

Of the four manned spaceflights, two each were by the United States and the Soviet Union. The American flights, Apollos 14 and 15, were both successful lunar–landing missions. The Soviets flew Soyuz 10 and 11, each involving the visit of a three-man crew to a space platform called Salyut 1. The Soyuz 11 mission accomplished the longest duration of man in space but claimed the lives of the three cosmonauts.

First of the manned flights, Apollo 14, was launched on Jan. 31 and commanded by Alan B. Shepard, Jr. Ten years earlier he had flown the first U.S. manned spacecraft but had not been up in the interim. His teammates were lunar-module pilot Edgar D. Mitchell and command-module pilot Stuart A. Roosa; both were space rookies.

Despite a series of minor difficulties en route, Apollo 14 made it to the moon and went into lunar orbit on Feb. 4. On the following day, Shepard and Mitchell descended to the lunar surface in the *Antares* landing module, becoming the fifth and sixth men to set foot on the moon. In the command module *Kitty Hawk,* Roosa continued to circle the moon in an orbit that dipped as low as 45,000 feet from the lunar surface.

At the Fra Mauro landing site in the rough lunar highlands, Shepard and Mitchell made two moonwalks totaling more than nine hours. On the first walk they remained in the vicinity of the lunar module, collecting soil and rock samples, photographing terrain features and deploying the ALSEP (Apollo Lunar Science Experiments Package), a $25,000,000 assortment of instruments designed to report data to earth after the astronauts' departure. The principal instruments were a seismometer, for a study of moonquakes, and a reflector to beam back to earth a laser–light ray triggered from an earth station. The latter instrument permits precise measurement of earth-moon distances over a long period for a study of earth's wobbling on its axis. In an additional experiment, Shepard detonated a series of very small explosive charges whose vibrations were recorded by earth stations to give scientists new information on the composition of the lunar crust.

On their second walk, Shepard and Mitchell made a mile-and-a-half round trip to Fra Mauro's Cone Carter, collecting more photographs, soil samples and rocks. On Feb. 6, after some 34 hours on the moon, the astronauts lifted off the surface in *Antares* and docked with the waiting *Kitty Hawk*. They brought with them 108 pounds of rock and soil samples. The return to earth was uneventful, and on Feb. 9 *Kitty Hawk* splashed down near Samoa, where the command module and crew were picked up by the aircraft carrier *New Orleans*. Mission time was just 2 minutes over 9 days.

The second lunar landing of the year, Apollo 15, was by far the most successful mission of the program from the standpoints of precision flight and scientific gain. Launched July 26, Apollo 15 was commanded by David R. Scott, a veteran of two previous spaceflights, and crewed by two rookies: James B. Irwin, pilot of the lunar module *Falcon;* and Alfred M. Worden, pilot of the command module *Endeavour*. Apollo 15 went into lunar orbit on July 29, and on July 30 Scott and Irwin landed alongside the moon's mile-wide, 1,200-foot-deep Hadley Rille, near the towering Apennine Mountains, whose peaks reach as high as 15,000 feet. During a stay of 66 hours and 5 minutes on the moon, Scott and Irwin made three lunar-surface expeditions for photography, sample collection and other experiments, remaining outside their spacecraft a total of 18½ hours.

Making its debut on Apollo 15 was the lunar rover, a wire–wheeled, battery–powered dune buggy capable of carrying the two astronauts and a variety of tools and experimental devices, including a TV camera and an umbrellalike antenna. In the rover, Scott and Irwin were able to range far from their landing site to collect samples from a number of locales with differing characteristics. On their three treks, they covered 17½ miles and acquired 171 pounds of samples. A tool innovation was a lunar drill, with which the astronauts were able to dig several feet into the lurain and extract core samples of the subsurface. They also set up another ALSEP station to join the two left by previous Apollo crews.

On Aug. 2, Scott and Irwin left the moon in the *Falcon* and flew to rendezvous with Worden and *Endeavour* waiting in orbit. Apollo 15 spent an additional two days in lunar orbit while the crew photographed and mapped the lunar surface. Additionally, the astronauts deployed a 78.5–pound subsatellite designed to remain in orbit and radio scientific data for a year. On Aug. 4, *Endeavour* was blasted out of lunar orbit and into homebound trajectory. The spacecraft reentered the atmosphere on Aug. 7 in a path that took it to splashdown north of the Hawaiian island of Oahu, where the recovery ship, the helicopter carrier *Okinawa*, was waiting. Apollo 15 ended on a tense note when

For the future: the reusable manned space shuttle will place unmanned satellites in earth orbit and deliver supplies to orbiting spacecraft. Go-ahead on development of the shuttle was given early in 1972.

only two of the three descent parachutes opened fully; the two, however, lowered the command module to a safe, if slightly harder than usual, impact. Longest of the Apollo lunar missions, Apollo 15 took more than 12 days from launch to splashdown.

A preliminary to the Soviet Union's manned-spaceflight activity was the Apr. 19 launch of Salyut 1, a 17½-ton unmanned space laboratory designed for a long stay in orbit and repeated visits by crews. On Apr. 23, the U.S.S.R. launched the first team of visitors in Soyuz 10; the crew comprised commander Vladimir Shatalov, engineer Aleksei Yeliseyev and "orbital station engineer" Nikolai Rukavishnikov. The last was on his first spaceflight, and his companions were making their second trips into space. The cosmonauts guided Soyuz 10 to a docking with Salyut 1 on Apr. 24, then transferred to the prototype space station, orbiting at an average altitude of 125 miles. The linked spacecraft, together weighing some 55,-000 pounds, provided 3,500 cubic feet of living and working area. Apparently the Soyuz 10 mission was intended only as a checkout of Salyut systems and the docking apparatus, for the three cosmonauts returned to earth on Apr. 25, having spent 5½ hours in the laboratory.

The second visit to Salyut began on June 6 with the launch of Soyuz 11, crewed by Georgi Dobrovolsky, Vladislav N. Volkov and Viktor I. Patsayev; Volkov had previously flown a Soyuz

mission, his crewmates were first-timers. A day later, Soyuz 11 docked with Salyut, and the cosmonauts transferred to the laboratory. One of their first acts was to fire the propulsion system to adjust the altitude of the linked Soyuz/Salyut to an average of about 155 miles, permitting a longer time in space. In the 65½-foot-long space station, the cosmonauts performed a variety of scientific experiments for almost 23 days, breaking the space endurance record of 425 hours established by the crew of Soyuz 9 a year earlier. Then, on June 30, the crew detached Soyuz 11 and started the return to earth. Soyuz 11 made what appeared to be a normal, safe reentry and descent, but communication with the cosmonauts was lost during the descent. The spacecraft was found intact, but all three cosmonauts were dead; analysis showed that death resulted from loss of cabin pressurization due to a leak in the hatch system. It was the third spacecraft tragedy. The U.S.S.R. had earlier lost cosmonaut Vladimir Komarov when the descent parachute of his Soyuz 1 spacecraft fouled during descent. The other tragedy, claiming three lives as did Soyuz 11, occurred on Jan. 27, 1967, when Virgil I. Grissom, Edward H. White and Roger B. Chaffee were killed in a cabin fire during a prelaunch test of Apollo 1.

Salyut 1 remained in orbit another 3½ months, but if there had ever been plans for additional crew visits they were canceled after the tragedy. Salyut was permitted to "decay" —drop into the atmosphere—and, since it was not designed for recovery, it burned from the friction heat of reentry on Oct. 11.

The most comprehensive exploration of Mars yet attempted began Nov. 13 when the U.S. Mariner 9 swept into orbit around the planet. Mariner was the surviving member of a two-spacecraft team launched in May; the companion Mariner 8 was lost on launch. Designed to provide 15 times as much planetary data as all previous Marscraft combined, Mariner 9 left the earth on May 30 and flew a 248,000,000-mile elliptical path to its encounter with Mars. Mariner 9, weighing 2,272 pounds, was equipped with two TV cameras for photomapping Mars and its two moons, plus instruments for acquiring detailed data on both the Martian atmosphere and the surface of the planet. In addition, it carried instruments to measure Mars' gravitational field, the planet's orbit around the sun, and the orbits of the moons, Phobos and Deimos, around the planet.

Mariner 9 encountered Mars at a velocity of slightly more than 11,000 mph. A 15–minute 15–second burn of the spacecraft's rocket engine slowed the craft to orbital velocity of 8,600 mph; Mariner 9 thus became the first spacecraft to go into orbit around another planet. A later, 6–second burn of the engine adjusted the orbit so that Mariner 9 was flying an elliptical path that took it to an apoapsis (high point in orbit) of 10,650 miles and a periapsis (low point) of 863 miles; in this orbit the craft was making 1 revolution every 12 hours.

The initial pictures returned to earth by Mariner 9 showed little planetary detail because of a raging dust storm which was expected to continue for several weeks; some scientists regarded this as a research bonus, for later comparison with clear pictures will permit study of Martian atmospheric disturbances. In its second week in orbit, Mariner returned the first photo ever taken of the tiny (6–mile–diameter) moon Deimos. Mariner was planned for a 90–day basic mission, during which it was to photomap some 70 per cent of the Martian surface and to take a number of pictures of the two moons. NASA scientists hoped, however, that the cameras and instruments would continue to function long beyond the planned mission lifetime. It was estimated that the spacecraft would orbit the planet for 17 years.

Mariner 9 was joined in the Mars exploration by two Soviet spacecraft, Mars 2 and 3, launched May 19 and May 28. Because their departure velocity was lower than that of Mariner 9, the two Soviet craft traveled less rapidly en route. The first of the five-ton probes, Mars 2, encountered the planet and began orbiting on Nov. 27; Mars 3 arrived Dec. 3 and also achieved orbit. Each of the spacecraft ejected a landing capsule, designed as a "soft lander," equipped with parachute and retro-rockets to control the rate of descent and with basic life-search instrumentation. The Mars 2 lander apparently crashed; the Mars 3 capsule touched down on the surface, but its signals terminated almost immediately. The Martian storm was blamed for the losses. The two basic spacecraft, however, continued to orbit and to send back Mars data.

On Nov. 17, after four days of Mariner 9 orbital operations, NASA sent details of the spacecraft's findings to the Soviet Academy of Sciences. This marked the initial step in a new program of U.S./U.S.S.R. space cooperation that goes far beyond the earlier agreement, which was confined largely to exchange of space–meteorological data. During the year, a series of Joint Working Group meetings· produced agreements covering expansion of the weather program to include coordination with respect to ground-receiving equipment; continued exchange of lunar samples and other lunar information; exchange of planetary data; and establishment of a joint sounding–rocket program in 1973–74. Approved in principle was the development of compatible docking equipment for manned spacecraft, so that spacecraft of either nation could dock with the other's earth–orbiting space stations. Discussions continued toward possible expansion of manned space cooperation.

In other space activity, the Soviet Union continued its unmanned exploration of the moon. Lunokhod 1, the robot laboratory deposited on the moon by Luna 17 in November 1970, continued to move about the lunar surface under earth command, performing a variety of scientific experiments. Although designed for only a 3–month lifetime, Lunokhod remained active more than 10 months, until Oct. 4 when its nuclear power generator ceased functioning. Lunokhod 1 qualified as one of the outstanding successes of unmanned space exploration. It moved 6.5 miles, mapped 95,000 square yards of the lunar surface, took more than 20,000 photographs, tested the soil at 500 sites and performed on–the–spot chemical analyses of soil constituents in 25 locales.

On Sept. 2, the U.S.S.R. launched Luna 18, a spacecraft similar to the Luna 17 which carried Lunokhod, and Western observers believe that the new mission was intended for delivering another Lunokhod. Luna 18 successfully achieved lunar orbit, but on Sept. 11

made what the Soviets described as an "unlucky" landing, and communication was lost. On Sept. 28, the Soviets sent Luna 19 into lunar trajectory, but U.S.S.R. officials indicated from the start that it was not designed as a lunar lander. The spacecraft went into lunar orbit on Oct. 3, and at year–end was still returning data to earth.

In 1971 the U.S.S.R. successfully launched three additional satellites to join the Meteor weather–observation network. Meteor 7, 8 and 9 were launched respectively on Jan. 20, Apr. 17 and July 16.

Most of the other Soviet space activity was grouped in the catchall Cosmos category of unmanned spacecraft. It includes scientific satel-

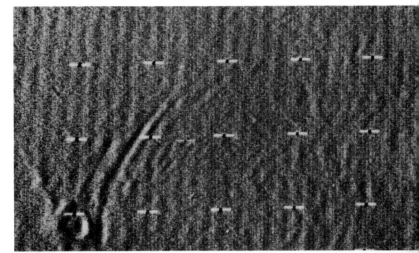

Mariner 9 began orbiting the planet Mars on Nov. 13. Its two television cameras transmitted photos of the planet back to earth as the craft approached Mars (r), Mars' moon Phobos (below, l) and a 70-mile-diameter crater near Nodus Gordii (below, r).

Photos NASA

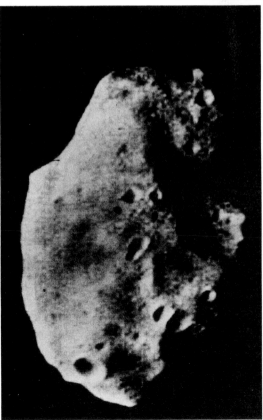

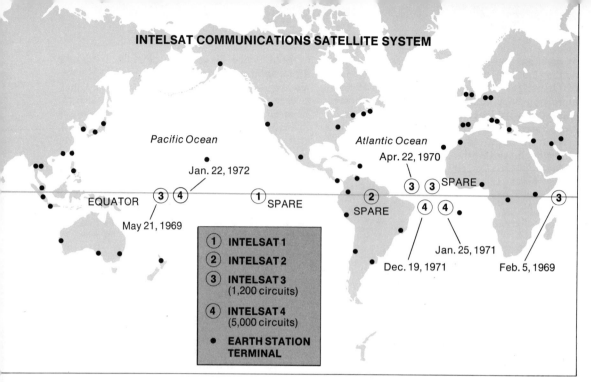

INTELSAT COMMUNICATIONS SATELLITE SYSTEM

Pacific Ocean

Jan. 22, 1972

EQUATOR ③ ④ ① SPARE

May 21, 1969

Atlantic Ocean

Apr. 22, 1970

③ ③ SPARE

② ④ ④

SPARE

Jan. 25, 1971

Dec. 19, 1971   Feb. 5, 1969

③

① INTELSAT 1
② INTELSAT 2
③ INTELSAT 3
(1,200 circuits)
④ INTELSAT 4
(5,000 circuits)
● EARTH STATION
TERMINAL

lites, military systems, experimental–applications satellites, and advanced technology experiments, including some in connection with Soyuz/Salyut. A highlight of the Cosmos program was Cosmos 393, launched Jan. 26: It marked the 1,000th space mission by all nations. On two occasions—May 7 and Oct. 7—the U.S.S.R. launched 8 Cosmos packages on a single booster. Cosmos satellites were orbited at the rate of 6 to 7 a month, a rate slightly higher than that of the 1970 record year.

Aside from the Apollo and Mariner missions, U.S. civil space activity was at a low ebb, averaging only about one launch a month, several of them cooperative programs with other nations. Included were three applications satellites, one of which failed. The failure was a weather satellite of the Tiros family, the first unsuccessful spacecraft in 22 meteorological-satellite launches. It would have been the second of a new, advanced series of metsats carrying the designation NOAA (for National Oceanic and Atmospheric Administration, which operates the network). Launched Oct. 21, the satellite failed to achieve orbit. The other applications satellites were Intelsat 4's for the global commercial comsat network, the first launched on Jan. 25, the second on Dec. 19, and the third on Jan. 22, 1972. The Intelsat 4's were the first of this advanced type of communication satellite to go into service; weighing more than 1,500 pounds, each Intelsat 4 is capable of handling an average of 5,000 circuits simultaneously.

NASA's major scientific satellite was OSO–7, the seventh in a series of Orbiting Solar Observatories. Launched Sept. 28, the satellite initially went into improper orbit and began tumbling, but it was "rescued" by radio command signals from the earth-control station, and all six of the spacecraft's experiments went into operation. OSO–7 was reporting data on a variety of solar phenomena, particularly solar flares and streamers, the latter mysterious rays in the faint outer layer of the solar atmosphere, photographed for the first time.

Other major programs included IMP–I, launched Mar. 13, and the Explorer 45 Small Scientific Satellite, launched from the Italian-operated San Marco launch platform in the Indian Ocean off Kenya on Nov. 15. IMP–I was the eighth in a series of Interplanetary Monitoring Platforms; it was operating in a highly elliptical orbit that took it as high as 125,000 miles from earth. The spacecraft's mission was to study energetic particles, solar plasma, magnetic fields, and astronomical phenomena, and also to test a new computer. Primary objective of the Small Scientific Satellite was to investigate the causes of large-scale magnetic disturbances associated with solar flares.

The U.S. military space program continued to decline in terms of launch activity, dropping to about 2 a month from the preceding year's 3. As in past years, most of the activity was of a classified nature, but the Department of Defense launched about 8 reconnaissance satellites, at least 1 missile–detection system and 2 or more communications–monitoring satellites. Among the unclassified programs were a series of Orbiting Vehicles; military/scientific spacecraft; and the first 2 satellites of a new military comsat system. The last, launched together on Nov. 3, were part of the DoD Phase II Defense Satellite Communications System, in which 6 large, high–capacity satellites will eventually replace the 26 smaller spacecraft in the currently operational Initial Defense Satellite Communications System. The Phase II satellites operate in synchronous orbit at 22,300 miles altitude; they weigh 1,150 pounds each and measure 9 by 13 feet.

In the area of international cooperative projects, the United States participated in major programs with the United Kingdom, Canada, France, Italy and West Germany, and with a greater number of nations in sounding–rocket programs. The Soviet Union announced the formation, on Nov. 15, of Intersputnik, the communist equivalent of the Western world's Intelsat satellite–communications network; initial membership comprised Bulgaria, Cuba, Czechoslovakia, East Germany, Hungary, Mongolia, Poland, Rumania and the U.S.S.R. The European Launcher Development Organization (ELDO), a consortium of Western European nations, experienced its fourth failure in as many attempts to launch a satellite by means of its Europa launch vehicle. Fired from the French Space Center at Kourou, French Guiana (South America), on Nov. 5, the Europa II rocket plunged into the Atlantic when its first and second stages failed to separate (the three previous oribtal attempts in 1968–70 had been with the smaller Europa I). Another try with Europa II was set for 1972.

The United Kingdom became the world's sixth space-capable nation; that is, one that has demonstrated it can orbit a home-built spacecraft by means of a home-built launch vehicle. (The United Kingdom had previously orbited a number of satellites, but with U.S. launch assistance.) On Oct 28, from the Woomera Test Range in Australia, the United Kingdom used its Black Arrow launch vehicle to send into orbit a 145-pound satellite named *Prospero*, a package containing both scientific and advanced technology experiments. Britain thus joined a select group of space-capable nations that comprises, chronologically, the U.S.S.R., the United States, France, Japan and the People's Republic of China.

The other nations of the group were also active during the year. Japan's Institute of Space and Aeronautical Science, a division of Tokyo University, launched the nation's second and third satellites following an initial success in 1970. Using the new Mu–4S launch vehicle, Japan sent into orbit on Feb. 16 from the Uchinoura Space Center a 138.6–pound test satellite named *Tansei* (Light Blue). With the same booster, the Japanese on Sept. 28 orbited the nation's first real scientific satellite, weighing 145 pounds and named *Shinsei* (New Star). On Mar. 3, Red China launched its second satellite, tentatively coded China 2, from a launch base identified by Western sources as Shangcheng–Tzu, near the Sino–Mongolian border. The new satellite was believed to be in the same weight category as 1970's China 1 (380 pounds), but no information was available on the launch vehicle employed. France, the third most active space nation, launched its seventh independent satellite, the D-2A, first of a new series of scientific satellites designed for solar ultraviolet research and for analyzing the distribution of hydrogen in the earth's atmosphere. The D-2A was launched Apr. 15 from Kourou by a Diamant B launch vehicle.

JAMES J. HAGGERTY
Free-Lance Writer
Author, *Apollo Lunar Landing*

Britain's first technological satellite, "Prospero," is launched by a Black Arrow rocket from the Woomera Test Range in Australia, on Oct. 28.

SPAIN

Although there were some gestures toward liberalizing government policies and the opposition grew stronger during 1971, the Franco regime held to its tight clamp on freedom of speech, of assembly and of association. A young lawyer, Alejandro Rojas Marcos, leader of the opposition to Franco in Seville, was arrested in March because he had accused the Government of talking about liberalism while frustrating it. Impatience was growing over the fact that the Constitution promulgated in 1967 —the "organic law of the state"—had still to be put into effect.

Instead, a law was proposed in the Cortes (Parliament) that would give greater power to mayors, governors, the police and the national Government to fine "offenders of public order" —that is, dissidents—from $14 up to $14,000. In effect, it would make the police a political pressure group. It drew strong protests in Madrid. Military courts were already imposing stiff fines on civilian offenders.

In September, after 17 psychiatrists refused to go home from the Francisco Franco Medical Center, in protest against the planned reduction of psychiatric services there, a doctors' sit-in spread to all of Spain (they continued to carry on their duties) until almost 2,000 of them were demonstrating against authoritarian, old-fashioned medical practices.

Yet, on Sept. 29, in an election for about a fifth of the Cortes members, only some half of the eligible voters bothered to go to the polls. At that, the only two candidates who had expressed opposition to the Government were elected.

Prince Juan Carlos, Franco's designated successor, himself began to show some independence. In a speech to Basques, at Guernica, he emphasized the monarchy without mentioning the regime, and omitted any reference to his pledge to perpetuate it.

In what was said to be the largest opposition gathering in Spain since the civil war (1936–39), about three hundred Catalonians, calling themselves the Assembly of Catalonia, met in secret to draft a program of resistance to bring down the regime and block the succession of the Prince.

Liberalism was being supported by the Vatican and, on the whole, by the Spanish Catholic Church. The struggle between the regime and the Church centered on a proposed new concordat (the last was in 1953). A majority of the 81-member Spanish Conference of Bishops objected to the new agreement on the grounds that it would do little to loosen the ties between church and state. In June, only three weeks after Madrid's Archbishop Casimiro Morcillo died, the Vatican appointed a moderate, Vicente Cardinal Enrique y Tarancon, Apostolic Administrator of Madrid-Alcala (later Archbishop of Madrid) to prevent the most important see in Spain from coming under the control of the extreme right-wing Msgr. Jose Guerra Campos. Further, a two thirds majority of an assembly of bishops and priests called for an end to church-state links and for establishing social and economic justice. A smaller majority apologized for the role of the Church in the civil war.

Spain achieved the fastest economic growth rate of any Western European country. In 1962–71 the yearly per capita income rose from $290 to $900. The aim was to raise the figure to $1,000 at least by the end of 1972. Tourism remained extremely important. In the period January–August 1971, some 20,000,000 visitors came, 11.2 per cent more than in the same period in 1970.

However, on the negative side, industrial production increased by only 4 to 5 per cent in 1971. During the 1960's it had achieved an annual growth rate of 15 per cent. In addition, the rise in the cost of living was officially estimated at 8 per cent, compared with a 1970 increase of 2 per cent.

Both Foreign Minister Gregorio Lopez Bravo and Prince Juan Carlos (with his wife, Princess Sofia) made extensive visits to Latin America. A great effort was being made to strengthen and expand the commercial, political and cultural ties between Spain and the Latin American nations. At the same time, Spain was edging toward increased trade with the Soviet Union and possible normal diplomatic relations.

On June 6, the anniversary of Franco's civil-war victory, the celebrations were attended by Admiral Thomas H. Moorer, chairman of the U.S. Joint Chiefs of Staff. On July 18, the 35th anniversary of the uprising led by Franco that began the civil war, U.S. Vice-President Spiro Agnew and his wife, on a world diplomatic tour, were guests of Franco. Earlier, Prince Juan Carlos had met with President Nixon during a visit to the United States.

SPAIN

Area: 194,844 sq. mi.
Population: 33,600,000
Capital: Madrid
Government: Francisco Franco, chief of state—1939
Gross National Product: $32,300,000,000
Foreign trade: exports, $2,387,000,000; imports, $4,715,000,000
Armed forces: 301,000

SPORTS

Pan-Am Games

In midsummer every four years the attention of many sports fans in the United States is diverted from baseball and golf to the Pan-Am Games. Thus it was in 1971.

Interest in the Games in the United States is less than overwhelming. Many think of the event as a tune-up for the Olympic Games, which come the following year. Other Americans, however—especially those south of the United States—regard the Pan-Am events as opportunities to show that their powerful neighbor is far from invincible. Individual triumphs are savored and at times regarded as political victories. So, although U.S. athletes dominated the 1971 Pan-Am Games in Cali, Colombia, almost as thoroughly as they had in 1967 in Winnipeg, Canada, there was much joy afterward among Latin Americans. The United States had been defeated in two sports it had invented: baseball and basketball!

Perhaps the story of the basketball setback is indicative of how smaller nations strive—sometimes together—to play giant-killer. The first shock to the U.S. men's basketball team came when Cuba topped the Yanks, 73–69. It was just the second time in Pan-Am history that the United States had lost a hardwood game. Brazil, Cuba and the United States were grouped in one section of the preliminary round, and after the United States downed Brazil in overtime, the future of the U.S. quintet had to be settled by a final game between Cuba and Brazil. Under a complicated scoring system, if Brazil were to defeat Cuba by more than five points, Brazil and the United States would advance to the finals with survivors of other eliminations. If Cuba topped Brazil, it would be Cuba and the United States.

As the United States players watched, Brazil outplayed the Cubans and had a 9-point lead with 1 minute to go, 73–64. Then Brazil coach Edson Bispo Dos Santos called a time-out. Brazil scored no more. Bispo's players fouled the Cubans, and the Cubans closed the gap with free throws. With 10 seconds left a free throw made it 73–68—a 5-point difference—and the game ended. The United States was eliminated because Brazil had won by exactly the margin needed. Brazil went on to win the basketball gold medal. U.S. officials referred to the outcome as "fishy."

There were smiles from the spectators, or perhaps laughs, when the U.S. baseball team

John Howard of Springfield, Mo., is the first U.S. cyclist to win a gold medal at Pan-Am Games.

committed 4 errors and lost to Cuba, 4–3. The Yanks, who were college players, then dropped a 5–4 decision to the Dominican Republic. Cuba won the gold medal in baseball.

In most other forms of competition, however, the United States outclassed its Latin opponents. On Aug. 4, for instance, the United States captured 16 of the 17 gold medals awarded.

Frank Heckl, a 6-foot-5 premedical student from USC, won a record 6 gold medals in swimming (3 individual and 3 relays). The United States took 14 of the 15 top awards in swimming and won both diving titles. Roxanne Pierce, a 16-year-old from Kenington, Md., took 4 medals—2 gold and 2 bronze—in women's gymnastics.

Of the 24 medals for track and field, 20 went to the United States. Just as the United States lost in a couple of its specialties, it also scored unexpected successes. John Howard, from Springfield, Mo., stunned the bicycle enthusiasts by taking the 122.5-mile road race. The United States captured 105 gold medals in all, plus 73 silver and 40 bronze, for a total of 218 points. Cuba was second with 30 gold medals and 105 points. Canada with 80 points was third.

BOB BROEG
Sports Editor, *St. Louis Post-Dispatch*

Auto Racing

The Triple Crown series, three 500-mile events, became a reality during the 1971 U.S. Auto Club season. However, no driver won more than one of the rich races.

Al Unser captured the Indianapolis 500 for the second straight year. But Mark Donohue took the first Pocono (Pa.) 500 and Joe Leonard, Unser's teammate, outlasted the field in the Ontario (Calif.) 500. Leonard, who also finished second at Pocono, drove consistently throughout the season and won the national driving title.

AUTO RACING

Grand Prix Winners
South African: Mario Andretti, U.S.
Spanish: Jackie Stewart, Scotland
Monaco: Jackie Stewart
Dutch: Jacky Ickx, Belgium
French: Jackie Stewart
British: Jackie Stewart
German: Jackie Stewart
Austrian: Jo Siffert, Switzerland
Italian: Peter Gethin, England
Canadian: Jackie Stewart
United States: François Cevert, France

The English-built McLaren cars, which have dominated all four years of Can-Am racing, made a big breakthrough with Indianapolis-type cars in 1971. Donohue won from the pole position at Pocono and also started on the pole at Ontario. Peter Revson, in another McLaren, captured the pole position at Indianapolis.

McLarens won 8 of 10 Can-Am events. Revson finished first and teammate Denis Hulme second in the final point standings.

Richard Petty, one of stock-car racing's all-time greats, pushed his earnings on the NASCAR circuit to over $1,000,000 during the season.

Scotland's Jackie Stewart won 6 of 11 Formula One races to nail his second world championship. However, tragedy once again hit the Grand Prix circuit. Mexico's Pedro Rodriguez and Jo Siffert of Switzerland were killed in racing accidents.

BOB COLLINS
Sports Editor
The Indianapolis Star

Baseball

The 1971 major-league baseball season was posted in history as the year of the Pittsburgh Pirates. They prevailed as National League pennant winners and World Series champions with twin comebacks. The Pirates lost the first game of the pennant play-off against the San Francisco Giants and the first two games of the World Series to the heavily favored Baltimore Orioles.

The Pirates began moving resolutely toward the pennant play-offs in April and May with the thunder of Willie Stargell's home-run bat. Stargell's hitting helped to offset soft spots in the Pittsburgh pitching staff. But, paradoxically, in the World Series, it was pitching that took the Bucs to victory over a Baltimore team that boasted four twenty-game winners.

Major league baseball activities were not confined to the playing field. The Curt Flood case, charging baseball with violation of U.S. antitrust laws, again became an important issue after it was dismissed in the lower courts. The U.S. Supreme Court agreed to review the decision of an appellate court. Thus there was the possibility that organized baseball would be deprived of its antitrust exemptions, including the reserve clause which binds a player to a certain team for as long as that team wants his services. Meanwhile, after a year of inactivity during which he had filed a $4,000,000 suit against the major leagues, Flood was lured back to baseball by the $100,000 salary offer of Robert E. Short, owner of the Washington

UPI

Wide World

The .414 hitting of Roberto Clemente (l) and the pitching of right-hander Steve Blass helped the Pittsburgh Pirates overcome a two-game deficit and win the 1971 World Series against Baltimore.

Senators. Short received the permission of the Phillies to sign Flood with the stipulation that it would not prejudice the player's continuing litigation against baseball. Flood stayed with the Senators barely more than a month, played poorly and quit the team without notice in May.

The Washington team also figured in another major development. The nation's capital was stripped of its franchise after 71 years as a charter-member city of the American League. Short was given permission to move the team to Arlington, Tex., midway between Fort Worth and Dallas, where it will be known as the Texas Rangers. Short claimed that Washington attendance was inadequate in view of the team's debts.

In the major managerial development of the year, Danny Murtaugh retired for health reasons as manager of the Pirates, following the World Series. Bill Virdon, Pirate coach and former outfielder, was named his successor. At Chicago, Cubs owner Phil Wrigley took a newspaper advertisement before the season's end to tell critics of Leo Durocher that Wrigley would not dismiss him. Durocher was rehired. The managers released were Cleveland's Al Dark, who was replaced in midseason by Johnny Lipton, who in turn was replaced by Ken Aspromonte as the 1972 manager, and Lefty Phillips. The California Angels dismissed Phillips; Del

Rice, minor-league manager of the year, was later named to the post.

The most-valuable-player honors were won in the National League by Joe Torre of the Cardinals, the league's batting champion (.363) and runs-batted-in leader (137), and in the American League the honor was captured by Oakland's new pitching sensation, Vida Blue. In his first full season, Blue compiled a 24–8 record. Oakland's left-hander also beat out Detroit's Mickey Lolich for the Cy Young Award.

While the World Series was a disappointment to the American League, it succeeded in ending eight years of domination by the National in the annual All-Star game. Despite three runs scored by the National Leaguers against Vida Blue in the first three innings, the AL prevailed, 6 to 4, chiefly on home runs hit by Frank Robinson, Reggie Jackson and Harmon Killebrew.

In only one of the four divisions of the two leagues was there much suspense in the pennant races. Baltimore demolished all opposition to finish 12 games ahead of Detroit in the AL East; Oakland won by 16 games in the AL West; Pittsburgh by 7 games in the NL East; and the Giants staved off a late rush by the Dodgers to win the NL West by 1 game. In the division play-offs, the Giants failed to win another game after beating Pittsburgh in the

BASEBALL

AMERICAN LEAGUE Final Standings	WON	LOST	PER CENT	GAMES BEHIND
Eastern Division				
Baltimore	101	57	.639	...
Detroit	91	71	.562	12
Boston	85	77	.525	18 -
New York	82	80	.506	21
Washington	63	96	.396	38½
Cleveland	60	102	.370	43
Western Division				
Oakland	101	60	.627	...
Kansas City	85	76	.528	16
Chicago	79	83	.488	22½
California	76	86	.469	25½
Minnesota	74	86	.463	26½
Milwaukee	69	92	.429	32

Baltimore defeated Oakland in play-offs

Batting Champion: Tony Oliva (.337) Minnesota
Cy Young Award: Vida Blue (24—8) Oakland
Home-Run Leader: Bill Melton (33) Chicago
Manager of the Year: Dick Williams, Oakland
Most Valuable Player: Vida Blue
Runs Batted In: Harmon Killebrew (119) Minnesota
Rookie of the Year: Chris Chambliss, Cleveland

NATIONAL LEAGUE Final Standings	WON	LOST	PER CENT	GAMES BEHIND
Eastern Division				
Pittsburgh	97	65	.599	...
St. Louis	90	72	.556	7
Chicago	83	79	.512	14
New York	83	79	.512	14
Montreal	71	90	.441	25½
Philadelphia	67	95	.414	30
Western Division				
San Francisco	90	72	.556	...
Los Angeles	89	73	.549	1
Atlanta	82	80	.506	8
Houston	79	83	.488	11
Cincinnati	79	83	.488	11
San Diego	61	100	.379	28½

Pittsburgh defeated San Francisco in play-offs

Batting Champion: Joe Torre (.363) St. Louis
Cy Young Award: Ferguson Jenkins (24–13) Chicago
Home-Run Leader: Willie Stargell (48) Pittsburgh
Manager of the Year: Walt Alston, Los Angeles
Most Valuable Player: Joe Torre
Runs Batted In: Joe Torre (137)
Rookie of the Year: Earl Williams, Atlanta

All-Star Game: American 6, National 4
World Series: Pittsburgh Pirates

MINOR LEAGUES

American Association: Indianapolis (East), Denver (West), Denver (play-offs)
International: Rochester, N.Y.
Pacific Coast: Tacoma (Northern), Salt Lake City (Southern), Salt Lake City (play-offs)

opener. Baltimore, for the third straight year, won its division honors in three straight games. The Orioles easily beat Oakland.

Roberto Clemente vied with Steve Blass, Pirates pitcher, as the outstanding performer in the World Series, a tribute to his leadership and .414 batting average in the series. Blass turned the tide for the Pirates after the Orioles had won the first two series games. He pitched a three-hitter in the third. In the decisive seventh game, Blass pitched a four-hitter to beat the Orioles, 2–1, with the help of a Clemente home run. In the final Baltimore used three of its four twenty-game winners—Mike Cuellar, Pat Dobson and Dave McNally.

As usual, National League attendance surpassed the American League's, 17,333,085 to 11,870,504. This represented an AL drop of 214,643 from the preceding season. The NL showed a gain of 670,887 over 1970, helped by the 802,976 increase at Philadelphia where fans flocked to the city's new stadium. The New York Mets led the majors in home attendance with 2,266,680 despite a down curve of 430,799 from the preceding season.

SHIRLEY POVICH
Sports Editor, *The Washington Post*

Basketball

For the basketball fan, the year 1971 went just as everyone had predicted. UCLA and the Milwaukee Bucks, to the surprise of no one, wound up as National Collegiate Athletic Association and National Basketball Association champions respectively. While the results of the National Invitation Tournament and the American Basketball Association championship followed the forecasts less closely, both the college and professional seasons saw many superb performances.

COLLEGE SEASON

NIT. Although the 1971 NIT lacked the excitement of the preceding year's tournament, which had featured Pete Maravich and the defensive play of Marquette, the contest provided an action-packed showcase for New York City fans. The tournament was very close and unpredictable until the final. In the final, Bill Chamberlain led North Carolina with his all-around floor play and fine defense as the Tar Heels ran roughshod over Georgia Tech. North Carolina all but humiliated Tech by a score of 84–66. Chamberlain, who scored a game high of 34 in the final and a total of 87 points in the tournament, was named most valuable player.

NCAA. For the fifth consecutive time and for the seventh time in eight years, the UCLA

Bruins won the national championship. Earlier, the Irish of Notre Dame, led by UPI's player of the year Austin Carr, had defeated the Bruins by seven points. Only this defeat marred an otherwise perfect season for UCLA.

As Kansas, UCLA, Western Kentucky and Villanova converged on Houston for the NCAA finals in the Astrodome, everyone expected the Bruins to win, but no one foresaw such excitement. In a semifinal, UCLA had all they could do to handle a determined hard-nosed Kansas team. It was only the tough defense of the Bruins that enabled them to come away with a 68–60 win. UCLA forced Kansas to shoot from the outside and limited them to a 40 per cent shooting performance. UCLA's big three, Henry Bibby, Sidney Wicks and Curtis Rowe, had 55 of the team's 68 points. The other star of the Bruins, Steve Patterson, was held to 6 points.

In the other semifinal, Villanova and Western Kentucky fought what was once called a "barn burner." It took Villanova two overtimes and a great defensive effort to come away with an exciting 3-point win, 92–89. The usually great outside shooting Hilltoppers could not find the range and hit only 39 of 105 shots from the floor for a "cool" 37 per cent. Western Kentucky held Villanova to 73 shots, but the Wildcats made 36 of them and added another 20 points from the foul line for the win.

In the final game, the Villanova Wildcats came to play. With a tight zone defense, the Wildcats held Wicks and Rowe to 7 and 8 points respectively, but once again the versatility of the Bruins reigned supreme as Steve Patterson came through. The 6-foot-10-inch center scored a game high of 29 points and led UCLA to a 68–62 win. Despite Villanova's loss, Howard Porter proved beyond a doubt why he was everyone's all-American choice as he led the Wildcats' offense with 25 points. The Bruins will be without Patterson, Wicks and Rowe in 1972; everyone wondered what coach Johnny Wooden would do without them.

PROFESSIONAL SEASON

NBA. The Milwaukee Bucks' combination of Lew Alcindor and Oscar Robertson proved to be unbeatable. During the NBA regular season the Bucks won 66 games and lost only 16. In addition, they won 12 of 14 play-off games. The addition of Robertson, acquired by the Bucks at the end of the 1970 season, transformed Milwaukee from a young, inexperienced ball

Baltimore's Wes Unseld simply watches as Milwaukee's Lew Alcindor goes over rim to score two. The Bucks won play-off finals in four straight.

"Sports Illustrated" photo by Heinz Kluetmeier © Time Inc.

club into a poised, powerful, confident team. They reminded many basketball experts of the famous Boston Celtics team of the 1960's.

The only unexpected occurrence in the NBA championship was the absence of the New York Knickerbockers from the final series. While Milwaukee easily handled San Francisco and Los Angeles in the initial play-off rounds, the other eventual finalist, the Baltimore Bullets, fought for their life. After beating the Philadelphia 76ers in seven games with limited service from all-pro Gus Johnson, the Bullets looked forward to their series with the reigning-champion Knicks. Still without Johnson at 100 per cent efficiency, the Bullets simply outfought the champs to win in seven games and thereby earned the right to meet the Bucks in the finals.

From the start, it was apparent that the Bullets had given their all in the New York series and simply did not have anything left for the rested Bucks. Milwaukee played a superb sagging defense, and the normally good-shooting Bullets could not hit. The Bullets became even more frustrated as Alcindor continually prevented them from penetrating for the easier lay-ups. On offense, Alcindor, the league's most valuable player, was superb. He exhibited a grace and versatility rarely seen in a big man. Robertson also contributed greatly to Milwaukee's four-game sweep of the Bullets. In a personal match-up with Baltimore star Earl Monroe, Robertson played unusually tough defense.

ABA. The younger American Basketball Association continued to make strides in attracting larger crowds to its arenas. Some 2,000,000 people paid to see ABA players exhibit their skills, an increase of about 25 per cent over the 1969–70 season.

In the ABA play-offs, the two favorites, Virginia, led by all-pro Charlie Scott, and Indiana, with the league's leading rebounder Mel Daniels, were upset by Utah and Kentucky.

The Colonels, with the league's leading scorer Dan Issel (29.8 points per game), went up against the Utah Stars. The Stars relied on former NBA great Zelmo Beaty for their stability. It was a great play-off series; when the final buzzer sounded, the Stars had edged the Colonels, 131–121. However, the Colonels could look forward to the next season. Earlier they had signed Artis Gilmore, Jacksonville's 7-foot-2-inch all-American, to a contract estimated at between $1,500,000 and $2,000,000. Gilmore and Issel together should make things rough for ABA front liners.

JACK TWYMAN
Basketball Commentator
American Broadcasting Company

BASKETBALL

COLLEGE

Conference Winners

Atlantic Coast: South Carolina
Big Eight: Kansas
Big Ten: Ohio State
Ivy League: Pennsylvania
Pacific Eight: UCLA
Southeastern: Kentucky
Southern: Furman
Southwest: TCU
West Coast Athletic: Pacific
Western Athletic: Brigham Young
Yankee: Massachusetts

PROFESSIONAL

National Basketball Association

Eastern Conference

Atlantic Division

	W	L	Pct.
New York	52	30	.634
Philadelphia	47	35	.573
Boston	44	38	.537
Buffalo	22	60	.268

Central Division

	W	L	Pct.
Baltimore	42	40	.512
Atlanta	36	46	.439
Cincinnati	33	49	.402
Cleveland	15	67	.183

Western Division

	W	L	Pct.
Milwaukee	66	16	.805
Chicago	51	31	.622
Phoenix	48	34	.585
Detroit	45	37	.549

Pacific Division

	W	L	Pct.
Los Angeles	48	34	.580
San Francisco	41	41	.500
San Diego	40	42	.488
Seattle	38	44	.463
Portland	29	53	.354

American Basketball Association

East Division

	W	L	Pct.
Virginia	55	29	.655
Kentucky	44	40	.524
New York	40	44	.476
Floridians	37	47	.440
Pittsburgh	36	48	.429
Carolina	34	50	.405

West Division

	W	L	Pct.
Indiana	58	26	.690
Utah	57	27	.679
Memphis	41	43	.488
Denver	30	54	.357
Texas	30	54	.357

ABA All-Star Game: East 126, West 122
ABA Coach of the Year: Al Bianchi, Virginia
ABA Most Valuable Player: Mel Daniels, Indiana
ABA Rookie of the Year: Dan Issel, Kentucky; Charlie Scott, Virginia
NBA All-Star Game: West 108, East 107
NBA Coach of the Year: Dick Motta, Chicago
NBA Most Valuable Player: Lew Alcindor, Milwaukee
NBA Rookie of the Year: Dave Cowens, Boston; Geoff Petrie, Portland

In New York City's Madison Square Garden, Mar. 8, Joe Frazier (r) wins a
15-round decision over Muhammad Ali for the world heavyweight title.

Boxing

Muhammad Ali dominated the year's boxing
scene both in the ring and out of it. He lost to
Joe Frazier in a torrid world heavyweight title
bout and was cleared of draft-dodging charges
by the U.S. Supreme Court.

The fight with Frazier, generally accepted as
the champion during Ali's three and a half
years of legal squabbles with the Government
over his draft status, was held in New York
City's Madison Square Garden on Mar. 8. It
enriched each of the gladiators by $2,500,000.
The Garden was filled, and millions of other
fans watched a closed-circuit-television production that was relayed around the world by satellite. Frazier, a stubby Philadelphia introvert
who relaxes with rock 'n' roll music, hammered
his way to a 15-round decision over Ali, an
arrogant product of Louisville, Ky., who gained
fame and wealth as Cassius Clay before he
converted to the Muslim faith. Total worldwide
receipts, never fully disclosed, zoomed above
the $20,000,000 mark, almost five times the
previous record of $4,747,690 taken in for a
Clay–Floyd Patterson encounter in 1963.

Ali strode into the ring wearing red trunks
with matching tassels on his shoes. Now 29, he
had sweated down to 215 pounds from the 240
he had weighed as a full-time minister. He
monopolized the attention of the crowd with
his antics while warming up. Frazier, dressed
in green and gold-brocaded trunks, sat quietly
in his corner. When the fight began, Ali set a
furious pace, but by the sixth round it was evi-

dent he was tiring. The 27-year-old Frazier began registering blows to Ali's head. In the 11th round Frazier followed a vicious smash to Ali's mouth with a crashing left to the midsection. The former champion's jaw appeared to be broken as he stalled through the 12th and 13th rounds, but he recovered enough to win the 14th. When Frazier connected with another left to the face in the final round, Ali dropped to the floor for a four-count. The Muhammad Ali bubble had burst. The decision that Frazier was the winner was unanimous.

The Supreme Court ruled on June 28 that Ali's conviction of being a draft dodger was illegal. The court said he was a true conscientious objector when he refused to be inducted into the armed services in 1967. By an 8–0 decision, the court held that the Kentucky draft board that ordered his induction had exceeded its authority. Ali had based his refusal on the Muslim condemnation of war and the killing of humans. He also insisted he was an active minister of that faith.

After a conviction in a lower court, the case was appealed; but Ali was stripped of his heavyweight title, and Frazier plodded to the top. The dethroned champion slipped into financial distress while continuing to preach. By Mar. 8, 1971, Ali had been suspended by the Muslims for having returned to the ring in 1970. He had won two tune-up fights.

Soon after winning his court battle, Ali registered a 12-round technical knockout over Jimmy Ellis, a boyhood friend from Louisville, in the Houston Astrodome on July 26.

Despite the enthusiasm and interest brought about by the Frazier-Ali affair, boxing in the United States showed little permanent recovery except in Los Angeles where Mexico's two world champions, welterweight Jose Napoles and bantamweight Ruben Olivares, are outstanding favorites.

New York's Madison Square Garden also was the scene when Ken Buchanan came from Scotland to successfully defend his world lightweight crown against Ismael Laguna of Panama. It was a gory bout that made the victor a hero in his homeland.

The world middleweight crown stayed with Carlos Monzon of Argentina, who scored a third-round technical knockout over Nino Benvenuti of Italy. Benvenuti was floored at the start of the third round. He bounded to his feet almost immediately, but his handlers threw in the towel to bring about a bizarre and confusing finish. Later, in another title defense, Monzon stopped Emile Griffith of New York.

HAROLD (SPIKE) CLAASSEN
Free-Lance Sportswriter

Football

If one word could be used to describe college and professional football in 1971, that word would be "run." Indeed, the running quarterback added a new dimension to offenses in the National Football League, while a contingent of hard-charging running backs assaulted the coveted 1,000-yard rushing plateau with uncommon frequency.

In the college ranks, the quarterback in the Wishbone Triple-Option offense set in motion a running attack that devastated enemy defenses and the record books.

Life quieted down in football, both amateur and professional. Unlike 1970, 1971 was marked by players who made headlines on the field, not off it. The NFL players, who went on strike in 1970, stayed on the job in 1971. And protests by college players, a reflection of the times perhaps, did not materialize in 1971 to as large a degree as in 1970.

Controversy did not rear its head in the year of the runner. People were too busy watching the exploits of their heroes, as crowds turned out in record numbers at NFL and college games. And players were too occupied fighting for honors in the increasingly competitive world of football.

PROFESSIONAL SEASON

In the NFL, upsets began the first week of the season and continued through the last week. Even the Super Bowl finalists, the Miami Dolphins and Dallas Cowboys, could not avoid getting upset, with the New England Patriots beating Miami and the New Orleans Saints surprising Dallas.

As usual, the NFL season opened with coaches getting hired and closed with coaches getting fired. Bob Hollway at St. Louis, George Allen at Washington, Dan Devine at Green Bay, Tommy Prothro at Los Angeles, Ed Hughes at Houston, Harvey Johnson at Buffalo and Nick Skorich at Cleveland were new head coaches. By the time the season ended, Hughes and Johnson were out, as were holdovers Lou Saban of Denver, Sid Gillman of San Diego, Jerry Williams of Philadelphia and Jim Dooley of Chicago.

Those were not the only changes in professional football. More and more NFL teams went to zone defenses and to running quarterbacks in the mold of Detroit's Greg Landry and Dallas's Roger Staubach.

These young quarterbacks, unlike the New York Giants' Fran Tarkenton, were runners, not just scramblers. This meant that they would gallop with the abandon of a fullback and baffle enemy defenses, which did not know how to

George Allen, who directed the Washington Redskins to a 9–4–1 season, is named Coach of the Year.

American Football Conference Championship: Paul Warfield, Miami's star wide receiver, evades Baltimore's safety Rick Volk and goes on to score game's first touchdown. Miami won 21–0.

Super Bowl VI: Dallas quarterback Roger Staubach (12) throws two touchdown passes and is named the game's outstanding player. Dallas routed Miami 24–3.

handle them. Instead of the traditional drop-back, pocket passers like Johnny Unitas and Bart Starr, the young quarterbacks with the ability to run—New Orleans' Archie Manning, New England's Jim Plunkett, Cincinnati's Virgil Carter, Miami's Bob Griese and Pittsburgh's Terry Bradshaw, along with Landry and Stau-bach—would look for a receiver, and then dash for yardage if one were not open.

The advent of the running quarterback, along with the increasing use of zone defenses, which took away long pass plays, were the NFL's two significant changes in 1971. Then, of course, there are the runners, who have always

---

FOOTBALL

COLLEGE

Final Coaches' Poll (UPI)

1. Nebraska
2. Alabama
3. Oklahoma
4. Michigan
5. Auburn
6. Arizona State
7. Colorado
8. Georgia
9. Tennessee
10. Louisiana State

Conference Winners

Atlantic Coast: North Carolina
Big Eight: Nebraska
Big Ten: Michigan
Ivy League: Dartmouth, Cornell
Mid-American: Toledo
Missouri Valley: Memphis
Pacific Eight: Stanford
Southeastern: Alabama
Southern: Richmond
Southwest: Texas
Western Athletic: Arizona State
Yankee: Connecticut, Massachusetts

Writers' Poll (AP)

Nebraska
Alabama
Oklahoma
Michigan
Auburn
Georgia
Colorado
Arizona State
Tennessee
Penn State

Bowl Games

Astro-Bluebonnet Bowl: Colorado 29, Houston 17
Cotton Bowl: Penn State 30, Texas 6
Gator Bowl: Georgia 7, North Carolina 3
Liberty Bowl: Tennessee 14, Arkansas 13
Orange Bowl: Nebraska 38, Alabama 6
Rose Bowl: Stanford 13, Michigan 12
Sugar Bowl: Oklahoma 40, Auburn 22
Sun Bowl: Louisiana State 33, Iowa State 15

PROFESSIONAL

National Football League Final Standings

American Football Conference

Eastern Division	WON	LOST	TIED	PER CENT
Miami	10	3	1	.769
*Baltimore	10	4	0	.714
N.Y. Jets	6	8	0	.429
New England	6	8	0	.429
Buffalo	1	13	0	.071
Central Division				
Cleveland	9	5	0	.643
Pittsburgh	6	8	0	.429
Houston	4	9	1	.308
Cincinnati	4	10	0	.286
Western Division				
Kansas City	10	3	1	.769
Oakland	8	4	2	.667
San Diego	6	8	0	.429
Denver	4	9	1	.308

National Football Conference

Eastern Division	WON	LOST	TIED	PER CENT
Dallas	11	3	0	.786
*Washington	9	4	1	.692
Philadelphia	6	7	1	.462
St. Louis	4	9	1	.308
N.Y. Giants	4	10	0	.286
Central Division				
Minnesota	11	3	0	.786
Detroit	7	6	1	.538
Chicago	6	8	0	.429
Green Bay	4	8	2	.333
Western Division				
San Francisco	9	5	0	.643
Los Angeles	8	5	1	.615
Atlanta	7	6	1	.538
New Orleans	4	8	2	.333

* Qualified for play-offs.

The Play-offs

Semifinals

Miami 27, Kansas City 24
Baltimore 20, Cleveland 3

Dallas 20, Minnesota 12
San Francisco 24, Washington 20

Finals

Miami 21, Baltimore 0

Dallas 14, San Francisco 3

Super Bowl

Miami 3

Dallas 24

Canada's Grey Cup: Calgary Stampeders

Rose Bowl: With 12 seconds remaining, Rod Garcia (14) kicks a 31-yard field goal to give the Stanford Indians a 13–12 win over Michigan.

Game of the Decade (I): Nebraska's Johnny Rogers returns kickoff as Cornhuskers defeat Oklahoma 35–31 and remain number one.

been around but never in so great a number. The best of the young crop was Green Bay rookie John Brockington, who led the National Conference with 1,105 yards. In all, there were five 1,000-yard runners, the others being the league leader Floyd Little of Denver, Miami's Larry Csonka, Detroit's Steve Owens and Los Angeles' Willie Ellison.

As for team performances, everything went pretty much according to form except in two incredible cases: Miami and Washington.

The Dolphins, in only their sixth season, found themselves in the play-offs after edging the Baltimore Colts—incumbent Super Bowl champions—for first place in the American Conference's Eastern Division. A young team, the Dolphins rose to prominence on the arm of quarterback Griese and the fleet legs of wide receiver Paul Warfield. Don Shula, their wily

coach, took them into the first round of the play-offs against a favored Kansas City team. In a game that went into two overtimes and lasted 82 minutes 40 seconds—longest in NFL history—the Dolphins won on a 37-yard field goal by Garo Yepremian, a balding Cypriot who kicks soccer style.

Then the Dolphins went back to Miami's Orange Bowl and won the AFC title by shutting out the Colts, who had gained the play-offs as the "wild card" team. In the Super Bowl in New Orleans, the Dolphins played the Cowboys, who beat both Minnesota and San Francisco to reach the world championship game.

Before a capacity crowd of 81,023 at Tulane Stadium, on Jan. 16, 1972, the Dallas Cowboys completely dominated the sixth Super Bowl game. The Cowboys outscored the Dolphins 24–3. The Dallas offensive team, led by Duane

Thomas, set a Super Bowl record for total yards rushing (252), while its defensive team completely stymied the Miami offense. A Dolphins fumble and interception led to a Dallas field goal and touchdown. Quarterback Staubach was named the game's most valuable player.

The Washington Redskins, under coach Allen, were the surprise team of 1971. Allen astutely traded for veterans to help the club and he built the Redskins into a contender. They won their first five games and looked as if they would win their first title in 26 years. But Washington faded, managing, however, to wind up as the National Conference's "wild card" team. The 49ers ended the Redskins' hopes in the first round of the play-offs.

COLLEGE SEASON

If the Redskins were the surprise team of the NFL, then Oklahoma was the surprise team of college football. Largely overlooked before the season, the Sooners rolled over opponents like a Sherman tank, chewing up large hunks of rushing yardage in the process. The Wishbone, Oklahoma's offensive weapon, enables the quarterback to have three options: the inside hand-off, the outside pitchout or the keeper. With crafty Jack Mildren at quarterback, the Sooners were able to run the offense better than any team in the nation.

Oklahoma was unbeaten and ranked second in the country on Thanksgiving Day, when it met Nebraska in what was billed as the "game of the decade." The Cornhuskers also were unbeaten and they were ranked number 1, with their defense tops among major colleges. Although the Sooners overpowered that Nebraska defense, the Cornhuskers had a pretty good offense themselves, led by quarterback Jerry Tagge, and Oklahoma was edged at home, 35–31.

When the bowl games came around, promoters were trying to think up a suitable title for the Nebraska-Alabama Orange Bowl game, since "game of the decade" had been used only weeks before. The Cornhuskers were still number 1, while the Crimson Tide had moved up to number 2. Both were undefeated. When the smoke cleared, the Cornhuskers had walked off the field with a 38–6 victory. Nebraska's Big Eight Conference compatriot, Oklahoma, easily beat Auburn in the Sugar Bowl, and the Big Eight's Colorado Buffaloes dumped Houston in the Bluebonnet Bowl, giving the conference reason to boast that it is the "best in the country."

BOB BROEG
Sports Editor, *St. Louis Post-Dispatch*

Golf

In one blazing four-week period of 1971, Lee Trevino laughed his way to the Open golf championships of three different countries, an accomplishment never before achieved in the long and sedate history of the sport.

Trevino, an obscure $35-a-week assistant pro in Texas less than a decade ago, began his historic splurge by defeating Jack Nicklaus by three strokes, 68–71, in a regulation 18-hole play-off for the United States crown June 21 on Merion's East Course at Ardmore, Pa. Two weeks later he ended Art Wall's chances in the Canadian Open on the first hole of a sudden-death play-off. Trevino then flew to England where he squeaked through to a one-stroke victory over the hat-tipping Lu Liang Huan of Taiwan for the British title.

Stricken with acute appendicitis while on a one-day fishing trip in mid-August, Trevino was operated on at 2 A.M. the following day. He recuperated fast enough to compete in the World Series of Golf at Akron, Ohio, on Sept. 11–12. Although Trevino finished last in the four-man field, he helped repulse the British for the Ryder Cup at St. Louis the following week.

Golf experts had seen 1971 as the year in which Nicklaus, rated by many as the greatest

---

GOLF

World Series of Golf: Charles Coody
PGA Team: Jack Nicklaus and Arnold Palmer
U.S. Match Play: DeWitt Weaver
World Match Play: Gary Player
World Cup: (team) United States; (individual) Jack Nicklaus
Ryder Cup: United States
U.S. Open (women): Mrs. JoAnne G. Carner
PGA (women): Kathrynne Whitworth
U.S. Amateur: Gary Cowan, Kitchener, Ont.
British Amateur: Steve Melnyk, Jacksonville, Fla.
Canadian Amateur: Dick Siderowf, Easton, Conn.
USGA Public Links: (team) Portland, Ore.; (individual) Fred Haney, Forest Grove, Ore.
Walker Cup: Great Britain
Curtis Cup (women): United States
U.S. Amateur (women): Laura Baugh, Long Beach, Calif.
NCAA: (team) University of Texas; (individual) Ben Crenshaw, University of Texas
Intercollegiate: (women-team) UCLA; (individual) Shelly Hamlin, UCLA
USGA Junior: Mike Brannan, Salinas, Calif.
USGA Junior (girls): Hollis Stacy, Savannah, Ga.

player ever, would become the first to win all four of pro golf's major titles—the U.S. and British Opens, the Masters and PGA—in a single season. The slimmed-down Ohioan appeared on his way when he cruised to the PGA crown at Palm Beach Gardens, Fla., in late February, making him the first to win all four glamour crowns twice. He one-putted 8 of the last 10 holes of his first round over the palm-dotted layout for a 69 and followed that with another 69 and a 70. He began the final day with a 4-stroke lead but zoomed over par on 3 of the first 5 holes. Gary Player, Tommy Bolt and Billy Casper all mounted challenges. Casper finished his stint at 283, five under par. Nicklaus, 6 under with 2 holes to go, sent a wedge to within five feet at 17 and sank the birdie putt. He won $40,000 first prize by 2 strokes.

After 54 holes in the Masters at Augusta, Ga., Apr. 8–11, Nicklaus and Charles Coody, who had won only 2 tournaments in 8 years on the tour, were deadlocked at 209. Going to the 15th on the last day, they trailed 23-year-old Johnny Miller of San Francisco. A spectacular chip by Coody, a former Air Force officer, on the 17th wrecked Nicklaus' dreams of a grand slam and he tied Miller for second. Nicklaus had three-putted four greens on the final round.

Now it was Trevino's turn. Virtual strangers were the leaders in the first three rounds of the U.S. Open on the deceptive East Course at Merion. Amateur Jim Simons, a Wake Forest student, led by two strokes after 54 holes. On the final round Trevino played precision golf until the last hole, where he sent his second shot 70 feet over the green for a bogey. He had just given his caddy a comic lecture for not offering him a club. Meanwhile, Nicklaus came through with phenomenal par-saving putts on 15, 16 and 17 to pull even with the happy-go-lucky Mexican-American.

The next morning the disconsolate Nicklaus was sitting under a tree, his head bowed. The chuckling Trevino approached, stopped, opened his bag and tossed an artificial snake at his rival. It brought laughter from everyone. The Ohioan went three over par on the first three holes. His wedge had betrayed him; the play-off was over; Trevino had won by three strokes.

Two weeks later Trevino bested Art Wall on the first hole of a sudden-death play-off for the Canadian Open title at Richelieu Valley near Montreal. They had deadlocked at 275 each over 72 holes.

Then it was on to Birkdale for the British Open, an event that the self-styled Super-Mex had frittered away in 1970. Holding a 1-stroke lead at the start of the final round, Trevino one-putted the first six holes and boasted a 5-stroke

Ken Regan from Camera 5

In 1971, Lee Trevino won British, Canadian and U.S. Opens, entertained the galleries with his antics and earned $231,202.97 in prize money.

edge over Lu as they made the turn. The Oriental shotmaker regained 2 by the 16th. Trevino's drive on 17 landed on a sandy knoll to the left of the fairway and he wound up with a double bogey. Lu holed out in par. Both came up with birdies on the last hole, and the American won by a single stroke.

HAROLD (SPIKE) CLAASSEN
Free-Lance Sportswriter

Horse Racing

Don Pedro Baptista's dream of winning the Triple Crown, with a $1,200 horse that nobody wanted, was racing's biggest story in 1971. The dream almost came true.

First, there was the Kentucky Derby. Canonero II's full record was not even available. He had done most of his racing in Caracas, Venezuela. He was so lightly regarded that he ran as a part of the mutuel field. Canonero II won the Kentucky Derby by 3¾ lengths, running the mile and a quarter at Churchill Downs in 2:03 1/5. A winning ticket paid $19.40.

Then, the Preakness. Railbirds still were snickering. They chuckled at trainer Juan Arias' technique of giving the three-year-old colt long gallops instead of short sprints. Canonero II set a speed record for the Preakness, winning the mile and three-sixteenths race at Pimlico in 1:54.

Now, the big chocolate-colored horse, which had been bought at the Keeneland Sales in his native Kentucky for $1,200, was odds-on favorite to become the first Triple Crown winner in 23 years. Baptista was offered $4,000,000 for him if he won.

Two thousand of Baptista's countrymen showed up at Belmont, waving Venezuelan flags. Baptista paid the air fare and lodging of 36 of them. The magic of Canonero II lured the biggest crowd in New York racing history, 82,694 to Belmont Park. The crowd wagered more than ever had been bet at a U.S. racetrack in a single day—$6,972,209. The 13 horses broke from the starting gate at 5:35 P.M. It was obvious that this would be the most important 2½ minutes in Baptista's life, in the life of the trainer and in that of jockey Gustavo Avila.

Mile and a half races are seldom won with the winner leading from wire to wire, but Avila, attempting to duplicate the Preakness win, shot Canonero II to the front. A lusty roar rocked the stands; Venezuelans waved their flags wildly. Baptista lit a cigarette and stood up. As the horses reached the backstretch, with Canonero II still on top, he threw the cigarette away. After the first six furlongs in 1:12 2/5 and the mile in 1:37, Canonero's lead diminished and Baptista lit another cigarette. A quarter mile from the finish, jockey Walter Blum gave Pass Catcher his head. The colt owned by Peter Kissel shot by Canonero II. Jim French and Bold Reason also went flying by.

Baptista smoked silently as the finish was recorded a hundred feet away from his box: Pass Catcher, Jim French, Bold Reason, Canonero II. For more than a half hour, Baptista sat in stunned silence. His countrymen did not bother him with condolences. They understood.

HORSE RACING

Kentucky Derby: Canonero II
Preakness: Canonero II
Belmont Stakes: Pass Catcher
Santa Anita Derby: Jim French
Wood Memorial: Good Behaving
Louisiana Derby: Northfields
Florida Derby: Eastern Fleet
Santa Anita Handicap: Ack Ack
Flamingo Stakes: Executioner
American Derby: Bold Reason
Hollywood Gold Cup: Ack Ack
Suburban Handicap: Twice Worthy
California Derby: Unconscious

Baptista finally broke the silence for two Louisville newspapermen. "Defeated horses never make history," he said. "I know how to win and I know how to lose. I am tranquil. I am satisfied. I believe the horse has run as well as he could." Alfred G. Vanderbilt, chairman of the board of the New York Racing Association, came around to shake Baptista's hand. "You made the day for us," said Vanderbilt. "It's the largest we've ever had." Baptista smiled and thanked him, through an interpreter, and sat down in his box. It was after 7 P.M. Baptista, noting that the cleaning crews were busy in the clubhouse, said: "Shall we go?" The Venezuelans were the last ones out.

Whether Canonero II would have won had he been in top shape is a point for argument. Trainer Arias said: "I saddled Canonero II for the Belmont with a tear in my eye. I knew he was not ready for the race. He had missed two days of training due to the infection in his right hind foot and the annoying skin rash. The infection was so bad a week before the race that I figured he would have to be withdrawn from the Belmont. However, when the infection responded to treatment, we decided to run the horse. Yet, I knew he was not right." Baptista sold the colt for $1,000,000 to Robert J. Kleberg, Jr. (King Ranch, Texas).

It was a big year for racing as far as money goes. Keeneland averaged a record $31,775 a head at its yearling sales, and Saratoga was not far behind with $30,541.

Ack Ack, owned by Mr. and Mrs. E. E. (Buddy) Fogelson, dominated the handicap horses. Drumtop, five-year-old mare owned by James B. Moseley and regarded as perhaps the finest grass-course specialist of her sex to race in the United States, beat colts in four big races. She bowed a tendon on Sept. 4, her last race.

DEAN EAGLE
Sports Editor
The Courier-Journal, Louisville, Ky.

Before 123,284 spectators at Churchill Downs, Louisville, Ky., May 1, Gustavo Avila rides Canonero II to a surprise victory in the Kentucky Derby. Canonero went on to win the Preakness but lost the Belmont Stakes.

With an erratic performance by their star, Bobby Orr (4), the Boston Bruins lost first round of Stanley Cup play-offs to Montreal. The Canadiens, who eventually won the Cup, were led by their veteran captain, Jean Beliveau (in red).

"Sports Illustrated" photo by Walter Iooss, Jr., © Time Inc.

Ice Hockey

In the spring of 1968, after the Montreal Canadiens had eliminated the Boston Bruins from the Stanley Cup play-offs in four straight games, Milt Schmidt, the Bruins' general manager, could hardly believe what he had seen. "They took everything away from us with their speed," he said in an awed voice. "They just wouldn't let us do anything." In 1969 Schmidt was disappointed again, though his Bruins carried the series to six games before being eliminated by the Canadiens.

But Schmidt was sure that things were going to be different when the two teams met again in the 1971 play-offs. The Canadiens had not even made the play-offs in 1970, and the Bruins had won the Stanley Cup. During the regular 1971 schedule, the powerful Bruins had finished in first place in the East Division and set a number of scoring records. They had scored 399 goals, more than any other team in league history; Phil Esposito had broken the individual scoring record with 76 goals in 78 games; the line of Esposito, Ken Hodge and Wayne Cashman had scored 140 goals, a new record for a unit; and the outstanding Bobby Orr had scored a total of 37 goals during the season, a new mark for a defenseman.

Who was going to beat them? The odds makers did not think the Canadiens, third-place finishers, had a chance, and they made the Bruins overwhelming favorites. Goaltending is admittedly the biggest single factor in play-off hockey. The Canadiens started Ken Dryden, a law student at McGill University who had been called up near the end of the season and had played only a few games in the NHL, in the nets. It was a desperate gamble, but it paid off.

To win a play-off series, a team that opens away from home must win at least one game in their opponents' rink. The Canadiens did the seemingly impossible by winning two games in Boston Garden, the second and the seventh, to provide the most dramatic upset in many years. Milt Schmidt was speechless. Phil Esposito said: "That Dryden was fantastic. I had my share of scoring chances, but he made one key save after another. He was the difference."

The Canadiens met the Minnesota North Stars, who had eliminated the St. Louis Blues, in the next series. It was supposed to be a cakewalk for the Canadiens, and when it was all square after the first four games, 2–2, the fans wondered if the first series against Boston had taken too much out of the Canadiens. But they pulled themselves together and won the next two games to take the series.

Meanwhile the Chicago Black Hawks, who had been shifted to the West Division when the league expanded to take in Buffalo and Vancouver at the start of the season, had eliminated the Philadelphia Flyers in four games and were now engaged in a torrid struggle for survival with the New York Rangers. This series went the limit, with the Black Hawks, led by Bobby Hull, winning the deciding game.

The Black Hawks were the ruling favorites in the final series against the Canadiens. Nerves were frayed, and after the Canadiens lost the fifth game in Chicago and the Black Hawks went ahead in the series, 3–2, Henri Richard called coach Al MacNeil "incompetent, the worst coach I ever played for." The Canadiens then won the next game in Montreal. Perhaps it was significant that Richard scored both the tieing and winning goals for the Canadiens in the seventh game in Chicago.

Veterans like Jean Beliveau and Frank Mahovlich, who had been on teams that had won the Stanley Cup in previous years, said this

victory had eclipsed all the others because they had been the "underdogs." The veterans played well, but the Conn Smythe Trophy, or MVP award, was awarded to the rookie goalie, Ken Dryden.

When it was all over, coach Al MacNeil's contract was not renewed for the 1971–72 season. The same thing happened to Harry Sinden in 1970 after he led the Boston Bruins to the Stanley Cup.

DINK CARROLL
Sports Columnist, *The Gazette,* Montreal

Soccer

In contrast to Brazil's exciting win in the 1970 World Cup final in Mexico, the 1970–71 soccer season was profoundly disappointing. For the first time in at least 12 years, the World Cup failed to set a pattern for the next four years. The world of soccer ignored the lesson of Mexico: that inspired attack can make up for the lack of a solid defense. In 1971, soccer players preferred to rely on cautious, defensive methods.

The Italians, humiliated in the World Cup final, still did not abandon the method that had so crippled their game: an extra defender behind the back four. In England, for only the second time this century, one team, the London Arsenal, won both the Cup and the League. Again defense was the watchword. In a European Cup final, Ajax of Holland scored early against the far less gifted Panathinaikos, Athens, and sat on its lead throughout the second half.

In June, Nacional de Montevideo defeated Estudiantes de la Plata in a play-off in Lima, Peru, to capture the South American Libertadores Cup. The match was characterized by outbreaks of violence. Earlier, New York Hota outscored the Los Angeles Yugoslavs, 6–4, to win the United States Challenge Cup.

Attendance at British League matches was down by 1,500,000. Two English clubs, Chelsea and Leeds United, won the Cup Winners Cup and European Fairs Cup respectively. England also won the European Youth Tournament.

Before an international television audience on July 18, Pele, the world's greatest soccer player, played his final game for Brazil's national team. He will continue to play for Santos, his professional club.

It was clear that world soccer had three urgent problems: too much defense, too much violence and too many games. Even the traditionally tireless English players complained.

BRIAN GLANVILLE
Chief Soccer Correspondent
The Sunday Times, London

ICE HOCKEY

COLLEGE
NCAA Championship: Boston University
PROFESSIONAL
National Hockey League
All-Star Game: West 2, East 1
Final Standings

East Division

	W	L	T	Pts.
Boston	57	14	7	121
New York	49	18	11	109
Montreal	42	23	13	97
Toronto	37	33	8	82
Buffalo	24	39	15	63
Vancouver	24	46	8	56
Detroit	22	45	11	55

West Division

	W	L	T	Pts.
Chicago	49	20	9	107
St. Louis	34	25	19	87
Philadelphia	28	33	17	73
Minnesota	28	34	16	72
Los Angeles	25	40	13	63
Pittsburgh	21	37	20	62
California	20	53	5	45

Stanley Cup: Montreal
Art Ross Trophy (scoring): Phil Esposito, Boston
Calder Trophy (rookie): Gil Perreault, Buffalo
Georges Vezina Trophy (goalie): Ed Giacomin, Gilles Villemure, New York
Hart Trophy (most valuable player): Bobby Orr, Boston
Lady Byng Trophy (sportsmanship): Johnny Bucyk, Boston
Norris Trophy (defense): Bobby Orr
Smythe Trophy (play-off performance): Ken Dryden, Montreal
WORLD CHAMPIONSHIP: Soviet Union

Swimming

Mark Spitz used to be an enigma, a young man who somehow failed to fulfill his enormous potential. But no more. Spitz, the 21-year-old who swims for Arden Hills Swim Club and Indiana University, set 3 world records in 1971 and won an unprecedented 4 individual events in the National AAU Long Course Championships at Houston.

Spitz broke his own record in the 100-meter butterfly, swimming a 55.1; topped Gary Hall's mark with 2:03.89 in the 200-meter butterfly; and wiped out Don Schollander's long-standing record in the 200-meter freestyle with a 1:54.2 clocking. Later, Mark lowered that mark to 1:53.5. He also helped Indiana to its fourth straight NCAA championship. (The 200-meter butterfly record was later lowered.)

Spitz was not the only star of the national college meet, where 10 U.S. and 14 NCAA records were set. Gary Hall won the 200- and 400-meter individual medleys.

Lanky Frank Heckl of USC won a record 6 gold medals as the United States dominated the Pan-American Games. He had also taken 3 titles in the Short Course nationals. John Kinsella won the Sullivan Award (America's greatest all-around amateur athlete).

Then there were the teen-age stars. Shane Gould, only 14, of Australia, established a world record (4:21.2) in the women's 400-meter freestyle, boosting her total to 3. Cathy Calhoun, just 13, displaced Debbie Meyer in the 1,500-meter freestyle with a 17:19.2 clocking. Deena Deardurff, also 13, set an American record in the AAU Short Course Championships, swimming 57.06 in the 100-yard butterfly.

Other world marks included: Ellie Daniel, 200-meter butterfly, 2:18.4; Ann Simmons, 800-meter freestyle, 8:59.37; Tom McBreen, 400-meter freestyle, 4:02.1; Hans Fassnacht, 200-meter butterfly, 2:03.3; Roland Matthes, 100-meter backstroke, 56.7, and 200-meter backstroke, 2:05.6; U.S. women's team, 400-meter medley relay, 4:27.3; U.S. women's team, 400-meter freestyle relay, 4:00.7; U.S. men's team, 400-meter medley relay, 3:50.4; U.S. men's team, 800-meter freestyle relay, 7:43.3. Among American record setters were Sue Atwood, Lynn Colella and Brian Job.

DWIGHT CHAPIN
Sportswriter, *Los Angeles Times*

Table Tennis

No sport gained front-page headlines in 1971 to the extent that table tennis did. Not only did Communist China participate in the 31st World Table Tennis Championships—for the first time in six years—but the U.S. table-tennis team accepted an invitation to compete in mainland China. British, Canadian, Colombian and Nigerian teams paid similar visits to Peking. In the months following, President Nixon announced that he too would journey to China, and a new term, "Ping-Pong diplomacy," crept into many vocabularies.

A total of 536 players and officials from 54 nations took part in the world championships held in Nagoya, Japan, in the spring. Interest centered on how the Chinese, the world's greatest players between 1959 and 1965, would rate. Led by Li Ching-kuang, China captured the Swaythling Cup (best men's team). The Japanese women's team defeated China, 3–1, for the Corbillon Cup (best women's team). Stellan Bengtsson of Sweden and Lin Hui-ching of China won the men's and women's singles respectively.

The 41st U.S. National Championships were held in Atlanta, Ga., in March. Dal Joon Lee of Parma, Ohio, and Connie Sweeris of Grand Rapids, Mich., gained the men's and women's singles. Sweden's Kjell Johansson and Bengtsson combined to win the Vanderbilt tournament.

At the national AAU championships in Houston, 21-year-old Mark Spitz sets a world record of 203.8 in the 200-meter butterfly.

Tennis

Abundant activity in 1971 confirmed tennis as the supergrowth game of the decade. Statisticians pointed out that Rod Laver won more prize money in 1969 through 1971 than golfing great Jack Nicklaus earned over the same period. In fact, Laver earned over $290,000 in 1971 alone, which pushed his lifetime earnings to over $1,000,000—a figure never before approached by any other tennis player. Laver performed his feats of gold gathering without capturing any of the traditional major titles.

But just as the traditional amateur game has been violently swept aside by the introduction of prize money and open tennis (1968), its sacrosanct tournament venues have been losing their once untouchable prestige. Since 1970, organized tennis has remained fragmented.

Texas oilman Lamar Hunt controls by contract 32 leading professionals, including Rod Laver, Ken Rosewall, Arthur Ashe and John Newcombe. He also owns less-known pros Graham Stillwell, Phil Dent and Allen Stone, who drastically reduce the overall quality of his players.

The other force, itself fragmented, is the world group of national tennis associations bound together by the International Lawn Tennis Federation (ILTF) which oversees the activities of the independent professionals (including Stan Smith, Ilie Nastase, Clark Graebner and Cliff Richey) who have no contractual obligations but maintain allegiance to their national associations. The independents do not offer overall strength at the top but do provide exciting young blood each year. Also there is the salutary proviso that if the athlete does not perform well, he will not get paid and may not be invited to the tournament the next week.

Both sides have enormous resources. The ILTF provides its own pot of gold through a $250,000 Grand Prix and a $300,000 U.S. indoor circuit. Lamar Hunt, on the other hand, has pieced together 20 tournaments with $1,000,000 in prizes. The result is that the players have become fat from the feuding. Sadly, the loser is the spectator who was told by the ILTF at the end of 1971 that the Open (those rare moments when contract pros and independent pros compete) might be a thing of the brief past because of Hunt's excessive financial demands at tournaments. The ILTF indirectly controls the world's major stadiums.

With the turmoil in tennis, it was, perhaps, fitting that the happiest moments of the year were without question provided by the 16-year-old sensation Chris Evert of Fort Lauderdale. The young amateur was the chief architect of a U.S. victory over England in the Wightman Cup. The following week she recorded a major triumph by capturing the Eastern Grass Court Championships. Chris saved the best for last. Unseeded at Forest Hills, she spotted three opponents a first set lead and then proceeded to stage one dramatic upset after another. The tiny Cinderella reached the semifinals before losing to Billie Jean King, the eventual winner in a match watched by the largest Friday crowd in Forest Hills history. At the other end of the age spectrum, Pancho Gonzales, 43, continued to demonstrate his mastery over age and younger opponents.

Stan Smith of Pasadena, Calif., emerged as the exciting new champion of 1971, reaching the finals at Wimbledon, winning the U.S. Open and the Pepsi Grand Prix.

EUGENE L. SCOTT
Former U.S. Davis Cup Player

TENNIS

Davis Cup: United States
Federation Cup (Women): Australia

WIMBLEDON CHAMPIONS
Men: John Newcombe, Australia
Women: Evonne Goolagong, Australia
Men's Doubles: Roy Emerson-Rod Laver, Australia
Women's Doubles: Mrs. Billie Jean King, Long Beach, Calif.; Rosemary Casals, San Francisco

U.S. OPEN CHAMPIONS
Men: Stan Smith, Pasadena, Calif.
Women: Mrs. Billie Jean King
Men's Doubles: John Newcombe-Roger Taylor, Britain
Women's Doubles: Rosemary Casals-Mrs. Judy Dalton, Australia

U.S. CLAY COURT CHAMPIONS
Men: Zeljko Franulovic, Yugoslavia
Women: Mrs. Billie Jean King
Men's Doubles: Jan Kodes, Czechoslovakia-Zeljko Franulovic
Women's Doubles: Mrs. Judy Dalton-Mrs. Billie Jean King

U.S. INDOOR CHAMPIONS
Men: Clark Graebner, New York
Women: Mrs. Billie Jean King

OTHER OPEN CHAMPIONS
Australian Men: Ken Rosewall, Australia
Australian Women: Mrs. Margaret Smith Court, Australia
Italian Men: Rod Laver, Australia
Italian Women: Virginia Wade, Great Britain
French Men: Jan Kodes
French Women: Evonne Goolagong

U.S. AMATEUR CHAMPIONS
Men: John Gardner, Australia
Men's Doubles: Gene Scott-Vitas Gerulaitis, New York

"Sports Illustrated" photo by Neil Leifer, © Time Inc.

In "dream mile" at third annual Martin Luther King, Jr., games, Marty Liquori of Villanova defeats world record holder Jim Ryun by a foot.

Track

Pat Matzdorf, a Wisconsin collegian, broke the world high-jump record in July. Matzdorf, a relative unknown, went 7–6¼ in the U.S.-Russian meet to help the Americans beat the Soviets, 126–110. The man who set the record of 7–5¾ in 1963 was Russian Valeri Brumel. Matzdorf's unexpected record was the high point of the outdoor season.

Rod Milburn of Southern University took ²⁄₁₀ of a second off the 120-yard high-hurdles record, covering the distance in 13 seconds flat. UCLA's John Smith bettered the 440-yard-dash mark of 44.7 set by Curtis Mills, with a 44.5 clocking.

Other outdoor records included 57–1 by Pedro Perez of Cuba in the triple jump; 250 feet 7.93 inches by Walter Schmidt of West Germany in the hammer throw; and three marks by European women—4:09.6 in the 1,500 meters by Karin Burneleit of East Germany, 6–3½ in the high jump by Ilona Gusenbauer of Austria and 212–10½ in the discus by Faina Melnik of Russia.

California was stripped of the 1970 NCAA championship for using an ineligible athlete, but the title returned to the West Coast in 1971, with UCLA topping USC.

Jay Silvester and Dr. Delano Meriwether, the Baltimore hematologist who runs in suspenders, missed records because of too much wind. Silvester threw the discus 230–11, and Meriwether ran the 100 in 9 seconds flat.

In the indoor season, the pole-vault record fell three times, with Kjell Isaksson of Sweden finally advancing the standard to 17–9. The shot-put record went twice, to Randy Matson at 67–10, then to Al Feuerbach at 68–11.

Kerry Pearce tied his own record of 8:27.2 in the two-mile, and Kerry O'Brien of Australia then broke it by running the fastest two-mile ever, 8:19.2. Belgium's Emile Puttemans later lowered the mark to 8:17.8.

Other new indoor records are: Lee Evans, 500-yard run, 54.4; Jean-Louis Ravelomanantsoa, 60-yard dash, 5.9; Rob Mitchell, 220-yard dash, 21.6; Villanova University, distance medley relay, 9:31.5; Tom Von Ruden, 1,000-meter run, 2:20.4; Pacific Coast Club, mile relay, 3:09.4.

Marty Liquori led Villanova to the NCAA indoor title.

Chi Cheng, the Taiwanese track star of 1970 who now lives in California, was awarded the second annual Tanqueray Sports Achievement Award. Chi Cheng is generally considered the world's foremost female athlete.

DWIGHT CHAPIN
Sportswriter, Los Angeles Times

Yachting

Although 1971 was not an America's Cup, Bermuda or Transatlantic Race year, it certainly did not lack in prestigious yachting events.

The Southern Ocean Racing Circuit, consisting of 6 distance races held each winter off the Florida coast and in the Bahamas, required a great amount of windward work. When all the points were tallied, Jakob Isbrandtsen's 60-foot sloop *Running Tide*, designed by Sparkman and Stephens, was overall winner. Class A and B yachts dominated the first 15 positions, with the Class E sloop *Smuggler* breaking the monopoly. A Scampi Class Half-Ton Cup Boat designed by Peter Norlin, *Smuggler* was sailed well by her young Swedish owner, Bengt Jornstedt, and four friends.

The year marked the first Cape Town to Rio Race with 15 countries participating. R. Knox-Johnson of Great Britain brought *Ocean Spirit* in first, but *Albatross II*, a Division III entry owned by J. Goodwin of South Africa, was first overall on corrected time.

In early February, Huey Long's *Ondine* set a new course record in the Buenos Aires-Rio Race. Though *Ondine* led a fleet that represented five nations, the Brazilian entry *Pluft*, sailed by Israel Klabin, captured the overall prize and first in Class A.

The presence of six 73-footers in the 69-boat fleet racing from San Pedro, Calif., to Honolulu brought added excitement and interest

---

YACHTING

KIEL WEEK

Flying Dutchman (108 entries)
  First: Keith Musto, England
  Second: Kurt Prenzeer, West Germany
Stars (52 entries)
  First: Stig Wennerstrom, Sweden
  Second: Pelle Petterson, Sweden
Dragons (66 entries)
  First: Aage Birch, Denmark
  Second: Heilmeier, West Germany
Solings (65 entries)
  First: Arved von Gruenewaldt, Sweden
  Second: Kadelbach, West Germany
Tempest (37 entries)
  First: Staartjes, Netherlands
  Second: Valentin Mankin, U.S.S.R.
Finns
  First: Thomas Jungblut, West Germany
Mallory Cup: John Kolius, Houston, Tex.
Sears Cup: Charles Scott, Annapolis Yacht Club
Prince of Wales Bowl: Terry Cronberg, MIT Nautical Association

The 1971 Transpac—from San Pedro, Calif., to Honolulu—begins July 4. The race was won in record time by "Windward Passage" (in foreground of photo).

Beckner Photo Service

to the 1971 Transpac. It got under way July 4. *Windward Passage*, designed by Alan Gurney and denied victory in 1969 because of a starting-line foul, was back to set the score straight. She did more than that. Mark Johnson not only brought her in first to finish off Diamond Head, but captured first overall, first in Class A and established a new course record of 9:09:06:48 (elapsed time). In a race that was marked by mainly light airs, this was an outstanding performance. No "A" boat had ever before swept a triple victory, in 26 Transpacs.

The Admiral's Cup, an international competition for ocean-racing teams, is run in midsummer every odd-numbered year in conjunction with Cowes Week and the Fastnet Race in England. In 1971, 14 countries fielded 3-boat entries which participated in the 225-mile Channel Race, two 30-mile day races during Cowes Week, and the 605-mile Fastnet. The British team—Arthur Slater's *Prospect of Whitby*, Prime Minister Edward Heath's *Morning Cloud* and R. C. Watson's *Cervantes IV*, all Sparkman and Stephens' designs—took the cup. The U.S. team placed second and the Australians third.

Though Ted Turner's *American Eagle* led the 218-boat fleet representing 17 nations in the Fastnet, Australia's Syd Fisher brought *Ragamuffin* in to capture overall honors and first in Class I. Six of the top 10 were designed by Sparkman and Stephens.

DIANE DURYEA
Yachting Magazine

SPORTS

Summary of Winners Not Included on Pages 397–418

ARCHERY—World Champions
Men: John Williams, Cranesville, Pa.
Women: Emma Gapchenko, U.S.S.R.

BADMINTON—U.S. Champions
Men: Muljadi, Indonesia
Women: Noriko Takagi, Japan

BOBSLEDDING—World Champions
Two-man: Italy
Four-man: Switzerland No. 2

BOWLING—American Bowling Congress Champions
All-events (classic): Gary Dickinson, Fort Worth, Tex.
All-events (regular): Al Cohn, Chicago
Doubles (classic): Bill Zuben-Barry Warshafsky, Chicago
Doubles (regular): Tony Maresca-Bill Haley, Mesa, Ariz.
Singles (classic): Al Cohn
Singles (regular): Victor Iwlew, Kalamazoo, Mich.
Team (classic): Chester Lio Investments, Houston
Team (regular): Carter Tool & Dye, Rochester, N.Y.

CANOEING—U.S. Champions
Canoe Singles (1,000 meters): Andy Weigand, Newport Beach, Calif.
Kayak Singles (1,000 meters): Tony Ralphs, Newport Beach, Calif.

CASTING—U.S. Champions
All-Distance Surf: Marion Hutson, Chesapeake, Va.
All-Distance Inland: B. L. Farley, San Antonio, Tex.

CURLING
U.S.: Edmore, N.D.
World: Canada

CYCLING
Amateur Bicycle League Sprints Champion: Gary Campbell, Paramount, Calif.
Tour de France: Eddy Merckx, France

DOGS—Best-in-Show Winners
International (Chicago): Ch. Chinoe's Adamant James, English springer spaniel
Westminster: Ch. Chinoe's Adamant James

FENCING—World Champions
Epée: Gregory Kriss, U.S.S.R.
Foil: Vasily Stankovich, U.S.S.R.
Saber: Michele Maffei, Italy

GYMNASTICS—U.S. National AAU Champions
All-around: Yoshiaki Takei, Georgia Southern G.C.
Team: New York A.C.

HANDBALL—U.S. Handball Association 4-Wall Champions
Singles: Paul Haber, Chicago
Doubles: Ray Neveau, Oshkosh, Wisc.; Simie Fein, Milwaukee

HORSESHOE PITCHING—World Champions
Men: Curt Day, Frankfurt, Ind.
Women: Ruth Hangen, Buffalo, N.Y.

ICE SKATING—World Champions
Men's Figure: Ondrej Nepela, Czechoslovakia
Women's Figure: Beatrix Schuba, Austria
Pairs: Irina Rodnina, Sergei Ulanov, U.S.S.R.
Men's Speed: Ard Schenk, Netherlands
Women's Speed: Nina Statkevich, U.S.S.R.

JUDO—U.S. National AAU Champions
Open: Roy Sukimoto, South Pacific Assoc.
Grand Champion: Douglass Nelson, Pacific Assoc.

LACROSSE
Club: Long Island A.C.
Intercollegiate: Cornell

MOTORCYCLING
U.S. Grand Champion: Dick Mann, Richmond, Calif.

PARACHUTING—U.S. Champions
Overall—Clay Schoelpple, Hartwood, Va.

ROWING
Intercollegiate R.A.: Cornell

RUGBY
World: South Africa
Canada: Ontario

SKIING
World Cup Champions
Men: Gustavo Thoeni, Italy
Women: Annamarie Proell, Austria
U.S. National Alpine Champions
Men's Slalom: Otto Tschudi, Denver U.
Men's Giant Slalom: Bob Cochran, Richmond, Vt.
Men's Downhill: Bob Cochran
Women's Slalom: Barbara Cochran, Richmond, Vt.
Women's Giant Slalom: Laurie Kreiner, Timmons, Ont.
Women's Downhill: Cheryl Bechdolt, Tahoe City, Calif.

SOFTBALL—American Amateur Association Champions
Men's Fast Pitch: Welty Way, Cedar Rapids, Iowa
Women's Fast Pitch: Raybestos Brakettes, Stratford, Conn.
Men's Slow Pitch: Piledrivers, Virginia Beach
Women's Slow Pitch: Gators, Fort Lauderdale

SURFING—U.S. Champions
All Round: Hal Sachs, San Juan Capistrano, Calif.
Men: David Nuuhiwa, Huntington Beach, Calif.
Women: Joyce Hoffman Langor, Del Mar, Calif.

VOLLEYBALL—U.S. Volleyball Assoc. Champions
Open: Santa Monica (Calif.) YMCA
Women: Los Angeles Renegades Red

WATER SKIING—World Champions
Overall: George Athanas, Kelowna, B.C.
Women's Overall: Christy Lynn Weir, McQueeney, Tex.

WRESTLING—U.S. National AAU Free-Style Champions
Unlimited: Greg Wojciechowski, Toledo, Ohio
Team: New York A.C.

Russell Reif from Pictorial

Possible help for New York State financial crisis: Off-track betting customers place their wagers.

STATES, U.S.

In 1971, civics and history textbooks still reminded students that the states once were considered the laboratories of American democracy. Many of the programs now carried out on the national level were first tried in the states: regulation of health and safety, unemployment insurance, minimum-wage laws. Many, if not most, U.S. national leaders were trained in their state governments. But in 1971, events continued to show that the states have lost their position as the main force and thrust in national affairs and national initiative.

Today there is hardly a state that is not literally engulfed by the needs and demands of its citizens. The growth in population, in urban sprawl and decay and in welfare has made it necessary for the states to have many more schools and colleges, more mental and general hospitals, greater staffs, more roads, more parks, bigger public-safety departments and much broader welfare budgets. As Prof.

Donald G. Herzberg of Rutgers University has written, "With state resources so hard pressed it is no wonder that there is little opportunity for state experimentation."

The demise of state power and influence is a matter that might be left for academic and even historical debate, on whether the states yielded because of lack of talent and will or whether events themselves gave rise to the power and influence of the Federal Government, through no fault of the states. The fact remains that during 1971 most states were in deep trouble trying to meet the demands of their citizens and that the root of their trouble was money—or, more precisely, the shortage of it. The U.S. Commerce Department estimated that in the fiscal year starting July 1, 1971, the governments of the 50 states would have a combined deficit totaling $6,200,000,000. It would be the sixth consecutive year of red-ink spending for the states, the Federal agency said. Commerce Department officials estimated that in the fiscal year, general tax receipts for the states were budgeted at a record $59,200,000,000, an increase of 15 per cent over the preceding year. This indicated not only a greater tax base but a greater effort by the states to increase taxes to meet ever-rising costs. Yet the expected rise in costs still exceeded the rise in revenues.

Despite a record showing political backlash against governors and state legislators who advocated higher taxes, state officials did act to raise taxes during 1971. The ferment in state capitols over levying or raising of income-tax rates at times reached fever pitch. There were intense debates over such levies in Connecticut, Massachusetts, Pennsylvania, Ohio and California among others. At year's end, 41 states had income taxes; and at one point in the year New Hampshire was the only state with neither an income tax nor a sales tax. New York State approved off-racetrack betting. Connecticut also approved off-track betting, and a state lottery.

With the states continuing to be strapped for money, governors led a growing effort to secure more funds from the Federal Government, not necessarily through more grant-in-aid programs but through direct sharing of revenues collected by Washington. This proposal is called revenue sharing, and in 1971 it again had the blessing of President Nixon. He called revenue sharing an integral part of "a new Federalism," and proposed sharing with the states $5,000,000,000 in general funds and $11,400,000,000 in special funds for broad categories, including education, health and welfare, urban development and mass transit. The proposal came in for intense debate. It was generally favored by governors and mayors (cities would get a big part of the shared monies). It also generated considerable opposition by those who contended that the states should and could do more for themselves, who argued that Nixon's plan would discourage states from bettering their affairs, and from those who contended that some states were doing well financially and thus should not get Federal help.

In the last group was Chairman Wilbur Mills (D-Ark.) of the tax-writing House Ways and Means Committee. It was Mills' opposition that helped to stall revenue-sharing legislation in the Congress. Then, in announcing his "new economic policy" in mid-August, Nixon proposed delaying revenue sharing for three months. This suggestion did not encourage Democratic leaders in Congress to push the legislation.

A nonpartisan citizens organization, the Citizens Conference on State Legislatures, released in 1971 the first comprehensive study of the 50 state legislatures. The study found the legislatures to be "the keystone of the American Federal system" but concluded they had not been meeting their responsibilities. The 14-month, $200,000 study did not attempt to measure the quality of legislation but based judgments on ability to function, size of staff, type of organization, accountability to the people as determined by the number of open sessions and treatment of minority members and relationship of legislators to lobbyists and private interests.

The study concluded that the legislatures lacked credibility and suffered from poor organization and practice. "State legislatures are heavily involved in making state policy," the report said. "It seems fairly obvious that, by and large, they have not been doing their job satisfactorily. The evidence is in the many 'crises' that beset American society. The fact that few people think of the state as a real source of answers to their problems presents further evidence. The state government is a gray area in the minds of most Americans." The study gave the top ten legislative rankings to California, New York, Illinois, Florida, Wisconsin, Iowa, Hawaii, Michigan, Nebraska and Minnesota. The bottom ten rankings, from the last on up, were Alabama, Wyoming, Delaware, North Carolina, Arkansas, Georgia, South Carolina, Arizona, Mississippi and Montana.

The study noted that there has been a movement for legislative reform and improvement in recent years; legislatures in Florida, Indiana and Connecticut were singled out for commendation. Some political commentators saw an improvement in the quality of men seeking governorships, and winning their elective con-

tests. A few states acted to improve and strengthen their consumer and environmental protection laws, and several states—led by Massachusetts—enacted "no fault" auto-insurance programs to simplify accident claims and trim driver costs. Several states even enacted statutes to curb "noise pollution"; North Dakota, for example, decreed limits on noise made by farm machinery, and Indiana acted to penalize excessive auto noise.

The states also acted quickly to ratify a constitutional amendment (the nation's 26th) giving the vote to 18, 19 and 20-year-olds. Then disputes arose as to where college students of those ages should be permitted to register to vote: from the homes of their parents or from their college residences. At year's end the issue seemed headed for the U.S. Supreme Court.

Another issue in the states during 1971 was that of remapping legislative districts, in line with population changes determined by the 1970 census and Supreme Court decisions requiring state legislative districts be drawn in accord with the court's "one man, one vote" rulings. Every state undertook the process of redistricting in time for the 1972 elections, and in 1971 many of the states accomplished this task. There were court challenges against some districting decisions (Kentucky, Alabama, Montana, New Jersey, Idaho, Louisiana, New Mexico, Virginia and Mississippi, among others, faced court tests), mostly on grounds that new district lines allowed too much deviation from the one-man, one-vote rule.

The Citizens Conference on State Legislatures (whose goal is to organize citizens' groups to push legislative reform) issued a report in 1971 outlining what it thought needs doing to improve state legislative performance. Among other things, the conference noted that:

Only 20 states provide office space for members of the legislature.

Only 20 states provide full-time professional assistance to legislative leaders during sessions.

Only 16 legislatures regularly record and publish committee votes.

Only 11 legislatures provide for the formal regulation of the flow of work through the legislature by a system of deadlines.

There is a wide range of salaries for state legislators: Rhode Island and North Dakota pay their legislators $5.00 a day for 60-day sessions, Rhode Island annually and North Dakota biennially. New Hampshire pays $200 every 2 years. California, at the other extreme, pays its legislators $19,200 a year.

ROBERT W. DIETSCH
Business-Economics Editor
Scripps-Howard Newspapers

Alabama. On Jan. 18, George C. Wallace was inaugurated, for the second time, as governor; and six elected Greene Co. black officials were sworn in, in Eutaw. ☐ State's antiriot law was declared unconstitutional on Apr. 9 by a Federal court. ☐ Under ancient public-nuisance statutes, State Attorney General Bill Baxley filed suit, on Apr. 26, charging 13 large Birmingham firms with endangering lives by polluting the air. ☐ Independent candidate James Robinson was elected mayor of Montgomery. ☐ Governor Wallace was charged with contempt of court on Aug. 25 for "flagrant violation" of court orders to stop interfering with school desegregation. ☐ From May 1 through Aug. 31, over 33,000 people, mostly black, were cut from state welfare rolls. ☐ As school opened on Sept. 8, Mobile Co. quietly began massive busing program. ☐ Rep. George Andrews (D) died Dec. 25.

Alaska. Preparations began in June for a five-megaton thermonuclear test, called Cannikin, in the Aleutian island of Amchitka, an uninhabited national wildlife refuge. The U.S. Supreme Court refused to order a delay, and the device was tested on Nov. 6. ☐ U.S. Interior Department reported on Jan. 13 that although the proposed 800-mi. oil pipeline across state would result in unavoidable environment damage, it should be built because of country's oil needs. Pending suits, however, kept the project stalled throughout 1971. ☐ On June 19, Alaska and a consortium of seven oil companies agreed on terms for a 380-mile road on North Slope. ☐ Just before it adjourned, the U.S. Congress passed a bill paying Alaska's natives—some 55,000 Eskimos, Indians and Aleuts—$962,500,000 and granting them 40,-000,000 acres of land. The legislation ended a 104-year-old land-claims dispute.

Arizona. By 1971 the "new town" of Lake Havasu City, where London Bridge was being re-erected, had a population of 8,000; and the promised lake had been created by damming the Colorado River. ☐ For the sunbaked, dry state in general there were prospects of both more river water and geothermal supplies (underground superheated water). ☐ In June, 24

About an hour after the Cannikin thermonuclear test in the Aleutian island of Amchitka, Nov. 6, Atomic Energy Commission Chairman James Schlesinger (r) and Maj. Gen. Edward B. Giller inspect the site. The blast, most powerful U.S. underground nuclear explosion ever, registered 7 on the Richter scale (below).

Photos UPI

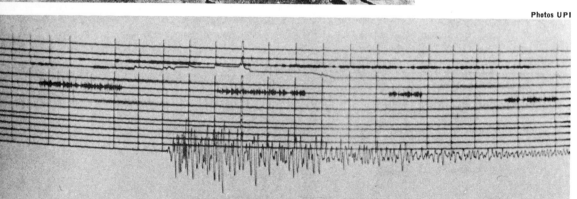

neighbors of the Tonto National Forest sued the Federal Government, charging that the use of defoliants in the forest had harmed their property and health.

Arkansas. The 1971 session of the state legislature reorganized Arkansas' executive branch into 13 cabinet-level departments; established a new code of ethics for legislative, executive and judicial officials; and increased the state's income tax. ☐ Gov. Dale Bumpers issued an executive order forming a Governor's Committee on Human Resources. ☐ In January, President Nixon announced that the biological-warfare facilities at Pine Bluff Arsenal would be converted into a center that will develop "better approaches to the understanding of what the data acquired from experimental animals means for man."

California. After vetoing $503,000,000 for education, welfare, medical care, and salary increases, Gov. Ronald Reagan (R) approved a $7,300,000,000 budget. The Governor also signed a welfare bill stiffening eligibility rules, setting residency requirements and tightening controls over the $2,100,000,000 system. ☐ Governor Reagan, a millionaire, attributed his failure to pay state income taxes in 1970 to "business reverses." ☐ Although under indictment, charged with violating a Federal law against interstate racketeering, San Francisco Mayor Joseph L. Alioto (D) was reelected. Pete Wilson was elected mayor of San Diego; and Sacramento Mayor Richard Marriott won a second term. Three seats on Berkeley's eight-member City Council were won by young candidates described as "radicals." ☐ A massive school-busing program to integrate San Francisco's school system got under way without violence. Earlier the system had been disrupted by a 19-day teachers strike. ☐ In February, Southern California suffered a devastating earthquake (*see also* Geology).

Colorado. Through 1953–66 the U.S. Atomic Energy Commission operated a uranium-ore processing mill in Grand Junction. After the mill closed, some 150,000 to 200,000 tons of sands (tailings), the waste from the uranium processing, were utilized in constructing concrete basements and building slabs. Late in 1971 there was evidence that structures, including homes and schools, built with the tailings had potential lethal levels of radioactivity. An investigation was planned. ☐ The $6,000,000 Denver Art Museum opened in the fall. ☐ The legislature passed a new criminal code, a consumer code and a no-fault divorce bill.

Connecticut. With a 1971 fiscal deficit of $261,-000,000, Connecticut faced a severe financial crisis. On Aug. 23, Gov. Thomas J. Meskill (R) signed a bill repealing the state's first personal income tax, passed earlier in 1971, and substituted a revenue package increasing the state sales tax to 6.5 per cent (highest in the nation). ☐ Other acts of the legislature defined the cir-

U.S. GOVERNORS

STATE	GOVERNOR	TERM EXPIRES
ALABAMA	George C. Wallace (D)	Jan. 1975
ALASKA	William A. Egan (D)	Dec. 1974
ARIZONA	Jack Williams (R)	Jan. 1975
ARKANSAS	Dale Bumpers (D)	Jan. 1973
CALIFORNIA	Ronald Reagan (R)	Jan. 1975
COLORADO	John A. Love (R)	Jan. 1975
CONNECTICUT	Thomas J. Meskill (R)	Jan. 1975
DELAWARE	Russell W. Peterson (R)	Jan. 1973
FLORIDA	Reubin Askew (D)	Jan. 1975
GEORGIA	Jimmy Carter (D)	Jan. 1975
HAWAII	John A. Burns (D)	Dec. 1974
IDAHO	Cecil Andrus (D)	Jan. 1975
ILLINOIS	Richard B. Ogilvie (R)	Jan. 1973
INDIANA	Edgar D. Whitcomb (R)	Jan. 1973
IOWA	Robert D. Ray (R)	Jan. 1973
KANSAS	Robert Docking (D)	Jan. 1973
KENTUCKY	Wendell Ford (D)	Dec. 1975
LOUISIANA	John J. McKeithen (D)	May 1972
MAINE	Kenneth M. Curtis (D)	Jan. 1975
MARYLAND	Marvin Mandel (D)	Jan. 1975
MASSACHUSETTS	Francis W. Sargent (R)	Jan. 1975
MICHIGAN	William G. Milliken (R)	Jan. 1975
MINNESOTA	Wendell R. Anderson (D)	Jan. 1975
MISSISSIPPI	William L. Waller (D)	Jan. 1976
MISSOURI	Warren E. Hearnes (D)	Jan. 1973
MONTANA	Forrest H. Anderson (D)	Jan. 1973
NEBRASKA	J. J. Exon (D)	Jan. 1975
NEVADA	D. N. O'Callaghan (D)	Jan. 1975
NEW HAMPSHIRE	Walter Peterson (R)	Jan. 1973
NEW JERSEY	William T. Cahill (R)	Jan. 1974
NEW MEXICO	Bruce King (D)	Jan. 1975
NEW YORK	Nelson A. Rockefeller (R)	Jan. 1975
NORTH CAROLINA	Robert W. Scott (D)	Jan. 1973
NORTH DAKOTA	William L. Guy (D)	Jan. 1973
OHIO	John J. Gilligan (D)	Jan. 1975
OKLAHOMA	David Hall (D)	Jan. 1975
OREGON	Tom McCall (R)	Jan. 1975
PENNSYLVANIA	Milton J. Shapp (D)	Jan. 1975
RHODE ISLAND	Frank Licht (D)	Jan. 1973
SOUTH CAROLINA	John C. West (D)	Jan. 1975
SOUTH DAKOTA	Richard S. Kneip (D)	Jan. 1973
TENNESSEE	Winfield Dunn (R)	Jan. 1975
TEXAS	Preston Smith (D)	Jan. 1973
UTAH	Calvin L. Rampton (D)	Jan. 1973
VERMONT	Deane C. Davis (R)	Jan. 1973
VIRGINIA	Linwood Holton (R)	Jan. 1973
WASHINGTON	Daniel J. Evans (R)	Jan. 1975
WEST VIRGINIA	Arch A. Moore, Jr. (R)	Jan. 1975
WISCONSIN	Patrick J. Lucey (D)	Jan. 1974
WYOMING	Stanley K. Hathaway (R)	Jan. 1973

cumstances under which wiretapping is permissible; reduced from 12 to 6 the number of jurors required in civil-trial cases; formed a department of the environment which consolidated the functions of various agencies and commissions; and established a new code of ethics for state-government employees.

Delaware. In June, Gov. Russell W. Peterson (R) signed a bill barring heavy industry from the coastline. □ A new tax program was approved by the legislature. □ The state's Family Court System was completely revised; and bills were passed establishing no-fault automobile insurance, prohibiting sex discrimination in housing and accommodations, increasing teachers' retirement and pension funds and also workmen's compensation benefits.

Florida. "To prevent potentially serious environmental damage," President Nixon ordered a halt to further construction of the Cross-Florida Barge Canal. □ More than two hundred miles of Tampa Bay and other Gulf coastal areas had severe outbreaks of red tide, caused by microorganisms that color seawater red and, in heavy concentration, kill fish. □ South Florida suffered a severe drought. □ In the spring a majority of the black students at the University of Florida resigned in protest against the university's racial policies. □ Racial unrest rocked Jacksonville for four days in June. □ In 1971 the legislature passed a tax-reform program, no-fault auto-insurance and no-fault divorce bills, and approved a Mar. 14 presidential primary. □ Miami Beach tourism declined by some 15 per cent.

Georgia. Jimmy Carter (D) was sworn in as governor on Jan. 12. In his inaugural address, the former peanut farmer stated: "I say to you quite frankly that the time for racial discrimination is over." □ Following the death of Sen. Richard Russell in January, David H. Gambrell (D) was appointed to fill the unexpired term. □ In Columbus, on June 21, a 20-year-old Negro youth was killed by a white detective. The incident aggravated racial tension in the city. Subsequently a biracial committee made charges of police brutality "by some black and white officers alike." □ In a referendum, Atlanta voters approved a new $1,300,000,000 rapid-transit system.

Hawaii. The state, particularly its sugar and pineapple industries, was severely hurt by a West Coast dock strike. □ A bill establishing a one-year-residency requirement for welfare recipients was signed by Gov. John Burns in

June. □ The 31-story, $62,000,000 Sheraton Waikiki, world's largest convention resort hotel, opened on Waikiki Beach.

Idaho. The Idaho legislature passed bills regulating surface mining and protecting the state's streams. Other legislative acts included a consumer-credit code and a consumer-protection code, an increase in the minimum wage, and a uniform probate code. □ The state's first annual general-fund budget, authorized by the legislature in 1970, called for expenditures totaling $125,300,000. □ Sen. Len B. Jordan (R) said that he would not seek reelection in 1972.

Illinois. Cook County State Attorney Edward V. Hanrahan and 13 aides were indicted by a grand jury on charges of conspiring to obstruct an investigation of the killing by police of two Black Panther leaders in 1969. □ Three Federal judges heard testimony that top Illinois Democrats, including former Gov. Otto Kerner, had received substantial profits in racetrack stocks. In December, Kerner, three former state officials and a business associate were named in a 19-count indictment, involving the racetrack stocks. □ Some $800,000 in unexplained cash was found among the personal effects of Paul Powell (D), Illinois secretary of state who died in 1969. □ A Federal court declared the state's 97-year-old abortion law unconstitutional. □ The legislature approved state aid for Catholic schools; a $900,000,000 bond issue for downstate highways, urban mass transit and airports; no-fault auto insurance; and a one-year-residency requirement for welfare recipients. □ Chicago Mayor Richard J. Daley (D) was elected to a fifth term. □ Rep. Charlotte Reid (R) was appointed to the Federal Communications Commission. Her House seat was vacant as 1971 ended.

Indiana. Gov. Edgar Whitcomb signed legislation prohibiting the sale (effective Jan. 1, 1972) of detergents with more than 12 per cent phospate and (effective Jan. 1, 1973) of detergents with more than 3 per cent phospate. The legislature also removed many state jobs from political patronage and increased the salaries of most elected state officials. □ Gary Mayor Richard D. Hatcher (D) and Indianapolis Mayor Richard G. Lugar (R) were reelected.

Iowa. Before adjourning in June, the state legislature reduced the number of judicial districts from 18 to 8; gave the Chemical Technological Review Board power to restrict or ban hazardous pesticides; reduced to one year the penalty for the illegal possession of drugs for personal use; and ordered a safety-inspection test for all automobiles before registration.

Kansas. Wichita's City Commission passed a fair-housing ordinance prohibiting discrimination in the sale, rental, advertising and financing of housing. □ Gov. Robert Docking signed a bill permitting nonprofit organizations to hold bingo games. □ When the worst blizzard of the century swept south-central Kansas in February, Air Force planes dropped bales of food to some seventy thousand stranded cattle in five counties.

Kentucky. Calling his campaign a first step in the "dump Nixon" movement, Lt. Gov. Wendell Ford (D) was elected governor. The voters also approved a Homestead Amendment exempting from property taxes the first $6,500 in assessed valuation of a home owned by a person 65 years of age or older. □ Rep. John Watts (D) of the sixth Congressional district died in September. In a special election, William P. Curlin, Jr. (D) was elected to fill the unexpired term. □ Outgoing Gov. Louis B. Nunn signed a bill regulating mine drainage.

Louisiana. After nine months of investigation, the Louisiana Legislative Mafia Investigating Committee concluded that, although there was some corruption, the state government was not controlled by the underworld. The committee had been appointed following an article in *Life* magazine in April 1970. □ In May, State Attorney General Jack P. F. Gremillion and two codefendants were found not guilty of fraud and conspiracy charges. □ Voters approved a $3,500,000 bond issue for constructing a new Orleans Parish prison. In September some 200 prisoners in the old jail rioted, resulting in damage of some $15,000.

Maine. Although a referendum proposition repealing the corporate and personal state income taxes was defeated, voters approved a $4,000,-000 bond issue for loans to higher-education students. □ A Human Rights Commission was created to look into the possibility of discrimination in housing, employment and public accommodations. □ The state hourly minimum wage was increased to $1.80.

Maryland. William O. Mills, a Democrat who had switched to the Republican Party in December 1970, was elected to the House of Representatives seat formerly held by the new Secretary of the Interior, Rogers C. B. Morton. □ The 1971 legislature approved a budget of $1,800,000,000 for fiscal 1972; assumed com-

UPI

Following a "dump Nixon" campaign, Lt. Gov. Wendell Ford is elected governor of Kentucky.

plete school-construction costs; increased legislators' yearly salaries to $11,000; and established a Commission on the Status of Women as well as a Joint Committee on Ethics for legislators. □ William D. Schaefer (D), a Baltimore city councilman from 1955, was elected mayor of Baltimore.

Massachusetts. Stating that "at its best, a lottery can produce only incidental usable funds for public purposes," Gov. Francis W. Sargent (R) vetoed a state-lottery bill. However, the legislature overrode the veto, and the lottery was scheduled to go into operation in the spring of 1972. □ The Governor signed bills extending no-fault auto insurance to cover property damage; providing for a sentence of life imprisonment for anyone convicted of detonating a bomb resulting in death; and increasing the state minimum wage to $1.75 per hour. □ In Boston's mayoralty race, Mayor Kevin White (D) won a second term, defeating Rep. Louise Day Hicks (R).

Michigan. School integration dominated Michigan news in 1971. In Pontiac, six Ku Klux Klan members were charged with the bombing of ten school buses, intended to help achieve a court-ordered school-integration plan. □ In Detroit, a U.S. judge said that the city's school system was deliberately segregated. □ Gov.

William G. Milliken (R) signed a bill lowering the age of majority from 21 to 18 in almost all fields. ☐ A 50 per cent (from 2.6 per cent to 3.9 per cent) increase in the state's personal income tax went into effect on Aug. 1.

Minnesota. In January the Minnesota Supreme Court ruled that Lt. Gov. Rudolph G. Perpich acted illegally when, in presiding over the opening session of the state Senate, he acted so as to give control of the Senate to his own Democratic-Farmer-Labor Party. Subsequently, the Republican-oriented Conservative Party gained control of the legislative body. ☐ Gov. Wendell R. Anderson (D) signed a tax plan, including a 30 per cent increase in individual income taxes. ☐ Minneapolis Mayor Charles S. Stenvig won a second term.

Mississippi. Running as an independent, Charles Evers, the black mayor of Fayette, was unsuccessful in his bid for the governorship. On Nov. 2 he was defeated by William L. Waller, 44-year-old Democratic lawyer. A total of 284 blacks ran for office; 40 were elected on Nov. 2. Democrats retained control of both houses of the state legislature. ☐ Gov. John Bell Williams issued an executive order withholding state funds from the Jackson school system, which had complied with a Federally ordered desegregation plan. ☐ Acting under a Federal court order, the Internal Revenue Service revoked the tax-exempt status of 23 Mississippi academies for failing to enforce nondiscriminatory admission policies. ☐ In Drew three white men were charged with the murder of an 18-year-old Negro girl. ☐ Eleven members of the Republic of New Africa were charged with the murder of a Jackson policeman and with treason.

Mississippi's newly elected Gov. William Waller delivers victory speech to campaign workers.

UPI

Missouri. Throughout 1971, Missouri celebrated the 150th anniversary of its statehood. ☐ The 1971 legislature made permanent the one-year income-tax increase, enacted in 1970; increased aid to public schools, by $70,000,000, and the salaries of state employees; created the Mined Land Conservation and Reclamation Commission; and authorized the sale of liquor by the drink on Sundays. ☐ The 12-member State Reorganization Commission called for a major reorganization of the state government.

Montana. Voters rejected a referendum proposition that would have reduced the 40 per cent income surtax to 10 per cent and substituted a 2 per cent sales-and-use tax. ☐ Gov. Forrest H. Anderson (D) announced that he would not seek reelection in 1972. ☐ It was the worst year in over a decade for prairie fires. The town of Oswego, in northeast Montana, was practically destroyed by such a fire.

Nebraska. In Lincoln, five women and four men were held on charges of plotting to blow up the Nebraska Capitol, a police station and a company building. ☐ Two members of the National Committee to Combat Fascism were found guilty of killing an Omaha policeman on Aug. 17, 1970. ☐ The legislature reapportioned the state's Supreme Court districts, approved a new statewide community-college system with the state assuming 75 per cent of the costs, and established an Environment Protection Agency.

Nevada. During the biennial legislative session, the salaries of state officials, including the governor, were increased; binding arbitration was called for in salary disputes involving state employees; five new district-court judges, a court administrator and an office of public defender were authorized; unemployment and disability benefits were raised; and a fair-housing law was passed. ☐ District Judge Richard Waters, Jr., ordered the Nevada Cement Company of Fernley to pay $1,850,000 in damages to 85 residents who had filed suit against the company for polluting the air.

New Hampshire. Gov. Walter R. Peterson, Jr.'s proposed 3 per cent state income tax was defeated in the legislature. ☐ The Governor and other state officials pushed efforts to preserve the state's natural environment as its population—particularly the number of vacationers generally and of people with second homes in the state—is increasing at a rapid rate. ☐ The home of Franklin Pierce, New Hampshire's only native son to become president, was saved from destruction.

A U.S. Senate committee hears testimony that the Four Corners Power Plant, in New Mexico, emits as much pollution as all of New York City.

New Jersey. A Federal grand jury indicted John V. Kenny, Hudson County Democratic leader, and three others on charges of extortion. Earlier, Jersey City Mayor Thomas J. Whelan had resigned after he was convicted with seven associates on Federal charges of extortion and conspiracy. In November, Dr. Paul Jordan, a Democrat who ran independently of the machine, was elected to fill Whelan's unexpired term. □ A bitter 11-week teachers' strike in Newark ended in April. □ The legislature voted to reimburse (up to $10,000) innocent victims of violent crimes; established a Pesticides Control Council and a Division of Consumer Affairs; reformed the state's divorce laws; passed a bill of rights for migrant farm workers; and set up a statewide system of drug-abuse and counseling clinics. □ A green-acres bond issue, providing $80,000,000 for the public acquisition of land for recreation and conservation, was approved by the voters, as was a $155,000,000 bond issue for higher-education buildings.

New Mexico. The city of Albuquerque was disrupted by 2 days of rioting—mainly by youngsters, including out-of-state hippies—in June; 41 persons were injured, and property damage was estimated at $3,000,000. □ The office of lieutenant governor became a full-time position with an annual salary of $15,000, and the salaries of other state officials were increased. □ Laws passed by the legislature provide that a person arrested on criminal charges must be brought to trial within six months or the charges are to be dropped, and created an Environment Improvement Agency with an appropriation of $1,800,000.

New York. On Nov. 2, voters rejected a $2,500,-000,000 transportation bond issue. □ In July, for the first time since December 1962, the state's unemployment rate exceeded 6 per cent. □ The 1971 legislature increased the state's sales tax from 3 to 4 per cent and the business tax by $168,000,000; cut the state's welfare and Medicaid programs; banned phosphate detergents; passed a one-year-residency requirement for welfare recipients (later declared unconstitutional); and increased aid to public and nonpublic schools. A subsequent special session passed a redistricting bill, but did not act on a $413,000,000 tax program before 1971 ended. □ Following one of the worst prison riots in history, $4,000,000 in emergency funds was allocated to repair Attica prison (*see also* Prison Reform).

North Carolina. In February, two persons were killed during racial hostilities in Wilmington.

Eight months later, the city suffered another outbreak of racial violence. ☐ The U.S. Supreme Court ruled that busing is a legal method of desegregating Charlotte's public-school system. ☐ The state government was reorganized, consolidating 317 agencies into 19 major departments. ☐ The age of majority was reduced to 18 years, except in certain areas. ☐ A scenic-rivers system and a pesticide board were approved.

North Dakota. On Dec. 15, the U.S. Air Force announced that 150 Minuteman 3 multiheaded missiles at Minot Air Force Base had been installed. ☐ Before it adjourned on Mar. 19, the legislature increased aid to education by $11,-000,000, funded a bonus for Vietnam veterans financed by a surtax on state income tax, raised the daily salary of legislative leaders and committee chairmen, and reorganized the state court system.

Ohio. On Dec. 7, charges against 20 persons indicted as a result of the Kent State University disorders of May 1970 were dropped for lack of evidence. In earlier trials, 2 defendants had pled guilty; 1 was found guilty on one count; charges against another were dismissed for lack of evidence; and a fifth defendant was acquitted. ☐ The legislature approved the state's first corporate and personal income tax, a political victory for Gov. John J. Gilligan. ☐ Ralph J. Perk became the first Republican in thirty years to be elected mayor of Cleveland.

Ohio Gov. John Gilligan advises Ronald Hooker, 19-year-old newly elected mayor of Newcomerstown, to "speak softly and carry a big gavel."
UPI

Oklahoma. At Catoosa in June, President Nixon took part in the dedication of the Arkansas River Navigation System. The public-works project makes Tulsa and its suburb Catoosa a seaport by connecting them with the Mississippi River. ☐ A major tax-reform program, increasing state revenues by an estimated $17,000,-000, was passed by the legislature. Other legislative acts included amendment of the unemployment-compensation laws and the State Clean Air Act to conform with Federal laws; increases in the hourly minimum wage and workmen's compensation benefits; and raising the minimum monthly teachers' salary to $500.

Oregon. The legislature passed bills requiring a deposit on all soft-drink and beer containers, effective Oct. 1, 1972; governing the location of nuclear-power plants; and allocating at least one per cent of state-highway funds for hiking and bicycling paths. ☐ Gov. Tom McCall (R) vetoed a bill regulating farm-workers unions. A boycott of Oregon's agricultural products had been threatened if McCall signed the bill.

Pennsylvania. Frank L. Rizzo, the "toughest cop in America," was elected mayor of Philadelphia. ☐ Reps. Robert J. Corbett and James G. Fulton died in 1971. H. John Heinz 3d was elected to fill Corbett's term; Fulton's House seat remained vacant as 1971 ended. ☐ A 2.3 per cent state income tax was enacted, as was a bill permitting restaurants to serve liquor on Sundays. A bill to aid families with children in parochial schools passed, replacing an earlier aid bill declared unconstitutional by the U.S. Supreme Court. ☐ In a landmark case, a three-judge Federal panel ordered Pennsylvania to provide free public-school education for all retarded children in the state. ☐ The State Human Relations Committee ordered Philadelphia and Pittsburgh public-school districts to "eliminate" racial imbalance. ☐ Philadelphia was hit by a transit strike; and Pittsburgh's newspapermen and teachers went on strike during the year.

Rhode Island. The 1971 legislature approved a $316,700,000 budget for fiscal 1972; passed a permanent personal income tax, amounting to 20 per cent of the Federal income tax; gave the governor the power to control extreme pollution; approved a one-year-residency requirement for welfare recipients; prohibited the display of indecent publications, pictures or articles at places of business frequented by minors; and authorized examination and treatment, without parental consent, of minors 18 to 21 years old for illness resulting from drug use.

South Carolina. With a promise to eliminate "any vestige of discrimination" from South Carolina's government, John C. West (D) was inaugurated governor on Jan. 19. □ George D. Hamilton, black welfare official, was appointed executive director of the newly formed Governor's Advisory Commission on Human Relations. □ Schools opened in Columbia under a new desegregation plan, including wide school busing, leaving about 13 per cent of the Negro population in all-black schools. □ A 20 per cent levy on X-rated films was authorized by the legislature; and teachers' salaries were increased by $300 annually. □ Mendel Jackson Davis, 28-year-old Democrat, was elected to the House of Representatives seat held for 29 years by the late L. Mendel Rivers. Davis is Rivers' godson and namesake.

South Dakota. During its two-month session, the legislature passed a $89,200,000 budget and special general funds totaling an additional $4,300,000 for fiscal 1972; created an Investment Council to direct investment of state funds; redistricted the state's Congressional and legislative districts; passed a consumer bill of rights; and increased workmen's compensation benefits. □ Gov. Richard F. Kneip's tax program was defeated.

Tennessee. In May, National Guardsmen were called to restore order in Chattanooga following a weekend of civil disorder. An unarmed black man was killed by police during the disturbance. In October scattered rock throwing and fire bombing broke out for several nights in Memphis. The unrest followed the beating and death of a 17-year-old Negro youth. Two months later, three sheriff's officers and a Memphis patrolman were charged with the death of the boy. Five others were indicted on lesser charges. □ Schools opened in Nashville under a court-ordered busing plan. □ Wyeth Chandler, a conservative councilman, was elected mayor of Memphis. John Franklin, a black educator and businessman, was elected health and education commissioner of Chattanooga.

Texas. State Attorney General Crawford C. Martin ruled that Gov. Preston E. Smith did not have the authority to ignore President Nixon's wage freeze as it applied to state employees. □ In the spring large sections of the state suffered prolonged drought. □ Wes Wise, an independent, was elected mayor of Dallas; and Houston mayor Louie Welch was reelected. □ As the year ended, the state's public-school financing system, based, as in most other states,

UPI

After beginning 1971 on the picket lines, Pittsburgh teachers accepted a $900 salary increase.

largely on property taxes, was declared unconstitutional. □ School-desegregation plans in Austin and Houston were rejected. □ A record $700,000,000 tax package was enacted. □ Voters approved sewer and college-construction bond issues. □ Although Governor Smith in most essentials accepted the budget approved by the legislature for fiscal 1972, he vetoed the budget for fiscal 1973. □ On Dec. 30 a jury in Baltimore, Md., District Court found Rep. John Dowdy (D-Tex., second district) guilty on eight counts of bribery, conspiracy and perjury.

Utah. Late in the year, two major milling and refinery operations in Utah announced that they would close, most likely resulting in serious effects on the state's industry and employment. □ The legislature increased the salaries of state employees, and workmen's compensation and unemployment benefits. □ In January, Gov. Calvin L. Rampton linked the death of 1,200 sheep in western Utah with a poisonous weed called halogeton, often mistakenly called locoweed.

Vermont. Following the death of Sen. Winston L. Prouty (R) on Sept. 10, Gov. Deane C.

A U.S. Department of Agriculture veterinarian observes the symptoms of Venezuelan equine encephalomyelitis, a sleeping-sickness virus spread by marsh mosquitoes, in a colt. During the summer, the disease killed some 2,500 horses in the Southwest, mainly in the state of Texas.

UPI

Davis (R) gave Rep. Robert T. Stafford (R) an interim appointment to the Senate. In a special election, early in 1972, Stafford was elected to fill the remaining five years of Prouty's term, and Richard Mallary (R) won election to the state's single House seat. □ The legislature gave 18-year-olds the right to vote, drink alcoholic beverages and make legal contracts, and granted state financial aid to parochial schools.

Virginia. In Norfolk a court-ordered school-busing plan—requiring a ratio of 55 per cent white to 45 per cent black students and doubling the number of children bused—went into effect in September. However, about 21 per cent of the white-student population had dropped out of the school system since the 1970–71 school year, a loss termed "unacceptable." Richmond too proceeded with a desegregation plan, increasing busing by about 50 per cent. □ On Nov. 2, Henry E. Howell, Jr., a populist-style Democrat turned independent, was elected lieutenant governor, to succeed the late J. Sargeant Reynolds.

Washington. With an unemployment rate of 13 per cent in Seattle, the U.S. Department of Agriculture authorized the use of both food distribution and food stamps in the city. □ The legislature lowered the age of majority to 18 years; legalized bingo games of nonprofit organizations; limited property-tax increases to 6 per cent annually; granted aid to students attending private colleges and universities; and created a land-planning commission.

West Virginia. While conservationists argued that strip-mining should be banned, and the mining and fuel industries opposed such a

move, the legislature imposed a 2-year halt to the issuing of state surface-mining permits in 22 of the state's 55 counties. □ The U.S. Supreme Court upheld West Virginia's law requiring the approval of 60 per cent of the voters in any referendum for bond issues or tax increases. □ Former Gov. William Wallace Barron was sentenced to prison (eligible for parole after four years) and fined $50,000 for bribing a Federal jury foreman in 1968.

Wisconsin. The state Supreme Court ruled that Wisconsin's compulsory-education law as it applies to the Amish people was unconstitutional. The State Attorney General announced that he would appeal the decision to the U.S. Supreme Court. □ In January a four-day strike by Milwaukee policemen was halted by court injunction. □ The University of Wisconsin and Wisconsin State University systems were merged, making the new institution the third largest university system in the nation. □ A three-judge Federal panel in Milwaukee ruled that it is unconstitutional for Wisconsin to grant tax exemptions to private organizations that discriminate racially in their membership policies. □ The legislature passed a bill requiring an annual legislative session.

Wyoming. Missing for ten days in July, Kevin Dye, a nine-year-old mentally retarded epileptic, was found alive and in "remarkably good" condition on Casper Mountain, near Casper. □ A Department of Administration and Fiscal Control replaced six agencies. In other legislative acts, state aid for the University of Wyoming and the state's community colleges was increased; the Criminal Code was revised; and the state's narcotic laws were amended to conform to Federal law.

SWEDEN

Sweden has the reputation of solving its labor conflicts peacefully, through arbitration and collective bargaining as well as a labor court. Nevertheless in early 1971 the country experienced one of the longest and most costly strikes in its whole history. Lasting from February to June, the strike originated in wage demands by white-collar workers employed by local governments and administrative units. It soon snowballed to encompass 50,000 workers, who in turn encountered lockouts by employers' organizations. Some 700,000 students in high schools, colleges and universities were given unexpected vacations when 25,000 teachers were locked out in February. The country's defense posture was also affected when 5,000 officers of the armed forces were locked out by the Collective Bargaining Office of the Government. Emergency powers were assumed by the Government in mid-March, which banned strikes for six weeks. Yet the conflict was not settled until June 22, when members of the striking unions received a 27.2 per cent increase in wages and benefits over a three-year period.

Discussions on Sweden's possible membership in the European Economic Community (Common Market) came to a sudden halt on Mar. 18, when the Government declared in effect that Sweden would not apply for full membership. It was pointed out that EEC membership, implying cooperation in foreign affairs as well as in economic and monetary fields, would not be compatible with Sweden's policy of nonalignment. At the same time it was announced that Sweden would welcome participation in cooperative arrangements within the scope of EEC, provided such cooperation would not limit Sweden's right of self-determination in areas that might affect its policy of neutrality. Sweden thus indicated interest in cooperation to strengthen free trade within Europe, and in membership in a customs union, including both industrial and agricultural products.

Carl Gustaf, grandson of 89-year-old King Gustaf VI Adolf and crown prince of Sweden, celebrated his 25th birthday on Apr. 30. Under the Swedish constitution, he came of age on that day and may now serve as regent if the King is unable to carry out the functions of his office.

Torsten Nilsson, who had served as a member of the Cabinet from 1945 and as foreign minister from 1962, resigned from that office on June 29. He was succeeded by the then minister of industry, Krister Wickman, whose position was taken over by Rune Johansson.

Gothenburg, Sweden's second largest city, marked its 350th anniversary with a Jubilee Week May 31–June 6. There were fireworks, a giant open-air variety show, and dancing in the streets.

The prestigious Swedish Academy on Mar. 12 elected Lars Forsell, well-known writer, to the seat formerly held by the late Sigfrid Siwertz, also a writer.

ERIK J. FRIIS
Editor, The American-Scandinavian Review

SWITZERLAND

The men of Switzerland approved a referendum on Feb. 7 giving women the vote in national elections. It was approved by a margin of 2 to 1, leaving tiny neighboring Liechtenstein as the only European country that denies women the vote.

Among the 1,698 candidates for the Nationalrat (lower house of Parliament) and the 44-seat Staenderat (upper house) were 268 women, among them nurses, airline hostesses and housewives. On Oct. 30 about 2,100,000 women, 60 per cent of the electorate, helped to send 11 women and 11 right-wing and antiforeigner candidates to Parliament. The conservative and antiforeign Republican Party picked up 7 seats in the 200-seat Nationalrat, and the allied National Action Party won 4 seats.

The pioneer woman member of Parliament was Mrs. Elisabeth Blunschy, a 49-year-old lawyer and Christian Democrat from the canton (province) of Schwyz. Ten other women followed her in winning seats.

The 4 major parties, which rule the neutral nation as a coalition, remained firmly in power with 162 seats, a loss of 5, and no major changes in policy were forecast.

Switzerland has no premier. The Government consists of a 7-man Federal council, aligned since 1959 on the "magic formula" of 2–2–2–1 portfolios allocated to the 4 largest parties: Socialist, Radical Democrat, Christian Democrat, and the Farmers, Tradesmen and Citizens.

The most heated political issue of the campaign was the presence of about a million foreigners in the country, many of them Italian

---

SWEDEN

Area: 173,649 sq. mi.
Population: 8,100,000
Capital: Stockholm
Government: Gustaf VI Adolf, king—1950; Olof Palme, prime minister—1969
Gross National Product: $31,200,000,000
Foreign trade: exports, $6,782,000,000; imports, $7,005,000,000
Armed forces: 750,000 (total mobilization strength)

seasonal workers. The Republicans and National Actionists called for sharp cutbacks in the number of non-Swiss residents. The proposal was defeated in a referendum. Zurich publisher James Schwarenbach, the Republican leader, argued that the presence of so many foreigners is changing the character and even the language of Switzerland. The Government contended that foreigners are needed to fill the growing demands of industry in this labor-short nation, which in September reported only 51 unemployed persons in the entire country.

Economically, 1971 was a year for clampdowns on domestic and international businessmen and bankers. The Government announced on May 10 that it was revaluing the (Swiss) franc by 7.07 per cent, the first change in its value since 1936. The measure followed a speculative run against the franc that totaled $600,000,000 on May 5 alone, a big factor in the rise of foreign reserves to $4,780,000,000.

The Finance Ministry imposed tighter controls effective Feb. 1 on about eighty foreign mutual-fund companies operating in Switzerland. The impetus for the move was the confidence-destroying crisis in 1970 that wracked the biggest of all so-called "offshore" funds, Investors Overseas Services Ltd. (IOS). The Swiss Banking Commission later banned IOS from using Switzerland as a base for selling mutual funds. U.S. expatriate Bernard Cornfeld, who pioneered the mutual-fund boom in Europe, ended his ties with IOS by selling his remaining holdings and resigning his remaining functions.

The Government also asked Parliament on Sept. 8 for full powers to defend the franc and discourage speculation by charging foreign depositors a "negative" interest. Switzerland has virtually no official exchange controls.

The 1972 budget was described as neutral because the difference between revenue and expenditure forecasts was a surplus of $44,610,-000, the second largest since 1964. Revenues were estimated at $2,488,000,000, up one sixth from 1971. One gloomy economic note: The cost of living increased by 7 per cent, a record for peacetime, over the 12 months ending June 30.

SWITZERLAND

Area: 15,941 sq. mi.
Population: 6,500,000
Capital: Bern
Government: Nello Celio, president—1972
Gross National Product: $20,500,000,000
Foreign trade: exports, $5,128,000,000; imports, $6,480,000,000
Armed forces: 600,000

On Apr. 23 the Swiss Supreme Court sentenced jet-engine expert Alfred Frauenknecht, 44, to 54 months' imprisonment on charges of spying for Israel. Frauenknecht admitted that he had sold Israeli agents some 200,000 secret documents enabling Israel to manufacture engines for Mirage-3 jets. He said he was able to obtain the documents through his job as officer of a Swiss company making the French-designed engines under license for the Swiss Air Force. The court confiscated $200,000 that Frauenknecht said he had been paid.

CHARLES W. BELL
News Editor, Rome Bureau
United Press International

TAIWAN

Nationalist China, which had claimed to be the government of mainland China for more than twenty years, lost its seat in the United Nations General Assembly, Security Council and other agencies in 1971. The immediate impact on Taiwan of the seating of Communist China in place of Chiang Kai-shek's Government was surprisingly slight. Part of the reason was the expanding economy and international trade of Taiwan, even with countries giving diplomatic recognition to Peking.

Foreign Relations. The claim to be the legitimate government of the mainland, accompanied by the threat to liberate mainland Chinese from communist rule, has dominated the foreign policy of Chiang Kai-shek's regime since it fled to Taiwan in 1949. Displaying remarkable flexibility and recuperative power in the wake of the historic UN ouster, the Taipei Government indicated that it would emphasize its foreign trade (three quarters that of far bigger Communist China) and its greater prosperity and higher living standards than the mainland's.

Taiwan's main foreign-policy concern following its UN setback was the future of the U.S. defense commitment to it. It was widely believed in Taipei that Washington's efforts to improve relations with Communist China (and U.S. presidential adviser Henry A. Kissinger's presence in Peking even as American UN diplomats were trying to line up votes for Taiwan in New York) led directly to Taiwan's ouster. Chiang Kai-shek himself, however, held off support for the Americans' "two Chinas" UN solution until the fall opening of the General Assembly. U.S. "pressure politics" on other UN delegations was largely an attempt to make up for lost time.

The American defense commitment to Taiwan, embodied in a 1954 treaty, was reaffirmed by Secretary of State William P. Rogers on

Without waiting for the vote by which Nationalist China was expelled from the UN, the Nationalist delegates walk out of the General Assembly Hall.

United Nations

Oct. 26. Nearly nine thousand U.S. servicemen were stationed on Taiwan in late 1971, half in support of the declining Vietnam war effort and the rest involved in various intelligence activities. Taipei's fear was that President Nixon's 1972 trip to Peking would result in a major reduction of the U.S. defense commitment to Taiwan, in fact if probably not in form.

Economy. Taiwan's economic development, rivaling that of Japan in annual growth rate in recent years, continued in 1971. Foreign investment declined 39 per cent in the first six months of 1971 (possibly reflecting an overexpansion of industry in 1970, when a record $139,000,-000 was invested in the country from abroad). The decline preceded the October anti-Taiwan UN vote, however, after which the Government announced a new record of $152,000,000 in foreign investment for the year.

Whether such foreign investment, a major factor in Taiwan's economic growth, would continue was problematical, particularly in the light of the possibility of political, if not military, efforts to extend Chinese Communist rule to the island.

Trade grew during the year, commerce with the United States reaching an estimated $200,-000,000 in 1971 (three times what it had been in 1969). The United States was the biggest customer for Taiwan's expanding textile industry, however, and fear mounted that American quotas on textiles might seriously undercut this key sector of the country's increasingly industrialized economy. There was less fear of the commercial consequences of the UN vote, in the light of such evidence as the two-thirds increase in trade with Canada following the latter's recognition of Peking.

Politics. Chiang Kai-shek's 84th birthday fell within a week following the UN ouster. Although the UN vote in no way immediately affected the short-term stability of Chiang's regime, the long-range implications were nonetheless there. The October vote seating Peking was followed by renewed reports, probably false, of discussions between Chiang's 62-year-old son and heir apparent, Chiang Ching-kuo, and Communist Chinese representatives.

Chiang's health was apparently no worse than in the preceding year, although it was not good. The 2,000,000 Chinese he had led from the mainland still controlled the apparatus of national government and defense, however, with the 14,000,000 native Taiwanese subjects.

Indigenous Taiwanese political opposition activity, all but impossible at home, seemed to show new life abroad, primarily in Japan and the United States, in the wake of the UN vote. But 500,000 men under arms, seemingly loyal to the Government, made the likelihood very remote of any locally based effort to give control of Taiwan to native elements.

RICHARD BUTWELL
Chairman, Department of Political Science
SUNY at Brockport

TAIWAN

Area: 13,885 sq. mi.
Population: 14,300,000
Capital: Taipei
Government: Chiang Kai-shek, president—1950; C. K. Yen, premier—1963
Gross National Product: $5,500,000,000
Foreign trade (1969): exports, $1,428,000,000; imports, $1,524,000,000
Armed forces: 540,000

TAXATION, U.S.

A standard complaint of economists is that the American governmental system works too slowly for changes in tax laws to be made in time for them to have the economic effects for which they should be designed. Complainers cite the long delay in 1967 and 1968 before enactment of the 10 per cent surcharge on income taxes, a delay that is widely thought to have contributed substantially to the inflation that followed. In 1971, however, Congress acted with unaccustomed speed in handing President Nixon substantially the same major tax legislation he had requested less than four months before. The difference could be traced to the nature of the request; in 1971, the economic prescription called not for raising taxes but for lowering them—and that is a prescription that Congress is ever eager to fill.

The tax legislation was part of the New Economic Policy announced by the President on Aug. 15, a package that included wage and price controls at home and a 10 per cent surtax on imports. The ninety-day freeze melted into a more fluid Phase 2, and the surtax disappeared entirely in the wake of the December currency realignment, leaving the tax part of the program as possibly its most permanent ingredient. The intent was clear: to stimulate the disappointing recovery from the 1969–70 recession and to make significant inroads in an unemployment rate that hovered around 6 per cent as 1971 ended.

The result was a comprehensive overhaul of United States tax law, coming unexpectedly soon after the historic revisions of the 1969 Tax Reform and Relief Act. What is more, the new bill went even further in reducing government revenues. When combined with changes in the depreciation rules under which business can write off its new capital equipment, rules that were liberalized by the Treasury and then slightly tightened by Congress, the year produced cumulative revenue losses of $114,000,000,000 over a ten-year period— more than twice as much red ink as is expected to come out of the 1969 act.

The compromise bill passed by the Democratic Congress on Dec. 9, and promptly signed by the President the following day, would reduce business and individual taxes $26,000,-000,000 by 1973, a sum that closely approximates Nixon's August request. The President praised the bill and warmly identified himself with it, though there was a noteworthy difference in emphasis from the original administration proposal, which would have concentrated more of the relief on industry and less on individual taxpayers. Either way, the bill was ex-

pected to have two results: a contribution to business improvement foreseen for 1972, and an addition to the certain Federal budget deficit.

For most taxpayers, the visible benefits began with an increase in the personal exemption from $650 to $750. Against the President's wishes, Congress made the first $25 of this increase retroactive to 1971. Low-income persons, who received a substantial portion of the benefits in the 1969 act, also were favored beneficiaries of Congress. The minimum standard deduction was raised from $1,000 to $1,300 in 1972. When combined with the exemption increase this meant that a couple with two children could have a tax-exempt income of $4,300. The objective was to remove from the tax rolls all persons at or below the expected 1972 official poverty levels.

Middle-income taxpayers were helped by raising, from 14 to 15 per cent, the portion of their adjusted gross income they can claim as an unitemized standard deduction. The ceiling for this deduction was put at $2,000. Another benefit for middle-class Americans, not to mention Women's Lib, was the allowance of up to $4,800 a year for child-care and household-service deductions by working couples and single persons with incomes of $18,000 a year or less.

Major corporate benefits began with repeal of the 7 per cent excise tax on automobiles. This had been requested by the President, but Congress threw in repeal of the 10 per cent excise on trucks weighing 10,000 pounds or less. The impact was viewed by some observers as creating "the Automobile Industry Relief Act of 1971." It did stimulate late-1971 sales in this import-harried industry. Business in general benefited from the reinstatement of the 7 per cent investment credit; it allows companies to subtract from their taxes 7 per cent of what they have spent on new machinery and equipment. Nixon would have preferred to have the credit set at a superstimulating 10 per cent for the first 12 months, but Congress feared that this would increase the boom-then-bust peril.

The combination of orthodox tax relief for the domestic economy and a dollar devaluation to bolster trade dimmed support for such earlier proposed remedies as a value-added tax, a sort of step-by-step sales tax that has been used by Europeans to make their export prices more competitive. At a time when economic theory called for lower taxes and deficit spending, the conventional political process proved more than adequate to deliver the goods.

LOUIS RUKEYSER
Economic Editor and News Commentator
American Broadcasting Company

"That's nice, someone thinks I'm cute! How about 'very'?"

"Who's the dummy writing this show?"

"The proper way to say it is . . ."

"Boy, to get a compliment around here, you really have to work for it!"

"Judge" Bill Cosby ponders a problem in punctuation on "The Electric Company," to teach reading skills, by the creators of "Sesame Street"; funny cartoons made important points even as they kept children amused.

TELEVISION

Commercial network television was on the defensive in the United States in 1971. The attack on its established ways began Jan. 2 when the predicted ban on cigarette advertising finally went into effect, costing the industry more than $200,000,000 a year. The onslaught was heightened in the fall when a government ruling reduced the amount of prime time granted each network in the new season by a half hour nightly, with only a few weekly exceptions. This ruling also went ahead on schedule and cost the major broadcast organizations another small fortune.

Then along came a book, *Television: The Business Behind the Box,* by a prestigious industry writer, Les Brown, video editor of *Variety,* the show-biz bible. Its assessments and revelations concerning broadcast personalities and policies earned the book wide national publicity and considerable praise, and caused more displeasure at the networks though outwardly they tried to pooh-pooh Brown's study.

As a topper, and probably most significantly, the networks were steadily subjected to withering criticism from influential sources reaching high into the Government, where Vice-President Agnew had for some time been firing blasts against certain aspects of news coverage and the people who guide it. Video has long been used to criticism about almost anything, from almost anyone, and has learned to react coolly. In addition, the continuing criticism in 1971 from groups demanding reforms in children's programing was accepted, and even acted on in the form of new, upgraded shows for youngsters. But the strain between the networks and government critics and their allies was unrelieved.

At times it was a war of nerves. In March, for instance, a White House source let it be known that President Nixon was unhappy with network coverage of the Vietnam issue. The sources said the Government believed its actions were clearly explained but that the networks were not listening. Top network executives, meanwhile, made speeches all over the place emphasizing the importance of freedom of expression, and it was no secret whom they regarded as their antagonists.

For example, in the furor over the publication of the controversial Pentagon Papers, ABC President Elton Rule stated: "Once again an alarm has sounded for the public's right to know. This time it is not television that is under attack but the print medium. Government attempts to suppress publication of the Vietnam papers by *The New York Times* and *The Washington Post* are further examples of the highest official pressure against the guarantees of the First Amendment."

That was in June. In a speech in October, Rule told the Radio-Television News Directors Association: "Because broadcasting stations are licensed, there are those who feel that broadcast journalists should function with greater restraints than those who work in other media. I see no justification for this thinking. The guarantee of the First Amendment must apply equally to all journalists in this nation."

As for the Nixon administration, Agnew and other influential critics of television news, there was no doubt they were making an effective case for themselves with the public and had many supporters. Even some top broadcast newsmen differed on the subject of intimidation. Walter Cronkite, for instance, in speaking to the Senate constitutional rights subcommittee inquiring into the state of freedom of the press, said: "Broadcast news today is not free. . . . Because it is operated by an industry that is beholden to the Government for its right to exist, its freedom has been curtailed by fiat, by assumption and by intimidation and harassment." He asked Congress for an end to government control over licensing of broadcasting.

On the other hand, David Brinkley said: "As for intimidation, there is none that I know of. . . . Anyone who can't stand criticism should not go into journalism, as I think anyone who can't stand criticism should not go into politics."

When all was said and done, though, despite the brave words by the networks and their vows to resist whatever intimidation might arise, the plain and simple fact was that most commercial network documentaries and news specials in 1971 were on the exceptionally tame side. Perhaps it was a coincidence, but to many it appeared that discretion was being used overtime in a highly sensitive period. In a year that included such significant events as the Attica prison tragedy, CBS–TV, for example, was scheduling documentaries on such subjects as John Dillinger, a gangster who was killed nearly four decades ago, and the surrender that ended the Civil War.

The networks reacted defensively in other ways too. Because of the loss of cigarette advertising, the reduction of their prime-time hours and the overall tight economy, they resorted in the new fall season to a retarded kind of programing that reached into their past, involved the least risk and seemed certain to attract the most viewers in a safe, mass way. What they did, in short, was emphasize hardaction, formula tales that showed little originality, and also brought back some of the violence in programing that had been purposely avoided since the assassinations of Martin Luther King, Jr., and Robert F. Kennedy had left the public with a severe distaste for unmotivated mayhem on video.

In fairness, one could not entirely blame the networks for playing it wholly safe financially in order to protect their stock-market investors. For the Government's cutback on prime time forced the networks into a corner—that is, into bread-and-butter programing—and, predictably, failed in its noble but naive intentions. The idea of the cutback was to encourage local and independent operators, and perhaps to bring forth a cultural upswing. Instead, the substitutes for what the networks used to provide in those suddenly open hours were mainly cheap, imitative, routine shows. In turn, the networks, stripped of the income these hours used to bring, cut back on experimental efforts, on dramas and on other "soft" but worthwhile programs that might be offbeat.

To their credit, the networks and their news departments did take a few steps to assure the public that they were still aware of their larger responsibilities. Despite the knowledge that news documentaries usually draw low ratings, NBC-TV and CBS-TV both scheduled monthly, two-hour, prime-time public affairs series. NBC-TV's was called *Chronolog,* and was simply the old *First Tuesday* series with a new title. The other monthly, two-hour news program was *CBS Reports.*

The Government's prime-time cutback also caused a hassle that aroused the ire of many owners of television stations. The problem arose when it appeared that prime time would begin, as usual, at 7:30 P.M. Eastern time nightly and end at 10:30, a half hour earlier than usual. What was generally downplayed by some key executives was that this meant most national programing would end by 9:30 P.M. in much of the country's midsection. Suddenly, many network affiliate stations complained about having prime time end at such an hour in midwestern and mountain states—an hour so early that it meant a probable loss of audiences, business and income at the peak of key evening viewing time. Finally, 8 to 11 P.M. Eastern time was settled on as the general prime-time spread.

But many impartial industry experts felt the cutback rule had so many negative aspects, and so few good ones, that the Government would be wise to rescind it after seeing for a while that it was just not working.

In such a defensive year for the commercial video networks, fairness dictates that they deserve some credit as well for trying to come up with improved children's programing to replace the moronic Saturday morning cartoons that had so upset parents' groups and others. What the networks did, however, was to try, in one form or another, to copy the enormously successful noncommercial television series for children, *Sesame Street*. Furthermore, being essentially profit-oriented, the commercial net-

NBC

Hugh Downs, Barbara Walters and Joe Garagiola, on the "Today" show, visited Rumania in May.

George C. Scott, Colleen Dewhurst and Barry Sullivan made Arthur Miller's "The Price" outstanding.

NBC

works simply did not seem geared to handle programing for youngsters as comfortably as they could handle situation comedies. The result was that, despite good intentions, such new network efforts of ABC-TV's *Curiosity Shop* and NBC-TV's *Take a Giant Step* were boring and imitative and gained hardly any following.

On the other hand, the noncommercial Children's Television Workshop, which created *Sesame Street,* stayed right in the groove with its second major series effort, *The Electric Company.* It arrived in the fall to try to help improve the reading of youngsters in the second, third and fourth grades—roughly, ages 7 through 10. Using clever and entertaining devices to put across reading lessons, *The Electric Company,* a daily half-hour series on the noncommercial video network, employed a regular repertory company that included Bill Cosby and Rita Moreno. The show gained immediate high praise.

In his controversial book, however, Les Brown had just about as little praise for noncommercial television as he did for the frankly commercial networks. He accused the non-

Family-situation hit "All in the Family" aimed to ridicule bigotry in the person of Carroll O'Connor, who played the outrageous father.

commercial video operators of playing ball with their benefactors in commercial television. He added that public television was "more interested in prestige and in the sources of its operating monies than in the attentions of the lower classes. . . . Superior television, and not a self-congratulating cultural service, should be the goal of public television. . . . [It] must embrace light entertainment, if for no other reason than to attract the television multitudes and to give the lie to its being a snob service."

As for commercial television, Brown wrote: "NBC, CBS and ABC would rather associate with big business than with any other kind, least of all show business." Also: "It was not through oversight that the networks, and local stations, did not for years produce programs of specific interest to the black population. The ghetto Negro was not a target audience for most advertisers because, generally speaking, he was a low-income citizen with scant buying power." Also: "When a writer establishes a controversial situation in television it is usually just to be intriguing; invariably the matter is resolved in a routine law-and-order way. One way or another the Establishment prevails over the dissident or the dropout."

Curiously, in a year when the networks were defensive and therefore exceptionally conservative in most programing, the biggest new hit of the entertainment series was a controversial CBS-TV show, *All in the Family,* a situation comedy about a bigot. Some industry cynics felt one reason for its success was that many viewers may well have been agreeing with his opinions as well as laughing at them. However if video had at least loosened up in this one sensitive area, there were bitter complaints in another: That many star Negro athletes do not get the same break in making commercials that their white counterparts do.

In keeping with their programing conservatism, the networks put on roughly twenty series with law-enforcement themes in the new fall season. They were easy to do, lent themselves to hard action and violence, and capitalized on mass sentiment for law and order. But another attempt at "safe" programing—the use of big movie-star names in new series—was a costly blunder. In the early fall ratings, performers like Shirley MacLaine, Anthony Quinn, Tony Curtis, Glenn Ford, James Garner and Rod Taylor registered from mediocre to disastrous in the popularity of their own series. They did not offer much quality either. James Stewart improved later.

There were other 1971 trends aimed at capturing an audience the networks coveted for its money-spending power: the younger, urban-oriented audience. Pursuing these viewers, desirable to advertisers as consumers, the networks eliminated numerous rural comedy series like *The Beverly Hillbillies, Mayberry R.F.D.* and *Hee Haw;* updated new weekly Westerns so they had a turn-of-the-century flavor; and introduced many anthology shows with movielike appeal. Top novels were purchased and put on, or prepared, as multipart presentations. Baseball joined football in seeking a regular nighttime television following.

The year's commercial entertainment highlights included Dick Cavett's second 90-minute show with Fred Astaire; the Tony Awards telecast, which offered great moments from Broadway's musical past; George C. Scott in Arthur Miller's *The Price;* Carrie Snodgress as a self-denying social worker in a two-hour teleplay, *The Impatient Heart;* Mia Farrow as a self-destructive starlet in a 90-minute original, *Goodbye, Raggedy Ann;* Ed Sullivan's special presenting memorable segments from his 23 years of televised vaudeville; and a 90-minute musical cartoon, *The Point,* written by pop composer Harry Nilsson and narrated by Dustin Hoffman.

Late in the year, commercial video offered *Beethoven's Birthday: A Celebration in Vienna with Leonard Bernstein; The Homecoming,* with Patricia Neal in a depression-era tale of a rural mountain family; and *The Snow Goose,* with Richard Harris in Paul Gallico's story of a lonely, embittered artist whose life is changed when he cares for a wounded bird. After almost ten years, Julie Andrews and Carol Burnett joined in their second delightful special, *Julie and Carol at Lincoln Center.*

The noncommercial network also had notable entries. For example, the *Hollywood Television Theatre* presented John Dos Passos' *U.S.A.,* in which Joan Hackett was unforgettable in a recitation about the life of Isadora Duncan; and *Poet Game,* about a hard-drinking Irish writer trying to come to terms with himself on an American lecture tour. In addition, there was a six-part *NET Playhouse* series in which the 1930's were recalled through the works of major playwrights and film makers.

Furthermore, noncommercial video introduced a stimulating new series, *The Great American Dream Machine,* which looked at life in the United States through a combination of documentary and theatrical devices. And an entry called *Masterpiece Theatre* scheduled major dramas, some multipart, that included *The First Churchills* and works by Balzac, Henry James, Tolstoi, Dostoevski, and Thackeray. For early 1972, meanwhile, the same network scheduled a 26-week series of movie

NET

In the British import "The First Churchills," John Neville, as young Churchill, dallies with Moira Redmond as the Duchess of Cleveland.

classics, *Film Odyssey*—with, naturally, no interruptions for advertisements.

On the documentary side, commercial television's excessive tameness was all too clear, but worthwhile projects emerged nonetheless. CBS-TV had a three-parter, *Justice in America,* about the nation's courts; and a two-parter, *POW's—Pawns of War,* concerning U.S. fighting men held in North Vietnam. ABC-TV presented *When Johnny Comes Marching Home,* about Vietnam veterans facing unemployment back in America; and *Alcoholism: Out of the Shadows,* which dealt with the disease of problem drinkers. NBC-TV offered *They've Killed President Lincoln!* a dramatized documentary about the 1865 assassination. Another offbeat entry, CBS-TV's *Search for the Goddess of Love,* traced a woman's controversial archeological quest for the famous, long-lost statue of Aphrodite.

David Brinkley stepped down in 1971 as anchorman of NBC-TV's nightly news (John Chancellor took over), and Hugh Downs quit as host of the same network's *Today* show (Frank McGee replaced him). The *Today* show also originated from communist Rumania for a week, and the networks went all out on coverage of the Apollo moon missions and the Southern California earthquake. Here and there the home medium had its moments, but in sum it could have used more vibrations from within in 1971.

RICK DU BROW
Television Critic, United Press International

THAILAND

Intensified communist insurgency and unexpected great-power shifts gave the Thai political leadership major concern and were a key factor in a reshaping of the Government near the year's end.

Politics. Proclamation of martial law by Premier (and Marshal) Thanom Kittikachorn on Nov. 17 ended Thailand's limited experiment with partly elected political institutions. The Constitution, promulgated in 1968 after ten years' preparation, was abrogated and Parliament and Cabinet dissolved. The lower house of the legislature (the other chamber of which was appointed) had been elected only in 1969, after more than a decade in which there had been no national voting.

The nonviolent political act, which ousted some top political figures, was followed by the establishment of a 16-man junta (headed by Thanom) and the creation of a new Revolutionary Party (the only political party permitted). The move reflected the growing strength of Army chief Gen. Praphas Charusathien, prepared the way for Praphas to succeed Thanom as the country's leader, and mirrored the dissatisfaction of Praphas with Parliamentary criticism of the Government.

Insurgency. Communist insurrectionary activity, which had begun in the middle 1960's and later seemed to be checked, was bolstered by the establishment of secure base areas in the north and northeast. The number of insurgents totaled less than 5,000, but their impact was increas-

THAILAND
Area: 198,456 sq. mi.
Population: 37,400,000
Capital: Bangkok
Government: Bhumibol Adulyadej, king—1946; Thanom Kittikachorn, chairman, National Executive Council—1971
Gross National Product: $6,790,000,000
Foreign trade: exports, $698,000,000; imports, $1,252,000,000
Armed forces: 175,000

ingly felt. Rocket and mine ambushes were staged with skill by Chinese-supported tribal rebels in the north, while the murder of officials and destruction of police stations increased in the northeast.

The establishment of martial law was partly justified by the Government in terms of worsening security conditions.

Foreign Relations. Surprised by American efforts to reach an understanding with Communist China and fearing abandonment by Washington in the wake of general U.S. military disengagement from Vietnam and other parts of Asia, Thailand also probed the possibility of reconciliation with the Chinese. There was no response from Peking, but Foreign Minister Thanat Khoman was nonetheless ousted in the November power shift (largely because Praphas opposed a *rapprochement* with China).

More than 5,000 Thai fought on the Government's side in Laos, and full support was given the American and South Vietnamese presence in Cambodia. Thai bases used for U.S. bombing missions over Laos and Vietnam were cut back from 6 to 5, but 32,000 Thai military personnel (down from a high of 48,000) remained in Indochina.

Economy. Thailand's economic growth, which had averaged 8 per cent a year in the 1960's, slowed down as Vietnam war-related U.S. military spending in the country declined, and export markets for traditional Thai products such as rice weakened. Foreign-exchange reserves continued to decline (though the mid-year figure, $941,000,000, was still strong). The budget for the fiscal year beginning Oct. 1 included an 8.8 per cent cut in economic-development spending and showed a 7.5 per cent increase in expenditure for internal security. The United States announced that it would seek to help the Thai by increasing its economic aid from $24,000,000 (1970–71) to $40,000,-000 (1971–72).

RICHARD BUTWELL
Chairman, Department of Political Science
State University of
New York College at Brockport

Field Marshal Thanom explains that Parliament's failure to approve budget, and pressure to recognize Communist China led to Nov. 17 coup.

Wide World

"The Basic Training of Pavlo Hummel" introduced a brilliant new U.S. playwright, David W. Rabe.

THEATER

It is not true that the history of the American theater in 1971 was, in effect, the history of one man, Joseph Papp. But there were moments when it seemed to be. In the course of the year, Papp solved most of his financial problems by selling his building, the Public Theater (originally the Astor Library), which now houses five small theaters, to the City of New York for more than $2,000,000 and arranged to have it leased back to himself for a modest annual fee. He discovered the most interesting new American playwright of the last several years, David Rabe, who showed himself, in his two abrasive plays, *The Basic Training of Pavlo Hummel* and *Sticks and Bones* (both of them at the Public), to be the only dramatist capable of writing effectively on the most serious American issue, the war in Vietnam. Papp presented at his annual summer Shakespeare Festival in Central Park a delightful musical adaptation of *The Two Gentlemen of Verona* (eliminating the first word of Shakespeare's title) and, later in the year, turned it into a Broadway hit. He sponsored two new theater magazines, *Performance* and *Scripts,* put out by the former editors of *The Drama Review.* He announced that he would, in 1972, send his productions to Washington and found something like a national theater. His designs on Washington seemed quixotic, but, obviously, Papp is not a man to be underestimated.

Papp's discovery of Rabe confirmed the truism that the best new American writing talent will not make its debut on Broadway. In 1970, the Pulitzer Prize and the New York Drama Critics Circle Award went, each for the first time, to off-Broadway plays. The same thing happened again in 1971, the Pulitzer Prize going to Paul Zindel's *The Effect of Gamma Rays on Man-in-the-Moon Marigolds* (a play of 1970 that won the Drama Critics Award the year before), and the Drama Critics Award for the best American play to John Guare's *The House of Blue Leaves.* (The Drama Critics Circle voted David Storey's *Home,* an English play presented on Broadway in 1970, the best play in all categories.) And if an American playwright of great promise appeared who was even newer than Rabe, he was Michael Weller, whose plays have not yet been seen in Manhattan. Weller has been living in London, and his plays have been staged there. Near the end of 1971, his one-act comedy *And Now There's Just the Three of Us* was done by the adventurous Chelsea Theater Center of Brooklyn, and his longer play *Moonchildren* (originally entitled *Cancer*) was presented at the Arena Stage in Washington. These two productions were scheduled for off-Broadway and Broadway respectively in 1972.

Neil Simon wrote one more hit comedy for Broadway, *The Prisoner of Second Avenue* (directed by Mike Nichols), about a man and

Lee Grant and Peter Falk, as husband and wife, suffer city-living horrors in Neil Simon's painfully funny "The Prisoner of Second Avenue."

his wife in Manhattan who suffer every conceivable disaster including the theft of their possessions and the loss of their jobs but doggedly persist in remaining the captives of urban blight. Simon's touch was as sure as ever now that he had wisely decided to halt his halfhearted efforts at writing problem plays.

But surely the future lies with such young writers as Rabe, Weller, Guare and Terrence McNally. Rabe's *The Basic Training of Pavlo Hummel* provides an unsparing analysis of an American recruit hardened to viciousness in Vietnam. In Rabe's *Sticks and Bones*, a more conscientious veteran comes home and faces a vacuous, "typically American" family right out of a television-situation comedy.

While Rabe has an inclination toward black humor, Weller's skill is more generally comedic. His *And Now There's Just the Three of Us* hilariously exposes a braggart who pretends to great sexual virtuosity. More seriously, *Moonchildren* shows young people who are so exasperated by their elders' hypocrisy that they can communicate only in put-ons and practical

jokes. In addition to writing *The House of Blue Leaves*, a black comedy compacted of such elements as a failed songwriter whose soldier son wants to assassinate the Pope, Guare contributed the lyrics of *Two Gentlemen of Verona* and collaborated on its book.

McNally, who has written some brilliant one-act plays, contributed an engaging but uneven off-Broadway comedy, *Where Has Tommy Flowers Gone?* (first seen at the Yale Repertory Theater earlier in the year), in which a light-footed adventurer unwillingly acquires responsibilities.

Musical comedies dominated the Broadway season. The principal commercial hits were *No, No, Nanette*, a 1925 musical revived and slightly revised with Ruby Keeler and Patsy Kelly in the cast to catch nostalgic movie fans; and *Jesus Christ Superstar*, a rock opera (score by Andrew Lloyd Webber, lyrics by Tim Rice) of English origin that began life as a popular record and became a super-production directed by Tom O'Horgan. *No, No, Nanette* led a nostalgic tendency reflected by a revival of the 1940's musical *On the Town* and by a new musical about former Ziegfeld Follies girls. *Follies* displayed its nostalgic bias by prominently casting such former film actresses as Alexis Smith and Yvonne De Carlo. While James Goldman's book told a conventional story, Stephen Sondheim's songs and the direction of Michael Bennett and Harold Prince projected nostalgia effectively and thus earned *Follies* its "best musical" award from the Drama Critics Circle. *Jesus Christ Superstar* followed by a few months an off-Broadway musical about the life of Christ, *Godspell* (music and lyrics by Stephen Schwartz). By its good will, good humor, and simplicity, it made *Superstar*, when it arrived, seem all the more garish and overdone.

The only other Broadway musical clearly destined for commercial success was the ebullient *Two Gentlemen of Verona* (directed by Mel Shapiro, book by Guare and Shapiro, lyrics by Guare, and music by Galt MacDermot, the composer of *Hair*). It benefited greatly from Jonelle Allen's uninhibited performance as Silvia. Among those less warmly received were *Lovely Ladies, Kind Gentlemen*, an adaptation of *The Teahouse of the August Moon; 70, Girls, 70*, which featured elderly shoplifters, some of them septuagenarians—hence the title; *Ain't Supposed to Die a Natural Death*, Melvin Van Peebles' astringent portrait of life in Harlem; and *Metamorphoses* (directed by Paul Sills and adapted from Ovid by Arnold Weinstein), which accompanied *Story Theater* in 1970.

The only general pattern revealed by the straight, nonmusical plays on Broadway was the increasing economic difficulty of survival. Only *The Prisoner of Second Avenue* and *Lenny* could pass for smash hits. *Lenny*, by Julian Barry, directed by Tom O'Horgan, who also composed a musical score for it, was a disturbing evocation of the life of the late Lenny Bruce. His irritant words and ideas offended audiences in the 1950's but are commonplace enough today. Cliff Gorman played the title role with unflagging wit and energy.

Also seen on Broadway were Paul Zindel's *And Miss Reardon Drinks a Little,* a sketch of three school-teacher sisters, highlighted by Estelle Parsons' portrait of one of them; Edward Albee's *All Over,* directed by John Gielgud, an extended, wandering conversation among the survivors of a wealthy man who is dying offstage; Abe Burrows' *Four on a Garden,* originally described as based on a French play by Pierre Barillet and Jean Pierre Gredy, four one-acters that gave Carol Channing and Sid Caesar a few—too few—opportunities for their characteristic clowning; and George Furth's *Twigs,* consisting of four sketches that were of no interest except as exercises for an accomplished actress, Sada Thompson. Molière's *The School for Wives,* in an admirable new verse translation by Richard Wilbur, was stylishly performed, especially by Brian Bedford in the leading role.

British importations on Broadway included Peter Brook's vigorous, iconoclastic Royal

Rock, lyricism and West Indies patter contributed to a joyous "Two Gentlemen of Verona." Jonelle Allen was Silvia and Clifton Davis, Valentine.

Ruby Keeler leads the chorus line in a radiant revival of the 1920's musical "No, No, Nanette."

Friedman-Abeles

A Passion play in the current idiom, the spectacular hit "Jesus Christ Superstar" was criticized less for irreverence than for cheapness.

Shakespeare Company production of *A Midsummer Night's Dream; Old Times,* Harold Pinter's enigmatic but rewarding study of a marriage that is shaken by a visit from the wife's girl friend of twenty years before, with the intruder particularly well played by Rosemary Harris; Christopher Hampton's *The Philanthropist,* a fine comedy that is, essentially, Molière's *The Misanthrope,* turned inside out and made to deal with a man (expertly played by Alec McCowen) who suffers for his reluctance to condemn anyone or anything; and Alan Ayckbourn's *How the Other Half Loves,* a comedy of marital infidelity, Americanized for Broadway but nevertheless unsuited to the talents of Phil Silvers, who took the lead.

The revivals at Lincoln Center tended to be high-minded but unexciting: Synge's *The Playboy of the Western World,* Ibsen's *An Enemy of the People* (in Arthur Miller's adaptation), Sophocles' *Antigone* and Schiller's *Mary Stuart.* Highlights of the livelier series at Lincoln Center's smaller Forum Theater were A. R. Gurney Jr.'s discursive play about changing life in Buffalo, *Scenes from American Life;* and Friedrich Dürrenmatt's farcical adaptation, *Play Strindberg,* of Strindberg's *The Dance of Death.* A new arrangement for middle-sized theaters, smaller than Broadway but larger than off-Broadway, made two superior Ibsen revivals possible, *A Doll's House* and *Hedda Gabler,* both starring Claire Bloom, who shone as Nora.

In addition to *Godspell* and the plays by Guare, Rabe and McNally, the high spots of the off-Broadway season were Father Daniel Berrigan's *The Trial of the Catonsville Nine* (previously seen in Los Angeles), a documentary play about antiwar agitators; O'Neill's *Long Day's Journey into Night,* understandingly directed by Arvin Brown; *The James Joyce Memorial Liquid Theater* (another importation from Los Angeles), not so much a theater as a communal effort at gently inducing the audience to join in fun and games. Dale Wasserman's *One Flew Over the Cuckoo's Nest* (based on Ken Kesey's novel of the same name), a revival of an anti-establishment play of eight years earlier, now found an enthusiastic audience among the young. *The Proposition,* a program of satire, much of it improvised, came from Boston. *Touch,* a sympathetic rock musical, showed the making of a commune.

The Tyrone Guthrie Theater of Minneapolis surmounted its economic problems by presenting successful revivals of *The Taming of the Shrew* and Rostand's *Cyrano de Bergerac* (in a new translation by Anthony Burgess), both staged by its new artistic director, Michael Langham. The best-liked production at the American Shakespeare Festival Theater of Stratford, Conn., was not Shakespeare but O'Neill's *Mourning Becomes Electra,* with Sada Thompson. Similarly, when a highly regarded production from the Stratford Festival of Ontario was scheduled for Broadway (early in 1972), it was not Shakespeare but a turn-of-the-century French farce, Georges Feydeau's *Le Dindon*, translated as *There's One in Every Marriage*.

Noteworthy among London's plays in 1971, in addition to *Old Times*, were three dramatizations of conflict between father and son: Peter Nichols' *Forget-me-not Lane*, surely the best and most graceful of the three; John Mortimer's *A Voyage Round My Father*, in which Alec Guinness appeared; and David Mercer's *After Haggerty*. Other plays of interest included Simon Gray's *Butley* (which Harold Pinter directed), about a quarrelsome schoolmaster; John Osborne's *West of Suez*, in which an aged English writer, played by Ralph Richardson, discourses endlessly while visiting an emerging tropical nation; Jack Good's *Catch My Soul* (a late arrival of 1970), a rock version of *Othello;* Adrian Mitchell's *Tyger* (at the National Theater), a musical "celebration of William Blake"; and David Storey's *The Changing Room*, about football players. Paul Scofield lent his personal distinction to the two National Theater productions in which he appeared, Carl Zuckmayer's *The Captain of Köpenick* and Pirandello's *The Rules of the Game*. Michael Redgrave was seen in London in a frail vehicle, William Trevor's *The Old Boys*, and John Gielgud at the Chichester Festival in Shaw's *Caesar and Cleopatra*.

Peter Brook took a company of actors from his International Center for Theater Research in Paris to the Shiraz Festival in Iran, where they performed *Orghast,* a play by the English poet Ted Hughes in Greek, Latin, Avestan and an artificial language called "Orghast."

Leading European productions included: in France, Ariane Mnouchkine's *1789*, a documentary drama of that year that put the audience in the middle of the action, and two

Seymour Krawitz & Co.

Pinter's dazzling new play "Old Times" starred Rosemary Harris, Robert Shaw and Mary Ure.

pantomime plays by an American, Robert Wilson's *Prologue* and *Deafman's Glance*, which had been seen only briefly in New York but created a sensation in Paris; in Germany, Peter Weiss's historical play *Hölderlin* and the extraordinary two-part revival of Ibsen's *Peer Gynt* by the *Schaubühne* of West Berlin; in Italy, Ignazio Silone's study of a medieval pope, *The Story of a Humble Christian;* and, in the Soviet Union, Yuri Lyubimov's long-awaited production of *Hamlet* at the Taganka Theater of Moscow.

HENRY POPKIN
Drama Critic, *The Herald* (N.Y.)
Professor of English, SUNY at Buffalo

International Center of Theater Research

Spoken in Orghast, an artificial language—deliberately created to sound foreign and yet interesting— the play of the same name, drawing on Greek myths, was given at the fifth annual Festival of the Arts in Shiraz, Iran.

TRADE

Financially, the year 1971 was one of the most cataclysmic in World War II history, preparing the way for the chance of a new beginning in world trade in 1972, particularly for the United States.

The most dramatic development in 1971 trade policy was President Richard M. Nixon's Aug. 15 announcement of measures designed to deal with the problems of U.S. inflation, unemployment and chronic balance-of-payments deficits. U.S. concern grew throughout the year as the trade balance, beset by rising imports and distorted by lingering dock strikes, continued its decline to a new low, with signs pointing along the way to the first U.S. trade deficit since 1888. Final figures showed that through the year, imports exceeded exports in the United States by $2,000,000,000. In the same period in 1970, the United States showed a surplus of $2,700,000,000.

Briefly, the aspects of the President's economic program that affected American trading partners included the following: (1) suspension of the international convertibility of the U.S. dollar into gold; (2) a temporary 10 per cent surcharge on U.S. imports; (3) proposals for a job-development investment tax credit for business, excluding foreign purchases; and (4) a proposal to provide tax deferral for earnings from export sales through the creation of Domestic International Sales Corporations (known as DISC).

The immediate and ultimate results of the surprise U.S. move were far-reaching and, in fact, led to basic changes in the very foundation of world monetary order. U.S. trading partners were quick to protest the new economic policy, particularly the import surcharge and the so-called "Buy American" feature of the program which limited the investment credit to U.S. property.

Increasingly, the Common Market countries and Japan—the other major economic powers —argued that the only final solution to the monetary crisis was for the United States to devalue the dollar against gold. At last, after a series of high-level meetings of financial officials of the top industrial countries of the world—the so-called Group of Ten—agreement was reached late in December on a new system of fixed exchange rates. The United States agreed to devalue the dollar by 8.57 per cent by raising the price of gold from $35 an ounce to $38 an ounce. The rise in the price of gold hinged on trade concessions to be offered by other countries and it also had to have Congressional approval, expected in early 1972. The subsequent realignment of exchange rates

resulted in upward revaluations of many foreign currencies in varying amounts, including the German mark, up more than 13 per cent, and the Japanese yen, up almost 17 per cent. It was also agreed that the new rates would be maintained within a new range of 2.5 per cent either side of parity, or a total of 5 per cent.

The Group of Ten agreement ushered in a new era in international monetary operations, the mainstay of world trade. The old system was essentially negotiated between Great Britain and the United States and accepted by their other trading partners at Bretton Woods, N.H., in 1944. The Bretton Woods system worked on the basis of fixed exchange rates, with each country's currency pegged in price to the U.S. dollar.

The new exchange rates were a partial answer to the U.S. problem of a diminishing balance of payments—long a complaint of other countries. Now goods sold abroad would cost more in terms of U.S. dollars, and thus an improvement in the U.S. trade balance was expected. As part of the monetary package agreement, the United States pledged to remove at once the 10 per cent import surcharge and "Buy American" provisions of the investment-tax credit, measures that were opposed by U.S. trading partners as overly protectionist.

U.S. Trade Legislation. The protectionist effort in 1970 to set U.S. quotas on shoes and textiles, and potentially on other types of imports, was not matched by a comparable single drive in 1971. However, there was no lack of trade legislation for Congress to consider. More than 350 trade and related bills were introduced in the 92d Congress. Of these, over a hundred were import-quota bills for specific product groups, and the rest were general orderly marketing bills, applicable when imports surpass stated levels of domestic consumption. Congress also voted to extend the authority of the U.S. Export-Import Bank and to grant it more leeway in its operations to assist U.S. sales abroad.

As 1971 ended, the Nixon administration was working out a new economic and trade program that it planned to send to Congress in 1972. The proposals included a stronger import adjustment assistance program, export expansion, encouragement of technological research, and authority to negotiate tariff and nontariff barrier reductions.

Textile Import Agreement. The impasse over textile imports into the United States from the major Asian suppliers was alleviated in October when agreement was reached with the Japanese Government on limiting shipments. Similar agreements were negotiated with Hong Kong,

Taiwan, South Korea and other Far Eastern textile sources. The agreements apply to woolen and synthetic textiles and will allow an annual increase in the noncotton textile categories of from 5 to 7.5 per cent. This import growth rate, however, apparently is somewhat larger than the growth in the U.S. textile market. Commerce Department experts estimated the market growth in man-made fibers as averaging no more than 3 per cent in recent years.

Common Market. In November, the British Parliament approved Britain's entry into the European Economic Community (EEC) by a target date of 1973. The decision ended a decade of doubt and two French vetoes and paved the way for a third world power to rival the United States and the Soviet Union on economic grounds at first, and perhaps eventually as a political union (*see also* European Economic Community).

A year-end EEC report warned that member countries faced dim economic prospects in 1972 because of uncertainty in international monetary and economic affairs. The report noted that the volume of exports to nonmember countries increased very little during the second quarter of 1971, despite a temporary improvement in the economic situation in the United States, the United Kingdom and Canada.

East-West Trade. Estimates of 300,000,000 potential customers in Eastern Europe and another 700,000,000 in Communist Asia sparked growing interest in expanding East-West trade. Enthusiasm was heightened by rising standards of living in Eastern Europe, including the U.S.S.R., and the slight trend toward liberalization in some of the communist economies.

Aware of the Eastern market, as well as the political potential, President Nixon in April announced a major program easing travel and trade between the United States and the People's Republic of China. The President issued a lengthy list of nonstrategic items, ranging from wheat and automobiles to some industrial equipment, which were now authorized for sale to mainland China. The Chinese export list appeared to parallel closely a similar list of exports to the Soviet Union which has been in existence for some time. If experience with the U.S.S.R. is a valid criterion, the new trade with mainland China will not have significant commercial value for U.S. industry. In 1970, U.S. exports to Russia totaled $118,-500,000, a small portion of the American total of $40,000,000,000 in trade with other countries. U.S. officials said that they expected trade with China would make up a similarly small portion of total exports, at least in the next few years.

There were also hints that the United States may soon drop all significant restrictions on exports to the Soviet Union as a result of Secretary of Commerce Maurice H. Stans' November visit to that country. Meeting with top Soviet officials, Stans reported that the Soviets expressed interest in U.S. machine tools, consumer goods, agricultural products and computer software. The United States was said to be looking into possible purchases of natural gas, oil, copper, pulp, paper and minerals. The Russians consider the main obstacles to more expansive U.S.-Soviet trade to be the absence of most-favored-nation treatment for the Soviet Union and a lack of U.S. credits to finance Soviet imports from the United States. Stans said that he expected trade with Russia to run in the billions of dollars if U.S.-Soviet relations continue to improve.

Developing Countries. Although the plan fell short of the expectations of the developing countries, the establishment in 1971 of a general system of trade preferences in their favor nevertheless represented a major change of attitude on the part of the industrialized world. The plan calls for the industrialized nations to accord tariff reductions (amounting to duty-free entry in some cases) to imports of specified manufactured and semimanufactured goods from developing countries. Although safeguard mechanisms exist, so that those countries extending the preferences may amend or even suspend their offers, UNCTAD (United Nations Conference on Trade and Development) will keep a close watch on such activities.

Review and Outlook. All the major flows of world trade expanded in 1970, but expected totals for 1971 were less promising. The annual report of the General Agreement on Tariffs and Trade (GATT) noted that a sharp acceleration in the combined gross national product of industrial countries during the first half of 1971 was not fully matched in trade development. In the early months of the year, the value of imports and exports of industrial countries was growing at an annual rate of 12 to 13 per cent, indicating a rate of increase in volume below the 16.5 per cent level of 1970. The currency realignment and the questions of trade concessions to be negotiated by the United States and foreign trading partners create even greater uncertainties regarding world trade in 1972. However, the fact that accord was reached demonstrates that the major nations are determined to take the path of cooperation rather than economic nationalism.

DEANNE E. NEUMAN
Managing Editor, *International Trade Reporter*
The Bureau of National Affairs, Inc.

A new mecca for tourists, especially those with children, is Walt Disney World at Orlando, Fla., which features a delectable fairy-tale castle.

TRAVEL

Agony, ecstasy and confusion were common emotions in the world of travel in 1971. Whole-sale fare cuts by international airlines sent more than 500,000 young Americans fanning out around the world. The sight of so many young people having so much fun for so little money sparked a near mutiny among airline passengers over thirty years old. The threat of a general price war caused panic in the board-rooms of hard-pressed U.S. airlines. Returning travelers frightened their friends with tales of countries where U.S. dollars did not seem welcome anymore. And, caught in the middle, U.S. travel agents teetered on the edge of a collective nervous breakdown.

While most people were watching the sky the passenger train staged a modest comeback, and Red China gingerly put out a thin welcome mat for Americans.

As Geoffrey Chaucer long ago noted, spring is the season when "men do go on pilgrimage." The spring of 1971 echoed to considerable speculation on whether the modern pilgrims called tourists would be so affected by the economic recession that they would resist their vernal wanderlust and stay home in their thousands.

Airlines, faced with the task of filling their cavernous 747's with fare–paying bodies and hard hit by the decline in business travel and the mounting competition from nonscheduled charter airlines, began wooing the young traveler.

Sabena, the Belgian airline, kicked off the war for the youthful passenger by finding a way around the International Air Transport Asso-ciation agreement setting student fares. IATA, the self-regulatory organization to which most major airlines belong, allows members to deviate from the agreement when ordered by their governments. Sabena—government-owned—received an order to cut fares on New York–Brussels flights to $220, competitive with charters.

Other lines followed suit and began cutting youth fares as well. Alitalia, which offered the best buy—$199 round trip between Rome–Milan and the U.S. East Coast—was threatened with legal action by the U.S. Civil Aeronautics Board. But Alitalia and its fare prevailed. Icelandic, the "Hippy Hoppy" airline favored by young travelers for its no-frills, bargain-basement flights to Europe, came up with the lowest youth fare; $175 round trip, off-season, between New York and Luxembourg.

It worked. Students flocked to Europe (Copenhagen was the "in" city in 1971) to roam, ramble, love and learn. Despite all the dire predictions, more Americans were going to Europe than ever before. At the height of the tourist season, in August, the U.S. Passport Office reported that the volume of passport applications was up 23 per cent over 1970.

Spring also saw the first of several currency scares, with the value of the dollar fluctuating downward in the world money market. U.S. tourists, used to spending dollars as easily overseas as at home, were startled to find the "almighty dollar" refused by some shops and banks because the exchange rate was uncertain. (The dollar was finally devalued in December 1971, which would make foreign travel more

A new cruise ship, the beautiful "Sea Venture," glides past Manhattan skyscrapers. On the New York-Bermuda run, she caters to the still strong lure of cruises.

Flagship Cruises Inc.

expensive for United States tourists in 1972.)

The American Express Company followed a policy of cashing traveler's checks in dollars at the rate at which they were purchased, but some travelers who had to cash currency suffered a loss. Wary travelers began leaning on their credit cards or buying traveler's checks in other currencies, such as Swiss francs.

The youthful exodus made airlines happy, but not the middle–aged stay–at–homes who could not raise the fare to go frolic in Europe. (A Gallup poll indicated that while 54 per cent of those in the 21–to–34 age group have flown, only 46 per cent of those in the 35–49 group and 40 per cent of those over 50 have been in an airplane.)

A champion of the overcharged and middle–aged emerged in Elizabeth Ann Gallagher of Phoenix, Ariz. Miss Gallagher, 27, sat beside her 23-year-old sister on a flight to Rome. Because she was two years over the youth-fare limit, the trip cost her $707, her sister only $199. Charging discrimination because of age, she sued Alitalia for $1,500,000.

Sensing that although youth must be served so should everybody else, airlines began making conciliatory gestures to the middle-aged and elderly with talk of senior-citizen fares and "advance–purchase" plans offering savings to the solid citizen who could pay his full fare ninety days in advance.

For a time, it seemed that airline passengers would be the happy beneficiaries of cutthroat competition to see who would offer the lowest excursion fares on the North Atlantic run. Lufthansa, the German carrier, at first refused to accept the new IATA fare schedule. However, in November, Lufthansa joined the other IATA members in agreeing to lower the 22–45–day round–trip, middle–season excursion fare between New York and London from $272 to $220. Similar cuts were decided upon for some other transatlantic round trips, all to go into effect on Apr. 1, 1972.

Confusion over exchange rates and ticket prices gave travel agents gray hairs and may have made some travelers stay home. Tourism was off in the Caribbean, Florida and Hawaii, but this was generally blamed on the economy. In contrast, Israel, despite uncertain conditions in the Middle East, registered a 40 per cent increase in tourism, passing the half–million mark for the first time.

A new tourist destination emerged in 1971: Red China. The opening of a People's Republic of China Embassy in Ottawa, Canada, the announcement that President Nixon planned a state visit to Peking, and the admission of Communist China to the United Nations focused attention on that country and made it the goal of many American travelers. The Red Chinese were not very receptive to visa applications but indicated that they would let "special interest groups" in if they came via Canada.

AMTRAK, the federally sponsored corporation trying to breathe new life into U.S. passenger–train service stole a leaf from the airlines' book and began offering new equipment, lower fares and even pretty girls as hostesses to lure travelers back to the tracks.

WILLIAM A. DAVIS
Travel Editor, *The Boston Globe*

TRUDEAU, PIERRE ELLIOTT

On Jan. 5, 1971, Canada's well-traveled Prime Minister left Ottawa on another globe-girdling tour. This time he visited Pakistan, India, Singapore, Indonesia, Ceylon and Iran. At the Commonwealth head-of-government conference in Singapore, he played a leading role in preventing a breakup of the British Commonwealth on the question of British arms sales to South Africa. By the end of the year, there was a marked change in the image—never very accurate, in any case—of Pierre Elliott Trudeau as the international playboy-statesman.

On Mar 4, with no advance publicity and no fanfare, the 51-year-old bachelor married 22-year-old Margaret Sinclair in a Roman Catholic ceremony in North Vancouver. The bride, one of five daughters of a former Liberal cabinet minister, and a political-science graduate of British Columbia's Simon Fraser University, had met Trudeau three years earlier in Tahiti. The secrecy about the marriage was so complete that newspapers were reporting Trudeau's absence on a "skiing vacation" on the day of the wedding. The couple quickly established an extremely private domestic life in Ottawa, contributing little to the social life of the capital. Their first child, a son, Justin Pierre, was born on Christmas day.

After a trip to the Soviet Union in May, accompanied by his wife, the Prime Minister devoted his time increasingly to Canada's economic problems. At a news conference in July, he conceded that efforts to control inflation had contributed to unemployment and that this had cost his Government "a substantial amount of popularity." He said that he would cancel tentative plans for visits to Africa, France and China and stay at home during the coming year to explain government policy to the public.

Trudeau was expected to call his second general election in 1972. His Liberal Government has enjoyed a comfortable majority in the House of Commons since the "Trudeaumania" election of 1968.

Canadian-American relations occupied much of the Prime Minister's attention in the last half of 1971. In Canada, he was criticized in some quarters for talking in Moscow about the "overpowering presence" of the United States in Canada and the threat posed by this to "our national identity from a cultural, economic and perhaps even military point of view." When President Nixon's import surcharge threatened to aggravate Canada's already difficult unemployment problem, Trudeau said that Americans "don't seem to realize what they are doing to Canadians."

In October, he asked during a press interview if the United States wanted to "try and buy up as much of the world as possible."

"You know this is real Marxist theory about imperialism being the last phase of capitalism," he said. "I don't think the Americans are deliberately trying to do that, but here we have a test case with Canada. . . ."

The difficult state of Canada-U.S. relations prompted a meeting in December between Prime Minister Trudeau and President Nixon, despite a previous commitment by Nixon to visit Ottawa in the spring of 1972. The Canadian leader came away from Washington reassured that "it is neither the intention nor the desire of the United States that the economy of Canada become so dependent on the United States in terms of a deficit-trading pattern that Canadians will inevitably lose independence of economic decision."

PETER DESBARATS
Ottawa Editor, *The Toronto Star*

TURKEY

In 1971 the Turkish Republic experienced its most difficult year since 1960, when the armed forces overthrew the Government of Adnan Menderes in order to prevent a betrayal of the principles of Kemal Atatürk. On Mar. 12, 1971, after student violence and urban terrorism on an unprecedented scale had brought the country to the brink of anarchy, senior military commanders issued a memorandum demanding that Premier Suleyman Demirel resign or accept a military take-over. The memorandum accused Demirel of failure to carry out needed reforms and of laxity in dealing with violence. On Apr. 26 martial law was imposed as a key condition of continued civilian leadership. Hundreds of people, including the bulk of Turkey's student and intellectual leadership, were arrested and held for questioning or trial. The mass arrests halted at least temporarily a spiral of urban violence marked by spectacular bank robberies and kidnapings, the most serious being the kidnap-murder in May of Israeli Consul General Ephraim Elrom in Istanbul as "an agent of American imperialism."

TURKEY

Area: 301,381 sq. mi.
Population: 36,500,000
Capital: Ankara
Government: Cevdet Sunay, president—1966; Nihat Erim, premier—1971
Gross National Product: $8,200,000,000
Foreign trade: exports, $589,000,000; imports, $886,000,000
Armed forces: 508,500

Following Demirel's resignation the four major political parties agreed on a compromise coalition Cabinet headed by Professor Nihat Erim, a law professor and parliamentary deputy from the Republican People's Party, which was accepted by the military. The Cabinet included five ministers from Demirel's Justice Party and several nonpolitical "technocrats." With a vote of confidence from Parliament the Erim Government began the painful process of fashioning a reform program. Meanwhile separate trials before special military courts for the arrested members of gangs belonging to *Dev Genc* (Revolutionary Youth Movement), an offshoot of the outlawed Turkish People's Liberation Army advocating violent revolution to change the Constitution and overcome American "imperialism," resulted in a number of death sentences. Unfortunately the military authorities often failed to distinguish between subversion and legitimate political differences. Some cases were dismissed for lack of legal evidence; and the arrest of persons for making "negative" propaganda or allegedly advocating Kurdish separatism or communism was sharply criticized.

Social unrest and dissatisfaction among political leaders with the pace of reforms produced another governmental crisis in October. The five Justice Party ministers resigned from the Cabinet. Personal hostility between Erim and Demirel surfaced as the latter accused the Premier of being the "chief culprit in a front of hate." In turn Demirel was charged with profiteering while in office and making negative propaganda, both being criminal offenses had they been followed up by an official investigation. Although a show of unity was restored during the state visits of Vice-President Agnew and Queen Elizabeth, it was clear that progress in such key reform areas as land distribution, education and equitable taxation remained contingent on the cooperation of the Justice Party with the Erim Government. Even such a relatively nonpolitical issue as the establishment of state-owned drugstores roused a storm of Parliamentary debate as opponents charged that the act would violate basic rules for Turkey's mixed economy and bring on socialism.

The economy remained sluggish as foreign investors were reluctant to plunge into Turkish political discord. Agricultural production increased 30 per cent due to excellent harvests, but the gains and a 7 per cent jump in industrial output were offset by inflation and population growth estimated at 2.6 per cent. A long-overdue pay raise for the 750,000 civil servants and devaluation of the lira from 9 to 15 per $1.00 were additional inflationary factors.

On Dec. 3, after more than half his Cabinet had resigned, Erim resigned for the second time. (He had quit temporarily on Oct. 27.) The 14 resigning ministers claimed that the drastic reforms demanded by the military leaders could not be carried out under the current political conditions.

However, in mid-December, Erim formed a more moderate Government "in complete understanding" with the military leaders.

WILLIAM SPENCER
Professor of History
The Florida State University

UNION OF SOVIET SOCIALIST REPUBLICS

In 1971, Leonid I. Brezhnev, general secretary of the Soviet Communist Party, accumulated enough power and prestige to stand above and apart from his colleagues in the "collective leadership" that succeeded Nikita S. Khrushchev. So unmistakable was his rise that President Georges Pompidou, without risking contradiction, could welcome Brezhnev to France as "the highest authority in the Soviet Union." As he was confirmed as his nation's undisputed leader, Brezhnev sought to identify himself with an internal policy that gave the impression of favoring the long-neglected Soviet consumer, and a foreign policy emphatically oriented toward peaceful coexistence with rival capitalist states.

The demonstration of his primacy began on the first day of the year. In a break with the practice established after Khrushchev ouster in 1964, Brezhnev appeared on television to deliver the leadership's traditional New Year's greeting. Under the previous arrangement a joint message from Brezhnev, President Nikolai V. Podgorny and Premier Aleksei N. Kosygin was read by a studio announcer. In a regime more conscious of ceremony than most, this was intended to symbolize that the men who had ousted Khrushchev and had ended his drive for a "cult of personality"—with all its attendant abuses—were standing together in balance as equals. The fact that Brezhnev alone now spoke for the former conspirators was a clear sign that he had gained a decisive step on them. It was considered especially important since the 24th Congress of the Communist Party of the Soviet Union (CPSU) was due to begin in Moscow at the end of March. Congresses are customarily times for stocktaking and confirming changes in relations among the nation's rulers and the interest groups they represent.

A year late, the Congress opened on Mar. 30. If it was not quite the "historic event" the

Leonid Brezhnev, number one man of U.S.S.R.'s "collective leadership," delivers speech to 24th Congress of the Soviet Communist Party.

official press claimed it to be, the gathering of the party's supreme body was easily the most significant item on the political calendar. The tasks before the 4,943 delegates were to select a new Central Committee (which in turn names the Politburo), approve the outlines of the new five-year plan, and reflect on the state of the Soviet Union and its ruling party. The centerpiece of the Congress was the General Secretary's report, whose delivery took a full six hours. It reviewed state and party activity since the 23d Congress in 1966, and offered a program to run until the next gathering. Predictably, Brezhnev viewed the period of his stewardship as one of "great successes," and he appeared confident about the future. His report was followed by a "debate"—a parade of delegates who said they approved of it.

All this was according to the script. What struck the foreign specialists and alert readers of *Pravda* was the amount and degree of praise the delegates reserved for Brezhnev personally. Not since the Khrushchev era had anyone heard that kind of lavish public acclaim for the person of a Soviet official. Five years before, delegates had referred simply to "Comrade Brezhnev's report" or had recalled something "as Comrade Brezhnev has said." At the 24th Congress, delegates graded the General Secretary's report as "incisive," "brilliant" or "eminently instructive." And Brezhnev himself was found to be a "tireless worker" and "profoundly knowledgeable."

For a Turkmenian party leader, Brezhnev deserved gratitude for his "fatherly concern for the Turkmen people." Kirghizian First Secretary Turdakun Usubaliyev discovered the General Secretary's "great organizational and political activities." A Moldavian official was captivated by Brezhnev's "unbending will to do as much as possible in the name of the working people." It was left to the milkmaid, K. I. Smirnova, to admit she had "tears of joy and pride in my eyes" when she heard the report of "our dear Leonid Ilyich."

When the fortnight of turgid oratory was over, several things had happened that pointed to the further consolidation of Brezhnev's position atop the hierarchy. The Central Committee was enlarged; the Politburo was packed with Brezhnev supporters; and the party's inner Secretariat was armed with a tool to purge the membership.

The Central Committee appointed by the delegates was expanded from 195 to 241 full members. Identified among the newcomers were the General Secretary's clients from the party apparatus. Brezhnev's allies from the police and the Army also gained influence. The Central Committee produced a Politburo larger by 4 members, 3 of them being Brezhnev protégés. While this was certain to strengthen Brezhnev's hand on the ruling body, specialists could not agree on whether the addition of these men guaranteed the General Secretary a majority on all issues. An affirmative answer would imply that he had acquired as much power as Khrushchev enjoyed at his peak.

Finally, the Congress instructed the Central Committee to conduct the first "exchange" of party cards in 17 years. This Brezhnev proposal, adopted despite some signs of reserve on the part of other leaders, will allow the Secretariat to weed out undesirables from among the 13,810,089 full members and 645,232 probationary members of the party. Procedure requires that each member submit his old card to a review board—in effect, he resigns. If found "worthy" he is issued a new card. Stalin used this method effectively to purge opponents, reducing party membership from 2,200,000 to 1,400,000 in the 1930's. The potential advantages for Brezhnev, as head of the party Secretariat, scarcely need emphasis.

The only surprise, at a Congress carefully staged to avoid the unexpected, was revealed at its conclusion when Brezhnev read out the 15 names of the Politburo members, listing them in order of rank. Podgorny, an early Brezhnev rival, displaced Kosygin in the No. 2 spot. Kosygin's fall to third position could signal the Premier's long-rumored retirement and his replacement by Dmitry S. Polyansky, a first deputy premier and Politburo member. Other losers of status were Alexander N. Shelepin and Gennady I. Voronov. Once considered a candidate for supreme power, Shelepin, former secret-police chief, has been stripped of one power base after another and has shown himself incapable of preventing the purge of his followers. In Brezhnev's ranking, Shelepin dropped from seventh to eleventh place, or last among the old members. Punished for his frequent offstage criticism of official farm policy, Voronov slipped from fifth to tenth in the hierarchy. His ouster as premier of the Russian Federation (R.S.F.S.R.) in July was a further blow, probably portending his removal from the Politburo altogether. Mikhail S. Solomentsev, Voronov's successor as R.S.F.S.R. premier, was nominated for that post by Brezhnev and was approved, East European Communists reported, over Kosygin's opposition.

That no one lost his Politburo seat in all this shuffling of status and role was eloquent testimony to the fact that the regime, as if traumatized by the methods of Stalin and Khrushchev, has made stability as much a fetish as it has made "monolithic unity" an official myth. Most things are done cautiously, conservatively. This was as true of the new economic plan covering the years 1971–75 as of everything else.

It was widely believed that top-level disagreement, hidden from public view, delayed the final drafting of the plan, and that this had caused the Party Congress to be convoked a year behind the statutory schedule. Ranged on one side in the dispute, it was felt, were advocates of consumer welfare and partisans of Kosygin's "indicative planning" reform. Against them were the supporters of hypercentralized control of an economy strongly biased toward heavy industry. When the draft directives of the ninth five-year plan were finally published on Feb. 14, it appeared that the reformers had been routed, although a slight shift of emphasis in the consumer's favor had been allowed. Overall, the targets were quite modest. National income under the plan was to rise between 37 and 40 per cent. This compared with the 41 per cent growth achieved in the preceding plan. Gross industrial output was to grow by between 42 and 46 per cent, a postwar low. Agricultural

Believed part of the Soviet fleet in the Mediterranean, Soviet Krivak class destroyer is equipped with complex radar installations and surface-to-surface missile launchers (forward).

Muscovites of all ages enjoy a rare thrill in the Soviet Union—an amusement-park ride. During the summer, millions of Russians visited the international carnival, Attraksion 71. Most of the 60 features were purchased, from 10 Western nations, by the Ministry of Culture.

Tass from Sovfoto

production may have been targeted a little ambitiously at 22 per cent. Total investment (36–40 per cent) was to be slightly below the 42 per cent attained under the eighth plan.

Most noteworthy were the new guidelines for producer goods (Group A) and consumer goods (Group B). Never since the adoption of the first five-year plan, in 1929, had the rate of growth for consumer goods exceeded that for producer goods. It had been an article of faith that defense-related industries must be favored. Although Group B had been growing slightly faster since 1968, much was made of the fact that this state of affairs was now policy, written into the plan. Editorials in *Pravda* and *Izvestia* expounded at length on the concern of the party and Government for the well-being of the Soviet citizen. Brezhnev said the time had passed when people must "accept privations and hardships." On one occasion he went so far as to speak of "saturating the market with consumer goods."

Under closer scrutiny the figures revealed that no basic change in priorities had yet been made and that there was nothing to justify Brezhnev's promise of "saturation," at least not before 1976. Kosygin's emphasis on increased productivity as the basis for more consumer goods meant that the worker, instead of getting a larger share of the national cake, was being offered a part of any additional cake he might create by his own labor. According to current estimates, Group A accounts for something on the order of four fifths of Soviet industrial output, Group B the rest. If the maximum-

growth targets provided in the plan for the two sectors are applied—45 per cent for producer goods and 48 per cent for consumer goods—the resulting proportions remain exactly the same: 80–20. Put in another way, given the immense existing base for producer goods, the growth rate for Group B could not have been pegged any lower without the consumer sector actually losing ground.

Even if the plan as drafted could not fulfill the expectations raised by the Soviet communications media, the fact remained that the country's leaders felt compelled to stress consumer welfare as a national aim. To the extent that there will be more goods of better quality, it can be attributed partly to the Polish uprisings of December 1970 which were linked directly to shortages of consumer items. Soviet leaders were reported to have been alarmed by the revolt, and there was speculation that they may have amended the economic blueprint, hoping to forestall the spread of that kind of disturbance to the Soviet Union. The attempt to "sell" the idea of a better deal for the Soviet consumer was also tied to a foreign-policy aim and dovetailed neatly with a well-orchestrated "peace offensive" begun in 1971.

Both were intended to impress the West with Russia's good intentions. A threat from the Soviet Union would appear less menacing if national policy was directed toward "butter" rather than "guns." Similarly, it was not by chance that the state budget for 1972 showed no increase in defense outlays for the second year in a row. Even communist specialists privately discounted that claim, pointing to a sharp rise in the allocation for "science" where a great deal of defense spending is customarily hidden. As indicators these factors were called upon to play a supporting role in the "peace program" announced by Brezhnev at the Congress. Among the "basic concrete tasks" of Soviet foreign policy, Brezhnev included treaties banning nuclear, chemical and bacteriological weapons; an end to nuclear testing; a five-power nuclear disarmament conference; a world disarmament conference; the end of "colonial regimes"; abolition of both NATO and the Warsaw Pact; dismantling of all foreign bases; "mutually advantageous cooperation" with all states; and repudiation of the "threat or use of force." Much of this was simply warmed over from earlier "peace offensives." Some was patently disingenuous.

Brezhnev reaffirmed elsewhere in his report the doctrine that bears his name, which was used to justify the Soviet-led invasion of Czechoslovakia in 1968. What Moscow did, Brezhnev said, "we were bound to do by our class duty, loyalty to socialist internationalism, and concern for the interests of our states and the future of socialism and peace in Europe." He declared in effect that he would do it again.

While the General Secretary's Western audience received the bulk of the "program" skeptically, it showed interest in his statement that "we stand for a reduction of armed forces and armaments in areas where military confrontation is especially dangerous, above all in Central Europe." It sounded like a response to NATO's mid-1968 call for discussions on mutual and balanced force reductions (MBFR). But NATO allies were not certain, and said so.

A modest plaque marks the grave of Nikita Khrushchev, who died Sept. 11. Only the former Premier's family, some friends and foreign newsmen attended the burial ceremony in a small cemetery near the Kremlin.
UPI

In contrast, a televised military funeral is held for the three Soyuz 11 cosmonauts, who died for lack of oxygen as their space capsule was returning to earth. Government, military and scientific leaders attend service.
Tass from Sovfoto

In a speech at Tbilisi on May 14, Brezhnev scolded them for trying to judge "the wine without sampling it." He said any vague points could "readily be eliminated," and he invited NATO to "taste the proposal, which, translated into diplomatic language, signifies to start negotiations." On Oct. 6 the Western allies gave former NATO Secretary-General Manlio Brosio a mandate to begin exploratory talks with the Soviet Union about MBFR. Although NATO had hoped that the discussions could begin by mid-November, at year's end the Soviets had yet to invite Brosio to Moscow.

It was generally agreed that force-reduction talks would be held separately from the European Security Conference the Soviets pushed with redoubled vigor in 1971. They pressed for the start of multilateral preparations so the conference could be convoked in Helsinki before the end of 1972. With military questions excluded, the Soviets began referring to the proposed gathering as the All-European Conference on Security and Cooperation, and began suggesting that such topics as air pollution could be made to fit into the agenda. Apart from the desire to gain *de facto* recognition for East Germany by all the European states and the two North American nations that would attend, Moscow's real purpose for the conference was made no clearer. At year's end it appeared that the gathering could be expected no sooner than 1973, unless the Soviet Union abandoned its insistence on linking Bonn's ratification of the 1970 Moscow treaty with completion of the big-four Berlin agreement of Sept. 3, 1971.

Nor did Soviet policy makers ignore their relations with the United States. Though Washington was perceived as Russia's main adversary, the Soviets continued their dialogue with the Americans. On May 20 the two governments jointly announced a procedural breakthrough in the bilateral negotiations to limit strategic armaments (SALT). The atmosphere was dramatically affected by President Nixon's announcement on July 15 that he would go to Peking, raising the awful prospect for Moscow that its two big-power rivals were begin-

ning to collude. Surprised, the Soviets reacted slowly. They began first by summoning Mongolia and all the Warsaw Pact allies, except Rumania, to the Crimea on Aug. 2 to plan counterstrategy. Toward China propaganda attacks were intensified, while Nixon received and accepted an invitation to visit Moscow in May 1972. Whether or not it was because of the China move, things began to loosen up in other bilateral dealings. In November, Maurice Stans became the first U.S. secretary of commerce to visit the Soviet Union. In his discussions with officials, including Kosygin, there was talk of a tenfold increase in trade turnover by 1975 that would make the United States Russia's principal trading partner in the capitalist world.

The Nixon attempt at *rapprochement* with China clearly shook the complacent Soviet leadership. If only for the sake of motion, Brezhnev, Podgorny and Kosygin left for diplomatic missions abroad. Brezhnev, who emerged as the main Soviet foreign-policy spokesman, went to see Tito in September, and in October was received with chief-of-state honors in France. Podgorny went to North Vietnam, India and Burma. Kosygin, now relegated to secondary tasks in foreign affairs, was sent to Algeria, Morocco, Denmark and Norway.

The Indians, too, were disturbed by the U.S. move toward China. To them it meant a loosening of ties between New Delhi and Washington. Drawing conclusions from Chinese support for Pakistan, the Indians dusted off an old draft treaty and on Aug. 9 signed a pact of "friendship and cooperation" with Russia. Thus, in the December conflict, the Indians moved against Pakistan with Soviet backing. The pact also allowed the Soviets to extend their southern line of expansion, which runs through the Middle East and Asia.

There was no evidence to suggest that the Soviet Union had altered its foreign-policy objectives in 1971. These were assumed to be primarily concerned with Europe where the maximum aim was felt to be the "Finlandization," or neutralization, of the Continent. Short of that, the Soviets were attempting to gain treaty recognition of the territorial *status quo* in Europe. Militarily the Soviets seemed to want nuclear parity, or, as they termed it, "equal security," with the United States through negotiations, without interrupting their weapons building in the meantime. Economically they made little effort to disguise their desire to gain access to Western technology as well as favorable long-term development credits.

STEPHENS BROENING
News Editor, Moscow Bureau
The Associated Press

U.S.S.R.

Area: 8,649,512 sq. mi.
Population: 245,000,000
Capital: Moscow
Government: Leonid I. Brezhnev, Communist Party secretary—1964; Aleksei N. Kosygin, premier—1964; Nikolai V. Podgorny, president of presidium—1965
Gross National Product: $490,000,000,000
Foreign trade: exports, $12,800,000,000; imports, $11,739,000,000
Armed forces: 3,375,000

At Conservative Party conference in Brighton in October, strong enthusiasm is obvious for Britain to join the European Economic Community.

UPI

UNITED KINGDOM

The year 1971 opened with a summit meeting of leaders of the Commonwealth in Singapore (Jan. 14–22)—31 heads of government or their deputies—at which the association formed upon the ashes of the British Empire came perilously close to dissolution. The issue was Prime Minister Edward Heath's decision to sell frigates and naval helicopters to South Africa. In the event, the Commonwealth did not break up.

Then, as the year drew to a close, Foreign Secretary Sir Alec Douglas-Home returned from Salisbury, Rhodesia (Nov. 25), with the terms of a settlement he had reached on the Government's behalf with the "rebel" former colony's Prime Minister Ian Smith. In the British view it marked a decisive change of direction for Rhodesia, away from a policy of racial apartheid and toward black rule. Yet it would clearly renew the strain on the Commonwealth, for it was impossible to tell how long black-majority rule would be in coming.

In May there was a formal reconciliation between the British and French governments when Heath and President Georges Pompidou met in Paris. It was followed by successful negotiation of terms for Britain's entry into the European Economic Community (the Common Market) at Luxembourg in June and the passage through Parliament in October of the motion to accept the terms in principle.

At home the Government had gone a considerable way toward implementing the "quiet revolution" spoken of by Heath in 1970. He vowed "to change the course of history for this nation—nothing less." Chancellor of the Exchequer Anthony Barber, on Mar. 30, announced the first thoroughgoing reform of the British tax system in fifty years, together with cuts in income tax, purchase taxes and the Selective Employment Tax. He followed this up in July with further substantial measures of reflation, adding nearly $3,000,000,000 to the total purchasing power in a year, the largest single such boost to it anyone could remember.

Employment Minister Robert Carr pushed through his massive Industrial Relations Bill, which was given the royal assent on Aug. 5. It set up a new Industrial Relations Commission, a new Code of Industrial Practice, and new judicial institutions with the aim of improving industrial relations in Britain. It introduced, for the first time in British labor history, the idea of a sixty-day "cooling-off period" in emergency strike situations, and a mandatory strike ballot where the support of a majority of employees is in doubt or where a dispute threatens others, not involved, with serious unemployment.

Meanwhile British trade continued to expand until the final quarter of the year. The nation's official reserves reached a record postwar level, at above $5,500,000,000. The balance-of-payments surplus was running at an annual rate of $1,600,000,000.

Yet the Government was unpopular. The Labor Party, although split down the middle by the Common Market issue, was running from 6 to 10 per cent ahead in the public-opinion polls. The same polls revealed little enthusiasm for the EEC; although after Parliament had accepted the deal in principle, a slight majority for entry became visible. The trade-union movement decided to fight the Industrial Relations Bill to the end, and ordered member unions not to register under it. Industrial output

At Newry, a center of violent unrest on the Ulster border, a woman demonstrator is moved on forcibly by British soldiers.

was static, manufacturing investment falling and inflation still rampant. Unemployment rose to a new post-World War II high, exceeding the 1,000,000 mark. And the situation in Northern Ireland almost daily became more dangerous.

Constitutionally part of the United Kingdom since a rebellion against Britain and an Irish civil war in 1919–20, the six predominantly Protestant counties of the north (Ulster) are nevertheless claimed as part of the territory of the Republic of Ireland. A "Unionist" government, however, has been in power in the north for fifty years, the union it supports being that with Great Britain instead of with the predominantly Roman Catholic Republic to the south. Discrimination against Catholics in the north had led to bitter intercommunity strife in previous years, and this escalated into something approaching terror in 1971. The British Army, reinforced to 14,000 men, had earlier been brought in to keep the peace between the religious communities. It now became the target of stones and homemade bombs, from the people of the Catholic ghettos, and of bullets from automatic weapons and rifles fired by snipers of the "provisional wing" of the illegal Irish Republican Army. A large quantity of arms from Czechoslovakia, allegedly intended for the IRA provisionals, was intercepted by the Netherlands police at the Amsterdam airport, and some from the United States at Cork by the Irish police.

Violence escalated still further when the government of Brian Faulkner, who had taken over the Unionist leadership from James Chichester-Clark in March, imposed a policy of internment without trial for terrorist suspects on Aug. 9. From March to Aug. 9 there had

been an average of 2 serious bomb explosions in Belfast or Londonderry per day. Twenty shops, taverns and banks owned by Protestants had been blown up and more than 100 civilians injured. From Aug. 9 to the end of November there were 400 more bombings. Twenty-six more British soldiers were killed and 110 wounded. Ten unarmed policemen of the Royal Ulster Constabulary were murdered.

The Army and police, however, began to get a considerable flow of intelligence information from internees. Charges of torture and brutality in obtaining this information were investigated by a special commission under Sir Edmund Compton, the Northern Ireland ombudsman, or people's attorney. They were found not proven, although considerable ill treatment of prisoners was substantiated. The intelligence provided resulted in some fifty of the top men in the IRA "provisionals" being detained and in the location of substantial caches of arms.

Irish Prime Minister John Lynch flew to London twice to see Heath and both met Faulkner as efforts to restore community peace accelerated. Lynch urged Britain to assume direct rule of Northern Ireland, an idea that met with stubborn resistance from both Faulkner and Heath. Faulkner sought to bring in Catholics to head government committees at Stormont Castle, the seat of Ulster's provincial government and parliament. All members of opposition parties walked out, however. A general Catholic boycott of provincial and local government affairs was decreed.

In November, British Opposition Leader Harold Wilson toured Ulster, seeing members of both communities and all factions. Wilson also visited Dublin. The result was the formation of a new Labor policy on Ulster, which most people hoped could be made bipartisan. British policy had been nonparty until then. The Unionists were politically affiliated with the British Conservatives, but it was a Labor government that had guaranteed the Protestants that no change would be made in their status without their consent in 1949 and, again, in 1967.

On Nov. 25 Wilson put forward entirely new proposals looking toward solving the problem by uniting all Ireland, with the new state thus founded entering the Commonwealth and accepting the British sovereign as head of the Commonwealth. He nevertheless repeated the guarantee that no change would be made in the border without the consent of the provincial parliament at Stormont Castle or of the majority of the people. He also insisted that the campaign of violence must end. That done, he proposed a constitutional commission representing Britain, Northern Ireland and the Republic to frame a new political system for a united Ireland in 15 years' time. The parliamentary Labor Party voted the same evening to end the bipartisan policy on the Irish problem that had been a feature of politics in Westminster for fifty years.

The Labor Party itself came under severe political strain, largely as a result of the Common Market vote. Having first declared he would "put the whips on"—would require Tories to attend and vote the government line —Heath in the end decreed a free vote for Conservatives. This put Labor in a predicament. Official policy was no vote against entry. Labor's whips stayed on. But 69 Labor members, including deputy leader Roy Jenkins, voted with the Government. Prime Minister Heath had a majority of 112.

The division within the Labor Party polarized into a straight conflict between the left and right wings. Jenkins, supported by the Right, barely scraped in again in fresh elections for the deputy leadership. He won 140 votes. Left-wing candidate Michael Foot received 126. Twenty-three Labor members abstained. To all appearances the party was split straight down the middle.

The development more or less guaranteed Heath a majority for all the legislation necessary for entering Europe. The hope was to get everything cleared away for Britain's official entry on Jan. 1, 1973.

In a practical sense, however, fresh difficulties appeared that would make it unexpectedly difficult for Britain to keep fully to the negotiated timetable. The major one was the appearance of severe structural unemployment in British industry. It appeared to be of a kind

UNITED KINGDOM

Area: 94,212 sq. mi.
Population: 56,300,000
Capital: London
Government: Elizabeth II, queen—1952; Edward Heath, prime minister—1970
Gross National Product: $121,000,000,000
Foreign trade: exports, $19,351,000,000; imports, $21,724,000,000
Armed forces: 380,900

that cannot be cured by the manipulation of demand. A second was the potentially inflationary effect of introducing the Value-Added Tax, Europe's rolling turnover tax, which would increase prices over a very wide range of goods that had borne no sales or other tax.

During the whole of 1971 it looked as though the effect of Heath's "quiet revolution" would be to make more difficult the nation's two most difficult economic problems, inflation and unemployment.

The Rolls-Royce company, the greatest name in British engineering, was allowed to go into liquidation. It was the victim of a fixed-price contract for a breakthrough aero engine in a

Workers from bankrupt Rolls-Royce company march on House of Commons in London to protest government plans to nationalize it.

Pictorial Parade Inc.

time of constantly increasing costs. A new company was formed and a new contract signed for the Lockheed TriStar RB-211 engines; but in regard to employment, the damage was done.

Another important firm to go bankrupt was the Upper Clyde Shipbuilding consortium, formed by the previous Labor Government to save shipbuilding on the upper reaches of the Clyde and to maintain the level of employment there. The consortium got through $100,000,-000 of public money in three years with little or nothing to show for it. Following the bankruptcy, the shipyard workers, led by two communist shop stewards, James Airlie and James Reid, took over the four yards involved and ran them successfully for a period of several months. Yet it was always clear that in the end there would never again be enough shipbuilding work in these upper reaches to keep four yards going.

The British Steel Corporation, which remained nationalized, lost $50,000,000 by midyear. The year-end results, it was officially stated, "would be substantially worse." Experiences like these, together with mounting unemployment, forced the Government to reconsider its policy on government spending. By the end of 1971 all the cuts in spending announced in 1970 had been restored and a program of additional expenditures was prepared.

In its social policies the Government was working toward a situation where it is people who are subsidized, when that is necessary, rather than things or services. The logical cli-

Prime Minister Edward Heath walks in procession at Oxford, to receive an honorary degree.

max to this is a form of negative income tax. It was under consideration. Meanwhile a new Family Income Supplement was introduced to eradicate family poverty, and a completely new housing policy was introduced. Here again tenants would be subsidized instead of housebuilding and rents. The concept of "fair rents" was to apply to public as well as private housing. All who could afford to pay these rents were to do so. Those who could not were to get an income supplement to enable them to do so. The current drawback to this scheme, which eventually would greatly stimulate housebuilding by making it profitable, was that there would be large rent increases over a considerable period of years for millions in rented public housing.

As part of the policy of making people "stand on their own two feet," and to pay the economic price for all the services they want, the Government also increased the price of meals at public, or state, schools, removed the privilege of free milk at school for children over the age of seven, and imposed a small charge for admission to national museums, which previously had been free.

Pensions were introduced for the first time for all, including those over eighty years of age who had not qualified during their working life for the state retirement pension. A new national scheme was prepared that eventually would provide two pensions for everyone, a basic one paid by the state and an earnings-related pension paid either by private employers or by a state "reserve scheme."

It was decided to build London's third international airport on reclaimed land at Foulness, at the northern extremity of the Thames estuary, instead of inland in the countryside of Buckinghamshire.

Britain's currency changed in February from the pounds, shillings and pence that had been familiar for more than 1,000 years to decimals. One hundred new pence make a pound sterling. The change was made easily, and the British accommodated themselves to the new coinage rapidly. It was, however, to some extent inflationary. In using the pound as the standard, instead of ten shillings (as in Australia and South Africa), the British more than doubled the value of their smallest coin and triggered off proportionately very large increases in prices at the lower end of the scale.

A start was made on turning British industry, and eventually the whole country, from yards, feet, inches and pounds avoirdupois to the metric system.

Foreign Affairs. Next to the agreement on terms for entry into the EEC, the most important de-

On 31st floor of London's Post Office Tower, workmen repair damage left by bomb explosion Oct. 31.

velopment in foreign affairs was the expulsion of 115 Soviet diplomats and trade officials. They were accused of engaging in espionage and other undiplomatic acts. Soviet reprisals were minimal, and it was felt that a new and more evenly balanced intelligence setup had been established between the two countries.

The total withdrawal of British forces from the Far East ordered by Labor was countermanded. A new five-nation combined force will be maintained in Southeast Asia, with units from Britain, Australia and New Zealand, Singapore and Malaysia. However, almost total withdrawal from the oil sheikdoms of the Middle East was agreed to.

The way was cleared for normal relations with Communist China; Great Britain voted for the inclusion in the United Nations.

After Libya nationalized the British Petroleum Co.'s properties there and removed all Libyan assets from British banks, late in 1971, Britain ousted Libya from the sterling area.

Queen Elizabeth, Prince Philip and Princess Anne visited Canada in May. Special security guards protected the Queen as she drove to and from the airport; as they did later, when she opened the new session of Parliament in November, because of a supposed IRA threat of assassination.

The experiment with British standard time was abandoned, at least for the present, on a free vote of Parliament. Britain reverted to Greenwich mean time during the winter, and British summer time, one hour in advance. Entry into the EEC could bring Britain back again to standard time, which is kept throughout the Common Market countries, perhaps in 1973.

See also European Economic Community

JOHN ALLAN MAY
Chief, London Bureau
The Christian Science Monitor

Service is suspended as Britain's first nation-wide postal strike begins at midnight Jan. 19.

Retiring UN Secretary-General U Thant extends congratulations to his successor, Kurt Waldheim, 53-year-old former Austrian foreign minister.

UNITED NATIONS

There used to be a custom of giving a distinguishing name to each session of the General Assembly. If followed in 1971, the session probably would have been known as the Assembly of Realities. For in its tumultuous closing weeks, delegate after delegate called on the world organization to face the "reality" of the global situation.

Among the realities confronting the United Nations during its 26th General Assembly session and during much of 1971 were these:

War between India and Pakistan. Three vetoes by the Soviet Union, in close support of Mrs. Indira Gandhi's New Delhi Government,

"Oh, I suppose it's reasonable to expect a few small changes"

Le Pelley in "The Christian Science Monitor" © TCSPS

prevented the Security Council from adopting even a simple cease-fire resolution. Transferred to the Assembly under the 1950 "uniting for peace" mechanism cofathered by Dean Acheson and John Foster Dulles, to enable the United Nations to act when the Council is paralyzed by a veto, a 104–11 vote for cease-fire-and-withdrawal on the subcontinent had no effect on the fighting.

After the Indian Army, with the support of native guerrillas, had captured Dacca, effectively splitting East Pakistan from West Pakistan, and India recognized the rebel Bengali state of Bangladesh, the Council approved a resolution framed along humanitarian lines.

The United States found itself politically aligned with Communist China on Pakistan's side against the Soviet-Indian alliance based on a treaty signed between those two countries earlier in the year.

Mainland China, after a 21-year struggle carried on by others in its name, won the Chinese seat in the United Nations. The United States, effective for two decades in retaining the seat for Generalissimo Chiang Kai-shek's Chinese Nationalists, futilely argued the "reality" that the Taiwan (Formosa) Government represented 14,000,000 persons, which made it one of the larger members of the United Nations.

The vote to seat Communist China, with its one fourth of the earth's population, swept aside U.S. arguments and demanded the expulsion of Chiang's representatives from the United Nations and all its organs. The Chinese, with a face-saving dramatic touch, walked out of the Assembly for good just before the vote was taken.

There were repercussions two months later when Assistant Secretary-General Agha Abdul Hamid, in charge of the Office of Public Information, acting on protests by the Peking delegation and with the approval of Secretary-General Thant, ordered representatives of the Nationalist Chinese Central News Agency to vacate their UN office and surrender their accreditation on less than a day's notice. This brought protests from press organizations in many parts of the world that the United Nations was suppressing freedom of information.

The organization teetered on the brink of financial bankruptcy. At least twice during the year, payday was threatened when Controller Bruce Turner (of New Zealand) found insufficient funds in the till. A payment by France saved the payday once, and one by the United States another time.

Despite this, the General Assembly approved a record budget of $213,124,410, an increase

UNITED NATIONS MEMBERSHIP

SECURITY COUNCIL MEMBERS AND TERMS

ARGENTINA	until Dec. 31, 1972	INDIA	until Dec. 31, 1973	SUDAN		until Dec. 31, 1973
BELGIUM	until Dec. 31, 1972	ITALY	until Dec. 31, 1972	U.S.S.R.		permanent
CHINA	permanent	JAPAN	until Dec. 31, 1972	UNITED KINGDOM		permanent
FRANCE	permanent	PANAMA	until Dec. 31, 1973	UNITED STATES		permanent
GUINEA	until Dec. 31, 1973	SOMALIA	until Dec. 31, 1972	YUGOSLAVIA		until Dec. 31, 1973

MEMBER NATIONS AND CHIEF REPRESENTATIVES

AFGHANISTAN	Abdur-Rahman Pazhwak	LEBANON	Edouard Ghorra
ALBANIA	Sami Baholli	LESOTHO	Mooki V. Molapo
ALGERIA	Abdellatif Rahal	LIBERIA	Nathan Barnes
ARGENTINA	Carlos Ortiz de Rozas	LIBYA	Mahmood Suleiman Maghribi
AUSTRALIA	Laurence McIntyre	LUXEMBOURG	André Philippe
AUSTRIA	vacant	MALAGASY REPUBLIC	Blaise Rabetafika
BAHRAIN	Salman M. Al-Saffar	MALAWI	Nyemba W. Mbekeani
BARBADOS	Waldo E. Waldron-Ramsey	MALAYSIA	H. M. A. Zakaria
BELGIUM	Edouard Longerstaey	MALDIVE ISLANDS	vacant
BHUTAN	Sangye Penjor	MALI	Seydou Traore
BOLIVIA	Walter Guevara Arze	MALTA	Joseph Attard Kingswell
BOTSWANA	T. J. Molefhe	MAURITANIA	Moulaye El Hassen
BRAZIL	Sergio Armando Frazão	MAURITIUS	Radha Krishna Ramphul
BULGARIA	Guero Grozev	MEXICO	Alfonso Garcia Robles
BURMA	U Lwin	MONGOLIA	Mangalyn Dugersuren
BURUNDI	Nsanze Terence	MOROCCO	Mehdi Mrani Zentar
BYELORUSSIAN S.S.R.	Vitaly S. Smirnov	NEPAL	Padma B. Khatri
CAMBODIA (KHMER REP.)	Khim Tit	NETHERLANDS	Robbert Fack
CAMEROON	Michel Njine	NEW ZEALAND	John Vivian Scott
CANADA	Yvon Beaulne	NICARAGUA	Guillermo Sevilla-Sacasa
CENTRAL AFRICAN REP.	Michel Adama-Tamboux	NIGER	Georges M. Condat
CEYLON	Hamilton S. Amerasinghe	NIGERIA	Edwin Ogebe Ogbu
CHAD	Homsala Ouangmotching[a]	NORWAY	Edvard Hambro
CHILE	Humberto Diaz Casanueva	OMAN	Ahmed Macki
CHINA	Huang Hua	PAKISTAN	Agha Shahi
COLOMBIA	Augusto Espinosa	PANAMA	Aquilino E. Boyd
CONGO (BRAZZAVILLE)	Nicolas Mondjo	PARAGUAY	Miguel Solano Lopez
COSTA RICA	Jose Luis Molina	PERU	Javier Perez de Cuellar
CUBA	Ricardo Alarcon Quesada	PHILIPPINES	Narciso G. Reyes
CYPRUS	Zenon Rossides	POLAND	Eugeniusz Kulaga
CZECHOSLOVAKIA	Zdenek Cernik	PORTUGAL	Antonio de Medeiros Patricio[a]
DAHOMEY	Wilfrid de Souza	QATAR	Hassan Kanel
DENMARK	Otto R. Borch	RUMANIA	Gheorghe Diaconescu
DOMINICAN REPUBLIC	Luis Raul Betances	RWANDA	Fidèle Nkundabagenzi
ECUADOR	Leopoldo Benites	SAUDI ARABIA	Jamil M. Baroody
EGYPT	Mohammed Hassan El-Zayyat	SENEGAL	Médoune Fall
EL SALVADOR	Reynaldo Galindo Pohl	SIERRE LEONE	Ismael B. Taylor-Kamara
EQUATORIAL GUINEA	Primo J. Esono Mica	SINGAPORE	Shunmugam Jayakumar
ETHIOPIA	Yohannes Tseghe	SOMALIA	Abdulrahim A. Farah
FIJI	Semesa K. Sikivou	SOUTH AFRICA	C. F. G. von Hirschberg
FINLAND	Max Jakobson	SPAIN	Jaime de Pinies
FRANCE	Jacques Kosciusko-Morizet	SUDAN	Kamal Mustafa
GABON	Jean Davin	SWAZILAND	Mboni Naph Dlamini
GAMBIA	vacant	SWEDEN	Olof Rydbeck
GHANA	Richard M. Akwei	SYRIAN ARAB REP.	George J. Tomeh
GREECE	Dimitri S. Bitsios	TANZANIA	Salim Ahmed Salim
GUATEMALA	Rafael E. Castillo-Valdes	THAILAND	Anand Panyarachun
GUINEA	El Hadj Abdoulaye Toure	TOGO	Michel Eklo
GUYANA	Frederick H. Talbot	TRINIDAD-TOBAGO	Eustace E. Seignoret
HAITI	Jean Coradin	TUNISIA	Rachid Driss
HONDURAS	Roberto Martinez Ordoñez	TURKEY	Umit H. Bayulken
HUNGARY	Károly Szarka	UGANDA	Grace S. Ibingira
ICELAND	Hannes Kjartansson	UKRAINIAN S.S.R.	Mikhail S. Polyanichko
INDIA	Samar Sen	UNION OF ARAB	Adnan Pachachi
INDONESIA	J. B. P. Maramis	EMIRATES	
IRAN	Fereydoun Hoveyda	U.S.S.R.	Yakov A. Malik
IRAQ	Talib El-Shibib	UNITED KINGDOM	Colin Crowe
IRELAND	Cornelius C. Cremin	UNITED STATES	George H. Bush
ISRAEL	Yosef Tekoah	UPPER VOLTA	Tensoré Paul Rouamba
ITALY	Piero Vinci	URUGUAY	Augusto Legnani
IVORY COAST	Siméon Ake	VENEZUELA	Andres Aguilar M.
JAMAICA	Keith Johnson	YEMEN	Yahya H. Geghman
JAPAN	Toru Nakagawa	YEMEN, PEOPLE'S DEM.	Abdul Malek Ismail
JORDAN	Baha Ud-Din Toukan	YUGOSLAVIA	Lazar Mojsov
KENYA	Joseph Odero-Jowi	ZAIRE	André Fernand Mandi
KUWAIT	Abdalla Yaccoub Bishara	ZAMBIA	Vernon J. Mwaanga
LAOS	Prince Khammao		

[a] chargé d'affaires

of about 11 per cent above the 1971 figure. The major money powers did not lend their support to adoption of the budget.

Actually, the United States, acting on the basis of a nongovernmental committee report prepared under the chairmanship of former U.S. Ambassador Henry Cabot Lodge, served notice that it wanted its share of UN costs reduced from 31.52 per cent to a maximum of 25 per cent annually.

Congress threatened to cut U.S. voluntary contributions to the specialized agencies and such funds as those for Palestinian refugees. A cutoff of U.S. funds for the International Labor Organization (ILO) raised serious issues for the entire UN family.

The United Nations found itself with a tired, ailing and discouraged Secretary-General. U Thant of Burma, who succeeded to the job on Nov. 3, 1961, following the death of Dag Hammarskjöld of Sweden in a plane crash in Africa, declared in January that he would not stand for reelection when his second five-year term expired Dec. 31. U.S. Ambassador George Bush—given the UN post when he lost election to the Senate in a Texas race President Nixon had persuaded him to resign his House of Representatives seat to enter—took Thant seriously from the start. But most of the other great powers hoped the Burmese diplomat could be persuaded to stay.

Not until December did the big powers get together to discuss a successor. The situation obviously was complicated by the arrival of mainland China, unsophisticated in UN politics, on the scene.

The secretary-general is elected by the General Assembly upon recommendation of the Security Council. In two private meetings, no nominee attaining the nine favorable votes required for approval escaped the veto of at least one of the big five members. Finally, on Dec. 21—the day the Assembly had set for its adjournment—China withheld the veto it had used against him and enabled the council to approve the candidacy of Kurt Waldheim, former Austrian foreign minister whose UN experience dated back 13 years, and who had lost his country's presidency by 3 per cent of the vote earlier in the year.

Waldheim received 11 favorable votes. Ambassador Carlos Ortiz de Rozas of Argentina received 12 but was vetoed; Ambassador Max Jakobson of Finland 9, but was vetoed. The ballot was secret and in a closed meeting of the Council. Diplomatic sources, claiming that China previously had vetoed Waldheim, said the Soviet Union cast the vetoes against Ortiz de Rozas and Jakobson.

The war in the Middle East showed signs of erupting anew. President Anwar al-Sadat of Egypt ostentatiously rattled his saber and Premier Golda Meir and Defense Minister Moise Dayan of Israel replied in kind.

Egypt accepted and Israel rejected—or perhaps accepted with too many conditions—suggestions of UN special envoy Gunnar V. Jarring for a peace settlement, and his Security Council-mandated mission was suspended in March. The Assembly, following a full-dress debate that was heavily overshadowed by the Indo-Pakistani war, asked Jarring to resume his mission on the basis of Council Resolution 242, adopted on Nov. 22, 1967, outlining broad terms for Middle East peace. But Jarring, after preliminary talks in New York with top Egyptian and Israeli diplomats, returned to his regular post as Swedish ambassador to Moscow, promising an early return to his Mideastern assignment.

Upsetting predictions that the Chinese Communist entry into the United Nations would be low-key and self-effacing, Peking's Deputy Foreign Minister Chiao Kuan-hua and Ambassador Huang Hua launched a new cold war immediately upon their arrival. The difference was that it was no longer an exclusive Moscow-Washington word conflict but a vicious exchange of vocabularies and polemics between the Russian and Chinese Communists. UN wits said the Communists were "washing their dirty Lenin in public."

The world organization in 1971 ran the gamut of its perennial subjects with little more or less success on any than in previous years.

It moved against Israel's "urban renewal" of the Old City of Jerusalem. It ranted against colonialism and demanded decolonization of Portuguese and South African territories. It urged a ban on weapons on the seabeds. It discussed disarmament in all its aspects and approved a treaty to outlaw biological weapons. It sought to reinforce sanctions against the white-supremacy Government of Rhodesia but was undermined when Congress authorized the U.S. purchase of chrome from Rhodesia. It saw its Secretary-General of a decade felled for the second time with an ulcer, eventually to retire without realizing his ambition of ending the Vietnam war, bridging the East-West gap or putting the UN on a firm financial basis.

It debated at length the desirability of ministates but admitted five of them—Bhutan, Bahrain, Qatar, Oman and the United Arab Emirates—raising its membership to 132 countries.

BRUCE W. MUNN
Chief UN Correspondent
United Press International

UNITED STATES

According to the Chinese calendar, 1971 was a year of the Pig, a time to be down to earth, to root about for fresh answers to vexing problems, but also a year fat with the promise of rewarded diligence. Such was 1971 for the United States. In foreign affairs, in economic matters and even in governmental structure, the nation entertained some ambitious proposals for solving some monumental difficulties. And while not every move met with success or applause, ideas were planted in the public mind that offered hope of fruition later.

As history so often records, the initiative for public debate on these questions was supplied by the one person who, by his very position, is best able to lead a break with the past—the President. Richard Milhous Nixon, in his third year of office, wasted little time in seizing upon several such opportunities in 1971.

Before January was out, he had boldly called upon Congress to reverse the steady growth of the Federal apparatus. He proposed in his State of the Union Message to "change the framework itself" by consolidating 7 of 11 cabinet departments. He called for a return to the cities and states of $16,000,000,000 in Federal taxes so they could solve some problems at local levels. He saw his breathtaking program as the basis for "a new American Revolution—a peaceful revolution in which power would be turned back to the people."

In the summer, presidential initiative again surprised the nation and the world. Nixon disclosed in July that he had been secretly planning a visit to the People's Republic of China for early 1972 to see Party Chairman Mao Tse-tung and Premier Chou En-lai. The news set off worldwide reverberations. It signaled an end of 25 years of anti-Peking diplomacy and acts by Washington. U.S. allies were caught unawares, and some were upset. At home, most liberals and independents approved, but anti-communist conservatives were angered and worried.

Sen. Edmund S. Muskie talks to a crowd of attentive Florida university students. As the leading (end of 1971) Democratic contender for the presidency, he will test his strength in crucial March 1972 Florida primary.

The John F. Kennedy Center for the Performing Arts, on the north bank of the Potomac River in Washington, embraces a 2,200-seat Opera House, a 2,575-seat Concert Hall and a theater named for the late President Eisenhower.

Fletcher Drake

Presidential adviser Henry Kissinger poses with his staff and Chinese hosts before the Summer Palace, near Peking, on second visit to China.

The White House

Then in August came the summer's second surprise. Nixon imposed a ninety-day freeze on wages, prices and rents, slapped a 10 per cent surcharge tax on imported goods, and asked Congress for a big package of tax-relief measures—all in the name of stopping inflation and the country's slide into recession.

Nixon took the initiative once more in autumn. He announced plans to visit the Soviet Union in May 1972, a trip that would make him the first American president to go there. And he set up semipermanent government machinery, including a pay board and a price commission, to administer economic controls when the freeze expired Nov. 13.

As important as all these developments were, they were not the only things that held America's attention in 1971.

A severe earthquake shook Southern California on Feb. 9, leaving 64 dead and hundreds injured. It forced 80,000 people to be evacuated when a dam in the San Fernando Valley sprang a leak and threatened to send nearly 7,000,000,000 gallons of water over the land. Scores of fires erupted; a veterans hospital collapsed; and major highways were closed. On the Golden State Freeway, pavement slabs tilted five feet above the roadbed.

In early March, a powerful bomb exploded in the U.S. Capitol in the dark hours before dawn, causing an estimated $200,000 damage but hurting no one. The blast came thirty minutes after an anonymous telephone caller had protested the Indochina war. The crime remained unsolved despite Federal investigations.

America's fancy was captured again by 1971 astronautical exploits. Apollo 14's crew landed on the moon in February, and Apollo 15 made another lunar landing in late July, each time titillating TV viewers with excellent pictures of the moon's terrain and their exploration of it. They brought back rock samples and borings that scientists used to learn more about the moon's age and composition. But the moon magic seemed to be fading nonetheless. When the three Apollo 14 astronauts visited the Capitol upon their return, less than half the members of the House of Representatives showed up.

Indochina continued to be very much on the minds of the American people and of Nixon as well. Administration policy was one of continuing U.S. troop withdrawals, massive efforts to improve the go-it-alone capabilities of the South Vietnamese Army, and fruitless negotiating sessions in Paris with Hanoi and the Vietcong. But there was no clear hint as to when and where it would all end.

In February, Nixon authorized a South Vietnamese "incursion" into Laos, supported by U.S. artillery and air power on the border. Perhaps because of the uproar over the use of American troops in Cambodia in 1970, U.S. soldiers were not used inside Laos in this operation. Once again, the administration made claims that the Laotian operation was necessary to cut off enemy supply lines threatening the safety of troops inside Vietnam. But heavy fighting forced the South Vietnamese to flee in near-panic conditions. Nixon was moved to tell

the country that "we cannot say that this is an operation that should be judged a failure."

Six antiwar activists were charged with plotting to blow up the heating plants of some Washington government buildings and then to kidnap the President's chief foreign-policy adviser, Henry A. Kissinger. The FBI said the alleged plot was directed by Father Philip Berrigan from his cell in Lewisburg (Pa.) penitentiary where he was serving time for an earlier antiwar conviction.

Perhaps the most visible symbol of an embittered and divided nation was First Lt. William L. Calley, Jr. He was convicted on Mar. 29 and sentenced to life in prison for the premeditated murder of 22 unarmed Vietnamese men, women and children during the "Mylai 4 massacre" three years before. The longest court-martial in American history generated a torrent of telegrams and letters to Nixon, the Pentagon, Calley, public officials, newspapers and TV stations everywhere. A majority thought the verdict unjust. Some veterans sided with Calley; groups organized rallies and started petitions seeking clemency. Some state legislatures entertained bills seeking presidential intervention. Some local draft boards in Arkansas, Florida, Michigan, Montana, Wyoming and Kansas resigned, and others said they would not draft boys to fight if they might get court-martialed for obeying orders. "It just doesn't seem right," said Vice-President Spiro T. Agnew.

At the peak of the public anguish, Nixon intervened by ordering Calley released from the

Paul Conklin

Youthful war protesters sit on the grounds of the Capitol in Washington during week-long, placid demonstration at the end of April.

stockade at Fort Benning, Ga., to house arrest until all his appeals to higher courts were decided. Furthermore, Nixon said, he personally would review the conviction and make the final decision about Calley's fate. Not everybody cheered the President's move. Army professionals and the military prosecutor in the case privately or publicly accused Nixon of meddling. The suggestion was that he was doing it for political motives.

Later in the year, in another court-martial, Calley's company commander, Capt. Ernest Medina, was acquitted of charges of murder and assault at Mylai. Medina subsequently resigned from the Army. He testified later that he had "lied" to Col. Oran Henderson about the extent of the killings at Mylai.

Henderson, sent in to investigate massacre reports, was himself under court-martial for allegedly whitewashing the tragedy in his report to Army brass. Henderson was cleared.

In April, Nixon told the nation over TV that he would remove another 100,000 troops from Vietnam before Dec. 1. In mid-November, the President announced further cutbacks that would reduce U.S. ground troops in Vietnam to 139,000 by Feb. 1, 1972. This was proof, he said, that he was indeed winding down the war and the end was "in sight." But the President declined to say when all Americans would be out of there, reiterating that he would have to keep a force in Vietnam until Hanoi released American POW's and possibly until the enemy agreed to a cease-fire in Laos and Cambodia as well as in Vietnam. To hammer the point, Nixon sent U.S. bombers over North Vietnam for five days after Christmas.

War foes staged 17 days of protest in the capital in May as thousands of young militants poured in, determined to "shut down the Government." Washington's helmeted police moved effectively to block that threat, arresting nearly 12,000 in demonstrations downtown and on Capitol Hill. The mass arrests triggered complaints of denial of free speech and assembly, and while the President defended the policy and encouraged other cities to do likewise, the Washington courts disagreed. All but a handful or two of those arrested were exonerated or saw the authorities drop the charges against them.

In October, the Nixon administration was embarrassed by its inability to keep at least one opposition candidate in the South Vietnam presidential election campaign. Unopposed President Nguyen Van Thieu, bowing to domestic and U.S. pressure, finally agreed to let his people vote yes or no on whether he should continue in office. As the Nixon administration desired, Thieu won handsomely. But the whole affair underscored the difficulty of attempting to impose American-style democracy on an Oriental country.

Perhaps the biggest national uproar over Vietnam was triggered June 13 when *The New York Times* began publishing the Pentagon Papers. They were an unusual set of secret documents and memos written by top government officials about U.S. policy in Vietnam during the Kennedy-Johnson administrations. The U.S. government went into court to halt the publication, contending irreparable injury to the national interest. In short order, parts of the documents began appearing in *The Washington Post, The Boston Globe, Chicago Sun-Times* and other papers. The Government took the *Post* and the *Globe* to court too.

The self-admitted purveyor of the secret study, later accused of stealing and misusing government documents, turned out to be a former Pentagon defense researcher, Daniel Ellsberg. A teacher and policy analyst at Massachusetts Institute of Technology, in Cambridge, Mass., Ellsberg said he provided the Pentagon documents to the newspapers because he had become totally disillusioned with a war he had once totally supported. He felt that the country had been tricked into a war it could not win.

Before the furor was over, the U.S. Supreme Court had held emergency sessions and ruled 6 to 3 on June 30 that the First Amendment protected the newspapers against prior restraint by the Government on the publication of the documents. But the newspapers' victory was a narrow one; some said it was even "hollow" because there were hints in the various opinions of the nine justices that there might be a future occasion when press freedom could be constitutionally limited in some way or other.

The White House never spelled out precisely why it feared publication of the Pentagon Papers, but that was disclosed later in a copyrighted *Detroit News* story. The documents, the paper quoted government sources as saying, contained details on current negotiations with the enemy and explicit information about U.S. spy-plane overflights across Communist China. What the Nixon administration could not say in court argument in June came out publicly on July 15.

That was the day Nixon informed an astonished world that he would visit Peking before May 1972 to talk with Red Chinese leaders "to seek the normalization of relations between the two countries and exchange views on questions of concern to both sides." Moreover, Nixon disclosed that Kissinger had met secretly

Dennis Brack, Black Star

Some three thousand guests, including former President Johnson and his wife, attend the dedication of the Johnson Library in Austin, Tex.

in Peking on July 9–11 to lay the groundwork for the Nixon trip. Had the Pentagon Papers' account of U.S. spying on Red China surfaced during June, administration officials feared that the embarrassed Chinese would have had to cancel plans then being made for Kissinger's trip to Peking and the anticipated Nixon visit.

The global reaction to Nixon's new pro-Peking stance was well-nigh incalculable, surprising even the White House with its intensity. Most profoundly disturbed were Japan, which had not been consulted in advance, and Russia, which suspected a Peking-Washington alliance against Moscow. The President sought to assure other nations that he was not trying to injure old allies or to upset delicate negotiations with the Soviets on nuclear-arms limitations and hopes for a mutual reduction of forces in Eastern and Western Europe. But the Nixon plans to visit mainland China, dates later scheduled as Feb. 21–28, 1972, clearly signaled a new era of triangular power politics involving the United States, the U.S.S.R. and the People's Republic of China.

The first serious repercussion came at the United Nations in New York. Over U.S. objections, the Nationalist Chinese regime on Taiwan was expelled from U.N. membership in tandem with the admission of mainland China. At the White House, Nixon was "shocked" by the UN action. But there was nothing he could do to change it.

Yet nothing occurred in all of 1971 that had more impact on Americans and the rest of the free world than the event that took place on a soft summer Sunday evening, Aug. 15. The President, in a TV broadcast from the White House, imposed an immediate ninety-day freeze on all wages, prices and rents, coupled with a plea to business to hold the line on dividends. He cut the dollar's anchor to the gold standard so it could float competitively on the world currency market. He clapped a 10 per cent tax surcharge on all goods imported into the United States. And he asked Congress for a package of tax-relief measures intended to spur consumer buying and industrial expansion.

In that twenty-minute address, a Republican President had boldly scrapped the traditional concept of free markets and free prices in favor of an economic battle plan that caught everyone by surprise, including members of his administration. Labor leaders and Democratic presidential aspirants, who had been complaining of

Television record of liftoff of lunar module "Falcon" (Apollo 15 mission) from moon surface: (from top) waiting for action; engine is fired and debris flies; descent stage alone is left.
NASA

a do-nothing Nixon, now were mumbling that maybe he was going too far.

"Dr. Nixon prescribes shock therapy," said *The New York Times.* One leading administration official observed that the President had "made a new economic policy out of all the things we had been saying weren't needed and couldn't work, and it turned the country around overnight."

Nixon embarked on his new course to bring under control three bogeymen of domestic prosperity: unemployment, inflation, and monetary speculators abroad who were diluting the dollar.

He said he had not wanted to do it, but that he had to. And most of the country seemed willing to give it a try. While AFL–CIO President George Meany complained that the Nixon program was biased against the workingman, polls showed that Americans generally approved the President's act. The stock market initially made the biggest one-day jump in prices in its history, a measure of the confidence that

wavered later in the year. Foreign governments, from Ottawa and London to Bonn and Tokyo, were thrown into confusion and consternation. And the more evident their unhappiness, the more American businessmen chortled about prospects of regaining trade lost to overseas competitors.

In mid-October, Nixon announced his Phase 2 strategy for keeping the lid on the economy after the freeze ended Nov. 13. It amounted to the creation of wage and price regulations of the kind, although not the degree, that the country had last experienced in World War II and the Korean war.

Two semiautonomous boards were created. The Pay Board, a tripartite body composed of 5 business, 5 labor and 5 public members, would regulate wages and salaries. While the AFL–CIO and the independent United Auto Workers and Teamsters Brotherhood were wary of participating, they went along after White House assurances that union members would not be discriminated against. The Pay

Wedding smiles at the White House: the just-married Mr. and Mrs. (Tricia Nixon) Edward Finch Cox and her parents beam for an unofficial portrait.

Relieved American troops being withdrawn from Vietnam file aboard ship for the long voyage home.

New York state troopers march on Attica prison to quell revolt and rescue hostages. In the resulting tragic clash, 32 inmates and 11 hostages died.

Daniel Ellsberg, who released the Pentagon Papers, accepts a declassified stamp from admirers.

Board set 5.5 per cent as the average allowable boost in wages. To govern prices, a 7-member, all-public Price Commission was established. It set a price-increase guideline of 2.5 per cent. The problem, as both bodies soon found out, was to keep wages and prices somewhere near those marks. To set administration policy, Nixon devised the Cost of Living Council of top government officials headed by Treasury Secretary John B. Connally.

The President counted heavily on voluntary compliance by companies, workers and the public to make the new economic program work. Instead of a big new Federal bureaucracy to police the system, the Internal Revenue Service was ordered to supervise performance at the local levels in addition to its time-honored task of collecting taxes. The 1,500 biggest U.S. companies had to "prenotify" the Price Commission of price increases. Really little merchants had to worry only about complaints and spot checks by IRS field offices.

Additionally, Nixon called upon Congress to give him legislative authority to continue controls, if necessary, into 1973. This was ironic on two counts. First, the original authority the President utilized had been given to him in 1970 by a Democratic Congress that intended only to embarrass him politically. Second, in seeking longer-range permission, Nixon not only made clear that he was serious about the first peacetime controlled economy but also that he

had discarded his old Republican hang-up over using governmental power to regulate the marketplace. Congress responded with alacrity, the Democratic majority in some instances voting more controls than the White House wanted.

The big question, of course, was whether the controls would work and, if they did, how long it would take before the economy again could be unshackled. Knowing Nixon's interest in a second term, most observers felt that the President would find a way to declare the plan a partial success and scrap some of the regulations before the 1972 November election. Even so, Federal management of the economy will be "continuing for a long time"—at least well into 1973, predicted Paul W. McCracken, the outgoing chairman of Nixon's Council of Economic Advisers, at year's end.

Just before Christmas, Nixon came up with another of his "surprises." He commuted the 13-year prison sentence of former Teamsters Union President James R. Hoffa. Behind bars since 1967 on convictions for jury tampering and mail fraud, Hoffa was freed on condition that he refrain from all union activity and report regularly to a Federal probation officer in Detroit. Washington speculated that Hoffa and the Teamsters Union might be in Nixon's corner in the 1972 presidential campaign.

For the 435 members of the House of Representatives and the 100 members of the U.S. Senate, 1971 was less than illustrious. While

President Nixon and Interior Secretary Rogers Morton discuss claims of Alaskan natives to ancestral lands with Alaska Sen. Theodore F. Stevens (far r) and Donald R. Wright (far l), president of Alaska Federation of Natives. On Dec. 15, Nixon signed bill making restitution.

UPI

Congress gave Nixon almost everything he asked for in terms of controls over the economy and a new tax bill, it took little action on his "New American Revolution," and it balked him and even itself on foreign affairs.

Three times the Senate passed an amendment to set a deadline on troop withdrawal from Vietnam. But each time, the proposal by Montana's Sen. Mike Mansfield, Democratic majority leader, was watered down and eventually defeated in the House.

And, after 25 years of routine approval, in 1971 the Senate refused to pass a foreign-aid bill. Finally, on the last day of the 1971 session,

LEGISLATION

Major bills passed by the First Session of the 92d Congress and signed by the President

SUBJECT	PURPOSE
SOCIAL SECURITY	Increases Social Security benefits by 10 per cent retroactive to Jan. 1, 1971. Signed Mar. 17. Public Law 92–5.
PASSPORTS	Authorizes the U.S. Postal Service to collect a fee of $2.00 for processing a passport application. Signed May 14. Public Law 92–14.
EMERGENCY EMPLOYMENT	Authorizes $2,250,000,000 to provide unemployed persons with public-service jobs. Signed July 12. Public Law 92–54.
PUBLIC WORKS AND ECONOMIC DEVELOPMENT	Authorizes $4,000,000,000 to extend the Public Works and Economic Development Act of 1965 and the Appalachian Regional Development Act of 1965. Signed Aug. 5. Public Law 92–65.
LOCKHEED AIRCRAFT CORPORATION LOAN	Approves a government-guaranteed private bank loan of $250,000,000 to the Lockheed Aircraft Corporation. Signed Aug. 9. Public Law 92–70.
BOAT SAFETY	Establishes safety requirements, including minimum safety construction standards, for pleasure boating. Signed Aug. 10. Public Law 92–75.
SELECTIVE SERVICE SYSTEM	Extends the military draft until June 30, 1973; calls on the president to set a "date certain" for withdrawal of all U.S. forces from Indochina, subject to the release of all U.S. prisoners of war. Signed Sept. 28. Public Law 92–129.
SUGAR QUOTAS	Extends for three years the law adjusting sugar quotas for foreign and domestic producers. Signed Oct. 14. Public Law 92–138.
HEALTH TRAINING	Assists in financing the training of medical personnel. Signed Nov. 18. Public Law 92–157.
TAXATION	Approves a 7 per cent tax credit for investment; repeals the automobile excise tax; raises the personal annual income-tax deduction to $675

it authorized a temporary extension of the 1971 program. But the real fight, over a bill separating military aid from economic assistance, was put off until 1972.

Congress scrapped Federal support for the supersonic transport plane, leaving the field to Britain, France and the Soviet Union. Ecologists in Congress contended that the SST would hurt the environment; conservatives argued that it was a waste of money. Nixon, badly disappointed, promised to revive the SST issue in 1972.

After months of infighting, Congress finally approved a two-year extension of the military draft. The Nixon administration also persuaded Congress to lend $250,000,000 to the Lockheed Aircraft Corp. to keep it out of bankruptcy, a move opponents claimed set a bad precedent in the defense industry.

Congress took limited action on the social front. It appropriated $1,600,000,000 for a massive attack on cancer through a separate Federal agency; and it authorized the creation of a network of government-financed day-care centers for children of working mothers. But Nixon vetoed the latter on grounds, raised by conservatives, that such a program would undermine America's family fabric.

The lawmakers wrangled all year over political-campaign financing. Senate Democrats,

aware of their party's $9,000,000 debt, voted a tax-bill amendment permitting taxpayers to contribute one dollar to a national fund that would bankroll all party campaigning. Republicans, with no visible money worries, opposed it. Nixon threatened to veto his own tax bill if the campaign checkoff plan was in it. In the end, the Democrats gave in. They delayed the effect of their amendment until 1976. Nixon accepted the compromise, confident that the whole matter would surely be redrafted by Congress before then.

A new Secretary of Agriculture, Earl Butz, dean of Purdue University, was confirmed by the Senate in November after a brief skirmish. Butz was picked by Nixon to succeed the retiring Clifford Hardin, but farm-belt lawmakers of both parties charged that Butz was too closely allied with giant food and feed companies to look after the interests of ordinary farmers.

There were leadership changes within Congress too. Rep. Carl Albert, diminutive Oklahoma Democrat, was elected Speaker of the House, succeeding the retired Rep. John W. McCormack of Massachusetts. Rep. Hale Boggs, Louisiana Democrat, took Albert's old place as majority floor leader. On the Senate side, West Virginia's Robert Byrd staged a minor coup by defeating Massachusetts' Sen.

	for 1971 and to $750 for 1972; permits any taxpayer to allocate $1.00 of tax money to help fund presidential elections beginning with the 1976 campaign. Signed Dec. 10. Public Law 92–178.
ANIMAL PROTECTION	Protects, manages and controls wild, free-roaming horses and burros on public lands. Signed Dec. 15. Public Law 92–195.
ALASKA LAND	Ends a 104-year-old land dispute by paying Alaska's natives $962,500,000 and granting them 40,000,000 acres of land. Signed Dec. 18. Public Law 92–203.
DEFENSE DEPARTMENT	Appropriates $70,518,463,000 for the Department of Defense for fiscal 1972. Signed Dec. 17. Public Law 92–204.
NATIONAL PARKS	Establishes the Capitol Reef National Park in Utah. Signed Dec. 18. Public Law 92–207.
ECONOMIC STABILIZATION	Approves a one-year extension, until Apr. 30, 1973, of the president's authority to control wages and prices, and adjusts statutory pay systems of Federal employees. Signed Dec. 22. Public Law 92–210.
CANCER RESEARCH	Authorizes a $1,600,000,000 three-year cancer-research plan. Signed Dec. 23. Public Law 92–218.
SOCIAL SECURITY— WELFARE REFORM	Pays lump-sum death benefits when the body of a soldier presumed killed in Vietnam is not found; extends Medicaid benefits to include services covered by Immediate Care Facilities (ICF's); guarantees that some 600,000 needy Americans will be covered by 1969 Social Security increases; requires all able-bodied welfare recipients to register for jobs or job training. Signed Dec. 28. Public Law 92–223.
UNEMPLOYMENT BENEFITS	Extends for 13 weeks the unemployment-compensation benefits in states that have had an unemployment rate of 6.5 per cent or more for 13 weeks. Signed Dec. 29. Public Law 92–224.
26TH AMENDMENT TO THE CONSTITUTION	Lowers voting age in all elections to 18 years. Ratified June 30.

Political upset: West Virginia Sen. Robert Byrd defeats Massachusetts Sen. Edward M. Kennedy for the post of Senate majority whip.

Edward M. Kennedy in a Democratic caucus fight over the majority whip's job, the No. 2 spot in the Democratic hierarchy. But the loss did little to diminish Kennedy's luster as a 1972 presidential prospect; it even gave him more time for speech-making around the country.

It is a rare year in Washington when school issues do not crop up to plague the Government—and 1971 was no exception. The U.S. Supreme Court upheld the concept of massive busing of pupils to integrate Southern schools. Chief Justice Warren E. Burger, a Nixon appointee of 1969, wrote the Court's opinion. It said that school officials must use all available tools to end segregation—including busing and the redrawing of district boundaries. It was an important decision because it undercut the old concept of the "neighborhood school." Burger declared that the busing remedy for segregation "may be administratively awkward, inconvenient and even bizarre" but must be applied anyway. The White House responded in lukewarm fashion. While saying that the Government would uphold the "law of the land," Nixon said he would sanction only a minimum of busing.

The busing furor reached a crescendo late in the year when several Federal judges in Northern cities began handing down opinions calling for the use of buses to mix pupils of mainly black schools in the central cities with pupils of mainly white schools in their suburbs. In a switch of past sentiment, Northern liberals

began teaming up with Southern conservatives in favor of a constitutional amendment prohibiting that kind of cross-district integration. The fuss was certain to recur in 1972, with no clue as to how it might be resolved.

On another school issue, the Supreme Court bucked the White House once more by prohibiting some forms of state aid for parochial schools. Again through an opinion by Chief Justice Burger, the high court struck down Pennsylvania and Rhode Island laws authorizing payment for teachers' salaries in church-related schools. Burger said this was an "excessive entanglement between government and religion."

Congress, for its part, became embroiled in a major controversy over a proposed constitutional amendment to permit prayer in public schools, something outlawed several years before by the Supreme Court as a breach of the wall separating church and state. The pro-prayer plan, in spite of substantial grass-roots support from fundamentalist Protestants, failed of the required two-thirds House approval.

Against this backdrop, fate provided Nixon with an opportunity rare for a president who has been in the White House less than three years.

Two justices of the Supreme Court resigned because of ill health: the highly respected Hugo L. Black and John M. Harlan. The Republican President, trying to turn the Court around, had already named two: Burger in 1969 and Harry Blackmun, another conservative, in 1970. Now he had the chance to name two more to the nine-man panel. After much suspense and a quarrel with the American Bar Association, Nixon picked Lewis F. Powell, Jr., prominent 64-year-old lawyer from Richmond, Va., and William H. Rehnquist, a conservative 47-year-old assistant attorney general from Arizona. The Senate, after lengthy hearings, confirmed both appointees. With four men of his choosing on the Supreme Court, Nixon appeared to have come a long way toward achieving a more limited, less activist approach to social and political questions by the nation's highest tribunal.

With Congress' adjournment in mid-December, Nixon was free to grab the public spotlight with preparations for his 1972 trips to mainland China and Russia. The President held "mini-summit meetings" with the heads of five allied countries: Canada, France, Great Britain, West Germany and (in January 1972) Japan.

The most significant was his session in the Portuguese Azores with French President Georges Pompidou. Nixon agreed to devalue

UNITED STATES

Area: 3,615,123 sq. mi.
Population: 208,557,735
Capital: Washington, D.C.
Government: Richard M. Nixon, president—1969
Gross National Product: $1,060,800,000,000
Foreign trade: exports, $45,924,000,000; imports, $48,072,000,000
Armed forces: 3,161,000

the American dollar in exchange for a promise that the European Common Market would ease restrictions against the sale of U.S. products. A few days later, Nixon announced the lifting of the 10 per cent surtax on imported goods. Both decisions reflected a new American concept of its position in the world of commerce. For the first time since World War II, the United States was saying that it could no longer do business with the rest of the world on terms that gave other nations an advantage. Collectively, they had reached the point where their aggressive trade and monetary practices were hurting American businessmen and workers alike. From now on, Nixon made clear, the United States would scramble for its share of the world market while protecting its own particular interests at home.

Washington's hopes for a relatively peaceful December were shattered when full-scale war broke out between India and Pakistan. The White House reacted angrily against India, blaming it for provoking the conflict, and cutting off all U.S. aid to the world's largest democracy. Democratic leaders as well as India and its chief backer, the Soviet Union, criticized the United States. They contended that Nixon was siding with Pakistan in spite of its "slaughter" of thousands of East Pakistanis seeking a greater measure of self-rule.

They argued further that the administration was backing Pakistan because Nixon did not want to irritate Communist China, Pakistan's other chief supporter, for fear that it might rub out his upcoming trip to Peking. Adding to the administration's discomfort were the disclosures of columnist Jack Anderson concerning secret White House meetings in which Nixon aides talked of ways to help Pakistan and thwart India. The United States proved unable to stem the war. India's Army "liberated" East Pakistan. A new nation, Bangladesh, was created, giving Nixon the future problem of deciding whether to ignore or to recognize the new country.

Considering all the surprises of 1971, Year of the Pig, scarcely anyone dared predict tranquility for the people of the United States in 1972. Another presidential election was in the offing. The Vietnam war, while winding down, was still not over. Controls on wages, prices and rents might be eased in 1972—if inflation and unemployment ceased to be problems. A ban on the use of nuclear weapons was a possibility—if Washington and Moscow came to terms.

Halfway around the globe, meanwhile, China prepared for 1972 and its first visit by an American president. It would be the Year of the Rat, the beginning of a new lunar cycle in the Orient. According to the ancients, it is ofttimes a very good year indeed.

J. F. terHORST
Chief, Washington Bureau
The Detroit News

UPI

Two priests and a former priest leave a U.S. court with Federal marshals after being held on $50,000 bond on charges that they (with the Rev. Philip Berrigan and two others) conspired to kidnap presidential adviser Henry Kissinger.

VEHICLES, ALL-TERRAIN

The all-terrain vehicle, or ATV, can be any one of several recreational vehicles powered by engines burning fossil fuels. Since 1966 these vehicles have evolved from a curiosity to a fad, and from there to a $1,000,000,000 industry providing outdoor activity for millions. At the same time, however, those enjoying ATVs are being exposed to injury and even death at rates attributable to few recreation forms in the past, save gladiatorial contests. In addition, vast stretches of North America's landscape are being exposed to permanent ecological damage. And huge segments of wildlife, from the micro-organic up, are finding essential elements of their life cycles destroyed.

The most common of the ATV are the snowmobile and the dune buggy. The snowmobile can carry 1 to 4 persons across relatively level stretches of snow at speeds in excess of 50 miles per hour by means of a wide power-driven belt stretching the length of the vehicle. The dune buggy is a lightweight vehicle, usually adapted from a small conventional passenger car, which can negotiate the fluctuating terrain of beach or desert by means of exceptionally wide, doughnut-shaped tires.

Variations on these two basic designs can include vehicles with 2 tracks; with 6, 8 or even 12 wheels; with a one-piece body, or an articulated or segmented body which twists in response to the undulations of the ground. The common denominator is invariably, through the use of tracks or soft, wide tires, less ground weight per square inch than with conventional vehicles. This ensures reasonably unhampered passage over soft terrain, such as snow, swamp or sand, or over highly irregular terrain, such as heavily wooded areas or rock-strewn slopes.

Most ATVs can be traced back about a decade to use in industry: mines, logging camps and oil fields. At the same time that these designs were being perfected, the pastime of converting old cars, or jalopies, to essentially nonfunctional uses expanded to include the rebuilding of small cars to adapt to beach and desert. The popularity of both vehicles increased as it was found that ideally they suit the needs of sportsmen, campers, ranchers and, in some cases, physicians and rescuers.

Once the market expanded to reach these new possible consumers, it was an obvious and easy step to begin offering the vehicles to the group that is now the biggest market of all: those bent on recreation or vacations.

A racing dune buggy churns up a cloud of sand. Such vehicles can move over very rough, uneven terrain and may tear away dune-holding grasses.

Snowmobiles are meant for winter transport; the noisy vehicles require little driving skill and can be extremely dangerous if handled carelessly.

The best-documented estimate placed sales of powered recreation vehicles at 155,000 units in 1960, and at 1,800,000 units in 1970. Direct and related consumer spending in this area amounted to $73,000,000 in 1960, and nearly $1,000,000,000 in 1970. Records from individual states and Canadian provinces are imprecise but tend to verify the above growth rate. In the mid-1960's, snowmobiles were a rarity in New York State. In 1971, the first year in which registration was required, some 144,000 snowmobiles were recorded. According to official records, the number of snowmobiles in Ontario grew from 5,000 in 1965 to 113,289 in March 1970, an increase of more than 20 times. Snowmobiles registered in Michigan in the 1969–70 season totaled 39,233. A year later the number had grown to 90,841.

California estimated it had 25,000 dune buggies in 1968. An estimate for early 1971 was 115,000. Similar growth rates in dune-buggy sales are attested to in most coastal states and provinces. Proportionately an even greater growth in snowmobile sales is estimated in the snow-belt area of the United States and the lower provinces of Canada.

Factors contributing to this growth are varied. The increase in leisure time is significant. Disposable personal income is rising at a slightly faster rate than inflation; and income, after covering the essentials of housing, food and clothing, is growing even faster. So there is more money left to spend on recreation. ATVs cost between $800 and $3,000, well within the reach of a fancier with access to short-term credit.

Suburbanization and the extensive network of superhighways across North America have opened new sections of heretofore untouched beaches and forests. ATVs qualify marginally as a sport. An infinitely greater number can now drive around in ATVs, which require virtually no motor skill or body coordination, than can participate in such physically demanding activities as skiing and surfing. Finally, there is the factor of a renewed interest in nature, spawned by ecological concern for the natural resources of the continent. ATVs permit increased access to greater areas of untouched woodland, beach and desert.

Ironically it is the last factor that is fueling the greatest outcry against the ATV. The

An amphibious ATV roars like a motorcycle, looks like a bathtub, weighs from 400 to 600 pounds and can cost from $1,000 up to $1,600.

vehicles are destroying the very wonders of nature that they take their riders to see. Snowmobiling is usually carried out over loosely defined trails. As the vehicles give the drivers an illusion of freedom, they are frequently driven with little restraint. They ramble beyond the defined trails and kill new perennial plant forms struggling to survive a second, third or fourth winter. Snowmobile trails in many sections of the United States border on farms. Private property is therefore often violated, with permanent damage done to plant life as well as out-structures.

As for the trail itself, snowmobile traffic may significantly alter the soil-temperature regime by compacting natural snow cover. This changes the snow's insulative property and subsequently alters organic-matter decomposition. With trails cutting into new areas of snow cover, deer and other wild animals are forced to retreat, cut off from part of their normal food supply.

Dune buggies, it is said, tear away the foundation for the dune grasses that are the beach's sole bastion against erosion by the sea. Regulations banning the use of dune buggies above the high-tide mark or diagonally across the face of a dune have been established in many parts of the United States, but enforcement has thus far remained pretty much a hit-or-miss proposition.

Of more immediate ecological concern is the noise made by ATVs. The noise of a snowmobile is so loud that if it were operated in an industrial plant it would be in violation of Federal law. Property owners along snowmobile trails protest against the noise unceasingly. The person with a more legitimate grievance is the snowmobile's own operator. A recent study showed that prolonged exposure to snowmobile noise can lead to partial but permanent hearing loss. Exposure, it was concluded, should be limited to 30-minute spans. Two-hour rides are not uncommon.

The danger of accidental death is acute. The National Safety Council reported that 94 persons died in snowmobile accidents in the 1970–71 season, with 420 persons injured. The preceding year 84 died and 306 were injured. In many states, accidents involving ATVs are routinely reported as road accidents and do not yet gain separate classification.

The industry responsible for production of ATVs hopes that through education of drivers and the passage of new, reasonable laws, controlling where and how ATVs are used, mortality rates will decline to a level commensurate with the anticipated increase in sales.

JAMES WARGO
Bureau Chief, Detroit, Mich.
McGraw-Hill World News

VETERANS

Congress appropriated $10,935,756,000 for the Veterans Administration in the 1971–72 fiscal year, $291,000,000 more than President Nixon requested and $1,026,000,000 more than was voted in the previous year.

It was by far the largest allotment ever allowed VA. Donald E. Johnson, the VA head, said this budget would provide compensation payments for 2,700,000 veterans and survivors of deceased veterans for service-connected disabilities; pension payments for 1,080,277 non-service-connected disabled veterans, widows and children; educational and training assistance to 1,800,000 veterans and 63,000 sons, daughters and wives; guaranteed monthly home loans for 32,000 veterans; continuation of a life-insurance program covering 8,700,000 veterans and active-duty servicemen; hospital care for 900,000 veterans; outpatient medical treatment involving more than 8,000,000 visits; and guardianship of the estates of 831,000 minors and incompetents.

The increase voted by Congress over the President's request was designated for improved medical care of veterans. Thus the law-makers indicated, as they had in adding extra medical funds for the preceding year, that they were dissatisfied with the care being given veterans and their dependents. Johnson, in reply to a question from Sen. John O. Pastore (D-R.I.), chairman of the subcommittee handling the VA appropriations bill, insisted that the sum sought by the administration was adequate to furnish good medical care. However, Sen. Alan Cranston (D-Calif.) noted that the administrator had made the same response a year earlier and yet had used the additional funds provided at the time. Cranston, chairman of the Health and Hospitals Subcommittee of the newly created Senate Committee on Veterans Affairs, said that Johnson gave the answer under constraint by Nixon's Office of Management and Budget. Cranston said the administration was not seeking any funds to add urgently needed doctors, nurses and other personnel to crowded VA hospitals. Johnson stressed that VA planned to open three new hospitals in the fiscal year, bringing the total to 168, and that there would be no closings. His staff conceded, however, that the staffing ratio in VA institutions was less than that in

Testifying before a U.S. Senate committee, veterans leader and former Navy officer John F. Kerry, thrice wounded, pleads: "How do you ask a man to be the last to die in Vietnam. . . . to die for a mistake?"

MR. FULBRIGHT

private hospitals. One survey of VA psychiatric hospitals made during the year revealed that thousands of patients passed their days rarely seeing a psychiatrist, that there was a critical shortage of registered nurses, and that many of the wards lacked such amenities as air conditioning.

The standing Senate Committee on Veterans Affairs, created in the 1970 Congressional reorganization act after a long fight, began operations in January at the outset of the 92d Congress. Sen. Van Hartke (D-Ind.) was named chairman; four other Democrats and four Republicans were appointed to the panel. However, the committee originated no major legislation in its first year. Most of its hearings were devoted to oversight of VA activities.

The American Legion, at its annual convention in Houston, Tex., Aug. 27–Sept. 2, elected John H. Geiger, Des Plaines, Ill., as its new national commander. The legion adopted resolutions deploring what it said were attempts to undermine the work of J. Edgar Hoover, director of the Federal Bureau of Investigation, and opposing efforts to tie the release of U.S. prisoners of war in North Vietnam to a specific date for withdrawal of all American troops from Indochina. At its national convention in Dallas, Tex., Aug. 13–20, the Veterans of Foreign Wars chose Joseph L. Vicites of Uniontown, Pa., as its new commander in chief. The organization adopted resolutions calling for substantial increases in both compensation and pension payments for veterans and urged Congress to reassess what it called "deteriorating U.S. military capabilities" as compared with Russian military strength.

JOSEPH W. HALL, JR.
Senate Staff, Washington Bureau
The Associated Press

WELFARE

In 1835, Alexis de Tocqueville wrote: "There are two incentives to work: the need to live and the desire to improve the conditions of life. Experience has proven that the majority of men can be sufficiently motivated to work only by the first of these incentives. The second is only effective with a small minority . . . A law which gives all the poor a right to public aid, whatever the origin of their poverty, weakens or destroys the first stimulant and leaves only the second intact."

However one might view this gloomy assessment, the fact is that in 1971 American law "which gives all the poor a right to public aid" came under roiling debate as never before. Law giving taxpayer money to the indigent is gen-

erally described as welfare. Such law is nothing new in the United States: From the earliest colonial times, towns and villages recognized an obligation to help the needy when family assistance and neighborly help was absent or insufficient. Almshouses and a loosely knit poor-relief system sprang up. But it was not until the great depression of the 1930's that Federal law was enacted to create a bank of social-insurance programs to help meet the risks not only of poverty but of old age, unemployment, child dependency and physical impairment. The principal statute carrying out these programs was the Social Security Act of 1935. In 1971, 36 years after Social Security was enacted, events showed that America still was not prepared to fully and finally embrace the principle that in the United States there is a basic constitutional and human "right to welfare."

In the broadest sense, welfare encompasses a variety of public assistance: not only aid to the aged, infirm and poor but aid to veterans and even the unemployed. There is little or no controversy over assistance to the aged (more than 25,000,000 Americans over the age of 62 collect Social Security pensions today), the blind, dependent children and persons in need of vocational rehabilitation. What remains in deep controversy is the program popularly associated with welfare: assistance to families with dependent children (AFDC). To most Americans, this is what welfare is all about, giving taxpayer money—or "relief money"—to the poor, and especially the poor who have children.

Public and political disenchantment with welfare is closely linked to the sharp increase in recipients and costs. A decade ago, welfare costs totaled $4,300,000,000. In the fiscal year ending on June 30, 1971, the Department of Health, Education, and Welfare (HEW) reported that welfare costs totaled a record $16,300,000,000, 27 per cent more than a year earlier. Relief rolls in the year went up 17 per cent, to 14,300,000 persons. In many big cities, about 1 in 10 persons was on welfare. There were more persons on welfare in New York City (1,200,000 in midyear) than there were total residents in Baltimore. In Baltimore, 15.2 per cent of the population was on welfare, and in Philadelphia 14.8 per cent, St. Louis 14.7 per cent, San Francisco 14.2 per cent, Washington, D.C., 10.5 per cent, Denver 10.1 per cent and New Orleans 14.8 per cent.

Welfare costs are generally shared fifty-fifty by the Federal Government and the states, with some help in a few cases from the cities and counties. There was little doubt that wel-

Able-bodied New York welfare recipients are put to work helping to keep Central Park tidy. To explode some popular welfare myths, Nixon administration issued figures given in the chart.

fare costs were fast propelling many state and local governments down the steep slide to bankruptcy. The business doldrums during the year intensified the welfare crisis. The slow economic pace of business drove ever more clients onto the welfare rolls while inflation magnified the cost to governments and diminished the value of welfare payments to the recipient.

Why the sharp increase in welfare rolls? More unemployment in the last two years. But the basic, longer range reason is attributed to the historic migration of rural families (mostly from the South) to urban areas, where parents are unable to find jobs because of lack of opportunities, lack of skills or racial prejudice. When without private income, these persons "go on the dole." A third reason is the growing militancy of the poor, who demand their "rights to welfare," and in so doing, of course, irritate many persons who think of all welfare recipients as lazy, shiftless and content to breed children out of wedlock. (Indeed, such conceptions are more myth than fact. Surveys show that less than one per cent of welfare recipients cheat, that the great majority of AFDC families

WELFARE FACTS

The largest racial group among welfare families is white.

WHITE 49%
BLACK 46%
OTHER 5%

Less than one per cent of welfare recipients are able-bodied unemployed males.

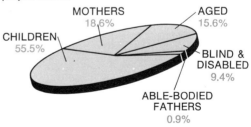

CHILDREN 55.5%
MOTHERS 18.6%
AGED 15.6%
BLIND & DISABLED 9.4%
ABLE-BODIED FATHERS 0.9%

A sizable majority of the more than 7 million children in welfare families were born in wedlock.

BORN IN WEDLOCK 68%
BORN OUT OF WEDLOCK 32%

have no more than three children and that the average length on the dole today for most families is less than in the 1960's. Surveys also show that relatively few AFDC families include an employable male; most families are headed by women with young children.)

It is generally acknowledged that welfare in the United States is a maddening mix of compassion and callous bureaucracy. The welfare system actually consists of 54 state and territorial operations, each with its own requirements, regulations and payment formulas. Benefits range from $840 a year in Mississippi to more than $4,000 a year in New York and New Jersey. There is more than a smattering of racial prejudice behind the mounting antipathy toward welfare, for while blacks constitute about 12 per cent of the population they represent almost 50 per cent of AFDC families. And in the big cities the percentage of blacks on welfare rolls is even greater: 96 per cent in Washington, D.C., and nearly 80 per cent in Detroit. In New York City, 90 per cent of the AFDC load is black or Puerto Rican.

In 1971, President Nixon (who in a September speech to the Detroit Economic Club called the nation's welfare system a "national disgrace") repeated his proposal for sweeping changes in welfare: He would give individuals and families a minimum annual income (a guaranteed annual income, although the President did not use that phrase), he would allow workers to earn outside income up to a point and still get part of their guaranteed income and he would require that the poor accept employment and training. Instead of a welfare system, the President said, the nation would practice "workfare." President Nixon had made his radical proposal first in 1969, and the Congress—and the nation—had debated the idea long and hard in 1970. So it did again in 1971.

The House of Representatives, in midyear, passed the workfare measure, 288 to 132, wrapping in it an increase in Social Security benefits and taxes and a tightening of Medicare and Medicaid regulations. The most significant section called for a national income floor of $2,400 for a family of four (a guaranteed income of $2,400, in other words) and for continued Federal minimum-income assistance, in tapering amounts, to families earning outside income until a maximum of $4,320 was reached. The Federal Government alone would guarantee such income, but states were to remain free to supplement these amounts if they wished.

Also under the House bill, families with employable members temporarily out of work would be required to register for work or for work training; the only exclusions would be persons too ill or too incapacitated and mothers with very young children. These "welfare work rules" were the subject of intense debate, with some critics contending that the rules were too rigid, that training would be too costly, that mothers should not be separated from their children. Nonetheless, the work requirement passed the House easily, and the welfare measure went to the Senate.

There, as was the case in 1970 (the House had enacted a welfare reform measure then too), the Senate stalled. Its Finance Committee, chaired by Sen. Russell Long (D-La.), showed no great enthusiasm for welfare reform. Then, in August, President Nixon, while calling the welfare-reform proposal the "most important piece of social legislation in 35 years," asked that his welfare bill be postponed one year. A work-requirement bill sped through Congress, however, and Nixon signed it on Dec. 28.

While the Congress stalled, the decade-long liberalization and expansion of welfare programs seemed to be drawing to an end. As costs continued to mount, as the nation continued in the grip of economic doldrums and as popular sentiment swung against welfare, state after state trimmed welfare programs, tightening up on eligibility rules and reducing benefits. New York State required a person to live in the state for one year before becoming eligible for welfare; the courts upset that requirement, but the state then made it a rule that recipients had to pick up welfare checks in person, instead of getting them through the mail. The idea was to eliminate fraud. More than a dozen other states cut the level of welfare, reducing the number of persons eligible for aid: Alabama, Arizona, California, Delaware, Georgia, Illinois, Kentucky, Louisiana, New Hampshire, Nevada, New Jersey, New Mexico, Pennsylvania, Hawaii, Texas and Washington among them. The result was that in the last months of 1971 there were slight declines in the number of welfare recipients and in welfare costs.

Thus events in 1971 showed that in the minds of many Americans there remains a Puritan belief that poverty is the result of a person's private moral failings rather than unavoidable circumstances arising out of a complex society and less-than-flourishing economy. Virtually all other free Western countries years ago came to terms with the realities of poverty. But in the last third of the twentieth century, the "right to welfare" remained a controversial issue in the United States.

ROBERT W. DIETSCH
Business-Economics Editor
Scripps-Howard Newspapers

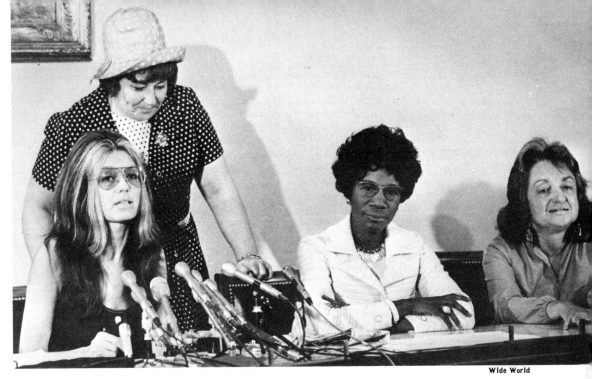

Wide World

Organizers of the National Women's Political Caucus confer: (from left) writer Gloria Steinem; Rep. Bella Abzug (D-N.Y.), standing; Rep. Shirley Chisholm (D-N.Y.); and Women's Liberation advocate Betty Friedan.

WOMEN

Despite widely held world opinion that American women are the richest, best-educated, most pampered women on the planet, a Harris poll taken in 1971 showed that they were unhappy and confused. More than half the women questioned (57 per cent) agreed that "Women are right to be unhappy with their role in American society, but wrong in the way they're protesting." Sixty-two per cent agreed that "If women don't speak up for themselves and confront men on their real problems, nothing will be done about them."

To help remedy this, two important American women's groups were organized in 1971 with headquarters in Washington, D.C. They shared a major goal: To promote passage of the proposed amendment to the United States Constitution which says "Equality of rights under the law shall not be denied or abridged by the United States or any state on account of sex."

On Feb. 1, Women United opened its offices with the endorsement of such influential power blocs as the Republican and Democratic political parties and the United Automobile Workers' union.

On July 10, the National Women's Political Caucus was formed. Caucus organizers included Rep. Bella Abzug (D-N.Y.), elected to Congress in November 1970 on a platform of women's rights and an end to the Vietnam war, and Rep. Shirley Chisholm (D-N.Y.), the first black woman elected to Congress.

But on June 22, the U.S. House of Representatives' Judiciary Committee voted to add two new provisions to the so-called Equal Rights Amendment. One would exempt women from compulsory military service, and the other would allow the fifty states to keep their restrictive, protective labor laws for women.

"This kills the bill," said its chief sponsor, Rep. Martha Griffiths (D-Mich.). Both Women United and the National Women's Political Caucus members concurred. If the women could not get an amendment to end all laws they found "discriminatory," there was a single law they could use to argue specific cases in court of discrimination against women.

The first women's cases argued under President Lyndon B. Johnson's landmark 1964 Civil Rights Act were decided in 1971 by high courts. On Jan. 25, the U.S. Supreme Court ruled that the Martin Marietta Corp. had violated that law by refusing to hire Mrs. Ida Phillips, of Florida, because she had preschool-age children. On Apr. 19, the Appeals Court of Georgia ruled that Mrs. Lorena W. Weeks had been denied a job promotion because of her sex. Her employer, Southern Bell Telephone and Telegraph Co., was ordered to pay her $31,000 in back pay. It represented the amount of salary she lost in being passed over for promotion.

In 1971 the Roper Organization conducted a survey to determine the effects of Women's Liberation on U.S. society. A representative group of American men and women was asked a series of questions about women. Some of the questions and answers follow:

	EVERYONE	MEN	WOMEN
Women should get equal pay with men for doing the same job			
Agree	88%	86%	89%
Disagree	9	12	7
Don't Know	3	2	4
Women are discriminated against and treated as second-class citizens			
Agree	24	24	24
Disagree	70	71	69
Don't Know	6	5	7
Women should have equal job opportunity with men			
Agree	73	71	74
Disagree	23	25	21
Don't Know	4	4	5
Working women should have free/low-cost child care centers			
Agree	65	61	68
Disagree	27	30	25
Don't Know	8	9	7
Men's clubs and lodges should be required to admit women			
Agree	19	25	13
Disagree	72	67	76
Don't Know	9	8	11
Wife should be breadwinner if better wage earner than husband			
Agree	16	22	10
Disagree	76	69	83
Don't Know	8	9	7
If a woman can play football as well as a man she should be on the team			
Agree	38	42	33
Disagree	57	54	61
Don't Know	5	4	6

The U.S. Census Bureau's 1971 population survey showed that American women's median income in 1970, for full-time work, had increased 7.1 per cent over the preceding year, up to almost 60 per cent of men's wages. Full-time women workers earned a median wage of $5,440, but the median income of full-time black women workers fell considerably short of this. The U.S. Government defines "poverty" as a yearly wage below $3,800 for a family of four.

Around the world, women's status remained much the same as it had been—except in Switzerland, where women were given suffrage on Feb. 7.

Europe's leading feminist, Simone de Beauvoir, 63, emerged from her secluded life in Paris on Apr. 5, when her signature appeared on a petition signed by 343 prominent Frenchwomen, declaring "I have undergone an abortion." The petition was aimed at abolishing a Napoleonic law that makes abortion punishable by up to two years in prison.

Prominent German women followed suit the first week in June. Actresses Romy Schneider and Senta Berger were among the 374 women who called for the repeal of an 1871 law making abortion punishable by up to two years in prison.

On May 22, 43 Irish feminists defied a 1935 Irish Republic ban on contraceptives by bringing them into the Roman Catholic Republic. Crossing the frontier into Northern Ireland, where birth control is legal, they purchased the devices there. On the return trip, customs officials at Dublin's Connolly railway station confiscated contraceptives from a few women, then gave up when the remaining women threw their contraband to hundreds of cheering feminists waiting across the barrier.

"Equality—ha!" said an attractive woman architect in Moscow. "It's just a cover-up for enslavement!" Her complaint stemmed from the fact that 80 per cent of Russian women aged 15 to 79 work, and most have low-paying jobs. Women outnumber Russian men by 19,-000,000 and do much of the manual labor in U.S.S.R., such as coal mining, bricklaying, and road work. A Leningrad survey showed that women have half the leisure time that Russian men do and one hour's less sleep at night. Nevertheless, Russian women make up a large percentage of some professions: 85 per cent of all physicians are women; nearly 50 per cent of all judges are women.

In Spain, women have few legal rights. They remain under parental authority until age 25; wives cannot work, open a bank account or a business, or sign rental contracts without their husband's permission. But by Apr. 1971, a small number of women had begun to work quietly to modify these laws. Dr. Aurora Gutierrez, 44, an educator and former nun, has achieved some influence among young Spaniards as a spokesman for women's rights. One obstacle to the formation of women's-rights groups is that meetings of more than 19 people are banned in Spain.

In Africa there were no strong women's-liberation movements. In June, Constance Morris, Liberian-born World Bank economist, explained. "We cannot afford to have women's liberation because it is a divisive force. All of the forces of colonialism have not yet disappeared, and men and women must work together." Nevertheless, a number of African women are gaining wide influence.

Some of the world's women leaders passed milestones in 1971. Sirimavo Bandaranaike, 55, the world's first woman prime minister (1960), continued as Ceylon's leader in that troubled country. Britain's Queen Elizabeth II turned 45 and began her 20th year as queen. In India the ruling New Congress Party of Indira Gandhi, 53, was returned to power by the world's largest electorate (275,000,000). A new Cabinet with Mrs. Gandhi as prime minister was sworn in on Mar. 18. Israel's Golda Meir, 73, survived two no-confidence votes in the Knesset (Parliament) and remained premier. She declined the marriage proposal of a 73-year-old American businessman, and on Feb. 1 was chosen Israel's "Man of the Year."

JEANNETTE SMYTH
Reporter ("Style" Staff)
The Washington Post

A London demonstration calls out largest number of militant women since suffragette days.

The Senate's first girl pages, Ellen McConnell (short hair) and Paulette Desell, are sponsored by Senators Percy (R-Ill.) and Javits (R-N.Y.).

In Michigan, newly eligible students are permitted to register and vote from their college residences—here at the University of Michigan.

YOUTH

The academic year 1970–71 was surprisingly quiet on college and university campuses across the United States. This was in sharp contrast to the preceding year, during which there had been massive student protests over the U.S. incursion into Cambodia and the killings at Kent State and Jackson State.

A variety of reasons have been given for this new quietude, some of them contradictory. It has been argued that students saw the hopelessness of trying to bring about change through demonstrations and thus turned inward to a form of personal privatism. On the other hand, it has been argued that immediate reasons for protest have been measurably lessened through actions of educational and governmental authorities: The granting of a greater voice for students in academic decision-making, reform of the draft law, the withdrawal of substantial numbers of American troops from Vietnam, and enactment of the Constitutional amendment granting the vote to 18-year-olds.

It has also been contended that the absence of a broad-based student-protest movement in 1970–71 was a reaction to radical violence. Among the small revolutionary-youth population there was a new emphasis on bombings and extralegal disruptions: The destruction of the Army Mathematics Research Center at the University of Wisconsin, causing the death of a 33-year-old physicist; possibly the explosion of a bomb in the U.S. Capitol; and the Washington Mayday demonstration.

Characterizing the attitudes of some 40,000,-000 young Americans, of whom nearly 6 per cent are in military service, over 50 per cent attend school, and nearly 40 per cent are in the work force or looking for work, can be at best only impressionistic and selective. Yet for the vast majority of young people the year 1971 seemed to mark a return to more traditional behavior patterns. Attendance was up at football games and other collegiate sports events; beer drinking was "in" again as a popular pastime; a new cult of "nostalgia" appeared, recalling the styles and pop heroes of the 1950's. There was an upsurge of interest in religion, though not necessarily through the organized church; and college bookstores reported a brisk sale for such works as Dr. David Reuben's *Everything You Always Wanted to Know about Sex.*

Among white youth there was a lessening of interest in civil rights as a cause. It may have been in part a result of an awakening pluralism in American society. As blacks and other ethnic groups tended to emphasize their uniqueness and special heritages, there were less room for and acceptance of whites within the movement. However, among ethnic youth, particularly the Mexican-Americans, there were signs of an increased militancy.

The cause that seemed to replace civil rights among white youth was ecology. But this remained a predominantly middle-class concern. A White House Youth Conference Report on the Environment found relatively little interest in the issue among the poor or minority youth and concluded that awareness of the environmental crisis rose as one moved up the economic ladder.

Politically, the big question remained how and how much youth would respond in the 1972 presidential election. For the first time there would be 11,000,000 new voters between the ages of 18 and 21. Historically, young voters have the poorest turnout record at the polls of any age group. Only about ⅓ of the eligible 18-, 19- and 20-year-olds voted in the 1964 and 1968 presidential elections, according to the U.S. Census Bureau. Despite much national publicity for "The Princeton Plan"—dismissing classes, to allow students to work in the 1970 election—relatively few took advantage of the opportunity. Opinion polls, also, showed that none of the 1972 presidential aspirants had a strong appeal to youth. On the other hand, a Gilbert Youth Research Survey revealed that 85 per cent of young people said that they planned to vote, and this combined

Waving a Bible, the Rev. Arthur Blessit, California youth leader, heads a "march of Jesus" past tawdry Times Square, N.Y., movie houses.

Bill Stanton, Magnum

In a surge of joy and loving-kindness, members of the Jesus Movement take part in a mass baptism in the surf at Long Beach, Calif.

Don Rutledge, Black Star

At the White House Conference on Youth, which became snowbound in Estes Park, Col., a cluster of the 1,500 delegates debates a paper.

with the novelty of voting for the first time, suggests that youth now has the potential to influence a close election. Moreover, if young people are permitted to vote from their college addresses (rather than their parents' homes), it is conceivable that they will have a potent impact on local elections.

Drug abuse—primarily a disease of the young—received heightened national attention. Another Gilbert Survey stated that about 30 per cent of the young people in its sample used drugs at some time. Yet it was primarily the prevalence of drug abuse among American troops in Vietnam that led to a greatly expanded Federal program under the direction of Dr. Jerome Jaffe.

The year 1971 also saw President Nixon convene the White House Conference on Youth, bringing together a cross section of 1,000 youths (ages 14 to 24) with 500 institutional leaders. The major recommendations of the conference included replacing the draft with an all-volunteer Army; withdrawal of U.S. troops from Vietnam by Dec. 31, 1971; legalization of marijuana (with a strong dissent from the black delegates); a graduated guaranteed annual income; strong opposition to racism, and support for cultural diversity; and a variety of proposals that would give young people a greater voice in the decisions that affect their lives, including the lowering of the age of legal majority to 18.

If the delegates to the White House Conference on Youth accurately reflected the views of their age group, then the number one concern of American youth in 1971 was to end the war in Southeast Asia. Still, as Harvard Professor Graham Allison wrote in *Foreign Policy,* 1970–71 winter issue, "Problems of foreign policy (with the exception of Vietnam) are not what young Americans think about, care about, or hope to spend their public lives doing something about. The public policy issues of greatest concern to them are domestic. . . ."

One of the more unexpected results of the conference was that there were very few issues on which the delegates were divided by age. Only on the questions of the legalization of marijuana and the so-called Peoples' Peace Treaty, a special cause of the National Student Association, were there appreciable differences between young people and older people in the pattern of voting.

This was in keeping with the findings released in 1971 of the "Youth in Transition Project" at the University of Michigan. This national sampling of 2,200 young men concluded, "Young people are dissatisfied with government in a number of ways. . . . But we do not take this to be evidence for a generation gap, since adults are also increasingly dissatisfied with government. . . . Perhaps the greater differences between youth and adults lie in their [youth's] willingness (and opportunities)

A fisherman ignores the sleeping young people in an Amsterdam (the Netherlands) park. The swarm of young, almost penniless visitors that descended on the city in the summer of 1971 was permitted to camp in the park to avoid the riots that had broken out in 1970.

UPI

to engage in activist demonstrations of their dissatisfaction, thus providing the illusion of a larger gap between the generations than in fact exists."

It was not just on issues of national importance that youth and adults appeared to be coming together. Harris Polls during 1971 showed that opinion was converging even on such questions as rock music and hippies. As Dr. Robert Wood, the president of the University of Massachusetts, stated, "One is less inclined to rant at one's kids when telephone linemen and stockbrokers alike have long hair and sideburns; when hockey players wear beads; and when suburban housewives go about in boots and no bras." It is this apparent fascina-

tion with youth culture that raised *The Greening of America* to the top of the best-seller list and produced such box-office successes as *Easy Rider, Five Easy Pieces* and *Woodstock*.

While there has always been a gap between generations to the extent that each age group has its own history and set of experiences, perhaps 1971 was the year in which the American people began to discover that the popularized "generation gap," that supposedly unbridgeable gulf of alienation, has—like the report of Mark Twain's death—been greatly exaggerated.

STEPHEN HESS
National Chairman, White House
Conference on Children and Youth

Although a commune may include married couples and children, many members join a commune as an alternative to the "nuclear" family.

Dennis Stock, Magnum

President and Mrs. Tito meet with Pope Paul VI at the Vatican, Mar. 29. Afterward, Tito said that the views of Yugoslavia and the papal state on major issues were "close or identical."

UPI

YUGOSLAVIA

To the world at large, President Tito remained the most conspicuous Yugoslav presence. Less visible were the changes at work.

Foreign Affairs. Two successive if related themes were evident in Yugoslavia's relations with the outside world in 1971. The first was the continuing strain in Yugoslav-Soviet relations. It was primarily a result of Yugoslav awareness of Soviet pressures and supposed manipulation of domestic and foreign foes. This was widely interpreted as evidence of Soviet interest in reincorporating Yugoslavia, in part or totally, in the Soviet bloc after President Tito, age 79, leaves the scene. Possibly also the Soviet moves grew out of Soviet fears of increasing Chinese as well as Western influence in the Balkans. The second theme involved efforts to find a safe place for small, nonaligned and awkwardly located countries like Yugoslavia in the new, more complex world order that seems likely after the dramatic changes in the relations among the Great Powers and the overall balance of power that began to emerge in mid-1971.

Efforts to improve Yugoslav-Soviet relations took Yugoslav Foreign Minister Mirko Tepavac to Moscow at the end of February. In March a delegation of the League of Communists of Yugoslavia headed by Mijalko Todorovic attended the 24th Congress of the Communist Party of the Soviet Union. For a time these steps had no visible positive effects. The Soviet press continued to criticize Yugoslavia's foreign and domestic policies, while the Yugoslavs continued to accuse a sometimes tactfully un-

specified foreign power of interference, of conspiracies with antiregime elements, and of "unbelievable pressures" (Tito in a May Day speech), including military maneuvers near Yugoslavia's borders.

In September, however, Soviet party chief Leonid Brezhnev came to Yugoslavia in an effort to calm the atmosphere on the Balkan flank of his European diplomatic peace offensive. In public, he said that the Soviet Union had no intention of intervening militarily in the Balkans, that there was no such thing as a Soviet doctrine of "limited sovereignty" for communist states (with which the occupation of Czechoslovakia had been justified since 1968). He also said, however, that the Yugoslav form of communism was not acceptable to the Soviet Union, although he signed a declaration reaffirming Soviet recognition of the sovereignty, independence and equality of Yugoslavia and the right of every communist state to determine its own form of socialism.

The Yugoslavs continued to pursue good relations and diplomatic reassurance in the nonaligned world and the West. To this end Presi-

---

YUGOSLAVIA

Area: 98,766 sq. mi.
Population: 20,504,516
Capital: Belgrade
Government: Josip Broz Tito, president—1953; Dzemal Bijedic, premier—1971
Gross National Product: $11,800,000,000
Foreign trade: exports, $1,679,000,000; imports, $2,874,000,000
Armed forces: 233,000

dent Tito again embarked on a personal diplomatic offensive of his own. On Oct. 28 he was received at the White House in Washington with special courtesy and attention. Following his first formal state visit to the United States, he made a state visit to Canada and an unofficial visit to London. The trip west had been preceded by an intensive series of talks with other heads of state attending the 2,500th-anniversary festivities of Iran at Persepolis, and with Indian and Egyptian leaders in New Delhi and Cairo. Still earlier, in June, Foreign Minister Tepavac had paid an official visit to Peking, and the subsequent improvement in Sino-Yugoslav relations brought accusations in the Soviet bloc press that China was building an anti-Soviet "Bucharest-Belgrade-Tirana axis."

In October the Yugoslavs conducted large-scale and widely publicized military maneuvers to advertise the effectiveness of their concept of "popular defense." It is a novel combination of regular and irregular warfare designed to give a small country a defense strategy that makes long-term resistance to invasion by a Great Power credible.

Domestic Affairs. A series of 21 amendments to the Federal Constitution, adopted in July after a lengthy and sometimes heated discussion, drastically reduced the power and competence of the Federal Government, legislature and administration. It virtually converted multinational Yugoslavia into a confederation of six republics and two autonomous provinces. The Federal apparatus retains responsibility only for foreign policy, defense, and economic instruments necessary for guaranteeing a "unified market." The amendments require the consent of all the republics and provinces for many kinds of decisions. A collective presidency was established, consisting of three delegates from each republic and two from each province. President Tito remained president of the Federation and 23d member of this collective head of state. After his retirement or death its chairmanship will rotate annually.

While many of the amendments were concerned with defining and expanding the Yugoslav concept of "social self-management," most attention and controversy focused on the new role of the republics as explicitly "sovereign" and "national" states, and on the conflicts among Yugoslavia's principal nationalities. The amendments were designed to relieve the latter, but the accompanying debate dramatically aggravated them.

The political leadership of Croatia, historically in the forefront of the struggle against "Serbian centralism," was the principal focus of mutual accusations that others were placing national interests before socialism. A closed-door meeting of the Federal presidium of the League of Communists at the end of April, subsequent condemnations of nationalism by all regional leaders including the Croats, and the tireless speeches and travels of President Tito in sensitive areas calmed the atmosphere temporarily. At the end of November, however, a nationalist-led strike by students at Croatia's Zagreb University precipitated a major political crisis. Accused by Tito of pandering to nationalists and separatists and of "rotten liberalism" in the face of a "counterrevolution," the three top Croatian Communist leaders were forced to resign. A massive purge of the Croatian party began. At the end of the year, the nation's political atmosphere was one of nervous apprehension.

Economic Developments. The Federal Government was virtually paralyzed as it awaited agreement on its future powers and on specific measures. Inflation, recession in many sectors continued along with a rapidly growing foreign-trade deficit. Increasingly critical was the problem of enterprise illiquidity, in which few companies could pay their bills or meet their payrolls, that accompanied the investment boom. This had ended the general recession of 1967–68 and put the growth rate back to about 6 per cent and began to reduce unemployment. The dinar was devaluated in January 1971 (from 12.50 to 15 dinars to U.S.$1.00), but did not produce expected results. A second devaluation (to 17 dinars to U.S.$1.00) followed. In the first eight months of 1971, exports amounted to only 7 per cent above the same 1970 levels, but imports were up 24 per cent, generating a record balance-of-trade deficit of 17,926,000,000 dinars ($1,195,000,000) as of Oct. 1. The official cost-of-living index rose 14 per cent in the same period, while nominal personal incomes in the socialist sector showed a 22 per cent increase (to 1,499 dinars, or $100, a month). Industrial production was up 11 per cent, and employment outside agriculture 5 per cent, but 672,000 Yugoslavs, 3.3 per cent of the total and 17 per cent of the employed population, were working abroad.

Responsible authorities and unpaid workers complained of an economic crisis, but the number of new passenger cars on Yugoslav roads in 1971 was obviously greater than the 158,000 (a 28 per cent increase) added in 1970.

Preliminary results of the April 1971 decennial census showed a total population of 20,504,516, an increase of 10.5 per cent since the last census, in 1961.

DENNISON RUSINOW
American Universities Field Staff

ZOOLOGY

As if attempting suicide, thirty whales swim onto beach at Gasparilla Island, Fla. Teen-agers rode all but two to safety in Gulf of Mexico.

Mike, the only spectacled (white circles around eyes) bear ever raised to cubhood in North America, stays close to his mother in St. Louis Zoo.

Photos UPI

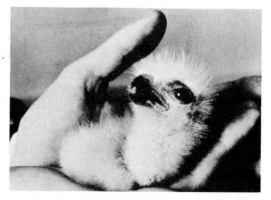

Just out of the egg, red-tailed hawk chick is first bird of prey to be successfully hatched from egg fertilized by artificial insemination.

Another bald eagle is found dead in Wyoming. Bald eagles face imminent extinction as ranchers may destroy them as threats to livestock.

Surgery on Tara, a 2-ton elephant: In a 2-hour operation, Sydney University (Australia) veterinarians remove an abdominal tumor, as big as a child's football, that could have led to Tara's death. She recovered in a few days.

Mazinda, a baby white rhinoceros, nurses shortly after his birth in Whipsnade Zoo, Bedfordshire, first white rhino to be born in Britain. His mother, known simply as No. 19, was already pregnant when she arrived from South Africa.

"London Daily Express"

Day-old Bengal tiger cubs, each still blind and weighing about two pounds, are placed in nursery incubator at Lincoln Park Zoo, Chicago. Their nervous mother was not taking proper care of them.

UPI

Friends—an orphaned baby seal, found washed up on the beach at North Bend, Ore., gets tender loving care and companionship from family pet dog. They share the dog's bed.

UPI

Dead pelicans give warning that Lake Nakuru, Kenya, is becoming polluted. Among the greatest of African wildlife refuges, lake is famous for its vast flocks of flamingos and other water birds.

Keystone

INDEX

Italicized numbers indicate illustrated pages.

A

Abortion 292, 486
Abrams, Creighton, U.S. gen. 228
Abzug, Bella, U.S. rep. *485*
Accelerators, nuclear *355–57*
Accidents, auto insurance 239
Acheson, Dean, U.S. off. *152*
ACTION, U.S. agency 62
Admiral's Cup yacht race 418
Advertising 62–63
Afghanistan 63
Africa, black *64–69*
   Benin mask *94*
   Christian churches 384
   city growth 136
   map *66*
   South Africa, Rep. of *389*
   women 487
Africa, North 80, *82, 83,* 84
"African Queen," boat *345*
Aged persons
   health care 28–29, *30–31,* 32
Aging, conference on *70–71,* 72
Agnew, Spiro, U.S. vice-pres. 73, *213,* 396, 435
Agriculture *73–74,* 75–76, 186, *189*
   Afghanistan 63
   Communist China *16*
   Europe, W. 50
   farmers' vacations, Norway 333
   Latin America 264–65
   pesticides, use of 185
   Poland 359
Ailey, Alvin, dance co. *150*
Air bags, car safety 103
Airbuses 107
Air-cushion trains 379
Air pollution 136, *181–82,* 196
Alabama 422
Alaska *422, 477*
   nuclear-weapons testing 182, 184
Albania 58, 76
Albert, Carl, U.S. House Speaker 76
Alberta *124*
   Citadel Theatre 129
Albuquerque, N.M. 427
Alcindor, Lew (U.S. basketball) *401–02*
Alexander, Lloyd, U.S. writer *285*
Algeria 195, 198
Ali, Muhammad, U.S. boxer 270, 272, *403–04*
Alioto, Joseph L., S.F. may. 58, 423
Allen, George, U.S. football coach *405,* 408
Allen, Gordon, U.S. sculp. *93*
Allen, Jonelle, U.S. act. *443*
Allen, Rae, U.S. act. *373*
Allen, Robert Thomas, Can. writer 130–31
Allende, Salvador, Chil. pres. *259,* 264–65
All in the Family, TV show *438*
All-terrain vehicles *478–80*
Aluminum production 237

Ambassadors and envoys (list) to and from U.S. 77
Amchitka Is., Alaska, nuclear test 182, 184, *422*
American Ballet Theater 149
American Legion 482
American Library Association 276
   awards 370
Amin, Idi, Uganda leader *64,* 65, 68
Amish people 430
Amnesty International 361
Amsterdam, Neth. 180, *491*
Amtrak, U.S. railroad 52, 137, 379, 449
Andean Pact (S. Amer.) 260
Anderson, Forrest H., Mont. gov. 426
Anderson, Lynne, U.S. pop. mus. 323
Angola 362
Animals see Zoology
Anthropology *78–79*
ANZUK def. pact 325
Apartheid, S. African policy 389
Apollo missions, U.S. space *205–07,* 390–91, 467, *470*
Applebaum, Louis, Can. comp. 129
Arab Republic of Egypt see Egypt
Arab states *80–84,* 109, 378
   list and map *81*
Aragon, Louis, Fr. writer 281
Arana, Carlos, Guat. pres. 263
Archeology *85–86*
Archer, Thomas, Can. music critic 130
Archery 419
Architecture *87–88*
   awards 369
   prison *364–65*
Argentina 50, 178, *259–61,* 380
Arizona *422–23*
Arkansas *160,* 423
Armed forces
   veterans, U.S. *481–82*
   See also Defense; Navy etc.
Armstrong, Louis, U.S. jazzman *154*
Army, U.S. 158
Arnold, Ralph, U.S. art. *93*
Arts *89–96*
   architecture *87–88*
   Canada *127–31*
   dance *149–51*
   music *317–23*
   photography *351–54*
   prizes and awards 369
   theater *441–45*
   thefts in Italy 246
   See also Literature
Asexual reproduction 110
Asia
   city growth 136
   See also Indochina and names of countries
Assad, Hafez al-, Syria pres. *82,* 83
Astronomy *97–99*
   Orbiting Solar Observatories 394
Aswan High Dam, Egypt 48

Atherosclerosis 334
Atomic power see Nuclear energy
Attica prison, N.Y. State 365–66, *472*
Auctions, art *89–90,* 91–92
Austin, Texas
   L. B. Johnson Library 88, *276, 469*
Australia *100–02,* 276, 387
   McMahon, William, p.m. 286–87
   Tidbinbilla Nature Reserve *343*
Austria 57, 102
Automobiles *103–05,* 169
   insurance 239
   pollution controls 181–82
   safety 62, *139*
Auto racing 398
Auto trains *379–80*
Aviation *106–08,* 324, 448–49, 475
   flight phobia 290–91
   France 195
   skyjacking 147
   US supersonic transport 50
Avila, Gustavo, Venez. jockey *410–11*
Awami League, E. Pak. 337, *339–40*

B

Badminton 419
Baez, Joan, U.S. folk singer 323
Bahrain, Persian Gulf nation 109
Bakr, Ahmad Hassan, Iraq pres. 83
Balance of payments
   United States 168
Balance of trade 446
   United States 168
Ballet see Dance
Baltimore Orioles 398–99
Banda, Hastings K., Malawi pres. 55, *65*
Bandaranaike, Sirimavo, Ceylon p.m. *134–35,* 487
Banff Festival, Canada 127, 129
Bangladesh (E. Pak.) 225, *323,* 337, *338–39,* 340, 462
Banking, Switzerland 432
Banzer, Hugo, Bol. pres. *261–* 62
Baptista, Don Pedro, Venez. race-horse owner 410
Barnes, E. L., U.S. arch. *95*
Barron, Wm. Wallace, U.S. pol. 430
Barrow, Errol, Barbados p.m. 132
Barzel, Rainer, W. Ger. pol. 211
Baseball 398, *399,* 400
Basic Training of Pavlo Hummel, The, play *441–42*
Basketball 400, *401,* 402
Baudouin, king of Belg. 109, *247*
Bauxite mines 266
Bears, spectacled *494*

Income
  ethnic minorities, U.S., of
    309, 311
  guaranteed-annual, U.S. 484
  retirement 70
  taxes, U.S. 420–21, 434
India *179*, 180, *223–26*, 298,
    462, 477
  agriculture 73
  elections 50
  Pakistan, conflict with 337,
    338–39, 340
Indiana 424
Indians, American, U.S. *307*,
    311, 348
Indochina 158–60, *227–33*,
    467–69, 472
  antiwar youth protest, U.S.
    490
  Korean troops in 252
  prisoners of war *367–68*
  refugees 303–04
  Thailand forces in 440
  war veterans, U.S. *481*
  See also Cambodia; Laos;
    Vietnam
Indonesia 234, 324
Industry 234–35, *236–38*
  advertising 62–63
  automobiles *103–05*
  aviation *106–08*
  Canada 118, 121
  China *14*, 20
  computers *139–40*
  consumer affairs *141–43*
  corporation taxes, U.S. 434
  environment pollution *181*,
    184–85
  fashion *34–39*
  fuels and energy 196–*97*,
    198–*99*
  Germany, W. *212*
  Japan 250
  labor *254–56*, 257–58
  mining 306
  New Zealand 325
  publishing *375–77*
  Puerto Rico 378
  Soviet Union 453–54
  United Kingdom 459–60
  vehicles, all-terrain *478–80*
  See also Trade; Transporta-
    tion
Inflation
  Canada 120, 257
  United States 169–70, 173,
    466, 471, 473
  Yugoslavia 493
Ingres in Rome, art exhibit 96
Insecticides 356
Insects, juvenile hormone 356
Insurance
  automobile 239
  crime 145–46
  health 30–32
Integration, school, U.S. 175,
    177
Intelsat, communications satel-
    lite 394
Interest rates, U.S. 171
International Association of
    Orientalist Librarians 276
International Federation of Li-
    brary Associations 276

Intersputnik, comm. satellite-
    communications network
    395
Interstellar molecules 99
Iowa *45*, 424–25
Iran *85*, 240–*41, 445*
Iraq 82, 83
Ireland, Northern 50, 57–58,
    242, *458–59*
Ireland, Rep. of 188, 242
  women, status 486
Irish Republican Army (IRA)
    242
Iron and steel industry 235, 286
  Communist China *14*
  labor 255–*56*
Irwin, James, U.S. astronaut
    207, 390
Islam 381
Israel 55, *84*, 243–*44*, 464
  immigrants 304
Italy 188, 244–*46*
  engineering projects 179
  labor 258
  railroads 380
  soccer 413
  volcanic eruption, *205*
Ivory Coast 65–66

J

Jackson, Glenda, Brit. act. 313,
    316
Jaffe, Jerome, U.S. psych. 294
Jagan, Cheddi, Guyana pol.
    266
Jamaica (island) 133
James Bay Develop. Corp. 120
Jamison, Judith, U.S. dancer
    150
Japan *167*, 169–70, *247–51*,
    253
  engineering projects 180
  industry *104*, 105, 235–36
  labor 257
  railroads 380
  religion 384
  return of Ryukyu Isls. 53, 250
  shipping 386–87, 388
  space capability 395
  stock transactions by com-
    puter 139–40
Jaroszewicz, Piotr, Pol. p.m.
    359
Jarring, Gunnar V., Swed. dip.
    464
Javits, Jacob, U.S. sen. *31*
Jazz 323
Jean, grand duke of Luxem-
    bourg 286
Jerusalem, Israel 244–*45*
Jesus Christ Superstar, musi-
    cal 321–22, 442, *444*
Jesus revival 381–82, 384, *489*
Jews, migration of 245, 304
Joffrey Ballet 149–50
John, Elton, Eng. pop. mus.
    322
Johnson, Ben, U.S. act. 313
Johnson, James Weldon, U.S.
    writer *277*
Johnson, Lyndon Baines, Li-
    brary 88, *276, 469*
Johnson, Philip, U.S. arch. 87

Johnson, Uwe, Germ. writer
    281–82
Jonas, Franz, Aus. pres. 102
Jones, Bobby, U.S. golfer *157*
Jordan, Len B., U.S. sen. 424
Jordan, Paul, Jersey City may.
    427
Jordan 54, *80, 84*, 245
Journalism
  prizes and awards 369–71
  See also Publishing
Juan Carlos, Prince (Spain)
    396
Judaism 383–84
Judo 419
Juliana, Neth. sovereign 211,
    234, 324
Juvenile literature *283–85*
  awards 370

K

Kahn, Louis I., U.S. arch. 88
Kaiser Found. of Calif. 32
Kane, Paul, Can. artist *128*, 131
Kansas 425
Karjalainen, Ahti, Finn. p.m.
    190
Kaunda, Kenneth, Zambia pres.
    64, *65*, 66
Keeler, Ruby, U.S. dancer 442–
    43
Kekkonen, Urho, Finn. pres.
    190
Kelly, Patsy, U.S. act. *373*
Kennedy, Edward M., U.S. sen.
    30
Kennedy, John F., Center, D.C.
    149, *317, 466*
Kent St. U., Ohio, case 428
Kentucky *425*
Kentucky Derby, race 410–*11*
Kerner, Otto, U.S. pol. 424
Kerry, John F., U.S. Vietnam
    vet. *481*
Khrushchev, Nikita S., late
    Sov. leader *152*, 451, *455*
Kidnaping, of diplomats 48, 49,
    53
King, Billie Jean, U.S. tennis
    415
Kissinger, Henry, U.S. pres.
    adviser 12, *466*, 469–70
Klassen, Elmer T., U.S. post.
    gen. *363*
Kluane Game Sanctuary, Yukon
    342
Knapp (Whitman) Commission,
    N.Y. 147
Kollek, Teddy, Jerusalem
    mayor *244*
Komocsin, Zoltan, Hung. pol.
    221
Korea, N. and S. 230, 252–53
Koster, Samuel W., U.S. Army
    officer 48, 159
Kosygin, A. N., Sov. p.m. 57,
    116, 118–19, 451, 453–54,
    456
Kotch, film *315–16*
Krag, Jens Otto, Den. p.m.
    161–*62*
Kreisky, Bruno, Aus. chan. 57,
    102

Trade (cont.)
 Hong Kong 218
 Israel 245
 Italy 245
 Japan 249–50
 Korea 253
 Latin America 259–60, 263
 Malaysia 287
 Mexico 302
 New Zealand 325
 Taiwan 432–33
 United Kingdom 457
 United States 470, 477
Traffic see Transportation
Trains see Railroads
Transpac yacht race *418*
Transportation
 aging, for 72
 automobiles *103–05*
 aviation *106–08*
 cities 136–*37*
 computers, use of 139
 highways 214–*15*
 new-town, U.S. *88*
 railroads 379–80
 rapid mass 42, *43*
 shipping 385, *386–87*
 vehicles, all-terrain *478–80*
 Warsaw, Poland *360*
Travel *448–49*
 air fares 108
 cruises 387
 Greece 214
 Mexico 302
 parks, national *341–44*
 Puerto Rico 378
Trenches, deep-sea 336
Trevino, Lee, Mex.-Amer. golfer
  408–*09*
Trial of the Catonsville Nine,
  The, play 444
Trinidad/Tobago 132, 266
Trintignant, Louis, Fr. act. 314
Trixie, life-saving dog *345*
Trojan, Women, The, film *315–
  16*
Trudeau, Margaret (Mrs. P.E.)
  121
Trudeau, Pierre E., Can. p.m.
  116–18, *121,* 450
Tsinghua Univ., China 20
Tuchman, Barbara, U.S. writer
  278, 279
Tunisia 82–83
Tunnels 180
Tupamaros, Urug. terrorist
  group 267
Turbo Train 379
Turkey *164, 236,* 450–51
 bans growing of opium
  poppies 294
 diplomat kidnaping 53
Two Gentlemen of Verona,
  musical 441–*43*

U

Uganda *64,* 65, 68
Ulbricht, Walter, E. Ger. leader
  210–*11*
Ulster see Ireland, Northern
Underwater archeology 86
Unemployment 106, *108,* 256–
  58

Canada 117, 119–20
United Kingdom 458–59
U.S. cities 136
UNESCO library sponsorship
  276
Union of Arab Emirates 84
Union of Soviet Socialist
  Republics see Soviet
  Union
Unions, labor *254–56,* 257–58
United Arab Republic see
  Egypt
United Kingdom *167,* 179, 186–
  87, 188, *457–61*
 labor 257–58
 Malta bases 287–*88*
 new towns 137–38
 ocean-dumping law 182
 railroads 380
 Rhodesia proposals 67–*68*
 shipping 387
 soccer 413
 Soviet agents expelled 56
 space capability *395*
 women's lib demon. *487*
 See also Ireland, Northern
United Nations *47,* 59, 162–63,
  192, 234, 245, *432–33,*
  462–64
 list of members 463
 refugees work 303
United States 244–45, 330–31,
  464, *465–77*
 agriculture *73, 74,* 75
 campaign spending 113–*15*
 Canada, relations with *116–*
  18
 China policy 51
 consumer affairs *141–43*
 defense 158, *159–*60
 drug-abuse prevention 294
 economy *167–72*
 education *173–77*
 Environmental Protection
  Agency 184–85
 forces in Korea 252
 foreign aid *191–92*
 fuels and energy 196–98
 health care 28–29, *30–31,* 32
 highways 215
 housing 138, *219–20*
 Indochina conflict *227–33*
 industry 234–*38*
 influence in Caribbean 132
 Japan, relations with 247,
  249–*50*
 labor *254–56*
 migration 304
 national parks *341,* 344
 Nixon, Richard M., 325, *326–*
  27
 Okinawa, return to Japan 53
 population 136
 postal service *363–*64
 shipping 386–87
 space exploration 390, 392,
  393, 394–95
 states *420–30*
 Taiwan, relations with 432–
  33
 taxation 434
 trade 446–47
Universities see Education
University without Walls 176

Updike, John, U.S. writer *278*
Urban environments *87–88,*
  136–*38*
Ure, Mary, Brit. act. *445*
Uruguay 56, 267
Utah 429

V

Vancouver, B.C., *122*
Vargas, Julio Sanchez, Mex.
  atty. gen. *301*
Vatican see Catholicism
Vehicles, all-terrain *478–80*
Velasco, Jose Maria, Ecuador
  pres. 265
Velasco, Juan, Peru pres. 266–
  67
Velazquez, Span. art. *89,* 92
Venereal disease *289–90*
Venezuela 198, 267
Venice, Italy, pollution 182
Venice (Calif.) Redevelop. Proj.
  179
Vermont 429–30
Veterans, war, U.S. *481–82*
 drug abuse 293
Victim (of crime) compensation
  145–46
Victimless crime, U.S. 146–47
Victor, Wilma L., U.S. Indian
  affairs off. *348*
Vienna prison, Ill. 366
Vietnam, N. and S. 79, *227–31,*
  233
 drug abuse in 293
 Mylai 52, 59, 158–59, *467–68*
Violence, criminal, U.S. 145–46
Virginia 430
Viroid, organism 291–92
Viruses 292
VISTA, U.S. 62
Volcanoes *205,* 246
Volkov, Vladislav N., Sov.
  cosmonaut 391
Volleyball *133,* 419
Vorster, John, So. Africa p.m.
  64–65
Vote, right to 49
Voting age, U.S. 53, 270, 489

W

Wages and salaries 254–55,
  257–58
 controls, U.S. 167, 169, 235,
  466, 471, 473
 teachers, U.S. 174
Waldheim, Kurt, UN sec.-gen.
  462, 464
Walker Art Gallery, Minneap-
  olis 95
Wallace, George C., Ala. gov.
  422
Waller, William, Miss. gov. *426*
Walters, Barbara, U.S. TV *437*
Warfield, Paul (U.S. football)
  405, 407
Warren, J. H., Can. off. *116*
Warsaw, Poland *360*
Warsaw Pact countries 330,
  385, 455–56
Washington, D.C., see Dist. of
  Col.